L = real money demand function
M = money supply
$MC(I)$ = marginal cost of investment
$MB(I)$ = marginal benefit of investment
MPC = marginal propensity to consume
MP_K = marginal product of capital
MP_N = marginal product of labour
$MRS_{x,y}$ = marginal rate of substitution of x for y
$MRT_{x,y}$ = marginal rate of transformation of x for y
N = employment
NFP = net factor payments
NL = number not in the labour force
NX = net exports
P = price level
P^* = foreign price level
PPF = production possibilities frontier
R = nominal interest rate
S = aggregate savings
S^p = private savings
S^g = government savings
T = current taxes
$TOT_{a,b}$ = terms of trade, or world price of a in terms of b
TR = aggregate transfers from the government
U = utility function (Chapter 4)
U = unemployment (Chapter 15)
V = present value of profits (Chapter 7)
V = velocity of money (Chapter 9)
$V_e(w)$ = welfare of a worker with a job paying real wage w
V_u = welfare of an unemployed worker
W = nominal wage
Y = aggregate real income
Y^d = disposable income
Y^T = trend level of output
π = profits

Notes

- Primes denote future variables; for example, C' denotes the future level of aggregate consumption.
- A superscript d denotes demand; for example, N^d is labour demand.
- A superscript s denotes supply; for example, N^s is labour supply.
- In Chapter 8, lowercase letters are variables in per-worker terms.

CANADIAN EDITION

macroeconomics

STEPHEN D. WILLIAMSON

University of Iowa

PEARSON

Addison
Wesley

Toronto

National Library of Canada Cataloguing in Publication

Williamson, Stephen D.
    Macroeconomics / Stephen D. Williamson. — Canadian ed.

Includes index.
ISBN 0-321-17054-7

1. Macroeconomics. I. Title.

HB172.5.W55 2003   339   C2003-904950-7

Vice President, Editorial Director: Michael J. Young
Acquisitions Editor: Gary Bennett
Marketing Manager: Steve McGill
Developmental Editor: Maurice Esses
Production Editor: Jennifer Handel
Copy Editor: Rodney Rawlings
Proofreader: Nicole Mellow
Production Coordinator: Deborah Starks
Page Layout: Hermia Chung
Art Director: Mary Opper
Cover Design: Michelle Bellemare
Cover Image: Masterfile

Statistics Canada information is used with the permission of the Minister of Industry, as Minister responsible for Statistics Canada. Information on the availability of the wide range of data from Statistics Canada can be obtained from Statistics Canada's Regional Offices, its World Wide Web site at http://www.statcan.ca, and its toll-free access number 1-800-263-1136. The Statistics Canada CANSIM II database can be accessed at http://cansim2.statcan.ca/cgi-win/CNSMCGI.EXE.

Printed and bound in the United States of America.

1 2 3 4 5   08 07 06 05 04

PEARSON
Addison
Wesley

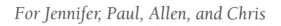

For Jennifer, Paul, Allen, and Chris

BRIEF CONTENTS

CONTENTS

CHAPTER 5 A Closed-Economy One-Period Macroeconomic Model 120

PART 4

Money and Business Cycles 287

CHAPTER 9 A Monetary Intertemporal Model: The Neutrality of Money, Long-Run Inflation, and Money Demand 288

PREFACE

This book follows a modern approach to macroeconomics by building macroeconomic models from microeconomic principles. As such, it is consistent with the way that macroeconomic research is conducted today.

This approach has three advantages. First, it allows deeper insights into economic growth processes and business cycles, the key topics in macroeconomics. Second, an emphasis on microeconomic foundations better integrates the study of macroeconomics with approaches that students learn in courses in microeconomics and in field courses in economics. Learning in macroeconomics and microeconomics thus becomes mutually reinforcing, and students learn more. Third, in following an approach to macroeconomics that is consistent with current macroeconomic research, students will be better prepared for advanced study in economics.

The First Canadian Edition

Good macroeconomic theory is sufficiently general that it can be used to understand economic problems and policy in any country. Thus, the chapter order and structure of the U.S. edition has been retained for this Canadian edition. At the same time, additional material has been added in Chapters 12 and 13 to reflect the importance of open-economy models to the Canadian economy. And, as we note on page xxiv in our discussion of the flexibility of this book, Chapter 12 can be covered immediately following Chapter 7, and Chapter 13 can be covered immediately following Chapter 9, without any loss of continuity.

Certain features of Canadian macroeconomic data and institutions are important for Canadian macroeconomists to know. Therefore, while maintaining a global perspective, we have incorporated Canadian data and applications to illustrate key points and applications throughout this Canadian edition, especially in the *Theory Confronts the Data* sections and the *Macroeconomics in Action* boxes. At the end of each chapter, we have also provided a completely new set of *Working with the Data* problems based on data from Statistics Canada.

Finally, for this Canadian edition, we have increased the number of *Problems* at the end of each chapter, and we have added *Problems* in the *Mathematical Appendix*.

Structure

The text begins in Part 1 with an introduction and study of measurement issues. Chapter 1 describes the approach taken in the book and the key ideas students should come away with. It previews the important issues that will be addressed throughout the book, along with some recent issues in macroeconomics, and the highlights of how these will be studied. Measurement is discussed in Chapters 2 and 3, first with regard to gross domestic product, prices, savings, and wealth, and then with regard to business cycles. In Chapter 3, we develop a set of key business cycle facts that will be used throughout the book, particularly in Chapters 10 and 11 where we investigate how alternative business cycle theories fit the facts.

Our study of macroeconomic theory begins in Part 2. In Chapter 4, we study the behaviour of consumers and firms in detail. In the one-period model developed in Chapter 5, we use the approach of capturing the behaviour of all consumers and all firms in the economy with a single representative consumer and a single representative firm. The one-period model is used to show how changes in government spending and total factor productivity affect aggregate output, employment, consumption, and the real wage.

In Part 3, we first use the theory of consumer and firm behaviour developed in Part 2 to construct in Chapter 6 a two-period model that can be used to study consumption–savings decisions and the effects of government deficits on the economy. The two-period model is then extended to include investment behaviour in the real intertemporal model of Chapter 7. This model serves as the basis for much of what is done in the remainder of the book. In Chapter 8, we develop economic growth theory, and study two key models of economic growth: the Solow growth model and a model of endogenous growth.

In Part 4, we include monetary phenomena in the real intertemporal model of Chapter 7, so as to construct a monetary intertemporal model. This model is used in Chapter 9 to examine the effects of changes in the money supply on the economy and the effects of inflation. Then, in Chapters 10 and 11, we study Keynesian and equilibrium theories of the business cycle. These theories are compared and contrasted, and we examine how alternative business cycle theories fit the data and how they help us to understand recent business cycle behaviour in Canada.

Part 5 is devoted to international macroeconomics. In Chapter 12, the models of Chapters 5 and 7 are used to show what benefits accrue from international trade, how changes in the relative prices of imports and exports affect the economy, and what determines the current account surplus. Then, in Chapter 13, we show how exchange rates are determined, and we investigate the roles of fiscal and monetary policy in an open economy that trades goods and assets with the rest of the world.

Finally, Part 6 examines some important topics in macroeconomics. In Chapter 14, we study in more depth the role of money in the economy and the functions of the private banking system and the central bank. Then, in Chapter 15, we study the determinants of unemployment and two models of unemployment: the search model and the efficiency wage model. In Chapter 16, we see how central banks can cause inflation, either because they do not correctly understand the relationship between real macroeconomic activity and inflation, or because they cannot commit themselves to a low-inflation policy. We also demonstrate in this chapter how inflation has been reduced over the past 20 years in Canada, New Zealand, and Argentina.

Features

Several key features enhance the learning process and illuminate critical ideas for the student. The intent is to make macroeconomic theory transparent, accessible, and relevant.

REAL-WORLD APPLICATIONS

Applications to current and historical problems are emphasized throughout in two running features. The first is a set of **Theory Confronts the Data** sections, which show how macroeconomic theory comes to life in matching (or sometimes falling short of matching) the characteristics of real-world economic data. A sampling of some of these sections includes the effects of taxes on consumption in Canada, the effects of the increase in government spending during World War II, and the macroeconomic impact of increases in energy prices. The second running feature is a series of **Macroeconomics in Action** boxes. These real-world applications relating directly to the theory encapsulate ideas from front-line research in macroeconomics and the history of economic thought, and they aid students in understanding the core material. Some of the subjects examined in these boxes are forecasting at the Bank of Canada, the interprovincial sharing of the tax burden, and East Asian growth miracles.

ART PROGRAM

Graphs and charts are plentiful in this book, as visual representations of macroeconomic models that can be manipulated to derive important results, and for showing the key features of important macro data in applications. To aid the student, graphs and charts use a consistent two-colour system that encodes the meaning of particular elements in graphs and of shifts in curves.

END-OF-CHAPTER SUMMARY AND LIST OF KEY TERMS

Each chapter wraps up with a summary of the key ideas contained in the chapter, followed by a glossary of the chapter's key terms. The key terms are listed in the order in which they appear in the chapter, and they are highlighted in bold type where they first appear.

QUESTIONS FOR REVIEW

These questions are intended as self-tests for students after they have finished reading the chapter material. The questions relate directly to ideas and facts covered in the chapter, and answering them will be straightforward if the student has read and comprehended the chapter material.

PROBLEMS

The end-of-chapter problems will help the student in learning the material and applying the macroeconomic models developed in the chapter. These problems are intended to be challenging and thought-provoking.

WORKING WITH THE DATA PROBLEMS

These problems guide the student in making use of the data that can be accessed online from the Text Enrichment Website accompanying this text. The database is a comprehensive set of Canadian macroeconomic data, which can be used to understand the chapter material and to gain a deeper knowledge of macroeconomic data and phenomena.

NOTATION

For easy reference, definitions of all variables used in the text are provided on the inside of the front cover.

MATHEMATICS AND MATHEMATICAL APPENDIX

In the body of the text, the analysis is mainly graphical, with some knowledge of basic algebra required; calculus is not used. However, for students and instructors who desire a more rigorous treatment of the material in the text, a **Mathematical Appendix** develops the key models and results more formally, assuming a basic knowledge of calculus and the fundamentals of mathematical economics. This advanced material is reinforced with problems.

Flexibility

This book was written to be used by instructors with different preferences and with different time allocations. The core material, recommended for all instructors, is the following:

Chapter 1   Introduction

Chapter 2   Measurement

Chapter 3   Business Cycle Measurement

Chapter 4   Consumer and Firm Behaviour: The Work–Leisure Decision and Profit Maximization

Chapter 5   A Closed-Economy One-Period Macroeconomic Model

Chapter 6   A Two-Period Model: The Consumption–Savings Decision and Ricardian Equivalence

Chapter 7   A Real Intertemporal Model with Investment

Some instructors find measurement issues uninteresting, and may choose to omit parts of Chapter 2, though at the minimum instructors should cover the key national income accounting identities. Parts of Chapter 3 can be omitted if the instructor chooses not to emphasize business cycles, but some important concepts are introduced here that are generally useful in later chapters, such as the meaning of correlation and how to read scatter plots and time series plots.

Though the text has an emphasis on micro foundations, Keynesian analysis is featured prominently. For example, we study a Keynesian sticky wage business cycle model in Chapter 10, examine a Keynesian coordination failure model in Chapter 5, and look at a type of Mundell-Fleming open economy model in Chapter 13. Chapter 15 also looks at the efficiency wage model. However, those instructors who choose to ignore Keynesian analysis can do so easily. Instructors can choose to emphasize economic growth or business cycle analysis, or they can give their course an international focus. As well, it is possible to deemphasize monetary factors. As a guide, the text can be adapted as follows:

FOCUS ON OPEN-ECONOMY MODELS

Chapters 12 (International Trade in Goods and Assets) and 13 (Money in the Open Economy) can be moved up in the sequence. Chapter 12 can follow Chapter 7, and Chapter 13 can follow Chapter 9.

FOCUS ON EQUILIBRIUM MODELS

Omit Chapter 10 (Keynesian Business Cycle Theory: The Sticky Wage Model).

FOCUS ON ECONOMIC GROWTH

Include Chapter 8 (Economic Growth), and consider dropping Chapter 10 and Chapter 11 (Market-Clearing Models of the Business Cycle), depending on time available.

FOCUS ON BUSINESS CYCLES

Drop Chapter 8, and include Chapters 9 (A Monetary Intertemporal Model: The Neutrality of Money, Long-Run Inflation, and Money Demand), 10, and 11.

FOCUS ON REAL FACTORS

Much of Chapter 9 can be omitted for those not interested in the macroeconomic effects of monetary factors. All the material after Chapter 9 can be handled with a basic knowledge of the money demand function and money neutrality.

ADVANCED MATHEMATICAL TREATMENT

Add material as desired from the Mathematical Appendix.

Supplemental Materials

The following materials that accompany the main text will enrich the intermediate macroeconomics course for instructors and students alike.

INSTRUCTOR'S RESOURCE CD-ROM

To facilitate the teaching of the course, the **Instructor's Resource CD-ROM** provides the following material for each chapter of the textbook.

- **Teaching Goals** that give an overview of the chapter
- **Classroom Discussion Topics** that explore ideas and questions to foster class participation
- **Chapter Outlines** that can be used to prepare overhead transparencies
- **Textbook Question Solutions** that provide answers to all the Questions for Review and solutions to all the Problems in the textbook
- **Multiple-Choice Questions** that form a Test Item File of questions (with answers), which can be incorporated into class tests

TEXT ENRICHMENT WEBSITE (WWW.PEARSONED.CA/WILLIAMSON)

A special **Text Enrichment Website** (www.pearsoned.ca/williamson) has been created for students and instructors. It provides data from Statistics Canada for the **Working with the Data** problems in the textbook. The data are organized into 5 large collections: daily, monthly, quarterly, annual, and detrended quarterly. The site also includes electronic files of all the Figures and Tables in the textbook.

Acknowledgments

For this Canadian edition, I am grateful to the following economists who provided formal reviews. Their observations and suggestions were very helpful.

David Andolfatto (Simon Fraser University)

Niels Anthonisen (Mount Allison University)

Douglas Curtis (Trent University)

Swapan Dasgupta (Dalhousie University)

Oliver Franke (Athabasca University)

Muhammed Kabir (University of New Brunswick, Saint John)

Ron Kneebone (University of Calgary)

Marc Lavoie (University of Ottawa)

Igor Livshits (The University of Western Ontario)

Leigh MacDonald (The University of Western Ontario)

Nurlan Turdaliev (McGill University)

Xiaopeng Yin (University of Windsor)

Special thanks go to Maurice Esses, Gary Bennett, Jennifer Handel, Rodney Rawlings, Michelle Bellemare, and all the people at Pearson Education Canada who provided so much help and encouragement.

Stephen D. Williamson

About the Author

Stephen Williamson is the Chester A. Phillips Professor of Financial Economics in the Department of Economics, Tippie College of Business, University of Iowa, and is a Visiting Scholar at the Federal Reserve Bank of Richmond. He attended Merwin Greer Public School, Dale Road Junior High School, and Cobourg District Collegiate Institute East in Cobourg, Ontario, received a B.Sc. (Honours, Mathematics) and an M.A. in Economics from Queen's University in Kingston, Ontario, and his Ph.D. from the University of Wisconsin–Madison. He has held academic positions at Queen's University and the University of Western Ontario, and has worked as an economist at the Federal Reserve Bank of Minneapolis and the Bank of Canada. Professor Williamson has been an academic visitor at the Federal Reserve Banks of Atlanta, Kansas City, Minneapolis, and Cleveland, and the Board of Governors of the Federal Reserve System in Washington, D.C. He has also been a long-term visitor at the University of Tilburg, the Netherlands, the London School of Economics, the University of Edinburgh, and Victoria University of Wellington, New Zealand. Professor Williamson has published scholarly articles in the *American Economic Review*, the *Journal of Political Economy*, the *Quarterly Journal of Economics*, the *Review of Economic Studies*, the *Journal of Economic Theory*, and the *Journal of Monetary Economics*, among other prestigious economics journals. His research, focused mainly on macroeconomics, monetary theory, and the theory of financial intermediation, has been supported by the National Science Foundation, the Lynde and Harry Bradley Foundation, and the Social Sciences and Humanities Research Council of Canada. Professor Williamson lives in Iowa City, Iowa, with his spouse Jennifer Gibson, his three sons Paul, Allen, and Chris, and Marco the Portuguese water dog.

PART

1

Introduction and Measurement Issues

Part I contains an introduction to macroeconomic analysis and a description of the approach in this text of building useful macroeconomic models based on microeconomic principles. We discuss the key ideas that will be analyzed, and some current issues that the macroeconomic theory developed in Parts II–VI will help us to understand. Then, to lay a foundation for what is done later, we explore how the key variables relating to macroeconomic theory are measured in practice. Finally, we analyze the key empirical facts concerning business cycles. These facts will prove useful in Parts II–VI in showing the successes and shortcomings of macroeconomic theory in explaining real-world phenomena.

CHAPTER 1

Introduction

This chapter frames the approach to macroeconomics that we take in this book, and it foreshadows the basic macroeconomic ideas and issues that we will develop in future chapters. We first discuss what macroeconomics is, and we then go on to look at the two phenomena that are of primary interest to macroeconomists, economic growth and business cycles, in terms of twentieth-century Canadian economic history. Then, we explain the approach this book takes—building macroeconomic models with microeconomic principles as a foundation—and discuss the issue of disagreement in macroeconomics. Finally, we explore the key lessons that we will learn from macroeconomic theory in this book, and we discuss how macroeconomics helps us understand recent and current issues.

What Is Macroeconomics?

Macroeconomists are motivated by large questions, by issues that affect many people and many nations of the world. Why are some countries exceedingly rich while others are exceedingly poor? Why are most Canadians so much better off than their parents and grandparents? Why are there fluctuations in aggregate economic activity? What causes inflation? Why is there unemployment?

Macroeconomics is the study of the behaviour of large collections of economic agents. It focuses on the aggregate behaviour of consumers and firms, the behaviour of governments, the overall level of economic activity in individual countries, the economic interactions among nations, and the effects of fiscal and monetary policy. Macroeconomics is distinct from microeconomics in that it deals with the overall effects on economies of the choices that all economic agents make, rather than of the choices of individual consumers or firms. Since the 1970s, however, the distinction between microeconomics and macroeconomics has blurred, for microeconomists and macroeconomists now use much the same kinds of tools. That is, the **economic models** that macroeconomists use, consisting of descriptions of consumers and firms, their objectives and constraints, and how they interact, are built up from microeconomic principles, and these models are typically analyzed and fit to data using methods similar to those used by microeconomists. What continues to make macroeconomics distinct, though, is the issues on which it focuses, particularly **long-run growth** and **business cycles**. Long-run growth refers to the increase in a nation's productive capacity and average standard of living that occurs over a long period of time, whereas business cycles are the short-run ups and downs, or booms and recessions, in aggregate economic activity.

The approach in this book will be to consistently build up macroeconomic analysis from microeconomic principles. There is some effort required in taking this type of approach, but the effort is well worth it. The result will be that you better understand how the economy works, and how to improve it.

Gross Domestic Product, Economic Growth, and Business Cycles

To begin our study of macroeconomic phenomena, we must first understand what facts we are trying to explain. The most basic set of facts in macroeconomics has to do with the behaviour of aggregate economic activity over time. One measure of aggregate economic activity is **gross domestic product (GDP)**, which is the quantity of goods and services produced within a country's borders during some specified period of time. GDP also represents the aggregate quantity of income earned by those who contribute to production in a country. In Figure 1.1 we show real GDP per capita for Canada for the period 1926–2001. This is a measure of aggregate output that adjusts for inflation and population growth, and the unit of measure is 1997 dollars per person.

The first observation we can make concerning Figure 1.1 is that there has been sustained growth in per capita GDP during the twentieth century. In 1926, the average income for a Canadian was about $6700 (1997 dollars), and this grew to more than $33 000 (1997 dollars) in 2001. Thus, the average Canadian became almost five times richer in real terms over the course of 75 years, which is quite remarkable! The second important observation from Figure 1.1 is that, while growth in per capita real GDP was sustained over long periods of time in Canada during the period 1926–2001, this growth was certainly not steady. Growth was higher at some times than at others, and there were periods over which per capita real GDP declined. These fluctuations in economic growth are business cycles.

Two key, though unusual, business cycle events in Canadian economic history that show up in Figure 1.1 are the Great Depression and World War II, and these events dwarf any other twentieth-century business cycle events in Canada in terms of the magnitude of the short-run change in economic growth. During the Great Depression, real GDP per capita dropped from a peak of $7546 (1997 dollars) per person in 1928 to a low of $4976 (1997 dollars) per person in 1933, a decline of about 34%. At the peak of war production in 1944, GDP had risen to $11 151 (1997 dollars) per person, an increase of 124% from 1933. These wild gyrations in aggregate economic activity over a 16-year period are as phenomenal, and certainly every bit as interesting, as the long-run sustained growth in per capita GNP that occurred from 1926 to 2001. In addition to the Great Depression and World War II, Figure 1.1 shows other business cycle upturns and downturns in the growth of per capita real GNP in Canada that, though less dramatic than the Great Depression or World War II, represent important macroeconomic events in Canadian history.

Figure 1.1 thus raises the following fundamental macroeconomic questions, which will motivate much of the material in this book:

1. What causes sustained economic growth?

2. Could economic growth continue indefinitely, or is there some limit to growth?

3. Is there anything that governments can or should do to alter the rate of economic growth?

4. What causes business cycles?

5. Could the dramatic decreases and increases in economic growth that occurred during the Great Depression and World War II be repeated?

6. Should governments act to smooth business cycles?

In analyzing economic data to study economic growth and business cycles, it often proves useful to transform the data in various ways, so as to obtain sharper insights. For economic time series that exhibit growth, such as per capita real GDP in Figure 1.1, a useful transformation is to take the natural logarithm of the time series. To show why this is useful, suppose that y_t is an observation on an economic time series in period t; for example, y_t could represent per capita real GDP in year t, where $t = 1926, 1927,$

FIGURE 1.1

Per Capita Real GDP for Canada for 1926–2001 (1997 dollars)

Per capita real GDP is a measure of the average level of income for a Canadian resident. Two unusual, though key, events in the figure are the Great Depression, when there was a large reduction in living standards for the average Canadian, and World War II, when per capita output increased greatly.

Source: Adapted from the Statistics Canada CANSIM database, Series v3860085, V1, and from the Statistics Canada publication *Historical Statistics of Canada*, Catalogue 11-516, 1983, Series F33–55, A1.

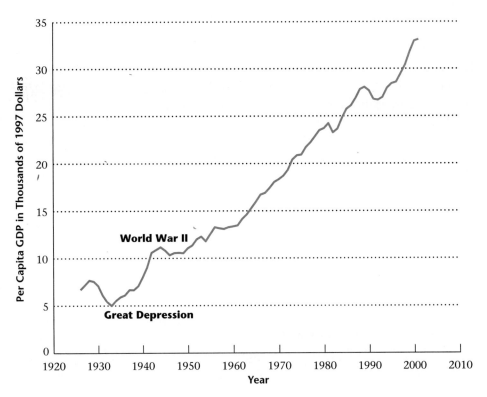

1928, etc. Then, the growth rate from period $t - 1$ to period t in y_t can be denoted by g_t, where

$$g_t = \frac{y_t}{y_{t-1}} - 1.$$

Now, if x is a small number, then $\log(1 + x) \cong x$, that is, the natural logarithm of $1 + x$ is approximately equal to x. Therefore, if g_t is small,

$$\log(g_t + 1) \cong g_t$$

or

$$\log\left(\frac{y_t}{y_{t-1}}\right) \cong g_t$$

or

$$\log y_t - \log y_{t-1} \cong g_t.$$

Since $\log y_t - \log y_{t-1}$ is the slope of the graph of the natural logarithm of y_t between periods $t - 1$ and t, it follows that *the slope of the graph of the natural logarithm of a time series y_t is a good approximation to the growth rate of y_t when the growth rate is small.*

In Figure 1.2 we graph the natural logarithm of real per capita GDP in Canada for the period 1926–2001. As explained above, the slope of the graph is a good approximation

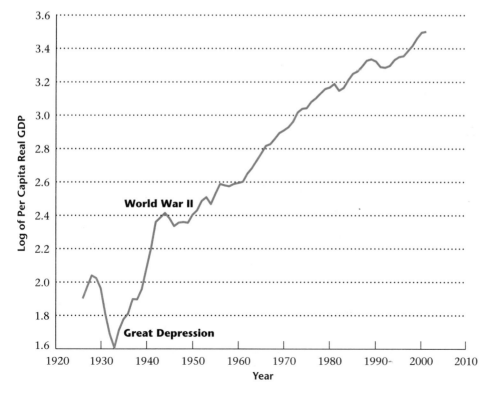

FIGURE 1.2

Natural Logarithm of Per Capita GDP

Here, the slope of the graph is approximately equal to the growth rate of per capita GNP. Excluding the Great Depression and World War II, the growth rate of per capita GNP is remarkably close to being constant during this period. That is, a straight line would fit the graph fairly well.

Source: Adapted from the Statistics Canada CANSIM database, Series v3860085, V1, and from the Statistics Canada publication *Historical Statistics of Canada*, Catalogue 11-516, 1983, Series F33–55, A1.

to the growth rate of real per capita GDP, so that changes in the slope represent changes in the growth rate of real per capita GDP. It is striking that in Figure 1.2, except for the Great Depression and World War II, a straight line would fit the graph quite well. That is, over the period 1926–2001 (again, except for the Great Depression and World War II), growth in per capita real GDP has been "roughly" constant at about 2.2% per year.

A second useful transformation to carry out on an economic time series is to separate the series into two components: the growth or **trend** component, and the business cycle component. For example, the business cycle component of real per capita GDP can be captured as the deviations of real per capita GDP from a smooth trend fit to the data. In Figure 1.3 we show the trend in the log of real per capita GDP as a coloured line,[1] while the log of actual real per capita GDP is the black line. We then define the business cycle component of the log of real per capita GDP to be the difference between the black line and the coloured line in Figure 1.3. The logic behind this decomposition of real per capita GDP into trend and business cycle components is that it is often simpler and more productive to consider separately the theory that explains trend growth and the theory that explains business cycles, which are the deviations from trend.

FIGURE 1.3

Natural Logarithm of Per Capita GDP and Trend

Sometimes it is useful to separate long-run growth from business cycle fluctuations. In the figure, the black line is the log of per capita GDP, while the coloured line denotes a smooth growth trend fit to the data. The deviations from the smooth trend then represent business cycles.

Source: Adapted from the Statistics Canada CANSIM database, Series v3860085, V1, and from the Statistics Canada publication *Historical Statistics of Canada*, Catalogue 11-516, 1983, Series F33–55, A1.

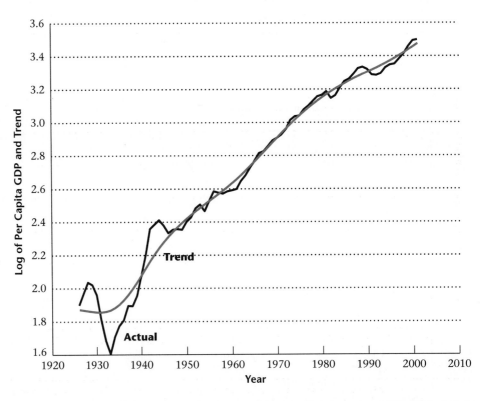

---

[1]Trend GDP was computed using a Hodrick-Prescott filter, as in E. Prescott, 1986, "Theory Ahead of Business Cycle Measurement," *Federal Reserve Bank of Minneapolis Quarterly Review*, Fall.

In Figure 1.4 we show only the percentage deviations from trend in real per capita GDP. Note in Figure 1.4 that the Great Depression and World War II represent enormous deviations from trend in real per capita GDP relative to anything else during the time period shown in the figure. During the Great Depression the percentage deviation from trend in real per capita GDP was about −25%, whereas the percentage deviation from trend was close to 20% during World War II. In the period after World War II, which is the focus of most business cycle analysis, the deviations from trend in real per capita GDP are at most about ±5%.[2]

Macroeconomic Models

Economics is a scientific pursuit involving the formulation and refinement of theories that can help us better understand how economies work and how they can be improved. In some sciences, such as chemistry and physics, theories are tested through laboratory experimentation. In economics, experimentation is a new and growing activity, but for most economic theories experimental verification is simply impossible. For example,

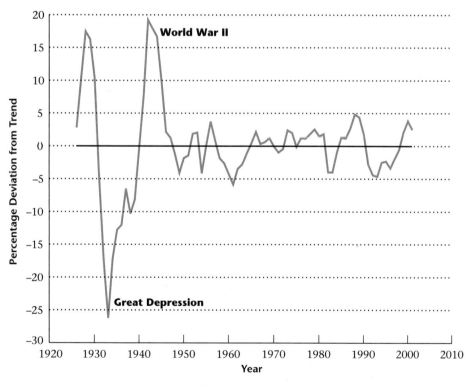

FIGURE 1.4

Percentage Deviations from Trend in Per Capita GDP
The Great Depression and World War II represent extremely large deviations from trend relative to post–World War II business cycle activity.

Source: Adapted from the Statistics Canada CANSIM database, Series v3860085, V1, and from the Statistics Canada publication *Historical Statistics of Canada*, Catalogue 11-516, 1983, Series F33–55, A1.

[2]Note that the extremely large deviation from trend in real per capita GNP in the late 1920s is principally a statistical artifact of the particular detrending procedure used here, which is akin to drawing a smooth curve through the time series. The presence of the Great Depression forces the growth rate in the trend to decrease long before the Great Depression actually occurs.

suppose an economist constructs a theory that implies that Canadian output would drop by half if there were no Toronto Stock Exchange. To evaluate this theory, we could shut down the Toronto Stock Exchange for a year to see what would happen. Of course, we know in advance that the Toronto Stock Exchange plays a very important role in helping the Canadian economy function efficiently, and that shutting it down for a year would likely cause significant irreparable damage. Thus, it is extremely unlikely that the experiment would be carried out. In macroeconomics, most experiments that could be informative are simply too costly to carry out, and in this respect macroeconomics is much like meteorology or astronomy. In predicting the weather or how planets move in space, meteorologists and astronomers rely on **models**, which are artificial devices that can replicate the behaviour of real weather systems or planetary systems, as the case may be.

Just like researchers in meteorology or astronomy, macroeconomists use models, which in our case are organized structures to explain long run economic growth, why there are business cycles, and what role economic policy should play in the macro-economy. All economic models are abstractions. They are not completely accurate descriptions of the world, nor are they intended to be. The purpose of an economic model is to capture the essential features of the world needed for analyzing a particular economic problem. To be useful then, a model must be simple, and simplicity requires that we leave out some "realistic" features of actual economies. For example, a road map is a model of a part of the earth's surface, and it is constructed with a particular purpose in mind, to help motorists guide themselves through the road system from one point to another. A road map is hardly a realistic depiction of the earth's surface, as it does not capture the curvature of the earth, and it does not typically include a great deal of information on topography, climate, and vegetation. However, this does not limit the map's usefulness; it serves the purpose for which it was constructed, and does so without a lot of extraneous information.

To be specific, the basic structure of a macroeconomic model is a description of the following features:

1. The consumers and firms that interact in the economy
2. The set of goods that consumers wish to consume
3. Consumers' preferences over goods
4. The technology available to firms for producing goods
5. The resources available

In this book, the descriptions of the above five features of any particular macroeconomic model will be provided in mathematical and graphical terms.

Once we have a description of the main economic actors in a model economy (the consumers and firms), the goods consumers want, and the technology available to firms for producing goods from available resources, we want to then use the model to make predictions. This step requires that we specify two additional features of the model. First, we need to know what the goals of the consumers and firms in the model are. How will consumers and firms behave given the environment they live in? In all the models we will use in this book, it is assumed that consumers and firms **optimize**—

that is, they do the best they can given the constraints they face. Second, we must specify how consistency is achieved in terms of the actions of consumers and firms. In economic models, this means that the economy must be in **equilibrium**. Several different concepts of equilibrium are used in economic models, but the one that we will use almost universally in this book is **competitive equilibrium**. In a competitive equilibrium, we assume that goods are bought and sold on markets in which consumers and firms are price-takers; they behave as if their actions have no effect on market prices. The economy is in equilibrium when market prices are such that the quantity of each good offered for sale (quantity supplied) is equal to the quantity that economic agents want to buy (quantity demanded), in each market.

Once we have a working economic model, with a specification of the economic environment, optimizing firms and consumers, and a notion of equilibrium, we can then begin to ask the model questions.[3] One way to think of this process is that the economic model is an experimental apparatus, and we want to attempt to run experiments using this apparatus. Typically, we begin by running experiments for which we know the answers. For example, suppose that we build an economic model so that we can study economic growth. The first experiment we might like to run is to determine, by working through the mathematics of the model, using graphical analysis, or running the model on a computer, whether in fact the model economy will grow. Further, will it grow in a manner that comes close to matching the data? If it does not, then we want to ask why, and to determine whether it would be a good idea to refine the model in some way, or to abandon it altogether and start over.

Ultimately, once we are satisfied that a model reasonably and accurately captures the economic phenomenon we are interested in, we can start running experiments on the model for which we do *not* know the answers. An experiment we might want to conduct with the economic growth model is to ask, for example, how historical growth performance would have differed in Canada had the level of government spending been higher. Would aggregate economic activity have grown at a higher or a lower rate? How would this have affected the consumption of goods? Would economic welfare have been higher or lower?

In keeping with the principle that models should be simple and designed specifically for the problem at hand, we will not stick to a single all-purpose model in this book. Instead, we will use an array of different models for different purposes, though these models will share a common approach and some of the same principal building blocks. For example, sometimes it will prove useful to build models that do not include international trade, macroeconomic growth, or the use of money in economic exchange, whereas at other times it will prove crucially important for the issue at hand that we explicitly model one, two, or perhaps all of these features.

Generally, macroeconomic research is a process whereby we continually attempt to develop better models, along with better methods for analyzing those models. Economic models continue to evolve in a way that helps us better understand the economic forces

---

[3]The following description of macroeconomic science is similar to that provided by Robert Lucas in "Methods and Problems in Business Cycle Theory," reprinted in *Studies in Business Cycle Theory,* 1981, MIT Press, pp. 271–296.

that shape the world we live in, so that we can promote economic policies that will make society better off.

Microeconomic Principles

This book emphasizes building macroeconomic models on sound microeconomic principles. Since the macroeconomy consists of many consumers and firms, each making decisions at the micro level, macroeconomic behaviour is the sum of many microeconomic decisions. It is not immediately obvious, however, that the best way to construct a macroeconomic model is to work our way up from decision making at the microeconomic level. In physics, for example, there is often no loss in ignoring micro behaviour. If I throw a brick from the top of a five-storey building, and if I know the force that I exert on the brick and the force of gravity on the brick, then Newtonian physics will do a very accurate job of predicting when and where the brick will land. However, Newtonian physics ignores micro behaviour, which in this case is the behaviour of the molecules in the brick.

Why is it that there may be no loss in ignoring the behaviour of molecules in a brick, but that ignoring the microeconomic behaviour of consumers and firms when doing macroeconomics could be devastating? Throwing a brick from a building does not affect the behaviour of the molecules within the brick in any way that would significantly change the trajectory of the brick. Changes in government policy, however, will generally alter the behaviour of consumers and firms in ways that significantly affect the behaviour of the economy as a whole. Any change in government policy effectively alters the features of the economic environment in which consumers and firms must make their decisions. To confidently predict the effects of a policy change in terms of aggregate behaviour, we must analyze how the change in policy will affect individual consumers and firms. For example, if the federal government changes the income tax rate, and we are interested in the macroeconomic effects of this policy change, the most productive approach is first to use microeconomic principles to determine how a change in the tax rate will affect an individual consumer's labour supply and consumption decisions, on the basis of optimizing behaviour. Then, we can aggregate these decisions to arrive at a conclusion that is consistent with how the individuals in the economy behave.

Macroeconomists were not always sympathetic to the notion that macro models should be microeconomically sound. Indeed, before the **rational expectations revolution** in the 1970s, which generally introduced more microeconomics into macroeconomics, most macroeconomists worked with models that did not have solid microeconomic foundations, though there were some exceptions.[4] The argument that macroeconomic policy analysis could be done in a sensible way only if microeconomic behaviour is taken seriously was persuasively expressed by Robert E. Lucas Jr. in a journal article published in 1976.[5] This argument is often referred to as the **Lucas critique**.

---

[4]See M. Friedman, 1968, "The Role of Monetary Policy," *American Economic Review* 58, 1–17.

[5]See R. E. Lucas, 1976, "Econometric Policy Evaluation: A Critique," *Carnegie-Rochester Conference Series on Public Policy* 1, 19–46.

Disagreement in Macroeconomics

There is little disagreement in macroeconomics concerning the general approach to be taken to construct models of economic growth. The Solow growth model,[6] studied in Chapter 8, is a widely accepted framework for understanding the economic growth process, and newer **endogenous growth models**, which model the economic mechanism determining the rate of economic growth and are covered in Chapter 8, have been well received by most macroeconomists. This is not to say that disagreement has been absent from discussions of economic growth in macroeconomics, only that the disagreement has not generally been over basic approaches to modelling growth.

The study of business cycles in macroeconomics, however, is another story. As it turns out, there is much controversy among macroeconomists concerning business cycle theory and the role of the government in smoothing business cycles over time. In Chapters 10 and 11 we study four competing theories of the business cycle.

The first theory is traditional **Keynesian** theory, captured in the Keynesian sticky wage model in Chapter 10. In this model, business cycles arise because wages are sufficiently inflexible that supply is not always equal to demand in the labour market. Traditional Keynesian macroeconomists are influenced by a line of work dating back to J. M. Keynes's *General Theory of Employment, Interest, and Money,* published in 1936. Keynesians argue that business cycles are caused primarily by shocks to the aggregate demand for goods and services, and that the government can and should play an active role in smoothing out business cycles.

The second theory is the **money surprise theory** of Milton Friedman[7] and Robert Lucas,[8] developed in the late 1960s and early 1970s. In the money surprise theory, monetary factors are the primary cause of business cycles, but the government should not play an active role in smoothing out cycles, as this will only make matters worse.

The third approach is **real business cycle theory**, initiated by Edward Prescott and Finn Kydland in the early 1980s.[9] Real business cycle theory is similar to the money surprise theory in that it implies that government policy aimed at smoothing business cycles is at best ineffective and at worst detrimental to the economy's performance. However, real business cycle theorists argue that business cycles are caused primarily by shocks to the economy's technological ability to produce goods and services.

The fourth business cycle theory we will study is the **Keynesian coordination failure theory**, which is a more modern approach to Keynesian ideas. In the coordination failure approach, business cycles can be caused by waves of self-fulfilling optimism and pessimism, and government policy may be effective in smoothing out business cycles.

This book seeks to take an objective view of all these competing theories of the business cycle. In Chapters 10 and 11, we will study the key features of each of the above four theories of the business cycle, and we will evaluate the theories in terms of how their predictions match the data.

---

[6]See R. Solow, 1956, "A Contribution to the Theory of Economic Growth," *Quarterly Journal of Economics* 70, 65–94.

[7]See M. Friedman, 1968, "The Role of Monetary Policy," *American Economic Review* 58, 1–17.

[8]See R. Lucas, 1972, "Expectations and the Neutrality of Money," *Journal of Economic Theory* 4, 103–124.

[9]F. Kydland and E. Prescott, 1982, "Time to Build and Aggregate Fluctuations," *Econometrica* 50, 1345–1370.

What Do We Learn from Macroeconomic Analysis?

At this stage, it is useful to map out some of the basic insights that can be learned from macroeconomic analysis, and which will be developed in the remainder of this book. These are the following:

1. *What is produced and consumed in the economy is determined jointly by the economy's productive capacity and the preferences of consumers.* In Chapters 4 and 5, we will develop a one-period model of the economy, which specifies the technology for producing goods from available resources, the preferences of consumers over goods, and how optimizing consumers and firms come together in competitive markets to determine what is produced and consumed.

2. *In free market economies, there are strong forces that tend to produce socially efficient economic outcomes.* Social inefficiencies can arise, but they should be considered unusual. The notion that an unregulated economy peopled by selfish individuals could result in a socially efficient state of affairs is surprising, and this idea goes back at least as far as Adam Smith's *The Wealth of Nations*, written in the eighteenth century. In Chapter 5, we will show this result in our one-period model, and we explain the circumstances under which social inefficiencies can arise in practice.

3. *A tax cut is not a free lunch.* When the government reduces taxes, this increases current incomes in the private sector, and it may seem that this implies that people are wealthier and may want to spend more. However, if the government reduces taxes and holds its spending constant, it must borrow more, and the government will have to increase taxes in the future to pay off this higher debt. Thus, future incomes in the private sector must fall. In Chapter 6, we show that there are circumstances where a current tax cut will have no effects whatsoever; the private sector is no wealthier, and there is no change in aggregate economic activity.

4. *What consumers and firms anticipate for the future will have an important bearing on current macroeconomic events.* In Chapters 6 and 7, we consider two-period models in which consumers and firms make dynamic decisions; consumers save for future consumption needs, and firms invest in plant and equipment so as to produce more in the future. If consumers anticipate, for example, that their future incomes will be high, they will want to save less in the present and consume more, and this will have important implications for current aggregate production, employment, and interest rates. If firms anticipate that a new technological innovation will come on line in the future, this will make them more inclined to invest today in new plant and equipment, and this will in turn also affect aggregate production, employment, and interest rates. Consumers and firms are forward-looking, in ways that matter for current aggregate economic activity and for government policy.

5. *Improvements in a country's standard of living are brought about in the long run by technological progress.* In Chapter 8, we study economic growth models, which give us a framework for understanding the forces that account for growth. These models show that growth in aggregate output can be produced by growth in a country's capital stock, growth in the labour force, and technological progress. In the long run, however, growth in the standard of living of the average person will come to

a stop unless there are continuous technological improvements. Thus, economic well-being ultimately cannot be improved simply by constructing more machines and buildings; economic progress depends on continuing advances in knowledge.

6. *In the long run, inflation is caused by growth in the money supply.* **Inflation**, the rate of growth in the average level of prices, can vary over the short run for many reasons. Over the long run, however, the rate at which the central bank (the **Bank of Canada** in Canada) causes the stock of money to grow determines what the inflation rate is. We will study this process in Chapter 9.

7. *Business cycles are similar, but they can have many causes.* In Chapter 3, we show that there are strong regularities in how aggregate macroeconomic variables fluctuate over the business cycle. In Chapters 10 and 11, we will also study several theories that can potentially explain business cycles. The fact that there are several business cycle theories to choose from does not mean that only one can be right and all the others are wrong, though some may be more right than others. Potentially, all of these theories shed some light on why we have business cycles and what can be done about them.

8. *Countries gain from trading goods and assets with each other, but trade is also a source of shocks to the domestic economy.* Economists tend to support the lifting of trade restrictions, as free trade allows a country to exploit its comparative advantage in production and thus make its citizens better off. However, the integration of world financial and goods markets implies that events in other countries can cause domestic business cycles. In Chapters 12 and 13, we will explore how changes in goods prices and interest rates on world markets affect the domestic economy

9. *Money takes many forms, and having it is much better than not having it. Once we have it, however, changing its quantity ultimately does not matter.* What differentiates money from other assets is its value as a medium of exchange, and having a medium of exchange makes economic transactions much easier in developed economies. Currently in Canada, there are several assets that act as a medium of exchange, including Canadian currency, transactions deposits at banks, and travellers' cheques. In Chapters 9 and 14, we will explore the role of money in the economy. One important result in Chapter 9 is that a one-time increase in the money supply, brought about by the central bank, has no long-run effect on any real economic magnitudes in the economy; it will only increase all prices in the same proportion.

10. *There is nothing inherently bad about unemployment. There will always be unemployment in a well-functioning economy.* Unemployment is measured as the number of people who are not employed and are actively seeking work. Since all of these people are looking for something they do not have, unemployment might seem undesirable, but the time unemployed people spend searching for jobs is in general well spent from a social point of view. It is economically efficient for workers to be well matched with jobs, in terms of their skills, and if an individual spends a longer time searching for work, this increases the chances of a good match. In Chapter 15, we explore the determinants of the aggregate unemployment rate, in terms of two theories of unemployment, **search theory** and **efficiency wage theory**. Search theory explains unemployment in terms of the costs of searching for job offers,

while efficiency wage theory posits that workers are unemployed due to an excess supply of labour brought about when firms pay high wages to induce their workers not to shirk.

11. *There may be a short-run tradeoff between aggregate output and inflation, but no such tradeoff exists in the long run.* In some countries and for some historical periods, a positive relationship appears to exist between the deviation of aggregate output from trend and the inflation rate. This relationship is called the **Phillips curve**, and in general the Phillips curve appears to be a quite unstable empirical relationship. The Friedman–Lucas money surprise model, discussed in Chapter 11, provides an explanation for the observed Phillips curve relationship. It also explains why the Phillips curve is unstable and does not represent a long-run *tradeoff* between output and inflation that can be exploited by government policymakers. In Chapter 16, we explore the importance of commitment on the part of central bank policymakers in explaining recent inflation experience in Canada.

Understanding Recent and Current Macroeconomic Events

Part of the excitement of studying macroeconomics is that it can make sense of recent and currently unfolding economic events. In this section, we will give an overview of some recent and current issues, and how we can understand them better using macroeconomic tools.

THE PRODUCTIVITY SLOWDOWN

A measure of productivity in the aggregate economy is **total factor productivity**, which captures the level of productivity of all factors of production, which will typically be capital and labour in this book. Total factor productivity is important, as economic growth theory tells us that growth in total factor productivity is what determines growth in living standards in the long run. In Figure 1.5 we plot the log of total factor productivity for Canada, measured as the log of the Solow residual (to be introduced in Chapter 4). Here, we show the log of total factor productivity, since then the slope of the graph will denote the growth rate in total factor productivity. The key features of Figure 1.5 are that total factor productivity grew at a high rate during the 1960s and 1990s, and growth slowed down from the early 1970s until the mid-1980s. The period from the early 1970s until the mid-1980s is referred to as the **productivity slowdown**.

What caused the productivity slowdown, and what led to the resurgence in productivity growth in the late 1980s and 1990s? If we can understand this behaviour of aggregate productivity, we might be able to avoid productivity slowdowns in the future, and to bring about larger future increases in our standard of living. One potential explanation for the productivity slowdown is that it simply reflects a measurement problem. Estimates of economic growth during the productivity slowdown period could have been biased downward for various reasons, which would also cause productivity growth to be biased downward. This explanation seems quite unexciting, but economic measurement generally is imperfect. Economists have to be very careful in tempering

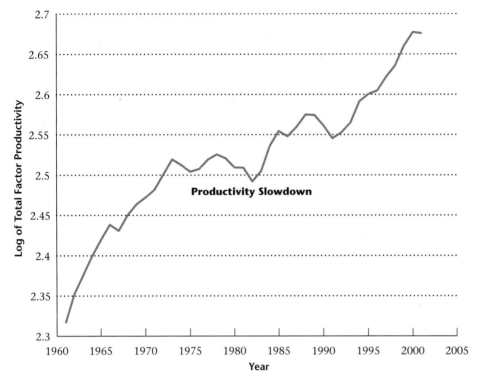

FIGURE 1.5

Natural Logarithm of Total Factor Productivity

Total factor productivity is the level of productivity of all factors of production. Since the graph is of the log of total factor productivity, the slope of the graph is approximately the growth rate in total factor productivity. A key feature in the figure is the productivity slowdown, which we see as a decrease in the slope of the graph beginning in the early 1970s and continuing into the mid-1980s.

Source: Adapted from the Statistics Canada CANSIM database, Series v3860085, v2461119, v3822183, v1078498, and from the Statistics Canada publication *Historical Statistics of Canada*, Catalogue 11-516, 1983, Series D175–189.

their conclusions with a thorough knowledge of the data they are studying. A more exciting potential explanation for the productivity slowdown, and the subsequent increase in productivity growth, is that this is symptomatic of the adoption of new technology. Modern information technology began to be introduced in the late 1960s with the wide use of high-speed computers. In learning to use computer technology, there was a temporary adjustment period, which could have slowed down productivity growth from the early 1970s until the mid-1980s. By the mid-1980s, however, according to this story, it had been discovered how to embody new information technology in personal computers, and the 1990s saw further uses for computer technology via the Internet. Thus, the productivity slowdown could have been due to the costs of adjusting to new technology, with productivity growth rebounding as information technology became widely diffused through the economy. We will explore these issues further in Chapter 8.

GOVERNMENT INCOME, GOVERNMENT OUTLAYS, AND THE GOVERNMENT DEFICIT

In Figure 1.6 we show total government income (the black line; this primarily includes taxes) and government outlays (the coloured line; this includes government expenditures on goods and services, transfers, and interest on the public debt) by all levels of government (federal, provincial, and municipal) in Canada from 1961 to 2002 as percentages of gross domestic product. Note the broad upward trend in both income and

FIGURE 1.6

**Total Government Income
(black line) and Outlays
(coloured line) in Canada,
as Percentages of GDP**

Of particular note is the gap
that opens up between
spending and taxes in the late
1970s, representing a government deficit. The gap closes
in the 1990s, and in the late
1990s spending falls below
taxes, and so there is a
positive government surplus.

Source: Adapted from the Statistics
Canada CANSIM database, Series
v498316, v498326.

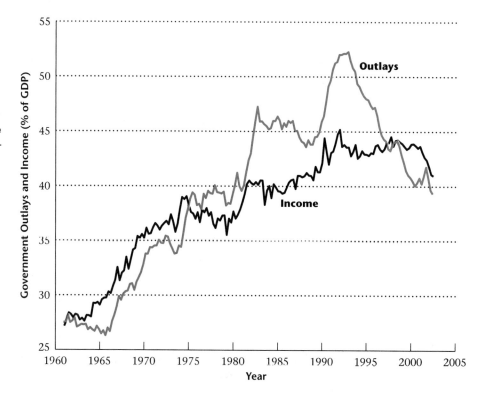

outlays. Total income was about 27% of GDP in 1961, and this increased to a high of almost 45% of GDP in the early 1990s, while outlays rose from about 27% of GDP in 1961 to a high of more than 50% of GDP in the early 1990s. These trends generally reflect an increase in the size of government in Canada relative to the aggregate econ-omy over this period. However, since the early 1990s, a decrease in the size of govern-ment is reflected in declines in outlays and income, with the decrease in outlays being quite substantial.

What ramifications does a larger government have for the economy as a whole? How does higher government spending and taxation affect private economic activity? We show in Chapters 4 and 6 that increased government activity in general causes a **crowding-out** of private economic activity. That is, the government competes for resources with the rest of the economy. If the size of the government increases, then through several economic mechanisms there is a reduction in the quantity of spending by private firms on new plant and equipment, and there is a reduction in private con-sumption expenditures.

An interesting feature of Figure 1.6 is that governments in Canada sometimes spent more than they received, and sometimes the reverse was true. Just as is the case for private consumers, the government can in principle spend more than it earns by borrowing and accumulating debt, and it can earn more than it spends and save the difference, thus reducing its debt. Figure 1.7 shows the total **government surplus** or total **government saving**, which is the difference between income and outlays. From

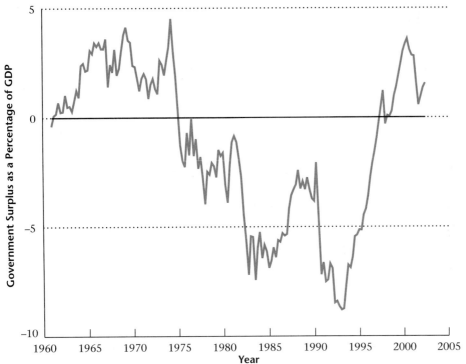

FIGURE 1.7

The Total Government Surplus in Canada, as a Percentage of GDP

Of particular note is the trend decrease that occurs in the government surplus until the early 1990s, with the government surplus being negative for most of the period since the mid-1970s. The government surplus increases through most of the 1990s and becomes positive in the late 1990s.

Source: Adapted from the Statistics Canada CANSIM database, Series v498316, v498086.

the figure, the government surplus was positive from 1961 until the mid-1970s, but from 1975 until the late 1990s, the surplus was negative. When there is a negative government surplus, we say that the government is running a deficit; the **government deficit** is the negative of the government surplus. The largest government deficit over this period was more than 8% of GDP, in the early 1990s. It was not until the late 1990s that there was again a positive government surplus; in 2000, the government surplus had reached about 3% of GDP.

What are the consequences of government deficits? We might think, in a manner similar to popular conceptions of household finance, that accumulating debt (running a deficit) is bad, whereas reducing debt (running a surplus) is good, but at the aggregate level the issue is not so simple. One principal difference between an individual and the government is that when the government accumulates debt by borrowing from its citizens, then this is debt that we as a nation owe to ourselves. Then, it turns out that the effects of a government deficit depend on what the source of the deficit is. Is the government running a deficit because taxes have decreased or because government spending has increased? If the deficit is due to a decrease in taxes, then the government debt that is issued to finance the deficit will have to be paid off ultimately by higher future taxes. Thus, running a deficit in this case implies that there is a redistribution of the tax burden from one group to another; one group has its current taxes reduced while another has its future taxes increased. Under some circumstances, these two groups might essentially be the same, in which case there would be no consequences of having the government run a deficit. This idea, that government deficits do not matter under some conditions, is called the **Ricardian equivalence theorem**, and we will study it in Chapter 6. In the case where a government deficit results from higher government spending, then there are always implications for aggregate economic activity, as discussed earlier in terms of the crowding-out of private spending. We will examine the effects of government spending in Chapters 5 and 7.

INFLATION

Inflation, as mentioned earlier, is the rate of change in the average level of prices, where the average level of prices is referred to as the **price level**. One measure of the price level is the consumer price index, which is essentially the price of the set of goods bought by the "average" consumer. In Figure 1.8 we show the inflation rate, the black line in the figure, as the percentage rate of increase (from 12 months previously) in the consumer price index. The inflation rate remained low from 1956 until the early 1970s, and then began climbing, reaching peaks of more than 10% per year in the mid-1970s and early 1980s. The inflation rate then declined steadily, to about 0% in the late 1990s.

Inflation is economically costly, but the low recent rates of inflation we are experiencing are certainly not viewed by the public or by policymakers as being worthy of much attention. However, it is certainly useful to understand the causes of inflation, its costs, and why and how inflation was reduced in Canada. There are good reasons to

FIGURE 1.8

Inflation and Money Growth
Macroeconomic theory tells us that growth in the money supply causes inflation in the long run. The figure is broadly consistent with this, in that the money growth rate (the coloured line) tracks the inflation rate (the black line) reasonably well, at least until the mid-1990s. There is substantial short-run variation in the inflation rate and money growth that appears to be unrelated, and money growth is quite erratic after 1995.

Source: Adapted from the Statistics Canada CANSIM database, Series v735319, v37145.

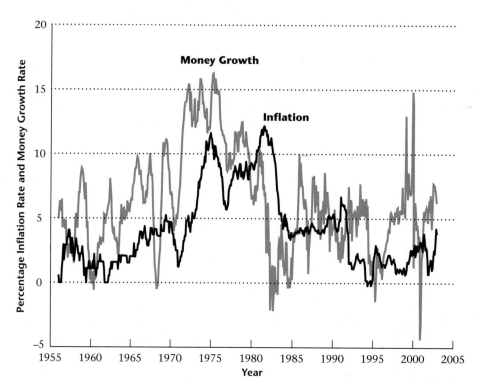

think that the inflation experience of the 1970s and early 1980s, or worse, could be repeated. As mentioned in the previous section, the inflation rate is explained in the long run by the rate of growth in the supply of money. Without money supply growth, prices cannot continue to increase, and higher money supply growth implies that there is more and more money chasing a given quantity of goods. This will ultimately cause prices to be bid up at a higher rate. In Figure 1.8 we show the inflation rate and the rate of money growth (measured as the percentage rate of growth in the monetary base, a narrow monetary aggregate) from 1956 until 2002. The inflation rate is represented by the black line, while the money growth rate is represented by the coloured line. Here, it is clear that the short-run relationship between the rate of inflation and the rate of money growth is not a tight one; there are many short-run ups and downs in the rate of money growth that are not reflected in similar movements in the inflation rate, and vice versa. Thus, there must be other factors that explain short-run movements in the rate of inflation, in addition to changes in the money growth rate. However, the broad trends in money growth in Figure 1.8 match the broad trends in the inflation rate. Money growth increases, on trend, until the mid-1970s, and then falls, as does the inflation rate, though money growth behaviour is quite erratic from the early 1980s on. The long-run effects of money growth on inflation are explored in Chapter 9, and we study the short-run effects of nonmonetary factors on the price level in Chapters 10 and 11.

Long-run inflation is costly, in that it tends to reduce employment, output, and consumption, as we will show in Chapter 9. However, since inflation is caused in the long run by money growth, the central bank determines the long-run inflation rate through its control of the rate at which the money supply grows. Why would the central bank want to generate inflation if it is costly? In Chapter 16, we explore the answer to this question, with recent experience in Canada as a backdrop. Surprise increases in the rate of inflation can cause short-run increases in employment and output, and the central bank might be tempted to generate these short-run surprises, either because it has not learned the consequences of long-run inflation, or because there is a failure of the central bank to commit itself to long-run actions. In Chapter 16, we will study the importance of central bank learning and commitment for the behaviour of inflation.

INTEREST RATES

Interest rates are important, as they affect many private economic decisions, particularly the decisions of consumers as to how much they will borrow and lend, and the decisions of firms concerning how much to invest in new plant and equipment. Further, movements in interest rates are an important element in the economic mechanism by which monetary policy affects real magnitudes in the short run. In Figure 1.9 we show the behaviour of the short-term **nominal interest rate** (the black line) in Canada over the period 1962–2002. This is the interest rate in money terms on 3-month federal government Treasury Bills, which are essentially riskless short-term government securities. In 1962, the short-term nominal interest rate was about 3%, but it rose on trend through the 1960s and 1970s, reaching a high of more than 20% in 1980. Since then, the nominal interest rate has declined on trend, and it was below 2% in 2001.

What explains the level of the nominal interest rate? Observant readers will recall that the trends in the inflation rate discussed in the previous subsection were very similar

FIGURE 1.9

**The Nominal Interest Rate
and the Inflation Rate**

Macroeconomic theory tells
us that the nominal interest
rate and the inflation rate are
positively related. In the figure,
the nominal interest rate,
which is the 3-month Treasury
bill rate (a short-term interest
rate on federal government
securities) tends to track the
ups and downs in the inflation
rate.

Source: Adapted from the Statistics
Canada CANSIM database, Series
v122531, v735319.

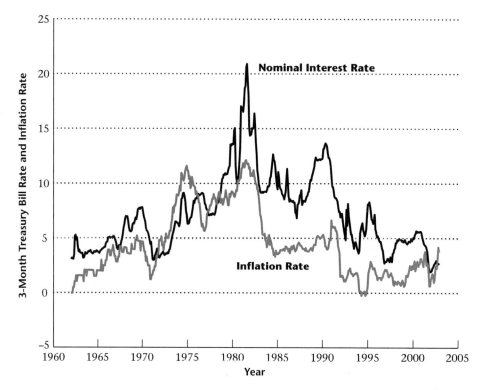

over the period 1962–2002 to the trends in the nominal interest rate, and we have
plotted the inflation rate as the coloured line along with the nominal interest rate in
Figure 1.9 to show this. Observe also that several of the peaks in inflation, around 1970,
in the mid-1970s, around 1980, and around 1990, are coupled with peaks in the nominal interest rate. Thus, the nominal interest rate tends to rise and fall with the inflation
rate. Why is this? Economic decisions are based on real rather than nominal interest
rates. The **real interest rate**, roughly speaking, is the nominal interest rate minus the
expected rate of inflation. That is, the real interest rate is the rate that a borrower expects
to have to repay, adjusting for the inflation that is expected to occur over the period of
time until the borrower's debt is repaid. If Allen obtains a one-year car loan at an interest rate of 9%, and he expects the inflation rate to be 3% over the next year, then he
faces a real interest rate on the car loan of 6%. Now, since economic decisions are based
on real interest rates rather than nominal interest rates, market forces will tend to determine the real interest rate. Therefore, as the inflation rate rises, the nominal interest rate
will tend to rise along with it. In Chapters 7 and 9, we will study the determination of
real and nominal interest rates in the long run, and the relationship between real and
nominal rates.

In Figure 1.10 we plot an estimate of the real interest rate, which is the nominal
interest rate minus the actual rate of inflation. Thus, this would be the actual real interest rate if the inflation rate over the next three months were the same as the inflation
rate over the previous year. Consumers and firms cannot correctly anticipate the actual

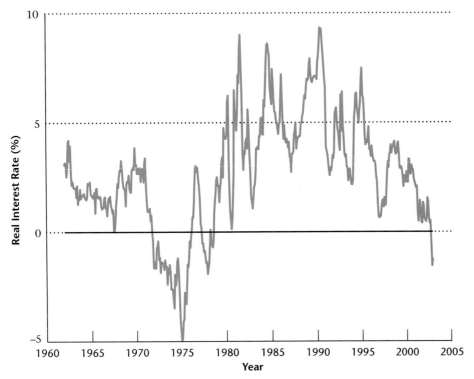

FIGURE 1.10

Real Interest Rate

The figure shows a measure of the real interest rate, which here is the short-term nominal interest rate minus the actual rate of inflation. Monetary policy can have a short-run effect on the real interest rate; for example, the high real interest rates in the 1980s are often attributed to tight monetary policy.

Source: Adapted from the Statistics Canada CANSIM database, Series v122531, v735319.

inflation rate. However, given that inflation does not change too much from quarter to quarter, their forecasts will be fairly accurate, and our estimate of the real interest rate will have a reasonably small measurement error. Note that the real interest rate fluctuates a great deal over time. The real rate has sometimes been negative, falling as low as almost −5% in 1975. Since the late 1970s, the real interest rate has been positive, except in 2002 when it again dipped below zero.

In the short run, the real interest rate is affected by monetary policy, though there is some disagreement among macroeconomists concerning why the central bank can control the real interest rate, and for how long it can do so. We can give the following interpretation to the path of the real interest rate from the mid-1970s to 2002 in Figure 1.10. First, the real interest rate was low in the mid-1970s because the Bank of Canada was causing the money supply to grow at a high rate—that is, monetary policy was expansionary and accommodating. As a result of the high inflation caused by this high money growth, the Bank of Canada embarked on a contractionary course in the early 1980s, reducing money supply growth and causing the real interest rate to rise. Since the mid-1980s, the Bank of Canada has remained seriously concerned about the possibility that high inflation could reemerge, and it has for the most part maintained a nonaccommodating monetary policy stance, which has caused the real interest rate to be historically high. During the 1990s, the real interest rate has decreased on trend, indicating a more accommodating monetary policy. In Chapters 10 and 11, we will study some theories of the business cycle that explain how the central bank can influence the real interest rate in the short run. While the rate of money growth may affect real interest rates in the long run, monetary policy is aimed not at setting the long-run real interest rate, but at determining long-run inflation while staying in tune with the short-run effects of monetary policy.

ENERGY PRICES AND MACROECONOMIC ACTIVITY

The price of energy in Canada, which is influenced to a high degree by the world price of crude oil, has played an important role in recent macroeconomic history in Canada, and it is currently a key factor in Canadian macroeconomic policy. In Figure 1.11 we plot the relative price of energy, measured as the industry price index for petroleum and coal products divided by the consumer price index. A higher relative price of energy implies that the price of energy rises for firms relative to the prices of other inputs to production, which will imply that firms will substitute away from energy and toward these other inputs. As a result, the productivity of firms will tend to fall, and this will have negative consequences for aggregate economic activity.

In Figure 1.11, there was a particularly sharp rise in the relative price of energy in 1974, caused by a restriction of oil output by OPEC (the Organization of Petroleum Exporting Countries). In Figure 1.12 we can see the result, which was a significant drop in real GDP below trend in 1973–75. In the early 1980s, there was an even more substantial increase in the relative price of energy (shown in Figure 1.11). Perhaps surprisingly, in Figure 1.12 there was not an immediate drop in real GDP below trend, but

FIGURE 1.11

The Relative Price of Energy, Measured as the Producer Price of Petroleum Products Divided by the Consumer Price Index

Two key events represented in the figure are the effects of the large increases in oil prices brought about by OPEC in 1973–74 and in the late 1970s.

Source: Adapted from the Statistics Canada CANSIM database, Series v735319, v3822650, v83718.

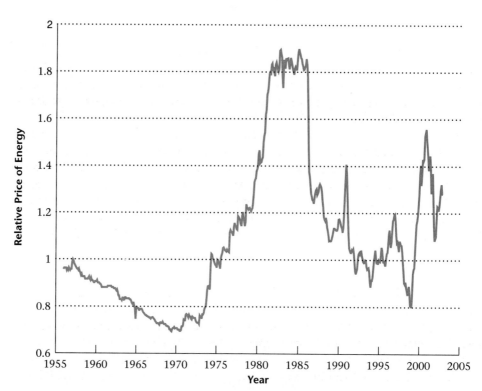

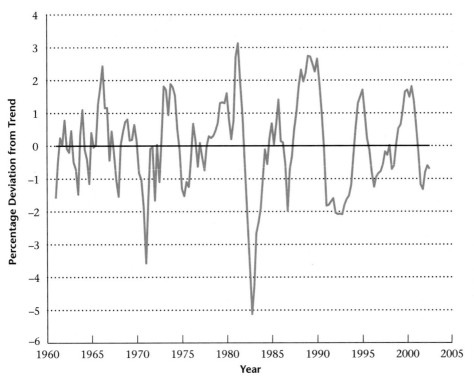

FIGURE 1.12

Percentage Deviations from Trend in Real GDP

Here, we are looking for the effects of changes in the relative price of energy. This clearly shows in the recession in 1973–75, which corresponds to the energy price hike that occurred at about the same time. However, the early 1980s recession shows up much later than the earlier large increase in the relative price of energy (see Figure 1.11).

Source: Adapted from the Statistics Canada CANSIM database, Series v1992067.

there was a large decrease in real GDP below trend that occurred somewhat later. Whereas the mid-1970s business cycle downturn is commonly attributed to the increase in the relative price of energy, the early 1980s downturn is often attributed to tight monetary policy (recall our discussion of Figure 1.10), though high energy prices may have played a role.

In the late 1980s, the relative price of energy returned to levels close to those of the early 1960s (see Figure 1.11), but an increase occurred in 2000, and this recent increase appears to have contributed to a dip below trend in real GDP in 2001–2002. Increases in energy prices do not have as strong a negative impact in Canada as in other countries, such as the United States, since high energy prices tend to increase domestic Canadian oil and gas production. However, there are significant negative effects of higher energy prices on Canadian manufacturing, construction, and agriculture.

TRADE AND THE TWIN DEFICITS

As the technology for transporting goods and information across countries has advanced and government-imposed impediments to trade have been reduced Canada has become a more open economy. That is, trade in goods and in assets between Canada and the rest of the world has increased. The change in the flow of goods and services between Canada and the rest of the world is shown in Figure 1.13, where we plot Canadian exports (the black line) and imports (the coloured line) as percentages of GDP from

FIGURE 1.13

**Exports and Imports of Goods
and Services for Canada, as
Percentages of GDP**
The increase in both imports
and exports reflects a general
increase in world trade.

Source: Adapted from the Statistics
Canada CANSIM database, Series
v199206, v1992063, v1992067.

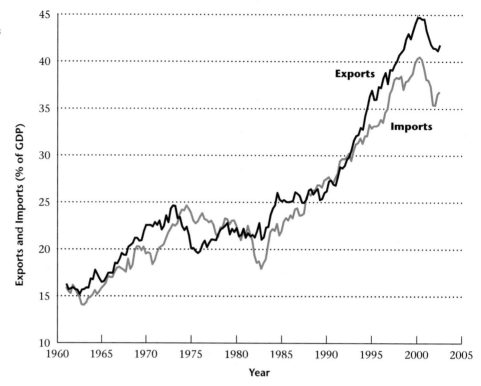

1961 to 2002. Canadian exports increased from about 16% of GDP in 1962 to almost 45% of GDP in 2000, while imports increased from about 16% in 1962 to 40% in 2000. As mentioned in the previous section, more trade has a positive effect on general economic welfare, as it allows countries to specialize in production and exploit their comparative advantages. However, more trade could also expose a given country to the transmission of business cycle fluctuations from abroad, though this need not necessarily be the case.

While the level of trade with the outside world is important in terms of aggregate economic activity and how it fluctuates, the balance of trade also plays an important role in macroeconomic activity and macroeconomic policymaking. One measure of the balance of trade is the **current account surplus**, which is **net exports** of goods and services (exports minus imports) plus **net factor payments** (net income from abroad). In Figure 1.14 we have graphed the current account surplus for Canada for the period 1961-2002, as a percentage of GDP. Canada had a current account deficit for most of this period (the current account surplus was usually negative), but the current account moved into surplus in the late 1990s.

Why is the current account surplus important? When the current account surplus in Canada is negative, there is a **current account deficit**, and the quantity of goods and services purchased abroad by domestic residents is greater than the quantity of domestic goods and services purchased by foreigners. To finance this current account deficit, residents of Canada and/or the Canadian government must be borrowing abroad. Is it

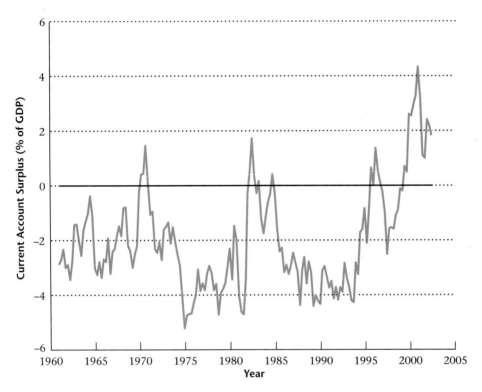

FIGURE 1.14
Current Account Surplus for Canada, 1961-2002
The figure shows the current account surplus for 1961–2002, which is exports of goods and services minus imports of goods and services plus net factor payments from foreigners, here plotted as a percentage of GDP. Canada ran a current account deficit for much of this period, but began to run a surplus in the late 1990s.

Source: Adapted from the Statistics Canada CANSIM database, Series v114532, v498086.

a bad idea for a country to run a current account deficit? This need not be the case, for two reasons. First, just as it may make sense for an individual to borrow so as to smooth his or her flow of consumption over time, it may also be beneficial for a country to borrow in the short run by running a current account deficit so as to smooth aggregate consumption over time. Second, persistent current account deficits may make sense if the associated foreign borrowing is used to finance additions to the nation's productive capacity that will allow for higher future living standards.

What accounts for movements over time in the current account surplus? One important influence on the current account surplus is government spending. When the government increases its spending, holding taxes constant, this will increase the government deficit, which needs to be financed by increased government borrowing. If the private sector does not save more, so as to increase its lending to the government, then the increased government borrowing will be done abroad, and it will show up as an increase in the current account deficit. Thus, an increase in the government deficit can be coupled with an increase in the current account deficit so that there are **twin deficits**. In Figures 1.7 and 1.14 we can see a tendency for a government surplus (deficit) to be reflected in a current account surplus (deficit). This regularity is empirically pronounced after the mid-1970s.

We will study international trade, the determinants of the current account surplus, and other issues associated with international business cycles and international financial relations in Chapters 12 and 13.

UNEMPLOYMENT

In the previous section we explained how the phenomenon of unemployment need not represent a problem, since unemployment is in general a socially useful search activity that is necessary, though perhaps painful to the individuals involved. As macroeconomists, we are interested in what explains the level of unemployment, and what the reasons are for fluctuations in unemployment over time. If we can understand these features, we can go on to determine how macroeconomic policy can be formulated so that labour markets work as efficiently as possible.

In Figure 1.15 we show the unemployment rate in Canada for the period 1976–2002. Two important features can be observed. First, the unemployment rate fluctuates significantly; it is not unusual for it to move up or down by four or five percentage points within a year or two. Second, since the mid-1980s, there was a trend decrease in the unemployment rate, as can be noted in the fact that the unemployment rate decreases after the mid-1980s from peak-to-peak and from trough-to-trough. What explains these features of the data?

There are four factors affecting unemployment that can explain essentially all of the observed behaviour of the unemployment rate in Figure 1.15: aggregate economic activity, the structure of the population, government intervention, and sectoral shifts. First, in general the unemployment rate fluctuates inversely along with aggregate economic activity; when aggregate output is above trend, then the unemployment rate tends to be low. Second, the population structure affects the unemployment rate, as workers in different age cohorts tend to behave differently in the labour market. For example,

FIGURE 1.15

The Unemployment Rate in Canada, 1976–2002

The unemployment rate is affected by aggregate economic activity, the structure of the population, government intervention, and sectoral shifts.

Source: Adapted from the Statistics Canada CANSIM database, Series v2062815.

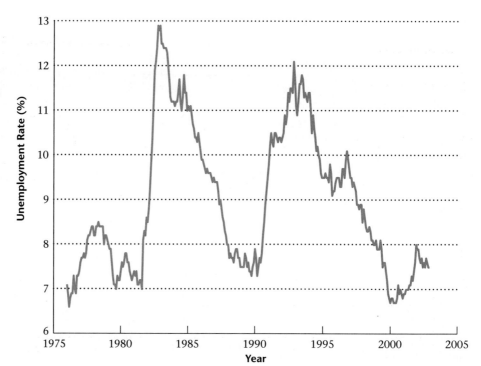

younger workers have a weaker attachment to jobs than older workers, and they tend to experience more frequent episodes of unemployment as they change jobs early in their careers. Third, government intervention affects the unemployment rate, particularly through the unemployment insurance system. For example, more generous unemployment compensation implies that the cost of searching for a job is reduced, and unemployed workers will then tend to search longer, increasing the unemployment rate. Fourth, sectoral shifts are long-run changes that occur in the sectoral structure of production. For example, in Canada there has recently been a shift from the manufacturing sector of the economy to the services sector. This kind of sectoral shift tends to displace workers from the declining sector, and they need to acquire new skills and to spend time searching to find jobs in the expanding sector of the economy. Therefore, the greater the extent of sectoral shifts occurring in the economy, the higher the unemployment rate.

The fact that the unemployment rate has tended to decrease since the mid-1980s, as observed in Figure 1.15, is probably due mainly to changes in the population structure. The postwar baby boom generation entered the labour force mainly between the late 1960s and 1980, so that the working age population became more youthful through the 1970s, which would tend to push the unemployment rate up. Then, as the baby boom generation aged through the 1980s and 1990s, the unemployment rate tended to fall. The unemployment rate fluctuated from 1976 to 2002 mainly due to fluctuations in aggregate economic activity. In Figure 1.16 we show deviations from trend in real GDP (in percentage terms) as the coloured line, and deviations from trend in the

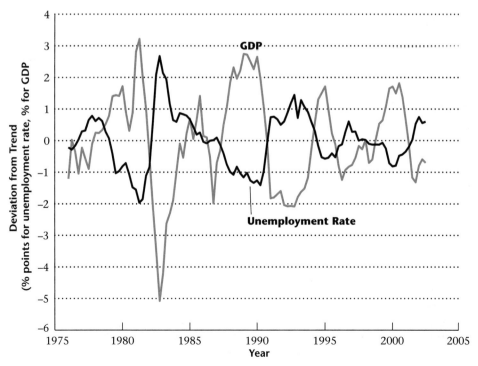

FIGURE 1.16

Deviations from Trend in the Unemployment Rate (black line) and Percentage Deviations from Trend in Real GDP (coloured line)

Of particular note in the figure is that the unemployment rate tends to be high (low) relative to trend when real GDP is low (high) relative to trend.

Source: Adapted from the Statistics Canada CANSIM database, Series v1992067, v1062815.

unemployment rate (in percentage points) as the black line. Clearly, when GDP is above (below) trend, the unemployment rate tends to be below (above) trend.

We will study determinants of the unemployment rate and theories of unemployment in Chapter 15.

Chapter Summary

This chapter set out the basic approach to macroeconomics taken in this book, and presented an overview of the ideas and issues that we will study in later chapters. Modern macroeconomics analyzes issues associated with long-run growth and business cycles, using models that are built up from microeconomic principles. During the period 1926–2002, Canada experienced long-run sustained growth in per capita gross domestic product; we also observed that gross domestic product exhibits business cycle fluctuations about a smooth long-run trend. Two unusual but important events in Canadian economic history were the Great Depression and World War II. The primary questions of interest to macroeconomists involve the causes of long-run growth and business cycles, and the appropriate role for government policy in influencing the performance of the economy. Macroeconomists rely mainly on abstract models to draw conclusions about how the world works, because it is usually very costly or impossible to experiment with the real economy. A good macroeconomic model is simple, while retaining all of the features essential for addressing the macroeconomic issue for which the model was intended. The models we will construct and use in this book are ones where price-taking consumers and firms optimize given the constraints they face, and where the actions of consumers and firms are consistent in a competitive equilibrium. Building models from microeconomic principles is important, because this will more often give us the correct answers to questions regarding the effects of changes in economic policy. There is relatively little disagreement among macroeconomists concerning approaches to modelling growth, but there are contentious issues in business cycle modelling, between Keynesian macroeconomists and those who argue for non-Keynesian alternative explanations for business cycles. In this chapter, we discussed 11 ideas that are the key insights that we will learn in this book. Then, we looked at seven important recent and current issues that the macroeconomic models in this book will help us to analyze and understand. These issues were the productivity slowdown; government income, government outlays, and the government deficit; inflation; interest rates; energy prices and macroeconomic activity; trade and the twin deficits; and unemployment.

Key Terms

economic model: A description of consumers and firms, their objectives and constraints, and how they interact.

long-run growth: The increase in a nation's productive capacity and average standard of living that occurs over a long period of time.

business cycles: Short-run ups and downs, or booms and recessions, in aggregate economic activity.

gross domestic product (GDP): The quantity of goods and services produced within a country's borders during some specified period of time.

trend: The smooth growth path around which an economic variable cycles.

models: Artificial devices that can replicate the behaviour of real systems.

optimize: The process by which economic agents (firms and consumers) do the best they can given the constraints they face.

equilibrium: The situation in an economy when the actions of all the consumers and firms are consistent.

competitive equilibrium: Equilibrium in which firms and households are assumed to be price-takers, and market prices are such that the quantity supplied equals the quantity demanded in each market in the economy.

rational expectations revolution: Macroeconomics movement that occurred in the 1970s, introducing more microeconomics into macroeconomics.

Lucas critique: The idea that macroeconomic policy analysis can be done in a sensible way only if microeconomic behaviour is taken seriously.

endogenous growth models: Models that describe the economic mechanism determining the rate of economic growth.

Keynesian: Describes macroeconomists who are followers of J. M. Keynes, and who see an active role for government in smoothing business cycles.

money surprise theory: In this theory, developed by Milton Friedman and Robert Lucas, monetary factors are the primary cause of business cycles, and the government should not be active in smoothing cycles.

real business cycle theory: This theory, initiated by Finn Kydland and Edward Prescott, implies that business cycles are caused primarily by shocks to technology and that the government should play a passive role over the business cycle.

Keynesian coordination failure theory: A modern incarnation of Keynesian business cycle theory positing that business cycles are caused by self-fulfilling waves of optimism and pessimism, which may be countered with government policy.

inflation: The rate of change in the average level of prices over time.

Bank of Canada: The central bank of Canada.

search theory: Theory that explains unemployment in terms of the costs of searching for job offers.

efficiency wage theory: Theory positing that workers are unemployed due to an excess supply of labour brought about when firms pay high wages to induce their workers not to shirk.

Phillips curve: A positive relationship between the deviation of aggregate output from trend and the inflation rate.

total factor productivity: The productivity of all factors of production.

productivity slowdown: The period of low productivity growth occurring from the early 1970s until the mid-1980s.

crowding-out: The process by which government spending reduces private sector expenditures on investment and consumption.

government surplus: The difference between taxes and government spending.

government saving: Identical to the government surplus.

government deficit: The negative of the government surplus.

Ricardian equivalence theorem: Theory asserting that a change in taxation by the government has no effect.

price level: The average level of prices.

nominal interest rate: The interest rate in money terms.

real interest rate: Approximately equal to the nominal interest rate minus the expected rate of inflation.

current account surplus: Exports minus imports plus net factor payments to domestic residents from abroad.

net exports: Exports of goods and services minus imports of goods and services.
net factor payments: These are the payments received by domestic factors of production from abroad, minus the payments to foreign factors of production from domestic sources.
current account deficit: Situation in which the current account surplus is negative.
twin deficits: The phenomenon by which a government deficit (surplus) is reflected in a current account deficit (surplus).

Questions for Review

1. What are the primary defining characteristics of macroeconomics?

2. What makes macroeconomics different from microeconomics? What do they have in common?

3. How much richer was the average Canadian in 2001 than in 1926?

4. What are two striking business cycle events in Canada during the last 80 years?

5. List six fundamental macroeconomic questions.

6. In a graph of the natural logarithm of an economic time series, what does the slope of the graph represent?

7. What is the difference between the trend and the business cycle component of an economic time series?

8. Explain why experimentation is difficult in macroeconomics.

9. Why should a macroeconomic model be simple?

10. Should a macroeconomic model be an exact description of the world? Explain why or why not.

11. What are the five elements that make up the basic structure of a macroeconomic model?

12. Why can macroeconomic models be useful? How do we determine whether or not they are useful?

13. Explain why a macroeconomic model should be built from microeconomic principles.

14. What are the four theories of the business cycle that we will study?

15. What are two possible causes of the productivity slowdown?

16. What is the principal effect of an increase in government spending?

17. Why might a decrease in taxes have no effect?

18. What is the cause of inflation in the long run?

19. Explain the difference between the nominal interest rate and the real interest rate.

20. What effect does an increase in the relative price of energy have on aggregate economic activity?

21. How are the government surplus and the current account surplus connected?

22. What are four factors that determine the quantity of unemployment?

Problems

1. Consider the following data on real GDP per capita in Canada:

Year	Canadian Real GDP per Capita (1997 Dollars)
1950	$11 037
1960	13 356
1970	18 312
1980	23 697
1990	27 686
1995	28 431
1996	28 582
1997	29 480
1998	30 412
1999	31 786
2000	32 921
2001	33 080

  a. Calculate the percentage growth rates in real GDP per capita in each of the years 1996 through 2001, from the previous year.
  b. Now, instead of calculating the annual percentage growth rates in the years 1996 through 2001 directly, use as an approximation $100 \times (\log y_t - \log y_{t-1})$, where y_t is real per capita GDP in year t. How close does this approximation come to the actual growth rates you calculated in part (a)?
  c. Repeat parts (a) and (b), but now calculate the percentage rates of growth in real per capita GDP from 1950 to 1960, from 1960 to 1970, from 1970 to 1980, from 1980 to 1990 and from 1990 to 2000. In this case, how large an error do you make by approximating the growth rate by the change in the log? Why is there a difference here relative to parts (a) and (b)?
  d. During what decade from 1950 to 2000 was growth in real per capita GDP the highest? When was it the lowest?

2. Suppose that you had the special powers to travel in time and to carry out any experiment you wanted on the economy. If you could turn back the clock to the time of the Great Depression, what experiment would you like to run on the Canadian economy? Why?

3. Give an example of a model that is used in some area other than economics, other than the road-map example explained in this chapter. What is unrealistic about this model? How well does it perform its intended function?

4. Explain how increases in the relative price of energy may have been a cause of the productivity slowdown, with reference to Figures 1.5 and 1.11.

5. Why do you think government outlays would increase during a recession, as happened in the early 1980s and early 1990s? (See Figure 1.6.)

6. Explain why the total government deficit in Canada was eliminated in the late 1990s, in terms of the behaviour of government income and government outlays.

7. Does Figure 1.8 make you suspicious of the claim that a high rate of inflation is caused by a higher rate of money growth? Why or why not?

8. Why do you think the real interest rate was low during the recession in the mid-1970s?

9. After 2000 the current account surplus increased. Relate this increase to what happened to exports and imports at the time.

10. In Figure 1.15, note that the unemployment rate tends to increase at a much higher rate than the rate at which it decreases. Suggest a reason for this. Why do you think the unemployment rate in Canada was very low at the end of the 1990s?

Working with the Data

1. Graph gross domestic product (GDP) and gross national product (GNP) in 1997 dollars. Is there much difference in these two measures of aggregate economic activity for Canada?

2. Total government expenditures consist of expenditures by the federal government and by provincial and municipal governments. Calculate and graph the ratio of federal government expenditures to total government expenditures. Has the federal government become larger or smaller relative to provincial and municipal governments over time?

3. Using the consumer price index as a measure of the price level, calculate and graph the annual inflation rate for 1969 to 2002. Calculate this as the percentage increase in the CPI from December to December (the annual inflation rate for 1999 would be the percentage increase in the CPI from December 1998 to December 1999). In addition, calculate and graph on the same chart the percentage annual increase in M1++ (a measure of the money supply) for the same years. How does your picture differ from Figure 1.8?

CHAPTER 2

Measurement

Economics is built on the twin pillars of measurement and theory. Measurements of the performance of the economy motivate macroeconomists to build simple models that can organize our thinking about how the economy works. For example, surveys of consumer prices done every year can tell us something about how prices change over time and, coupled with observations on other economic variables, can help us to develop theories that explain *why* prices change over time. Meanwhile, economic theory can better inform us about the most efficient ways to carry out economic measurement. For example, theories of consumer behaviour can tell us something about the appropriate way to use the prices of consumer goods to derive a price index that is a good measure of the price level.

   Our goal in this chapter is to understand the basic issues concerning how key macro-economic variables are measured. These key macroeconomic variables will play the most important roles in the economic models that we will construct and study in the remainder of this book. In particular, in the rest of this chapter we will examine the measurement of GDP and its components, and the measurement of prices, savings, wealth, capital, and labour market variables.

Measuring GDP: The National Income and Expenditure Accounts

The chief aim of national income accounting is to obtain a measure of the total quantity of goods and services produced for the market in a given country over a given period of time. For many issues in macroeconomics (though by no means for all), the measure of aggregate economic activity we are interested in is **gross domestic product (GDP)**, which is the dollar value of final output produced during a given period of time within the borders of Canada. GDP is published on a quarterly basis by Statistics Canada as part of the **National Income and Expenditure Accounts (NIEA)**.

   There are three approaches to measuring GDP, each of which is incorporated in some way in NIEA. All three approaches will give exactly the same measure of GDP, provided there are no errors of measurement in using any of these approaches. The three approaches are the **product approach**, the **expenditure approach**, and the **income approach**. We will discuss each approach in turn, using an example.

In our running example, we consider a simplified economy consisting of a corn producer, a hog producer, consumers, and a government. To keep things simple, suppose that the corn producer can magically cause corn to sprout from the ground (so we do not need to worry about inputs of fertilizer, pesticides, fuel for farm machinery, etc.), and in the current year produces 1 million tonnes of corn, which are sold for $20.00 per tonne, yielding total revenue of $20 million. The corn producer also pays wages of $5 million to its workers (who are the consumers in this economy), $0.5 million in interest on a loan to some consumers, and $1.5 million in taxes to the government. The relevant data for the corn producer are shown in Table 2.1.

TABLE 2.1 **Corn Producer**

Total revenue	$20 million
Wages	$ 5 million
Interest on loan	$ 0.5 million
Taxes	$ 1.5 million

Of the 1 million tonnes of corn produced, 0.6 million tonnes go to the hog producer, who grows hogs using corn as feed. The remaining 0.4 million tonnes are bought by the consumers. Again, all corn is sold at $20 per tonne. Note that corn is serving two roles in this economy. First, it is an **intermediate good**, a good that is produced and then used as an input to another production process—here, the hog production process. Second, it is a final consumption good, in that corn is purchased by consumers. The hog producer produces 20 million kilograms of hogs during the year, and sells all these hogs to consumers at $1.50 per kilogram. The total cost of feed corn for the hog producer is $12 million, and the hog producer pays its workers $4 million in wages and the government $3 million in taxes. Data for the hog producer are provided in Table 2.2.

TABLE 2.2 **Hog Producer**

Total revenue	$30 million
Cost of feed corn	$12 million
Wages	$ 4 million
Taxes	$ 3 million

Next, we need to calculate after-tax profits for each of the producers. After-tax profits in this example are simply

After-tax profits = Total revenue − Wages − Interest − Cost of intermediate inputs − Taxes

Therefore, from Tables 2.1 and 2.2 above, we calculate after-tax profits in Table 2.3.

TABLE 2.3 **After-Tax Profits**

Corn producer	$13 million
Hog producer	$11 million

The government collects taxes and then uses all of this tax revenue to pay government workers (some of the consumers) to build a bridge. Suppose the workers cut down trees from public land to build a wooden bridge, so that we neglect the material inputs. Let's say the government collects $1 million in taxes from consumers, then the total taxes collected will be $5.5 million (i.e., $4.5 million from producers and $1 million from consumers). The data for the government are as shown in Table 2.4.

TABLE 2.4 **Government**

Tax revenue	$5.5 million
Wages	$5.5 million

Consumers work for the producers and for the government, earning total wages of $14.5 million. They receive $0.5 million in interest from the corn producer, pay $1 million in taxes to the government, and they also receive after-tax profits of $24 million from the producers, since some of the consumers own all the production units. Data for the consumers are shown in Table 2.5.

TABLE 2.5 **Consumers**

Wage income	$14.5 million
Interest income	$ 0.5 million
Taxes	$ 1 million
Profits distributed by producers	$24 million

Now, given the above data for this simple economy, we will examine how GDP would be calculated using the three different national income accounting approaches.

THE PRODUCT APPROACH TO MEASURING GDP

The product approach to NIEA is also called the **value-added** approach. This is because the main principle in the product approach is that GDP is calculated as *the sum of value added to goods and services in production across all productive units in the economy.* To calculate GDP using the product approach, we want to add the value of all goods produced in the economy, and then subtract the value of all intermediate goods used in production to obtain total value added. If we did not subtract the value of intermediate goods used in production, we would be double-counting. In our example, we do not want to count the value of the corn used in hog production as part of GDP.

In the example, the corn producer does not use any intermediate goods in production, so value added in producing corn, which is the corn producer's total revenue, is $20 million. For the hog producer, however, valued added is total revenue minus the value of the corn used in production; thus, total value added for the hog producer is $18 million. For government production, we have a problem, because the bridge the government built was not sold at market prices. Standard practice here is to value the bridge at the cost of the inputs to production. Here, the only input to production was labour, so the total value added for the government is $5.5 million. Therefore, total value added, or GDP, is $43.5 million. The GDP calculation using the product approach is summarized in Table 2.6.

TABLE 2.6 **GDP Using the Product Approach**

Value added—corn	$20 million
Value added—hogs	$18 million
Value added—government	$ 5.5 million
GDP	$43.5 million

THE EXPENDITURE APPROACH

In the expenditure approach, we calculate GDP as *total spending on all final goods and services production in the economy.* Note again that we do not count spending on intermediate goods. In the NIEA, total expenditure is calculated as

$$\text{Total expenditure} = C + I + G + NX,$$

where C denotes expenditures on consumption, I is investment expenditure (i.e., expenditure on goods that are produced but not consumed during the period under consideration), G is government expenditure, and NX is net exports—that is, total exports of Canadian goods and services minus total imports into Canada. We add exports because this includes goods and services produced within Canada. Imports are subtracted because, in general, each of C, I, and G includes some goods and services that were produced abroad, and we do not want to include these in Canadian GDP.

In our example, there is no investment, no exports, and no imports, so that $I = NX = 0$. Consumers spend $8 million on corn and $30 million on hogs, so that $C = \$38$ million. For government expenditures, again we count the $5.5 million in wages spent by the government as if the government had purchased the bridge as a final good at $5.5 million, and so $G = \$5.5$ million. Therefore, calculating GDP using the expenditure approach, we get

$$GDP = C + I + G + NX = \$43.5 \text{ million.}$$

The GDP calculation using the expenditure approach is shown in Table 2.7. Note that we obtain the same answer calculating GDP this way as using the product approach, as we should.

TABLE 2.7 **GDP Using the Expenditure Approach**

Consumption	$38 million
Investment	0
Government expenditures	$ 5.5 million
Net exports	0
GDP	$43.5 million

THE INCOME APPROACH

To calculate GDP using the income approach, we want to *add up all incomes received by economic agents contributing to production.* Incomes will include the profits made by firms. In the NIEA, incomes include compensation of employees (wages, salaries, and benefits), corporate profits, net interest, net income of farm operators and unincorporated businesses, taxes less subsidies on factors of production, taxes less subsidies on products, government business enterprise profits before taxes, inventory valuation adjustment, and depreciation. Depreciation represents the value of productive capital (plant and equipment) that wears out during the period we are considering. Depreciation is taken out when we calculate profits, and so it needs to be added in again when we compute GDP. The inventory valuation adjustment enters for a similar reason.

In the example, we need to include the wage income of consumers, $14.5 million, as a component of GDP. In addition, we need to count the profits of producers. If we do this on an after-tax basis, total profits for the two producers are $24 million. Next, we add the interest income of consumers (this is net interest), which is $0.5 million. Finally, we need to add the taxes paid by producers to the government, which are essentially government income. This amount is $4.5 million. Total GDP is then $43.5 million, which of course is the same answer that we obtained for the other two approaches. The calculation of GDP using the income approach is summarized in Table 2.8.

TABLE 2.8 **GDP Using the Income Approach**

Wage Income	$14.5 million
After-tax profits	$24 million
Interest income	$ 0.5 million
Taxes	$ 4.5 million
GDP	$43.5 million

Why do the product approach, the expenditure approach, and the income approach yield the same GDP measure? This happens because the total quantity of output, or value added, in the economy is ultimately sold, thus showing up as expenditure, and what is spent on all output produced is income, in some form or other, for someone in the economy. If we let Y denote total GDP in the economy, then Y is total aggregate output, and it is also aggregate income. Further, it is also true as an identity that aggregate income equals aggregate expenditure, or

$$Y = C + I + G + NX.$$

This relationship is sometimes referred to as the **income–expenditure identity**, as the quantity on the left-hand side of the identity is aggregate income, and the right-hand side is the sum of the components of aggregate expenditure.

AN EXAMPLE WITH INVENTORY INVESTMENT

One component of investment expenditures is inventory investment, which consists of any goods that are produced but are not consumed during the current period. Stocks of inventories consist of inventories of finished goods (e.g., automobiles that are stored on the lot), goods in process (e.g., automobiles still on the assembly line), and raw materials.

Suppose in our running example that everything is identical to the above, except that the corn producer produces 1.3 million tonnes of corn instead of 1 million, and that the extra 0.3 million tonnes is not sold but is stored as inventory. In terms of the value-added approach, GDP is the total value of corn produced, which is now $26 million, plus the value of hogs produced, $30 million, minus the value of intermediate goods used up in hog production, $12 million, plus value added by the government, $5.5 million, for total GDP of $49.5 million. Note that we value the corn inventory at the market price of corn in the example. In practice, this need not be the case; sometimes the book value of inventories carried by firms is not the same as market value, though sound economics says it should be.

Now, for the expenditure approach, $C = \$38$ million, $NX = 0$, and $G = \$5.5$ million as before, but now $I = \$6$ million, so GDP $= C + I + G + NX - \$49.5$ million. It may seem odd that the inventory investment of $6 million is counted as expenditure, since this does not appear to be expenditure on a final good or service. However, the convention is to treat the inventory investment here as if the corn producer bought $6 million in corn from itself.

Finally, in terms of the income approach, wage income to consumers is $14.5 million, interest income to consumers is $0.5 million, taxes are $4.5 million, as before, and total profits after taxes for the two producers are now $30 million (i.e., $19 million plus $11 million), for total GDP of $49.5 million. Here, we add the $6 million in inventories to the corn producer's profits, since this is an addition to the firm's assets.

AN EXAMPLE WITH INTERNATIONAL TRADE

To show what can happen when exports and imports come into the picture, we will take our original example and alter it slightly. Suppose that the hog producer imports 0.2 million tonnes of corn at $20 per tonne, in addition to the corn purchased from the domestic corn producer, and that all of this corn is used to feed hogs. The hog producer still produces 20 million kilograms of hogs but now sells 15 million kilograms to domestic consumers and exports 5 million kilograms, with all hogs selling as before at $1.50 per kilogram.

Here, following the value-added approach, the value added by the domestic corn producer is $20 million as before. For the hog producer, value added is the value of hogs produced, $30 million, minus the value of intermediate inputs, which is $16 million (i.e., $12 million plus $4 million), including the cost of imported corn. As before, total value added for the government is $5.5 million. Therefore, GDP is total value added for the two producers and the government, or $39.5 million.

Next, using the expenditure approach, consumption of corn by consumers is $8 million and hog consumption is $22.5 million, so that $C = \$30.5$ million. Government expenditures are the same as in the initial example, with $G = \$5.5$ million, and we have $I = 0$. The only exports are hogs, so that total exports are $7.5 million. The only imports are corn, so that total imports are $4 million. Thus, net exports are $NX = \$7.5$ million $- \$4$ million $= \$3.5$ million. We then have GDP $= C + I + G + NX = \$39.5$ million.

Finally, following the income approach, the wage income of consumers is $14.5 million, interest income of consumers is $0.5 million, and taxes are $4.5 million, as in the initial example. The after-tax profits of the corn producer are $13 million, also as before. The change here is in the after-tax profits of the hog producer, which are reduced by $4 million, the value of the imported corn, so that after-tax hog producer profits are $7 million. Total GDP is then $39.5 million.

GROSS NATIONAL PRODUCT (GNP)

At one time, **gross national product (GNP)** was used in Canada as the official measure of aggregate production. In line with international practice, however, the official measure is now GDP. GNP measures the value of output produced by domestic factors of production, whether or not the production takes place (as is the case for GDP) inside Canadian borders. For example, if an oil well in South America is owned and managed by Canadian residents, then the incomes accruing to Canadian factors of production include the managerial income and profits of this oil well, and this is included in Canadian GNP, but not in Canadian GDP. Similarly, if a Wal-Mart store in Saskatchewan has U.S. owners, the profits of the store would not be included in GNP, as these profits are not income for Canadian residents, but the profits would be included in GDP.

In practice, there is little difference between GDP and GNP in some countries, such as the United States. However, for Canada the difference is significant. Figure 2.1 shows GNP (the coloured line) and GDP (the black line) for Canada during the period 1961–2002. Clearly, GNP is typically significantly smaller than GDP in Canada. For example, in the third quarter of 2002, GDP was 2.23% higher than GNP. The reason for this difference is that a large fraction of productive plant and equipment in Canada is foreign-owned.

WHAT DOES GDP LEAVE OUT?

GDP is intended simply as a measure of the quantity of output produced and exchanged in the economy as a whole. However, sometimes GDP, or GDP per person, is used as a measure of aggregate economic welfare. There are at least two problems with this approach. The first is that aggregate GDP does not take into account how income is distributed across the individuals in the population. At the extreme, if one person in the economy has all the income and the rest of the people have no income, the average level of economic welfare in the economy would be very low. Second, GDP leaves out all nonmarket activity, such as work in the home. If people eat restaurant meals rather than eating at home, then GDP will rise, because there are now more services produced in the market than before. People should be better off as a result, since they had the option of eating at home but chose to go out. However, this increase in GDP exaggerates the increase in economic welfare, as GDP does not measure the value added when food is cooked at home.

GDP may be an inaccurate measure of welfare, but there are also some problems with GDP as a measure of aggregate output, two of which are as follows. First, economic activities in the so-called **underground economy** are, by definition, not counted in GDP. The underground economy includes any unreported economic activity. A high-profile example of underground activity is trade in illegal drugs; a low-profile example

FIGURE 2.1

GDP and GNP for Canada (1961–2002)

GNP is GDP plus payments from abroad to Canadian factors of production, minus payments to foreign factors of production for output produced in Canada. The figure shows that there is a significant difference between GNP and GDP in Canada. This is because the net factor payments flowing out of Canada are relatively large.

Source: Adapted from the Statistics Canada CANSIM database, Series v498086, v499688.

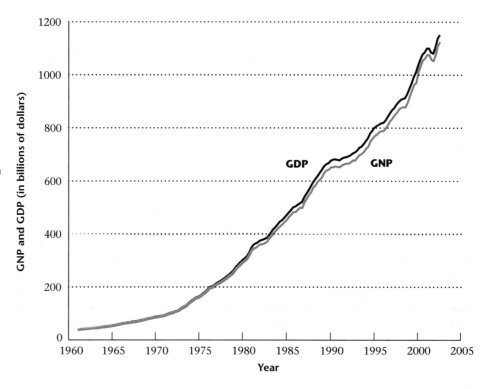

is the exchange of babysitting services for cash. Economic activity goes underground so as to avoid legal penalties and taxation, and underground activity often involves cash transactions. The size of the underground economy may indeed be significant in Canada, as evidenced by the fact that the quantity of Canadian currency held per Canadian resident was about $1250 at the end of 2002.[1] Clearly, most individuals engaged in standard market transactions do not hold this much currency. Further, this large quantity of Canadian currency in circulation does not reflect illegal transactions that take place in Canada using other currencies, particularly U.S. dollars.

A second problem in measuring GDP, which we encountered in our example, is how to count government expenditures. Most of what the government produces is not sold at market prices. For example, how are we to value roads, bridges, and national defence services? The solution in the NIEA, as in our example, is to value government expenditures at cost, that is, the payments to all of the factors of production that went into producing the good or service. In some cases, this could overvalue what is produced; for example, if the government produced something that nobody used, such as a highway to nowhere. In other cases, government production could be undervalued; for example, we might be willing to pay much more for health care than what it costs in terms of wages, salaries, materials, and so forth.

---

[1]*Bank of Canada Review* and Statistics Canada CANSIM database, Series v1.

THE COMPONENTS OF AGGREGATE EXPENDITURE

Typically, particularly in constructing economic models to understand how the economy works, we are interested mainly in the expenditure side of the NIEA. Here, we will consider each of the expenditure components in more detail. Table 2.9 gives the GDP components for 2001.

Consumption Consumption expenditures are the largest expenditure component of Canadian GDP, accounting for 56.8% of GDP in 2001 (see Table 2.9). **Consumption** is expenditure on consumer goods and services during the current period, and the components of consumption are durable goods, semi-durable goods, nondurable goods, and services. Durable goods include household appliances, furniture, and video equipment, while examples of semi-durables are clothing, window coverings, and footwear. Nondurable goods include food, electricity, and fuel, whereas services are intangible items such as haircuts and hotel stays. Note that some items included in consumption are clearly not consumed within the period. For example, if the period is one year, an automobile may provide services to the buyer for ten years or more, and is therefore not a consumption good, but might economically be more appropriately considered an investment expenditure rather than consumption expenditure when it is bought. Note that the purchase of a used car or other used durable good is not included in GDP, but the services provided (e.g., by a dealer) in selling a used car would be included.

Investment In Table 2.9, investment expenditures were 16.8% of GDP in 2001. **Investment** is expenditure on goods that are produced but not consumed during the current period. There are two types of investment. These are **fixed investment**, which is production of capital, such as plant, equipment, and housing, and **inventory investment**,

TABLE 2.9 **Gross Domestic Product for Canada for 2001**

Component of GDP	$ Billions	% of GDP*
GDP	1092.2	100
Consumption	620.8	56.8
Durables	84.8	7.8
Semi-durables	54.4	5.0
Nondurables	149.4	13.7
Services	332.0	30.4
Investment	184.0	16.8
Nonresidential	137.8	12.6
Residential	52.2	4.8
Change in inventories	−6.0	−0.5
Government expenditures	231.1	21.1
Government consumption	204.5	18.7
Government investment	26.6	2.4
Net exports	56.5	5.2
Exports	473.0	43.3
Imports	−416.5	−38.1

Source: Statistics Canada, CANSIM database, Table 380-0002.
*Percentages do not add up to 100 because of rounding.

which consists of goods that are essentially put into storage. The components of fixed investment are *nonresidential investment* and *residential investment*. Nonresidential investment adds to the plant, equipment, and software that make up the capital stock for producing goods and services. Residential investment—housing—is also productive, in that it produces housing services.

Though investment is a much smaller fraction of GDP than consumption is, investment plays a very important role in business cycles. Investment is much more variable than consumption or GDP, and some components of investment also tend to lead the business cycle. For example, an upward or downward blip in housing investment tends to precede an upward or downward blip in GDP. We will study this phenomenon further in Chapter 3.

Net Exports As exports were greater than imports in 2001, Canada ran a trade surplus in goods and services with the rest of the world—that is, **net exports** were positive (see Table 2.9). Net exports, at 5.2% of GDP, represent a significant component of Canadian production. Exports were 43.3% of GDP in 2001 while imports were 38.1% of GDP. Thus, trade with the rest of the world in goods and services is very important to the Canadian economy, as we noted in Chapter 1.

Government Expenditures **Government expenditures**, which consist of expenditures by federal, provincial, and municipal governments on final goods and services, were 21.1% of GDP in 2001, as seen in Table 2.9. The main components of government expenditures are *government consumption* (18.7% of GDP in 2001), and *government investment* (2.4% of GDP in 2001). In the NIEA we make the important distinction between government consumption and government gross investment, just as we distinguish between private consumption and private investment. An important point is that the government spending included in the NIEA is only the expenditures on final goods and services. This does not include **transfers**, which are very important in the government budget. These outlays essentially transfer purchasing power from one group of economic agents to another, and they include such items as payments under Old Age Security and the Canada Pension Plan as well as benefits under the Employment Insurance System. Transfers are not included in GDP, as they are simply money transfers from one group of people to another—in other words, income redistribution rather than income creation.

Nominal and Real GDP and Price Indices

While the components of GDP for any specific time period give us the total dollar value of goods and services produced in the economy during that period, for many purposes we would like to make comparisons between GDP data in different time periods. Such comparisons can tell us something about growth in the productive capacity of the economy over time, and about growth in our standard of living. However, one obstacle is that the average level of prices changes over time, so that part of the increase in GDP that we typically observe is due to inflation. In this section, we show how to adjust for this effect of inflation on the growth in GDP, and in so doing we arrive also at a measure of the price level and the inflation rate.

A **price index** is a weighted average of the prices of a set of the goods and services produced in the economy over a period of time. If the price index includes prices of all goods and services, then that price index is a measure of the general **price level**, or the average level of prices across all goods and services. We use price indices to measure the **inflation rate**, which is the rate of change in the price level from one period of time to another. If we can measure the inflation rate, we can also determine how much of a change in GDP from one period to another is purely *nominal*, and how much is *real*. A **nominal change** in GDP is a change in GDP that occurred only because the price level changed, whereas a **real change** in GDP is an increase in the physical quantity of output.

REAL GDP

To see how real GDP is calculated in the NIEA, it helps to consider an example. Imagine an economy in which the only goods produced are apples and oranges. In year 1, 50 apples and 100 oranges are produced, and the prices of apples and oranges are $1 and $0.80, respectively. In year 2, 80 apples and 120 oranges are produced, and the prices of apples and oranges are $1.25 and $1.60, respectively. These data are displayed in Table 2.10.

TABLE 2.10 **Data for Real GDP Example**

	Apples	*Oranges*
Quantity in year 1	50	100
Price in year 1	$1.00	$0.80
Quantity in year 2	80	120
Price in year 2	$1.25	$1.60

Using the product approach, the calculation of nominal GDP in each year is straightforward here, as there are no intermediate goods. In year 1, nominal GDP = ($1 × 50) + ($0.80 × 100) = $130, and in year 2 we have nominal GDP = ($1.25 × 80) + ($1.60 × 120) = $292. Therefore, the percentage increase in nominal GDP from year 1 to year 2 is $(\frac{292}{130} - 1) \times 100\% = 124.6\%$; that is, nominal GDP more than doubled from year 1 to year 2.

Now, the question is, how much of this increase in nominal GDP is accounted for by inflation, and how much by an increase in the real quantity of aggregate output produced? Until recently, the practice in Canadian NIEA was first to choose a base year, and then to calculate real GDP using these base year prices. That is, rather than multiplying the quantities produced in a given year by current year prices (which is what we do when calculating nominal GDP), we multiply by base year prices to obtain real GDP. In the example, suppose that we use year 1 as the base year. Then, real GDP in year 1 is the same as nominal GDP for that year, since year 1 is the base year. That is, year 1 real GDP is $130. Now, for year 2 real GDP, we use year 2 quantities and year 1 prices to obtain real GDP in year 2 = ($1 × 80) + ($0.80 × 120) = $176. Therefore, the percentage increase in real GDP from year 1 to year 2, using year 1 as the base year, is $(\frac{176}{130} - 1) \times 100\% = 35.4\%$. Alternatively, suppose that we use year 2 as the base year.

Then, year 2 real GDP is the same as year 2 nominal GDP, which is $292. Year 1 GDP, using year 1 quantities and year 2 prices = ($1.25 × 50) + ($1.60 × 100) = $222.50. According to this calculation, the percentage increase in GDP from year 1 to year 2 is $(\frac{292}{222.5} - 1) \times 100\% = 31.2\%$.

A key message from the example is that the choice of the base year will matter for the calculation of GDP. If year 1 is used as the base year, then the increase in real GDP is 35.4%, and if year 2 is the base year, real GDP is calculated to increase by 31.2%. The reason the choice of the base year matters in the example, and in reality, is that the relative prices of goods change over time. In our example, the relative price of apples to oranges is $\frac{1.00}{\$0.80} = 1.25$ in year 1, and this relative price is $\frac{\$1.25}{\$1.60} = 0.78$ in year 2. Therefore, apples became cheaper relative to oranges from year 1 to year 2. If relative prices had remained the same between year 1 and year 2, then the choice of the base year would not matter. In calculating real GDP, the problem of changing relative prices would not be too great in calculating GDP close to the base year (say 1993 or 1994 relative to a base year in 1992), since relative prices would typically not change much over a short period of time. Over many years, however, the problem could be severe, for example, in calculating real GDP in 2002 relative to a base year in 1982.

The solution to this problem, adopted in the NIEA, is to use a **chain-weighting** scheme for calculating real GDP, which is essentially like using a rolling base period. The actual chain-weighting scheme used in the NIEA is too complicated to discuss in detail here, but for illustration we will provide an example that closely approximates actual chain-weighting. In our chain-weighting scheme, to calculate the percentage increase in GDP from one year to the next, the prices that are used are the average prices for the two years. In the example, we would take the average price for apples over year 1 and year 2, which is $1.125, and the average price for oranges, which is $1.20, and calculate real GDP in year 1 = ($1.125 × 50) + ($1.20 × 100) = $176.25, and real GDP in year 2 = ($1.125 × 80) + ($1.20 × 120) = $234.00. Then, according to our chain-weighting method, the percentage increase in real GDP from year 1 to year 2 is $(\frac{234}{176.25} - 1) \times 100\%$ = 32.8%. Note that the measure of real GDP growth we obtain here is different from what came from using either year 1 or year 2 as a base year.

In our illustrative chain-weighting approach, the percentage change in real GDP for two adjacent periods (say, 1995 and 1996) is calculated using the average prices for the two years; then for the next two adjacent periods (1996 and 1997), the percentage change in real GDP is calculated using the average prices for those two years, and so forth. In this sense, annual GDP is "chained" together in terms of the base year prices that are used. Chain-weighting should in principle give a more accurate measure of the year-to-year, or quarter-to-quarter, changes in real GDP.

How much difference there is between real and nominal GDP depends on how high the inflation rate is. If the inflation rate is very high, then nominal GDP will grow at a much higher rate than real GDP. In Figure 2.2 we graph nominal GDP (the black line) and real GDP (the coloured line) for the period 1961–2002. Here, real GDP was calculated using the chain-weighting technique, and it is measured in chained 1997 dollars.[2]

---

[2]When real GDP is calculated for many years using the chain-weighting technique, real GDP is scaled so that all years are comparable, in this case in 1997 dollars.

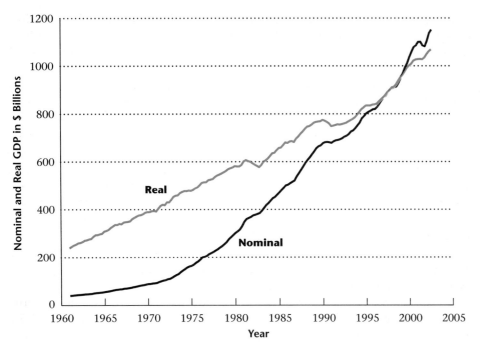

FIGURE 2.2
Nominal GDP (black line) and Chain-Weighted Real GDP (coloured line) for the Period 1961–2002
Note that the two time series cross in 1997 because real GDP is measured in 1997 dollars. The growth rate in real GDP is smaller than the growth rate for nominal GDP because of positive inflation over this period.

Source: Adpated from the Statistics Canada CANSIM database, Series v498086, v1992067.

Thus, real GDP is the same as nominal GDP in 1997, where the two time series cross. Since the inflation rate was positive, and was particularly high in the 1970s, real GDP grows in Figure 2.2 at a lower rate than does nominal GDP.

MEASURES OF THE PRICE LEVEL

There are two commonly used measures of the price level. The first is the **implicit GDP price deflator**, and the second is the **consumer price index (CPI)**. The implicit GDP price deflator is measured as

$$\text{Implicit GDP price deflator} = \frac{\text{Nominal GDP}}{\text{Real GDP}} \times 100.$$

Here, multiplying by 100 just normalizes the price deflator to 100 in the base year (if there is one). For the example above, the price deflator we calculate would depend on whether we use year 1 or year 2 as a base year, or compute chain-weighted GDP. We give the results in Table 2.11. Note in Table 2.11 that the answers we get for the percentage rate of inflation between year 1 and year 2 depend critically on how we measure real GDP.

TABLE 2.11 Implicit GDP Price Deflators, Example

	Year 1	Year 2	% Increase
Year 1 = base year	100	165.9	65.9
Year 2 = base year	58.4	100	71.2
Chain-weighting	73.8	124.8	69.1

The alternative measure of the price level, the CPI, is not as broadly based as the implicit GDP price deflator, since it includes only goods and services that are purchased by consumers. Further, the CPI is a fixed-weight price index, which takes the quantities in some base year as being the typical goods bought by the average consumer during that base year, and then uses those quantities as weights to calculate the index in each year. Thus, the CPI in the current year would be

$$\text{Current year CPI} = \frac{\text{Current year total expenditures}}{\text{Current year total expenditures at base year prices}} \times 100.$$

In the example, if we take year 1 as the base year, then the year 1 (base year) CPI is 100, and the year 2 CPI is $\frac{222.5}{130} \times 100 = 171.2$, so that the percentage increase in the CPI from year 1 to year 2 is 71.2%.

In practice, there can be substantial differences between the inflation rates calculated using the implicit GDP price deflator and those calculated using the CPI. Figure 2.3 shows the GDP deflator inflation rate (the black line) and CPI inflation rate (the coloured line), calculated quarter by quarter, for Canada over the period 1961–2002. Note that the two measures of the inflation rate track each other broadly, but the CPI inflation rate tends to be somewhat more volatile than the GDP deflator inflation rate. At times, there can be substantial differences between the two measures. These differences in inflation rate measures could matter greatly for contracts that are geared to the inflation rate, or for the formulation of monetary policy, where close attention is paid to inflation performance.

FIGURE 2.3

Inflation Rate Calculated from the CPI (coloured line), and Calculated from the Implicit GDP Price Deflator (black line) for the Period 1961–2002.

These measures are broadly similar, but at times there can be substantial differences.

Source: Adapted from the Statistics Canada CANSIM database, Series v1997756, v735319.

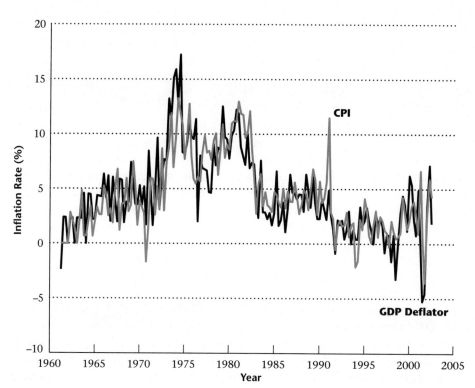

PROBLEMS WITH MEASURING REAL GDP AND THE PRICE LEVEL

As we saw above, particularly in how the implicit GDP price deflator is derived, the measurement of real GDP and the measurement of the price level are intimately related. If a particular measure of real GDP underestimates the growth in real GDP, the rate of inflation will be overestimated. In practice, there are three important problems with measuring real GDP and the price level.

The first problem was mentioned above, which is that relative prices change over time. We showed how chain-weighting corrects this problem in the measurement of real GDP, and therefore corrects for the bias that relative price changes would introduce in the measurement of inflation using the implicit GDP price deflator. Changes in relative prices can also introduce severe bias in how the CPI measures inflation. When there is a relative price change, consumers typically will purchase less of the goods that have become more expensive and more of those that have become relatively cheap. This is what is represented in the previous example, where apples became cheaper relative to oranges in year 2, and the ratio of apples consumed to oranges consumed increased. In computing the CPI, the implicit assumption that consumers do not change their buying habits when relative price changes occur is clearly false. As a result, goods that become relatively more expensive receive a higher weight than they should in the CPI, and therefore the CPI-based measure of the rate of inflation will be biased upward. This is, in fact, a serious policy issue (see the box Macroeconomics in Action 2.1). Since some federal transfer payments, including Canada Pension Plan and Old Age Security payments, are indexed to the CPI, and therefore an upward bias in CPI inflation would also commit the federal government to higher transfer payments. This would in turn increase the size of the federal government budget deficit. Also, federal income tax brackets are geared to CPI inflation. Upward bias in CPI inflation causes tax revenues to fall, increasing the government deficit. Rather than the rate of increase in the CPI, a more accurate measure of the rate of inflation in consumer goods is the implicit consumption price deflator, which is the price deflator (see Macroeconomics in Action 2.1).

A second problem in measuring real GDP concerns the changes in the quality of goods over time. Consider the case of 2002 vintage cars versus 1952 vintage cars. Clearly, the price of a new car in 2002 was much higher than the price of a new car in 1952, but the 2002 car is very different from the 1952 car. In 2002, most cars sold in Canada had computerized devices to monitor engine performance, automatic transmissions, power windows, air bags, seatbelts, and CD players, none of which were standard equipment (or in some cases even invented) in 1952. In a sense, the 2002 car is "more car," since its quality is higher, and so some of the increase in price from 1952 to 2002 simply represents the fact that the buyer is receiving more in exchange for his or her money. To the extent that NIEA does not compensate for changes in quality over time, growth in real GDP will be biased downward and inflation will be biased upward.

A third problem is how measured GDP takes account of new goods. For example, personal computers were introduced in the early 1980s, and they did not exist in the NIEA before then. Clearly, we cannot make a straightforward calculation of real GDP growth from the 1970s to the 1980s, as there were no prices existing for personal computers in the 1970s. If the NIEA does not correctly take account of the fact that the new personal computers that were introduced (initially at very high prices) were a huge

Price Indices and Monetary Policy in Canada

In February 1991, the Bank of Canada adopted inflation targets as an explicit objective for monetary policy. Other central banks in the world, including the Bank of England, the Reserve Bank of New Zealand, the Swedish Riksbank, and the Reserve Bank of Australia, have similar targets.

If a central bank adopts inflation targeting as a goal, an important consideration is the choice of the measure of inflation to use in the targeting procedure. First, the measure of inflation used should be easily understood and observed by the public, so that the performance of the central bank in meeting its goals can be readily evaluated. Second, the measure should accurately reflect actual inflation in the economy. Third, the measure of inflation should be easily controlled by the central bank.

The inflation rate that was chosen for the Bank of Canada to target was the 12-month rate of increase in the consumer price index (CPI). The CPI certainly meets the criterion of being easily understood and observed by the public. Statistics Canada reports the CPI on a monthly basis, and these reports are typically widely reported in the news media. However, as pointed out in this chapter, the rate of change in the CPI is a biased measure of inflation. The Boskin Commission, which studied the CPI in the United States in the mid-1990s, found that the rate of change in the U.S. consumer price index tended to be about one percentage point higher than the actual inflation rate.[1] In Canada, the upward bias in inflation using the CPI is thought to be about 0.5 percentage points.

There are many factors other than monetary policy that cause the CPI to change from month to month. For example, the CPI might spike upward because of a drought that results in a shortage of food and higher food prices, because the government increases sales taxes, or because of a temporary shortage of crude oil on world markets. The Bank of Canada may not wish to respond to these temporary increases in the rate of inflation, as they are likely to be reversed before monetary policy could have any effect on the rate of inflation. As a result, in addition to targeting the CPI rate of inflation, the Bank of Canada monitors a "core" measure of the inflation rate, which is the CPI rate of inflation

quality advance over old-fashioned calculators and slide rules, then this could bias downward the measure of real GDP growth and bias upward the measure of the inflation rate.

Savings, Wealth, and Capital

While the components of GDP in the NIEA measure aggregate activity that takes place within the current period, another key aspect of the economy that is of interest to macroeconomists is aggregate productive capacity, and how aggregate savings adds to this productive capacity. In this section we will explore, by way of several accounting identities, the relationships among savings, wealth, and capital.

An important distinction in economics is between *flows* and *stocks*. A **flow** is a rate per unit time, whereas a **stock** is the quantity in existence of some object at a point in time. In the NIEA, GDP, consumption, investment, government spending, and net exports are all flows. For example, GDP is measured in dollars spent per period. In con-

neglecting effects on inflation that are judged to be temporary.[2]

The current measure of the core price level used by the Bank of Canada is what was previously known as CPIX. This price index leaves out the eight components of expenditure in the CPI for which prices are most volatile. These components are fruit, vegetables, gasoline, fuel oil, natural gas, intercity transportation, tobacco, and mortgage interest costs. As well, CPIX adjusts the CPI for the effects of indirect taxes such as sales and excise taxes. While the use of this more narrow measure perhaps has some merit, there are some drawbacks as well. First, what is to stop the Bank of Canada from focusing the public's attention on particular measures of inflation that put the Bank's performance in a favourable light? We need to be aware of the natural tendency of central bankers to hide information. Second, the particular goods which have the most volatile prices during the current year may not be the same ones having volatile prices next year, or ten years from now, necessitating continuous changes in the measure of core inflation. Note that the Bank of Canada changed its measure of the core price level to CPIX from CPIXFET in May 2001.

What other choices does the Bank of Canada have in trying to measure and target inflation? The Bank could monitor the CPI rather than some core measure of the price level and, in light of the limitations of the CPI, widen its inflation targets. Alternatively, the Bank could try using a different measure of the price level. For example, one possibility is to use the implicit GDP price deflator, which has the advantage of not being biased to the degree that the CPI is, but has the disadvantage of including some goods, such as government-provided goods and services, which do not have market prices that can be affected by monetary policy. In the United States, some proponents of inflation targeting argue that a good measure of the inflation rate is the rate of change in the implicit consumption deflator. The implicit consumption deflator is calculated similarly to the implicit GDP deflator, but is measured as the ratio of nominal consumption expenditures to real consumption expenditures.

---

[1]See M. Boskin, E. Deulberger, R. Gordon, Z. Griliches, and D. Jorgensen, 1996, "Toward a More Accurate Measure of the Cost of Living," *Final Report of the Senate Finance Committee*.

[2]See T. Macklem, 2001, "A New Measure of Core Inflation," *Banh of Canada Review*, Autumn, pp. 3–12.

---

trast, the quantity of housing in existence in Canada at the end of a given year is a stock. In the following, we will see that national saving is a flow, while the nation's wealth is a stock. In particular, national saving is the flow that is added to the stock of the nation's wealth in each year. A classic analogy is the example of water flowing into a bathtub, where the quantity of water coming out of the faucet per minute is a flow, whereas the quantity of water in the bathtub at any point in time is a stock.

Savings can mean very different things, depending on whether we are referring to the private (nongovernment) sector, the government, or the nation as a whole. For the private sector, to determine savings we first need to start with what the private sector has available to spend, which is **private disposable income**, denoted Y^d. We have

$$Y^d = Y + NFP + TR + INT - T,$$

where Y is GDP, NFP is net factor payments from abroad to Canadian residents, TR is transfers from the government to the private sector, INT is interest on the government debt, and T is taxes. Recall that GNP is $Y + NFP$. What the private sector saves is simply what it has available to spend minus what it consumes, and so letting S^p denote **private sector saving**, we have

$$S^p = Y^d - C = Y + NFP + TR + INT - T - C.$$

What the government has available to spend is its tax revenue, T, minus TR, minus INT, and what it consumes is government expenditures, G. Thus, **government saving** S^g is given by

$$S^g = T - TR - INT - G.$$

Government saving is the **government surplus**, and the government surplus is equal to the negative of the **government deficit**, denoted D, or

$$D = -S^g = -T + TR + INT + G,$$

which is just government outlays minus government receipts.

If we add private saving and government saving, we obtain **national saving**,

$$S = S^P + S^g = Y + NFP - C - G,$$

which is GNP minus private consumption, minus government consumption. Since the income–expenditure identity gives $Y = C + I + G + NX$, we can substitute for Y in the above equation to obtain

$$\begin{aligned} S &= Y + NFP - C - G \\ &= C + I + G + NX + NFP - C - G \\ &= I + NX + NFP. \end{aligned}$$

Thus, national saving must equal investment plus net exports plus net factor payments from abroad. The quantity $NX + NFP$ is the **current account surplus** with the rest of the world, which we will denote CA; thus, we have

$$S = I + CA.$$

The current account surplus is a measure of the balance of trade in goods with the rest of the world. The above identity reflects the fact that any domestic savings not absorbed by domestic investment must be shipped outside the country in the form of goods and services.

As a flow, national saving represents additions to the **nation's wealth** (the stock of assets held by the country as a whole). Since $S = I + CA$, wealth is accumulated in two ways. First, wealth is accumulated through investment, I, which is additions to the nation's **capital stock**. The capital stock is the quantity of plants, equipment, housing, and inventories in existence in an economy at a point in time. Second, wealth is accumulated through current account surpluses, CA, since a current account surplus implies that Canadian residents are accumulating claims on foreigners. The current account surplus, CA, represents increases in claims on foreigners. If goods are flowing from Canada to other countries, then these goods must be paid for with a transfer of wealth from outside Canada to Canadian residents. The current account surplus is then a flow, while the quantity of claims on foreigners in existence in Canada at a particular point in time is a stock.

Labour Market Measurement

The labour market variables we will focus on here are those measured in the monthly survey carried out by Statistics Canada. In this survey, the population aged 15 and older is divided into three groups: the **employed**—those who worked part-time or full-time during the past week; the **unemployed**—those who were not employed during the past week, but actively searched for work at some time during the last four weeks; and **not in the labour force**—those who are neither employed or unemployed. Thus, the labour force is the employed plus the unemployed.

Of key interest in analyzing the results of the household survey are the **unemployment rate**, measured as

$$\text{Unemployment rate} = \frac{\text{Number unemployed}}{\text{Labour force}},$$

and the **participation rate**, measured as

$$\text{Participation rate} = \frac{\text{Labour force}}{\text{Total working age population}}.$$

The unemployment rate is potentially useful as a measure of **labour market tightness**, which is the degree of difficulty firms face in hiring workers. However, there are two ways in which the unemployment rate might mismeasure labour market tightness. First, some people, referred to as **discouraged workers**, are not counted in the labour force and have stopped searching for work, but actually wish to be employed. Thus, during a long recession, when the level of aggregate economic activity is depressed for a long duration, it is possible that the unemployment rate might fall only because some unemployed people have become discouraged and stopped looking for work. In this circumstance, labour market tightness would not really have increased with the decrease in the unemployment rate, but we might be fooled into thinking so.

The second factor that could cause the unemployment rate to be a bad measure of labour market tightness is that the unemployment rate does not adjust for how intensively the unemployed are searching for work. Thus, it could be the case that when the unemployment rate is high, the unemployed do not search very hard for work, because they think their chances of success are low. For example, each worker might spend only one or two hours per day trying to find work. However, when the unemployment rate is low, the unemployed might be searching very hard, because their prospects for success seem good. For example, each worker might search eight or ten hours per day. If this were the case, we might actually think of a high unemployment rate as being associated with high labour market tightness and a low unemployment rate as being associated with low labour market tightness. For example, if a firm is looking to hire, it is more difficult to find workers if the unemployed are not looking hard for work.

The Help-Wanted Index and the Beveridge Curve

An alternative to the unemployment rate as a measure of labour market tightness is the labour market vacancy rate. The vacancy rate is the number of jobs that employers wish to fill divided by the total labour force. In Canada, Statistics Canada publishes the Help-Wanted Index (HWI), a monthly measure of the number of printed job postings in Canada. To obtain the Help-Wanted Index, Statistics Canada counts the number of help-wanted ads in 22 metropolitan-area newspapers in Canada every month. A measure of the Canadian vacancy rate can then be obtained by taking the ratio of the HWI to the total labour force.

There are two key problems with the HWI as a measure of unfilled jobs. First, the index does not include help-wanted ads in all newspapers, or from a survey of newspapers, but only from those in the selected metropolitan areas. If job vacancies in rural areas vary systematically relative to those in urban areas, the HWI will be biased. Second, the HWI measures only newspaper advertising, but employers have many other ways of getting information to potential job candidates. For example, Internet communication has become increasingly important in recent years, and job information for many occupations is currently available electronically.

Suppose, however, that we accept the ratio of the HWI to total labour force as a reasonable measure of the vacancy rate. We should then observe that this measure of the vacancy rate is high when the labour market is tight, and low when the labour market is not tight. Thus, we would tend to observe that the vacancy rate is high (low) when the unemployment rate is low (high). This inverse relationship between the vacancy rate and the unemployment rate was observed by John Beveridge in the 1940s, and is called the "Beveridge Curve." In Figure 2.4, we show a scatter plot of the vacancy rate in Canada (measured as the ratio of the HWI to the labour force) versus the unemployment rate for the years 1981–2002. Clearly, there is an inverse relationship between the two. The Beveridge curve is the downward-sloping curve, shown in colour, that best fits the points in the figure. Stephen Nickell, Luca Nunziata, Wolfgang Ochel, and Glenda Quintini studied Beveridge curves for OECD countries from the 1960s to the 1990s.[1] They argue that changes in labour market institutions caused Beveridge curves in these countries to shift over time. A more detailed analysis of the data in Figure 2.4 would likely indicate that there were factors during the period 1981–2002 that caused the Beveridge curve to shift.

For another way of measuring labour market tightness, see the box Macroeconomics in Action 2.2.

Partly because of problems in interpreting what movements in the unemployment rate mean, macroeconomists often focus attention on the level and growth rate of employment when they analyze the implications of labour market activity. Indeed, many of the models we will analyze in this book do not explain the behaviour of unemployment. However, we will study some explanations for unemployment in Chapters 10 and 15.

So far, we have learned how aggregate economic activity is measured in the NIEA, how nominal GDP can be decomposed to obtain measures of real GDP and the price level, what the relationships are among savings, wealth, and capital, and what the key measurement issues in the labour market are. In the next chapter we will deal with busi-

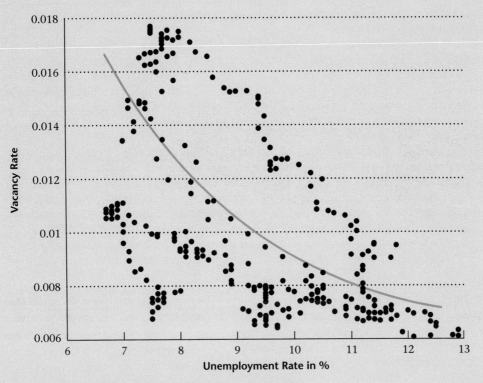

FIGURE 2.4   Beveridge Curve for Canada, 1981–2002

[1]See Stephen Nickell, Luca Nunziata, Wolfgang Ochel, and Glenda Quintini, July 2001, "The Beveridge Curve, Unemployment and Wages in the OECD from the 1960s to the 1990s," Ideas, RePEc (Research Papers in Economics) site ideas.repec.org/p/cep/cepdps/0502.html, accessed July 4, 2003.

ness cycle measurement, and derive a set of key business cycle facts that will help focus our study of macroeconomic theory beginning in Chapter 4.

Chapter Summary

This chapter focused on the measurement of gross domestic product (GDP) and its components, and the measurement of the price level, savings, wealth, capital, and labour market variables. We first discussed how GDP is measured in the National Income and Expenditure Accounts (NIEA) of Canada. GDP can be measured using the product approach, the expenditure approach, or the income approach, which will each yield the same quantity of GDP in a given period if there is no measurement error. GDP must be used carefully as a measure of aggregate welfare, because it leaves out home production. Further, there are problems with GDP as a measure of aggregate output, due to the existence of the underground economy and because government output is difficult to measure.

It is useful to distinguish how much of nominal GDP growth is accounted for by inflation, and how much is growth in real GDP. Two approaches to measuring real GDP are choosing a base year and chain-weighting. The latter is the current method used in the NIEA. Chain-weighting corrects for the bias that arises in real GDP calculations when a base year is used and relative prices change over time. Problems with real GDP measurement arise because it is difficult to account for changes in the quality of goods over time and because new goods are introduced and others become obsolete.

Private saving is private disposable income minus consumption, while government saving is government receipts minus government spending and transfers. The government surplus is equal to government saving. National saving is the sum of private and government saving and is equal to investment expenditures plus the current account surplus. National saving is just the accumulation of national wealth, which comes in the form of additions to the capital stock (investment) and additions to domestic claims on foreigners (the current account surplus).

The labour market variables we focus on are those measured in the monthly survey of Statistics Canada. The working age population consists of the employed, the unemployed (those searching for work), and those not in the labour force. Two key labour market variables are the unemployment rate and the participation rate. The unemployment rate is sometimes used as a measure of labour market tightness, but care needs to be taken in interpreting the unemployment rate in this way.

Key Terms

gross domestic product (GDP): The dollar value of final output produced during a given period of time within a country's borders.

National Income and Expenditure Accounts (NIEA): The official Canadian accounts of aggregate economic activity, which include GDP measurements conducted by Statistics Canada.

product approach: The approach to GDP measurement that determines GDP as the sum of value added to goods and services in production across all productive units in the economy.

expenditure approach: The approach to GDP measurement that determines GDP as total spending on all final goods and services production in the economy.

income approach: The approach to GDP measurement that determines GDP as the sum of all incomes received by economic agents contributing to production.

intermediate good: A good that is produced and then used as an input in another production process.

value added: The value of goods produced, minus the value of intermediate goods used in production.

income–expenditure identity: $Y = C + I + G + NX$, where Y is aggregate income (output), C is consumption expenditures, I is investment expenditures, G is government expenditures, and NX is net exports.

gross national product (GNP): $GNP = GDP +$ Net factor payments to Canadian residents from abroad.

underground economy: All unreported economic activity.

consumption: Goods and services produced and consumed during the current period.

investment: Goods produced in the current period but not consumed in the current period.

fixed investment: Investment in plant, equipment, and housing.

inventory investment: Goods produced in the current period that are set aside for future periods.

net exports: Expenditures on domestically produced goods and services by foreigners (exports), minus expenditures on foreign-produced goods and services by domestic residents (imports).

government expenditures: Expenditures by the federal, provincial, and municipal governments on final goods and services.

transfers: Government outlays that are transfers of purchasing power from one group of private economic agents to another.

price index: A weighted average of prices of some set of goods produced in the economy during a particular period.

price level: The average level of prices across all goods and services in the economy.

inflation rate: The rate of change in the price level from one period to another.

nominal change: The change in the dollar value of a good, service, or asset.

real change: The change in the quantity of a good, service, or asset.

chain-weighting: An approach to calculating real GDP that uses a rolling base year.

implicit GDP price deflator: Nominal GDP divided by real GDP, all multiplied by 100.

consumer price index (CPI): Current-year total expenditures, divided by current-year total expenditures at base year prices, all multiplied by 100.

flow: A rate per unit time.

stock: Quantity in existence of some object at a point in time.

private disposable income: GDP plus net factor payments, plus transfers from the government, plus interest on the government debt, minus taxes.

private sector saving: Private disposable income minus consumption expenditures.

government saving: Taxes minus transfers, minus interest on the government debt, minus government expenditures.

government surplus: Identical to government saving.

government deficit: The negative of the government surplus.

national saving: Private sector saving plus government saving.

current account surplus: Net exports plus net factor payments from abroad.

national wealth: The stock of assets held by the country as a whole.

capital stock: The quantity of plant, equipment, housing, and inventories in existence in an economy at a point in time.

employed: In the Statistics Canada monthly household survey, those who worked part-time or full-time during the past week.

unemployed: In the Statistics Canada monthly household survey, those who were not employed during the past week, but actively searched for work at some time during the last four weeks.

not in the labour force: In the Statistics Canada household survey, those who are neither employed or unemployed.

unemployment rate: The number of unemployed divided by the number in the labour force.

participation rate: The number in the labour force divided by the working-age population.

labour market tightness: The degree of difficulty firms face in hiring workers.

discouraged workers: Those who are not counted in the labour force and have stopped searching for work, but actually wish to be employed.

Questions for Review

1. What are the three approaches used to measure GDP?

2. Explain the concept of *value added*.

3. Why is the income–expenditure identity important?

4. What is the difference between GDP and GNP?

5. Is GDP a good measure of economic welfare? Why or why not?

6. What are two difficulties in the measurement of aggregate output using GDP?

7. What is the largest expenditure component of GDP?

8. What is investment?

9. What are government transfers? Explain why they are not included in GDP.

10. Why does the base year matter in calculating real GDP?

11. Explain what *chain-weighting* is.

12. Explain three problems in the measurement of real GDP.

13. What are the differences and similarities among private sector saving, government saving, and national saving?

14. What are the two ways in which national wealth is accumulated?

15. Give two reasons why the unemployment rate may mismeasure the degree of labour market tightness.

Problems

1. Assume an economy where there are two producers: a wheat producer and a bread producer. In a given year, the wheat producer grows 3 million tonnes of wheat, of which 2.5 million tonnes are sold to the bread producer at $30 per bushel, and 0.5 million tonnes are stored by the wheat producer to use as seed for next year's crop. The bread producer produces and sells 100 million loaves of bread to consumers for $3.50 per loaf. Determine GDP in this economy during this year using the product and expenditure approaches.

2. Assume an economy with a coal producer, a steel producer, and some consumers (there is no government). In a given year, the coal producer produces 15 million tonnes of coal and sells it for $5 per tonne. The coal producer pays $50 million in wages to consumers. The steel producer uses 25 million tonnes of coal as an input into steel production, all purchased at $5 per tonne. Of this, 15 million tonnes of coal comes from the domestic coal producer, and 10 million tonnes is imported. The steel producer produces 10 million tonnes of steel and sells it for $20 per tonne. Domestic consumers buy 8 million tonnes of steel, and 2 million tonnes are exported. The steel producer pays consumers $40 million in wages. All profits made by domestic producers are distributed to domestic consumers.
   a. Determine GDP using (i) the product approach, (ii) the expenditure approach, and (iii) the income approach.
   b. Determine the current account surplus.
   c. What is GNP in this economy? Determine GNP and GDP in the case where the coal producer is owned by foreigners, so that the profits of the domestic coal producer go to foreigners and are not distributed to domestic consumers.

3. Assume an economy with two firms. Firm A produces wheat and firm B produces bread. In a given year, firm A produces 5000 tonnes of wheat, sells 2000 tonnes of wheat to firm B at $30 per tonne, exports 2500 tonnes of wheat at $30 per tonne, and stores 500 tonnes as inventory. Firm A pays $50 000 in wages to consumers. Firm B produces 50 000 loaves of

bread, and sells all of it to domestic consumers at $2 per loaf. Firm B pays consumers
$20 000 in wages. In addition to the 50 000 loaves of bread consumers buy from firm B,
consumers import and consume 15 000 loaves of bread, and they pay $1 per loaf for this
imported bread. Calculate gross domestic product using (a) the product approach, (b) the
expenditure approach, and (c) the income approach.

4. In year 1 and year 2, there are two products produced in a given economy: computers and
   bread. Suppose that there are no intermediate goods. In year 1, 20 computers are produced
   and sold at $1000 each, and in year 2, 25 computers are sold at $1500 each. In year 1,
   10 000 loaves of bread are sold for $1 each, and in year 2, 12 000 loaves of bread are sold
   for $1.10 each.
   a. Calculate nominal GDP in each year.
   b. Calculate real GDP in each year and the percentage increase in real GDP from year 1 to
      year 2 using year 1 as the base year. Next, do the same calculations using the chain-
      weighting method.
   c. Calculate the implicit GDP price deflator and the percentage inflation rate from year 1 to
      year 2 using year 1 as the base year. Next, do the same calculations using the chain-
      weighting method.
   d. Suppose that computers in year 2 are twice as productive as computers in year 1. How
      does this change your calculations in parts (a)–(c)? Explain any differences.

5. Assume an economy where only broccoli and cauliflower are produced. In year 1, 500 million kilograms of broccoli are produced and consumed and its price is $0.50 per kilogram,
   while 300 million kilograms of cauliflower are produced and consumed and its price is $0.80
   per kilogram. In year 2, 400 million kilograms of broccoli are produced and consumed and
   its price is $0.60 per kilogram, while 350 million kilograms of cauliflower are produced and
   its price is $0.85 per kilogram.
   a. Using year 1 as the base year, calculate the GDP price deflator in years 1 and 2, and cal-
      culate the rate of inflation between years 1 and 2 from the GDP price deflator.
   b. Using year 1 as the base year, calculate the CPI in years 1 and 2, and calculate the CPI rate
      of inflation. Explain any differences in your results between parts (a) and (b).

6. In some countries, price controls exist on some goods, which set maximum prices at which
   these goods can be sold. Indeed, Canada experienced a period of wage and price controls in
   the 1970s, under the Anti-Inflation Board. Sometimes the existence of price controls leads
   to the growth of black markets, where goods are exchanged at prices above the legal maxi-
   mums. Carefully explain how price controls present a problem for measuring GDP and for
   measuring the price level and inflation.

7. Consider an economy with a corn producer, some consumers, and a government. In a given
   year, the corn producer grows 3 million tonnes of corn, and the market price for corn is $50
   per tonne. Of the 3 million tonnes produced, 2 million tonnes are sold to consumers, 0.5
   million are stored in inventory, and 0.5 million are sold to the government to feed the army.
   The corn producer pays $60 million in wages to consumers and $20 million in taxes to the
   government. Consumers pay $10 million in taxes to the government, receive $10 million in
   interest on the government debt, and receive $5 million in Canadian Pension Plan payments
   from the government. The profits of the corn producer are distributed to consumers.
   a. Calculate GDP using (i) the product approach, (ii) the expenditure approach, and (iii) the
      income approach.
   b. Calculate private disposable income, private sector saving, government saving, national
      saving, and the government deficit. Is the government budget in deficit or surplus?

8. Consider the identity

$$S^P - I = CA + D,$$

where S^P is private sector saving, I is investment, CA is the current account surplus, and D is the government deficit.

a. Show that the above identity holds.

b. Explain what the above identity means.

9. Suppose that the government deficit is 10, interest on the government debt is 5, taxes are 40, government expenditures are 30, consumption expenditures are 80, net factor payments are 10, the current account surplus is –5, and national saving is 20. Calculate the following (not necessarily in the order given):

a. Private disposable income

b. Transfers from the government to the private sector

c. Gross national product

d. Gross domestic product

e. The government surplus

f. Net exports

g. Investment expenditures

10. Explain how each of the following would affect (i) the degree of difficulty firms face in hiring workers, (ii) the measured unemployment rate, and (iii) the measured help-wanted index.

a. The number of newspapers in metropolitan areas increases.

b. An increasing number of firms post job listings on the Internet rather than taking out ads in newspapers.

c. Unemployment insurance benefits increase.

d. Some unemployed people become discouraged and stop searching for work.

e. Agriculture grows relative to manufacturing.

Working with the Data

1. Calculate consumption of durables, consumption of nondurables, consumption of semi-durables and consumption of services as percentages of total consumption, and plot these time series. Comment on the changes that have taken place over time in the consumption of services relative to durables, semi-durables, and nondurables.

2. Macroeconomists sometimes study the behaviour of the consumer price index, leaving out food, indirect taxes, and energy prices. Calculate the year-to-year inflation rate (December to December) in percentage terms using the consumer price index (all items) and using the consumer price index excluding food, energy, and the effects of indirect taxes. Plot the two inflation rates and comment on the differences. Why would we want to neglect food, indirect taxes, and energy in our calculation of the CPI? Why would we *not* want to neglect these items?

3. Plot the stocks of capital, fixed residential capital, and fixed nonresidential capital over time. Comment on the movements in these time series and the proportion of each component of capital in the total.

4. Plot national savings, total investment expenditures, and the current account surplus over time. Comment on how these time series move together over time, with reference to the last equation in the section "Savings, Wealth, and Capital" in this chapter.

CHAPTER 3

Business Cycle Measurement

Before we go on to build models of aggregate economic activity that can explain why business cycles exist and what, if anything, should be done about them, we must understand the key features that we observe in economic data that define a business cycle. In this chapter, we move beyond the study of the measurement of gross domestic product, the price level, savings, and wealth, which we covered in Chapter 2, to an examination of the regularities in the relationships among aggregate economic variables as they fluctuate over time.

We will show that business cycles are quite irregular, in that they are unpredictable; macroeconomic forecasters often have a difficult time predicting the timing of a business cycle upturn or downturn. However, business cycles are quite regular in terms of comovements, which is to say that macroeconomic variables move together in highly predictable ways. We will focus separately on the components of real GDP, nominal variables, and labour market variables.

This chapter describes a set of key business cycle facts concerning comovements in Canadian macroeconomic data. In Chapters 4–7 and 9, we will use these facts to show how our models can make sense of what we observe in the data. Then, in Chapters 10 and 11, we will use the key business cycle facts to help us evaluate alternative theories of the business cycle.

Regularities in GDP Fluctuations

The primary defining feature of **business cycles** is that they are *fluctuations about trend in real gross domestic product*. Recall from Chapter 1 that we represent the trend in real GDP with a smooth curve that closely fits actual real GDP, with the trend representing that part of real GDP that can be explained by long-run growth factors. What is left over, the deviations from trend, we take to represent business cycle activity.

In Figure 3.1 we show idealized business cycle activity in real GDP, with fluctuations about a long-run trend. In the figure, real GDP is represented by the black line, while the trend is represented by the coloured line. There are **peaks** and **troughs** in real GDP, a peak being a relatively large positive deviation from trend, and a trough a relatively large negative deviation from trend. Peaks and troughs in the deviations from trend in real GDP are referred to as **turning points**. In a manner analogous to wave motion in the physical sciences, we can think of the maximum deviation from trend in Figure 3.1 as the **amplitude**

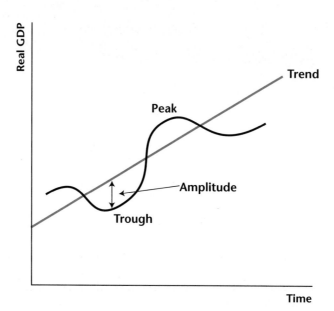

of the business cycle, and the number of peaks in real GDP that occur per year as the **frequency** of the business cycle.

Next, in Figure 3.2 we show the actual percentage deviations from trend in real GDP for Canada over the period 1961–2002. A series of positive deviations from trend culminating in a peak represents a **boom**, whereas a series of negative deviations from trend culminating in a trough represents a **recession**. In Figure 3.2, we have marked four important recent recessions: the 1974–75, 1981–82, 1990–92, and 2001–02 recessions. The 1974–75 recession was relatively mild, with a negative deviation from trend of less than 2%, while the 1981–82 recession was relatively severe, with a negative deviation from trend in excess of 5%. In the 1990–92 recession, the negative deviation from trend was fairly moderate, at about 2%, and the 2001–02 recession was also relatively mild.

An examination of Figure 3.2 indicates a striking regularity, which is that the deviations from trend in real GDP are **persistent**. That is, when real GDP is above trend, it tends to stay above trend, and when it is below trend, it tends to stay below trend. This feature is quite important in terms of economic forecasting over the short run; persistence implies we can fairly confidently predict that if real GDP is currently below (above) trend, it will be below (above) trend several months from now. Other than being persistent, however, the deviations from trend in real GDP are actually quite irregular. There are three other features to note from Figure 3.2:

1. The time series of deviations from trend in real GDP is quite choppy.

2. There is no regularity in the amplitude of fluctuations in real GDP about trend. Some of the peaks and troughs represent large deviations from trend, whereas other peaks and troughs represent small deviations from trend.

3. There is no regularity in the frequency of fluctuations in real GDP about trend. The length of time between peaks and troughs in real GDP varies considerably.

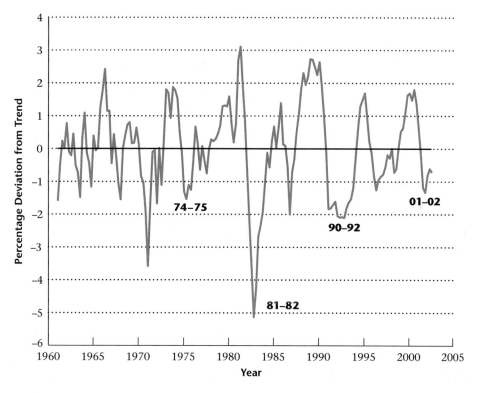

FIGURE 3.2

Percentage Deviations from Trend in Real GDP, 1961–2002
Of particular note are the four most recent recessions, in 1974–75, 1981–82, 1990–92, and 2001–02.

Source: Adapted from the Statistics Canada CANSIM database, Series v1992067.

Though deviations from trend in real GDP are persistent, which makes short-term forecasting relatively easy, the above three features imply that longer-term forecasting is difficult. The choppiness of fluctuations in real GDP will make these fluctuations difficult to predict, while the lack of regularity in the amplitude and frequency of fluctuations implies that it is difficult to predict the severity and length of recessions and booms. Therefore, predicting future fluctuations in real GDP by looking only at past real GDP is much like attempting to forecast the weather by looking out the window. If it is sunny today, it is likely that it will be sunny tomorrow (weather is persistent), but the fact that it is sunny today may give us very little information on whether it will be sunny one week from today. (See Macroeconomics in Action 3.1 for a discussion of forecasting at the Bank of Canada.)

Comovement

While real GDP fluctuates in irregular patterns, macroeconomic variables exhibit strong regularities. We refer to these patterns in fluctuations as **comovement**. Robert Lucas once remarked that "with respect to qualitative behavior of comovements among [economic time] series, business cycles are all alike."[1]

---

[1]See R. Lucas, 1980, "Understanding Business Cycles," in *Studies in Business Cycle Theory*, MIT Press, p. 218.

Forecasting at the Bank of Canada

In Canada, macroeconomic forecasting is done in the Department of Finance and the Bank of Canada in Ottawa, by provincial governments, and by private firms, such as the Conference Board of Canada, that sell forecasts to governments and businesses. There are essentially three approaches to macroeconomic forecasting: judgmental forecasting, structural forecasting, and statistical forecasting.

Judgmental forecasters gather various kinds of information and data from official and unofficial sources, and then forecast future macroeconomic activity on the basis of their own informal judgment about how the economy works. A judgmental forecaster does not use sophisticated statistical methods or macroeconomic theory in a rigorous way, but instead relies on his or her own "gut feelings" about where the economy is headed.

Structural forecasting is done using an explicit macroeconomic model constructed using macroeconomic theory. The types of models used vary considerably but those developed in the 1960s and 1970s, one of which was the RDX2 model constructed at the Bank of Canada, consisted of several hundred equations that captured the relationships among several hundred macroeconomic variables. The original RDX2 model was adapted for use as a forecasting tool in the Research Department of the Bank of Canada in the late 1970s. This adapted model was called RDXF. A forecast using the RDXF model typically involved work by a team of people who fine-tuned the model before the forecast, with a forecast generated as a computer simulation of the model's predictions for future macroeconomic activity.

Statistical forecasting is a reaction to structural forecasting. It arose when some macroeconomists thought forecasting models had simply gotten out of hand. They argue that typical structural macroeconomic forecasting models are so large and complicated that no one actually understands how they work. Further, as they argue, a forecasting exercise with a large team of forecasters typically degenerates into an exercise wherein members of the team supply "add factors" to the model to make the results conform to their own judgment of how the forecast should look. At worst, then, the model is not allowed to make predictions, but is simply a device for enforcing national income accounting identities (e.g., the income–expenditure identity). As is argued, the forecast is then judgmental, and not a model forecast at all. An example of a statistical model is the Bayesian Vector Autoregression (or BVAR) model developed at the Federal Reserve Bank of Minneapolis in the 1970s and 1980s. Related models are sometimes used at the Bank of Canada, sometimes in a hybrid form that mixes a structural approach with a vector autoregression.[1] As well, the Bank of Canada has experimented with a statistical forecasting approach called a *factor model*.[2]

Large structural models are unwieldy, and they can only be of limited use for policy analysis because they are not always consistently grounded in theory. In response to these problems, in the 1980s and 1990s the Bank of Canada developed smaller models for forecasting and policy analysis that make use of some of the machinery from modern macroeconomic theory. The first of these models was the Small Annual Model (SAM), intended for longer-term forecasting and policy analysis.[3] A second model, constructed during the 1990s, was the Quarterly Projection Model (QPM). This model in part uses a "calibration" approach, as is done in the real business cycle models that will be discussed in Chapter 11. One of the policy exercises carried out with the QPM was an evaluation of how the economy would behave under alternative types of behaviour on the part of the Bank of Canada.[4]

[1]See K. Moran and V. Dolar, 2002, "Estimated DGE Models and Forecasting Accuracy: A Preliminary Investigation with Canadian Data," Bank of Canada working paper 2002-18,

available at **www.bankofcanada.ca/en/res/wp02-18.htm**, accessed July 10, 2003.

[2]See M. Gosselin and G. Tkacz, 2001, "Evaluating Factor Models: An Application to Forecasting Inflation in Canada," Bank of Canada working paper 2001-18, available at **www.bankofcanada.ca/en/res/wp01-18.htm**, accessed July 10, 2003.

[3]See D. Rose and J. Selody, 1985, "The Structure of the Small Annual Model," Bank of Canada Technical Report No. 40.

[4]See J. Armour, B. Fung, and D. Maclean, 2002, "Taylor Rules in the Quarterly Projection Model," Bank of Canada working paper 2002-1, available at **www.bankofcanada.ca/en/res/wp02-1.htm**, accessed July 10, 2003.

Macroeconomic variables are measured as **time series**; for example, real GDP is measured in a series of quarterly observations over time. When we examine comovements in macroeconomic time series, typically we look at these time series two at a time, and a good starting point is to plot the data. Suppose, for example, that we have two macroeconomic time series and we would like to study their comovement. We first transform these two time series by removing trends, and we will let x and y denote the percentage deviations from trend in the two time series. One way to plot x and y is in time series form, as in Figure 3.3. What we want to look for first in the time series plot is a pattern of **positive correlation** or **negative correlation** in x and y. In Figure 3.3(a), there is positive correlation between x and y: x is high when y is high, and x is low when y is low. That is, one economic time series tends to be above (below) trend when the other economic time series is above (below) trend. In Figure 3.3(b) x and y are negatively correlated: x is high (low) when y is low (high).

Another way to plot the data is as a **scatter plot**, with x on the horizontal axis and y on the vertical axis. In Figure 3.4, each point in the scatter plot is an observation on x and y for a particular time period. Here, whether x and y are positively or negatively correlated is determined by the slope of a straight line that best fits the points in the

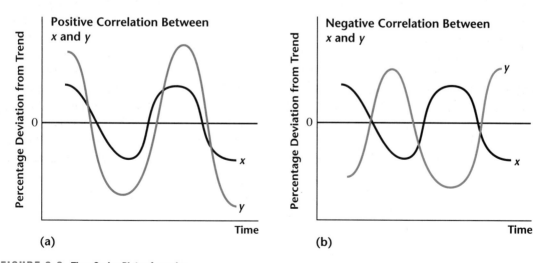

(a)   **(b)**

FIGURE 3.3 Time Series Plots of x and y

(a) Two time series that are positively correlated: when x is high (low), y tends to be high (low). (b) Two time series that are negatively correlated: when x is high (low), y tends to be low (high).

FIGURE 3.4

Scatter Plots of *y* and *x*

(a) *x* and *y* are positively
correlated. (b) *x* and *y* are
negatively correlated.
    (c) *x* and *y* are uncorrelated.

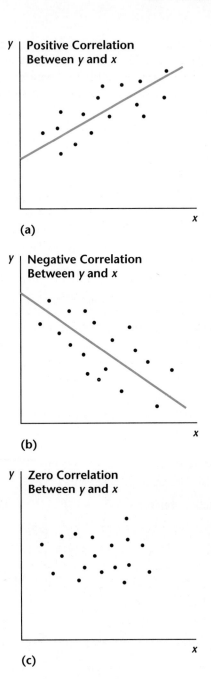

(a)

(b)

(c)

scatter plot. The top panel of Figure 3.4 shows a positive correlation between x and y, the middle panel a negative correlation, and the bottom panel a zero correlation. For example, in the Canadian population, if we plotted cigarettes smoked per year against the incidence of lung cancer, we would observe a positive correlation, and if we plotted the level of good cholesterol in the blood against the incidence of heart disease, we would observe a negative correlation.

Macroeconomists are often primarily interested in how an individual macroeconomic variable comoves with real GDP. An economic variable is said to be **procyclical** if its deviations from trend are positively correlated with the deviations from trend in real GDP, **countercyclical** if its deviations from trend are negatively correlated with the deviations from trend in real GDP, and **acyclical** if it is neither procyclical nor countercyclical. As an example of comovement between two macroeconomic time series, we will consider real GDP and real imports for Canada over the period 1961–2002. In Figure 3.5 we plot the percentage deviations from trend in real GDP (the coloured line) and real imports (the black line) in time series form. There is a distinct pattern of positive correlation in Figure 3.5; when GDP is high (low) relative to trend, imports tend to be high (low) relative to trend. This positive correlation also shows up in the scatter plot in Figure 3.6, where we show a graph of observations of percentage deviations from trend in imports versus percentage deviations from trend in GDP. Note that a straight line fit to the points in Figure 3.6 would have a positive slope.

A measure of the degree of correlation between two variables is the **correlation coefficient**. The correlation coefficient between two variables, x and y, takes on values between −1 and 1. If the correlation coefficient is 1, then x and y are **perfectly positively correlated**, and a scatter plot of observations on x and y will fall on a positively sloped straight line. If the correlation coefficient is −1, x and y are **perfectly negatively correlated**, and a scatter plot would consist of points on a negatively sloped straight line. If the correlation coefficient is 0, x and y are uncorrelated. In the example above,

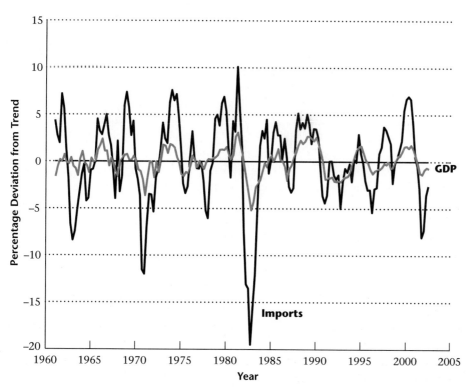

FIGURE 3.5

Imports and GDP for Canada, 1961–2002

This figure, as an example, shows the time series of percentage deviations from trend in real imports (the black line) and real GDP (the coloured line) for Canada for the period 1961–2002. Imports and GDP are clearly positively correlated, so imports are procyclical.

Source: Adapted from the Statistics Canada CANSIM database, Series v1992067, v1992063.

FIGURE 3.6

Scatter Plot of Imports and GDP for Canada, 1961–2002

This figure shows the same data as Figure 3.5, but in scatter plot rather than time series form. We again observe the positive correlation between imports and GDP, as a positively sloped straight line would best fit the scatter plot; and again, imports are procyclical.

Source: Adapted from the Statistics Canada CANSIM database, Series v1992067, v1992063.

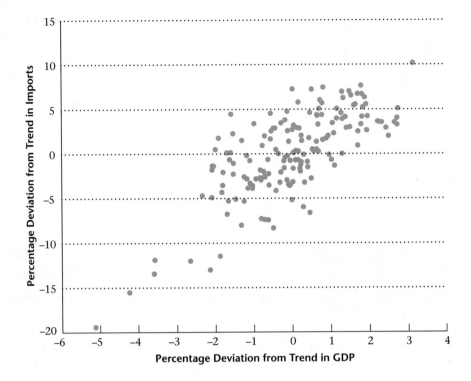

the percentage deviations from trend in real GDP and real imports have a correlation coefficient of 0.74, indicating positive correlation.

An important element of comovement is the leading and lagging relationships that exist in macroeconomic data. If a macroeconomic variable tends to aid in predicting the future path of real GDP, we say that it is a **leading variable**, whereas if real GDP helps to predict the future path of a particular macroeconomic variable, that variable is said to be a **lagging variable**. In Figure 3.7 we show idealized time series plots of the percentage deviations from trend in real GDP and two variables, x and y. In part (a) of the figure, variable x is a leading variable, whereas in (b) variable y is a lagging variable. A **coincident variable** is one which neither leads nor lags real GDP.

If it is known that some set of macroeconomic variables all tend to be leading variables, this information can be very useful in macroeconomic forecasting, as timely information on leading variables can then be used to forecast real GDP. One way to use this information is to construct a macroeconomic model, grounded in economic theory, that incorporates the relationships between leading variables and real GDP, which can then be used for forecasting. However, some economists argue that forecasting can be done simply by exploiting past statistical relationships among macroeconomic variables to project into the future. A very simple form of this approach is the construction and use of the **composite index of business leading indicators** (or **index of leading indicators** for short). This index is a weighted average of macroeconomic variables that has been found to do a good job of predicting future real GDP. Watching the index of leading economic indicators can sometimes provide useful information for forecasters, partic-

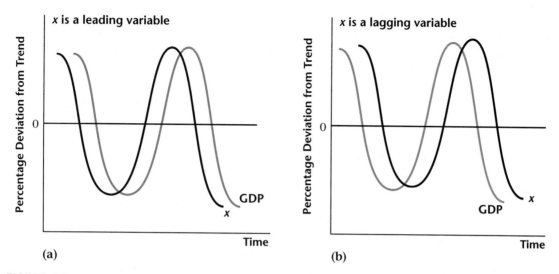

(a)

(b)

FIGURE 3.7 Leading and Lagging Variables

In (a), x is a leading variable, as its peaks and troughs tend to precede those of real GDP. In (b), x is a lagging variable, as the peaks and troughs in real GDP tend to lead those in x.

ularly with respect to the turning points in aggregate economic activity. In Figure 3.8 we show a plot of the percentage deviations from trend in real GDP (the coloured line)

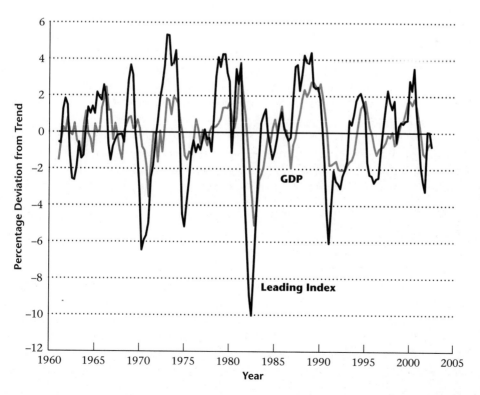

FIGURE 3.8

Percentage Deviations from Trend in Real GDP (coloured line) and the Composite Index of Business Leading Indictors (black line), 1961–2002

The index is a weighted average of leading variables and so, not surprisingly, it tends to lead real GDP.

Source: Adapted from the Statistics Canada CANSIM database, Series v1992067, v7687.

and in the index of leading indicators (the black line). Note that the index of leading economic indicators tends to track real GDP fairly closely, but with a lead. In particular, turning points in the index of leading economic indicators in Figure 3.8 tend to fall before turning points in real GDP.

Finally, there are key regularities in terms of the variability of economic variables over the business cycle. As we will see, some macroeconomic variables are highly volatile, while others behave in a very smooth way relative to trend. These patterns in variability are an important part of business cycle behaviour that we would like to understand. A measure of cyclical variability is the **standard deviation** of the percentage deviations from trend. For example, in Figure 3.5, imports are much more variable than GDP. The standard deviation of the percentage deviations from trend in imports is more than twice that for GDP.

Next we will examine some key macroeconomic variables and will evaluate for each whether they are (i) procyclical or countercyclical; (ii) leading or lagging; and (iii) more or less variable relative to real GDP. These facts will then make up the set of important business cycle regularities that we would like to explain using macroeconomic theory.

The Components of GDP

In Figure 3.9 we show the percentage deviations from trend in real aggregate consumption (the black line) and real GDP (the coloured line). Clearly, the deviations from

FIGURE 3.9

Percentage Deviations from Trend in Real Consumption (black line) and Real GDP (coloured line) for Canada, 1961–2002

From the figure, we can observe that consumption is procyclical, coincident, and less variable than GDP.

Source: Adapted from the Statistics Canada CANSIM database, Series v1992067, v1992044.

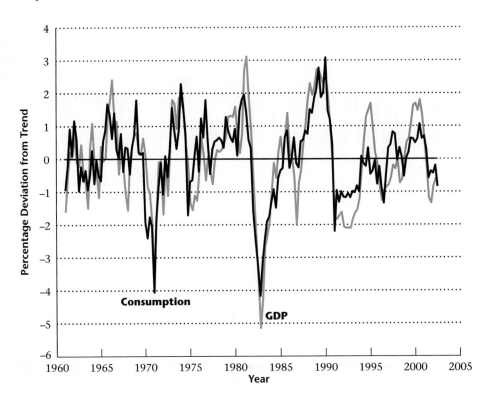

trend in consumption and in GDP are highly positively correlated, in that consumption tends to be above (below) trend when GDP is above (below) trend; these two time series move very closely together. The correlation coefficient between the percentage deviation from trend in real consumption and the percentage deviation from trend in real GDP is 0.82, which is greater than zero, so consumption is procyclical. There appears to be no discernible lead/lag relationship between real consumption and real GDP in Figure 3.9—the turning points in consumption do not appear to lead or lag the turning points in real GDP. Thus, consumption is a coincident variable.

From Figure 3.9, note that consumption is less variable than GDP, in that the deviations from trend in consumption tend to be smaller than those in GDP. In Chapter 6 we will study the theory of consumption decisions over time, and this theory will explain why consumption tends to be smoother than GDP. For the data displayed in Figure 3.9, the standard deviation of the percentage deviations in real consumption is 85.0% of that for real GDP. This is a more precise measure of what our eyes tell us about Figure 3.9, which is that consumption is smoother than GDP.

The percentage deviations from trend in real investment (the black line) and real GDP (the coloured line) are plotted in Figure 3.10. As with consumption, investment is procyclical, since it tends to be above (below) trend when GDP is above (below) trend. The correlation coefficient between the percentage deviations from trend in investment and those in GDP is 0.80. There is no tendency for investment to lead or lag GDP from Figure 3.10, and so investment is a coincident variable. However, it is well known that some components of investment, in particular residential investment

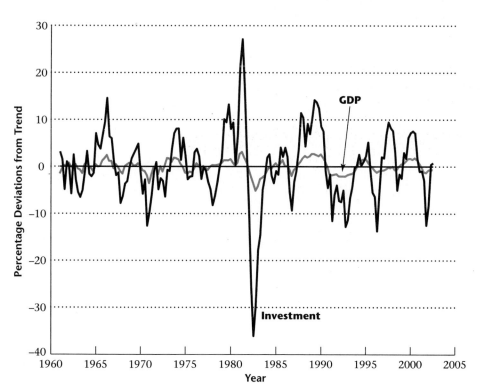

FIGURE 3.10

Percentage Deviations from Trend in Real Investment (black line) and Real GDP (coloured line) for Canada, 1961–2002

We can observe from the figure that investment is procyclical, coincident, and more variable than GDP.

Source: Adapted from the Statistics Canada CANSIM database, Series v1992052, v1992057, v1992067.

and inventory investment, tend to lead the business cycle. In contrast to consumption, investment is much more volatile than is GDP. This is indicated in Figure 3.10, where the deviations from trend in investment tend to be much larger than those for GDP. The standard deviation of the percentage deviations from trend in investment is 564.8% of what it is for GDP. Given that some components of investment lead GDP and that it is highly volatile, investment can play a very important role over the business cycle.

Nominal Variables

The correlation between money prices and aggregate economic activity has long been of interest to macroeconomists. In the 1950s, A. W. Phillips[2] observed that there was a negative relationship between the rate of change in money wages and the unemployment rate in the United Kingdom, a relationship that came to be known as the **Phillips curve**. If we take the unemployment rate to be a measure of aggregate economic activity (as we will see in Chapter 15, the unemployment rate is a strongly countercyclical variable; when real GDP is above trend, the unemployment rate is low), then the Phillips curve captures a positive relationship between the rate of change in a money price (the money wage) and the level of aggregate economic activity. Since Phillips made his initial observation, "Phillips curve" has come to be applied to any positive relationship between the rate of change in money prices or wages, or the deviation from trend in money prices or wages, and the deviation from trend in aggregate economic activity. As we will see in Chapters 11 and 16, observed Phillips curves are notoriously unstable—that is, they tend to shift over time—and there are sound theories to explain this instability. However, a regularity in the 1961–2002 period is the negative correlation between deviations of the price level from trend and deviations of GDP from trend, observed in the scatter plot in Figure 3.11. We might think of this as a **reverse Phillips curve**, as there is a negative rather than a positive correlation between the price level and real GDP, with the correlation coefficient for the data in Figure 3.11 being –0.18. Thus, over the period 1961–2002, the price level is a countercyclical variable, though it is not strongly countercyclical.

Note from Figure 3.12 that the price level (the black line) is about as variable as real GDP (the coloured line); the standard deviation of the percentage deviations from trend in the price level is 101.0% of that for GDP. Also, the price level tends to be much smoother than most asset prices. For example, the average price of shares traded on the Toronto Stock Exchange is highly variable relative to the money prices of goods and services. In Figure 3.12 there appears to be no tendency for the price level to lead or lag real GDP, so that the price level appears to be coincident.

Whether the price level is procyclical or countercyclical, and whether it is a leading or a lagging variable, it can play an important role in resolving debates concerning the causes of business cycles, as we will see in Chapters 10 and 11. In contrast to the 1961–2002 Canadian data examined above, it appears that the price level was a pro-

---

[2]See A. Phillips, 1958, "The Relationship Between Unemployment and the Rate of Change in Money Wages in the United Kingdom, 1861–1957," *Economica* 25, 283–299.

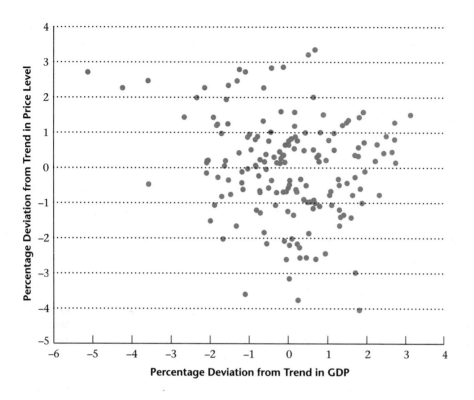

FIGURE 3.11

Scatter Plot for the Percentage Deviations from Trend in the Price Level (the Implicit GDP Price Deflator) and Real GDP for Canada, 1961–2002

The figure shows a negative correlation between the two for 1961–2002. Therefore, the price level is countercyclical for the period 1961–2002. The figure captures a reverse Phillips curve relationship.

Source: Adapted from the Statistics Canada CANSIM database, Series v1992067, v1997756.

cyclical variable over some periods of history in some countries, for example, during the period between the World Wars in Canada. Also, note that an alternative interpretation of Figure 3.12 is that the price level is a procyclical and lagging variable. That is, when real GDP is above (below) trend, the price level tends to be above (below) trend about two years later. However, without other evidence to guide us, we will stick to the interpretation that the price level is a countercyclical coincident variable in the Canadian data for 1961–2002.

In addition to Phillips curve relationships and reverse Phillips curve relationships, a key element of the comovement between nominal variables and aggregate economic activity is the positive correlation between deviations from trend in the nominal money supply and deviations from trend in real GDP. The money supply is a measure of the nominal quantity of assets used in making transactions in the economy. Depending on the measure of money under consideration, the money supply in Canada can include currency in circulation and transactions accounts at chartered banks and other depository institutions. In Figure 3.13 we show the percentage deviations from trend in a measure of the money supply (the black line) and in real GDP (the coloured line) over the period 1961–2002.[3] The procyclical nature of the money supply is fairly pronounced, with the correlation coefficient for the data in Figure 3.13 being 0.36. Another

---

[3]The money supply measure used here is the *monetary base*, a narrow measure of money. In Chapters 8 and 14, we will discuss the measurement of the money supply in more detail.

FIGURE 3.12

Price Level and GDP for Canada, 1961–2002

This figure shows the time series plot of the same data as in Figure 3.11. Here, we see that the price level (the black line) is countercyclical, coincident, and about as variable as real GDP (the coloured line).

Source: Adapted from the Statistics Canada CANSIM database, Series v1992067, v1997756.

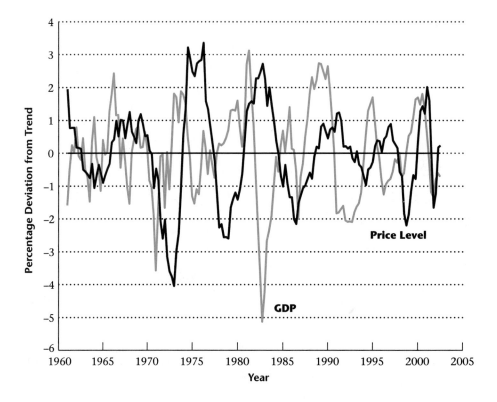

important observation concerning the nominal money supply and real GDP is that money tends to be a leading variable, which we observe as a tendency for turning points in the money supply to lead turning points in GDP in Figure 3.13. This observation was emphasized by Milton Friedman and Anna Schwartz,[4] who studied the behaviour of the money supply and real GDP in the United States over the period 1867–1960.

The money supply is somewhat more variable than GDP, with the standard deviation of the percentage deviations from trend in the money supply being 124.4% of what it is for GDP. This can also be observed in Figure 3.13.

Labour Market Variables

The last business cycle regularities we will examine are those in labour markets, relating to the variables we will determine in the business cycle models in Chapters 10 and 11. First, in Figure 3.14 we show percentage deviations from trend in employment (the black line) and in real GDP (the coloured line) for the period 1976–2001. Clearly, the deviations from trend in employment closely track those in real GDP, and so employment

---

[4]See M. Friedman and A. Schwartz, 1963, *A Monetary History of the United States: 1867–1960*, Princeton University Press, Princeton, NJ.

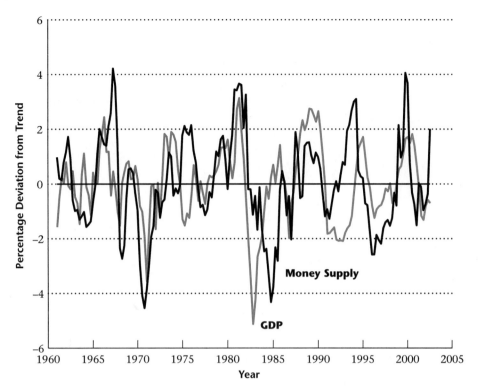

FIGURE 3.13

Percentage Deviations from Trend in the Money Supply (black line) and Real GDP (coloured line) for Canada, 1961–2002
Money is a procyclical and leading variable, and it is more variable than real GDP.

Source: Adapted from the Statistics Canada CANSIM database, Series v1992067, v37152.

is a procyclical variable. The correlation coefficient for the data in Figure 3.14 is 0.84. In terms of lead/lag relationships, we can observe a tendency in Figure 3.14 for turning points in employment to lag turning points in GDP, and so employment is a lagging variable. Employment is less variable than GDP, with the standard deviation of the percentage deviation from trend for employment being 90.8% of that for real GDP in Figure 13.14.

In the macroeconomic models we analyze, a key variable will be the market **real wage**, which is the purchasing power of the wage earned per hour worked. This is measured from the data as the average money wage for all workers, divided by the price level. The cyclical behaviour of the real wage will prove to be crucial in helping us discriminate among different theories of the business cycle in Chapters 10 and 11. The weight of empirical evidence indicates that the real wage is procyclical.[5] We do not show data on the aggregate real wage, as it is difficult to measure the relationship between real wages and real GDP by examining aggregate data. The key problem is that the composition of the labour force tends to change over the business cycle, which tends to bias the correlation between the real wage and real GDP. There is no strong evidence on whether the real wage is a leading or a lagging variable.

---

[5]For the evidence for the United States, see G. Solon, R. Barsky, and J. Parker, 1994, "Measuring the Cyclicality of Real Wages: How Important Is Composition Bias?" *Quarterly Journal of Economics*, February, 1–25.

FIGURE 3.14

Percentage Deviations from Trend in Employment (black line) and Real GDP (coloured line) for Canada, 1976–2001

Employment is procyclical, it is a lagging variable, and it is less variable than real GDP.

Source: Adapted from the Statistics Canada CANSIM database, Series v1992067, v159599, and from the Statistics Canada publication *Historical Statistics of Canada*, Catalogue 11-516, 1983, Series D175–189.

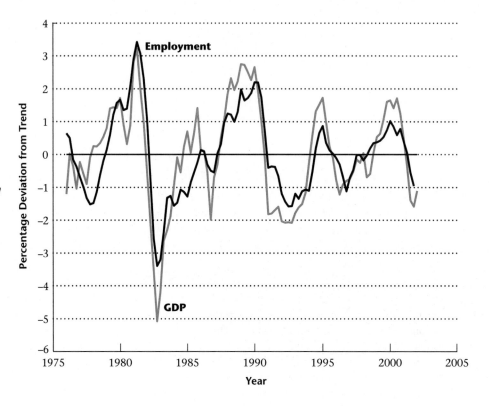

Comovement Summary

To summarize the business cycle facts discussed above, we present Tables 3.1 and 3.2. These, particularly Table 3.2, will prove very useful, particularly when we discuss the predictions of different theories of the business cycle in Chapters 10 and 11. A first test of the usefulness of macroeconomic theories is their ability to match what we see in macroeconomic data.

TABLE 3.1 Correlation Coefficients and Variability of Percentage Deviations from Trend

	Correlation Coefficient (GDP)	Std. Dev. (% of S.D. of GDP)
Consumption	0.82	85.0%
Investment	0.80	564.8
Price level	−0.18	101.0
Money supply	0.36	124.4
Employment	0.84	90.8

TABLE 3.2 **Summary of Business Cycle Facts**			
	Cyclicality	*Lead/Lag*	*Variability Relative to* GDP
Consumption	Procyclical	Coincident	Smaller
Investment	Procyclical	Coincident	Larger
Price level	Countercyclical	Coincident	Larger
Money supply	Procyclical	Leading	Larger
Employment	Procyclical	Lagging	Smaller
Real wage	Procyclical	?	—

We have concluded our study of measurement issues, in that we now know the basics of national income accounting, basic macroeconomic accounting identities, price measurement, labour market facts, and business cycle facts. In the next chapters, we will proceed to build useful macroeconomic models, starting with some basic microeconomic principles concerning the behaviour of consumers and firms.

Chapter Summary

This chapter discusses the main business cycle facts that we will use as a backdrop in our study of macroeconomic theory in the coming chapters. These facts will also be important in judging the performance of the business cycle theories in Chapters 10 and 11. The key business cycle facts relate to the deviations of important macroeconomic variables from their trends, and the comovements in these deviations from trend.

The most important business cycle fact is that real GDP fluctuates about trend in an irregular fashion. Though deviations from trend in real GDP are persistent, there is no observed regularity in the amplitude or frequency of fluctuations in real GDP about trend.

Business cycles are similar mainly in terms of the comovements among macroeconomic time series. Comovement can be discerned by plotting the percentage deviations from trend in two economic variables in a time series or in a scatter plot, or by calculating the correlation coefficient between the percentage deviations from trend.

We are interested principally in how a particular variable moves about trend relative to real GDP (whether it is procyclical, countercyclical, or acyclical), whether it is a leading, lagging, or coincident variable (relative to real GDP), and how variable it is relative to real GDP. In terms of the components of GDP, consumption is procyclical, coincident, and less variable than real GDP, while investment is procyclical, coincident, and more variable than real GDP.

In the data set we examined here, the price level is a countercyclical variable (there is a reverse Phillips curve), it is coincident, and it is about as variable as GDP. The money supply is procyclical, leading, and more variable than real GDP. The fact that the money supply tends to lead real GDP was assigned much importance by Milton Friedman. In the labour market, employment is procyclical, lagging, and less variable than real GDP. The real wage, too, is procyclical. However, there is no consensus among macroeconomists on whether the real wage is a leading or lagging variable.

Key Terms

business cycles: Fluctuations about trend in real GDP.
peak: A relatively large positive deviation from trend in real GDP.

trough: A relatively large negative deviation from trend in real GDP.

turning points: Peaks and troughs in real GDP.

amplitude: The maximum deviation from trend in an economic time series.

frequency: The number of peaks in an economic time series that occur per year.

boom: A series of positive deviations from trend in real GDP, culminating in a peak.

recession: A series of negative deviations from trend in real GDP, culminating in a trough.

persistent: Describes an economic time series that tends to stay above (below) trend when it has been above (below) trend during the recent past.

comovement: How aggregate economic variables move together over the business cycle.

time series: Sequential measurements of an economic variable over time.

positive correlation: Relationship between two economic time series when a straight line fit to a scatter plot of the two variables has a positive slope.

negative correlation: Relationship between two economic time series when a straight line fit to a scatter plot of the two variables has a negative slope.

scatter plot: A plot of two variables, x and y, with x measured on the horizontal axis, and y measured on the vertical axis.

procyclical: Describes an economic variable that tends to be above (below) trend when real GDP is above (below) trend.

countercyclical: Describes an economic variable that tends to be below (above) trend when real GDP is above (below) trend.

acyclical: Describes an economic variable that is neither procyclical nor countercyclical.

correlation coefficient: A measure of the degree of correlation between two variables.

perfectly positively correlated: Describes two variables that have a correlation coefficient of 1.

perfectly negatively correlated: Describes two variables that have a correlation coefficient of -1.

leading variable: An economic variable that helps to predict future real GDP.

lagging variable: An economic variable that past real GDP helps to predict.

coincident variable: An economic variable that neither leads nor lags real GDP.

composite index of business leading indicators *or* index of leading indicators: A weighted average of leading macroeconomic variables, which is sometimes used to forecast the deviations of real GDP from trend.

standard deviation: A measure of variability. The cyclical variability in an economic time series can be measured by the standard deviation of the percentage deviations from trend.

Phillips curve: A positive correlation between a money price or the rate of change in a money price, and a measure of aggregate economic activity.

reverse Phillips curve: A negative correlation between a money price or the rate of change in a money price, and a measure of aggregate economic activity.

real wage: The purchasing power of the wage earned per hour worked.

Questions for Review

1. What is the primary defining feature of business cycles?

2. Besides persistence, what are three important features of the deviations from trend in GDP?

3. Explain why forecasting GDP over the long term is difficult.

4. Why are the comovements in aggregate economic variables important?

5. What did Robert Lucas say about the comovements among economic variables?

6. How can we discern positive and negative correlation in a time series plot? In a scatter plot?

7. Give a noneconomic example of two variables that are positively correlated and an example of two variables that are negatively correlated.

8. Why is the index of leading economic indicators useful for forecasting GDP?

9. What are the three features of comovement that macroeconomists are interested in?

10. Describe the key business cycle regularities in consumption and investment expenditures.

11. What are the key business cycle regularities with respect to the price level and the money supply?

12. Does a Phillips curve relationship exist in the data set that was studied in this chapter?

13. What are the key business cycle regularities in the labour market?

Problems

1. Consider the following data, which are observations on x and y over several periods of time.

Period	x	y
1	100	500
2	200	500
3	200	1000
4	100	1000
5	50	500
6	50	250
7	100	250

a. Construct a scatter plot of y against x. Are y and x positively correlated, negatively correlated, or uncorrelated? Explain your answer.

b. Now, construct a time series of y and x. Is y a leading, lagging, or coincident variable with respect to x? Explain your answer.

c. Do x and y exhibit persistence? Explain.

2. From Figure 3.2, determine how many booms and recessions occurred from 1961 to 1976, and from 1977 to 2002, and calculate the average strength of booms and the average severity of recessions from 1961 to 1976 and from 1977 to 2002. To do this, count as peaks and troughs only those deviations from trend that exceed ±1%. As a measure of the strength of a boom or the severity of a recession, use the percentage deviation from trend of real GDP at the peak or trough, respectively.

a. When were booms more frequent, from 1961 to 1976 or from 1977 to 2002?

b. When were recessions more frequent, from 1961 to 1976 or from 1977 to 2002?

c. When were booms stronger, from 1961 to 1976 or from 1977 to 2002?

d. When were recessions more severe, from 1961 to 1976 or from 1977 to 2002?

3. For each of the following sets of two variables, determine whether there is a positive or negative correlation, and explain your answer.

a. Volume of auto traffic and the auto accident rate

b. Average level of training of air traffic controllers and airplane crashes

c. Seatbelt use and deaths on the road

d. Use of pesticides and crop yields

e. Success as a politician and IQ

4. For each of the following sets of two variables, determine whether the second variable leads or lags the first, and explain your answer.
   a. (i) Strictness of environmental protection laws; (ii) cleanliness of rivers
   b. (i) Average height of the population; (ii) average nutrition level of the population
   c. (i) Rainfall in Montreal; (ii) rainfall in Toronto
   d. (i) Percentage of the population owning guns; (ii) average IQ of the population
   e. (i) Hours spent doing homework; (ii) GPA

5. Average labour productivity is measured as Y/N, where Y is aggregate output and N is employment. Average labour productivity is a procyclical variable. What does this tell us about the comovements of aggregate output and employment over the business cycle? Reconcile this with the key business cycle facts in Tables 3.1 and 3.2.

6. Consumption of durables is more variable relative to trend than consumption of semi-durables, and consumption of semi-durables is more variable relative to trend than consumption of nondurables and services. Speculate on why we observe these phenomena, and relate this to the key business cycle facts in Tables 3.1 and 3.2.

7. From Figure 3.5, we determined that real imports and real GDP were positively correlated. Suggest a reason for this, and discuss.

8. From Figure 3.8, is the index of leading indicators infallible? That is, do peaks and troughs in the index always predict peaks and troughs in real GDP? Explain.

Working with the Data

1. Calculate the year-to-year (December to December) percentage increase in the consumer price index, and then do a scatter plot of this against the unemployment rate (match the December 1996 unemployment rate with the percentage change in the CPI from December 1995 to December 1996, for example). Do you observe a positive correlation, a negative correlation, or a correlation that is essentially zero? Is there a Phillips curve relationship here, or a reverse Phillips curve?

2. Gross domestic product data is available in Canada on a monthly as well as quarterly basis. Calculate the percentage year-to-year (December to December) growth rates in the monthly gross domestic product and the percentage year-to-year growth rates in the money supply (M2++). Graph the growth in monthly gross domestic product and in the money supply using a time series plot and using a scatter plot.
   a. Are growth in monthly gross domestic product and in the money supply positively correlated or negatively correlated?
   b. Does one time series lead the other, or are they coincident?
   c. Are your answers to (a) and (b) consistent with what we observed in Figure 3.13? Explain.

3. Plot detrended GDP and detrended consumption of durables, detrended GDP and detrended consumption of semidurables, detrended GDP and detrended consumption of nondurables, and detrended GDP and consumption of services.
   a. What do you notice in these plots as compared to Figure 3.9 for GDP and total consumption and Figure 3.10 for GDP and investment?
   b. Provide an explanation for the your observations in part (a).

4. Plot detrended GDP and each of: detrended residential investment in structures, detrended nonresidential investment in structures, detrended investment in machinery and equipment, and inventory investment.

   a. Which of the components of investment shows the most (least) variability relative to GDP?

   b. What lead/lag patterns do you detect in the plots?

   c. Provide possible explanations for the patterns you detected in parts (a) and (b).

A One-Period Model of the Macroeconomy

The goal of Part II is to construct a working model of the macroeconomy that can be used to analyze some key macroeconomic issues. The basic building blocks of this model will be the microeconomic behaviour of consumers and firms. We therefore start in Chapter 4 by analyzing the behaviour of a representative consumer and a representative firm, with each making decisions over one period. The representative consumer's fundamental choice in this environment concerns how to allocate time between work and leisure, making himself or herself as well off as possible while obeying his or her budget constraint. The representative firm chooses how much labour it should hire so as to maximize profits. In Chapter 5, we will build consumer behaviour and firm behaviour into a one-period macroeconomic model, in which there is a government that can spend and tax. This model will then be used to show that, under ideal conditions, free market outcomes can be socially efficient, that government spending crowds out private consumption while increasing aggregate output, and that increases in productivity increase welfare, consumption, and aggregate output.

CHAPTER 4

Consumer and Firm Behaviour: The Work–Leisure Decision and Profit Maximization

Whereas Chapters 2 and 3 focused on how we measure variables of macroeconomic interest, we will now turn to the construction and analysis of a particular macroeconomic model. Recall that, in Chapter 1, we saw how a macroeconomic model is built from a description of consumers and their preferences over goods, and of firms and the technology available to produce goods from available resources. In this chapter, we focus on the behaviour of consumers and firms in a simple model environment *with only one time period*. One-period decision making for consumers and firms will limit the kinds of macroeconomic issues we can address with the resulting model. However, this simplification will make it easier to understand the basic microeconomic principles of consumer and firm optimization on which we will build in the rest of this book. Given that there is only one time period, consumers and firms will make **static**, as opposed to **dynamic**, decisions. Dynamic decision making involves planning over more than one period, as, for example, when individuals make decisions concerning how much to spend today and how much to save for the future. Dynamic decisions will be analyzed in Part III.

With regard to consumer behaviour, we will focus on how a consumer makes choices concerning the tradeoff between consuming and working. For the consumer, consuming more goods comes at a cost: the consumer must work harder and will enjoy less leisure time. Primarily, we are interested in how a consumer's work–leisure choice is affected by his or her preferences and by the constraints he or she faces. For example, we want to know how a change in the market wage rate and in the consumer's nonwage income affects his or her choices concerning how much to work, how much to consume, and how much leisure time to take. For the firm, we focus on how the available technology for producing goods and the market environment influence the firm's decision concerning how much labour to hire during the period.

As was discussed in Chapter 1, a fundamental principle that we adhere to here is that consumers and firms *optimize*. That is, a consumer wishes to make himself or herself as well off as possible given the constraints he or she faces. Likewise, a firm acts to maximize profits, given market prices and the available technology. The optimization principle is a very powerful and useful tool in economics, and it helps in sharpening the predictions of economic models. Given optimizing behaviour by consumers and firms, we can then analyze how these economic agents will respond to changes in the environment they live in. For example, we will show how consumers and firms change their labour supply and labour demand, respectively, in response to a change in the market wage rate, and how consumers respond to a change in taxes. The knowledge we build up in this chapter concerning these optimal responses will be critical in the next chapter, where we study what happens in the economy as a whole when there is an important shock to the system, for example, a large increase in government spending or a major new invention.

The Representative Consumer

To begin, we will consider the behaviour of a single representative consumer, who will act as a stand-in for all of the consumers in the economy. We will show how to represent a consumer's preferences over the available goods in the economy, and how to represent the consumer's budget constraint, which tells us what goods it is feasible for the consumer to purchase given market prices. We then put preferences together with the budget constraint to determine how the consumer will behave given market prices, and how he or she responds to a change in nonwage income and to a change in the market wage rate.

THE REPRESENTATIVE CONSUMER'S PREFERENCES

It will prove simplest to analyze consumer choice, and will be adequate for the issues we will want to address in this chapter and the next, to suppose that there are two goods that consumers desire. The first is a physical good, which we can think of as an aggregation of all consumer goods in the economy, or measured aggregate consumption. We will call this the **consumption good**. The second good is **leisure**, which is any time spent not working in the market. Thus, in terms of our definition, leisure could include recreational activities, sleep, and work at home (cooking, yard work, housecleaning).

For macroeconomic purposes, it proves convenient to suppose that all consumers in the economy are identical. In reality, of course, consumers are not identical, but for many macroeconomic issues diversity among consumers is not essential to addressing the economics of the problem at hand, and considering it will only cloud our thinking. Identical consumers will in general behave in identical ways, and so we need only analyze the behaviour of one of these consumers. Further, if all consumers are identical, the economy will behave *as if* there were only one consumer, and it is therefore convenient to write down the model as having only a single **representative consumer**. We must recognize, however, that the representative consumer in our macroeconomic model plays the role of a stand-in for all consumers in the economy.

A key step in determining how the representative consumer makes choices is to show how we can capture the preferences of the representative consumer over leisure and consumption goods by a **utility function**, written as

$$U(C, l),$$

where U is the utility function, C is the quantity of consumption, and l is the quantity of leisure. We will refer to a particular combination of consumption and leisure—for example, (C_1, l_1), where C_1 is a particular consumption quantity and l_1 is a particular quantity of leisure—as a **consumption bundle**. The utility function represents how the consumer ranks different consumption bundles. That is, suppose that there are two different consumption bundles, representing different quantities of consumption and leisure, denoted (C_1, l_1) and (C_2, l_2). We say that (C_1, l_1) is *strictly preferred* by the consumer to (C_2, l_2) if

$$U(C_1, l_1) > U(C_2, l_2);$$

(C_2, l_2) is strictly preferred to (C_1, l_1) if

$$U(C_1, l_1) < U(C_2, l_2);$$

and the consumer is indifferent between the two consumption bundles if

$$U(C_1, l_1) = U(C_2, l_2).$$

It is useful to think of $U(C, l)$ as giving the level of happiness, or utility, that the consumer receives from consuming the bundle (C, l). Note, however, that the actual level of utility is irrelevant; all that matters for the consumer is what the level of utility is from a given consumption bundle *relative* to another one.

To use our representation of the consumer's preferences for analyzing macroeconomic issues, we must make some assumptions concerning the form that preferences take. These assumptions are useful for making the analysis work, and they are also consistent with how consumers actually behave. We will assume that the representative consumer's preferences have three properties: more is preferred to less; the consumer likes diversity in his or her consumption bundle; and consumption and leisure are normal goods. We will discuss each of these in turn.

1. *More is always preferred to less.* A consumer always prefers a consumption bundle that contains more consumption, more leisure, or both. This may appear unnatural, since it seems that we can get too much of a good thing. For example, consuming too much of one good may sometimes make one worse off, as when we overeat. However, in terms of general consumption goods, the average consumer in Canada today consumes far more than the average consumer 200 years ago would have dreamed possible, and it certainly seems that the average consumer today in Canada would like to consume more if it were feasible. Indeed, even the extremely wealthy appear to desire more than they have.

2. *The consumer likes diversity in his or her consumption bundle.* To see that this is a natural property of consumer preferences, consider a consumer who, instead of

consuming consumption goods and leisure, is making a decision about where to eat lunch during the week. Lynn can go to one of two restaurants to eat lunch, one of which serves only hamburgers, while the other serves only tuna sandwiches. One choice open to Lynn is to eat a hamburger for lunch on each day of the week, and another choice is to eat tuna sandwiches all week. Suppose that Lynn is indifferent between these two choices. However, if she has a preference for diversity, Lynn would prefer to alternate between restaurants during the week rather than eat at one place every day. In the case of our representative consumer, who is choosing among consumption bundles with different combinations of consumption goods and leisure, a preference for diversity means that, if the consumer is indifferent between two consumption bundles, then some mixture of the two consumption bundles will be preferable to either one. At the extreme, suppose that the consumer is indifferent between a consumption bundle that has 6 units of consumption and no leisure and another bundle that has no consumption goods and 8 units of leisure. Then, a preference for diversity implies that the consumer would prefer a third consumption bundle, consisting of half of each of the other bundles, to having either of the other consumption bundles. This preferable third consumption bundle would have 3 units of consumption goods and 4 units of leisure.

3. *Consumption and leisure are normal goods.* A good is **normal** for a consumer if the quantity of the good that he or she purchases increases when income increases. For example, meals at high-quality restaurants are a normal good for most people; if our income increases, we tend to eat out more in good places. In contrast, a good is **inferior** for a consumer if he or she purchases less of that good when income increases. An example of an inferior good is food from Denny's; most people would tend to eat less at Denny's as their income increases. In our model, then, given that consumption and leisure are normal goods, the representative consumer will purchase more consumption goods and increase his or her leisure time when income increases. This seems intuitively appealing; if, for example, you received a windfall increase in your income, perhaps through an inheritance, you would probably want to consume more goods as well as taking more vacation time (leisure). In practice, the behaviour of consumers is consistent with consumption and leisure being normal goods.

While we will postpone discussion of property 3 of the representative consumer's preferences until we have more machinery to analyze how the consumer behaves, our next step will be to show how we represent properties 1 and 2 graphically. It is helpful to consider the representative consumer's preferences using a graphical representation of the utility function, called the **indifference map**. The indifference map is a family of **indifference curves**.

DEFINITION
An *indifference curve* connects a set of points, with these points representing consumption bundles among which the consumer is indifferent.

Figure 4.1 shows two indifference curves. In the figure, I_1 is an indifference curve, and two points on the indifference curve are (C_1, l_1) (point B) and (C_2, l_2) (point D). Since these two consumption bundles lie on the same indifference curve, we must have $U(C_1, l_1) = U(C_2, l_2)$. That is, being indifferent implies that the consumer obtains the same level of happiness from each consumption bundle. Another indifference curve is I_2. Since indifference curve I_2 lies above indifference curve I_1, and we know more is preferred to less, consumption bundles on I_2 are strictly preferred to consumption bundles on I_1. For example, consider point A, which represents a consumption bundle with the same quantity of leisure as at point B, but with a higher quantity of the consumption good. Since more is preferred to less, A is strictly preferred to B.

An indifference curve has two key properties:

1. An indifference curve slopes downward.

2. An indifference curve is convex, that is bowed in toward the origin.

Since the indifference map is just the graphical representation of preferences, it should not be surprising that the properties of the indifference curve are related to the properties of preferences, 1 and 2, described above. In fact, property 1 of an indifference curve follows from property 1 of preferences (more is always preferred to less), and property 2 of an indifference curve follows from property 2 of preferences (the consumer likes diversity in his or her consumption bundles).

To see why the fact that indifference curves slope downward follows from the fact that more is preferred to less, consider Figure 4.2. At point A, consumption is C_1 and leisure is l_1. Suppose that we now consider holding the quantity of leisure constant for the consumer at l_1 and reduce the consumer's quantity of consumption to C_2, so that the consumer now has the consumption bundle represented by point D. Since more is

FIGURE 4.1

Indifference Curves

The figure shows two indifference curves for the consumer. Each indifference curve represents a set of consumption bundles among which the consumer is indifferent. Higher indifference curves represent higher welfare for the consumer.

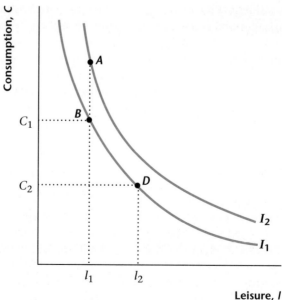

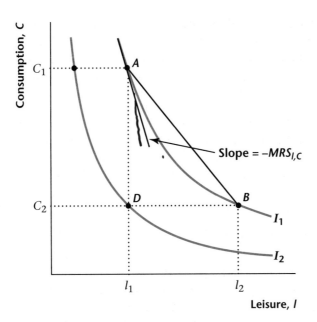

FIGURE 4.2

Properties of Indifference Curves

Indifference curves are downward-sloping because more is preferred to less. A preference for diversity implies that indifference curves are convex (bowed in toward the origin). The slope of an indifference curve is the negative of the marginal rate of substitution.

preferred to less, point D must be on a lower indifference curve (indifference curve I_2) than is point A (on indifference curve I_1). Now we can ask how much leisure we would have to add to l_1, holding consumption constant at C_2, to obtain a consumption bundle B such that the consumer is indifferent between A and B. Point B must lie below and to the right of point A since, if we are taking consumption goods away from the consumer, we need to give him or her more leisure. Thus, the indifference curve I_1 is downward-sloping because more is preferred to less.

To understand why the convexity of the indifference curve follows from the preference of the representative consumer for diversity, it is useful to introduce the following concept.

DEFINITION

The marginal rate of substitution of leisure for consumption, denoted $MRS_{l,C}$ is the rate at which the consumer is just willing to substitute leisure for consumption goods.

We have

$$MRS_{l,C} = -[\text{The slope of the indifference curve passing through } (C, l)].$$

To see why the marginal rate of substitution is minus the slope of the indifference curve, consider consumption bundles A and B in Figure 4.2. There, the rate at which the consumer is willing to substitute leisure for consumption in moving from A to B is the ratio $\frac{C_1 - C_2}{l_2 - l_1}$, or minus the slope of the line segment AB. Minus the slope of AB tells us how much consumption we need to take away for each unit of leisure added as we move from A to B, with the consumer being just indifferent between A and B. If we imagine choosing a point like point B on the indifference curve I_1 below point A but closer and closer to A, then as the distance between that point and A becomes small, the rate at which the consumer is willing to substitute leisure for consumption between A and the chosen point is the marginal rate of substitution, which is minus the slope of the indifference curve at point A (or minus the slope of a tangent to the indifference curve at A).

Suppose, for example, that Marla can choose how many weeks of vacation to take each year, and that she currently works 50 weeks in the year and takes two weeks of vacation, so that her leisure time is two weeks. To keep things simple, suppose Marla consumes only coconuts, so that we can measure her consumption in coconuts. Currently, she eats 500 coconuts per year. If Marla were to take one more week of vacation per year, she would be just as happy as she is now if she were to give up 50 coconuts per year. This implies that Marla's marginal rate of substitution of leisure for consumption, given her current consumption bundle of 500 coconuts of consumption and two weeks of leisure, is 50 coconuts per week.

Stating that an indifference curve is convex (property 2 of the indifference curve) is identical to stating that the marginal rate of substitution is diminishing. That is, note that the indifference curve in Figure 4.2 becomes flatter as we move down the indifference curve from left to right, that is, as the consumer receives more leisure and less of the consumption good. Thus, minus the slope of the indifference curve becomes smaller as leisure increases and consumption decreases. In other words, the marginal rate of substitution is diminishing. As we increase the quantity of leisure and reduce the quantity of consumption, the consumer needs to be compensated more and more in terms of leisure time to give up another unit of consumption. The consumer requires this extra compensation because of a preference for diversity.

To give a concrete example of a preference for diversity in terms of a consumption–leisure choice, suppose that Allen sleeps 8 hours in every 24-hour period, and so has 112 hours per week to split between work and leisure. Consider two situations. In the first, Allen takes 10 hours of leisure per week and works 102 hours, and in the second he takes 102 hours of leisure per week and works 10 hours. In the first circumstance, Allen is willing to give up much more consumption expenditure in exchange for one extra hour of leisure than in the second case.

THE REPRESENTATIVE CONSUMER'S BUDGET CONSTRAINT

Now that we know something about the representative consumer's preferences, we must also specify his or her constraints and objectives in order to predict what he or she will do. We will assume that the representative consumer behaves **competitively**. Here, competitive behaviour means that the consumer is a *price-taker*; he or she treats market prices as being given, and acts as if his or her actions have no effect on those prices. This is certainly an accurate description of reality if the consumer is small relative to the market, but of course this is not literally true if there is only one consumer. Recall, however, that the single representative consumer is a stand-in for all the consumers in the economy. Even though it is obvious that real economies do not have only one consumer, a real economy can still behave *as if* there were a single representative consumer.

An important assumption that we make at this stage is that there is no money in this economy. That is, there is no government-supplied currency to be used in exchange, and no banks through which people can conduct transactions—for example, through chequing accounts. For some macroeconomic issues, the complication of introducing money will not add anything to our analysis, and is best left out. Later, however, in Chapters 9–11, we begin to analyze the role that money plays in the macroeconomy, so that we can address issues such as the effects of inflation and the conduct of monetary policy.

An economy without monetary exchange is a **barter** economy. In a barter economy, all trade involves exchanges of goods for goods. There are only two goods here: consumption goods and time. When time is used at home, we call it leisure time, and when time is exchanged in the market, we call it work—more explicitly, labour time. Any trades in this economy must involve exchanges of labour time for consumption goods, or vice versa. The consumer is assumed to have h hours of time available, which can be allocated between leisure time, l, and time spent working (or labour supply), denoted by N^s. The **time constraint** for the consumer is then

$$l + N^s = h, \tag{4.1}$$

which states that leisure time plus time spent working must sum to total time available.

The Consumer's Real Disposable Income Having specified how the representative consumer allocates time between work and leisure, we can describe the consumer's real disposable income, which is wage income plus dividend income minus taxes.

Labour time is sold by the consumer in the labour market at a price w in terms of consumption goods. That is, one unit of labour time exchanges for w units of consumption goods. Therefore, w is the **real wage**, or the wage rate of the consumer in units of purchasing power. Throughout, the consumption good will play the role of **numeraire**, or the good in which all prices and quantities will be denominated. In actual economies, money is the numeraire, but in our barter economy model, the choice of numeraire is arbitrary. We choose the consumption good as numeraire, as this is a common convention.

If the consumer works N^s hours, then his or her real wage income will be wN^s, which is expressed in units of the consumption good. The second source of income for the consumer is profits distributed as dividends from firms. We will let π be the quantity of profits, in real terms, that the consumer receives. In our model, firms have to be owned by someone, and this someone must be the representative consumer. Therefore, any profits earned by firms must be distributed to the representative consumer as income, which we can think of as dividends. Thus, we will refer to π as real **dividend income**.

Finally, the consumer pays taxes to the government. We will assume that the real quantity of taxes is a **lump-sum** amount T. A lump-sum tax is a tax that does not depend in any way on the actions of the economic agent who is being taxed. In practice, no taxes are lump-sum; for example, the quantity of sales taxes we pay depends on the quantity of taxable goods that we buy, and our income taxes depend on how much we work. Taxes that are not lump-sum have important effects on the effective prices that consumers face in the market. For example, an increase in the sales tax on gasoline increases the effective price of gasoline for consumers relative to other goods. This change in the effective relative price of gasoline will in turn affect the demand for gasoline and for other goods. These distorting effects of taxation are important, but we will confine attention to lump-sum taxation for now, as this is simpler.

Real wage income plus real dividend income minus taxes is the consumer's real disposable income, and this is what the consumer has available to spend on consumption goods.

The Budget Constraint Now that we know how the representative consumer can allocate time between work and leisure, and what his or her real disposable income is, we can derive the consumer's budget constraint algebraically, and show it graphically.

We can view the representative consumer as receiving his or her real disposable income, and spending it in the market for consumption goods. What actually happens, however, is that the consumer receives income and pays taxes in terms of consumption goods, and then he or she decides how much to consume out of this disposable income. Since this is a one-period economy, which implies that the consumer has no motive to save, and because the consumer prefers more to less, all disposable income is consumed, so that we have

$$C = wN^s + \pi - T, \tag{4.2}$$

or total real consumption equals real disposable income. Equation (4.2) is the consumer's **budget constraint**. Now, substituting for N^s in (4.2) using (4.1), we get

$$C = w(h - l) + \pi - T. \tag{4.3}$$

The interpretation of Equation (4.3) is that the right-hand side is real disposable income, while the left-hand side is expenditure on consumption goods, so that total market expenditure is equal to disposable income.

Alternatively if we add wl to both sides of (4.3), we get

$$C + wl = wh + \pi - T. \tag{4.4}$$

An interpretation of Equation (4.4) is that the right-hand side is the implicit quantity of real disposable income the consumer has, and the left-hand side is implicit expenditure on the two goods, consumption and leisure. On the right-hand side of (4.4), since the consumer has h units of time, with each unit of time valued in real terms according to the market real wage w, and $\pi - T$ is real dividend income minus taxes, the total quantity of implicit real disposable income is $wh + \pi - T$. On the left-hand side of (4.4), C is what is spent on consumption goods, while wl is what is implicitly "spent" on leisure. That is, w is the market price of leisure time, since each unit of leisure is forgone labour, and labour time is priced at the real wage w. Thus, $C + wl$ is implicit real expenditure on consumption goods and leisure.

To graph the consumer's budget constraint, it is convenient to write Equation (4.4), in slope–intercept form, with C as the dependent variable, to get

$$C = -wl + wh + \pi - T, \tag{4.5}$$

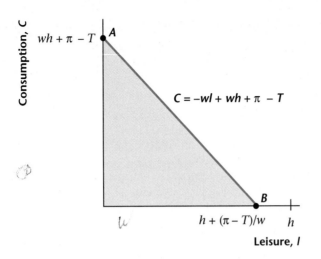

FIGURE 4.3

Representative Consumer's Budget Constraint ($T > \pi$)

The figure shows the consumer's budget constraint for the case where taxes are greater than the consumer's dividend income. The slope of the budget constraint is $-w$, and the constraint shifts with the quantity of nonwage real disposable income, $\pi - T$. All points in the shaded area and on the budget constraint can be purchased by the consumer.

so that the slope of the budget constraint is: $-w$, and the vertical intercept is $wh + \pi - T$. In Figure 4.3 we graph the budget constraint, Equation (4.5), as the line AB. Here, we have drawn the budget constraint for the case where $T > \pi$, so that dividend income minus taxes, $\pi - T$, is negative. Further, by setting $C = 0$ in Equation (4.5) and solving for l, we can get the horizontal intercept, $h + \frac{\pi - T}{w}$. The vertical intercept is the maximum quantity of consumption attainable for the consumer, which is what is achieved if the consumer works h hours and consumes no leisure. The horizontal intercept is the maximum number of hours of leisure that the consumer can take and still be able to pay the lump-sum tax.

Figure 4.4 shows what the consumer's budget constraint looks like in the case where $T < \pi$, in which case dividend income minus taxes, $\pi - T$, is positive. Here, the budget constraint is somewhat unusual, as it is kinked; the slope of the budget con-

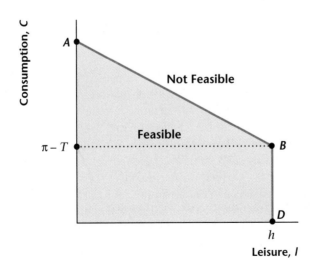

FIGURE 4.4

Representative Consumer's Budget Constraint ($T < \pi$)

The figure shows the consumer's budget constraint when taxes are less than dividend income. This implies that the budget constraint is kinked. The examples we study will always deal with this case, rather than the one where taxes are greater than dividend income. Consumption bundles in the shaded region and on the budget constraint are feasible for the consumer; all other consumption bundles are not feasible.

straint is $-w$ over its upper portion, and the constraint is vertical over its lower portion. There is a kink in the budget constraint because the consumer cannot consume more than h hours of leisure. Thus, at point B we have $l = h$, which implies that the number of hours worked by the consumer is zero. Points along BD all involve the consumer working zero hours and consuming some amount $C \leq \pi - T$—that is, the consumer always has the option of throwing away some of his or her dividend income. Even though the consumer does not work at point B, we have $C = \pi - T > 0$, as dividend income exceeds taxes. In what follows, we will always consider the case where $\pi - T > 0$, as this is the more complicated case (because of the kink in the consumer's budget constraint), and because ultimately it will not make any difference for our analysis whether we look only at the case $\pi - T > 0$ or $\pi - T < 0$.

The representative consumer's budget constraint tells us what consumption bundles are feasible for him or her to consume given the market real wage, dividend income, and taxes. In Figure 4.4, consumption bundles in the shaded region inside and on the budget constraint are feasible; all other consumption bundles are infeasible.

CONSUMER OPTIMIZATION

We have now described the representative consumer's preferences over consumption and leisure, and determined the budget constraint that tells us what combinations of consumption and leisure are feasible. Our next step is to put preferences together with the budget constraint so as to analyze how the representative consumer will behave.

To determine what choice of consumption and leisure the consumer will make, we will assume that the consumer is **rational**. Rationality in this context means that the representative consumer knows his or her own preferences and budget constraint and can evaluate which feasible consumption bundle is best for him or her. Basically, we are assuming that the consumer can make an informed optimization decision.

DEFINITION

The optimal consumption bundle is the point representing a consumption–leisure pair that is on the highest possible indifference curve, and is on or inside the consumer's budget constraint.

Consider Figure 4.5, and note that we are considering only the case where $T < \pi$, since ignoring the case where $T > \pi$ will not matter. We want to demonstrate why point H, where indifference curve I_1 is just tangent to the budget constraint ABD, is the optimal consumption bundle for the consumer. First, the consumer would never choose a consumption bundle inside the budget constraint because the consumer prefers more to less. For example, consider a point like J in Figure 4.5, which lies inside the budget constraint. Clearly, point F, which is on the budget constraint, is strictly preferred by the consumer to J since the consumer gets more consumption at point F than at J, while receiving the same quantity of leisure. Further, the consumer would not choose any points along BD other than B; B is preferred to any point on BD because more consumption goods are preferred to fewer consumption goods.

In considering the consumer's optimization problem, given the above we can restrict attention solely to points on the line segment AB in Figure 4.5. Which of these

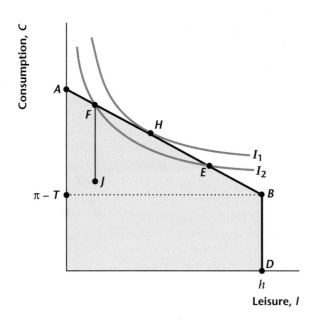

FIGURE 4.5

Consumer Optimization

The consumption bundle represented by point *H*, where an indifference curve is tangent to the budget constraint, is the optimal consumption bundle for the consumer. Points inside the budget constraint, such as *J*, cannot be optimal (more is preferred to less), and points such as *E* and *F*, where an indifference curve cuts the budget constraint, also cannot be optimal.

points will the consumer choose? Given the assumptions we have made about the representative consumer's preferences, we are guaranteed that there is a single consumption bundle on *AB* that is optimal for the consumer: the point at which an indifference curve is tangent to *AB*. Why is this the best the consumer can do? Again, consider Figure 4.5. At a point like *F*, minus the slope of the indifference curve passing through *F*, or $MRS_{l,C}$, is greater than minus the slope of the budget constraint at *F*, which is equal to *w*. Alternatively, at *F* the rate at which the consumer is willing to trade leisure for consumption is greater than the rate at which the consumer can trade leisure for consumption in the market, or $MRS_{l,C} > w$. Thus, the consumer would be better off if he or she sacrificed consumption for more leisure by moving from point *F* in the direction of *H*. Note that, in so doing, the consumer will move to successively higher indifference curves, which is another indication that he or she is becoming better off. Similarly, at point *E* in Figure 4.5, the indifference curve is flatter than the budget constraint, so that $MRS_{l,C} < w$. Thus, moving from point *E* toward point *H* implies that the consumer substitutes leisure for consumption and moves to higher indifference curves, becoming better off as a result. At point *H*, where an indifference curve is just tangent to the budget constraint, the rate at which the consumer is willing to trade leisure for consumption is equal to the rate at which leisure trades for consumption in the market, and thus the consumer is at his or her optimum. In other words, when the representative consumer is optimizing, we have

$$MRS_{l,C} = w, \qquad (4.6)$$

or the marginal rate of substitution of leisure for consumption is equal to the real wage. Note, in (4.6), that this optimizing, or marginal, condition, takes the following form: marginal rate of substitution of leisure for consumption equals the **relative price** of leisure in terms of consumption goods. In general, the relative price of a good *x* in terms of a good y is the number of units of y that trade for a unit of x. It is generally true that *consumer optimization in competitive markets will imply that the consumer sets the marginal rate of substitution of any good x for any other good y equal to the relative price of x in terms of y*. We will use this fact in later chapters.

Given the way we have drawn the budget constraint in Figure 4.5, there seems no obvious reason that the highest indifference curve could not be reached at point B, in which case the consumer would choose to consume all his or her time as leisure, as in Figure 4.6. However, this could not happen when we take account of the interaction of consumers and firms—it would imply that the representative consumer would not work, in which case nothing would be produced, and therefore the consumer would not have anything to consume. The assumption that the consumer always wishes to consume some of both goods (the consumption good and leisure) will prevent the consumer from choosing either point A or point B in Figure 4.5.

The assumption that the representative consumer behaves optimally subject to his or her constraints will be very powerful in giving us predictions about what the consumer does when his or her budget constraint changes, or when his or her preferences change. Is it plausible to assume that a consumer makes optimizing decisions? In our own lives, we can generally think of many occasions on which we did not make optimal decisions. For example, suppose Jennifer is self-employed and can choose how much vacation to take every year. Suppose that, for ten years, Jennifer takes two weeks of vacation every summer. One year, by chance, she takes three weeks of vacation, and finds that she is much happier than before. We might imagine this happening not because Jennifer's preferences or budget constraint changed, but because she does not really know her own preferences without experimenting with different consumption–leisure combinations. This would violate the assumption of rationality that we have made for the representative consumer, who always knows exactly what his or her pref-

FIGURE 4.6

The Representative Consumer Chooses Not to Work

The consumer's optimal consumption bundle is at the kink in the budget constraint, at *B*, so that the consumer does not work ($l = h$). This is a situation that cannot happen, taking into account consistency between the actions of the consumer and of firms.

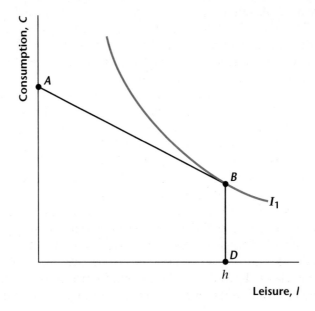

erences are. The defence for using optimizing behaviour for consumers as a fundamental principle in our models is that mistakes by the consumer are not likely to persist for a long time. Eventually, people learn how to behave optimally, and what is important, particularly in terms of macroeconomic models, is that people on average behave optimally, not that each individual in the economy always does so. Further, if we were to abandon optimization behaviour, there would be many possible alternatives, and it would be extremely difficult to get our models to make any predictions at all. While there is typically only one way to behave optimally, there are many ways in which individuals can be stupid!

How Does the Representative Consumer Respond to a Change in Real Dividends or Taxes? Recall from Chapter 1 that a macroeconomic model, once constructed, can be used to conduct "experiments," somewhat like the experiments conducted by a chemist or a physicist using a laboratory apparatus. Now that we have shown how the representative consumer makes choices about consumption and leisure, we are interested as economists in how the consumer will respond to changes in the economic environment he or she faces. We will carry out two experiments on the representative consumer. The first will be to change his or her real dividend income minus taxes, $\pi - T$, and the second will be to change the market real wage w that he or she faces. In each case, we will be interested in how these experiments affect the quantities of consumption and leisure chosen by the representative consumer.

We will first look at a change in real dividend income minus taxes, or $\pi - T$, which is the component of real disposable income that does not depend on the real wage w. In changing $\pi - T$, we hold w constant. A change in $\pi - T$ could be caused either by a change in either π or T, or both. For example, an increase in π could be caused by an increase in the productivity of firms, which in turn results in an increase in the dividends that are paid to the consumer. Similarly, if T decreases, this represents a tax cut for the consumer, and disposable income increases. In any case, we will think of the increase in $\pi - T$ as producing a **pure income effect** on the consumer's choices, since prices remain the same (w remains constant) while disposable income increases.

For the case where $\pi > T$, we will consider an increase in $\pi - T$ (recall that the $\pi < T$ case will not be fundamentally different). In Figure 4.7 suppose that initially $\pi = \pi_1$ and $T = T_1$, and then there are changes in π and T so that $\pi = \pi_2$ and $T = T_2$ with $\pi_2 - T_2 > \pi_1 - T_1$. Recall that the vertical intercept of the budget constraint is $wh + \pi - T$, so that initially the budget constraint of the consumer is ABD, and with the increase in $\pi - T$, the constraint shifts out to FJD. Note that FJ is parallel to AB, since the real wage has not changed, leaving the slope of the budget constraint $(-w)$ identical to what it was initially. Now suppose that initially the consumer chooses point H, where the highest indifference curve I_1 is reached on the initial budget constraint, and we have $l = l_1$ and $C = C_1$. When $\pi - T$ increases, which consumption bundle will the consumer choose? We have the consumer choosing point K, where the indifference curve I_2 is tangent to the new budget constraint. At point K, we have $l = l_2$ and $C = C_2$, so that consumption and leisure are both higher. Why would this necessarily be the case? Indeed, we could draw indifference curves that are consistent with more being preferred to less and a preference for diversity—which could have

FIGURE 4.7

**An Increase in the
Consumer's Dividend
Income**

Initially the consumer chooses
H, and when dividend income
rises (or taxes fall) this shifts
the budget constraint out in a
parallel fashion (the real wage,
which determines the slope of
the budget constraint, stays
constant). Consumption and
leisure both increase, as both
are normal goods.

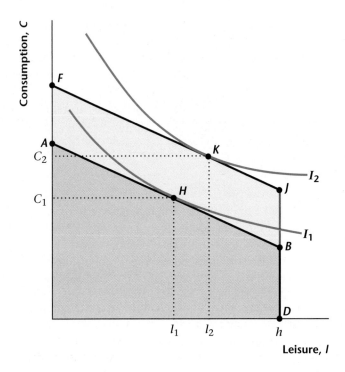

consumption falling or leisure falling—when income increases. Recall, however, that
we assumed earlier in this chapter that consumption and leisure are normal goods. This
means that, if we hold the real wage constant, an increase in income will imply that the
representative consumer will choose more consumption and more leisure, as is the case
in Figure 4.7.

To see why it is natural to assume that consumption and leisure are both normal
goods, consider a consumer, Paula, who receives a windfall increase in her income from
winning a lottery. It seems likely that, as a result, Paula will spend more on consumption goods and take more vacation time, thus working less and increasing leisure time.
This would happen only if Paula's preferences have the property that consumption and
leisure are normal goods.

The assumption that consumption and leisure are both normal implies that higher
nonwage disposable income increases consumption and reduces labour supply. Thus,
for example, given lower real taxes, consumers will spend more and work less. The
increase in income is given in Figure 4.7 by the distance *AF,* but the increase in consumption, $C_2 - C_1$, is less than *AF.* Though nonwage income increases, wage income
falls since the consumer is working less. The reduction in income from the decrease in
wage income will not completely offset the increase in nonwage income, as consumption
has to increase because it is a normal good.

**The Representative Consumer and Changes in the Real Wage: Income and
Substitution Effects** The second experiment we will examine is to change the real

wage faced by the representative consumer, holding everything else constant. In studying how consumer behaviour changes when the market real wage changes, we have some interest in how the consumer's quantity of consumption is affected, but we are perhaps most concerned with what happens to leisure and labour supply. In elementary economics, we typically treat supply curves as being upward-sloping, in that the quantity of a good supplied increases with the market price of the good, holding everything else constant. Labour supply, however, is different. Although it is straightforward to show that the quantity of consumption goods chosen by the consumer increases when the real wage increases, labour supply, N^s, may rise *or* fall when the real wage rises. Part of this section will focus on why this is the case.

In considering how the behaviour of the consumer changes in response to a change in the real wage w, we hold constant real dividends π and real taxes T. We do the experiment in this way to remove the pure income effect on consumer behaviour that we studied in the previous subsection. Consider Figure 4.8, where initially the budget constraint is ABD, and an increase in the real wage w causes the budget constraint to shift out to EBD. Here, note that EB is steeper than AB since the real wage has increased, but the kink in the budget constraint remains fixed at B, as nonwage disposable income, $\pi - T$, is unchanged. Initially, the consumer chooses point F, where indifference curve I_1 is tangent to the initial budget constraint. Here, $l = l_1$ and $C = C_1$. When the real wage increases, the consumer might choose a point like H, where indifference curve I_2 is tangent to the new budget constraint. As Figure 4.8 is drawn, leisure remains unchanged at l_1, and consumption increases from C_1 to C_2. What we want to show is that, given that

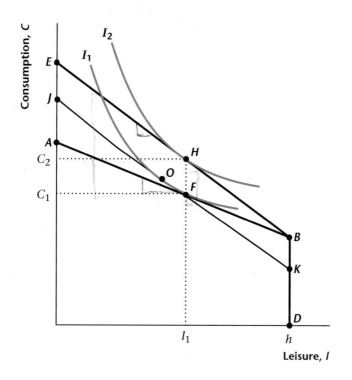

FIGURE 4.8

Increase in the Real Wage Rate—Income and Substitution Effects

An increase in the real wage shifts the budget constraint from *ABD* to *EBD*. The kink in the constraint remains fixed, and the budget constraint becomes steeper. Consumption must increase, but leisure may rise or fall, because of opposing substitution and income effects. The substitution effect is the movement from *F* to *O*; the income effect is the movement from *O* to *H*.

consumption and leisure are normal goods, consumption must increase but leisure may increase or decrease in response to an increase in the real wage. To understand why this is the case, we need to introduce the concepts of **income effect** and **substitution effect**.

The effects of an increase in the real wage on the consumer's optimal choice of consumption and leisure can be broken down into an income effect and a substitution effect as follows. First, given the new higher real wage, suppose that we take away dividend income from the consumer or increase taxes until he or she chooses a consumption bundle O that is on the initial indifference curve I_1. Thus, given the increase in the real wage, we have taken real disposable income away from the consumer so that he or she is just indifferent between the consumption bundle chosen (point O) and the initial consumption bundle (F). It is as if the consumer now faces the budget constraint JKD. The movement from F to O is a pure substitution effect in that it just captures the movement along the indifference curve in response to the increase in the real wage. The real wage increases, so that leisure has become more expensive relative to consumption goods, and the consumer substitutes away from the good that has become more expensive (leisure) to the one that has become relatively cheaper (consumption). Therefore, the substitution effect of the real wage increase is for consumption to increase and for leisure to decrease, and so the substitution effect is for labour supply, $N^s = h - l$, to increase.

Now, the movement from O to H is then a pure income effect, as the real wage stays the same as the budget constraint shifts out from JKD to EBD, and nonwage income increases. Since both goods are normal, consumption increases and leisure increases in moving from O to H. Thus, when the real wage increases, the consumer can consume more consumption goods and more leisure, since the budget constraint has shifted out. On net, then, consumption must increase, since the substitution and income effects both act to increase consumption. However, there are opposing substitution and income effects on leisure, so that it is ultimately unclear whether leisure will rise or fall. Therefore, an increase in the real wage could lead to an increase or a decrease in labour supply N^s.

To understand the intuition behind this result, assume Alex is working 40 hours per week and earning $15 per hour, so that his weekly wage income is $600. Now suppose that Alex's wage rate increases to $20 per hour and that he is free to set his hours of work. On the one hand, because his wage rate is now higher, the cost of taking leisure has increased, and Alex may choose to work more (the substitution effect). On the other hand, he could now work 30 hours per week, still receive $600 in wage income per week, and enjoy 10 more hours of free time (the income effect), so that Alex may choose to reduce his hours of work.

While some of the analysis we will do, particularly in Chapter 5, will involve work with indifference curves, it is sometimes useful to summarize consumer behaviour with supply and demand relationships. In Chapter 7 and in later chapters, it will often prove useful to work at the level of supply and demand curves in different markets. Then, an important relationship will be the **labour supply curve**, which tells us how much labour the representative consumer wishes to supply given any real wage. To construct the labour supply curve, one could imagine presenting the representative consumer with different real wage rates, and asking what quantity of labour the consumer would choose to supply at each wage rate. That is, suppose $l(w)$ is a function that tells us how much leisure the consumer wishes to consume, given the real wage w. Then, the labour supply curve is given by

$$N^s(w) = h - l(w).$$

Now, since the effect of a wage increase on the consumer's leisure choice is ambiguous, we do not know whether labour supply is increasing or decreasing in the real wage. Assuming that the substitution effect is larger than the income effect of a change in the real wage, labour supply will increase with an increase in the real wage, and the labour supply schedule will be upward-sloping as in Figure 4.9. Furthermore, we know that, since the quantity of leisure increases when nonwage disposable income increases, an increase in nonwage disposable income will shift the labour supply curve to the left, that is, from N^s to N^s_1 as shown in Figure 4.10. In analysis where we work with supply and demand relationships, we will typically assume that the substitution effect of an increase in the real wage dominates the income effect, so that the labour supply curve is upward-sloping, as in Figure 4.9.

An Example: Consumption and Leisure are Perfect Complements An example of consumer optimization that we can work out in a straightforward way, both algebraically and graphically, is the case where the representative consumer's preferences have the **perfect complements** property. Goods are perfect complements for the consumer if he or she always wishes to consume these goods in fixed proportions. In practice, there are many cases of goods that are perfect complements. For example, right shoes are almost always consumed one-to-one with left shoes, in that a right shoe is typically not much good without the left shoe. Also, cars and tires are usually consumed in fixed proportions of one to four (ignoring the spare tire, of course).

If consumption and leisure are perfect complements, the consumer always wishes to have $\frac{C}{l}$ equal to some constant, or

$$C = al, \qquad (4.7)$$

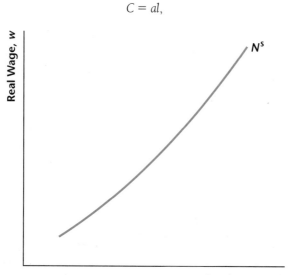

FIGURE 4.9

Labour Supply Curve

The labour supply curve tells us how much labour the consumer wishes to supply for each possible value for the real wage. Here, the labour supply curve is upward-sloping, which implies that the substitution effect of an increase in the real wage is larger than the income effect for the consumer.

FIGURE 4.10

Effect of an Increase in Dividend Income or a Decrease in Taxes

The labour supply curve shifts to the left when dividend income increases or taxes fall, due to a positive income effect on leisure for the consumer.

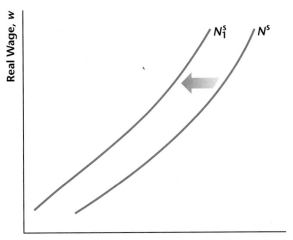

where $a > 0$ is a constant. With perfect complements, the indifference curves of the consumer will be L-shaped, as in Figure 4.11, with the right angles of the indifference curves falling along the line $C = al$. At a point such as E on indifference curve I_2, adding more consumption while holding leisure constant will simply make the consumer indifferent, as will adding more leisure while holding consumption constant. The consumer can be better off only if he or she receives more of both goods. Note that perfect complements preferences do not satisfy all the properties for preferences that we assumed in general. More is not always preferred to less, as the consumer is not better off with more of one good unless he or she has more of the other good as well. However, the consumer does have a preference for diversity, but of a very dramatic sort. That is, as we move downward along the indifference curve, the slope does not become flatter in a smooth way, but goes instantly from vertical to horizontal.

The optimal consumption bundle for the consumer will always be along the line $C = al$, as in Figure 4.11, where the budget constraint is ABD and the consumer optimizes by choosing a point F on the budget constraint and on the highest indifference curve, which is point F. Algebraically, the quantities of consumption and leisure must solve (4.7) and must also satisfy the budget constraint

$$C = w(h - l) + \pi - T. \tag{4.8}$$

Now, Equations (4.7) and (4.8) are two equations in the two unknowns, C and l, with $a, w, h, \pi,$ and T given. We can solve these two equations for the two unknowns by substitution to get

$$l = \frac{wh + \pi - T}{a + w},$$

$$C = \frac{a(wh + \pi - T)}{a + w}.$$

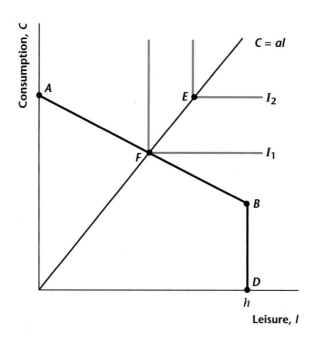

FIGURE 4.11

Perfect Complements
When consumption and leisure are perfect complements for the consumer, indifference curves are L-shaped with right angles along the line $C = al$, where a is a constant. The budget constraint is ABD, and the optimal consumption bundle will always be on the line $C = al$.

As you see, leisure and consumption increase with nonwage disposable income $\pi - T$, and we can also show that consumption and leisure both increase when the real wage w increases. Note that with perfect complements there are no substitution effects. Further, if a increases, so that the consumer prefers more consumption relative to leisure, then as seems obvious the consumer will choose more of C and less of l at the optimum.

We will use perfect complements preferences in examples in Chapter 6. Another simple example dealt with in the problems at the end of this chapter is the case where preferences have the **perfect substitutes** property. In this case, the marginal rate of substitution is constant and the indifference curves are downward-sloping straight lines.

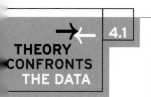

THEORY CONFRONTS THE DATA

4.1

Income and Substitution Effects and Labour Supply in Canada

In Figures 4.12 and 4.13 we examine some empirical evidence on the behaviour of the real wage rate in manufacturing and average hours worked in manufacturing for the period 1961–2002. The real wage rate is measured as the average wage in dollars divided by the consumer price index, and it corresponds to the real wage rate w in our model. Likewise, average hours worked in manufacturing per week corresponds to $N^s = h - l$ in the model. To use the theory of the representative consumer in this chapter to address what we see in Figures 4.12 and 4.13, we need to assume that the main factor affecting labour supply for the average worker in manufacturing over this period was changes in the real wage. This is not a bad assumption in this context, as the primary source of income for manufacturing workers should be wage income (i.e., we do not need to worry about the possibility that nonwage income may have changed significantly over this period for some consumers), and neglecting changes in taxes probably is not too harmful.

In Figure 4.12 we observe a trend increase in the real wage rate from 1961 until sometime in the late 1970s. Indeed, over that period, the real wage rate rose by about 60% (note that we have adjusted the real wage so that it equals 100 at the beginning of the sample). The real wage then stayed roughly constant, with some variation, from the late 1970s until 2002. Figure 4.13 shows that, from 1961 until the late 1970s, average hours decreased from more than 40 hours per week to about 38.5 hours per week. After the late 1970s, average hours per week fluctuated somewhat, but there was no strong upward or downward trend. This evidence is consistent with the existence of an income effect on labour supply stronger than the substitution effect. Thus, labour supply decreased from 1961 until the late 1970s as the real wage increased, and remained roughly constant from the late 1970s on, when the real wage was roughly constant.

The key point is that the observations on the real wage and hours worked might appear puzzling if we were to analyze the data in terms of a standard upward-sloping supply curve for labour. However, given the deeper knowledge of labour supply that comes from an analysis of income and substitution effects, these observations are not puzzling at all. This is not to say that we can explain *anything* in terms of labour market observations by appealing to opposing income and substitution effects. A careful analysis of the data would require that our explanations for what we see in Figures 4.12 and 4.13 be quantitatively consistent, and consistent with other kinds of evidence about labour market behaviour.

FIGURE 4.12

Real Wage in Manufacturing, for Canada, 1961–2002

An upward trend in real wages until the late 1970s corresponds to a decrease in average hours worked in manufacturing over the same period. This can be explained by a tendency over this period for the income effect to exceed the substitution effect.

Source: Adapted from the Statistics Canada CANSIM database, Series v75659, v256166, v1590642.

FIGURE 4.13

Average Hours per Week in Manufacturing for Canada, 1961–2002

Average hours worked in manufacturing decrease on trend until the late 1970s, after which there is essentially no trend.

Source: Adapted from the Statistics Canada CANSIM database, Series v75536, v255604, v1600903.

The Representative Firm

In our model economy, consumers and firms come together to exchange labour for consumption goods. While the representative consumer supplies labour and demands consumption goods, we will turn now to the behaviour of firms, which demand labour and supply consumption goods. The choices of the firms are determined by the available technology and by profit maximization. As with consumer behaviour, we will ultimately focus here on the choices of a single, representative firm.

The firms in this economy own productive capital (plant and equipment), and they hire labour to produce consumption goods. We can describe the production technology available to each firm by a **production function**, which describes the technological possibilities for converting factor inputs into outputs. We can express this relationship in algebraic terms as

$$Y = zF(K, N^d),$$

where z is **total factor productivity**, Y is output of consumption goods, K is the quantity of capital input in the production process, N^d is the quantity of labour input measured as total hours worked by employees of the firm, and F is a function. Since this is a one-period or static (as opposed to dynamic) model, we treat K as being a fixed input to production, and N^d as a variable factor of production. That is, in the short run, firms cannot vary the quantity of plant and equipment (K) they have, but they have flexibility in hiring and laying off workers (N^d). Total factor productivity z captures the degree of sophistication of the production process. That is, an increase in z will make both factors of production, K and N^d, more productive, in that, given factor inputs, higher z implies that more output can be produced.

For example, suppose that the above production function represents the technology available to a bakery. The quantity of capital, K, includes the building in which the bakery operates, ovens for baking bread, a computer for doing the bakery accounts, and other miscellaneous equipment. The quantity of labour, N^d, is total hours worked by all the bakery employees, including the manager, the bakers who operate the ovens, and the employees who work selling the bakery's products to customers. The variable z, total factor productivity, can be affected by the techniques used for organizing production. For example, bread could be produced either by having each baker operate an individual oven, using this oven to produce different kinds of bread, or each baker could specialize in making a particular kind of bread, and use the oven that happens to be available when an oven is needed. If the latter production method produces more bread per day using the same inputs of capital and labour, that method implies a higher value of z than the first method.

For our analysis, we need to discuss several important properties of the production function. Before doing this, we will need the following definition.

DEFINITION

The marginal product of a factor of production is the additional output that can be produced with one additional unit of that factor input, holding constant the quantities of the other factor inputs.

In terms of the production function above, there are two factor inputs, labour and capital. Figure 4.14 shows a graph of the production function, fixing the quantity of capital at some arbitrary value, K^*, and allowing the labour input, N^d, to vary. Some of the properties of this graph require further explanation. In the figure, the marginal

FIGURE 4.14

Production Function, Fixing the Quantity of Capital and Varying the Quantity of Labour

The marginal product of labour is the slope of the production function at a given point. Note that the marginal product of labour declines with the quantity of labour.

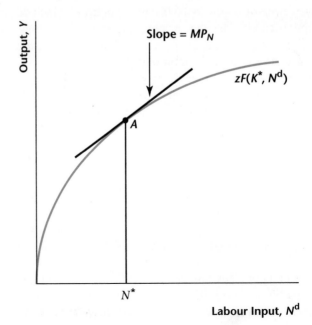

product of labour, given the quantity of labour N^*, is the slope of the production function at point A; this is because the slope of the production function is the additional output produced from an additional unit of the labour input when the quantity of labour is N^* and the quantity of capital is K^*. We will let MP_N denote the marginal product of labour.

Next, in Figure 4.15 we graph the production function again, but this time we fix the quantity of labour at N^* and allow the quantity of capital to vary. In Figure 4.15, the marginal product of capital, denoted MP_K, given the quantity of capital K^*, is the slope of the production function at point A.

The production function has five key properties, which we will discuss in turn.

1. *The production function exhibits constant returns to scale.* **Constant returns to scale** means that, given any constant $x > 0$, the following relationship holds:

$$xzF(K,N^d) = zF(xK, xN^d).$$

That is, if all factor inputs are changed by a factor x, output changes by the same factor x. For example, if all factor inputs double ($x = 2$), then output also doubles. The alternatives to constant returns to scale in production are **increasing returns to scale** and **decreasing returns to scale**. Increasing returns to scale implies that large firms (firms producing a large quantity of output) are more efficient than small firms, whereas decreasing returns to scale implies that small firms are more efficient than large firms. With constant returns to scale, a small firm is just as efficient as a large firm. Indeed, constant returns to scale means that a very large firm simply replicates, many times over, how a very small firm produces. Given a constant-returns-to-scale production function, the economy will behave in exactly the same way if there were many small firms producing consumption goods as it would if there were a few large firms, provided all firms behave competitively (they are

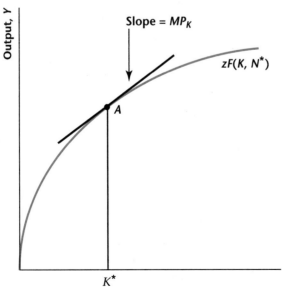

FIGURE 4.15
Production Function, Fixing the Quantity of Labour and Varying the Quantity of Capital
The slope of the production function is the marginal product of capital, and the marginal product of capital declines with the quantity of capital.

price-takers in product and factor markets). Given this, it is most convenient to suppose that there is only one firm in the economy, the **representative firm**—which (as with the representative consumer), it is helpful to think of as a convenient stand-in for many firms, all with the same constant-returns-to-scale production function. In practice, it is clear that in some industries decreasing returns to scale are important. For example, high-quality restaurant food seems to be produced most efficiently on a small scale. Alternatively, increasing returns to scale are important in the automobile industry, where essentially all production occurs in large-scale firms, such as the Ford Motor Company of Canada. This does not mean, however, that it is harmful to assume there exists constant returns to scale in production at the aggregate level, as in our model. Even the largest firm in the Canadian economy produces a small amount of output relative to Canadian GDP. The aggregate economy can exhibit constant returns to scale in aggregate production, even if this is not literally true for each firm in the economy.

2. *The production function has the property that output increases when either the capital input or the labour input increases.* In other words, the marginal products of labour and capital are both positive: $MP_N > 0$ and $MP_K > 0$. In Figures 4.14 and 4.15, these properties of the production function are exhibited by the upward slope of the production function. Recall that the slope of the production function in Figure 4.14 is the marginal product of labour and the slope in Figure 4.15 is the marginal product of capital. Positive marginal product is a quite natural property of the production function, as this states simply that more inputs yield more output. In the bakery example discussed previously, if the bakery hires more workers given the same capital equipment, it will produce more bread, and if it installs more ovens given the same quantity of workers, it will also produce more bread.

3. *The marginal product of labour decreases as the quantity of labour increases.* In Figure 4.14 the declining marginal product of labour is reflected in the concavity of the production function. That is, the slope of the production function in Figure 4.14, which is equal to MP_N, decreases as N^d increases. The following example helps to illustrate why the marginal product of labour should fall as the quantity of labour input increases. Suppose accountants work in an office building that has one photocopy machine, and suppose they work with pencils and paper but at random intervals need to use the photocopy machine. The first accountant added to the production process, Sara, is very productive—that is, she has a high marginal product—as she can use the photocopy machine whenever she wants. However, when the second accountant, Paul, is added, on occasion when Sara wants to use the machine she gets up from her desk, walks to the machine, and finds that Paul is using it. Thus, some time is wasted. Paul and Sara produce more than Sara alone, but what Paul adds to production (his marginal product) is lower than the marginal product of Sara. Similarly, adding a third accountant, Julia, will make for even more congestion around the photocopy machine, and Julia's marginal product will be lower than Paul's marginal product, which is lower than Sara's. Figure 4.16 shows the representative firm's marginal product of labour schedule. This is a graph of the firm's marginal product, given a fixed quantity of capital, as a function of the

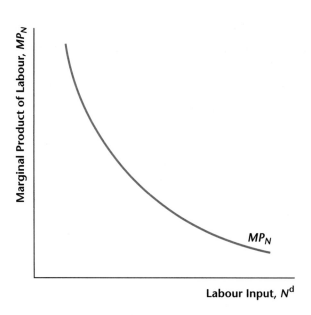

FIGURE 4.16

Marginal Product of Labour Schedule for the Representative Firm

The marginal product of labour declines as the quantity of labour used in the production process increases.

labour input. That is, this is the graph of the slope of the production function in Figure 4.14. Note that the marginal product schedule is always positive and that it slopes downward.

4. *The marginal product of capital decreases as the quantity of capital increases.* This property of the production function is very similar to the previous one, and it is illustrated in Figure 4.15 by the decreasing slope, or concavity, of the production function. In terms of the example above, if we suppose that Sara, Paul, and Julia are the accountants working in the office and imagine what happens as we add photocopy machines, we can gain some intuition as to why the decreasing-marginal-product-of-capital property is natural. Adding the first photocopy machine adds a great deal to total output, as Sara, Paul, and Julia now can duplicate documents that formerly had to be copied by hand. With three accountants in the office, however, there is congestion around the machine. This congestion is relieved with the addition of a second machine, so that the second machine increases output, but the marginal product of the second machine is smaller than the marginal product of the first machine, and so on.

5. *The marginal product of labour increases as the quantity of capital input increases.* To provide some intuition for this property of the production function, let's once again return to the example of the accounting firm. Suppose that Sara, Paul, and Julia initially have one photocopy machine to work with. Adding another photocopy machine amounts to adding capital equipment. This will relieve congestion around the copy machine, and make each of Sara, Paul, and Julia more productive, including Julia, who was the last accountant added to the workforce at the firm. Therefore, adding more capital increases the marginal product of labour, for each quantity of labour. In Figure 4.17 an increase in the quantity of capital from K_1 to K_2 shifts the marginal product of labour schedule to the right, from MP_N^1 to MP_N^2.

FIGURE 4.17

Adding Capital Increases the Marginal Product of Labour
For each quantity of the labour input, the marginal product of labour increases when the quantity of capital used in production increases.

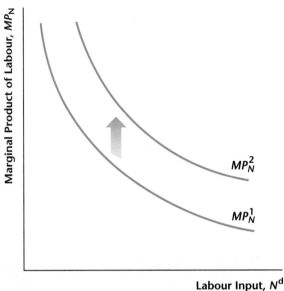

THE EFFECT OF A CHANGE IN TOTAL FACTOR PRODUCTIVITY ON THE PRODUCTION FUNCTION

Changes in total factor productivity, z, will be critical to our understanding of the causes of economic growth and business cycles, and so we must understand how a change in z alters the production technology. An increase in total factor productivity z has two important effects. First, since more output can be produced given capital and labour inputs when z increases, this shifts the production function up. In Figure 4.18, with the quantity of capital fixed at K^*, there is an upward shift in the production function when z increases from z_1 to z_2. Second, the marginal product of labour increases when z increases. This is reflected in the fact that the slope of the production function when $z = z_2$ in Figure 4.18 is higher than the slope given $z = z_1$, for any given quantity of the labour input, N^d. In Figure 4.19 the marginal product of labour schedule shifts to the right from MP_N^1 to MP_N^2 when z increases. Note that an increase in z has a similar effect on the marginal product of labour schedule as an increase in the capital stock (see Figure 4.17).

What could cause a change in total factor productivity? In general, an increase in z arises from anything that permits more output to be produced for given inputs. In the macroeconomy, there are many factors that can cause z to increase. One of these factors is technological innovation. The best examples of technological innovations that increase total factor productivity are changes in the organization of production or in management techniques. For example, the assembly line, introduced to automobile manufacturing by Henry Ford (see the box Macroeconomics in Action 4.1) brought about a huge increase in the quantity of Model T Fords that could be produced using the same quantities of capital equipment and workers. Some of the most important inventions of the twentieth century—for example, the personal computer—might more appropriately be considered to involve increases in the capital stock rather than

Henry Ford and Total Factor Productivity

The Ford Motor Company was founded in the United States in 1903 by Henry Ford and a financial backer, but Ford achieved only modest success until the introduction to the market of the Model T Ford in 1908. This car proved to be extremely popular, because it was light, strong, simple, and relatively easy to drive. Given the high demand for Model T cars, Henry Ford decided to increase output, but he did this not by simply replicating his existing production process through the construction of identical plants; rather, he increased total factor productivity, while also augmenting the capital and labour inputs in production. A key element of the total factor productivity increase was the introduction of the assembly line to automobile manufacturing. Henry Ford borrowed this idea from assembly lines used in the Chicago meat-packing industry. However, the general principle at work in the assembly line was known much earlier, for example by Adam Smith, the father of modern economics. In *The Wealth of Nations*, Smith discusses how production was organized in a pin factory, as an illustration of what he called the "division of labour":

> One man draws out the wire, another straightens it, a third cuts it … the important business of making a pin is, in this manner, divided into about eighteen distinct operations….[1]

Smith was impressed by how the specialization of tasks led to increased productivity in the manufacture of pins. More than a century later, Henry Ford's assembly line replaced an arrangement where automobiles were assembled by teams that each accumulated parts and completed a single automobile in a single location in the plant. Just as in the pin factory, Ford was able to exploit the gains from specialization that the assembly line permitted. Each worker performed only one specialized task, and therefore automobiles could be completed at a much higher rate.

The increase in total factor productivity at the Ford Motor Company was reflected in the fact that, in 1914, 13 000 workers produced 260 720 cars at Ford, while in the rest of the U.S. automobile industry 66 350 workers produced 286 770 cars. Thus, output per worker at Ford was almost five times that in the rest of the U.S. auto industry! We do not have measures of the size of the capital stock at Ford and elsewhere in the auto industry, so that there is a slim chance that the higher quantity of output per worker at Ford could have been due simply to higher capital per worker. However, it seems safe to say that total factor productivity at Ford Motor Company increased by a remarkable amount due to the innovations of Henry Ford, and these innovations were quickly imitated in the auto industry around the world.[2]

---

[1]See Adam Smith, *An Enquiry into the Nature and Causes of the Wealth of Nations*, Liberty Fund, Indianapolis, reprinted 1981, p. 15.
[2]See H. Ford, 1926, *My Life and Work*, Doubleday, Page and Co., New York; A. Nevins, 1954, *Ford: The Times, the Man, the Company*, Charles Scribner's and Sons, New York.

increases in z, since the new technology is embodied in capital equipment. A second factor that acts to increase z is good weather. Weather is especially important for production in the agricultural and construction sectors. For example, crop yields are higher, given factor inputs, if rainfall is higher (as long as it is not *too* high), and construction projects proceed more quickly if rainfall is lower. A third factor affecting z is government regulations. For example, if the government imposes regulations requiring that firms install pollution abatement equipment, this may be good for the welfare of the population, but it results in a decrease in z. This happens because pollution abatement equipment increases the quantity of the capital input in the production process, but

FIGURE 4.18

**Total Factor Productivity
Increases**
An increase in total factor
productivity has two effects:
More output is produced
given each quantity of the
labour input, and the marginal
product of labour increases
for each quantity of the
labour input.

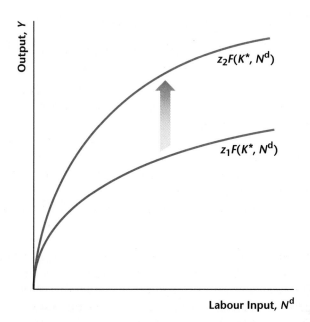

contributes nothing to measured output. Finally, an increase in the relative price of energy is often interpreted as a decrease in z. When the relative price of energy increases, firms use less energy in production, and this reduces the productivity of both capital and labour, thus causing a decrease in z. Major increases in the price of energy occurred in Canada in the 1970s and early 1980s, and particularly in 1973–74 and 1979–80, with important macroeconomic consequences that we will study in Chapters 5, 7, and 11.

FIGURE 4.19

**Effect of an Increase in Total
Factor Productivity on the
Marginal Product of Labour**
When total factor productivity
increases, the marginal product of labour schedule shifts
to the right.

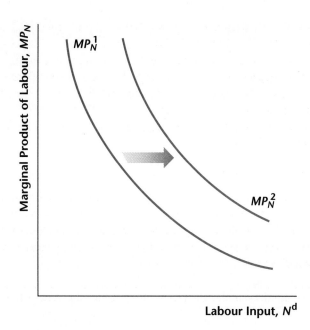

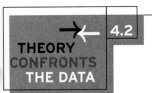

4.2 Total Factor Productivity and the Canadian Aggregate Production Function

So far we have assumed that the production function for the representative firm takes the form $Y = zF(K, N^d)$, where the function F has some very general properties (constant returns to scale, diminishing marginal products, etc.). When macroeconomists work with data to test theories, or when they want to simulate a macroeconomic model on the computer to study some quantitative aspects of a theory, they need to be much more specific about the form the production function takes. A very common production function used in theory and empirical work is the **Cobb-Douglas production function**. This function takes the form

$$Y = zK^a(N^d)^{1-a},$$

where a is a parameter, with $0 < a < 1$. The exponents on K and N^d in the function sum to 1 ($a + 1 - a = 1$), which reflects constant returns to scale. It will turn out that if there are profit-maximizing price-taking firms and constant returns to scale, then a Cobb-Douglas production function implies that a will be the share of national income that capital receives (in our model, the profits of firms), and $1 - a$ the share that labour receives (wage income before taxes) in equilibrium. What is remarkable is that, from the National Income and Expenditure Accounts of Canada, the capital and labour shares of national income have been roughly constant in Canada, which is consistent with the Cobb-Douglas production function. Given this, an empirical estimate of a is the average share of capital in national income, which from the data is about 0.3, or 30%, so a good approximation to the actual Canadian aggregate production function is

$$Y = zK^{0.3}(N^d)^{0.7}. \tag{4.9}$$

In Equation (4.9), the quantities Y, K, and N^d can all be measured. For example, Y can be measured as real GDP from the NIEA, K can be measured as the total quantity of capital in existence, built up from investment expenditures in the NIEA, and N^d can be measured as total employment, in the survey done by Statistics Canada. But how is total factor productivity z measured? Total factor productivity cannot be measured directly, but it can be measured indirectly, as a residual. That is, from Equation (4.9), if we can measure Y, K, and N^d, then a measure of z is the **Solow residual** (named after Robert Solow[1]), which is calculated as

$$z = \frac{Y}{K^{0.3}(N^d)^{0.7}}. \tag{4.10}$$

In Figure 4.20 we graph the Solow residual, calculated using Equation (4.10) and measurements of Y, K, and N^d as described above. Note that measured total factor productivity grows over time, and that it fluctuates about trend. In Chapters 8 and 11, we will see how growth and fluctuations in total factor productivity can cause growth and fluctuations in real GDP.

---

[1]See R. Solow, 1957, "Technical Change and the Aggregate Production Function," *Review of Economic Statistics* 39, 312–320.

FIGURE 4.20

The Solow Residual for Canada, 1961–2001

The Solow residual is a measure of total factor productivity, and it is calculated here using a Cobb-Douglas production function. Measured total factor productivity has increased over time, and it also fluctuates about trend, as shown.

Source: Adapted from the Statistics Canada CANSIM database, Series v3860085, v2461119, v3822183, v1078498, and from the Statistics Canada publication *Historical Statistics of Canada*, Catalogue 11-516, 1983, Series D175–189.

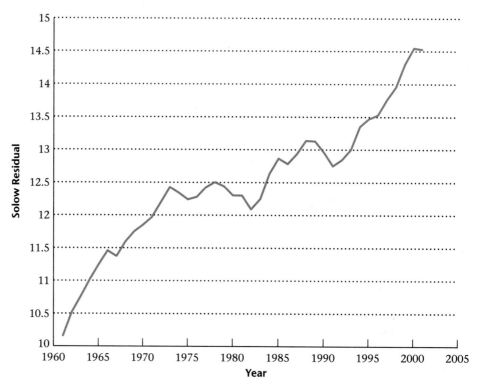

THE PROFIT MAXIMIZATION PROBLEM OF THE REPRESENTATIVE FIRM

Now that we have studied the properties of the representative firm's production technology, we can examine the determinants of the firm's demand for labour. Like the representative consumer, the representative firm behaves competitively, in that it takes as given the real wage, which is the price at which labour trades for consumption goods. The goal of the firm is to maximize its profits, given by $Y - wN^d$, where Y is the total revenue that the firm receives from selling its output, in units of the consumption good, and wN^d is the total real cost of the labour input, or total real variable costs. Then, substituting for Y using the production function $Y = zF(K, N^d)$, the firm's problem is to choose N^d to maximize

$$\pi = zF(K, N^d) - wN^d,$$

where K is fixed. Here, π is real profit. In Figure 4.21 we graph the revenue function, $zF(K, N^d)$, and the variable cost function, wN^d. Profit is then the difference between total revenue and total variable cost. Here, to maximize profits, the firm will choose $N^d = N^*$ in Figure 4.21. The maximized quantity of profits, π^*, is the distance AB in Figure 4.21. For future reference, note also that π^* is the distance ED, where AE is a line drawn parallel to the variable cost function. Thus, AE has slope w. At the profit-maximizing quantity of labour, N^*, *the slope of the total revenue function is equal to the slope of the total*

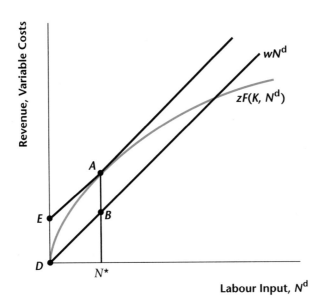

FIGURE 4.21

Revenue, Variable Costs, and Profit Maximization
$Y = zF(K, N^d)$ is the firm's revenue, while wN^d is the firm's variable cost. Profits are the difference between the former and the latter. The firm maximizes profits at the point where marginal revenue equals marginal cost, or $MP_N = w$. Maximized profits are the distance AB, or the distance ED.

variable cost function. But the slope of the total revenue function is just the slope of the production function, or the marginal product of labour, and the slope of the total variable cost function is the real wage w. Thus, the firm maximizes profits by setting

$$MP_N = w. \tag{4.11}$$

To understand the intuition behind Equation (4.11), note that the contribution to the firm's profits of having employees work an extra hour is the extra output produced minus what the extra input costs—that is, $MP_N - w$. Given a fixed quantity of capital, the marginal product of labour is very high for the first hour worked by employees, and the way we have drawn the production function in Figure 4.17, MP_N is very large for $N^d = 0$, so that $MP_N - w > 0$ for $N^d = 0$. Thus, it is worthwhile for the firm to hire the first unit of labour, as this implies positive profits. As the firm hires more labour, MP_N falls, and each additional unit of labour is contributing less to revenue, but contributing the same amount, w, to costs. Eventually, at $N^d = N^*$, the firm has hired enough labour so that hiring an additional unit will imply $MP_N - w < 0$, which in turn means that hiring an additional unit of labour will only cause profits to go down, and this cannot be optimal. Therefore, the profit-maximizing firm will choose its labour input according to Equation (4.11).

In our earlier example of the accounting firm, suppose that there is one photocopy machine at the firm, and output for the firm can be measured in terms of the clients the firm has. Each client pays $20 000 per year to the firm, and the wage rate for an accountant is $50 000 per year. Therefore, the real wage is $\frac{50,000}{20,000} = 2.5$ clients. If the firm has one accountant, it can handle 5 clients per year, if it has two accountants it can handle 9 clients per year, and if it has three accountants it can handle 11 clients per year. What is the profit-maximizing number of accountants for the firm to hire? If the

FIGURE 4.22

The Marginal Product of Labour Curve Is the Labour Demand Curve of the Profit-Maximizing Firm

This is true because the firm hires labour up to the point where $MP_N = w$.

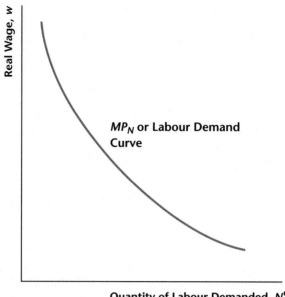

firm hires Sara, her marginal product is 5 clients per year. This exceeds the real wage of 2.5 clients, so it would be worthwhile for the firm to hire Sara. If the firm hires Sara and Paul, Paul's marginal product is 4 clients per year. This also exceeds the market real wage, and it would also be worthwhile to hire Paul. If the firm hires Sara, Paul, and Julia, Julia's marginal product is 2 clients per year, which is less than the market real wage of 2.5 clients. Therefore, it would be optimal to hire two accountants, Sara and Paul.

Our analysis tells us that the representative firm's marginal product of labour schedule, as shown in Figure 4.22, is the firm's demand curve for labour. This is because the firm maximizes profits for the quantity of labour input that implies $MP_N = w$. Therefore, given a real wage w, the marginal product of labour schedule tells us how much labour the firm needs to hire such that $MP_N = w$, and so the marginal product of labour schedule and the firm's demand curve for labour are the same thing.

In this chapter, we have determined the important elements of the microeconomic behaviour of a representative consumer and a representative firm. In the next chapter, we will put this behaviour together in a macroeconomic model that can be used to address some important macroeconomic issues. In this model, the consumer and the firm interact in markets, where the consumer supplies labour and demands consumption goods, and the firm demands labour and supplies consumption goods.

Chapter Summary

In this chapter, we studied the behaviour of the representative consumer and the representative firm in a one-period, or static, environment. This behaviour will be the basis for constructing a macroeconomic model that we can work with in Chapter 5. The representative consumer stands in for the large number of consumers that exist in the economy as a whole, and the representative firm stands in for a large number of firms.

The representative consumer's goal is to choose consumption and leisure to make himself or herself as well off as possible while respecting his or her budget constraint. More is always preferred to less and there is preference for diversity in consumption and leisure. The consumer is a price-taker: he or she treats the market real wage as given, and his or her real disposable income is real wage income plus real dividend income, minus real taxes. Graphically, the representative consumer optimizes by choosing the consumption bundle where an indifference curve is tangent to the budget constraint or, what is the same thing, the marginal rate of substitution of leisure for consumption is equal to the real wage.

Assuming consumption and leisure are normal goods, an increase in the representative consumer's income will lead to an increase in consumption and an increase in leisure, which means labour supply goes down. An increase in the real wage will lead to an increase in consumption, but it may cause leisure to rise or fall, because there are opposing income and substitution effects. Therefore, the consumer's labour supply may increase or decrease when the real wage increases.

The representative firm chooses the quantity of labour to hire to maximize profits, with the quantity of capital fixed in this one-period environment. The firm's production technology is captured by the production function, which has constant returns to scale, a diminishing marginal product of labour, and a diminishing marginal product of capital. Further, the marginal products of labour and capital are positive, and the marginal product of labour increases with the quantity of capital. An increase in total factor productivity increases the quantity of output that can be produced with any quantities of labour and capital, and it increases the marginal product of labour. When the firm optimizes, it sets the marginal product of labour equal to the real wage. This implies that the firm's marginal product of labour schedule is its demand curve for labour.

Key Terms

static decision: A decision made by a consumer or firm for only one time period.

dynamic decision: A decision made by a consumer or firm for more than one time period.

consumption good: A single good that represents an aggregation of all consumer goods in the economy.

leisure: Time spent not working in the market.

representative consumer: A stand-in for all consumers in the economy.

utility function: A function that captures a consumer's preferences over goods.

consumption bundle: A given consumption–leisure combination.

normal good: A good for which consumption increases as income increases.

inferior good: A good for which consumption decreases as income increases.

indifference map: A set of indifference curves representing a consumer's preferences over goods; has the same information as the utility function.

indifference curve: A set of points that represents consumption bundles among which a consumer is indifferent.

marginal rate of substitution: Minus the slope of an indifference curve, or the rate at which the consumer is just willing to trade one good for another.

competitive behaviour: Actions taken by a consumer or firm if market prices are outside its control.

barter: An exchange of goods for goods.

time constraint: Condition that hours worked plus leisure time sum to total time available to the consumer.

real wage: The wage rate in units of the consumption good.

numeraire: The good in which prices are denominated.

dividend income: Profits of firms that are distributed to the consumer, who owns the firms.

lump-sum tax: A tax that is unaffected by the actions of the consumer or firm being taxed.

budget constraint: Condition that consumption equals wage income plus nonwage income minus taxes.

rational: Describes a consumer who makes an informed optimizing decision.

optimal consumption bundle: The consumption bundle for which the consumer is as well off as possible while satisfying the budget constraint.

relative price: The price of a good in units of another good.

pure income effect: The effect on the consumer's optimal consumption bundle due to a change in real disposable income, holding prices constant.

income effect: The effect on the quantity consumed of a good of a price change, due to having effectively different income.

substitution effect: The effect on the quantity consumed of a good of a price change, holding the consumer's welfare constant.

labour supply curve: A relationship describing the quantity of labour supplied for each level of the real wage.

perfect complements: Two goods that are always consumed in fixed proportions.

perfect substitutes: Two goods with a constant marginal rate of substitution between them.

production function: A function describing the technological possibilities for converting factor inputs into output.

total factor productivity: A variable in the production function that makes all factors of production more productive if it increases.

marginal product: The additional output produced when another unit of a factor of production is added to the production process.

constant returns to scale: A property of the production technology whereby if the firm increases all inputs by a factor x, this increases output by the same factor x.

increasing returns to scale: A property of the production technology whereby if the firm increases all inputs by a factor x, this increases output by more than the factor x.

decreasing returns to scale: A property of the production technology whereby if the firm increases all inputs by a factor x, this increases output by less than the factor x.

representative firm: A stand-in for all firms in the economy.

Cobb-Douglas production function: A particular mathematical form for the production function that fits Canadian aggregate data well.

Solow residual: A measure of total factor productivity obtained as a residual from the production function, given measures of aggregate output, labour input, and capital input.

Questions for Review

All questions refer to the elements of the macroeconomic model developed in this chapter.

1. What goods do consumers consume in this model?

2. How are a consumer's preferences over goods represented?

3. What three properties do the preferences of the representative consumer have? Explain the importance of each.

4. What two properties do indifference curves have? How are these properties associated with the properties of the consumer's preferences?

5. What is the representative consumer's goal?

6. When the consumer chooses his or her optimal consumption bundle while respecting his or her budget constraint, what condition is satisfied?

7. How is the representative consumer's behaviour affected by an increase in real dividend income?

8. How is the representative consumer's behaviour affected by an increase in real taxes?

9. Why might hours worked by the representative consumer decrease when the real wage increases?

10. What is the representative firm's goal?

11. Why is the marginal product of labour diminishing?

12. What are the effects on the production function of an increase in total factor productivity?

13. Explain why the marginal product of labour curve is the firm's labour demand curve.

Problems

1. Use a diagram to show that if the consumer prefers more to less, then indifference curves cannot cross.

2. In this chapter, we showed an example where the consumer has preferences for consumption with the perfect complements property. Suppose, alternatively, that leisure and consumption goods are *perfect substitutes*. In this case, an indifference curve is described by the equation

$$u = al + bC,$$

where a and b are positive constants, and u is the level of utility. That is, a given indifference curve has a particular value for u, with higher indifference curves having higher values for u.
   a. Show what the consumer's indifference curves look like when consumption and leisure are perfect substitutes, and determine graphically and algebraically what consumption bundle the consumer will choose. Show that the consumption bundle the consumer chooses depends on the relationship between $\frac{a}{b}$ and w, and explain why.
   b. Do you think it likely that any consumer would treat consumption goods and leisure as perfect substitutes?
   c. Given perfect substitutes, is more preferred to less? Do preferences satisfy the diminishing marginal rate of substitution property?

3. Suppose that the government imposes a proportional income tax on the representative consumer's wage income. That is, the consumer's wage income is $w(1 - t)(h - l)$, where t is the tax rate. What effect does the income tax have on consumption and labour supply? Explain your results in terms of income and substitution effects.

4. Show that the consumer is better off with a lump-sum tax rather than a proportional tax on wage income (as in question 3) given that either tax yields the same revenue for the government. You will need to use a diagram to show this. *Hint:* The consumption bundle the consumer chooses under the proportional tax must be just affordable given the lump-sum tax.

5. Suppose that the representative consumer's dividend income increases, and his or her wage rate falls at the same time. Determine the effects on consumption and labour supply, and explain your results in terms of income and substitution effects.

6. Suppose that a consumer can earn a higher wage rate for working "overtime." That is, for the first q hours the consumer works, he or she receives a real wage rate of w_1, and for hours worked more than q he or she receives w_2, where $w_2 > w_1$. Suppose that the consumer pays no taxes and receives no nonwage income, and he or she is free to choose hours of work.
   a. Draw the consumer's budget constraint, and show his or her optimal choice of consumption and leisure.
   b. Show that the consumer would never work q hours, or anything very close to q hours. Explain the intuition behind this.
   c. Determine what happens if the overtime wage rate w_2 increases. Explain your results in terms of income and substitution effects. You will need to consider the case of a worker who initially works overtime, and a worker who initially does not work overtime.

7. Suppose that the government imposes a producer tax. That is, the firm pays t units of consumption goods to the government for each unit of output it produces. Determine the effect of this tax on the firm's demand for labour.

8. Suppose that the government subsidizes employment. That is, the government pays the firm s units of consumption goods for each unit of labour that the firm hires. Determine the effect of the subsidy on the firm's demand for labour.

9. Suppose that the firm has a minimum quantity of employment, N^*, that is, the firm can produce no output unless the labour input is greater than or equal to N^*. Otherwise, the firm produces output according to the same production function as specified in this chapter. Given these circumstances, determine the effects of an increase in the real wage on the firm's choice of labour input. As well, construct the firm's demand curve for labour.

10. Supposing that a single consumer works for a firm, the quantity of labour input for the firm, N, is identical to the quantity of hours worked by the consumer, $h - l$. Graph the relationship between output produced, Y, on the vertical axis and leisure hours of the consumer, l, on the horizontal axis, which is implied by the production function of the firm. (In Chapter 5, we will refer to this relationship as the *production possibilities frontier*.) What is the slope of the curve you have graphed?

11. Suppose a firm has a production function given by $Y = zK^{0.3}N^{0.7}$.
   a. If $z = 1$ and $K = 1$, graph the production function. Is the marginal product of labour positive and diminishing?
   b. Now, graph the production function when $z = 2$ and $K = 1$. Explain how the production function changed from part (a).
   c. Next, graph the production function when $z = 1$ and $K = 2$. What happened now?
   d. Given this production function, the marginal product of labour is given by $MP_N = 0.7zK^{0.3}N^{-0.3}$. Graph the marginal product of labour for $(z, K) = (1, 1)$, $(2, 1)$, $(1, 2)$, and explain what you get.

Working with the Data

1. The ratio of employment to the total population might be taken to be a measure of the fraction of time spent working by the average working age person in the population. This measure might correspond to the concept of employment, N, in our model.
   a. Calculate and plot the ratio of employment to the total population for the years 1961 through 2001.
   b. Comment on the movements over time in this ratio, with particular reference to the real wage data in Figure 4.12.

c. How would you tell a story about the income and substitution effects in labour supply decisions that would be consistent with this data?

d. Do you think that the ratio of employment to the total population is a good measure of average hours worked per person in the economy? Explain why or why not.

2. Using annual data on real gross domestic product, employment, and the total capital stock, calculate the Solow residual using a Cobb-Douglas production function for the years 1961 through 2001.

a. Calculate the percentage growth rate in the Solow residual for each of the years 1962 through 2001.

b. Calculate the percentage growth rate in real GDP for the years 1962 through 2001.

c. Plot the percentage growth rates in parts (a) and (b), and comment on the relationship between the two. What might explain this relationship?

3. An alternative measure of productivity to total factor productivity is *average labour productivity*, which is calculated as Y/N, where Y is aggregate output and N is employment. Calculate average labour productivity from annual data for 1961–2001, and compare this to your plot of the Solow residual for the same years as calculated in question 2. Comment on what you see in the two plots, and explain.

CHAPTER 5

A Closed-Economy One-Period Macroeconomic Model

In Chapter 4, we studied the microeconomic behaviour of a representative consumer and a representative firm. In this chapter, our first goal will be to take this microeconomic behaviour and build it into a working model of the macroeconomy. Then, we will use this model to illustrate how unconstrained markets can produce economic outcomes that are socially efficient. This social efficiency will prove to be useful in how we use our model to analyze some important macroeconomic issues. We will show how increases in government spending increase aggregate output and crowd out private consumption expenditures, and how increases in productivity can lead to increases in aggregate output and the standard of living.

We want to start our approach to macroeconomic modelling in this chapter by analyzing how consumers and firms interact in markets in a **closed economy**. This is a model of a single country that has no interaction with the rest of the world—it does not trade with other countries. It is easier to first understand how a closed economy works, and much of the economic intuition we will build up for the closed-economy case will carry over to an **open economy**, where international trade is allowed. Further, for many economic questions, particularly the ones addressed in this chapter, the answers will not be fundamentally different if we allow the economy to be open.

There are three different actors in this economy, the representative consumer who stands in for the many consumers in the economy who sell labour and buy goods, the representative firm that stands in for the many firms in the economy that buy labour and sell goods, and the government. We have already described the behaviour of the representative consumer and representative firm in detail in Chapter 4; it only remains to explain what the government does.

Government

The behaviour of the government here is quite simple. It wishes to purchase a given quantity of consumption goods, G, and finances these purchases by taxing the representative consumer. In practice, governments provide many different goods and services, including roads and bridges, national defence, air traffic control, and education. Which goods and services the government should provide is subject to both political and economic debate, but economists generally agree that the government has a special role to play in providing **public goods**, such as national defence, which are difficult or impossible for the private sector to provide. National defence is a good example of a public good, since it is difficult to get an individual to pay for it in a private market according to how much of it he or she uses.

To keep things as simple as possible, for now we will not be specific about the public goods nature of government expenditure. What we want to capture here is that government spending uses up resources, and we will model this by assuming that government spending simply involves taking goods from the private sector. Output is produced, and the government purchases an **exogenous** amount G of this output, with the remainder consumed by the representative consumer. An exogenous variable is determined outside the model, while an **endogenous** variable is determined by the model itself. Government spending is exogenous in our model, as we are assuming that government spending is independent of what happens in the rest of the economy. The government must abide by the **government budget constraint**, which we write as

$$G = T,$$

or government purchases equal taxes, in real terms.

Introducing the government in this way allows us to study some basic effects of **fiscal policy**. In general, fiscal policy refers to the government's choices over its expenditures, taxes, transfers, and borrowing. Recall from Chapter 2 that government expenditures are purchases of final goods and services, while transfers are simply reallocations of purchasing power from one set of individuals to another. Since this is a one-period economic environment, the government's choices are very limited, as described by the above government budget constraint. The government cannot borrow to finance government expenditures, since there is no future in which to repay its debt, and the government does not tax more than it spends, as this would imply that the government would foolishly throw goods away. The government budget deficit, which is $G - T$ here, is always zero. Thus, the only elements of fiscal policy we will study in this chapter are the setting of government purchases, G, and the macroeconomic effects of changing G. In Chapter 6, we will explore what happens when the government can run deficits and surpluses.

Competitive Equilibrium

Now that we have looked at the behaviour of the representative consumer, the representative firm, and the government, what remains in constructing our model is to show how consistency is obtained in the actions of all these economic agents. Once we have done this, we can use this model to make predictions about how the whole economy behaves in response to changes in the economic environment.

Mathematically, a macroeconomic model takes the exogenous variables, which for the purposes of the problem at hand are determined outside the system we are modelling, and determines values for the endogenous variables, as outlined in Figure 5.1. In

FIGURE 5.1

**A Model Takes Exogenous
Variables and Determines
Endogenous Variables**
Exogenous variables are
determined outside a macroeconomic model. Given the
exogenous variables, the
model determines the
endogenous variables. In
experiments, we are interested
in how the endogenous
variables change when there
are changes in exogenous
variables.

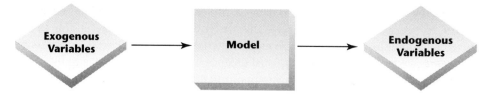

the model we are working with here, the exogenous variables are G, z, and K— that is, government spending, total factor productivity, and the economy's capital stock, respectively. The endogenous variables are C, N^s, N^d, T, Y, and w—that is, consumption, labour supply, labour demand, taxes, aggregate output, and the market real wage. Making use of the model is a process of running experiments in order to determine how changes in the exogenous variables will change the endogenous variables. By running these experiments, we hope to understand real-world macroeconomic events, and to say something about macroeconomic policy. For example, one of the experiments we will run on our model in this chapter is to change exogenous government spending, and then determine the effects on consumption, employment, aggregate output, and the real wage. An example of the phenomena this will help us to understand are the events that occurred in the economy during World War II, when there was a large increase in government spending.

By consistency we mean that, given market prices, demand is equal to supply in each market in the economy. Such a state of affairs is called a **competitive equilibrium**. Here, *competitive* refers to the fact that all consumers and firms are price-takers, and the economy is in *equilibrium* when the actions of all consumers and firms are consistent. When demand equals supply in all markets, we say that markets **clear**. In our model economy, there is only one price, which is the real wage w. We can also think of the economy as having only one market, on which labour time is exchanged for consumption goods. In this labour market, the representative consumer supplies labour and the representative firm demands labour. A competitive equilibrium is achieved when, given the exogenous variables G, z, and K, the real wage w is such that *the quantity of labour the consumer wishes to supply is equal to the quantity of labour the firm wishes to hire*. Also, note that the consumer's supply of labour is in part determined by taxes T and dividend income π. In a competitive equilibrium, T must satisfy the government budget constraint, and π must be equal to the profits generated by the firm.

A competitive equilibrium is a set of endogenous quantities, C (consumption), N^s (labour supply), N^d (labour demand), T (taxes), Y (aggregate output), and an endogenous real wage w, such that, given the exogenous variables G (government spending), z (total factor productivity), and K (capital stock), the following are satisfied:

1. The representative consumer chooses C (consumption) and N^s (labour supply) to make himself or herself as well off as possible subject to his or her budget constraint, given w (the real wage), T (taxes), and π (dividend income). That is, the representative consumer optimizes given his or her budget constraint, which is determined by the real wage, taxes, and the profits the consumer receives from the firm as dividend income.

2. The representative firm chooses N^d (labour demand) to maximize profits, with maximized output $Y = zF(K, N^d)$, and maximized profits $\pi = Y - wN^d$. The firm treats z (total factor productivity), K (the capital stock), and w (the real wage) as given. That is, the representative firm optimizes given total factor productivity, its capital stock, and the market real wage. In equilibrium, the profits that the representative firm earns must be equal to the dividend income that is received by the consumer.

3. The market for labour clears, that is, $N^d = N^s$. The quantity of labour that the representative firm wants to hire is equal to the quantity of labour the representative consumer wants to supply.

4. The government budget constraint is satisfied—that is, $G = T$. The taxes paid by consumers are equal to the exogenous quantity of government spending.

An important property of a competitive equilibrium is that

$$Y = C + G, \tag{5.1}$$

which is the income–expenditure identity. Recall from Chapter 2 that we generally state the income–expenditure identity as $Y = C + I + G + NX$, where I is investment and NX is net exports. In this economy, there is no investment expenditure, as there is only one period, and net exports are zero, as the economy is closed, so that $I = 0$ and $NX = 0$.

To show why the income–expenditure identity holds in equilibrium, we start with the representative consumer's budget constraint,

$$C = wN^s + \pi - T, \tag{5.2}$$

or consumption expenditures equal real wage income plus real dividend income minus taxes. In equilibrium, dividend income is equal to the firm's maximized profits, or $\pi = Y - wN^d$, and the government budget constraint is satisfied, so that $T = G$. If we then substitute in Equation (5.2) for π and T, we get

$$C = wN^s + Y - wN^d - G. \tag{5.3}$$

In equilibrium, labour supply is equal to labour demand, or $N^s = N^d$, which then gives us, substituting for N^s in Equation (5.3) and rearranging, the identity in Equation (5.1).

There are many ways to work with macroeconomic models. Modern macroeconomic researchers sometimes work with an algebraic representation of a model, sometimes with a formulation of a model that can be put on a computer and simulated, and sometimes with a model in graphical form. We will use the latter approach most often in this book. In doing graphical analysis, sometimes the simplest approach will be to work with a model in the form of supply and demand curves, with one supply curve and one demand curve for each market under consideration. As the number of markets in the model increases, this approach will become most practical, and in Chapters 7–11 and some later chapters, we will work mainly with models in the form of supply and demand curves. These supply and demand curves will be derived from the microeconomic behaviour of consumers and firms, as was the case when we examined labour supply and labour demand curves in Chapter 4, but the underlying microeconomic behaviour will not be explicit. For our analysis here, however, where exchange takes place between the representative consumer and the representative firm in only one market, it is relatively straightforward to be entirely explicit about microeconomic principles. The approach we will follow in this chapter is to study competitive equilibrium in our model by examining the consumer's and the firm's decisions in the same diagram, so that we can determine how aggregate consistency is achieved in competitive equilibrium.

We want to start first with the production technology operated by the representative firm. In a competitive equilibrium, $N^d = N^s = N$—that is, labour demand equals labour supply—and we will refer to N as employment. Then, as in Chapter 4, from the production function, output is given by

$$Y = zF(K, N), \tag{5.4}$$

and we graph the production function in Figure 5.2(a), for a given capital stock K. Note that, since the representative consumer has a maximum of h hours to spend working, N can be no larger than h, which implies that the maximum output that could be produced in this economy is Y^* in Figure 5.2(a).

Another way to graph the production function, which will prove very useful for integrating the firm's production behaviour with the consumer's behaviour, is to use the fact that, in equilibrium, we have $N = h - l$. Substituting for N in the production function (5.4), we get

$$Y = zF(K, h - l), \tag{5.5}$$

which is a relationship between output Y and leisure l, given the exogenous variables z and K. If we graph this relationship, as Figure 5.2(b), with leisure on the horizontal axis and Y on the vertical axis, then we get a mirror image of the production function in Figure 5.2(a). That is, the point $(l, Y) = (h, 0)$ in panel (b) of the figure corresponds to the point $(N, Y) = (0, 0)$ in panel (a). When the consumer takes all of his or her time as leisure, then employment is zero and nothing gets produced. As leisure falls in (b) from h, employment increases in (a) from zero, and output increases. In (b), when $l = 0$, the consumer is using all of his or her time for work and consuming no leisure, and the maximum quantity of output, Y^*, is produced. Note that, since the slope of the production function in panel (a) of the figure is MP_N, the marginal product of labour, the slope of the relationship in panel (b) is $-MP_N$, since this relationship is just the mirror image of the production function.

Now, since in equilibrium $C = Y - G$, from the income–expenditure identity, from (5.5) we get

$$C = zF(K, h - l) - G,$$

which is a relationship between C and l, given the exogenous variables z, K, and G. This relationship, graphed in Figure 5.2(c), is just the relationship in (b) shifted down by the amount G, since consumption is output minus government spending in equilibrium. The relationship is called a **production possibilities frontier** (**PPF**), and it describes

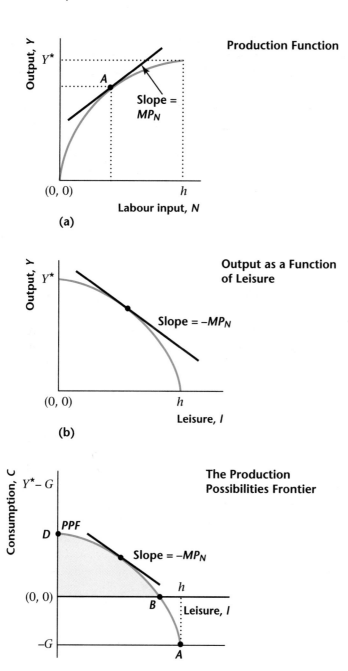

FIGURE 5.2

The Production Function and the Production Possibilities Frontier

Panel (a) shows the production function of the representative firm, while panel (b) shows the equilibrium relationship between the quantity of leisure consumed by the representative consumer and aggregate output. The relationship in (b) is the mirror image of the production function in (a). In (c), we show the production possibilities frontier (*PPF*), which is the technological relationship between *C* and *I*, determined by shifting the relationship in (b) down by the amount *G*. The shaded region in (c) represents consumption bundles that are technologically feasible to produce in this economy.

what the technological possibilities are for the economy as a whole, in terms of the production of consumption goods and leisure. Though leisure is not literally produced, all of the points in the shaded area inside the *PPF* and on the *PPF* in Figure 5.2(c) are technologically possible in this economy. The *PPF* captures the tradeoff between leisure and consumption that the available production technology makes available to the representative consumer in the economy. Note that the points on the *PPF* on *AB* are not feasible for this economy, as consumption is negative. Only the points on the *PPF* on *DB* are feasible, since here enough consumption goods are produced so that the government can take some of these goods and still leave something for private consumption.

As in Figure 5.2(b), the slope of the *PPF* in (c) is $-MP_N$. Another name for the negative of the slope of the *PPF* is the **marginal rate of transformation**. The marginal rate of transformation is the rate at which one good can be converted technologically into another; in this case, the marginal rate of transformation is the rate at which leisure can be converted in the economy into consumption goods through work. We will let $MRT_{l,C}$ denote the marginal rate of transformation of leisure into consumption. Then, we have

$$MRT_{l,C} = MP_N = -(\text{Slope of the } PPF).$$

Our next step will be to put the *PPF* together with the consumer's indifference curves, and to show how we can analyze a competitive equilibrium in a single diagram in Figure 5.3. In the figure, the *PPF* is given by the curve *HF*. From the relationship between the production function and the *PPF* in Figure 5.2, and given what we know about the profit-maximizing decision of the firm from Chapter 4, we can determine the production point on the *PPF* chosen by the firm, given the equilibrium real wage *w*. Namely, the representative firm chooses the labour input to maximize profits in equi-

FIGURE 5.3

Competitive Equilibrium

This figure brings together the representative consumer's preferences and the representative firm's production technology to determine a competitive equilibrium. Point *J* represents the equilibrium consumption bundle. *ADB* is the budget constraint faced by the consumer in equilibrium, with the slope of *AD* equal to the minus real wage, and the distance *DB* equal to dividend income minus taxes.

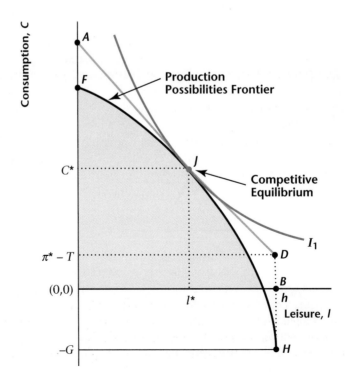

librium by setting $MP_N = w$, and so in equilibrium minus the slope of the *PPF* must be equal to w, since $MRT_{l,C} = MP_N = w$ in equilibrium. Therefore, if w is an equilibrium real wage rate, we can draw a line AD in Figure 5.3 that has slope $-w$ and is tangent to the *PPF* at point J, where $MP_N = w$. Then, the firm chooses labour demand equal to $h - l^*$ and produces $Y^* = zF(K, h - l^*)$, from the production function. Maximized profits for the firm are $\pi^* = zF(K, h - l^*) - w(h - l^*)$ (total revenue minus the cost of hiring labour), or the distance DH in Figure 5.3 (recall this from Chapter 4). Now, DB in Figure 5.3 is equal to $\pi^* - G = \pi^* - T$, from the government budget constraint $G = T$.

It is important to recognize that ADB in the figure is the budget constraint that the consumer faces in equilibrium, since the slope of AD is $-w$ and the length of DB is the consumer's dividend income minus taxes, where dividend income is the profits that the firm earns and distributes to the consumer. Since J represents the competitive equilibrium production point, where C^* is the quantity of consumption goods produced by the firm, and $h - l^*$ is the quantity of labour hired by the firm, it must be the case (as is required for aggregate consistency) that C^* is also the quantity of consumption goods that the representative consumer desires, and l^* is the quantity of leisure the consumer desires. This implies that an indifference curve (curve I_1 in Figure 5.3) must be tangent to AD (the budget constraint) at point J in Figure 5.3. Given this, in equilibrium at point J we will have $MRS_{l,C} = w$—that is, the marginal rate of substitution of leisure for consumption for the consumer is equal to the real wage. Since $MRT_{l,C} = MP_N = w$ in equilibrium, we have, at point J in Figure 5.3,

$$MRS_{l,C} = MRT_{l,C} = MP_N. \tag{5.6}$$

In other words, the marginal rate of substitution of leisure for consumption is equal to the marginal rate of transformation, which is equal to the marginal product of labour. That is, because the consumer and the firm face the same market real wage in equilibrium, the rate at which the consumer is just willing to trade leisure for consumption is the same as the rate at which leisure can be converted into consumption goods using the production technology.

The condition expressed in Equation (5.6) will be important in the next subsection in establishing the economic efficiency of a competitive equilibrium. The connection between market outcomes and economic efficiency will be critical in making the analysis of macroeconomic issues with this model simple.

Optimality

Now that we know what the characteristics of a competitive equilibrium are, from Figure 5.3, we can analyze the connection between a competitive equilibrium and economic efficiency. This connection will be important for two reasons. First, this will illustrate how free markets can produce socially optimal outcomes. Second, it proves to be much easier to analyze a social optimum than a competitive equilibrium in this model, and so our analysis in this section will allow us to use our model efficiently.

An important part of economics is analyzing how markets act to arrange production and consumption activities, and asking how this arrangement compares with some ideal or efficient arrangement. Typically, the efficiency criterion that economists use in evaluating market outcomes is **Pareto-optimality**. (Pareto, a nineteenth-century Italian economist, is famous for, among other things, his application of mathematics to economic analysis and introducing the concept of indifference curves.)

DEFINITION

A competitive equilibrium is Pareto-optimal if there is no way to rearrange production or to reallocate goods so that someone is made better off without making someone else worse off.

For this model, we would like to ask whether the competitive equilibrium is Pareto-optimal, but our job is relatively easy because there is only one representative consumer. We do not have to consider how goods are allocated across people. In our model, we can focus solely on how production is arranged to make the representative consumer as well off as possible. To construct the Pareto optimum here, we introduce the device of a fictitious social planner, a device commonly used to determine efficiency in economic models. The planner does not have to deal with markets, and he or she can simply order the representative firm to hire a given quantity of labour and produce a given quantity of consumption goods. The planner also has the power to coerce the consumer into supplying the required amount of labour. Produced consumption goods are taken by the planner, G is given to the government, and the remainder is allocated to the consumer. The planner is benevolent, and he or she chooses quantities so as to make the representative consumer as well off as possible. In this way, the planner's choices tell us what, in the best possible circumstances, could be achieved in our model economy.

The social planner's problem is to choose C and l, given the technology for converting l into C, to make the representative consumer as well off as possible. That is, the social planner chooses a consumption bundle that is on or within the production possibilities frontier (*PPF*), and that is on the highest possible indifference curve for the consumer. In Figure 5.4 the Pareto optimum is located at point B, where an indifference curve is just tangent to the *PPF*—curve AH. The social planner's problem is very similar to the representative consumer's problem of making himself or herself as well off as possible given his or her budget constraint. The only difference is that the budget constraint of the consumer is a straight line, while the *PPF* is concave (i.e., bowed out from the origin).

From Figure 5.4, since the slope of the indifference curve is minus the marginal rate of substitution, $-MRS_{l,C}$, and the slope of the *PPF* is minus the marginal rate of transformation, $-MRT_{l,C}$, or minus the marginal product of labour, $-MP_N$, the Pareto optimum has the property that

$$MRS_{l,C} = MRT_{l,C} = MP_N.$$

This is the same property that a competitive equilibrium has—or Equation (5.6). Comparing Figures 5.3 and 5.4, we easily see that the Pareto optimum and the competitive equilibrium are the same thing, since a competitive equilibrium is the point

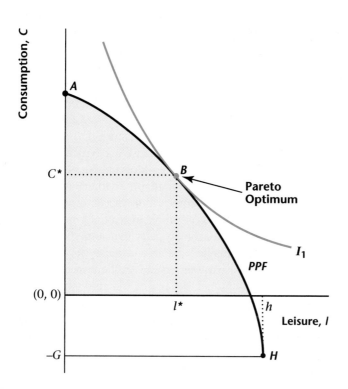

FIGURE 5.4
Pareto-Optimality
The Pareto optimum is the point that a social planner would choose, where the representative consumer is as well off as possible given the technology for producing consumption goods using labour as an input. Here, the Pareto optimum is *B*, where an indifference curve is tangent to the *PPF*.

where an indifference curve is tangent to the *PPF* in Figure 5.3, and the same is true of the Pareto optimum in Figure 5.4. A key result of this chapter is that, for this model, the competitive equilibrium is identical to the Pareto optimum.

There are two fundamental principles in economics that apply here, and these are the following:

DEFINITION

The *first fundamental theorem of welfare economics* states that, under certain conditions, a competitive equilibrium is Pareto-optimal.

DEFINITION

The *second fundamental theorem of welfare economics* states that, under certain conditions, a Pareto optimum is a competitive equilibrium.

The above two theorems are often referred to as the "first welfare theorem" and the "second welfare theorem." In our model, it is straightforward to see, from Figures 5.3 and 5.4, that the first and second welfare theorems hold, since there is one competitive equilibrium and one Pareto optimum, and they are clearly the same thing. In other kinds of economic models, however, showing whether the first and second welfare theorems hold can be hard work.

The idea behind the first welfare theorem goes back at least as far as Adam Smith's *The Wealth of Nations*. Smith argued that an unfettered market economy composed of self-interested consumers and firms could achieve an allocation of resources and goods that was socially efficient, as if an "invisible hand" were guiding the actions of individuals toward a state of affairs beneficial for all. (See Macroeconomics in Action 5.1.) The model we have constructed here has the property that a competitive equilibrium, or unfettered market outcome, is the same outcome that would be chosen by the invisible hand of the fictitious social planner.

The first welfare theorem is quite remarkable, since it appears to be inconsistent with the training we receive early in life, when we are typically encouraged to have empathy for others and to share our belongings. Most people value generosity and compassion, and so it certainly seems surprising that individuals motivated only by greed and profit maximization could achieve some kind of social utopia. Note, however, that if we consider economies with many consumers instead of a single representative consumer, a Pareto optimum might have the property that some people are very poor and some are very rich. That is, we may not be able to make the poor better off without making the rich worse off. At the extreme, a state of affairs where one person has all of society's wealth may be Pareto-optimal, but few would argue that this is a sensible way to arrange an economy. Pareto-optimality is a very narrow concept of social optimality. In some instances, society is interested in equity as well as efficiency, and there may be a tradeoff between the two.

SOURCES OF SOCIAL INEFFICIENCIES

What could cause a competitive equilibrium to fail to be Pareto-optimal? In practice, many factors can result in inefficiency in a market economy.

First, a competitive equilibrium may not be Pareto-optimal due to **externalities**. An externality is any activity for which an individual firm or consumer does not take account of all associated costs and benefits; externalities can be positive or negative. For example, pollution is a common example of a negative externality. Suppose that Disgusting Chemical Corporation (DCC) produces and sells chemicals, and in the production process generates a byproduct released as a gas into the atmosphere. This byproduct smells and is hazardous, and there are people who live close to DCC who are worse off as the result of the air pollution it produces. However, the negative externality that is produced in the form of pollution costs to the neighbours of DCC is not reflected in any way in DCC's profits. Therefore, DCC does not take the pollution externality into account in deciding how much labour to hire and the quantity of chemicals to produce. As a result, DCC will tend to produce more of these pollution-causing chemicals than is socially optimal. The key problem is that there is not a market on which pollution (or the rights to pollute) is traded. If such a market existed, private markets would not fail to produce a socially optimal outcome. This is because the people who bear the costs of pollution could sell the rights to pollute to DCC, and there would then be a cost to DCC for polluting, which DCC would take into account in making production decisions. Of course, such markets in pollution rights do not exist in practice, as it is hard to measure and monitor pollution, and very difficult to verify who bears its costs. In practice, the typical method used to correct a negative externality is regulation, which occurs in Canada at the federal, provincial, and municipal levels.

Adam Smith's Invisible Hand and the Former Soviet Union

In discussing the idea that private market forces could lead to socially efficient outcomes, Adam Smith argued in *The Wealth of Nations* that the owner of a private business,

> by directing that industry in such a manner as its produce may be of the greatest value, ... intends only his own gain, and he is in this, as in many other cases, led by an invisible hand to promote an end which was no part of his intention. Nor is it always the worse for the society that it was no part of it. By pursuing his own interest he frequently promotes that of the society more effectually than when he really intends to promote it. I have never known much good done by those who affected to trade for the public good. It is an affectation, indeed, not very common among merchants, and very few words need be employed in dissuading them from it.[1]

This statement of Smith's concerning the benefits to be had from a free market economy is even stronger than saying that a society of self-interested individuals can produce a socially efficient outcome. Smith appears to argue that, even if a group of individuals were given the power to decide what is in the public good, they would actually do worse in terms of general social welfare than private markets. This seems to be exactly the issue at stake in the case of the former Soviet Union, which was widely judged to have been extremely inefficient.

In the former Soviet Union, much economic activity was managed by way of central planning. That is, a group of planners in the Soviet government would make detailed decisions about the quantities of output that would be produced at different plants, where investment in new plant and equipment would take place, who would be employed where and in what capacity, and so on. The key problem with the Soviet system, however, was that the Soviet central planners knew much less about the economy than the social planner we invented to determine what was socially efficient in our model. For a planner to efficiently determine how production and consumption should take place in the economy, he or she

would need to know all the details about the available technologies for producing different goods, what resources are available, and the preferences of all consumers for all goods in existence. Collecting all of this information would clearly be impossible, and so it is not surprising that there were problems in the Soviet Union in running the economy efficiently. Examples of the types of problems that arose were that consumers had to wait in queues for goods that were short in supply, and firms did not always receive supplies of intermediate goods or raw materials in a timely way, so that production was interrupted.

One of the key features that makes market economies more efficient than centrally planned economies is that no one needs to acquire detailed information on production technologies and consumer preferences. The economy will generally operate efficiently if each producer and each consumer pays attention only to the signals that come from market prices. When the price of a particular good, oranges for example, is high, this reflects a scarcity. A central planner might react to a scarcity of oranges by directing that more oranges be produced, and by perhaps discouraging some consumers from eating oranges and encouraging them to eat apples instead. In a market economy, the high price of oranges would result in higher profits for the producers of oranges, which would make the production of oranges attractive for other would-be producers, and the supply of oranges would tend to increase.

Higher prices of oranges would also cause consumers to substitute away from oranges, perhaps to apples. A market economy can generally react much faster to a shortage of a good, and with the correct result. Market prices are a highly efficient device for effectively transmitting all of the relevant information to the producers and consumers in an economy. Often, trying to substitute organizational planning for market mechanisms can be a recipe for disaster.

---

[1]A. Smith, reprinted 1981, *An Enquiry into the Nature and Causes of the Wealth of Nations*, Liberty Fund, Indianapolis, p. 456.

A positive externality is a benefit other people receive for which no one is compensated. For example, suppose that DCC has an attractive head office designed by a high-profile architect in a major city. This building yields a benefit to people who can walk by the building on a public street and admire the fine architecture. These people do not compensate the firm for this positive externality, as it would be very costly or impossible to set up a fee structure for the public viewing of the building. As a result, DCC will tend to underinvest in its head office. Likely, the building that DCC would construct would be less attractive than if the firm took account of the positive externality. Therefore, positive externalities lead to social inefficiencies, just as negative externalities do, and the root cause of an externality is a market failure. It is too costly or impossible to set up a market to buy and sell the benefits or costs associated with the externality.

A second reason a competitive equilibrium may not be Pareto-optimal is that there are **distorting taxes**. In Chapter 4 we discussed the difference between a lump-sum tax, which does not depend on the actions of the person being taxed, and a distorting tax, which does. An example of a distorting tax in our model would be if government purchases were financed by a proportional wage income tax rather than by a lump-sum tax. That is, for each unit of real wage income earned, the representative consumer pays t units of consumption goods to the government, so that t is the tax rate. Then, wage income is $w(1 - t)(h - l)$, and the effective wage for the consumer is $w(1 - t)$. Then, when the consumer optimizes, he or she will set $MRS_{l,C} = w(1 - t)$, while the firm optimizes by setting $MP_N = w$. Therefore, in a competitive equilibrium

$$MRS_{l,C} < MP_N = MRT_{l,C},$$

so that the tax drives a "wedge" between the marginal rate of substitution and the marginal product of labour. Thus, Equation (5.6) does not hold, as required for a Pareto optimum, so that the first welfare theorem does not hold. In a competitive equilibrium, a proportional wage income tax will tend to discourage work (so long as the substitution effect of a change in the wage is larger than the income effect), and there will tend to be too much leisure consumed relative to consumption goods.

In practice, all real-world taxes, including sales taxes, the income tax, and property taxes, cause distortions; lump-sum taxes are, in fact, not feasible.[1] This does not mean, however, that having lump-sum taxes in our model is nonsense. The assumption of lump-sum taxation in our model is an appropriate simplification, because for most of the issues we will address, the effects of more realistic distorting taxation will be unimportant.

A third reason market economies do not achieve efficiency is that firms may not be price-takers. If a firm is large relative to the market, it can use its monopoly power to restrict output, raise prices, and increase profits. Monopoly power tends to lead to underproduction relative to what is socially optimal. There are many examples of

---

[1]This is because any lump-sum tax is large enough that someone cannot pay it. Therefore, some people must be exempted from the tax; but if this is so, people will alter their behaviour so as to be considered exempt. Thus, the tax will distort private decisions.

monopoly power in Canada. For example, Canadian telecommunications and auto-mobile manufacturing are each dominated by a few producers.

Since there are good reasons to believe that the three inefficiencies discussed above—externalities, tax distortions, and monopoly power—are important in modern economies, two questions arise. First, why should we analyze an economy that is efficient in the sense that a competitive equilibrium for this economy is Pareto-optimal? The reason is that, in studying most macroeconomic issues, an economic model with inefficiencies will behave much like an economic model without inefficiencies, so actually modelling all these inefficiencies would merely add clutter to our model. With the assumption of the equivalence of the competitive equilibrium and the Pareto optimum, determining the competitive equilibrium need only involve solving the social planner's problem and not the more complicated one of determining prices and quantities.

A second question that arises concerning real-world social inefficiencies is whether Adam Smith was completely off track in emphasizing the tendency of unrestricted markets to produce socially efficient outcomes. It might appear that the existence of externalities, tax distortions, and monopoly power should lead us to press for various government regulations to offset the negative effects of these inefficiencies. However, the tendency of unregulated markets to produce efficient outcomes is a powerful one, and sometimes the cost of government regulations, in terms of added waste, outweighs the gains, in terms of correcting private market failures. The cure can often be worse than the disease.

HOW TO USE THE MODEL

The key to using our model is the equivalence between the competitive equilibrium and the Pareto optimum. We need only draw a picture as in Figure 5.5, where we are essentially considering the solution to the social planner's problem. Here, the PPF is curve AH, and the competitive equilibrium (or Pareto optimum) is at point B, where an indifference curve, I_1, is tangent to the PPF. The equilibrium quantity of consumption is then C^*, and the equilibrium quantity of leisure is l^*. The quantity of employment is $N^* = h - l^*$, as shown in Figure 5.5, and the quantity of output is $Y^* = C^* + G$, as also shown in the figure. The real wage w is determined by minus the slope of the PPF, or minus the slope of the indifference curve I_1 at point B. The real wage is determined in this way because we know that, in equilibrium, the firm optimizes by setting the marginal product of labour equal to the real wage, and the consumer optimizes by setting the marginal rate of substitution equal to the real wage.

What we are primarily interested in now is how a change in an exogenous variable will affect the key endogenous variables C, Y, N, and w. The exogenous variables G, z, and K, which are government spending, total factor productivity, and the capital stock, respectively, will all alter the endogenous variables by shifting the PPF in particular ways. We will examine these effects and their interpretation in the next sections.

Figure 5.5 illustrates a key concept of this chapter in the clearest possible way. What is produced and consumed in the economy is determined entirely by the interaction of consumers' preferences with the technology available to firms. Though economic activity involves a complicated array of transactions among many economic actors,

FIGURE 5.5

Using the Second Welfare Theorem to Determine a Competitive Equilibrium

Since the competitive equilibrium and the Pareto optimum are the same thing, we can analyze a competitive equilibrium by working out the Pareto optimum, which is point B in the figure. At the Pareto optimum, an indifference curve is tangent to the PPF, and the equilibrium real wage is equal to minus the slope of the PPF and minus the slope of the indifference curve at B.

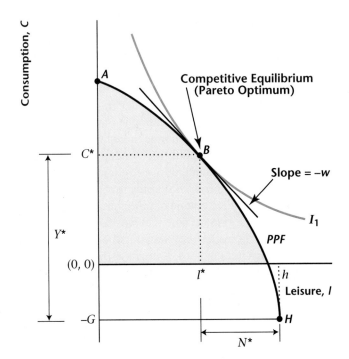

fundamentally aggregate economic activity boils down to the preferences of consumers, as captured by the representative consumer's indifference curves, and the technology of firms, as captured by the PPF. Both consumer preferences and the firm's technology are important for determining aggregate output, aggregate consumption, employment, and the real wage. A change in either indifference curves or the PPF will affect what is produced and consumed.

Working with the Model: The Effects of a Change in Government Purchases

Recall from Chapter 1 that working with a macroeconomic model involves carrying out experiments. The first experiment we will conduct here is to change government spending G, and ask what this does to aggregate output, consumption, employment, and the real wage. In Figure 5.6 an increase in G from G_1 to G_2 shifts the PPF from PPF_1 to PPF_2, where the shift down is by the same amount, $G_2 - G_1$, for each quantity of leisure, l. This shift leaves the slope of the PPF constant for each l. The effect of shifting the PPF downward by a constant amount is very similar to shifting the budget constraint for the consumer through a reduction in his or her nonwage disposable income, as we did in Chapter 4. Indeed, since $G = T$, an increase in government spending must necessarily increase taxes by the same amount, which will reduce the consumer's disposable income. It should not be surprising, then, that the effects of an increase in government spending essentially involve a negative income effect on consumption and leisure.

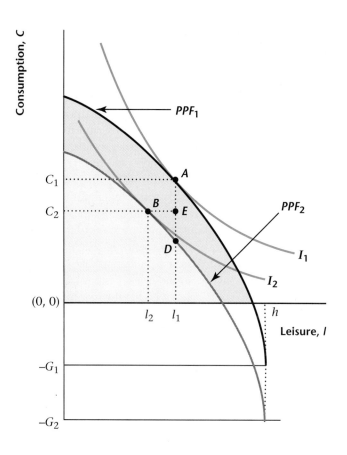

FIGURE 5.6
Equilibrium Effects of an Increase in Government Spending
An increase in government spending shifts the PPF down by the amount of the increase in G. There are negative income effects on consumption and leisure, so that both C and l fall, and employment rises, while output (equal to C + G) increases.

In Figure 5.6 the initial equilibrium is at point A, where indifference curve I_1 is tangent to PPF_1, the initial PPF. Here, equilibrium consumption is C_1, while the equilibrium quantity of leisure is l_1, and so equilibrium employment is $N_1 = h - l_1$. The initial equilibrium real wage is minus the slope of the indifference curve (or PPF_1) at point A. Now, when government spending increases, the PPF shifts to PPF_2, and the equilibrium point is at B, where consumption and leisure are both lower, at C_2 and l_2, respectively. Why do consumption and leisure decrease? This is because consumption and leisure are normal goods. Given the normal goods assumption, a negative income effect from the downward shift in the PPF must reduce consumption and leisure. Since leisure falls, then employment, which is $N_2 = h - l_2$, must rise. Further, since employment increases, the quantity of output must rise. We know this because the quantity of capital is fixed in the experiment, while employment has increased, and so the production function tells us that output must increase.

Now, the income–expenditure identity tells us that $Y = C + G$; therefore, $C = Y - G$, and so

$$\Delta C = \Delta Y - \Delta G,$$

where Δ denotes "the change in." Thus, since $\Delta Y > 0$, we have that $\Delta C > - \Delta G$, so that private consumption is **crowded out** by government purchases, but it is not completely crowded out due to the increase in output. In Figure 5.6 ΔG is the distance AD, and ΔC is the distance AE. While a larger government, reflected in increased government spending, results in more output being produced, because there is a negative income effect on leisure and therefore a positive effect on labour supply, a larger government reduces private consumption, through a negative income effect produced by the higher taxes required to finance higher government spending. As the representative consumer pays higher taxes, his or her disposable income falls, and in equilibrium he or she spends less on consumption goods, and works harder to support a larger government.

What happens to the real wage when G increases? In Figure 5.6 the slope of PPF_2 is identical to the slope of PPF_1 for each quantity of leisure, l. Therefore, since the PPF becomes steeper as l increases (the marginal product of labour increases as employment decreases), PPF_2 at point B is less steep than is PPF_1 at point A. Thus, since minus the slope of the PPF at the equilibrium point is equal to the equilibrium real wage, the real wage falls due to the increase in government spending. The real wage must fall, as we know that equilibrium employment rises, and the representative firm would hire more labour only in response to a reduction in the market real wage.

Now, a question we might like to ask is whether fluctuations in government spending are a likely cause of business cycles. Recall that in Chapter 3 we developed a set of key business cycle facts. If fluctuations in government spending are important in causing business cycles, it should be the case that our model can replicate these key business cycle facts in response to a change in G. The model predicts that, when government spending increases, aggregate output and employment increase, and consumption and the real wage decrease. One of our key business cycle facts is that exployment is procyclical. This fact is consistent with government spending shocks causing business cycles, since employment will always move in the same direction as aggregate output in response to a change in G. Additional business cycle facts are that consumption and the real wage are procyclical, but the model predicts that consumption and the real wage are countercyclical in response to government spending shocks. This is because, when G changes, consumption and the real wage always move in the direction opposite to the resulting change in Y. Therefore, government spending shocks do not appear to be a good candidate as a cause of business cycles. Whatever the primary cause of business cycles, it is unlikely to be the fact that governments change their spending plans from time to time. We will explore this idea further in Chapters 10 and 11.

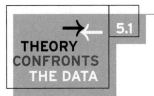

THEORY CONFRONTS THE DATA   5.1

Government Spending in World War II

Wars typically involve huge increases in government expenditure, and they therefore represent interesting "natural experiments" that we can examine as an informal empirical test of the predictions of our model. For example, a key economic effect on the Canadian economy of World War II, because it was so large, was an increase in the quantity of government purchases. During World War II, aggregate output was quickly channelled from private consumption to military uses. Figure 5.7 shows the natural logarithms of real GDP, real consumption expenditures, and real government expenditures for the period 1926–2001. Of particular note is the extremely large increase in government expenditures that occurred during World War II, which clearly swamps the small fluctuations in G about trend that happened before and after World War II. Clearly, GDP also increases above trend in the figure during World War II, and consumption dips somewhat below trend. Thus, these observations on the behaviour of consumption and output during World War II are consistent with our model, in that private consumption is crowded out somewhat and output increases. ⟐

Working with the Model: A Change in Total Factor Productivity

An increase in total factor productivity involves a better technology for converting factor inputs into aggregate output. As we will see in this section, increases in total factor productivity increase consumption and aggregate output, but there is an ambiguous effect on employment. This ambiguity is the result of opposing income and substitution effects on labour supply. While an increase in government spending essentially produces only an income effect on consumer behaviour, an increase in total factor productivity generates both an income effect and a substitution effect.

Suppose that total factor productivity z increases. As mentioned previously, the interpretation of an increase in z is as a technological innovation (a new invention or

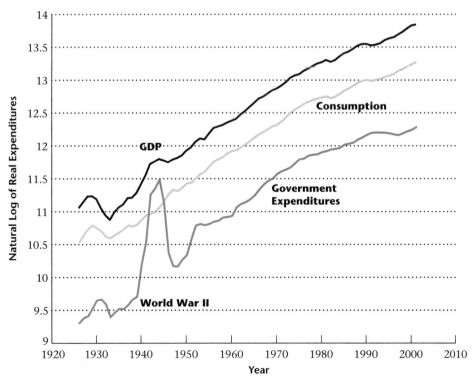

FIGURE 5.7

GDP, Consumption, and Government Expenditures for Canada, 1926 2001

During World War II, an increase in government spending is associated with an increase in aggregate output and a slight decrease in consumption from trend, as is consistent with our model.

Source: Adapted from the Statistics Canada CANSIM database, Series v3860085, v3860062, v3860067, v3860068, v3860069, and from the Statistics Canada publication *Historical Statistics of Canada*, Catalogue 11-516, 1983, Series F14–32.

an advance in management techniques), a spell of good weather, a relaxation in government regulations, or a decrease in the price of energy. The interpretation of the increase in z and the resulting effects depend on what we take one period in the model to represent relative to time in the real world. One period could be many years, in which case our model captures **long-run** effects; or one period could be just a month, a quarter, or a year, in which case it captures **short-run** effects. In macroeconomics the *short run* typically means a year or less, and the *long run* means more than a year. However, what is taken to be the boundary between the short run and the long run can vary considerably in different contexts.

The effect of an increase in z is to shift the production function up, as in Figure 5.8. Note that an increase in z not only permits more output to be produced given the quantity of labour input, but it increases the marginal product of labour for each quantity of labour input. That is, the slope of the production function increases for each N. In Figure 5.8, z increases from z_1 to z_2. We can show exactly the same shift in the production function as a shift outward in the *PPF* in Figure 5.9 from AB to AD. Here, more consumption is attainable given the better technology, for any quantity of leisure consumed. Further, the tradeoff between consumption and leisure has improved, in that the new *PPF* is steeper for any given quantity of leisure. That is, since MP_N increases, and the slope of the *PPF* is $-MP_N$, the *PPF* will be steeper when z increases.

Figure 5.9 allows us to determine all the equilibrium effects of an increase in z. Here, indifference curve I_1 is tangent to the initial *PPF* at point F. After the shift in the *PPF*, the economy will be at a point such as H, where there is a tangency between the new *PPF* and indifference curve I_2. What must be the case is that consumption increases in moving from F to H, in this case increasing from C_1 to C_2. However, leisure may increase or decrease, and here we have shown the case where it remains the same at l_1. Since $Y = C + G$ in equilibrium, and since G remains constant and C increases, there is an increase in aggregate output, and since $N = h - l$, employment is unchanged (but

FIGURE 5.8

Increase in Total Factor Productivity

An increase in total factor productivity shifts the production function up and increases the marginal product of labour for each quantity of the labour input.

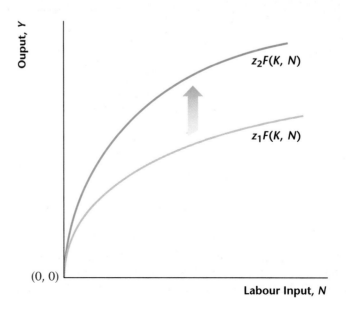

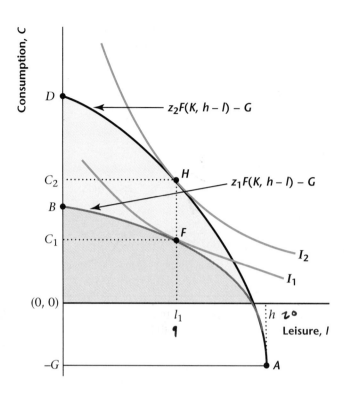

FIGURE 5.9
Competitive Equilibrium Effects of an Increase in Total Factor Productivity
An increase in total factor productivity shifts the *PPF* from *AB* to *AD*. The competitive equilibrium changes from *F* to *H* as a result. Output and consumption increase, the real wage increases, and leisure may rise or fall. Since employment is $N = h - l$, employment may rise or fall.

employment could have increased or decreased). The equilibrium real wage is minus the slope of the *PPF* at point *H* (i.e., $w = MP_N$). When we separate the income and substitution effects of the increase in z, we will show that the real wage must increase in equilibrium. In Figure 5.9 it is clear that the *PPF* is steeper at *H* than at *F*, so that the real wage is higher in equilibrium, but we will show how this must be true in general, even when the quantities of leisure and employment change.

To see why consumption has to increase, and why the change in leisure is ambiguous, we separate the shift in the *PPF* into an income effect and a substitution effect. In Figure 5.10, PPF_1 is the original *PPF*, and it shifts to PPF_2 when z increases from z_1 to z_2. The initial equilibrium is at point *A*, and the final equilibrium is at point *B* after z increases. The equation for PPF_2 is given by

$$C = z_2 F(K, h - l) - G.$$

Now, consider constructing an artificial *PPF*, called PPF_3, which is obtained by shifting PPF_2 downward by a constant amount. That is, the equation for PPF_3 is given by

$$C = z_2 F(K, h - l) - G - C_0.$$

Here, C_0 is a constant that is large enough so that PPF_3 is just tangent to the initial indifference curve I_1. What we are doing here is taking consumption (i.e., "income") away from the representative consumer to obtain the pure substitution effect of an increase in z. In Figure 5.10 the substitution effect is then the movement from *A* to *D*, and the

FIGURE 5.10
Income and Substitution
Effects of an Increase in
Total Factor Productivity
Here, the effects of an
increase in total factor
productivity are separated
into substitution and income
effects. The increase in total
factor productivity involves a
shift from PPF_1 to PPF_2. The
curve PPF_3 is an artificial PPF,
and it is PPF_2 with the income
effect of the increase in z
taken out. The substitution
effect is the movement from A
to D, and the income effect is
the movement from D to B.

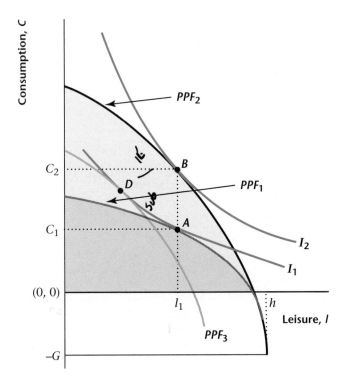

income effect is the movement from D to B. Much the same as when we considered income and substitution effects for a consumer facing an increase in his or her wage rate, here the substitution effect is for consumption to increase and leisure to decrease, so that hours worked increase. Also, the income effect is for both consumption and leisure to increase. As before, consumption must increase as both goods are normal, but leisure may increase or decrease because of opposing income and substitution effects.

Now, why must the real wage increase in moving from A to B, even if the quantities of leisure and employment rise or fall? First, the substitution effect involves an increase in $MRS_{l,C}$ (the indifference curve gets steeper) in moving along the indifference curve from A to D. Second, since PPF_2 is just PPF_3 shifted up by a fixed amount, the slope of PPF_2 is the same as the slope of PPF_3 for each quantity of leisure. As the quantity of leisure is higher at point B than at point D, the PPF is steeper at B than at D, and so $MRS_{l,C}$ also increases in moving from B to D. Thus, the real wage, which is equal to the marginal rate of substitution in equilibrium, must be higher in equilibrium when z is higher.

The increase in total factor productivity causes an increase in the marginal productivity of labour, which increases the demand for labour by firms, driving up the real wage. Workers now have more income given the number of hours worked, and they spend the increased income on consumption goods. Since there are offsetting income and substitution effects on labour supply, however, hours worked may increase or decrease. An important feature of the increase in total factor productivity is that the welfare of the representative consumer must increase. That is, the representative consumer must consume on a higher indifference curve when z increases. Therefore, increases in total factor productivity unambiguously increase the aggregate standard of living.

INTERPRETATION OF THE MODEL'S PREDICTIONS

Figure 5.9 tells a story about the long-term economic effects of long-run improvements in technology, such as those that have occurred since World War II in Canada. There have been many important technological innovations since World War II, particularly in electronics and information technology. Also, some key observations from post–World War II Canadian data are that aggregate output has increased steadily, consumption has increased, the real wage has increased, and hours worked per employed person have remained roughly constant. Figure 5.9 matches these observations in predicting that a technological advance leads to increased output, increased consumption, a higher real wage, and ambiguous effects on hours worked. Thus, if income and substitution effects roughly cancel each other out over the long run, the model is consistent with the fact that hours worked per person have remained roughly constant over the post–World War II period in Canada. There may have been many other factors in addition to technological change affecting output, consumption, the real wage, and hours worked over this period in Canadian history. However, our model tells us that empirical observations for this period are consistent with technological innovations having been an important contributing factor to changes in these key macroeconomic variables.

A second interpretation of Figure 5.9 is in terms of short-run aggregate fluctuations in macroeconomic variables. Could fluctuations in total factor productivity be an important cause of business cycles? Recall from Chapter 3 that three key business cycle facts are that consumption is procyclical, employment is procyclical, and the real wage is procyclical. From Figure 5.9, our model predicts that, in response to an increase in z, aggregate output increases, consumption increases, employment may increase or decrease, and the real wage increases. Therefore, the model is consistent with procyclical consumption and real wages, as consumption and the real wage always move in the same direction as output when z changes. However, employment may be procyclical or countercyclical, depending on the strength of opposing income and substitution effects. For the model to be consistent with the data requires that the substitution effect dominate the income effect, so that the consumer wants to increase labour supply in response to an increase in the market real wage. Thus, it is certainly possible that total factor productivity shocks could be a primary cause of business cycles, but to be consistent with the data requires that workers increase and decrease labour supply in response to increases and decreases in total factor productivity over the business cycle.

Some macroeconomists, the advocates of **real business cycle theory**, view total factor productivity shocks as the most important cause of business cycles. This view may seem to be contradicted by the long-run evidence that the income and substitution effects on labour supply of real wage increases appear to roughly cancel each other out in the post–World War II period. However, real business cycle theorists argue that much of the short-run variation in labour supply is due to **intertemporal substitution of labour**, which is the substitution of labour over time in response to real wage movements. For example, a worker may choose to work harder in the present if he or she views his or her wage as being temporarily high, while planning to take more vacation in the future. The worker basically "makes hay while the sun shines." In this way, even though income and substitution effects may cancel each other out in the long run, in the short run the substitution effect of an increase in the real wage could outweigh the income effect. We will explore intertemporal substitution further in Chapters 7 and 9–11.

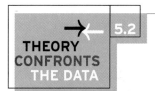

THEORY CONFRONTS THE DATA

5.2

Total Factor Productivity, Energy Prices, and the 1974–75 Recession

A decrease in total factor productivity, as mentioned in Chapter 4, can be caused by an increase in the price of energy. Such an increase occurred in 1973–74, when the Organization of Petroleum Exporting Countries (OPEC) brought about an increase in the world price of crude oil. Gradually, this increase in the price of oil was reflected in higher prices of fuel, electricity (as oil is used in power generation), and other final sources of energy. As discussed in Chapter 4, an increase in energy prices causes firms to use less energy in production, and this is reflected in a drop in the productivity of capital and labour. There is thus a drop in total factor productivity. While there are beneficial effects of an increase in the price of energy for Canada, since oil and gas production then became more profitable, energy price increases nevertheless have net adverse effects. The adverse negative effect on total factor productivity is commonly given as the cause of Canada's 1974–75 recession.

In Figure 5.11 we show the percentage deviations from trend in the Solow residual, calculated from aggregate Canadian data. The Solow residual, as discussed in Chapter 4, is a measure of total factor productivity. Note that the Solow residual dropped below trend at the time of the 1974–75 recession, which is consistent with the story that an increase in energy prices at that time resulted in a drop in total factor productivity. Further, in Figure 5.12 we show the percentage deviations from trend in real GDP and in employment. Clearly, as is consistent with our model, the drop in total factor productivity in 1974–75 was also associated with a drop in output and employment below trend. Figure 5.13 shows an inconsistency between the model and the data, in that consumption rises above trend during the 1974–75 recession, while the model predicts that consumption should fall when there is a negative shock to total factor productivity.

The 1974–75 recession in Canada was relatively mild, in terms of the size of the deviation from trend in GDP at that time relative to the 1981–82 or the 1991–92 recession (see Figure 5.12). This is related to the fact, mentioned above, that Canada experiences some positive macroeconomic effects from increases in energy prices. This situation implies that profits and employment increase in the oil and gas industry and government tax revenues rise. In the United States, which is a net importer of oil and natural gas (Canada is a net exporter of these commodities), there was a recession in 1973–75 that was much more severe than the 1974–75 recession in Canada.

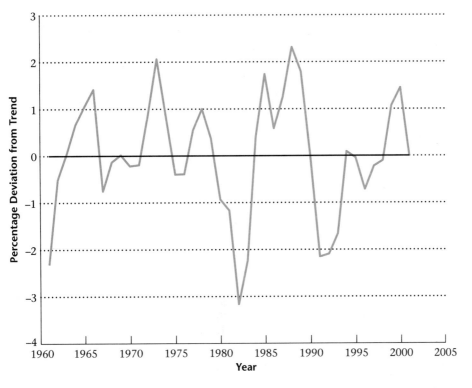

FIGURE 5.11

Deviations from Trend in the Solow Residual for Canada, 1961–2001

The figure shows the percentage deviations from trend in the Solow residual, a measure of total factor productivity. Of particular significance is that this measure of total factor productivity dropped below trend at the time of the 1973–75 recession, as is consistent with our model.

Source: Adapted from the Statistics Canada CANSIM database, Series v3860085, v2461119, v3822183, v1078498, and from the Statistics Canada publication *Historical Statistics of Canada*, Catalogue 11-516, 1983, Series D175–189.

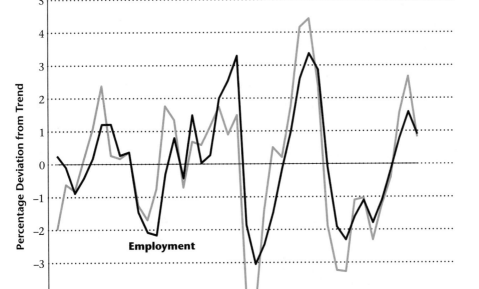

FIGURE 5.12

Employment and GDP for Canada, 1961–2001

Employment and aggregate output dropped below trend in the 1974–75 recession, in a manner consistent with our model.

Source: Adapted from the Statistics Canada CANSIM database, Series v3860085, v2461119, and from the Statistics Canada publication *Historical Statistics of Canada*, Catalogue 11-516, 1983, Series D175–189.

FIGURE 5.13

Consumption and GDP for Canada, 1961–2001

Consumption rose above trend during the 1974–75 recession, which is inconsistent with our model.

Source: Adapted from the Statistics Canada CANSIM database, Series v3860085, v3860062.

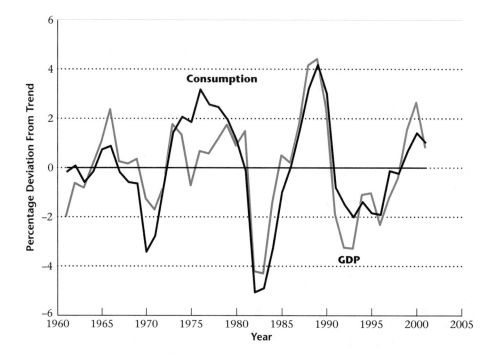

Now that we have gained some knowledge from a one-period model concerning how the macroeconomy functions, we can move on in Chapter 6 to study the intertemporal behaviour of consumers, and some issues associated with government budget deficits.

Chapter Summary

In this chapter, we took the consumer behaviour and firm behaviour developed in Chapter 4, added government behaviour, and constructed a complete one-period macroeconomic model. In a competitive equilibrium, the actions of the representative consumer, the representative firm, and the government must be mutually consistent, which implies that the market on which labour is exchanged for goods must clear, and the government budget constraint must hold. In a competitive equilibrium, we determined aggregate output, consumption, employment, taxes, and the real wage (the endogenous variables) given the capital stock, total factor productivity, and government spending (the exogenous variables). We demonstrated how to represent a competitive equilibrium in a single diagram, and we used this diagram to illustrate the equivalence between the competitive equilibrium and the Pareto optimum, which is an economically efficient state of affairs. We then showed how to use the model to study the effects on the economy of changes in government spending and in technology. An increase in government spending has a pure negative income effect on the representative consumer, so that employment increases and consumption decreases. Government spending thus crowds out private consumption, but not completely, as there is an increase in aggregate output. An increase in total factor productivity, which may arise from improved technology, leads to an increase in output, consumption, and the real wage, but employment may increase or decrease due to opposing income and substitution effects.

Key Terms

closed economy: An economy that does not trade with the rest of the world.

open economy: An economy that trades with the rest of the world.

public goods: Goods that are difficult or impossible for the private sector to provide, for example, national defence.

exogenous variable: A variable determined outside the model.

endogenous variable: A variable that the model determines.

government budget constraint: An equation describing the sources and uses of government revenues.

fiscal policy: The government's choices over government expenditures, taxes, transfers, and government borrowing.

competitive equilibrium: A state of the economy where prices and quantities are such that the behaviour of price-taking consumers and firms is consistent.

market clearing: When supply equals demand in a particular market or markets.

production possibilities frontier (PPF): The boundary of a set that describes what consumption bundles are technologically feasible to produce.

marginal rate of transformation: Minus the slope of the *PPF*, or the rate at which one good in the economy can be technologically exchanged for another.

Pareto-optimality: A state of the economy that cannot be improved on by making one consumer better off without making another worse off.

first fundamental theorem of welfare economics (or first welfare theorem): Result stating that, under certain conditions, a competitive equilibrium is Pareto-optimal.

second fundamental theorem of welfare economics (or second welfare theorem): Result stating that, under certain conditions, a Pareto optimum is a competitive equilibrium.

externality: The effect an action taken by an economic agent has on another economic agent or agents, where the agent performing the action does not take into account this effect on others.

distorting tax: A tax, such as an income tax, that creates a difference between the effective prices faced by buyers and sellers of some good.

crowding out: The displacement of private expenditures by government purchases.

short run: Typically describes macroeconomic effects that occur within a year's time.

long run: Typically describes macroeconomic effects that occur beyond a year's time.

real business cycle theory: A theory postulating that the primary cause of aggregate fluctuations is fluctuations in total factor productivity.

intertemporal substitution of labour: The substitution of labour over time by a worker in response to movements in real wages.

Questions for Review

All questions refer to the macroeconomic model developed in this chapter.

1. Why is it useful to study a closed-economy model?

2. What is the role of the government in the one-period closed-economy model?

3. Can the government run a deficit in the one-period model? Why or why not?

4. What are the endogenous variables in the model?

5. What are the exogenous variables in the model?

6. What are the four conditions that a competitive equilibrium must satisfy for this model?

7. What is the economic significance of the slope of the production possibilities frontier?

8. Why is the competitive equilibrium in this model Pareto-optimal?

9. Explain the difference between the first and second welfare theorems. Why is each useful?

10. Give three reasons why an equilibrium might not be Pareto-optimal.

11. What are the effects of an increase in government purchases?

12. Why does government spending crowd out private purchases?

13. What are the equilibrium effects of an increase in total factor productivity?

14. Explain why employment may rise or fall in response to an increase in total factor productivity.

Problems

1. Many negative externalities exist in cities. For example, a high concentration of automobile traffic in cities generates pollution and causes congestion, and both pollution and congestion are negative externalities. When a particular person decides to drive a car in a city on a given day, he or she does not take into account the negative effects that driving his or her car has in terms of pollution and deterring other drivers from reaching their destinations (congestion). Although negative externalities (including pollution and congestion) appear to abound in cities, people still prefer to live in cities (otherwise, cities would not exist). In economic terms, discuss the forces that cause people to prefer life in the city. How do these forces relate to whether market outcomes are economically efficient?

2. Suppose that the government decides to reduce taxes. In the model used in this chapter, determine the effects this will have on aggregate output, consumption, employment, and the real wage, and explain your results.

3. Faroffland is an island state that does not trade with the rest of the world. Unfortunately, the island of Faroffland is actively volcanic. A volcanic eruption destroys part of Faroffland's capital stock, though there is no loss of life (the representative consumer survives).
   a. Determine the effects on aggregate output, consumption, employment, and the real wage, with reference to income and substitution effects, and explain your results.
   b. Describe another type of event that would cause a decrease in a nation's capital stock. Interpret your results in terms of this other type of event.
   c. Do you think that changes in the capital stock are a likely cause of business cycles? Explain, with reference to your answers in parts (a) and (b) and the key business cycle facts described in Chapter 3.

4. Suppose that the government treats government expenditures G as a policy instrument, and suppose that the policy goal of the government is to stabilize consumption for the representative consumer. That is, whenever z changes in the economy, the government observes this, and changes G in such a way that C is the same before and after the change in z. Now, suppose that z falls.
   a. In what direction will the government need to change G in order to stabilize C when z falls?
   b. If the government stabilizes C when z falls, show that employment and aggregate output must fall, and that the representative consumer must be better off than before the decrease in z. Explain your results. You will need to show the income and substitution effects involved to solve the problem.

5. Suppose that the government's goal is to make GDP as large as possible, and that it sets out to accomplish this goal by manipulating the quantity of government purchases. Show using

a diagram that this type of government policy gives a very poor result for the economy as a whole, and discuss.

6. Suppose that total factor productivity, z, affects the productivity of government production just as it affects private production. That is, suppose that when the government collects taxes, it acquires goods that are then turned into government-produced goods according to $G = zT$, so that z units of government goods are produced for each unit of taxes collected. With the government setting G, an increase in z will imply that a smaller quantity of taxes are required to finance the given quantity of government purchases G. Under these circumstances, use a diagram to determine the effects of an increase in z on output, consumption, employment, and the real wage, treating G as given. Explain your results.

7. Suppose that the representative consumer's preferences change, in that his or her marginal rate of substitution of leisure for consumption increases for any quantities of consumption and leisure.
   a. Explain what this change in preferences means in more intuitive language.
   b. What effects does this have on the equilibrium real wage, hours worked, output, and consumption?
   c. Do you think that preference shifts like this might explain why economies experience recessions (periods when output is low)? Explain why or why not, with reference to the key business cycle facts in Chapter 3.

8. Suppose that government spending makes private firms more productive; for example, government spending on roads and bridges lowers the cost of transportation. This means that there will now be two effects of government spending, the first being the effects discussed in this chapter of an increase in G, and the second being similar to the effects of an increase in the nation's capital stock K.
   a. Show that an increase in government spending that is productive in this fashion could increase welfare for the representative consumer.
   b. Show that the equilibrium effects on consumption and hours worked of an increase in government spending of this type are ambiguous, but that output increases. You will need to consider income and substitution effects to show this.

Working with the Data

1. Calculate and plot the annual percentage growth rates in real GDP and in total real government purchases from 1961 to 2001. Calculate these growth rates from quarterly data, as percentage growth rates from four quarters previously.
   a. Does there appear to be any relationship between the growth rates in GDP and in government purchases?
   b. What does your answer to part (a) tell you about the role in business cycles of fluctuations in government purchases?

2. As a measure of the relative price of energy, calculate and plot the ratio of the price for petroleum and coal products to the producer price index for all finished goods, for 1961 through 2001. Comment on the movements over time in this index, particularly relative to the 1973–75 recession.

3. Calculate and plot the annual percentage change in average weekly hours in manufacturing for each year from 1961 to 2001. Calculate these percentage changes as December-to-December percentage growth rates. Comment on the relationship between these percentage growth rates and the percentage deviations from trend in real GDP, from Figure 5.12.

PART 3

Savings, Government Deficits, Investment, and Growth

In this part, we will explore the macroeconomics of intertemporal decisions and dynamic issues. We start in Chapter 6 by considering the consumption-savings decisions of consumers, building on our knowledge of consumer behaviour from Chapter 4. We then study the Ricardian equivalence theorem, which states that, under certain conditions, a change in the timing of taxes by the government will have no effects on real macroeconomic variables or on the welfare of consumers. A key implication of the Ricardian equivalence theorem is that a cut in taxes by the government is not a free lunch.

In Chapter 7, we use what was learned about the microeconomics of consumption-savings behaviour in Chapter 6, along with an analysis of the microeconomic principles of the intertemporal labour supply behaviour of consumers and the investment decisions of firms, to construct a complete intertemporal macroeconomic model. This model will be the basis for what we do in much of the remainder of this book. The model will be used in Chapter 7 to show the effects of changes in government spending and in total factor productivity on output, employment, consumption, investment, the real wage, and the real interest rate. As well, we will focus on the effects of expectations about the future on current events.

In Chapter 8, we will study the determinants of economic growth, using two models of the growth process: the Solow growth model and an endogenous growth model. Growth in the economy's productive capacity is in general driven by technological progress. The Solow model treats technological progress as being exogenous, while the endogenous growth model involves a serious treatment of the economic determinants of technical change.

CHAPTER 6

A Two-Period Model: The Consumption–Savings Decision and Ricardian Equivalence

This chapter focuses on **intertemporal decisions** and the implications of intertemporal decision making for how government deficits affect macroeconomic activity. Intertemporal decisions involve economic tradeoffs across periods of time. We will first analyze the microeconomic behaviour of a consumer who must make a dynamic **consumption–savings decision**. In doing so, we will apply what was learned in Chapter 4 concerning how a consumer optimizes subject to his or her budget constraint. We will then study a model with many consumers, and with a government that need not balance its budget and can issue debt to finance a government budget deficit. An important implication of this model is that the **Ricardian equivalence theorem** holds. This theorem states that there are conditions under which the size of the government's deficit is irrelevant, in that it does not affect any macroeconomic variables of importance or the economic welfare of any individual.

The consumption–savings decision involves intertemporal choice, as this is fundamentally a decision involving a tradeoff between current and future consumption. Similarly, the government's decision concerning the financing of government expenditures is an intertemporal choice, involving a tradeoff between current and future taxes. If the government decreases taxes in the present, it must borrow from the private sector to do so, which implies that future taxes must increase to pay off the higher government debt. Essentially, the government's financing decision is a decision about the quantity of government saving, or the size of the government deficit, making it closely related to the consumption–savings decisions of private consumers.

To study the consumption–savings decisions of consumers and the government's intertemporal choices, we will work in this chapter with a **two-period model**, which is the simplest framework for understanding intertemporal choice and dynamic issues. We will treat the first period in the model as the current period and the second period as the future period. In intertemporal choice, a key variable of interest is the **real interest rate**, which in the model is the interest rate at which consumers and the government can borrow and lend. The real interest rate determines the relative price of consumption in the future in terms of consumption in the present. With respect to consumer choice, we are interested in how savings and consumption in the present and in the future are affected by changes in the real interest rate and in present and future incomes. With respect to the effects of real interest rate changes, income and substitution effects will be important, and we can apply here what was learned in Chapters 4 and 5 about how to isolate income and substitution effects in a consumer's choice problem.

An important principle in the response of consumption to changes in income is **consumption smoothing**. That is, there are natural forces that cause consumers to wish to have a smooth consumption path over time, as opposed to a choppy one. Consumption-smoothing behaviour is implied by particular properties of indifference curves that we have already studied in Chapter 4. As well, consumption-smoothing behaviour has important implications for how consumers will respond in the aggregate to changes in government policies or other features of their external environment that affect their income streams.

It will remain true here, as in the one-period model studied in Chapter 5, that while an increase in government spending has real effects on macroeconomic activity, the Ricardian equivalence theorem establishes conditions under which the timing of taxation will not matter for aggregate economic activity. David Ricardo, for whom the Ricardian equivalence theorem is named, is best known for his work in the early nineteenth century on the theory of comparative advantage and international trade. Ricardian equivalence runs counter to much of public debate, which attaches importance to the size of the government deficit. We will explain why Ricardian equivalence is important in economic analysis, and why the Ricardian equivalence theorem is a useful starting point for thinking about how the burden of the government debt is shared. A key implication of the Ricardian equivalence theorem is that a tax cut is not a free lunch. A tax cut may not matter at all, or it may involve a redistribution of wealth within the current population or across generations.

To maintain simplicity and to retain focus on the important ideas in this chapter, our two-period model will leave out production and investment. In Chapter 7, we will reintroduce production and add investment decisions by firms so that we can understand more completely the aggregate determination of output, employment, consumption, investment, the real wage rate, and the interest rate.

A Two-Period Model of the Economy

A consumer's consumption–savings decision is fundamentally a decision involving a tradeoff between current and future consumption. By saving, a consumer gives up consumption in exchange for assets in the present, in order to consume more in the future. Alternatively, a consumer can dissave by borrowing in the present to gain more current consumption, thus sacrificing future consumption when the loan is repaid. Borrowing (or dissaving) is thus negative savings.

A consumer's consumption–savings decision is a dynamic decision, in that it has implications over more than one period of time, as opposed to the consumer's static work–leisure decision considered in Chapters 4 and 5. We will model the consumer's dynamic problem here in the simplest possible way, namely, in a two-period model. In this model, we will denote the first period as the *current period*, and the second period as the *future period*. For some economic problems, assuming that decision making by consumers takes place over two periods is obviously unrealistic. For example, if a period is a quarter, and since the working life of a typical individual is about 200 quarters, then a 200-period model might seem more appropriate. However, the results we consider in this chapter all generalize to more elaborate models with many periods or an infinite number of periods. The reason for studying models with two periods is that they are simple to analyze, while capturing the essentials of dynamic decision making by consumers and firms.

CONSUMERS

It will not cause any difficulties, in terms of what we want to accomplish with this model, to suppose that there are many different consumers rather than a single representative consumer. Therefore, we will assume that there are m consumers, where we can think of m being a large number. We will assume that each consumer lives for two periods, the current period and the future period. We will further suppose that consumers do not make a work–leisure decision in either period, but simply receive exogenous income. Assuming that incomes are exogenous allows us to focus attention on what we are interested in here: the consumer's consumption–savings decision. Let y be a consumer's real income in the current period, and y' be real income in the future period. Throughout, we will use lowercase letters to refer to variables at the individual level, and uppercase letters for aggregate variables. Primes will denote variables in the future period (e.g., y' denotes the consumer's future income). Each consumer pays lump-sum taxes t in the current period, and t' in the future period. Suppose that incomes can be different for different consumers, but that all consumers pay the same taxes. If we let a consumer's savings in the current period be s, then the consumer's budget constraint in the current period is

$$c + s = y - t, \tag{6.1}$$

where c is current period consumption. Here, (6.1) states that consumption plus savings in the current period must equal disposable income in the current period. Note that we assume that the consumer starts the current period with no assets. This will not matter in any important way for our analysis.

In (6.1), if $s > 0$ then the consumer will be a lender on the credit market, and if $s < 0$ the consumer will be a borrower. We will suppose that the financial asset that is traded in the credit market is a bond. In the model, bonds can be issued by consumers as well as by the government. If a consumer lends, he or she buys bonds; if he or she borrows, there is a sale of bonds. There are two important assumptions here. The first is that all bonds are indistinguishable, because consumers never default on their debts, so that there is no risk associated with holding a bond. In practice, different credit instruments are associated with different levels of risk. Interest-bearing securities issued by the government are essentially riskless, while corporate bonds may be risky if investors feel that the corporate issuer might default, and a loan made by a bank to a consumer may also be quite risky. The second important assumption is that bonds are traded directly in the credit market. In practice, much of the economy's credit activity is channelled through financial intermediaries, such as chartered banks. For example, when a consumer borrows to purchase a car, the loan is usually taken out at a chartered bank or other depository institution; a consumer typically does not borrow directly from the ultimate lender (in the case of a chartered bank, the ultimate lenders include the depositors at the bank). For the problems we will address with this model, it will simplify matters considerably, without any key loss in the insights we will get, to assume away credit risk and financial institutions like chartered banks. Credit risk and financial intermediation will be discussed in detail in Chapter 14.

In our model, one bond issued in the current period is a promise to pay $1 + r$ units of the consumption good in the future period, so that the real interest rate on each bond is r. Since this implies that one unit of current consumption can be exchanged in the credit market for $1 + r$ units of the future consumption good, the relative price of future consumption in terms of current consumption is $\frac{1}{1+r}$. Recall from Chapter 1 that in practice the real interest rate is approximately the nominal interest rate (the interest rate in money terms) minus the inflation rate. We will study the relationship between real and nominal interest rates in Chapter 9.

A key assumption here is that the real rate of interest at which a consumer can lend is the same as the real rate of interest at which a consumer can borrow. In practice, consumers typically borrow at higher rates of interest than they can lend at. For example, the interest rates on consumer loans are usually several percentage points higher than the interest rates on bank deposits, reflecting the costs for the bank of taking deposits and making loans. The assumption that borrowing and lending rates of interest are the same will matter for some of what we do here, and we will ultimately show what difference this makes to our analysis.

In the future period, the consumer has disposable income $y' - t'$, and receives the interest and principal on his or her savings, which totals $(1 + r)s$. Since the future period is the final period, the consumer will choose to finish this period with no assets, consuming all disposable income and the interest and principal on savings (we assume there are no bequests to descendants). We then have

$$c' = y' - t' + (1 + r)s, \tag{6.2}$$

where c' is consumption in the future period. Note in Equation (6.2) that if $s < 0$, the consumer pays the interest and principal on his or her loan (retires the bonds he or she issued in the current period) and then consumes what remains of his or her future period disposable income.

The consumer chooses current consumption and future consumption, c and c', respectively, and savings s to make himself or herself as well off as possible while satisfying the budget constraints (6.1) and (6.2).

The Consumer's Lifetime Budget Constraint We can work with diagrams similar to those used in Chapter 4 to analyze the consumer's work–leisure decision, if we take the two budget constraints expressed in Equations (6.1) and (6.2) and write them as a single lifetime constraint. To do this, we first use (6.2) to solve for s to get

$$s = \frac{c' - y' + t'}{1 + r}. \tag{6.3}$$

Then, substitute for s from (6.3) in (6.1) to get

$$c + \frac{c' - y' + t'}{1 + r} = y - t,$$

or rearranging,

$$c + \frac{c'}{1 + r} = y + \frac{y'}{1 + r} - t - \frac{t'}{1 + r}. \tag{6.4}$$

Equation (6.4) is the consumer's **lifetime budget constraint**, and it states that the **present value** of lifetime consumption ($c + \frac{c'}{1+r}$) equals the present value of lifetime income ($y + \frac{y'}{1+r}$) minus the present value of lifetime taxes ($t + \frac{t'}{1+r}$). The present value here is the value in terms of period 1 consumption goods. That is, $\frac{1}{1+r}$ is the relative price of period 2 consumption goods in terms of period 1 consumption goods, since a consumer can give up 1 unit of period 1 consumption goods and obtain $1 + r$ units of period 2 consumption goods by saving for one period. The problem of the consumer is now simplified, in that he or she chooses c and c' to make himself or herself as well off as possible, while satisfying the budget constraint (6.4) and given $r, y, y,' t$, and t'. Note that, once we have determined what the consumer's optimal consumption is in the current and future periods, we can determine savings, s, from the current-period budget constraint (6.1).

For a numerical example to illustrate present values, suppose that current income is $y = 110$ while future income is $y' = 120$. Taxes in the current period are $t = 20$, and taxes in the future period are $t' = 10$. Also suppose that the real interest rate is 10%, so that $r = 0.1$. In this example, the relative price of future consumption goods in terms of current consumption goods is $\frac{1}{1+r} = 0.909$. Here, when we discount future income and future taxes to obtain these quantities in units of current consumption goods, we will multiply by the discount factor 0.909. The fact that the discount factor is less than 1 indicates that having a given amount of income in the future is worth less to the consumer than having the same amount of income in the current period. The present discounted value of lifetime income is

$$y + y' \times \frac{1}{1 + r} = 110 + 120 \times 0.909 = 219.1,$$

and the present value of lifetime taxes is

$$t + t' \times \frac{1}{1 + r} = 20 + 10 \times 0.909 = 29.1.$$

Then, in this example, we can write the consumer's lifetime budget constraint from (6.4) as

$$c + 0.909c' = 190.$$

We will label the present value of lifetime disposable income, the quantity on the right-hand side of (6.4), as **lifetime wealth**, *we*, since this is the quantity of resources that the consumer has available to spend on consumption, in present-value terms, over his or her lifetime. We then have

$$we = y + \frac{y'}{1 + r} - t - \frac{t'}{1 + r} \qquad (6.5)$$

and we can rewrite (6.4) as

$$c + \frac{c'}{1 + r} = we. \qquad (6.6)$$

In Figure 6.1 we graph the consumer's lifetime budget constraint as expressed in Equation (6.6). Writing this equation in slope–intercept form, we have

$$c' = -(1 + r)c + we(1 + r). \qquad (6.7)$$

Therefore, in Equation (6.7) and in Figure 6.1, the vertical intercept, $we(1 + r)$, is what could be consumed in the future period if the consumer saved all of his or her current-period disposable income and consumed lifetime wealth (after earning the real interest rate r on savings) in the future period. The horizontal intercept in Equation (6.7) and Figure 6.1, we, is what could be consumed if the consumer borrowed the maximum amount possible against future period disposable income and consumed all of lifetime wealth in period 1. The slope of the lifetime budget constraint is $-(1 + r)$, which is determined by the real interest rate. Point E in Figure 6.1 is the **endowment point**, which is the consumption bundle the consumer gets if he or she simply consumes disposable income in the current period and in the future period—that is, $c = y - t$ and $c' = y' - t'$—with zero savings in the current period. You can verify by substituting $c = y - t$ and $c' = y' - t'$ in Equation (6.4) that the endowment point satisfies the lifetime budget constraint. Now, note that any point along BE in Figure 6.1 implies that $s \geq 0$, so that the consumer is a lender, since $c \leq y - t$. Also, a consumption bundle along AE in Figure 6.1 implies that the consumer is a borrower with $s \leq 0$.

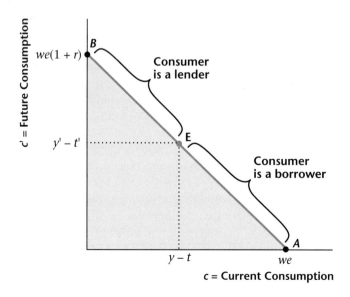

c′ = Future Consumption

$we(1 + r)$ ·B

Consumer is a lender

$y' - t'$ ·E

Consumer is a borrower

$y - t$ we

c = Current Consumption

FIGURE 6.1

Consumer's Lifetime Budget Constraint

The lifetime budget constraint defines the quantities of current and future consumption the consumer can acquire, given current and future income and taxes, through borrowing and lending on the credit market. To the northwest of the endowment point E, the consumer is a lender with positive savings; to the southeast of E, he or she is a borrower with negative savings.

Any point on or inside AB in the shaded area in Figure 6.1 represents a feasible consumption bundle, that is, a combination of current-period and future-period consumptions that satisfies the consumer's lifetime budget constraint. As may be clear by now, the way we will approach the consumer's problem here will be very similar to our analysis of the consumer's work–leisure decision in Chapter 4. Once we describe the consumer's preferences, and add indifference curves to the budget constraint as depicted in Figure 6.1, we can determine the consumer's optimal consumption bundle.

The Consumer's Preferences As with the consumer's work–leisure decision in Chapter 4, the consumption bundle chosen by the consumer, which here is a combination of current-period and future-period consumptions, is determined jointly by the consumer's budget constraint and his or her preferences. Just as in Chapter 4, we will assume that preferences have three properties, which are the following:

1. *More is always preferred to less.* Here, this means that more current consumption or more future consumption always makes the consumer better off.

2. *The consumer likes diversity in his or her consumption bundle.* Here, a preference for diversity has a specific meaning in terms of the consumer's desire to smooth consumption over time. Namely, the consumer has a dislike for consumption that is far from equal between the current period and the future period. Note that this does not mean that the consumer would always choose to have equal consumption in the current and future periods.

3. *Current consumption and future consumption are normal goods.* This implies that if there is a parallel shift to the right in the consumer's budget constraint, current consumption and future consumption will both increase. This is related to the consumer's desire to smooth consumption over time. If there is a parallel shift to the right in the consumer's budget constraint, this is because lifetime wealth *we* has increased. Given the consumer's desire to smooth consumption over time, any increase in lifetime wealth will imply that the consumer will choose more consumption in the present *and* in the future.

As in Chapter 4, we represent preferences with an indifference map, which is a family of indifference curves. A typical indifference map is shown in Figure 6.2, where the marginal rate of substitution of consumption in the current period for consumption in the future period, or $MRS_{c,c'}$, is minus the slope of an indifference curve. For example, $MRS_{c,c'}$ at point A in Figure 6.2 is minus the slope of a tangent to the indifference curve at point A. Recall that a preference for diversity, or diminishing marginal rate of substitution, is captured by the convexity in an indifference curve, which here also represents a consumer's desire to smooth consumption over time. On indifference curve I_1, at point A the consumer has a large quantity of current consumption and a small quantity of future consumption. He or she needs to be given a large quantity of current consumption to willingly give up a small quantity of future consumption (minus the slope of the indifference curve at A is small). Conversely, at point B the consumer has a small quantity of current consumption and a large quantity of future consumption. He or she needs to be given a large quantity of future consumption to give up a small quantity of current

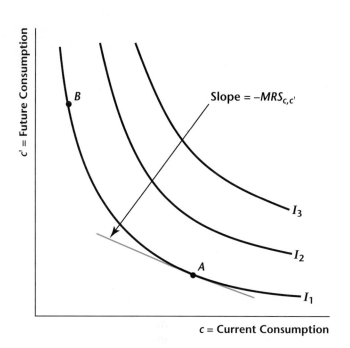

FIGURE 6.2

A Consumer's Indifference Curves

The figure shows the indifference map of a consumer. Indifference curves are convex and downward-sloping. Minus the slope of an indifference curve is the marginal rate of substitution of current consumption for future consumption.

consumption (minus the slope of the indifference curve is large). Thus, the consumer does not like large differences in consumption between the two periods.

As an example to show why consumption smoothing is a natural property for preferences to have, suppose that Sara is a consumer living on a desert island, and that she eats only coconuts. Suppose that coconuts can be stored for two weeks without spoiling, and that Sara has 20 coconuts to last for this week (the current period) and next week (the future period). One option that Sara has is to eat 5 coconuts this week and 15 coconuts next week. Suppose that Sara is just indifferent between this first consumption bundle and a second bundle that involves eating 17 coconuts this week and 3 coconuts next week. However, eating only 5 coconuts in the first week or only 3 coconuts in the second week leaves Sara rather hungry. She would in fact prefer to eat 11 coconuts in the first week and 9 coconuts in the second week, rather than either of the other two consumption bundles. Note that this third consumption bundle combines half of the first consumption bundle with half of the second consumption bundle. That is, $\frac{5+17}{2} = 11$ and $\frac{15+3}{2} = 9$. Sara's preferences reflect a desire for consumption smoothing, or a preference for diversity in her consumption bundle, that seems natural. In Table 6.1 we show the consumption bundles that Sara chooses among.

TABLE 6.1 **Sara's Desire for Consumption Smoothing**

	Week 1 Coconuts	Week 2 Coconuts	Total Consumption
Bundle 1	5	15	20
Bundle 2	17	3	20
Preferred bundle	11	9	20

Consumer Optimization As with the work–leisure decision we considered in Chapter 4, the consumer's optimal consumption bundle here will be determined by where an indifference curve is tangent to the budget constraint. In Figure 6.3 we show the optimal consumption choice for a consumer who decides to be a lender. The endowment point is at E, while the consumer chooses the consumption bundle at point A, where $(c, c') = (c^*, c'^*)$. At point A, it is then the case that

$$MRS_{c,c'} = 1 + r; \tag{6.8}$$

that is, the marginal rate of substitution of current consumption for future consumption (minus the slope of the indifference curve) is equal to the relative price of current consumption in terms of future consumption ($1 + r$, which is minus the slope of the consumer's lifetime budget constraint). Recall from Chapter 4 that Equation (6.8) is a particular case of a standard marginal condition that is implied by consumer optimization (at the optimum, the marginal rate of substitution of good 1 for good 2 is equal to the relative price of good 1 in terms of good 2). Here, the consumer optimizes by choosing the consumption bundle on his or her lifetime budget constraint where the rate at which he or she is willing to trade off current consumption for future consumption is the same as the rate at which he or she can trade current consumption for future consumption in the market (by saving). At point A in Figure 6.3, the quantity of savings is $s = y - t - c^*$, or the distance BD. Similarly, Figure 6.4 shows the case of a consumer who chooses to be a borrower. That is, the endowment point is E and the consumer chooses point A, where $(c, c') = (c^*, c'^*)$. Here, the quantity the consumer borrows in the first period is $-s = c^* - y + t$, or the distance DB.

In the next stage in our analysis, we consider some experiments that will tell us how the consumer responds to changes in current income, future income, and interest rates.

FIGURE 6.3

A Consumer Who Is a Lender
The optimal consumption bundle for the consumer is at point A, where the marginal rate of substitution (minus the slope of an indifference curve) is equal to $1 + r$ (minus the slope of the lifetime budget constraint). The consumer is a lender, as the consumption bundle chosen implies positive savings, with E being the endowment point.

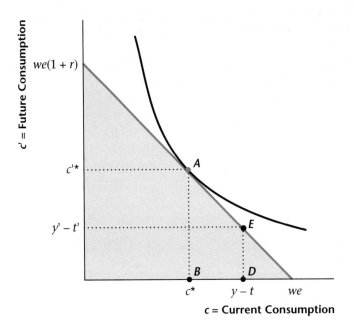

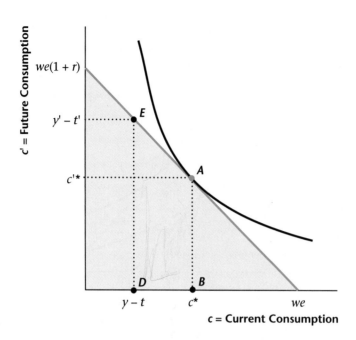

An Increase in Current-Period Income From Chapter 4, we know that an increase in a consumer's dividend income or a reduction in taxes amounts to a pure income effect, which will increase consumption and reduce labour supply. Here, we want to focus on how an increase in the consumer's current income will affect intertemporal decisions. In particular, we want to know the effects of an increase in current income on current consumption, future consumption, and savings. As we will show, these effects will reflect the consumer's desire for consumption smoothing.

Suppose that, holding the interest rate, taxes in the current and future periods, and future income constant, a consumer receives an increase in period 1 income. Asking the consumer's response to this change in income is much like asking how an individual would react to winning a lottery. In Figure 6.5 the initial endowment point is at E_1, and the consumer initially chooses the consumption bundle represented by point A. In this figure we have shown the case of a consumer who is initially a lender, but it will not make a difference for what we want to show if the consumer is a borrower. We will suppose that current-period income increases from y_1 to y_2. The result is that lifetime wealth increases from

$$we_1 = y_1 + \frac{y'}{1+r} - t - \frac{t'}{1+r}$$

to

$$we_2 = y_2 + \frac{y'}{1+r} - t - \frac{t'}{1+r},$$

and the change in lifetime wealth is

$$\Delta we = we_2 - we_1 = y_2 - y_1.$$

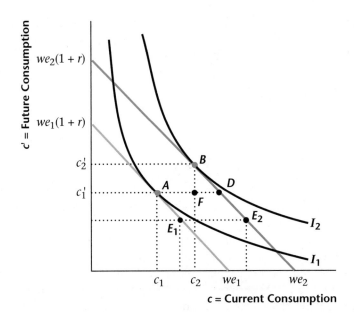

The effect is that the budget constraint shifts to the right by the amount $y_2 - y_1$, which is the distance $E_1 E_2$, where E_2 is the new endowment point. Note that the slope of the budget constraint remains unchanged, as the real interest rate is the same.

Since current-period consumption and future consumption are normal goods, the consumer will now choose a consumption bundle represented by a point like B, where consumption in both periods has risen from the previous values. Current consumption increases from c_1 to c_2, and future consumption increases from c'_1 to c'_2. Thus, if current income increases, the consumer wishes to spread this additional income over both periods and not consume it all in the current period. In Figure 6.5 the increase in current income is the distance AD, while the increase in current consumption is the distance AF, which is less than the distance AD. The change in the consumer's savings is given by

$$\Delta s = \Delta y - \Delta t - \Delta c, \tag{6.9}$$

and since $\Delta t = 0$, and $\Delta y > \Delta c > 0$, we have $\Delta s > 0$. Thus, an increase in current income causes an increase in consumption in both periods, and an increase in savings.

Our analysis tells us that any one consumer who receives an increase in his or her current income will consume more during the current period, but will also save some of the increase in income so as to consume more in the future as well. This behaviour, which arises because of the consumer's desire to smooth consumption over time, is certainly reasonable. For example, consider a consumer Paul, who is currently 25 years of age and wins $1 million in a lottery. Paul could certainly spend all his winnings on consumption goods within the current year and save nothing, but it would seem more sensible if he consumed a small part of his winnings in the current year and saved a substantial fraction in order to consume more for the rest of his life.

If all consumers act to smooth their consumption relative to their income, aggregate consumption should likewise be smooth relative to aggregate income. Indeed, this prediction of our theory is consistent with what we see in the data. Recall from Chapter 3 that real aggregate consumption is less variable than real GDP. The difference in variability between aggregate consumption and GDP is even larger if we take account of the fact that some of what is included in aggregate consumption is not consumption in the economic sense. For example, purchases of new automobiles are included in the NIEA as consumption of durables, but the purchase of a car might more appropriately be included in investment, since the car will yield a flow of consumption services over its lifetime. In the data, expenditures on consumer durables are much more variable than actual consumption, measured as the flow of consumption services that consumers receive from goods. In Figure 6.6 we show the percentage deviations from trend in the consumption of durables, in the consumption of nondurables and services, and in GDP for the period 1961–2002. Clearly, the consumption of durables is much more variable than aggregate income, while the consumption of nondurables and services is much less variable than income. Since the consumption of nondurables and services comes fairly close to measuring a flow of consumption services, the variability in this component of consumption reflects more accurately the tendency of consumers to smooth consumption.

Though aggregate data on consumption and income is clearly qualitatively consistent with consumption-smoothing behaviour on the part of consumers, macroeconomists

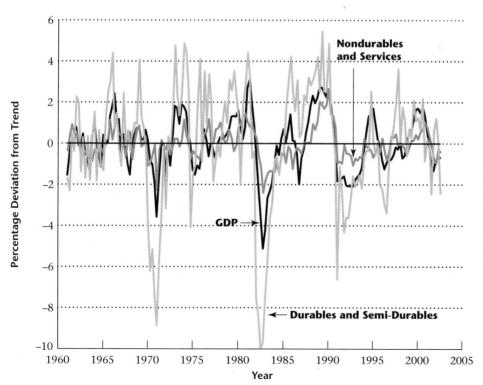

FIGURE 6.6

Percentage Deviations from Trend in GDP and Consumption, 1961–2002

Consumption of durables and semi-durables is much more variable than GDP, which is much more variable than consumption of nondurables and services. The consumption-smoothing behaviour of consumers is clearly reflected in the behaviour of non-durables and services.

Source: Adapted from the Statistics Canada CANSIM database, Series v1992069, v1992045, v1992046, v1992047, v1992048.

have been interested in the quantitative match between consumption theory and the data. The question is whether measured consumption is smooth *enough* relative to measured income to be consistent with theory. Generally, the conclusion from empirical work is that, while the theory points in the right direction, there is some **excess variability** of aggregate consumption relative to aggregate income. That is, while consumption is smoother than income, as the theory predicts, consumption is not quite smooth enough to tightly match the theory.[1] Thus, the theory needs some more work if it is to fit the facts. Two possible explanations for the excess variability in consumption are the following:

1. *There are imperfections in the credit market.* Our theory assumes that a consumer can smooth consumption by borrowing or lending at the market real interest rate r. In reality, consumers cannot borrow all they would like at the market interest rate, and market loan interest rates are typically higher than the interest rates at which consumers lend. As a result, in reality consumers may have less ability to smooth consumption than they do in the theory. We could refine the model by introducing credit market imperfections, but this would make the model considerably more complicated. We will further discuss credit market imperfections later in this chapter.

2. *When all consumers are trying to smooth consumption in the same way simultaneously, this will change market prices.* The consumption-smoothing theory we have studied thus far does not take into account the interaction of consumers with each other and with other sectors of the economy. All consumers may wish to smooth consumption over time, but aggregate consumption must fall during a recession because aggregate income is lower then, and similarly, aggregate consumption must rise in a boom. The way that consumers are reconciled to having high consumption when output is high, and low consumption when output is low, is through movements in market prices, including the market interest rate. Shortly, we will study how individual consumers react to changes in the real interest rate.

An Increase in Future Income While a consumer's response to a change in his or her current income is informative about consumption-smoothing behaviour, we are also interested in the effects on consumer behaviour of a change in income that is expected to occur in the future. Suppose, for example, that Jennifer is about to finish her college degree in four months, and she lines up a job that will start as soon as she graduates. On landing the job, Jennifer's future income has increased considerably. How would she react to this future increase in income? Clearly, this would imply that she would plan to increase her future consumption, but Jennifer also likes to smooth consumption, so that she should want to have higher current consumption as well. She can consume more currently by borrowing against her future income and repaying the loan when she starts working.

In Figure 6.7 we show the effects of an increase for the consumer in future income, from y'_1 to y'_2. This has an effect similar to the increase in current income on lifetime

---

[1]See, for example, R. Hall, 1989, "Consumption," in R. Barro, ed., *Modern Business Cycle Theory*, Harvard University Press, Cambridge, MA.

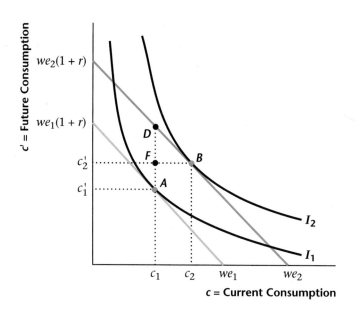

FIGURE 6.7

An Increase in Future Income
An increase in future income increases lifetime wealth from we_1 to we_2, shifting the life-time budget constraint to the right and leaving its slope unchanged. The consumer initially chooses point A, and he or she chooses B after the budget constraint shifts. Future consumption increases by less than the increase in future income, saving decreases, and current consumption increases.

wealth, with lifetime wealth increasing from we_1 to we_2, and shifting the budget constraint up by the amount $y'_2 - y'_1$. Initially, the consumer chooses consumption bundle A, and he or she chooses B after the increase in future income. Note again that both current and future consumption increase; current consumption increases from c_1 to c_2, and future consumption increases from c'_1 to c'_2. The increase in future consumption, which is the distance AF in Figure 6.7, is less than the increase in future income, which is the distance AD. This occurs because, as with the increase in current income, the consumer wants to smooth consumption over time. Rather than spend all the increase in income in the future, the consumer saves less in the current period so that current consumption can increase. The change in saving is given by Equation (6.9), where $\Delta t = \Delta y = 0$, and since $\Delta c > 0$, we must have $\Delta s < 0$—that is, savings decreases.

In the case of an expected increase in future income, the consumer acts to smooth consumption over time, just as when he or she receives an increase in current income. The difference is that an increase in future income leads to smoothing backward, with the consumer saving less in the current period so that current consumption can increase, whereas an increase in current income leads to smoothing forward, with the consumer saving more in the current period so that future consumption can increase.

Temporary and Permanent Changes in Income When a consumer receives a change in his or her current income, it matters a great deal for his or her current consumption–savings choice whether this change in income is temporary or permanent. For example, Allen would respond quite differently to receiving a windfall increase in his income of $1000, say by winning a lottery, as opposed to receiving a $1000 yearly salary increase that he expects to continue indefinitely. In the case of the lottery winnings, we might expect that Allen would increase current consumption by only a small amount, saving most of the lottery winnings to increase consumption in the future. If

Allen received a permanent increase in his income, as in the second case, we would expect his increase in current consumption to be much larger.

The difference between the effects of temporary and permanent changes in income on consumption was articulated by Milton Friedman in his **permanent income hypothesis**.[2] Friedman argued that a primary determinant of a consumer's current consumption is his or her permanent income, which is closely related to the concept of lifetime wealth in our model. Changes in income that are temporary yield small changes in permanent income (lifetime wealth), which have small effects on current consumption, whereas changes in income that are permanent have large effects on permanent income (lifetime wealth) and current consumption.

In our model, we can show the effects of temporary versus permanent changes in income by examining an increase in income that occurs only in the current period versus an increase in income occurring in the current period *and* the future period. In Figure 6.8 the budget constraint of the consumer is initially AB, and he or she chooses the consumption bundle represented by point H, on indifference curve I_1. Then, the consumer experiences a temporary increase in income, with current income increasing from y_1 to y_2, so that the budget constraint shifts out to DE. The real interest rate does not change, so that the slope of the budget constraint remains constant. The distance HL is equal to the change in current income, $y_2 - y_1$. Now, the consumer chooses point J on indifference curve I_2, and we know from our previous discussion that the increase in current consumption, $c_2 - c_1$, is less than the increase in current income, $y_2 - y_1$, as saving increases due to consumption-smoothing behaviour.

Now, suppose that the increase in income is permanent. We interpret this as an equal increase of $y_2 - y_1$ in both current and future income. That is, initially future income is y'_1 and it increases to y'_2 with $y'_2 - y'_1 = y_2 - y_1$. Now, the budget constraint is given by FG in Figure 6.8, where the upward shift in the budget constraint from DE is the distance LM, which is $y'_2 - y'_1 = y_2 - y_1$. The consumer now chooses point K on indifference curve I_3. At point K, current consumption is c_3. Given that current and future consumption are normal goods, current consumption increases from point H to point J and from point J to point K. Therefore, if income increases permanently, this has a larger effect on current consumption than if income increases only temporarily. Note that, if income increases only temporarily, there is an increase in saving, so that consumption does not increase as much as income. However, if there is a permanent increase in income, there need not be an increase in saving, and current consumption could increase as much as or more than income.

Why is it important that consumers will respond differently to temporary and permanent changes in their income? Suppose that the government is considering cutting taxes, and this tax cut could be temporary or permanent. For now, ignore how the government will go about financing this tax cut (we will consider this later in the chapter). If consumers receive a tax cut that increases lifetime wealth, then this will increase aggregate consumption. However, if consumers expect the tax cut to be temporary, the increase in consumption will be much smaller than if they expect the tax cut to be permanent.

---

[2]See M. Friedman, 1957, *A Theory of the Consumption Function*, Princeton University Press, Princeton, NJ.

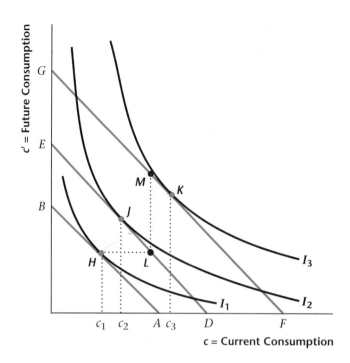

FIGURE 6.8
Temporary Versus Permanent Increases in Income
A temporary increase in income is an increase in current income, with the budget constraint shifting from *AB* to *DE*, and the optimal consumption bundle changing from *H* to *J*. When there is a permanent increase in income, current and future income both increase, and the budget constraint shifts from *AB* to *FG*, with the optimal consumption bundle changing from *H* to *K*.

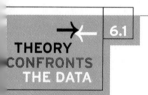

THEORY CONFRONTS THE DATA   6.1

Consumption Smoothing and the Stock Market

Thus far, our theory tells us that, in response to increases in their lifetime wealth, consumers will increase consumption, but in such a way that their consumption path is smoothed over time. One way in which consumers' wealth changes is through variation in the prices of stocks traded on organized stock exchanges, such as the Toronto Stock Exchange.

How should we expect aggregate consumption to respond to a change in stock prices? On the one hand, publicly traded stock is not a large fraction of national wealth. That is, a large fraction of national wealth includes the housing stock and the capital of privately held companies, which are not traded on the stock market. Therefore, even if there is a large change in stock prices, this need not represent a large change in national wealth. On the other hand, financial theory tells us that, when the price of a stock changes, we should expect this price change to be permanent.

Financial theory tells us (with some qualifications) that stock prices are **martingales**. A martingale has the property that the best prediction of its value tomorrow is its value today. In the case of a stock price, the best prediction of tomorrow's stock price is today's stock price. The reason that stock prices follow martingales is that, if they did not, then there would be opportunities for investors to make profits. That is, suppose that a stock price does not follow a martingale, and suppose first that the best forecast is that tomorrow's stock price will be higher than today's stock price. Then, investors would want to buy the stock today so as to make a profit by selling it tomorrow. Ultimately, this would force up the market price of the stock today, to the point where the price today is what it is expected to be tomorrow. Similarly, if the price of the stock today were greater than what the stock's price was expected to be tomorrow, investors would want to sell the stock today so they could buy it at a cheaper price tomorrow. In this case, investors' actions would force the current stock price down to the point where it was equal to its expected price tomorrow. Since the current price of a stock is the best forecast of its future price, any change in prices is a surprise, and this change in prices is expected to be permanent.

A change in the overall value of the stock market does not represent a change in a large fraction of national wealth, and this would tend to dampen the effect of price movements in the stock market on aggregate consumption. However, the fact that any change in stock prices is expected to be permanent will tend to amplify the effects of changes in stock prices, as we know that permanent changes in wealth have larger effects on consumption than do temporary changes in wealth. What do the data tell us? In Figure 6.9 we show a time series plot of the percentage deviations from trend in the Toronto Stock Exchange composite price index, and percentage deviations from trend in real consumption of nondurables and services. The data plotted are quarterly data for the period 1961–2002. Here, note in particular that the stock price index is highly volatile relative to consumption. On the one hand, deviations from trend in the stock price index of 10 to 20% are not uncommon, and the stock price index dipped more than 30% below trend in the 1980s. However, a close examination of Figure 6.9 will indicate that deviations from trend in the stock price index are positively correlated with deviations from trend in consumption. Figure 6.10 shows this more clearly, where we show the same data as in Figure 6.9, except in a scatter plot. The positively sloped line in Figure 6.10 is the best fit to the data in the scatter plot, indicating that the stock price and consumption are positively correlated.

The data indicate that the stock market is potentially an important channel for the effects of changes in wealth on aggregate consumption behaviour. The fact that consumption and stock prices move together is consistent with the notion that shocks to the financial system that are reflected in the prices of publicly traded stocks can cause significant movements in aggregate consumption. Though the value of publicly traded stock is not a large part of national wealth, the fact that stock price changes are expected to be permanent potentially contributes to the influence of the stock market on consumption behaviour.

An Increase in the Real Interest Rate To this point, we have examined how changes in a consumer's current income and future income affect his or her choices of consumption in the current and future periods. These are changes that shift the consumer's budget constraint but do not change its slope. In this subsection, we will study how the consumer responds to a change in the real interest rate, which will change the slope of the budget constraint. Changes in the market real interest rate will ultimately be an important part of the mechanism by which shocks to the economy, fiscal policy, and monetary policy affect real activity, as we will show in Chapters 9–11. A key channel for interest rate effects on real activity will be through aggregate consumption.

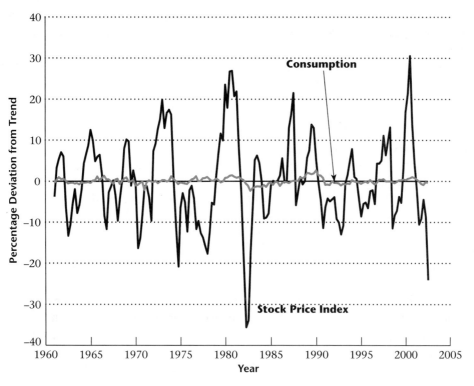

FIGURE 6.9
Stock Prices and Consumption of Nondurables and Services, 1961–2002
The graph shows that deviations from trend in stock prices (the black line) and in consumption of nondurables and services (the coloured line) are positively correlated. When there is a positive (negative) deviation from trend in stock prices, there tends to be a positive (negative) deviation from trend in consumption.

Source: Adapted from the Statistics Canada CANSIM database, Series v1992047, v1992048, v122620.

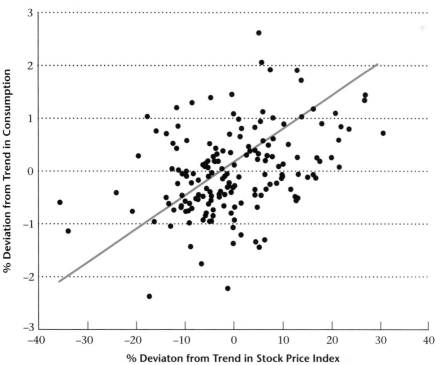

FIGURE 6.10
Scatter Plot of Percentage Deviations from Trend in Nondurable Consumption of Nondurables and Services Versus Percentage Deviations from Trend in a Stock Price Index
The coloured line represents the best statistical fit to the scatter plot. Since this line is positively sloped, the two variables are positively correlated.

Source: Adapted from the Statistics Canada CANSIM database, Series v1992047, v1992048, v122620.

Since $\frac{1}{1+r}$ is the relative price of future consumption goods in terms of current consumption goods, a change in the real interest rate effectively changes this intertemporal relative price. In Chapter 4, in the consumer's work–leisure choice problem, a change in the real wage was effectively a change in the relative price of leisure and consumption, and a change in the real wage had income and substitution effects. Here, in our two-period framework, a change in the real interest rate will also have income and substitution effects in its influence on consumption in the present and the future.

Suppose the consumer faces an increase in the real interest rate, with taxes and income held constant in both periods. Note first that this will make the budget constraint steeper, since the slope of the budget constraint is $-(1+r)$. Further, under the assumption that the consumer never has to pay a tax larger than his or her income, so that $y' - t' > 0$, an increase in r will decrease lifetime wealth we, as shown in Equation (6.5). Also from Equation (6.5), we have

$$we(1+r) = (y-t)(1+r) + y' - t',$$

and since $y > t$, there will be an increase in $we(1+r)$ when r increases. Therefore, we know that an increase in r will cause the budget constraint to pivot, as in Figure 6.11, where r increases from r_1 to r_2, resulting in a decrease in we from we_1 to we_2. We also know that the budget constraint must pivot around the endowment point E, since it must always be possible for the consumer to consume his or her disposable income in each period, no matter what the real interest rate is.

A change in r results in a change in the relative price of consumption in the current and future periods; that is, an increase in r causes future consumption to become cheaper relative to current consumption. A higher interest rate implies that the return on savings is higher, so that more future consumption goods can be obtained for a given sacrifice of current consumption goods. As well, for a given loan in the first period, the consumer

FIGURE 6.11

An Increase in the Real Interest Rate

An increase in the real interest rate causes the lifetime budget constraint of the consumer to become steeper and to pivot around the endowment point E.

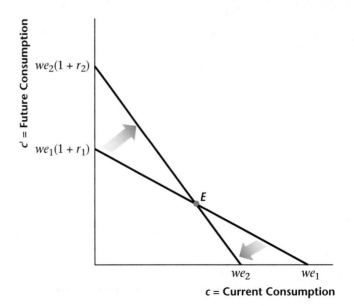

will have to forgo more future consumption goods when the loan is repaid. We can use what we learned about income and substitution effects in Chapter 4 to understand how an increase in the real interest rate will affect the consumer's behaviour. However, it turns out that the income effects of an increase in the real interest rate work in different directions for lenders and borrowers, which is what we want to show next.

First, let's consider the case of a lender. In Figure 6.12 consider a consumer who is initially a lender and faces an increase in the market real interest rate from r_1 to r_2. Initially, lifetime wealth is we_1, and this changes to we_2. The budget constraint pivots around the endowment point E. Initially, the consumer chose the consumption bundle A, and we suppose that the consumer chooses B after the increase in the real interest rate. To find the substitution effect of the real interest rate increase, we draw an artificial budget constraint FG, which has the same slope as the new budget constraint, and is just tangent to the initial indifference curve I_1. Thus, we are taking wealth away from the consumer until he or she is as well off as before the increase in r. Then, the movement from A to D is a pure substitution effect, and in moving from A to D future consumption increases and current consumption decreases, as future consumption has become cheaper relative to current consumption. The remaining effect, the movement from D to B, is a pure income effect, which causes both current-period and future-period

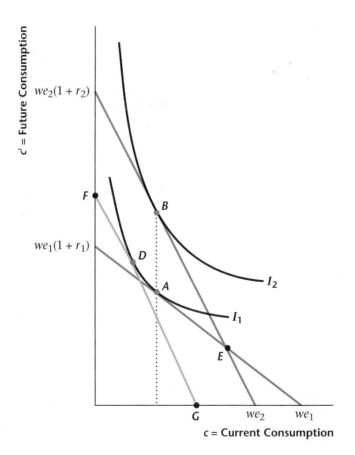

FIGURE 6.12

An Increase in the Real Interest Rate for a Lender
When the real interest rate increases for a lender, the substitution effect is the movement from A to D, and the income effect is the movement from D to B. Current consumption and saving may rise or fall, while future consumption increases.

consumption to increase (recall that we assumed that current and future consumption are normal goods). Therefore, future consumption must increase, as both the income and substitution effects work in the same direction. However, current-period consumption may increase or decrease, as the substitution effect causes current consumption to decrease, and the income effect causes it to increase. If the income effect is larger than the substitution effect, current consumption increases. Note that the effect on savings depends on the change in current consumption, as we are holding constant current disposable income. Thus, saving may increase or decrease. Saving increases if the substitution effect is larger than the income effect, and saving decreases otherwise. An increase in the real interest rate makes saving more attractive, since the relative price of future consumption is lower (the substitution effect), but it makes saving less attractive, since there is a positive income effect on period 1 consumption which will tend to reduce saving.

Consider the following example, which shows the intuition behind the income and substitution effects of a change in the real interest rate. Suppose Christine is currently a lender, whose disposable income in the current year is $40 000. She currently saves 30% of her current income, and she faces a real interest rate of 5%. Her income next year will also be $40 000 (in current-year dollars), and so initially she consumes $0.7 \times \$40\,000 = \$28\,000$ this year, and she consumes $\$40\,000 + (1 + 0.05) \times \$12\,000 = \$52\,600$ next year. Now, suppose that the real interest rate rises to 10%. How should Christine respond? If she continues to consume $28 000 in the current year and saves $12 000, she will have future consumption of $53 200, an increase over initial future consumption, reflecting the substitution effect. However, if she consumes the same amount next year, she can now save less in the current year to achieve the same result. That is, she could save $11 454 in the current year, which would imply that she could consume $52 600 next year. Then, she consumes $\$40\,000 - \$11\,454 = \$28\,546$, which is more than before, reflecting the income effect. What Christine will do depends on her own preferences and how strong the relative income and substitution effects are for her as an individual.

Now consider the effects of an increase in r for a borrower. In Figure 6.13, r increases from r_1 to r_2, and lifetime wealth changes from we_1 to we_2. The endowment point is at E, and the consumer initially chooses consumption bundle A; then, he or she chooses B after r increases. Again, we can separate the movement from A to B into substitution and income effects by drawing an artificial budget constraint FG, which is parallel to the new budget constraint and tangent to the initial indifference curve I_1. Therefore, we are essentially compensating the consumer with extra wealth to make him or her as well off as initially when facing the higher interest rate. Then, the substitution effect is the movement from A to D, and the income effect is the movement from D to B. Here, the substitution effect is for future consumption to rise and current consumption to fall, just as was the case for a lender. However, the income effect in this case is negative for both current consumption and future consumption. As a result, current consumption falls for the borrower, but future consumption may rise or fall, depending on how strong the opposing substitution and income effects are. Savings must rise as current consumption falls and current disposable income is held constant.

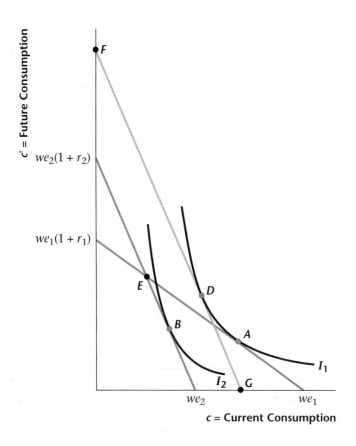

FIGURE 6.13

An Increase in the Real Interest Rate for a Borrower
When the real interest rate increases for a borrower, the substitution effect is the movement from A to D, and the income effect is the movement from D to B. Current consumption decreases, savings increases, and future consumption may rise or fall.

As an example, suppose that Christopher is initially a borrower whose income in the current year and next year is $40 000 (in current-year dollars). Initially, Christopher takes out a loan of $20 000 in the current year, so that he can consume $60 000 in the current year. The real interest rate is 5%, so that the principal and interest on his loan is $21 000, and he consumes $19 000 next year. Now, suppose alternatively that the real interest rate is 10%. If Christopher holds constant his consumption in the future, this must imply that his current consumption will go down, reflecting the negative income effect. That is, if he continues to consume $19 000 next year, given a real interest rate of 10%, he can borrow only $19 091 this year, which implies that his current-year consumption is $59 091.

For both lenders and borrowers, there is an **intertemporal substitution effect** of an increase in the real interest rate. That is, a higher real interest rate lowers the relative price of future consumption in terms of current consumption, and this leads to a substitution of future consumption for current consumption, and therefore to an increase in savings. In much of macroeconomics, we are interested in aggregate effects, but the above analysis tells us that there are potentially confounding income effects in determining the effect of an increase in the real interest rate on aggregate consumption. The population consists of many consumers, some of whom are lenders and some borrowers. Though consumption will decrease for each borrower when the real interest rate goes up, what happens to the consumption of lenders depends on the strength of opposing income and substitution effects. There is a tendency for the negative income effects on the consumption of borrowers to offset the positive income effects on the consumption of lenders, leaving us with only the substitution effects. However, there is no theoretical guarantee that aggregate consumption will fall when the real interest rate rises.

Tables 6.2 and 6.3 summarize the above discussion of the effects of an increase in the real interest rate.

An Example: Perfect Complements A convenient example to work with is the case where a consumer has preferences with the perfect complements property. Recall from Chapter 4 that if two goods are perfect complements they are always consumed in fixed proportions. In the case of current consumption and future consumption, the perfect complements property implies that the consumer will always choose c and c' such that

$$c' = ac, \tag{6.10}$$

where a is a positive constant. In Figure 6.14 the consumer's indifference curves, for example I_1 and I_2, are L-shaped with the right angles on the line $c' = ac$. Perfect complementarity is an extreme case of a desire for consumption smoothing. The consumer will never want to deviate from having current and future consumption in fixed proportions. The consumer's budget constraint is AB in the figure, which is described by the equation

$$c + \frac{c'}{1 + r} = we, \tag{6.11}$$

where

$$we = y - t + \frac{y' - t'}{1 + r}. \tag{6.12}$$

In Figure 6.14 the optimal consumption bundle will be at a point such as D, which is on the consumer's budget constraint, and also on the line $c' = ac$. Therefore, we can

TABLE 6.2 **Effects of an Increase in the Real Interest Rate for a Lender**

Current consumption	?
Future consumption	Increases
Current savings	?

TABLE 6.3 **Effects of an Increase in the Real Interest Rate for a Borrower**

Current consumption	Decreases
Future consumption	?
Current savings	Increases

solve algebraically for the current and future consumption c and c', respectively, by solving the two equations (6.10) and (6.11) for the two variables c and c', given r and we. Using substitution, we get

$$c = \frac{we(1 + r)}{1 + r + a}, \tag{6.13}$$

$$c' = \frac{awe(1 + r)}{1 + r + a}, \tag{6.14}$$

or substituting for we in (6.13) and (6.14) using (6.12), we obtain

$$c = \frac{(y - t)(1 + r) + y' - t'}{1 + r + a}, \tag{6.15}$$

$$c' = a\left[\frac{(y - t)(1 + r) + y' - t'}{1 + r + a}\right]. \tag{6.16}$$

Note in particular from (6.15) and (6.16) that current and future consumption increase with current income y, and with future income y'. The effects of a change in the interest rate r are more complicated, but essentially the effect of an increase in r on c and c' depends only on whether the consumer is a lender or a borrower. This is because there are no substitution effects when preferences have the perfect complements property. We will explore this further in the problems at the end of this chapter.

The Demand for Current Consumption Goods In later chapters, particularly Chapters 7 and 9–11, we will need to work with models that are specified at the level of supply and demand curves. It may sometimes be too complicated to be entirely explicit about consumers' preferences, particularly when we need to study the interaction among several markets in the economy. Thus, a less explicit but simpler approach will be necessary.

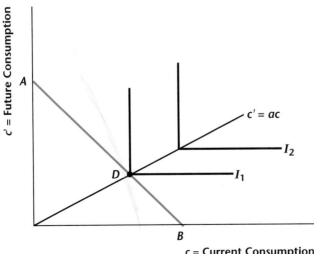

c' = Future Consumption

c' = ac

I₂

I₁

B

c = Current Consumption

One element of demand that will be useful in later chapters is consumers' demand for current consumption goods. From the above analysis, we know that an individual's demand for current consumption goods increases with either current or future income. Further, if we assume that the intertemporal substitution effect of an increase in the real interest rate dominates the income effect when a consumer is a lender, then an increase in the real interest rate will always cause the consumer's demand for current consumption goods to fall. Therefore, we can graph the demand for current consumption goods of an individual consumer, c^d, as a function of current income, as in Figure 6.15. Here, current income y is on the horizontal axis and current consumption c is on the vertical axis. Note that the curve c^d in the figure is upward-sloping. Further, since an increase in current income always produces a less than one-for-one increase in current consumption (given the consumption-smoothing motive, some of an increase in income is always saved), the slope of the c^d curve is less than 1, since this slope represents the increase in the consumer's current consumption that arises when current income increases by 1 unit. The slope of the c^d curve is defined to be the **marginal propensity to consume** or the **MPC**. We thus have $MPC < 1$. While we can say that the marginal propensity to consume must be less than 1, the MPC may vary with the level of income, depending on the consumer's preferences.

The consumer's demand for consumption c^d will shift with either a change in the real interest rate or a change in the consumer's future income. Under the assumption that the intertemporal substitution effect of a change in the real interest rate always dominates the income effect, the c^d curve will shift up, as in Figure 6.16, if the real interest rate falls, the present value of taxes decreases, or if future income for the consumer increases.

FIGURE 6.15

A Consumer's Demand for Current Consumption Goods, c^d, as a Function of Current Income

The slope of the c^d curve is the marginal propensity to consume, *MPC*, which is less than 1 for all *y*.

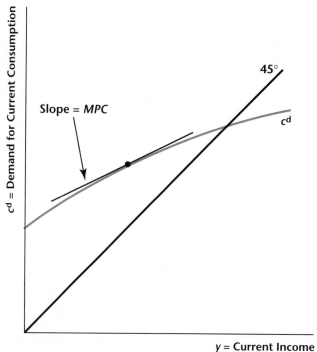

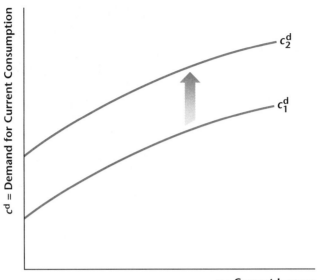

FIGURE 6.16

A Shift in a Consumer's Demand for Current Consumption

The c^d curve shifts up with a decrease in the real interest rate, a decrease in the present value of taxes, or an increase in future income.

Though we will not use the approach of Figures 6.15 and 6.16 in this chapter in our analysis, it will be applied in Chapters 7 and beyond.

GOVERNMENT

Now that we have studied how consumers behave, to complete our description of the model we need only describe what the government does. We can then explore the equilibrium effects of tax policy.

We will suppose that the government wishes to purchase G consumption goods in the current period and G' units in the future period, with these quantities of government purchases given exogenously. The aggregate quantity of taxes collected by the government in the current period is T. Recall that there are m consumers who each pay a current tax of t, so that $T = mt$. Similarly, in the future period total taxes are equal to T', and we have $T' = mt'$. The government can borrow by issuing bonds. Recall that government bonds and private bonds are indistinguishable, with these bonds all bearing the same real interest rate r. Letting B denote the quantity of government bonds issued in the current period, the government's current-period budget constraint is

$$G = T + B; \tag{6.17}$$

that is, government spending is financed through taxes and the issue of bonds. Put another way, the current-period government deficit, $G - T$, is financed by issuing bonds. In the future period, the government's budget constraint is

$$G' + (1 + r)B = T'. \tag{6.18}$$

The left-hand side of (6.18) is total government outlays in the future, consisting of future government purchases and the principal and interest on the government bonds issued in the current period. These government outlays are financed through future taxes, the quantity on the right-hand side of (6.18). Note that the government's budget constraints allow for the possibility that $B < 0$. If $B < 0$, this would imply that the government was a lender to the private sector, rather than a borrower from it. Note that in practice the government engages in direct lending to the private sector, and it also issues debt to private economic agents, so that it is a lender *and* a borrower.

Recall that, when we analyzed a consumer's budget constraint, we took the budget constraints for the current and future periods and collapsed them into a single lifetime budget constraint. Here, we can accomplish something similar, in taking the government's budget constraints expressed in Equations (6.17) and (6.18) and collapsing them into a single **government present-value budget constraint**. We obtain this constraint by first solving Equation (6.18) for B to get

$$B = \frac{T' - G'}{1 + r},$$

and then substituting in Equation (6.17) for B to get

$$G + \frac{G'}{1 + r} = T + \frac{T'}{1 + r}. \tag{6.19}$$

Equation (6.19) is the government present-value budget constraint, and it states that the present value of government purchases must equal the present value of taxes. This is similar to the consumer's lifetime budget constraint, which states that the present value of consumption is equal to the present value of lifetime disposable income. An interpretation of the government present-value budget constraint is that the government must eventually pay off all of its debt by taxing its citizens.

COMPETITIVE EQUILIBRIUM

Now that we have described the behaviour of the consumers and the government in our model, we can proceed with the final step in putting the model into working order, which is to specify how a competitive equilibrium is achieved.

The market in which the m consumers in this economy and the government interact is the credit market, a market in which consumers and the government can borrow and lend. In trading in the credit market, consumers and the government are effectively trading future consumption goods for current consumption goods. Recall that the relative price at which future consumption goods trade for current consumption goods is $\frac{1}{1+r}$, which is determined by the real interest rate r.

In a competitive equilibrium for this two-period economy, three conditions must hold:

1. Each consumer chooses first- and second-period consumption and savings optimally given the real interest rate r.

2. The government present-value budget constraint, Equation (6.19), holds.

3. The credit market clears.

The credit market clears when the net quantity that consumers want to lend in the current period is equal to the quantity that the government wishes to borrow. Letting

S^p denote the aggregate quantity of private savings—that is, the savings of consumers—the credit market equilibrium condition is

$$S^p = B, \tag{6.20}$$

or the aggregate quantity of private savings is equal to the quantity of debt issued by the government in the current period. Equation (6.20) also states that national saving, which is equal to aggregate private saving minus B, is equal to zero in equilibrium. Recall from Chapter 2 that a national income accounts identity states that $S^p + S^g = I + CA$, where S^g is government savings, I is investment, and CA is the current account surplus. Here, $S^g = -B, I = 0$ since there is no capital accumulation in this model, and $CA = 0$ since this is a closed economy model. Also recall that $S = S^p + S^g$, where S is national saving.

The equilibrium condition (6.20) implies that

$$Y = C + G, \tag{6.21}$$

where Y is aggregate income in the current period (the sum of incomes across all m consumers) and C is aggregate consumption in the current period (the sum of consumptions across all m consumers). Recall from Chapter 2 that Equation (6.21) is the income–expenditure identity for this economy, since there is no investment, and no interaction with the rest of the world (net exports equal zero). To see why Equation (6.21) follows from Equation (6.20), note that

$$S^p = Y - C - T; \tag{6.22}$$

that is, aggregate private saving is equal to current-period income minus aggregate current consumption, minus aggregate current taxes. Also, from the government's current-period budget constraint, Equation (6.17), we have

$$B = G - T. \tag{6.23}$$

Then, substituting in Equation (6.20) for S^p from Equation (6.22) and for B from Equation (6.23), we get

$$Y - C - T = G - T,$$

or, rearranging,

$$Y = C + G.$$

This result will prove to be useful in the next section, as the economy can be shown to be in a competitive equilibrium if *either* Equation (6.20) or Equation (6.21) holds.

The Ricardian Equivalence Theorem

From Chapter 5, recall that an increase in government spending comes at a cost, in that it crowds out private consumption expenditures. However, in Chapter 5, we could not disentangle the effects of taxation from the effects of government spending, since the government was unable to borrow in the model considered there. That is certainly not true here, where we can independently evaluate the effects of changes in government spending and in taxes.

What we want to show here is a key result in macroeconomics, called the Ricardian equivalence theorem. (See Macroeconomics in Action 6.1 on p. 183 for a discussion of the idea's origins.) This theorem states that a change in the timing of taxes by the government is neutral. By neutral, we mean that in equilibrium a change in current taxes, exactly offset in present-value terms by an equal and opposite change in future taxes, has no effect on the real interest rate or on the consumption of individual consumers. This is a very strong result, as it says that there is a sense in which government deficits do not matter, which seems to run counter to standard intuition. As we will see, however, this is an important starting point for thinking about why government deficits *do* matter, and a key message that comes from the logic of the Ricardian equivalence theorem is that *a tax cut is not a free lunch.*

DEFINITION

The Ricardian Equivalence Theorem

If current and future government spending are held constant, a change in current taxes with an equal and opposite change in the present value of future taxes leaves the equilibrium real interest rate and the consumptions of individuals unchanged.

To show why the Ricardian equivalence theorem holds in this model, we will follow these three steps:

1. Given current and future government expenditures and current and future taxes, we suppose that the economy is initially in a competitive equilibrium at a particular real interest rate. That is, given the market real interest rate, consumers choose current and future consumption and savings optimally, the government's present-value budget constraint holds, and the credit market clears.

2. We suppose that current taxes paid by consumers change from what they were in step 1, and that future taxes adjust so that the government's present-value budget constraint still holds.

3. We show that, given the equilibrium real interest rate from step 1, consumers now choose the same quantities of current-period and future-period consumptions as in step 1, and that the credit market clears. Therefore, the equilibrium is essentially unchanged from step 1, except that taxes are different and government saving and private saving change by equal and opposite amounts.

   Step 1: Suppose that the economy is initially in a competitive equilibrium with a real interest rate r^*, government purchases are G and G' in the current period and the future period, respectively, and each consumer pays taxes of t^* and t'^* in the current period and the future period, respectively. Suppose we consider a particular consumer, who chooses to consume c^* and c'^* in the current period and the future period, respectively, given the budget constraint he or she faces, which is

$$c + \frac{c'}{1 + r^*} = y + \frac{y'}{1 + r^*} - t^* - \frac{t'^*}{1 + r^*}, \tag{6.24}$$

and the government's present-value budget constraint is

$$G + \frac{G'}{1 + r^*} = T^* + \frac{T'^*}{1 + r^*}, \tag{6.25}$$

where T^* is aggregate current period taxes, with $T^* = mt^*$, and T'^* is aggregate future taxes, with $T'^* = mt'^*$. In a competitive equilibrium, the credit market clears, which implies that Equation (6.21) holds, or

$$Y = C^* + G, \tag{6.26}$$

where Y is current aggregate income, which is exogenous, and C^* is aggregate current consumption. Aggregate private saving is given by

$$S^{p*} = Y - C^* - T^*, \tag{6.27}$$

while government borrowing is

$$B^* = G - T^*. \tag{6.28}$$

Step 2: Suppose that current-period taxes increase by Δt for each consumer; that is, current taxes for each consumer are now $t^{**} = t^* + \Delta t$. Aggregate current taxes are then $T^{**} = T^* + m \Delta t$. For the government to satisfy its present-value budget constraint, it must then be the case that future taxes must change for each consumer. If t'^{**} is now the quantity of future taxes for each consumer, $T'^{**} = mt'^{**}$ is the aggregate quantity of future taxes. Supposing for now that the real interest rate remains unchanged in equilibrium (which we will show is the case), if the present-value government budget constraint, Equation (6.19), is to hold, then

$$G + \frac{G'}{1 + r^*} = T^{**} + \frac{T'^{**}}{1 + r^*}, \tag{6.29}$$

and so from Equations (6.25) and (6.29) we have $T'^{**} = T'^* - m \Delta t(1 + r)$. That is, if current taxes increase by $m \Delta t$, this means that the government issues $m \Delta t$ fewer bonds in the current period, which implies that the interest and principal that needs to be paid off with future taxes decreases by $m \Delta t(1 + r)$.

Step 3: What we wish to show now is that r^* is still the equilibrium real interest rate. First, note that we have set the new levels of current-period aggregate taxes, T^{**}, and future-period aggregate taxes, T'^{**}, so that the government present-value budget constraint, Equation (6.29), holds. This equation then implies that the present value of taxes paid by each consumer is

$$t^{**} + \frac{t'^{**}}{1 + r^*} = \frac{1}{m}\left(G + \frac{G'}{1 + r^*}\right). \tag{6.30}$$

That is, the present value of taxes for each consumer is just the per capita present value of government expenditures. An individual consumer's budget constraint, given the new values for present and future taxes, is then

$$c + \frac{c'}{1 + r^*} = y + \frac{y'}{1 + r^*} - t^{**} - \frac{t'^{**}}{1 + r^*}, \tag{6.31}$$

and substituting for the present value of taxes in Equation (6.31) using Equation (6.30), we get

$$c + \frac{c'}{1 + r^*} = y + \frac{y'}{1 + r^*} - \frac{1}{m}\left(G - \frac{G'}{1 + r^*}\right). \tag{6.32}$$

But then, substituting using Equation (6.25) for the present value of government spending in Equation (6.32), and noting that $mt^* = T^*$ and $mt'^* = T'^*$, we obtain

$$c + \frac{c'}{1 + r^*} = y + \frac{y'}{1 + r^*} - t^* - \frac{t'^*}{1 + r^*},$$

so that the consumer faces the same budget constraint before and after the change in taxes (see (6.24)), since the present value of taxes stays constant, leaving lifetime wealth constant for the consumer. As the consumer's budget constraint stays the same, he or she will make exactly the same choices before and after taxes change, that is $c = c^*$ and $c' = c'^*$. Since each consumer's consumption is unchanged in each period, aggregate consumption is the same in the current period before and after the change in taxes; therefore, it must still be the case that

$$Y = C^* + G,$$

and so the credit market remains in equilibrium. Therefore, since consumers are all optimizing, the government budget constraint holds, and the credit market clears, r^* must still be the equilibrium real interest rate.

We have shown that the change in taxes leaves the equilibrium real interest rate unchanged, and that consumers all choose the same consumption in the current and future periods. What does change, however, is the saving of consumers and of the government. For consumers, since income and consumption in the current period remain unchanged, the change in private saving is

$$\Delta S^P = T^* - T^{**} = -m\,\Delta t.$$

That is, the change in saving for a consumer is equal to minus the change in aggregate current taxes. For example, if $\Delta t < 0$, so that there is a tax cut for each consumer, the consumer will save the full amount of the tax cut in order to pay higher future taxes. For the government, since government spending remains the same in each period, the change in government borrowing will be $-m\,\Delta t$, so that the change in government saving is $m\,\Delta t$. Thus, government saving and aggregate private saving change by equal and opposite amounts, and so national saving (recall from Chapter 2 that national saving is the sum of private saving and government saving) does not change.

RICARDIAN EQUIVALENCE: A NUMERICAL EXAMPLE

To give a numerical example, assume an economy with 500 consumers who are all identical. Initially, the equilibrium real interest rate is 5%, and each consumer receives income of 10 units in the current period, and income of 12 units in the future period. In the current and future periods, each consumer initially pays taxes of 3 and 4 units, respectively. Lifetime wealth for each consumer is then

$$we = 10 - 3 + \frac{12 - 4}{1.05} = 14.61.$$

Suppose that each consumer initially finds it optimal to consume 6 units in the current period and 9.04 units in the future period. We can verify that this consumption bundle satisfies the consumer's lifetime budget constraint. That is,

$$6 + \frac{9.04}{1.05} = 14.61.$$

Then, each consumer saves $10 - 6 - 3 = 1$ in the current period, so that aggregate private saving is initially 500 units.

The government purchases 2000 units in the current period and 1475 units in the second period. Since aggregate taxes are 1500 in the current period and 2000 in the second period, the government borrows $B = 500$ in the current period. Thus, note that national saving is private saving plus government saving, or $500 - 500 = 0$. The government's present-value budget constraint holds as

$$2000 + \frac{1475}{1.05} = 1500 + \frac{2000}{1.05}.$$

Further, aggregate current income is 5000, while aggregate current consumption is 3000. This implies that $Y = C + G$, and so the credit market is in equilibrium.

Now, suppose that the government reduces taxes for each consumer in the current period to 2 units, and increases taxes for each consumer in the future period to 5.05 units. Suppose for now that the equilibrium real interest rate is unchanged at 5%. Then, the government's present-value budget constraint still holds, as

$$2000 + \frac{1475}{1.05} = 1000 + \frac{2525}{1.05}.$$

Further, lifetime wealth for each consumer is now

$$we = 10 - 2 + \frac{12 - 5.05}{1.05} = 14.61,$$

which is identical to lifetime wealth before the current tax cut, and so each consumer will still want to consume 6 units in the current period and 9.04 units in the future period. As a result, it must still be the case that $Y = C + G$—that is, the credit market clears. Therefore, 5% is still the equilibrium real interest rate, and each consumer's consumption decisions are unchanged.

Aggregate private saving has now increased by the amount of the tax cut, to 1000, and government saving has decreased by the amount of the tax cut, to -1000, with equilibrium national saving unchanged at 0.

RICARDIAN EQUIVALENCE: A GRAPH

We can show more generally how the Ricardian equivalence theorem works by considering the effects of a current tax cut on an individual consumer. Here, the consumer also faces an increase in taxes in the future, as the government must pay off the current debt issued to finance the tax cut. Suppose that a consumer initially faces taxes t^* and t'^* in the current period and future period, respectively. In Figure 6.17 he or she has an endowment point E_1, and chooses consumption bundle A. Now, suppose there is a tax cut in the current period, so that $\Delta t < 0$. Therefore, the government must borrow $m\,\Delta t$ more in period 1 to finance the larger current government deficit, and taxes must rise for each consumer by $-\Delta t(1 + r)$ in the future period to pay off the increased government debt. The effect of this on the consumer is that lifetime wealth we remains unchanged, as the present value of taxes has not changed. The budget constraint is unaffected, and the consumer will still choose point A in Figure 6.17. What will change is that the endowment point moves to E_2; that is, the consumer has more disposable income in the current period and less disposable income in the future period due to the tax cut in the current period. Since the consumer buys the same consumption bundle, what he or she does is to save *all* of the tax cut in the current period in order to pay the higher taxes that he or she will face in the future period.

Previously, when we looked at the effects of an increase in a consumer's current disposable income on current consumption, we determined that, because of the consumer's consumption-smoothing motive, some of the increase in disposable income would be saved. Thus, a temporary increase in disposable income would lead to a less than one-for-one increase in current consumption. In the real world, where individual consumption decisions are made over long horizons, any temporary increase in a consumer's disposable income should lead to a relatively small increase in his or her

FIGURE 6.17

Ricardian Equivalence with a Cut in Current Taxes for a Lender

A current tax cut with a future increase in taxes leaves the consumer's lifetime budget constraint unchanged, and so the consumer's optimal consumption bundle remains at A. The endowment point shifts from E_1 to E_2, so that there is an increase in saving by the amount of the current tax cut.

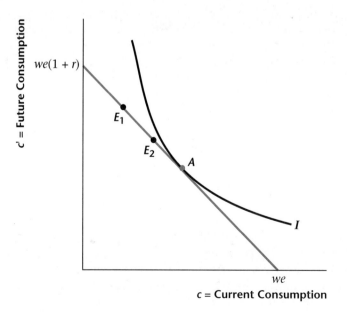

Was Ricardo a Ricardian?

The intellectual history of the Ricardian equivalence theorem contains some interesting lessons in how economic ideas originate, develop, and come to be accepted doctrine. Ricardian equivalence was introduced into modern thought by Robert Barro,[1] who argued that the timing of taxes may not matter, even in cases where we might think that future generations would bear the full burden of the government debt. If people care about their offspring, they would also effectively care about the tax liabilities of all their descendants, so that the relevant wealth variable for an individual would include all of these tax liabilities.

When a "new" idea comes along in economics, it often does not take long before some well-read economist will assert that the idea is not new, but can be found in the work of Keynes, Marx, Smith, Marshall, or some other key contributor to early economic thought. Such was the case with Barro's notion that the timing of taxes could be irrelevant. James Buchanan, in an article that took issue with Barro's analysis, chided Barro for ignoring the fact that David Ricardo had come up with the idea first.[2] Further, in his article Buchanan coined the term "Ricardian equivalence theorem," and Barro and others picked this up.[3]

David Ricardo is best known for his *Principles of Political Economy and Taxation*, published in 1817. While his theories of economic growth have not stood the test of time, his work on comparative advantage in international trade has had a lasting impact. Deep in a discussion of war finance in a piece called "Funding System,"[4] Ricardo pointed out the equivalence between two methods of financing government spending in wartime, with one method involving current taxation to finance government expenditure and the other involving debt issue. However, an article published by Gerald O'Driscoll in 1977 points out that Ricardo was actually doubtful that equivalence would hold in practice.[5] In Barro's theory, as in ours, consumers are forward-looking, and they rationally take account of the government's current actions for future taxation. However, Ricardo argued that consumers would not have the foresight to figure this out, and so would spend more if they received a current tax cut, even if this meant that their lifetime wealth was essentially unaffected. Thus, Ricardo may not have thought like a Ricardian at all!

Ultimately, it does not matter much whether the idea Barro exposited was originally Ricardo's, or what Ricardo might have thought of his own idea. Barro's statement of the Ricardian equivalence theorem is stated in the precise language of modern economics, in a persuasive manner that made it very clear what his point was. While Ricardo had many interesting and useful ideas, there is much in his writing that we would consider useless today, and reading his work carefully requires much patience. Indeed, it is unlikely that most readers would stumble on the significance of the Ricardian equivalence theorem in Ricardo's writings if they did not know beforehand that the idea was there.

---

[1]See R. Barro, 1974, "Are Government Bonds Net Wealth?" *Journal of Political Economy* 82, 1095–1117.

[2]See J. Buchanan, 1976, "Barro on the Ricardian Equivalence Theorem," *Journal of Political Economy* 84, 337–343.

[3]See for example R. Barro, 1989, "The Ricardian Approach to Government Deficits," *Journal of Economic Perspectives* 3, 37–54.

[4]See D. Ricardo, 1951, *Principles of Political Economy and Taxation, Works and Correspondence*, ed. Piero Straffa, Cambridge University Press, Cambridge.

[5]See G. O'Driscoll, 1977, "The Ricardian Nonequivalence Theorem," *Journal of Political Economy* 85, 207–210.

current income, in line with Friedman's permanent income hypothesis. Thus, the hypothesis would appear to imply that a temporary change in taxes will lead to a very small change in current consumption. The Ricardian equivalence theorem carries this logic one step further by taking into account the implications of a current change in taxes for future taxes. For example, because any current tax cut must be paid for with government borrowing, this borrowing implies higher future taxes to pay off the government debt. In making their lifetime wealth calculations, consumers recognize that the current tax cut is exactly offset by higher taxes in the future, and they save *all* of the current tax cut to pay the higher future taxes.

A key message from the Ricardian equivalence theorem is that *a tax cut is not a free lunch*. While a current tax cut can give all consumers higher current disposable incomes, and this seems like a good thing, consumers must pay for the current tax cut by bearing higher taxes in the future. Under the conditions studied in our model, the costs of a tax cut exactly offset the benefits, and consumers are no better off with the tax cut than without it.

RICARDIAN EQUIVALENCE AND THE BURDEN OF THE GOVERNMENT DEBT

At the individual level, debt represents a liability that reduces an individual's lifetime wealth. The Ricardian equivalence theorem implies that the same logic holds for the government debt, which the theorem tells us represents our future tax liabilities as a nation. The government debt is a burden in that it is something we owe to ourselves; the government must pay off its debt by taxing us in the future. In the model in which we explained the Ricardian equivalence theorem above, the burden of the debt is shared equally among consumers. In practice, however, many issues in fiscal policy revolve around how the burden of the government debt is shared, among the current population and between generations. To discuss these issues, we need to address the role played by four key assumptions in the above analysis of the Ricardian equivalence theorem.

1. The first key assumption is that when taxes change, in the experiment we considered above, they change by the same amount for all consumers, both in the present and in the future. For example, when a particular consumer received a tax cut in the current period, this was offset by an equal and opposite (in present-value terms) increase in taxes in the future. The present-value tax burden for each individual was unchanged. Now, if some consumers received higher tax cuts than others, lifetime wealth could change for some consumers, and this would necessarily change their consumption choices and could change the equilibrium real interest rate. In the future, when the higher debt is paid off through higher future taxes, consumers might share unequally in this taxation, so that the burden of the debt might not be distributed equally. The government can redistribute wealth in society through tax policy, and the public debate concerning changes in taxes often focuses on how these tax changes affect consumers at different income levels.

2. A second key assumption in the model is that any debt issued by the government is paid off during the lifetimes of the people alive when the debt was issued. In

practice, the government can postpone the taxes required to pay off the debt until long in the future, when the consumers who received the current benefits of a higher government debt are either retired or dead. That is, if the government cuts taxes, the current old receive higher disposable incomes, but it is the current young who will have to pay off the government debt in the future through higher taxes. In this sense, the government debt can be a burden on the young, and it can involve an intergenerational redistribution of wealth.

3. A third assumption made above was that taxes are lump-sum. In practice, as mentioned in Chapter 4, all taxes cause distortions, in that they change the effective relative prices of goods faced by consumers in the market. These distortions represent welfare losses from taxation. That is, if the government collects $1 million in taxes, the welfare cost to the economy will be something greater than $1 million, because of the distortions caused by taxation. The study of optimal taxation in public finance involves examining how large these welfare costs are for different kinds of taxes. For example, it could be that the welfare cost of income taxation at the margin is higher than the welfare cost of sales taxes at the margin. If the government taxes optimally, it minimizes the welfare cost of taxation, given the quantity of tax revenue it needs to generate. One of the tradeoffs made by the government in setting taxes optimally is that between current taxation and future taxation. The government debt represents a burden, in that the future taxes required to pay off the debt will cause distortions. Some work on optimal taxation by Robert Barro,[3] among others, shows that the government should act to smooth tax rates over time, so as to achieve the optimal tradeoff between current and future taxation.

4. A fourth key assumption made above is that there are **perfect credit markets**, in the sense that consumers can borrow and lend as much as they please, subject to their lifetime budget constraints, and they can borrow and lend at the same interest rate. In practice, consumers face constraints on how much they can borrow; for example, credit cards have borrowing limits, and sometimes consumers cannot borrow without collateral (as with mortgages and auto loans).[4] Consumers also typically borrow at higher interest rates than they can lend at. For example, the gap between the interest rate on a typical bank loan and the interest rate on a typical bank deposit can be 6 percentage points per annum or more. Further, the government borrows at lower interest rates than does the typical consumer. While all consumers need not be affected by **credit market imperfections**, to the extent that some consumers are credit-constrained, these credit-constrained consumers could be affected beneficially by a tax cut, even if there is an offsetting tax liability for these consumers in the future. In this sense, the government debt may not be a burden for some segments of the population; it may in fact increase welfare for these groups. We will explore this idea further in the next section.

---

[3]See R. Barro, 1979, "On the Determination of the Public Debt," *Journal of Political Economy* 87, 940–971.

[4]Collateral is the security a borrower puts up when the loan is made. If the borrower defaults on the loan, the collateral is seized by the lender. For a mortgage loan the collateral is the house purchased with it, and for an auto loan the collateral is the car purchased.

The Ricardian equivalence theorem captures a key reality: current changes in taxes have consequences for future taxes. However, there are many complications associated with real-world tax policy that essentially involve shifts in the distribution of taxation across the population, and in the distribution of the burden of the government debt. These complications are left out of our analysis of the Ricardian equivalence theorem. For some macroeconomic issues, the distributional effects of tax policy are irrelevant, but for other issues they matter a great deal. For example, if you were a macroeconomist working for a political party, how a particular tax policy affected the wealth of different consumers in different ways might be the key to your party's success. You would want to pay close attention to this detail. In Canada, an important element in the sharing of the burden of the debt is how this debt burden is distributed among provinces. See Macroeconomics in Action 6.2 for a discussion of this issue.

CREDIT MARKET IMPERFECTIONS AND CONSUMPTION

Here, we will show how a consumer who is credit-constrained can be affected by a change in taxes that would not have any effect on the consumer's choices if there were perfect credit markets. Consider a consumer who lends at a real interest rate r_1 and borrows at a real interest rate r_2, where $r_2 > r_1$. This difference in borrowing and lending rates of interest arises in practice, for example, when borrowing and lending is carried out through banks, and it is costly for banks to sort credit risks. If the bank borrows from lenders (depositors in the bank) at the real interest rate r_1, and it makes loans at the real interest rate r_2, the difference $r_2 - r_1 > 0$ could arise in equilibrium to compensate the bank for the costs of making loans. The difference between borrowing and lending rates of interest will lead to a more complicated lifetime budget constraint. As before, the current-period budget constraint of the consumer is given by Equation (6.1); but the future-period budget constraint is

$$c' = y' - t' + s(1 + r_1),$$

if $s \geq 0$ (the consumer is a lender), and

$$c' = y' - t' + s(1 + r_2),$$

if $s \leq 0$ (the consumer is a borrower). Going through the same mechanics as before to derive the consumer's lifetime budget constraint, we obtain

$$c + \frac{c'}{1 + r_1} = y + \frac{y'}{1 + r_1} - t - \frac{t'}{1 + r_1} = we_1, \tag{6.33}$$

if $c \leq y - t$ (the consumer is a lender), and

$$c + \frac{c'}{1 + r_2} = y + \frac{y'}{1 + r_2} - t - \frac{t'}{1 + r_2} = we_2, \tag{6.34}$$

if $c \geq y - t$ (the consumer is a borrower).

We graph the consumer's budget constraint in Figure 6.18, where AB is given by Equation (6.33) and has slope $-(1 + r_1)$, and DF is given by Equation (6.34) and has

The Interprovincial Sharing of the Tax Burden

In the two-period model studied in this chapter, each individual in the economy pays the same tax in the present and in the future. Of course, in practice the tax burden is different for different consumers depending on their incomes, the income tax deductions that they can claim, and the goods and services they consume, among other things. As well, the tax burden will differ across provinces. Provinces with higher average incomes and greater average consumption of goods and services will tend to pay higher taxes per capita to the federal government. If all provinces give consumers the same level of government services per capita, consumers in poorer provinces will be paying a larger fraction of their incomes in provincial taxes to support those services.

In Canada, there are three federally operated transfer programs whose aim is to equalize across provinces the tax burden of providing government services. The first is the Equalization Program, through which the federal government gives transfers to poorer provinces. The transfers are set at levels that will guarantee that residents of each province receive roughly the same level of government services with approximately the same level of per capita provincial taxes. The provinces are not restricted in how they may spend these transfer payments. During 2003–04, eight provinces will receive a total of about $10.5 billion in equalization transfers; the only provinces not receiving these transfers in 2003–04 are Alberta and Ontario (see **www.fin.gc.ca/fedprov/eqpe.html**).

The second program is the Canada Health and Social Transfer (CHST). This transfer from the federal government to the provinces is targeted specifically to health care, post-secondary education, social assistance, and social services. It takes the form of cash transfers and tax transfers, which are agreements by which the federal government reduces a particular tax while the provincial government increases the same tax by the amount of the federal tax reduction. In 2002–03, transfers under the CHST totalled $35.3 billion. Thus, these transfers are more than three times the size of equalization transfers. Further, under the February 2003 First Ministers' Accord, CHST transfers (now called CHT and CST for Canada Health Transfer and Canada Social Transfer, respectively) are scheduled to increase substantially (see **www.fin.gc.ca/fedprov/chse.html**).

The third program is Territorial Formula Financing (TTF). It entails annual unconditional transfers from the federal government to territorial governments, allowing them to provide approximately the same level of government services to territorial residents as residents of the provinces receive (see **www.fin.gc.ca/fedprov/tffe.html**).

Clearly, the above three programs were designed with equity in mind; they all tend to equalize government services and the tax burdens associated with providing those services across provinces. However, the cost of these programs is a loss in economic efficiency. Since the transfers support higher social assistance payments than would otherwise exist in destitute regions of the country, transfer programs tend to have adverse incentive effects. That is, they encourage those who are unemployed or employed in low-productivity jobs in poorer regions of the country to remain in those regions, rather than seeking employment in high-productivity jobs in more prosperous areas of the country. As a result, aggregate GDP will tend to be lower with these programs in place than it would be in their absence.

FIGURE 6.18

A Consumer Facing Different Lending and Borrowing Rates

When the borrowing rate of interest is higher than the lending rate, there is a kinked budget constraint, *AEF*, with the kink at the endowment point *E*.

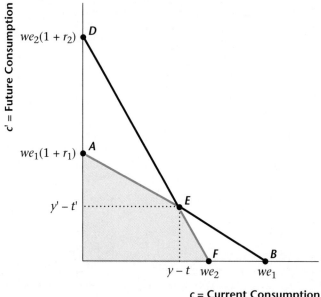

slope $-(1 + r_2)$. The budget constraint is *AEF*, where *E* is the endowment point. Thus, the budget constraint has a kink at the endowment point, because the consumer lends at a lower interest rate than he or she can borrow at.

In a world where there are many different consumers, all having different indifference curves and different incomes, and where each consumer has a kinked budget constraint as in Figure 6.18, there will be a significant number of consumers in the population whose optimal consumption bundle is the endowment point. For example, in Figure 6.19 the consumer faces budget constraint AE_1B, and the highest indifference curve on the budget constraint is reached at E_1, the endowment point. For this consumer, at the endowment point, the lending rate is too low to make lending worthwhile, and the borrowing rate is too high to make borrowing worthwhile.

Suppose in Figure 6.19 that the consumer receives a tax cut in the current period—that is, period 1 taxes change by $\Delta t < 0$—with a corresponding change of $-\Delta t(1 + r_1)$ in future taxes. This is the consumer's future tax liability implied by the tax cut, assuming that the interest rate that the government pays on its debt is r_1, the lending rate of interest. Assume that interest rates do not change. The effect of the change in current and future taxes is to shift the endowment point to E_2, and given the way we have drawn the consumer's indifference curves, the consumer now chooses E_2 as his or her optimal consumption bundle on indifference curve I_2. Since he or she chooses the endowment point before and after the tax cut, period 1 consumption increases by the amount of the tax cut, $-\Delta t$. Contrast this with the Ricardian equivalence result where the consumer would save the entire tax cut and consumption would be unaffected.

The reason that the consumer's consumption increases is that the government is effectively making a low interest loan available to him or her through the tax cut scheme.

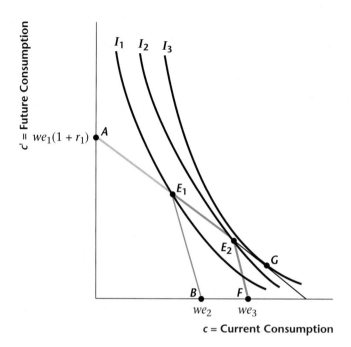

FIGURE 6.19

Effects of a Tax Cut for a Consumer with Different Borrowing and Lending Rates

The consumer receives a current tax cut, with a future increase in taxes, and this shifts the budget constraint from AE_1B to AE_2F. The consumer's optimal consumption bundle shifts from E_1 to E_2, and the consumer will consume the entire tax cut.

In Figure 6.19, the consumer would like to consume at point G if he or she could borrow at the interest rate r_1. Giving the consumer a tax cut of $-\Delta t$ with a corresponding future tax liability of $-\Delta t(1 + r_1)$ is just like having the government loan the consumer $-\Delta t$ at the interest rate r_1. Since the consumer would take such a loan willingly if it was offered, this tax cut makes the consumer better off.

Therefore, to the extent that credit market imperfections are important in practice, there can be beneficial effects of positive government debt. The government effectively acts like a bank that makes loans at below-market rates. If credit market imperfections matter significantly, then the people that are helped by current tax cuts are those who are affected most by credit market imperfections. This might suggest to us that tax policy could be used in this way to increase general economic welfare. However, tax policy is quite a blunt instrument for relieving perceived problems due to credit market imperfections. A preferable policy might be to target particular groups of people—for example, small businesses, farmers, or homeowners—with direct government credit programs. In fact, there are many such programs in place in Canada. In considering government credit policies, though, careful evaluation needs to be done to determine whether direct lending by the government is a good idea in each particular circumstance. There may be good reasons for a particular private market credit imperfection. For example, real loan interest rates may be high in a segment of the credit market because the costs of screening and evaluating loans are very high, and the government would face the same high costs. This would then imply that the government has no special advantage in offering credit to these borrowers, and it would be inefficient for the government to get into the business of lending to them.

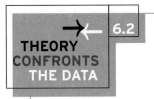

Ricardian Equivalence, Consumption, and Taxes

If the Ricardian equivalence theorem is a good description of reality, we might expect that fluctuations in taxes over time would have no effect on consumption. However, if credit market imperfections are important in practice, we would anticipate that taxes and consumption would be negatively correlated; increases (decreases) in taxes would tend to cause decreases (increases) in consumption.

Figure 6.20 is a time series plot of the percentage deviations from trend in the consumption of nondurables and services and in taxes for Canada over the period 1961–2002. Here, taxes are measured as total government income minus transfers, which corresponds closely to what taxes represent in the two-period model in this chapter. As is clearly discernible in Figure 6.20, taxes and consumption are in fact positively correlated, which appears to be consistent with neither the Ricardian equivalence theorem nor the existence of significant credit market imperfections. What is going on here?

To find a natural experiment in the data that would be useful as a test of the Ricardian equivalence theorem, we would need to find a historical example of an exogenous increase in taxes. Typically, most changes in taxes in the data are not exogenous. That is, there are usually factors simultaneously affecting both consumption and taxes, and the principal factor that does so is income. When aggregate income rises consumption tends to rise (fall), and taxes tend to rise (fall) as well. We already know from our study of consumption/savings behaviour in this chapter the reasons consumption rises with income. Why do taxes rise with income? First, as income increases, governments collect more revenue from the income tax, the goods and services tax, and provincial sales taxes, among other taxes. Second, transfers will tend to decrease as income rises, for example because employment insurance benefits fall. Transfers are simply a negative tax in the government budget.

As a result, the data in Figure 6.20 need not be interpreted as inconsistent with the Ricardian equivalence theorem. There is considerable debate in the literature about how good an approximation the theorem is to reality. In other countries there are historical events that appear to be consistent with Ricardian equivalence. For example, in 1992 there was a reduction in personal income tax withholding in the United States with no change in personal income tax liabilities. This was effectively a natural Ricardian experiment, and it seems to have led to no discernible change in aggregate consumption spending.[1]

[1]See S. Williamson, 2002, *Macroeconomics*, 1st ed., Addison-Wesley, Boston, MA, pp. 207–208.

Chapter Summary

In this chapter, we studied a two-period macroeconomic model, in order to understand the intertemporal consumption–savings decisions of consumers and the effects of fiscal policy choices concerning the timing of taxes and the quantity of government debt. In the model, there are many consumers, and each makes decisions over a two-period horizon where a consumer's incomes in the two periods are given, and the consumer pays lump-sum taxes in each period to

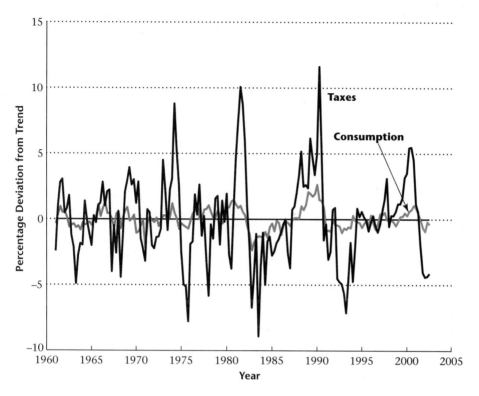

FIGURE 6.20

Taxes and Consumption of Nondurables and Services
The figure shows that detrended taxes and detrended consumption of nondurables and services are positively correlated, which appears to be inconsistent with Ricardian equivalence and with significant credit market imperfections.

Source: Adapted from the Statistics Canada CANSIM database, Series v498316, v498328, v1992047, v1992048, v498328.

the government. An important concept is the lifetime budget constraint of the consumer, which states that the present value of consumption over the consumer's two-period time horizon is equal to the present value of disposable income. The consumer's lifetime wealth is his or her present value of disposable income. A consumer's preferences have the property that more is preferred to less with regard to current and future consumption, there is a preference for diversity in current and future consumption, and current and future consumption are normal goods. A preference for diversity implies that consumers wish to smooth consumption relative to income over the present and the future. Consumption smoothing yields the result that, if income increases in the current period for a consumer, current consumption increases, future consumption increases, and current saving increases. If future income increases, consumption increases in both periods and current saving decreases. A permanent increase in income (when current *and* future income increase) has a larger impact on current consumption than a temporary increase in income (only current-income increases). If there is an increase in the real interest rate a consumer faces, there are income and substitution effects on consumption. Because an increase in the real interest rate causes a reduction in the price of future consumption in terms of current consumption, the substitution effect is for current consumption to fall, future consumption to rise, and current saving to rise when the real interest rate rises. For a lender (borrower), the income effect of an increase in the real interest rate is positive (negative) for both current and future consumption.

The Ricardian equivalence theorem states that changes in current taxes by the government that leave the present value of taxes constant have no effect on consumers' consumption choices or on the equilibrium real interest rate. This is because consumers change savings by an amount equal and opposite to the change in current taxes in order to compensate for the change in future taxes. Ricardian equivalence depends critically on the notion that the burden of the government debt is shared equally among the people alive when the debt is issued. The burden of the debt is not shared equally when: (i) there are current distributional effects of changes in taxes; (ii) there are intergenerational distribution effects; (iii) taxes cause distortions; or (iv) there are credit market imperfections.

Key Terms

intertemporal decisions: Decisions involving economic tradeoffs across periods of time.

consumption–savings decision: The decision by a consumer about how to split current income between current consumption and savings.

Ricardian equivalence theorem: This theorem, named for David Ricardo, states that changes in the stream of taxes faced by consumers that leave the present value of taxes unchanged have no effect on consumption, interest rates, or welfare.

two-period model: An economic model where all decision makers (consumers and firms) have two-period planning horizons, with the two periods typically representing the present and the future.

real interest rate: The rate of return on savings in units of consumption goods.

consumption smoothing: The tendency of consumers to seek a consumption path over time that is smoother than income.

lifetime budget constraint: Condition that the present value of a consumer's lifetime disposable income equals the present value of his or her lifetime consumption.

present value: The value, in terms of money today or current goods, of a future stream of money or goods.

lifetime wealth: The present value of lifetime disposable income for a consumer.

endowment point: The point on a consumer's budget constraint where consumption is equal to disposable income in each period.

excess variability: The observed fact that measured consumption is more variable than theory appears to predict.

permanent income hypothesis: A theory developed by Milton Friedman that implies a consumer's current consumption depends on his or her permanent income. Permanent income is closely related to lifetime wealth in our model.

martingale: An economic variable with the property that the best forecast of its value tomorrow is its value today. Finance theory implies that stock prices are martingales.

intertemporal substitution effect: Substitution by a consumer of a good in one time period for a good in another time period, in response to a change in the relative price of the two goods. The intertemporal substitution effect of an increase in the real interest rate is for current consumption to fall and future consumption to rise.

marginal propensity to consume (MPC): The increase in current consumption resulting from an increase of one unit in current income.

government present-value budget constraint: Condition that the present value of government purchases is equal to the present value of tax revenues.

perfect credit market: An idealized credit market in which consumers can borrow and lend all they want at the market interest rate, and the interest rate at which consumers lend is equal to the interest rate at which they borrow.

credit market imperfections: Constraints on borrowing, or differences between borrowing and lending rates of interest.

Questions for Review

All questions refer to the macroeconomic model developed in this chapter.

1. Why do consumers save?

2. How do consumers save in the two-period model?

3. What factors are important to a consumer in making his or her consumption–savings decision?

4. What is the price of future consumption in terms of current consumption?

5. Show how to derive the consumer's lifetime budget constraint from the consumer's current-period and future-period budget constraints.

6. What is the slope of a consumer's lifetime budget constraint?

7. What are the horizontal and vertical intercepts of a consumer's lifetime budget constraint?

8. If a consumer chooses the endowment point, how much does he or she consume in each period, and how much does he or she save?

9. What are the three properties of a consumer's preferences?

10. How is the consumer's motive to smooth consumption captured by the shape of an indifference curve?

11. What are the effects of an increase in current income on consumption in each period, and on savings?

12. Give two reasons that consumption is not as variable in the data as theory seems to predict.

13. What are the effects of an increase in future income on consumption in each period, and on savings?

14. What produces a larger increase in a consumer's current consumption, a permanent increase in the consumer's income, or a temporary increase?

15. What does theory tell us about how the value of stocks held by consumers should be related to consumption behaviour? Does the data support this?

16. What are the effects of an increase in the real interest rate on consumption in each period, and on savings? How does this depend on income and substitution effects and whether the consumer is a borrower or lender?

17. How does the government finance its purchases in the two-period model?

18. State the Ricardian equivalence theorem.

19. Give four reasons that the burden of the government debt is not shared equally in practice.

20. Does the existence of credit market imperfections imply that there is a useful role for government tax policy?

Problems

1. A consumer's income in the current period is $y = 100$, and income in the future period is $y' = 120$. He or she pays lump-sum taxes $t = 20$ in the current period and $t' = 10$ in the future period. The real interest rate is 0.1, or 10% per period.
   a. Determine the consumer's lifetime wealth.

    b. Suppose that current and future consumption are perfect complements for the consumer and that he or she always wants to have equal consumption in the current and future periods. Draw the consumer's indifference curves.

    c. Determine what the consumer's optimal first- and second-period consumption are, and what optimal saving is, and show this in a diagram with the consumer's budget constraint and indifference curves. Is the consumer a lender or a borrower?

    d. Now suppose that instead of $y = 100$, the consumer has $y = 140$. Again, determine optimal consumption in the first and second periods and optimal saving, and show this in a diagram. Is the consumer a lender or a borrower?

    e. Explain the differences in your results between parts (c) and (d).

2. Suppose that a consumer's future income increases, and the real interest rate increases as well. In a diagram, determine how the consumer's optimal choice of current consumption and future consumption changes, and how saving changes. Show how your results depend on income and substitution effects, and consider the case where the consumer is initially a lender, and where he or she is initially a borrower.

3. An employer offers his or her employee the option of shifting x units of income from next year to this year. That is, the option is to reduce income next year by x units and increase income this year by x units.

    a. Would the employee take this option (use a diagram)?

    b. Determine, using a diagram, how this shift in income will affect consumption this year and next year, and saving this year. Explain your results.

4. Consider the following effects of an increase in taxes for a consumer.

    a. The consumer's taxes increase by Δt in the current period. How does this affect current consumption, future consumption, and current saving?

    b. The consumer's taxes increase permanently, increasing by Δt in the current period and future period. Using a diagram, determine how this affects current consumption, future consumption, and current saving. Explain the differences between your results here and in part (a).

5. Suppose that the government introduces a tax on interest earnings. That is, borrowers face a real interest rate of r before and after the tax is introduced, but lenders receive an interest rate of $(1 - x)r$ on their savings, where x is the tax rate. Therefore, we are looking at the effects of having x increase from zero to some value greater than zero, with r assumed to remain constant.

    a. Show the effects of the increase in the tax rate on a consumer's lifetime budget constraint.

    b. How will the increase in the tax rate affect the optimal choice of consumption (in the current and future periods) and saving for the consumer? Show how income and substitution effects matter for your answer, and show how it matters whether the consumer is initially a borrower or a lender.

6. A consumer receives income y in the current period, income y' in the future period, and pays taxes of t and t' in the current and future periods respectively. The consumer can borrow and lend at the real interest rate r. This consumer faces a constraint on how much he or she can borrow, much like the credit limit typically placed on a credit card account. That is, the consumer cannot borrow more than x, where $x < we - y + t$, with we denoting lifetime wealth. Use diagrams to determine the effects on the consumer's current consumption, future consumption, and savings of a change in x, and explain your results.

7. A consumer receives income y in the current period, income y' in the future period, and pays taxes of t and t' in the current and future periods respectively. The consumer can lend at the

real interest rate r_1. The consumer is given two options. First, he or she can borrow at the interest rate r_1, but can only borrow an amount x or less, where $x < we - y + t$. Second, he or she can borrow an unlimited amount at the interest rate r_2, where $r_2 > r_1$. Use a diagram to determine which option the consumer will choose, and explain your results.

8. Assume a consumer who has current-period income $y = 200$, future-period income $y' = 150$, current and future taxes $t = 40$ and $t' = 50$, respectively, and faces a market real interest rate of $r = 0.05$, or 5% per period. The consumer would like to consume equal amounts in both periods; that is, he or she would like to set $c_1 = c_2$, if possible. However, this consumer is faced with a credit market imperfection, in that he or she cannot borrow at all—that is, $s \geq 0$.
   a. Show the consumer's lifetime budget constraint and indifference curves in a diagram.
   b. Calculate his or her optimal current-period and future-period consumption, and optimal saving, and show this in your diagram.
   c. Suppose that everything remains unchanged, except that now $t = 20$ and $t' = 71$. Calculate the effects on current and future consumption and optimal saving, and show this in your diagram.
   d. Now, suppose alternatively that $y = 100$. Repeat parts (a)–(c), and explain any differences.

9. Assume an economy with 1000 consumers. Each consumer has income in the current period of 50 units, and future income of 60 units, and pays a lump-sum tax of 10 in the current period and 20 in the future period. The market real interest rate is 8%. Of the 1000 consumers, 500 consume 60 units in the future, while 500 consume 20 units in the future.
   a. Determine each consumer's current consumption and current saving.
   b. Determine aggregate private saving, aggregate consumption in each period, government spending in the current and future periods, the current-period government deficit, and the quantity of debt issued by the government in the current period.
   c. Suppose that current taxes increase to 15 for each consumer. Repeat parts (a) and (b) and explain your results.

10. Suppose in our two-period model of the economy that the government, instead of borrowing in the current period, runs a government loan program. That is, loans are made to consumers at the market real interest rate r, with the aggregate quantity of loans made in period 1 denoted by L. Government loans are financed by lump-sum taxes on consumers in the current period, and we will assume that government spending is zero in the current and future periods. In the future period, when the government loans are repaid by consumers, the government rebates this amount as lump-sum transfers (negative taxes) to consumers.
   a. Write down the government's current-period budget constraint and its future-period budget constraint.
   b. Determine the present-value budget constraint of the government.
   c. Write down the lifetime budget constraint of a consumer.
   d. Show that the size of the government loan program (i.e., the quantity L) has no effect on current consumption or future consumption for each individual consumer, and that there is no effect on the equilibrium real interest rate. Explain this result.

Working with the Data

1. Calculate and plot the ratio of aggregate consumption to GDP, and plot this data as a time series. Comment on the features of your time series plot. What principle of consumption behaviour helps to explain what you see?

2. Calculate the value of real total government income by dividing current-dollar government income by the implicit GDP price deflator. Then, calculate the quarterly percentage change in total government receipts and the quarterly percentage change in real GDP, starting in 1961 until the end of 2002.

   a. In a scatter plot, plot the percentage change in real government income against the quarterly percentage change in real GDP.

   b. What do you see in the scatter plot in part (a)? Is there a positive or negative correlation between the two time series?

   c. Is this data consistent with the Ricardian equivalence theorem? Why or why not?

3. Calculate the relative price of housing as the new housing price index divided by the consumer price index. Then, calculate annual increases in the relative price of housing as the December-to-December percentage increase in this relative price, and plot this against the fourth-quarter-to-fourth-quarter increase in real spending on consumer nondurables and services.

   a. Do you notice a positive or negative correlation in the scatter plot?

   b. How is your observation in part (a) consistent or not with the theory of consumption behaviour in this chapter? Explain.

CHAPTER 7

A Real Intertemporal Model with Investment

This chapter brings together the microeconomic behaviour we have studied in the previous chapters to build a model that can serve as a basis for analyzing how macroeconomic shocks affect the economy. That model can be used for evaluating the role of macroeconomic policy. With regard to consumer behaviour, we have examined work–leisure choices in Chapter 4, and intertemporal consumption–savings choices in Chapter 6. Further, from the production side, in Chapter 4 we studied a firm's production technology and its labour demand decision, and then in Chapter 5 we showed how changes in total factor productivity affect consumption, employment, and output in the economy as a whole. In Chapter 6, we looked at the effects of choices by the government concerning the financing of government expenditure and the timing of taxes. In this chapter, we will add investment behaviour to the theory we are developing. This will allow us to complete a model of the *real* side of the economy. That is, the *real intertemporal model* we will construct in this chapter will show how real aggregate output, real consumption, real investment, employment, the real wage, and the real interest rate are determined in the macroeconomy. To predict *nominal* variables, we need to add money to the real intertemporal model, which will be done in Chapter 9. The *intertemporal* aspect of the model refers to the fact that both consumers and firms make intertemporal decisions, reflecting tradeoffs between the present and the future.

Recall from Chapter 2 that the defining characteristic of investment—expenditure on plants, equipment, and housing—is that it consists of the goods that are produced currently for future use in the production of goods and services. For the economy as a whole, investment represents a tradeoff between present and future consumption. Productive capacity that is used for producing investment goods could otherwise be used for producing current consumption goods, but today's investment increases future productive capacity, which means that more consumption goods can be produced in the future. To understand the determinants of investment, we must study the microeconomic investment behaviour of a firm, which makes an intertemporal decision regarding investment in the current period. When a firm invests, it forgoes current profits to have a higher capital stock in the future, which allows it to earn higher future profits. As we will show, a firm will invest more the lower its current capital stock, the higher its expected future total factor productivity, and the lower the real interest rate.

A key determinant of investment is the real interest rate, which represents the opportunity cost of investment. A higher real interest rate implies that the opportunity cost of investment is larger, at the margin, and so investment will fall. Movements in the real interest rate are an important channel by which shocks to the economy affect investment, as we will show in this chapter. Further, monetary policy may affect investment through its influence on the real interest rate, as will be shown in Chapters 9 to 11.

A good part of this chapter will involve model-building, and there are several important steps we will have to take before we can use this model to address some important economic issues. This will require some patience and work, but the payoff will arrive in the last part of this chapter, and continue through the remainder of this book, where this model will be the basis for our study of monetary factors in Chapter 9, business cycles in Chapters 10 and 11, and other issues in later chapters.

This chapter will focus on the macroeconomic effects on aggregate output, investment, consumption, the real interest rate, and labour market variables of aggregate shocks to government spending, total factor productivity, and the nation's capital stock. While we have studied elements of these effects in Chapters 5 and 6, there will be new insights in this chapter involving the effects on the interest rate and investment of these shocks, and the effects of permanent versus temporary shocks. For example, we will see that the effects of permanent changes in government spending can be quite different from those of temporary changes, and that shocks to the economy that are expected in the future can have important implications for how the economy performs in the present.

As in Chapters 4 and 5, we will work with a model that has a representative consumer, a representative firm, and a government, and for simplicity this model will ultimately be specified at the level of supply and demand curves. We will be able to capture the essential behaviour in this model economy by examining the participation of the representative consumer, the representative firm, and the government in two markets: the market for labour in the current period and the market for goods in the current period. The representative consumer will supply labour in the current labour market and will purchase consumption goods in the current goods market, while the representative firm will demand labour in the current labour market, supply goods in the current goods market, and demand investment goods in the current goods market. The government will demand goods in the current goods market in terms of government purchases.

The Representative Consumer

The behaviour of the representative consumer in this model will bring together the work–leisure choice from Chapter 4 with the intertemporal consumption behaviour from Chapter 6. That is, the consumer will make a work–leisure decision in each of the current and future periods, and he or she will make a consumption–savings decision in the current period.

The representative consumer works and consumes in the current period and the future period. He or she has h units of time in each period, and divides this time between work and leisure in each period. Let w denote the real wage in the current period, w' the real wage in the future period, and r the real interest rate. The consumer pays lump-sum taxes to the government of T in the current period and T' in the future period. His or her goal is to choose current consumption C, future consumption C', leisure time in the current and future periods, l and l', respectively, and savings in the current period, S^p, to make himself or herself as well off as possible, given his or her budget constraints in the current and future periods. The representative consumer is a price-taker who takes w, w', and r as given. Taxes are also given from the consumer's point of view.

In the current period, the representative consumer earns real wage income $w(h - l)$, receives dividend income π from the representative firm, and pays taxes T, so that his or her current-period disposable income is $w(h - l) + \pi - T$, just as in Chapter 4. As in Chapter 6, disposable income in the current period is then split between consumption and savings, and savings takes the form of bonds that earn the one-period real interest rate r. Just as in Chapter 6, savings can be negative, in which case the consumer borrows by issuing bonds. The consumer's current budget constraint is then

$$C + S^p = w(h - l) + \pi - T. \tag{7.1}$$

In the future period, the representative consumer receives real wage income $w'(h - l')$, receives real dividend income π' from the representative firm, pays taxes T' to the government, and receives the principal and interest on savings from the current period, $(1 + r)S^p$. Because the future period is the last period and since the consumer is assumed to make no bequests, all wealth available to the consumer in the future is consumed, so that the consumer's future budget constraint is

$$C' = w'(h - l') + \pi' - T' + (1 + r)S^p \tag{7.2}$$

Just as in Chapter 6, we can substitute for savings S^p in Equation (7.1) using Equation (7.2) to obtain a lifetime budget constraint for the representative consumer:

$$C + \frac{C'}{1 + r} = w(h - l) + \pi - T + \frac{w'(h - l') + \pi' - T'}{1 + r}. \tag{7.3}$$

This constraint states that the present value of lifetime consumption (on the left-hand side of the equation) equals the present value of lifetime disposable income (on the right-hand side of the equation). Note that a difference from the consumer's lifetime budget constraint in Chapter 6 is that the consumer in this model has some choice, through his or her current and future choices of leisure, l and l', over his or her lifetime wealth.

The representative consumer's problem is to choose C, C', l, and l' to make himself or herself as well off as possible while respecting his or her lifetime budget constraint, as given by Equation (7.3). We cannot depict this choice for the consumer conveniently in a graph, as the problem is four-dimensional (choosing current and future consumption and current and future leisure), while a graph is two-dimensional. It is straightforward, however, to describe the consumer's optimizing decision in terms of three marginal conditions we have looked at previously in Chapters 4 and 6. These are as follows:

1. The consumer makes a work–leisure decision in the current period, so that when he or she optimizes, we will have

$$MRS_{l,C} = w; \tag{7.4}$$

that is, the consumer optimizes by choosing current leisure and consumption so that the marginal rate of substitution of leisure for consumption is equal to the real wage in the current period. This is the same marginal condition as in the work–leisure problem for a consumer that we considered in Chapter 4. Recall that, in general, a consumer optimizes by setting the marginal rate of substitution of one good for another equal to the relative price of the two goods. In Equation (7.4), the current real wage w is the relative price of leisure in terms of consumption goods.

2. Similarly, in the future the consumer makes another work–leisure decision, and he or she optimizes by setting

$$MRS_{l',C'} = w'; \tag{7.5}$$

that is, at the optimum, the marginal rate of substitution of future leisure for future consumption must be equal to the future real wage.

3. With respect to his or her consumption–savings decision in the current period, as in Chapter 6, the consumer optimizes by setting

$$MRS_{C,C'} = 1 + r; \tag{7.6}$$

that is, the marginal rate of substitution of current consumption for future consumption equals the relative price of current consumption in terms of future consumption.

CURRENT LABOUR SUPPLY

Our ultimate focus will be on interaction between the representative consumer and the representative firm in the markets for current labour and current consumption goods. Therefore, we will be interested in the determinants of the representative consumer's supply of labour and his or her demand for current consumption goods.

First, we will consider the representative consumer's current supply of labour, which is determined by three factors—the current real wage, the real interest rate, and lifetime wealth. These three factors affect current labour supply as listed below.

1. *Current labour supply increases when the current real wage increases.* The consumer's marginal condition (7.4) captures the idea that substitution between current leisure and current consumption is governed by the current real wage rate w. Recall from Chapter 4 that a change in the real wage has opposing income and substitution effects on the quantity of leisure, so that an increase in the real wage could lead to an increase or a decrease in the quantity of leisure, depending on the size of the income effect. Here, we will assume that the substitution effect of a change in the real wage is always larger than the income effect, implying that leisure decreases and hours worked increases in response to an increase in the real wage. This might

seem inconsistent with the fact, pointed out in Chapter 4, that over the long run, income and substitution effects on labour supply appear to cancel. However, the model we are building here is intended mainly for analyzing short-run phenomena. As we argued in Chapter 4, the cancelling of income and substitution effects in the long run can be consistent with the substitution effect dominating in the short run, as we assume here.

2. *Current labour supply increases when the real interest rate increases.* The consumer can substitute intertemporally not only by substituting current consumption for future consumption, as we studied in Chapter 6, but by substituting current leisure for future leisure. In substituting leisure between the two periods, the representative consumer responds to the current price of leisure relative to the future price of leisure, which is $\frac{w(1 + r)}{w'}$. Here, w is the price of current leisure (labour) in terms of current consumption, w' is the price of future leisure in terms of future consumption, and $1 + r$ is the price of current consumption in terms of future consumption. Therefore, an increase in the real interest rate r, given w and w', results in an increase in the price of current leisure relative to future leisure. Assuming again that the substitution effect is larger than the income effect, the consumer will want to consume less current leisure and more future leisure. An example of how this **intertemporal substitution of leisure** effect works is as follows. Suppose that Paul is self-employed and that the market interest rate rises. Then Paul faces a higher return on his savings, so that if he works more in the current period and saves the proceeds, in the future he can both consume more and work less. It may be helpful to consider that leisure, like consumption, is a good. When the real interest rate increases, and if substitution effects dominate income effects for lenders, current consumption will fall (from Chapter 6), just as current leisure will decrease when the real interest rate increases and substitution effects dominate.

3. *Current labour supply decreases when lifetime wealth increases.* From Chapter 4, we know that an increase in current nonwage disposable income results in an increase in the quantity of leisure and a decrease in labour supply for the consumer, as leisure is a normal good. Further, in Chapter 6, we showed how income effects generalize to the intertemporal case in which the consumer chooses current and future consumption. That is, an increase in lifetime wealth will increase the quantities of current and future consumption chosen by the consumer. Here, when there is an increase in lifetime wealth, there will be an increase in current leisure, and thus a decrease in current labour supply, since current leisure is assumed to be normal. The key wealth effect for our analysis in this chapter is the effect of a change in the present value of taxes for the consumer. Any increase in the present value of taxes implies a decrease in lifetime wealth and an increase in current labour supply.

Given these three factors, we can construct an upward-sloping current labour supply curve as in Figure 7.1. Here, the current real wage w is measured along the vertical axis, and current labour supply N is on the horizontal axis. The current labour supply curve is labelled $N^s(r)$ to indicate that labour supply depends on the current real interest rate. If the real interest rate rises, say from r_1 to r_2, the labour supply curve will shift to the right, as in Figure 7.2, since labour supply will increase for any current real

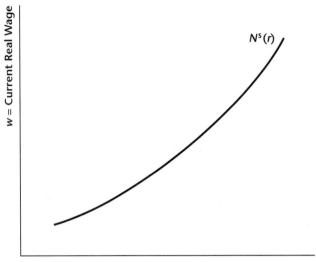

wage w. In Figure 7.3, an increase in lifetime wealth shifts the labour supply curve to the left from $N_1^s(r)$ to $N_2^s(r)$. Such an increase in lifetime wealth could be caused by a decrease in the present value of taxes for the consumer. Note in Figure 7.3 that the real interest rate is held constant as we shift the current labour supply curve to the left.

THE CURRENT DEMAND FOR CONSUMPTION GOODS

Now that we have dealt with the determinants of the representative consumer's current labour supply, we can turn to his or her demand for current consumption goods. The

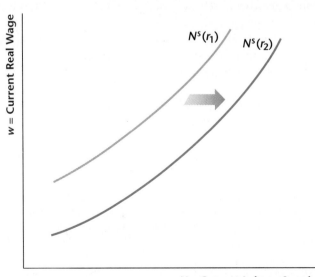

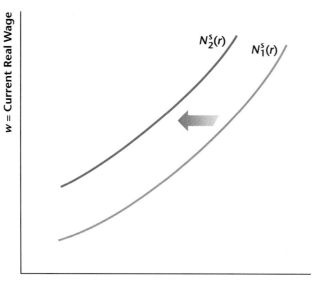

FIGURE 7.3

Effects of an Increase in Lifetime Wealth

More leisure is consumed in the present, due to an income effect, and the current labour supply curve shifts to the left.

w = Current Real Wage

$N_2^s(r)$ $N_1^s(r)$

N = Current Labour Supply

determinants of the demand for current consumption goods were studied in Chapter 6, where we showed that the primary factors affecting current consumption are lifetime wealth and the real interest rate. Further, lifetime wealth is affected by current income, and by the present value of taxes.

As in Chapter 6, we can construct a demand curve for current consumption by the representative consumer, as a function of current aggregate income Y, as shown in Figure 7.4. In the figure, the demand for consumption goods is on the vertical axis, and aggregate income is on the horizontal axis. We let $C^d(r)$ denote the demand curve

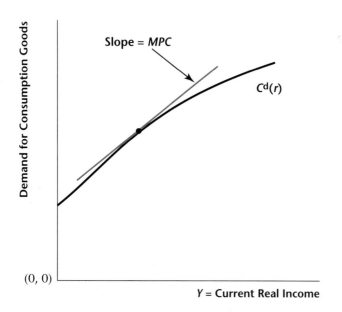

FIGURE 7.4

The Representative Consumer's Current Demand for Consumption Goods Increases with Income

The slope of the demand curve for current consumption is the marginal propensity to consume, *MPC*. We have *MPC* <1, since part of an increase in current income is saved.

Slope = *MPC*

$C^d(r)$

Demand for Consumption Goods

(0, 0)

Y = Current Real Income

FIGURE 7.5

**An Increase in the Real
Interest Rate from r_1 to r_2
Shifts the Demand for
Consumption Goods Down**

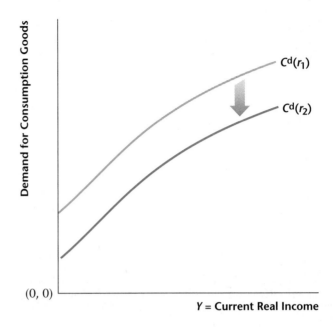

for current consumption goods, indicating the dependence of the demand for consumption on the real interest rate. Recall from Chapter 6 that the slope of the curve $C^d(r)$ in the figure is the *MPC* or marginal propensity to consume, which is the amount that current consumption increases when there is a unit increase in aggregate real income Y.

When there is an increase in the real interest rate, assuming again that the substitution effect of this increase dominates the income effect, there will be a decrease in the demand for current consumption goods due to the intertemporal substitution of consumption. In Figure 7.5, if the real interest rate increases from r_1 to r_2, the demand curve for current consumption shifts down from $C^d(r_1)$ to $C^d(r_2)$. Also, holding constant r and Y, if there is an increase in lifetime wealth, then, as in Figure 7.6, the demand curve for current consumption shifts up from $C_1^d(r)$ to $C_2^d(r)$. Such an increase in lifetime wealth could be caused by a decrease in the present value of taxes for the consumer, or by an increase in future income.

The Representative Firm

Now that we have covered the important features of the consumer's current labour supply and current consumption demand decisions, we can turn to the key decisions of the representative firm for the current labour market and the current goods market.

The representative firm, as in Chapter 4, produces goods using inputs of labour and capital. The key differences here are that output is produced in both the current period and future periods, and that the firm can invest in the current period by accu-

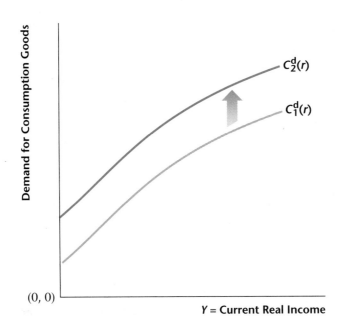

FIGURE 7.6

An Increase in Lifetime Wealth for the Consumer Shifts Up the Demand for Consumption Goods

mulating capital so as to expand future production capacity and produce more future output. In the current period, the representative firm produces output according to the production function

$$Y = zF(K, N), \tag{7.7}$$

where Y is current output, z is total factor productivity, F is the production function, K is current capital, and N is current labour input. Here, K is the capital with which the firm starts the current period, and this quantity is given. The production function F is identical in all respects to the production function we studied in Chapter 4.

Similarly, in the future period, output is produced according to

$$Y' = z'F(K', N'), \tag{7.8}$$

where Y' is future output, z' is future total factor productivity, K' is the future capital stock, and N' is the future labour input.

Recall from Chapter 2 that investment, as measured in the NIEA, is expenditure on plant, equipment, housing, and inventory accumulation. Here, we will model investment goods as being produced from output. That is, for simplicity we assume that it requires one unit of consumption goods in the current period to produce one unit of capital. The representative firm invests by acquiring capital in the current period, and the essence of investment is that something must be forgone in the current period in order to gain something in the future. What is forgone by the firm when it invests is current profits; that is, the firm uses some of the current output it produces to invest in capital, which becomes productive in the future. Capital also **depreciates** at the rate d when used, in that a fraction of the capital stock, d, wears out and becomes useless each period. Then, letting I denote the quantity of current investment, the future capital stock is given by

$$K' = (1 - d)K + I; \qquad (7.9)$$

that is, the future capital stock is the current capital stock net of depreciation, plus the quantity of current investment that has been added to the capital stock. Further, the quantity of capital left at the end of the future period is $(1 - d)K'$. Since the future period is the last period, it would not be useful for the representative firm to retain this quantity of capital, and so the firm will liquidate it. We will suppose that the firm can take the quantity $(1 - d)K'$, the capital left at the end of the future period, and convert it one-for-one back into consumption goods, which it can then sell. This is a simple way to model a firm's ability to sell off capital for what it can fetch on the secondhand market. For example, a restaurant that goes out of business can sell its used tables, chairs, and kitchen equipment in a liquidation sale.

PROFITS AND CURRENT LABOUR DEMAND

Now that we know how the firm produces output in the present and the future, and how investment can take place, we are ready to determine present and future profits for the firm. The goal of the firm will be to maximize the present value of profits over the current and future periods, and this will allow us to determine the firm's demand for current labour. For the representative firm, current profits in units of the current consumption good are

$$profits \qquad \pi = Y - wN - I, \qquad (7.10)$$

which is current output (or revenue) Y minus wages paid to workers in the current period, minus current investment. Note again that the firm can produce one unit of capital using one unit of output, so that each unit of investment decreases current profits by one unit. Future profits for the firm are

$$future \qquad \pi' = Y' - w'N' + (1 - d)K', \qquad (7.11)$$

which is future output minus wages paid to workers in the future, plus the value of the capital stock net of depreciation at the end of the future period.

   Profits earned by the firm in the current and future periods are paid out to the shareholders of the firm as dividend income in each period. There is one shareholder in this economy, the representative consumer, and the firm acts in the interests of this shareholder. That implies that the firm will maximize the present value of the consumer's dividend income, which serves to maximize the lifetime wealth of the consumer. Letting V denote the present value of profits for the firm, the firm will then maximize

$$V = \pi + \frac{\pi'}{1 + r} \qquad (7.12)$$

by choosing current labour demand N, future labour demand N', and current investment I.

   The firm's choice of current labour demand N affects only current profits π in Equation (7.10). As in Chapter 4, the firm will hire current labour until the current

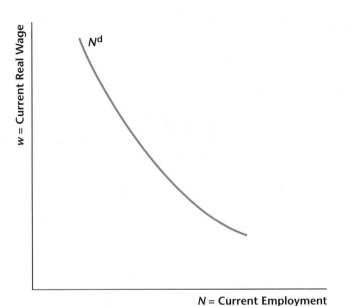

FIGURE 7.7

The Demand Curve for Current Labour Is the Representative Firm's Marginal Product of Labour Schedule

The curve slopes downward because the marginal product of labour declines as the labour input increases.

marginal product of labour equals the current real wage, that is, $MP_N = w$. Also as in Chapter 4, the demand curve for labour in the current period is identical to the marginal product of labour schedule, as the MP_N schedule tells us how much labour the firm needs to hire so that $MP_N = w$. In Figure 7.7 we show the representative firm's demand curve for labour, N^d, with the current real wage w on the vertical axis and the current quantity of labour N on the horizontal axis. Recall from Chapter 4 that the labour demand curve is downward-sloping because the marginal product of labour declines with the quantity of labour employed.

As in Chapter 4, the labour demand curve shifts with changes in total factor productivity z, or with changes in the initial capital stock K. A higher current level of total factor productivity z or a higher level of K will shift the labour demand curve to the right, for example, from N_1^d to N_2^d in Figure 7.8.

The firm chooses labour demand in the future period in a similar way to its choice of current-period labour demand. However, we will ignore this future choice in our analysis, as this will simplify our model in a way that makes the model's predictions clearer, while doing no harm.

THE REPRESENTATIVE FIRM'S INVESTMENT DECISION

Having dealt with the representative firm's labour demand decision, and given the firm's goal of maximizing the present value of its profits, we can proceed to a central aspect of this chapter, which is analyzing the investment choice of the firm.

The choice of investment by the representative firm will involve equating the marginal cost of investment with the marginal benefit of investment. We will let $MC(I)$ denote the **marginal cost of investment** for the firm, where

$$MC(I) = 1. \qquad (7.13)$$

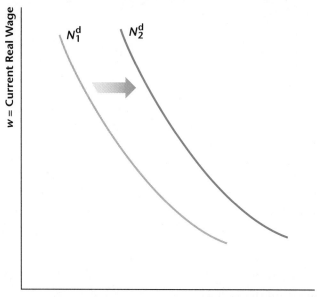

That is, the marginal cost of investment for the firm is what it gives up, in terms of the present value of profits, V, by investing in one unit of capital in the current period. This marginal cost is 1, as from Equations (7.12) and (7.10), an additional unit of current investment I reduces current profits π by one unit, which reduces the present value of profits V by one unit.

The **marginal benefit from investment**, denoted by $MB(I)$, is what one extra unit of investment in the current period adds to the present value of profits, V. In Equation (7.11), all the benefits from investment come in terms of future profits π', and there are two components to the marginal benefit. First, an additional unit of current investment adds one unit to the future capital stock K'. This implies that the firm will produce more output in the future, and the additional output produced is equal to the firm's future marginal product of capital, MP_K'. Second, each unit of current investment implies that there will be an additional $1 - d$ units of capital remaining at the end of the future period (after depreciation in the future period), which can be liquidated. Thus, one unit of additional investment in the current period implies an additional $MP_K' + 1 - d$ units of future profits π'. In calculating the marginal benefit of investment, we have to discount these future profits, and so we then have

$$MB(I) = \frac{MP_K' + 1 - d}{1 + r}. \tag{7.14}$$

The firm will invest until the marginal benefit from investment is equal to the marginal cost—that is, $MB(I) = MC(I)$—or from Equations (7.13) and (7.14),

$$\frac{MP_K' + 1 - d}{1 + r} = 1. \tag{7.15}$$

We can rewrite (7.15) as

$$MP'_K = r + d,$$

or

$$MP'_K - d = r. \tag{7.16}$$

Equation (7.16) states that the firm invests until the **net marginal product of capital**, $MP'_K - d$, is equal to the real interest rate. The net marginal product of capital, $MP'_K - d$, is the marginal product of capital after taking account of the depreciation of the capital stock. The intuition behind the **optimal investment rule**, (7.16), is that the opportunity cost of investing in more capital is the real rate of interest, which is the rate of return on the alternative asset in this economy. That is, in the model there are two assets: bonds traded on the credit market and capital held by the representative firm.

Effectively, the representative consumer holds the capital of the firm indirectly, since the consumer owns the firm and receives its profits as dividend income. From the consumer's point of view, the rate of return he or she receives between the current and future periods when the firm engages in investment is the net marginal product of capital. As the firm acts in the interests of the consumer, it would not be optimal for the firm to invest beyond the point where the net marginal product is equal to the real interest rate, as in Equation (7.16). This would imply that the consumer was receiving a lower rate of return on his or her savings than could be obtained by lending in the credit market at the real interest rate r. Thus, the real interest rate represents the opportunity cost of investing for the representative firm.

In Figure 7.9 we graph the firm's **optimal investment schedule**, with the real interest rate on the vertical axis and the demand for investment goods, I^d, on the horizontal axis. Given (7.16), the optimal investment schedule is the firm's net marginal product of capital. In the figure, if the real interest rate is r_1, the firm wishes to invest I_1, and if the real interest rate falls to r_2, investment will increase to I_2. Note the similarity here to the firm's current labour demand decision, as represented, for example, in Figure 7.7. When making its current labour demand decision, the relevant price to consider is the current real wage, and the firm hires labour until the marginal product of labour is equal to the real wage. In making its investment decision, the relevant price is the real interest rate, and the firm acquires capital (invests) until the net marginal product of capital is equal to the real interest rate.

Optimal investment I^d is determined in part by the market real interest rate r, as reflected in the negative slope of the optimal investment schedule in Figure 7.9. Also, the optimal investment schedule will shift due to any factor that changes the future marginal product of capital. Primarily, we will be interested in the following two types of shifts in the optimal investment schedule:

1. *The optimal investment schedule shifts to the right if future total factor productivity z' increases.* From Chapter 4, recall that an increase in total factor productivity will increase the marginal product of capital, for each level of the capital stock. Therefore, if total factor productivity is expected to be higher in the future, so that z' increases, this increases the future marginal product of capital, and the firm will

FIGURE 7.9

Optimal Investment Schedule for the Representative Firm

The optimal investment rule states that the firm invests until $MP'_K - d = r$. The future net marginal product schedule $MP'_K - d$ is the representative firm's optimal investment schedule, since this describes how much investment is required for the net marginal product of future capital to equal the real interest rate.

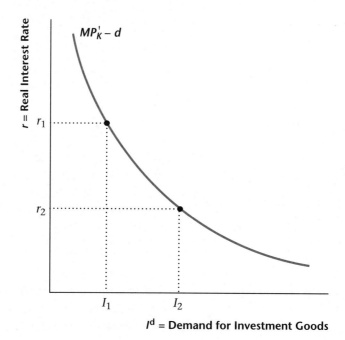

be more willing to invest during the current period. Higher investment in the current period leads to higher future productive capacity, so that the firm can take advantage of high future total factor productivity.

2. *The optimal investment schedule shifts to the left if the current capital stock K is higher.* A higher capital stock at the beginning of the current period implies, from Equation (7.9), that for a given level of current investment I, the future capital stock K' will be larger. That is, if K is larger, there is more of this initial capital left after depreciation in the current period to use in future production. Therefore, higher K implies that the future marginal product of capital, MP'_K, will decrease for each level of investment, and the optimal investment schedule will then shift to the left.

In Figure 7.10 we show a shift to the right in the optimal investment schedule, which could be caused either by an increase in future total factor productivity z', or by a lower current quantity of capital K. Note that the optimal investment schedule will also shift if the depreciation rate d changes, but it will be left to the reader to determine the resulting shift in the curve as a problem at the end of this chapter.

This theory of investment might explain why aggregate investment expenditures tend to be more variable over the business cycle than aggregate output or aggregate consumption. A key implication of consumer behaviour is smoothing; consumers wish to smooth consumption over time relative to their income, and this explains why consumption tends to be less variable than income. However, investment behaviour is not about smoothing, but about the response of the firm's investment behaviour to perceived marginal rates of return to investment. Provided the real interest rate and future total factor productivity vary sufficiently over the business cycle, our theory of the busi-

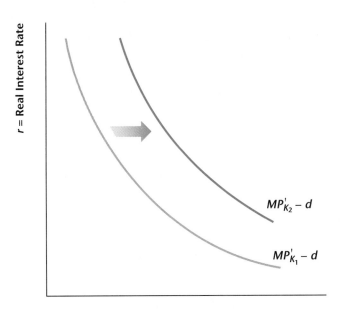

FIGURE 7.10

The Optimal Investment Schedule Shifts to the Right if Current Capital Decreases or Future Total Factor Productivity Is Expected to Increase

Either of these changes causes the future marginal product of capital to increase. The figure shows the effect of a decrease in current capital from K_1 to K_2.

I^d = **Demand for Investment Goods**

ness cycle can explain the variability in observed investment expenditures. That is, investment will be variable if the real interest rate is variable, causing movements along the optimal investment schedule in Figure 7.9, or if there is variability in future total factor productivity, causing the optimal investment schedule to shift over time.

Optimal Investment: A Numerical Example To make the firm's optimal investment decision more concrete, consider the following numerical example. Paula, a small-scale farmer, has an apple orchard, which has 10 trees in the current period—that is, $K = 10$. For simplicity, suppose that the quantity of labour required to operate the orchard does not depend on the number of trees Paula has, at least for the number of trees that Paula can plant on her land. In the current period, the 10 trees produce 100 kilograms of apples—that is, $Y = 100$. Paula can invest in more trees by taking some of the apples, extracting the seeds (which we assume makes the apples useless), and planting them. Very few of the seeds grow, and it takes 1 kilogram of apples to yield 1 tree that will be productive in the future period. The first extra tree that Paula grows will be on her best land, and therefore it will have a high marginal product, bearing a relatively large amount of fruit. The second tree will be planted on slightly worse land, and so will have a smaller marginal product, and so on. Every period, some trees die. In fact, at the end of each period, Paula loses 20% of her trees, and so the depreciation rate is $d = 0.2$. At the end of the future period, Paula can liquidate her trees. Since each kilogram of apples can produce a tree, it is possible to exchange 1 tree for 1 kilogram of apples on the open market, so that the liquidation value of a tree remaining in the future period, after depreciation, is 1 kilogram of apples. The real interest rate is 5%, or $r = 0.05$ in units of apples. Table 7.1 shows the quantity of future output that will

TABLE 7.1 **Data for Paula's Orchard**

$K' = $ Trees in Future	I	Y'	V	$MP_K - d$
8	0	95	196.57	—
9	1	98	199.19	2.8
10	2	100	200.86	1.8
11	3	101	201.57	0.8
12	4	101.5	201.81	0.3
13	5	101.65	201.71	−0.05
14	6	101.75	201.57	−0.1
15	7	101.77	201.35	−0.18

be produced when the number of trees Paula has in the future is 8, 9, 10, …, 15, as well as the associated level of investment, the present discounted value of profits (in units of apples), and the net marginal product of capital (trees) in the future.

From Table 7.1, note that the present value of profits is maximized when the number of trees in the future is 12, and the quantity of investment is 4 kilograms of apples. Also note that for each unit of investment from 1 to 4, the net marginal product of capital in the future is greater than the real interest rate, which is 0.05, but that the net marginal product of capital is less than 0.05 for each unit of investment above 4. Therefore, it is optimal to invest as long as the net marginal product of future capital is greater than the real interest rate.

Government

We have now shown how the representative consumer and the representative firm behave in the markets for current goods and current labour. It remains only to consider government behaviour, before we show how all these economic agents interact in a competitive equilibrium. Government behaviour is identical to what it was in Chapter 6. The government sets government purchases of consumption goods exogenously in each period. The quantity of government purchases in the current period is G, and in future government purchases are G'. The government finances government purchases in the current period through taxation and issuing government bonds in the current period. Then in the future, the government pays off the interest and principal on its bonds and finances future government spending through future lump-sum taxation. As in Chapter 6, the government must satisfy its present-value budget constraint,

$$G + \frac{G'}{1 + r} = T + \frac{T'}{1 + r}. \tag{7.17}$$

Competitive Equilibrium

Our analysis thus far has focused on the behaviour of the representative consumer, the representative firm, and the government in two markets, the current-period labour market and the current-period market for goods. In this real intertemporal model, the representative consumer supplies labour in the current-period labour market, and demands consumption goods in the current-period goods market. The representative firm demands labour in the current period, supplies goods in the current period, and demands investment goods in the current period. Finally, the government demands goods in the current period, in terms of government purchases.

Perceptive readers might wonder why we have neglected the future markets for labour and goods and the market for credit. Markets in the future are disregarded to make our model simple to work with, and this simplification will be essentially harmless at this level of analysis. As for the credit market, later in this chapter we will show that we have not actually neglected it, as equilibrium in the current-period goods market will imply that the credit market clears.

This section will show how a competitive equilibrium for our model, where supply equals demand in the current-period labour and goods markets, can be expressed in terms of diagrams. We will put together the labour supply and labour demand curves to capture how the labour market functions; then, we will derive an output supply curve that describes how the supply of goods is related to the real interest rate. Finally, we will derive an output demand curve, which describes how the sum of the demand for goods from the representative consumer (consumption goods), the representative firm (investment goods), and the government (government purchases) is related to the real interest rate. Putting the output demand and supply curves together in a diagram with the labour market will give us a working model, which will be used to address some key issues in macroeconomics in the following sections and in later chapters.

THE CURRENT LABOUR MARKET AND THE OUTPUT SUPPLY CURVE

First, we will consider how the market for labour in the current period works. In Figure 7.11(a), we show the labour demand curve for the representative firm, and the labour supply curve for the representative consumer, as derived in the previous sections, with the current real wage w on the vertical axis and the current quantity of labour, N, on the horizontal axis. Recall from earlier sections in this chapter that the labour supply curve slopes upward, as we are assuming that the substitution effect of an increase in the real wage dominates the income effect, and recall that the position of the labour supply curve depends on the real interest rate r. Also, we determined that an increase (decrease) in the real interest rate will cause an increase (decrease) in labour supply for each real wage w, and the labour supply curve will shift to the right (left). Given the real interest rate r, the equilibrium real wage in Figure 7.11(a) is w^* and the equilibrium quantity of employment is N^*, and from the production function in Figure 7.11(b), we determine the quantity of aggregate output supplied (given the real interest rate), which is Y^*. Recall from Chapter 4 that the position of the production function is determined by current total factor productivity z and by the current capital stock K. An increase in z or K would shift the production function up.

Our next step will be to use the diagrams in Figure 7.11 to derive an output supply curve, which describes how much output will be supplied by firms for each possible level for the real interest rate. In Figure 7.12(a), the labour supply curves for two different interest rates, r_1 and r_2, are shown, where $r_1 < r_2$. Thus, with the increase in the real interest rate, the current labour supply curve shifts to the right, the current

FIGURE 7.11

Determination of Equilibrium in the Labour Market Given the Real Interest Rate *r*

In (a), the intersection of the current labour supply and demand curves determines the current real wage and current employment, and the production function in (b) then determines aggregate output.

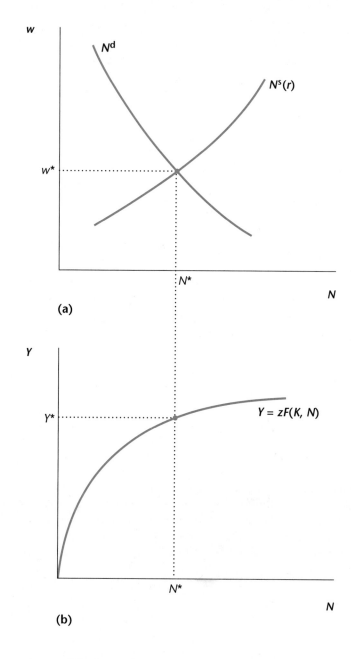

(a)

(b)

equilibrium real wage falls from w_1 to w_2, and current employment increases from N_1 to N_2. Further, current output increases from Y_1 to Y_2, in Figure 7.12(b), from the production function. We can then construct a curve, called the **output supply curve**, which is an upward-sloping curve consisting of all combinations of current output and real interest rates, (Y, r), for which the current labour market is in equilibrium. This curve is denoted Y^s in Figure 7.12(c). Note that two points on the Y^s curve are (Y_1, r_1) and (Y_2, r_2), since at real interest rate r_1 the labour market is in equilibrium when the

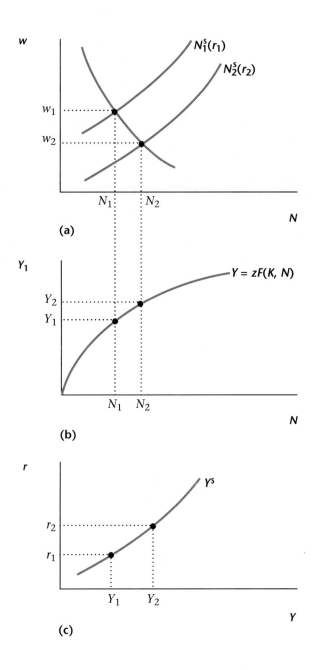

FIGURE 7.12
Construction of the
Output Supply Curve
The output supply curve Y^s is
an upward-sloping curve in
panel (c) of the figure,
consisting of real current
output and real interest rate
pairs for which the labour
market is in equilibrium.

representative firm produces current output Y_1, and at real interest rate r_2 the labour market is in equilibrium when the representative firm produces current output Y_2.

Shifts in the Output Supply Curve When we work with our real intertemporal model, it will be critical to know how changes in particular exogenous variables shift supply and demand curves. In this subsection, we will show how three factors—lifetime wealth, current total factor productivity, and the current capital stock—can shift the output supply curve. It turns out that the latter two factors have much the same effect, and so we will deal with these together.

The output supply curve will shift because of a shift in the current labour supply curve (not arising because of a change in the real interest rate; the output supply curve already takes this into account), because of a shift in the current labour demand curve, or because of a shift in the production function. From our analysis of consumer behaviour, we know that a change in lifetime wealth will shift the labour supply curve, whereas a change in either current total factor productivity or the current capital stock will shift the labour demand curve and the production function. We will deal with each of these shifts in turn.

Recall, from our earlier discussion in this chapter of the representative consumer's behaviour, that a decrease in lifetime wealth will reduce the consumer's demand for current leisure, due to an income effect. Therefore the consumer will supply more labour for any current real wage, and the labour supply curve will shift to the right. What would cause a reduction in lifetime wealth for the representative consumer? The key such factor of interest will be an increase in government spending, either in the present or in the future. From the present-value government budget constraint (7.17), any increase in government spending, either in the present or the future (that is an increase in G or G') must be reflected in an increase in the present value of taxes for the consumer, $T + \frac{T'}{1+r}$. Therefore an increase in G, in G', or in both, will result in an increase in the lifetime tax burden for the representative consumer. In Figure 7.13(a), this causes a shift to the right in the labour supply curve from $N_1^s(r_1)$ to $N_2^s(r_1)$, as there is a negative income effect on current leisure.

The shift to the right in the labour supply curve in Figure 7.13(a) implies that, for a given real interest rate, the equilibrium quantity of employment in the labour market is higher; that is, employment rises from N_1 to N_2 in Figure 7.13(a), given a particular real interest rate r_1. From the production function in Figure 7.13(b), output will rise from Y_1 to Y_2 given the real interest rate r_1. This will then imply that the output supply function shifts to the right, from Y_1^s to Y_2^s in 7.13(c). That is, output will be higher for each possible value for the real interest rate. The conclusion is that *an increase in G or G' shifts the labour supply curve to the right and shifts the output supply curve to the right, because of the income effect on labour supply.*

From Chapter 4, recall that an increase in total factor productivity or in the capital stock will shift the production function up, since more output can be produced for any level of the labour input, and the labour demand curve shifts to the right, since the marginal product of labour increases. In our model, an increase in current total factor productivity z, or in the current capital stock K, causes the production function to shift up. In Figure 7.14(b) we show the results of an increase in z from z_1 to z_2, but the effect of an increase in K would be identical. The labour demand curve shifts to the right in Figure 7.14(a), from N_1^d to N_2^d. As a result, given the real interest rate r_1, the equilibrium quantity of employment rises from N_1 to N_2. Therefore, from the production function in Figure 7.14(b), as employment is higher and z is higher, output increases from Y_1 to Y_2. The same effects (an increase in employment and output) would happen for any level of the real interest rate, which implies that the output supply curve in Figure 7.14(c)

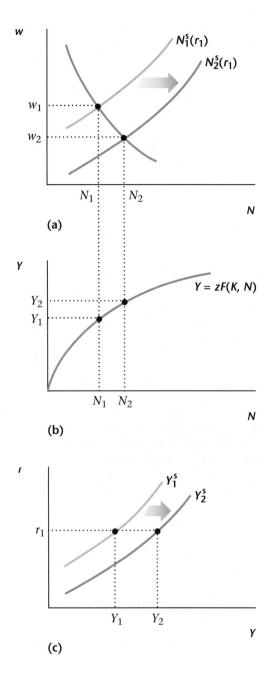

FIGURE 7.13

An Increase in Current or Future Government Spending Shifts the Y^s Curve
The increase in government spending increases the present value of taxes for the representative consumer, and current leisure falls, shifting the labour supply curve to the right in (a) and shifting the output supply curve to the right in (c).

must shift to the right. The results would be identical if there had been an increase in the current capital stock. The conclusion is that *an increase in z or K will cause the production function to shift up, the labour demand curve to shift to the right, and the output supply curve to shift to the right.*

FIGURE 7.14

An Increase in Current Total Factor Productivity Shifts the Y^s Curve

An increase in z increases the marginal product of current labour, shifting the labour demand curve to the right in (a). As well, the production function shifts up, so the ^{s} output supply curve shifts to the right in (c).

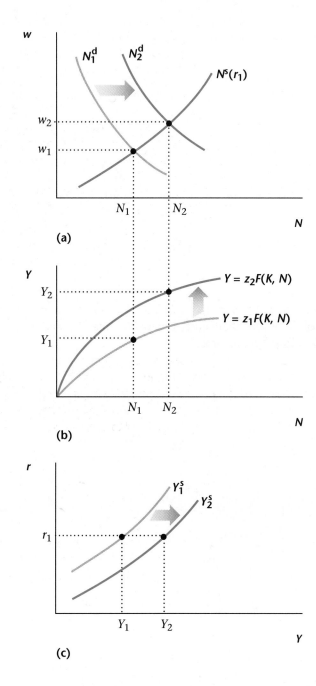

THE CURRENT GOODS MARKET AND THE OUTPUT DEMAND CURVE

Now that we understand how the current labour market works, and how the output supply curve is constructed, we can turn to the functioning of the current-period goods market and the construction of the output demand curve. This will then complete our model.

Total current aggregate income Y is the sum of the demand for current consumption goods by the representative consumer, $C^d(r)$, the demand for investment goods by the representative firm, $I^d(r)$, and government purchases of current goods, G:

$$Y = C^d(r) + I^d(r) + G. \tag{7.18}$$

Here, we use the notation $C^d(r)$ and $I^d(r)$ to reflect that the demand for current consumption goods and the demand for investment goods depend on the real interest rate r; this dependence is negative. Recall from our treatment of consumer behaviour earlier in this chapter that the demand for current consumption goods also depends on the lifetime wealth of the representative consumer, one component of which is current income. In Figure 7.15 we show the total demand for goods, the right-hand side of (7.18), as a function of current aggregate income Y. Since the demands for investment goods and government purchases do not depend on aggregate income, the slope of the curve $C^d(r) + I^d(r) + G$ in the figure is the marginal propensity to consume, MPC. What will be the equilibrium demand for current goods in the market, given the real interest rate r? This will be determined by the point at which the curve $C^d(r) + I^d(r) + G$ intersects the 45° line. Therefore, in Figure 7.15 the demand for current goods is Y_1, which is the quantity of aggregate income that generates a total demand for goods just equal to that quantity of aggregate income.

The next step is to construct the **output demand curve**, which is a negative relationship between current aggregate output and the real interest rate. In Figure 7.16(a), if the real interest rate is r_1, the current demand for goods is $C^d(r_1) + I^d(r_1) + G$. If the real interest rate were r_2 with $r_2 > r_1$, the current demand for goods will fall for each level of aggregate current income Y, as the demand for current consumption goods and

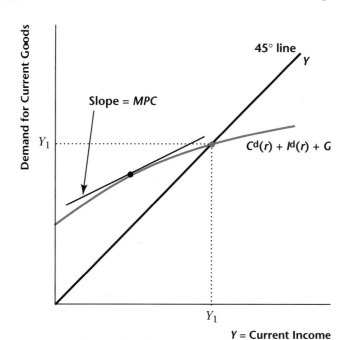

Y = Current Income

FIGURE 7.15

The Demand for Current Goods

This is an upward-sloping curve, as the demand for consumption goods increases with current income. The slope of the demand curve for current goods is the marginal propensity to consume (MPC).

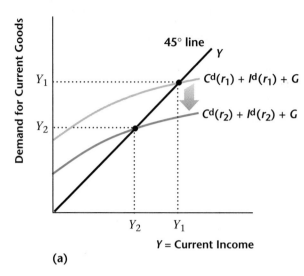

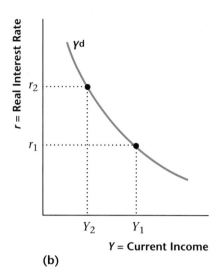

(a)   **(b)**

FIGURE 7.16

Construction of the Output Demand Curve

The output demand curve Y^d in (b) is a downward-sloping one describing the combinations of real output and the real interest rate for which the current goods market is in equilibrium.

for current investment goods will be lower. Thus, the demand for goods will shift down to $C^d(r_2) + I^d(r_2) + G$. As a result, the equilibrium quantity of goods demanded will fall from Y_1 to Y_2. Now, in Figure 7.16(b), we can construct a downward-sloping curve in a diagram with the real interest rate r on the vertical axis, and current aggregate income Y on the horizontal axis. This curve, Y^d, is the output demand curve, and a point on the curve, (Y, r), represents the level of demand for goods (output), Y, given the real interest rate r. Note that two points on the output demand curve are (Y_1, r_1) and (Y_2, r_2), corresponding to Figure 7.16(a).

Shifts in the Output Demand Curve Before we put all the elements of our real intertemporal model together—the output demand curve, the output supply curve, the production function, and the current labour supply and demand curves—we need to understand the important factors that will shift the output demand curve. The output demand curve will shift as the result of a shift in the demand for current consumption goods, $C^d(r)$, a shift in the demand for investment goods, $I^d(r)$, or a change in the current quantity of government purchases G. In Figure 7.17 we show the effects of an increase in G. In Figure 7.17(a), the demand for current goods shifts up when current government purchases increase from G_1 to G_2.[1] Then, given the real interest rate r_1, the quantity of current goods demanded will increase from Y_1 to Y_2. As a result, in Figure 7.17(b), the output demand curve shifts to the right from Y_1^d to Y_2^d; that is, the quantity of current goods demanded is higher for any real interest rate, including r_1. Other important factors that will shift the Y^d curve to the right, in a manner identical to the results for an increase in G in Figure 7.17, are the following:

- *A decrease in the present value of taxes shifts the Y^d curve to the right.* A decrease in the present value of taxes is caused by a reduction in current taxes, future taxes, or both. When this happens, the lifetime wealth of the representative consumer rises,

---

[1]The shift up in the demand for current goods includes the negative effect of the increase in the present value of taxes required to finance the increase in G.

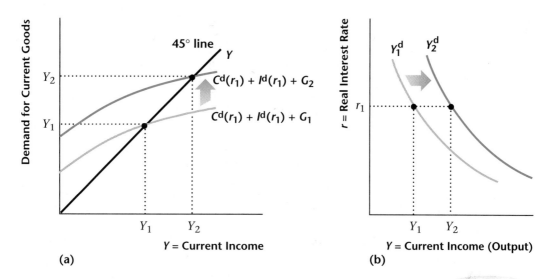

(a)   (b)

FIGURE 7.17

The Output Demand Curve Shifts to the Right if Current Government Spending Increases

The curve shifts in a similar manner if future income increases, if future total factor productivity increases, or if the current capital stock declines.

and therefore the demand for consumption goods, $C^d(r)$, increases, which causes a shift to the right in the output demand curve.

- *An increase in future income Y′ shifts the Y^d curve to the right.* If the representative consumer anticipates that his or her future income will be higher, then this is an increase in lifetime wealth, which causes $C^d(r)$ to increase and brings about a shift to the right in the output demand curve.

- *An increase in future total factor productivity z′ causes the Y^d curve to shift to the right.* If the representative firm expects total factor productivity to be higher in the future, this increases the firm's demand for investment goods, so that $I^d(r)$ increases. The output demand curve then shifts to the right.

- *A decrease in the current capital stock K causes the Y^d curve to shift to the right.* When there is a lower current capital stock, perhaps because of destruction, the demand for investment goods, $I^d(r)$, will increase for each r. As a result, the output demand curve will shift to the right.

THE COMPLETE REAL INTERTEMPORAL MODEL

We now have all the building blocks for our real intertemporal model, and so we can put them together and use the model to address some interesting economic issues. Our model is presented in Figure 7.18, where a competitive equilibrium consists of a state of affairs where supply equals demand in the current labour market in panel (a), and in the current goods market in panel (b). In Figure 7.18(a), N^d is the current labour demand curve, while $N^s(r)$ is the current labour supply curve, which shifts with the real interest rate r. The equilibrium real wage is given by w^*, and the equilibrium quantity of employment is N^*, where w^* and N^* are determined by the intersection of the demand and supply curves for current labour. Equilibrium output and the equilibrium real interest rate are Y^* and r^*, respectively, in Figure 7.18(b), and they are determined by the intersection of the output demand curve Y^d with the output supply curve Y^s.

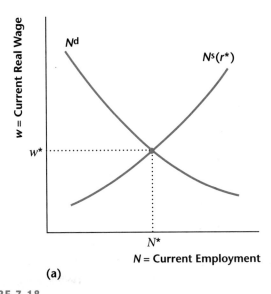
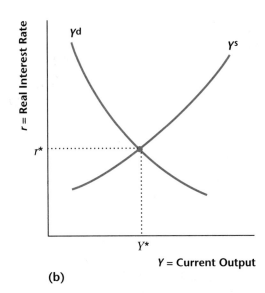

(a)   **(b)**

FIGURE 7.18

The Complete Real Intertemporal Model

(a) The current real wage and current employment are determined by the intersection of the current labour supply and demand curves, given the real interest rate. (b) Current aggregate output and the real interest rate are determined by the intersection of the output supply and demand curves.

To use the model to help us understand how the macroeconomy works, we will perform some experiments that involve changing the value of some exogenous variable or variables and asking how the solution of the model will change as a result. We will then show how we interpret the results in terms of real-world macroeconomic events. Our experiments will answer the following questions:

1. How does an increase in current government purchases, anticipated to be temporary, affect current macroeconomic variables?

2. How does an increase in government purchases expected to be permanent affect the macroeconomy?

3. What are the effects on current macroeconomic variables of a decrease in the current capital stock, brought about by a natural disaster or a war?

4. How does a temporary increase in total factor productivity affect macroeconomic variables, and how does this fit the key business cycle facts?

5. If total factor productivity is expected to increase in the future, how does this affect current macroeconomic variables?

Government Purchases Increase Temporarily: The Equilibrium Effects of an Increase in *G*

Two key messages in this chapter are (i) the macroeconomic effects of a shock to the economy depend on whether the shock is temporary or permanent and (ii) the effects of a shock to the economy expected in the future will have important macroeconomic effects in the current period. Both these messages will come through when we look at the effects of temporary and permanent changes in government purchases in this section and the next.

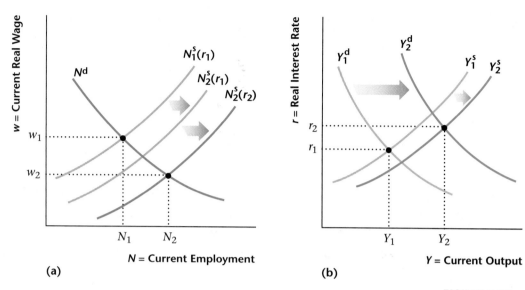

(a)

(b)

FIGURE 7.19

A Temporary Increase in Government Purchases
The increase in G shifts the labour supply curve to the right, the output supply curve to the right, and the output demand curve to the right. The real interest rate rises, and aggregate output increases in equilibrium. There is an additional shift to the right in the labour supply curve because of the increase in r, and so employment rises and the real wage falls in equilibrium.

We will model a temporary increase in government spending as an increase in G, the quantity of government purchases in the current period, leaving future government purchases G' unchanged. When would the government choose to increase its expenditures on goods and services temporarily? An important example is a war. Typically, wars are known to be temporary (though their length can be uncertain), and the government commits spending to the war effort that will not remain in place when the war is over. Sometimes, however, a change in government spending can be essentially permanent. For example, when the Canadian government established Medicare, this involved a commitment of resources that was as permanent as government commitments can be—no one expects national health care to be abolished in the future.

Before the increase in current government purchases G, in Figure 7.19, the economy is in equilibrium with a current real wage w_1, current employment N_1, current output Y_1, and real interest rate r_1. When G increases, this will have two effects, one on output supply and one on output demand. First, since an increase in G increases the present value of government spending, the present value of taxes must rise, from the present-value government budget constraint (7.17), and the representative consumer's lifetime wealth falls. As a result, leisure will decrease (leisure is a normal good) for the representative consumer, given the current real wage, and so the labour supply curve in Figure 7.19(a) shifts to the right from $N_1^s(r_1)$ to $N_2^s(r_1)$, and the output supply curve in Figure 7.19(b) shifts to the right from Y_1^s to Y_2^s. Second, the demand for consumption goods, $C_1(r)$, falls because of the drop in the consumer's lifetime wealth, and the demand for goods arising from government purchases increases, since G goes up. What happens on net to the demand for goods? We know that $MPC < 1$, that is, that the marginal propensity to consume is smaller than one. Thus, since for any real interest rate the present value of taxes increases by the increase in current government spending, the demand for current consumption goods must fall by less than government purchases rise. Therefore, the total demand for goods must rise for any real interest rate, and the output demand curve shifts to the right from Y_1^d to Y_2^d.

To determine all the equilibrium effects using the model, we start first with Figure 7.19(b). It is clear that current aggregate output must increase, as both the output demand and output supply curves shift to the right, and so Y increases from Y_1 to Y_2. It may appear that the real interest rate may rise or fall; however, there is strong theoretical support for an increase in the real interest rate. This is because the temporary increase in government spending should lead to only a small decrease in lifetime wealth for the consumer, which will produce small effects on labour supply and on the demand for consumption goods. Therefore, there should be only a small shift to the right in the Y^s curve, and the small decrease in demand for consumption goods will not greatly offset the increase in demand for goods coming from the increase in G, so that the shift to the right in Y^d will be relatively large. As a result, the real interest rate will rise, as in Figure 7.19(b).

Current consumption expenditure must fall, as lifetime wealth has decreased and the real interest rate has gone up. As well, investment expenditures must decrease, due to the increase in the real interest rate. Thus, both components of private expenditure (current consumption and investment) are crowded out by current government expenditure. Recall from Chapter 5, that when we analyzed the effects of an increase in government spending in a one-period model, without taking intertemporal substitution and investment into account, government spending crowded out only consumption expenditure. Since government spending is shown here to crowd out private investment expenditure, a further cost of government is that it reduces the economy's future productive capacity, as the future capital stock will be lower (than it otherwise would have been).

The next step is to work through the effects of the increase in the real interest rate for the labour market. In Figure 7.19(a), given the initial interest rate r_1, the labour supply curve shifts from $N_1^s(r_1)$ to $N_2^s(r_1)$. With an increase in the equilibrium real interest rate to r_2, the labour supply curve shifts further to the right, to $N_2^s(r_2)$. Therefore, the equilibrium real wage falls, from w_1 to w_2.

What this analysis tells us is that increased temporary government spending, while it leads to higher aggregate output, comes at a cost. With higher current government spending, the representative consumer consumes less and takes less leisure, and he or she also faces a lower real wage rate. Further, current investment spending is lower, which implies that the capital stock will be lower in the future, and the future capacity of the economy for producing goods will be lower.

Government Purchases Increase Permanently:
The Equilibrium Effects of an Increase in Both *G* and *G'*

It turns out that the macroeconomic effects of a permanent increase in government spending are quite different from those of a temporary increase in spending. Again, a good example of a permanent increase in government purchases is the establishment of a new government program, such as medicare.

To set up the problem, suppose that government spending increases permanently by the amount ΔG. That is, current government spending G increases from G_1 to $G_1 + \Delta G$,

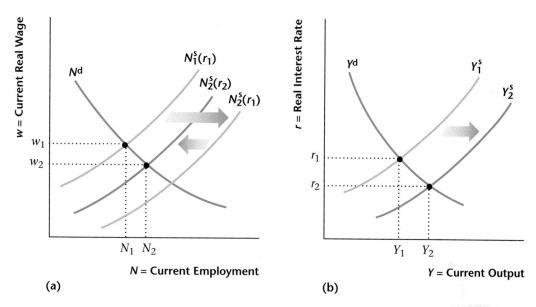

FIGURE 7.20

A Permanent Increase in Government Purchases

When government purchases increase permanently (G and G' increase), the labour supply curve shifts to the right, and the output supply curve shifts right. There is no shift in output demand, and the real interest rate falls, with aggregate output rising. There is a further shift to the left in the labour supply curve, and employment rises with the real wage falling in equilibrium.

and future government spending G' increases from G'_1 to $G'_1 + \Delta G$. Just as with a temporary increase in government purchases, there are two primary effects in the current period, which are the decrease in lifetime wealth for the representative consumer and the direct effect of an increase in current government purchases on the current demand for goods. In terms of the effect on output supply, from the present-value government budget constraint (7.17) the present value of taxes must rise for the consumer, given the real interest rate, because G and G' have increased. As a result, the lifetime wealth of the representative consumer goes down, which implies that he or she will consume less leisure and will work harder in the current period. Therefore, in Figure 7.20(a) the supply curve for current labour shifts to the right from $N_1^s(r_1)$ to $N_2^s(r_1)$, where r_1 is the initial real interest rate. Because of this shift in the labour supply curve, the output supply curve in Figure 7.20(b) will shift to the right from Y_1^s to Y_2^s.

The decrease in lifetime wealth for the consumer, in addition to affecting labour supply, will also cause a reduction in the consumer's current demand for consumption goods. At the same time, there is an increase in the demand for goods as a result of the increase in current government purchases. What, then, is the net impact on the current demand for goods? Milton Friedman's permanent income hypothesis, discussed in Chapter 6, implies that there would be no change in the demand for goods in the current period. That is, since government spending has increased permanently by ΔG, one way to finance this increase in spending would be for the government to increase taxes by ΔG in the present and the future. One way for the representative consumer to absorb the permanent increase in taxes would be to reduce his or her demand for consumption goods by ΔG in each of the current and future periods. In Friedman's language, the consumer's "permanent income" would decline by ΔG, and Friedman argued that the marginal propensity to consume out of permanent income is 1. This implies that the increase in the current demand for goods because of the increase in G and the decrease in the demand for goods because of the negative income effect on current consumption would exactly offset each other. This is what we have shown in Figure 7.20(b), where the output demand curve Y^d remains unaffected by the change in government purchases.

What is the impact of the permanent increase in government purchases on current variables in a competitive equilibrium? First, in Figure 7.20(b), the real interest rate must fall, from r_1 to r_2, and the quantity of aggregate output must rise, from Y_1 to Y_2. The decrease in the real interest rate results in an increase in investment expenditures. What happens to current consumption expenditures? There are two opposing effects here, in that the lifetime wealth of the consumer is affected negatively by the increase in government spending, but the decrease in the real interest rate will affect consumption positively. Whether consumption increases or decreases depends on how strong an intertemporal substitution effect there is on consumption (through the change in r), and on the size of the income effect on labour supply, which affects how much the Y^s curve shifts. An important key difference between the effects of a permanent and a temporary increase in government purchases on current macroeconomic activity is that the permanent increase does not have the same crowding-out effects as the temporary increase. With a permanent increase in government spending, investment expenditure rises rather than falls, and there is a positive effect on consumption from the decrease in the real interest rate. Note, however, that the crowding-out effect on consumption as the result of a reduction in the consumer's lifetime wealth is stronger when the increase in government purchases is permanent.

To determine the ultimate effects of the changes in government spending on the labour market, we need to consider the impact of the decrease in the equilibrium real interest rate. When the real interest rate decreases in equilibrium from r_1 to r_2, this will shift the current labour supply curve in Figure 7.20(a) to the left from $N_2^s(r_1)$ to $N_2^s(r_2)$, because of the intertemporal substitution effect on labour supply. How do we know that the shift to the left in the labour supply curve is smaller than the initial rightward shift in this curve? In equilibrium, we know from Figure 7.20(b) that aggregate output in the current period must increase. For this to happen, from the production function (7.7), employment N must increase in equilibrium, as total factor productivity z and the current capital stock K have not changed. Thus, the shifts in the labour supply curve are as shown in the figure, and so employment increases from N_1 to N_2 and the real wage falls from w_1 to w_2.

Does current aggregate output increase more because of a temporary increase in government spending or a permanent increase? As sometimes occurs when we use economic theory to analyze a particular issue, the answer is that it depends. With the cases of permanent and temporary increases in government spending, there are two positive effects on aggregate output: an output demand effect and an output supply effect. The output demand effect is larger with a temporary increase in government purchases, whereas the output supply effect is larger with a permanent increase. Therefore, whether output increases more or less when government purchases increase temporarily is determined by the relative strengths of the output demand effect and the output supply effect.

How does macroeconomic theory help us understand the effects of changes in government purchases on aggregate output, if the answer here is ambiguous? Theory *does* help, as we have isolated what the relevant effects depend on, and so we have clear direction from the theory concerning what to look for in terms of measurement and empirical work. To get a clear answer to our question, we would want to know the empirical effects of a change in lifetime wealth on the demand for consumption goods and on labour supply, among other things. This will help tell us about the size of the shifts in the output demand and output supply curves. The theory tells us what is important for answering the question, and as economists we can then proceed to find the information we need to obtain this answer. A more technical analysis of the problem by S. Rao Aiyagari, Lawrence Christiano, and Martin Eichenbaum.[2] shows that output will increase more when government spending increases permanently than when it increases temporarily.

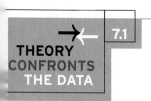

THEORY CONFRONTS THE DATA

7.1

Investment Spending During World War II

Recall that an example of a temporary increase in government purchases is what occurs during wartime. Here, we will consider the macroeconomic effects of the increase in government spending during World War II in Canada. In Chapter 5, we studied data for Canada showing that, during World War II when there was an extremely large increase in real government spending, aggregate real output increased and aggregate consumption declined. This is certainly consistent with the results from our model above, where we showed that a temporary increase in government purchases causes an increase in output because of an increase in labour supply, and a decrease in consumption because of a reduction in lifetime wealth and an increase in the real interest rate. In addition, our model predicts that investment spending will decrease during a war, and so it would be interesting to check this prediction against the data.

Figure 7.21 shows the natural logarithm of real investment expenditures in Canada from 1926 to 2001. Note the extremely large drop in investment spending that occurred during World War II. Indeed, other than the decrease in investment spending during the Great Depression, there are no deviations from trend in investment of comparable magnitude. Recall from Chapter 5 that the crowding-out effect of government spending on consumption that appeared in the data during World War II was quite small, in that consumption expenditures dipped only slightly during this period. The drop in investment spending in the figure is extremely large, however, indicating that the empirical crowding-out effect of a temporary increase in government purchases may be much larger for investment than for consumption.

Although the decrease in investment in World War II is consistent with our theory, it appears that this drop in investment did not occur through an increase in the real interest rate, as in our model. Therefore, our model cannot completely explain the behaviour of the macroeconomy during World War II. One possible explanation for the

---

[2]S. R. Aiyagari, L. Christiano, and M. Eichenbaum, 1992, "The Output, Employment, and Interest Rate Effects of Government Purchases," *Journal of Monetary Economics* 30, 73–86.

FIGURE 7.21

**Natural Log of Real
Investment, 1926–2001**

The figure indicates a large
drop in investment during
World War II, consistent with
the predictions of the real
intertemporal model.

Source: Adapted from the Statistics
Canada CANSIM database, Series
v3860070, v3860075, and from the
Statistics Canada publication *Historical
Statistics of Canada*, Catalogue 11-516,
1983, Series F21, F25.

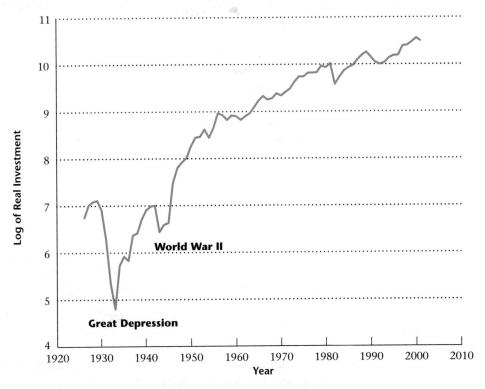

problem in fitting our model to the data is that, in contrast to our assumption of market-clearing prices in the model, during World War II there was much government control over prices and the distribution of goods and raw materials (e.g., through rationing). The large decrease in investment spending may have occurred in part because private producers of investment goods could not obtain material inputs (e.g., gasoline and cement) at any price.

The Equilibrium Effects of a Decrease in the Current Capital Stock, *K*

Over time, through investment, a nation adds to its capital stock, and this generally occurs slowly, as investment expenditure is typically quite small relative to the total capital stock. Thus, increases in capital do not contribute much to short-run fluctuations in aggregate output and employment. However, sometimes major reductions in the aggregate capital stock occur over a short period of time. For example, a war can leave a country with a much lower capital stock, as happened due to bombing in Germany, Great Britain, and Japan during World War II, and in Vietnam during the Vietnam War. The capital stock can also be reduced because of natural disasters such as ice storms (see Macroeconomics in Action 7.1) or hurricanes.

The Macroeconomic Effects of the 1998 Ice Storm in Eastern Canada

An unusually severe ice storm hit eastern Canada January 5–10, 1998, affecting large areas of eastern Ontario, Quebec, New Brunswick, and Nova Scotia. Precipitation fell mostly as freezing rain, with a total water equivalent of about 85 millimetres in Ottawa, 73 millimetres in Kingston, 108 millimetres in Cornwall, and 100 millimetres in Montreal. This was more than twice the precipitation that fell in any major ice storm in this area over the previous forty years.

This storm represented an important macro-economic shock to the Canadian economy, with the damage to the aggregate capital stock being quite significant. There was key damage to the electrical power grid, with the destruction of 120 000 kilometres of power lines and cables, 13 transmission towers valued at about $100 000 each, and 30 000 wooden utility poles valued at about $3000 each. Numerous homes and businesses were damaged by ice and falling trees. Total damages were estimated at more than $2 billion, which was essentially lost productive capital. As well, production was disrupted for several days, as workers could not get to work and equipment could not run in the absence of electricity.[1]

In spite of the widespread damage, there appears to have been no effects on aggregate economic activity. Aggregate output and employment seem not to have been affected. In particular, the percentage increase in real GDP (seasonally adjusted at annual rates) in Canada was 0.86% in fourth-quarter 1997, 1.28% in first-quarter 1998, and 0.26% in second-quarter 1998.[2] Thus, growth in real GDP was actually higher during the quarter the ice storm occurred than in the previous quarter or the following quarter. Our real intertemporal model is entirely consistent with this. While the ice storm disrupted macroeconomic activity, in that activity in manufacturing, services, and agriculture was partially shut down, there was also much activity to repair damage. In the language of our model, the capital stock was reduced, thus reducing productive capacity, the demand for labour, and employment, which would ultimately reduce output supply. However, there was an opposing effect, an increase in the demand for investment goods (repairs to the capital stock), which increased output demand, and in the 1998 ice storm this perhaps more than offset the negative effect on output of the reduced capital stock.

---

[1]See School of Natural Resources, University of Nebraska-Lincoln, "Ice Storm 1998 Eastern Canada," <snrs.unl.edu/amet451/bartlett/icecase.htm>, accessed July 10, 2003.

[2]Statistics Canada, CANSIM database, Series v1992067.

In this subsection, we examine the effects of an experiment in our model where the current capital stock K is reduced. While this experiment can be interpreted as capturing the effects of wars and natural disasters on the capital stock, there is an alternative interpretation in terms of "rich" and "poor" countries. That is, this experiment allows us to explore the differences between two economies: a rich economy, with a high capital stock, and a poor economy, with a low capital stock.

Now, suppose that the representative firm begins the current period with a lower capital stock K. This will affect both the supply and the demand for output. First, a

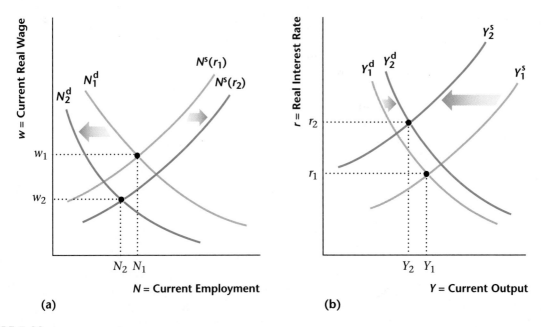

(a)   **(b)**

FIGURE 7.22

The Equilibrium Effects of a Decrease in the Current Capital Stock

If the current capital stock falls—for example, because of a natural disaster—the output demand curve shifts to the right and the output supply curve shifts to the left. The real interest rate rises, but current output may rise or fall.

decrease in K from K_1 to K_2 decreases the current marginal product of labour, which shifts the current demand for labour curve to the left from N_1^d to N_2^d in Figure 7.22(a). The output supply curve will then shift to the left, from Y_1^s to Y_2^s in Figure 7.22(b). Second, a decrease in K will increase investment by the firm, since the future marginal product of capital will be higher. This shifts the output demand curve to the right in Figure 7.22(b), from Y_1^d to Y_2^d. The result is that, in equilibrium, in Figure 7.22(b), the real interest rate must rise from r_1 to r_2, but the effect on current aggregate output is ambiguous, depending on whether the output supply effect is larger or smaller than the output demand effect. In the figure, we have drawn the case where the output supply effect dominates, so that current real output falls. Empirically, there may be circumstances, such as with natural disasters (see the box Macroeconomics in Action 7.1), where aggregate output may not fall.

In Figure 7.22 current consumption must fall, since the real interest rate has increased and current real income has decreased. The effects on investment appear to be ambiguous, since the decrease in K causes investment to increase, while the increase in the equilibrium real interest rate causes investment to fall. However, investment must rise, because less capital would otherwise cause ever-decreasing investment, which would be inconsistent with the fact that the marginal product of capital rises as the quantity of capital falls. That is, as the quantity of capital falls, the marginal product of capital rises, making the return on investment very high, so that ultimately investment must increase if the capital stock decreases.

Due to the increase in the real interest rate, there will be intertemporal substitution of leisure, with the representative consumer working harder in the current period for each current real wage w. Therefore, the labour supply curve shifts to the right in Figure 7.22(a), from $N^s(r_1)$ to $N^s(r_2)$. This reinforces the effect of the decrease in labour demand on the real wage, and so the real wage must fall, from w_1 to w_2. The equilibrium effect on the quantity of labour is ambiguous, since the effect on labour demand and on labour supply work in opposite directions on the quantity of employment. In Figure 7.22(a), we show employment falling from N_1 to N_2.

Now, suppose we interpret these results in terms of the macroeconomic effects of a natural disaster or a war that destroys part of the nation's capital stock. The model shows that there are two effects on the quantity of output. The lower quantity of capital implies that less output can be produced for a given quantity of labour input, which tends to reduce output. However, the lower quantity of capital acts to increase investment to replace the destroyed capital, which will tend to increase output. Theoretically, it is not clear whether output increases or decreases, and there appear to be empirical cases (see Macroeconomics in Action 7.1), where the output supply and output demand effects roughly cancel.

If we view the above results as predictions about how rich countries having high capital stocks should compare with poor countries having low capital stocks, the model fits some facts but not others. If the output demand effect is small and the effect of the real interest rate on labour supply is small, as in Figure 7.22, the model predicts that capital-rich countries should have relatively high output, relatively low real interest rates, relatively high employment, and relatively high real wages. Most of these predictions seem consistent with what we observe, except that rich countries typically do not have low real interest rates. Also, in U.S. post–World War II data, we see trend growth in real output, consumption, and the real wage. However, we do not see a trend decrease in the real interest rate, nor a decrease in investment. Thus, to explain some key facts about cross-country relationships and economic growth, there must be some factor other than differences in capital stocks (either across countries or over time) at work. As we will see in Chapter 8, the other factor that helps explain these key facts is differences across countries and over time in total factor productivity.

The Equilibrium Effects of an Increase in Current Total Factor Productivity, z

Temporary changes in total factor productivity are an important cause of business cycles. Recall from Chapter 4 that an increase in total factor productivity could be caused by good weather, a favourable change in government regulations, a new invention, a decrease in the relative price of energy, or any other factor that results in more aggregate output being produced with the same factor inputs.

The experiment we examine here in our real intertemporal model is to increase current total factor productivity z, and then determine the effects of this change on current aggregate output, the real interest rate, current employment, the current real wage, current consumption, and investment. If current total factor productivity increases, the marginal product of labour goes up for each quantity of labour input, and so in Figure 7.23(a) the demand for labour curve shifts to the right, from N_1^d to N_2^d. Therefore, in Figure 7.23(b), the output supply curve shifts to the right, from Y_1^s to Y_2^s, and in

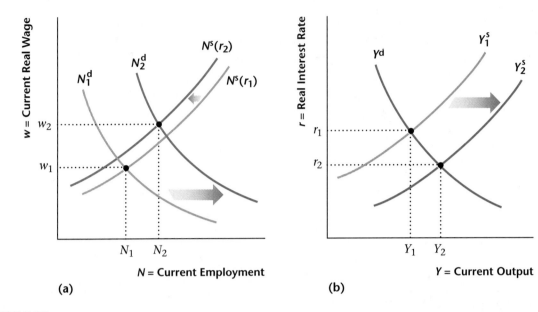

(a)   **(b)**

FIGURE 7.23

The Equilibrium Effects of an Increase in Current Total Factor Productivity

When total factor productivity increases temporarily, the output supply curve shifts to the right in (b), with the real interest rate falling and aggregate output rising. Investment and consumption rise, and employment and the real wage increase in (a).

equilibrium the quantity of output rises and the real interest rate must fall, from r_1 to r_2. The decrease in the real interest rate leads to increases in both consumption and investment and the increase in real income contributes to the increase in consumption.

In the labour market, the decrease in the real interest rate causes intertemporal substitution of leisure between the current and future periods, with current leisure increasing, and so the labour supply curve shifts to the left in Figure 7.23(a), from $N^s(r_1)$ to $N^s(r_2)$. In equilibrium, the real wage must increase from w_1 to w_2, but the net effect on the equilibrium quantity of employment is ambiguous. Empirically, however, the effect of the real interest rate on labour supply is small and, as in Figure 7.23(a), employment rises from N_1 to N_2.

When total factor productivity increases, this increases the current demand for labour, which raises the market real wage. With this increase, workers are willing to supply more labour, employment increases, and output increases. In the goods market, the increased supply of goods decreases the market real interest rate, which results in an increased demand for investment goods and consumption goods, so that the demand for goods rises to meet the increased supply of goods on the market.

From Chapter 3, recall that consumption, investment, employment, and the real wage are procyclical. Note that our real intertemporal model will predict these comovements in the data if the economy receives temporary shocks to total factor productivity. That is, since Figure 7.23 predicts that a temporary increase in total factor productivity increases aggregate output, consumption, investment, employment, and the real wage, the model predicts that consumption, investment, employment, and the real wage are procyclical, just as in the data. Thus, temporary shocks to total factor productivity are a candidate as a cause of business cycles. Indeed, the proponents of real business cycle theory, which we will study in detail in Chapter 11, argue that total factor productivity shocks are the most important cause of business cycles.

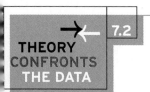

7.2

Changes in the Relative Price of Energy and Total Factor Productivity

Changes in the relative price of energy have been a key example in Canadian macroeconomic history of decreases in total factor productivity. We have already looked at the 1974–75 recession as an example of an economic downturn caused by an increase in energy prices.

Figure 7.24 shows a plot of the relative price of energy in Canada, measured as the industrial price of petroleum and coal products divided by the consumer price index. Note that there were three large increases in the price of energy occurring over the period in Figure 7.24, one in 1973–74, one in 1979–80, and one in 1999–2000. All these relative price increases can be traced to large increases in the world price of crude oil. During the first two periods, these increases were due primarily to reductions in the quantity of crude oil sold on world markets by OPEC (the Organization of Petroleum Exporting Countries). If indeed these changes in the relative price of energy can be interpreted as being total factor productivity shocks, our model predicts that at all three of these times we should have observed decreases in aggregate output, investment, employment, and consumption.

For each of these three large increases in the relative price of energy, a recession follows, as shown in Figure 7.25, with approximately similar timing in each case. The

FIGURE 7.24

The Relative Price of Energy in Canada

Note the large increases in 1973–74 and 1979–80, and the large decrease in 1985.

Source: Adapted from the Statistics Canada CANSIM database, Series v735319, v3822650, v83778.

FIGURE 7.25

Percentage Deviations from Trend in GDP for Canada

Note the negative deviations from trend in 1973–75, 1981–82, and 2001. In each case, the dip in real GDP was preceded by an increase in the relative price of energy.

Source: Adapted from the Statistics Canada CANSIM database, Series v1992067.

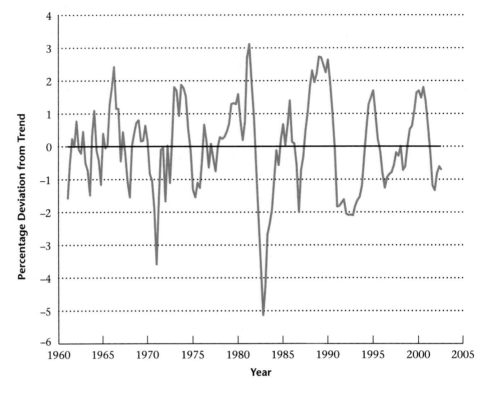

1973–74 energy price increase is followed by a decrease in real GDP from its peak above trend in late 1974 to a trough below trend in 1975. The 1979–80 energy price increase precedes a decrease in real GDP from its peak above trend in late 1980 to a trough below trend in 1982. Finally, the increase in the relative price of energy in 1999–2000 comes prior to a decrease in real GDP from a peak above trend in 2000 to a trough below trend in 2002. Though there are other factors that contributed to each of the business cycle downturns in question (in particular, monetary policy is typically thought to have played an important role in the 1981–82 recession), there is strong evidence that the increase in the relative price of energy was an important factor in each case.

Recall from Chapter 5 that the behaviour of consumption appears to be inconsistent with our theory for the 1974–75 recession, because real consumption expenditures were above trend at this time. However, consumption otherwise moves in line with real GDP in 1981–82 and 2000–02, which is consistent with the theory. As well, from Figure 7.26, investment is below trend during the 1974–75 recession, the 1981–82 recession, and the downturn in 2001–02, though the dip is small in 1974–75. In Figure 7.27, employment tracks real GDP closely[3]. Thus, the behaviour of investment and employment is broadly consistent with the theory following these three major increases in the relative price of energy.

---

[3]In Figures 7.25, 7.26, and 7.28, the data is quarterly for 1961–2002, whereas the data in Figure 7.27 is annual for 1961–2001. That is why a downturn in GDP below trend is not observed at the end of the time period in Figure 7.27, but it is in the other figures.

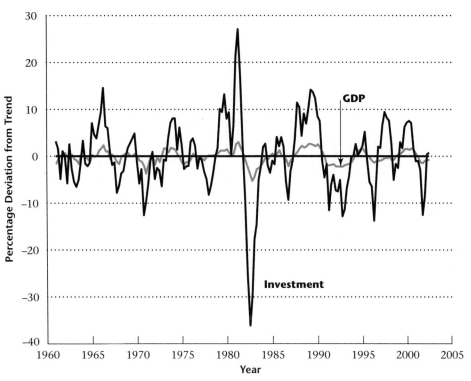

FIGURE 7.26

Percentage Deviations from Trend in Real Investment and Real GDP for Canada

Note the large negative deviations in 1974–75, 1981–82, and 2001.

Source: Adapted from the Statistics Canada CANSIM database, Series v1992057, v1992067.

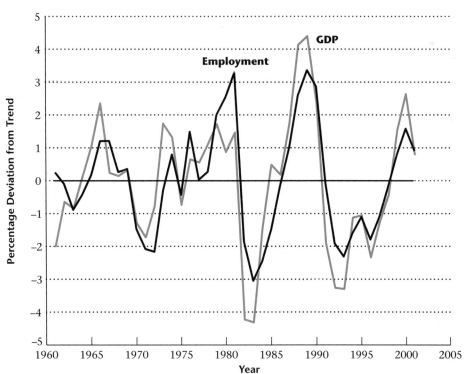

FIGURE 7.27

Percentage Deviations from Trend in Employment and Real GDP for Canada

Note the negative deviations from trend in 1974–75 and 1981–82.

Source: Adapted from the Statistics Canada CANSIM database, Series v2461119, v3860085, and from the Statistics Canada publication *Historical Statistics of Canada*, Catalogue 11-516, 1983, Series D175–189.

FIGURE 7.28

Percentage Deviations from Trend in Real Consumption and Real GDP for Canada

Note the large negative deviations in 1981–82 and 2001–02.

Source: Adapted from the Statistics Canada CANSIM database, Series v1992044, v1992067.

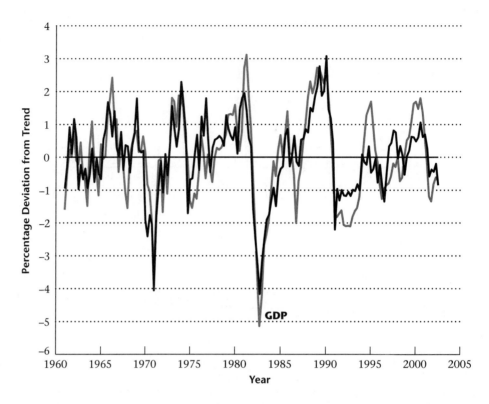

Note also that there is a substantial increase in real GDP above trend in Figure 7.25 in the late 1980s following the sharp decline in energy prices. This again is consistent with our theory, as we would expect a decrease in the relative price of energy to increase total factor productivity and cause real output to go up. However, we might expect there to be an asymmetry in the economy's response to positive and negative energy price changes, with output changing less in absolute value for a 1% decrease in the relative price of energy than output decreases for a 1% increase. When a positive shock occurs to the relative price of energy, the initial response of firms is to reduce the quantity of energy used in production, which reduces total factor productivity, and so output, employment, consumption, and investment decrease. If the relative price of energy remains high for a long time, firms eventually develop new technologies that economize on energy use. Once these technologies are in place, a temporary negative shock to the price of energy will not lead to a dramatic increase in the use of energy in production or to a large increase in total factor productivity. This is because new energy-efficient technologies are in use, and firms will not in the short run revert to older, less energy-efficient technologies.

The Equilibrium Effects of an Increase in Future Total Factor Productivity, *z′*

The anticipation of future events can have important macroeconomic consequences currently, as when an increase in total factor productivity is expected to happen in the

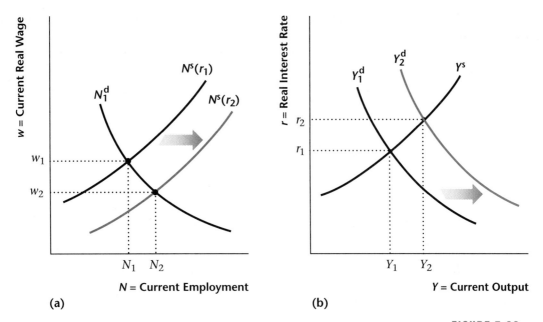

FIGURE 7.29

The Equilibrium Effects of an Increase in Future Total Factor Productivity

An anticipated increase in future total factor productivity shifts the output demand curve to the right, with current output and the real interest rate increasing in equilibrium. The real wage falls, and employment rises.

future. For example, firms might learn of a new invention, such as a new production process, which is not available currently but will come on line in the future. We will see that this shock will increase current investment, current output, and current employment, and reduce the real wage.

Suppose that z' increases. This implies that the future marginal product of capital increases for the representative firm, and so the firm will wish to invest more in the current period, which increases the demand for current goods, shifting the output demand curve to the right in Figure 7.29(b). In equilibrium, this implies that aggregate output increases from Y_1 to Y_2, and the real interest rate increases from r_1 to r_2. The increase in the real interest rate will then cause current consumption to fall though the increase in real income will tend to increase consumption, so consumption could rise or fall. In equilibrium, there are two effects on investment; the increase in z' causes investment to rise, and the increase in r causes it to fall. Therefore, investment may rise or fall, but the presumption here is that investment rises, as this was the initial source of the increase in the demand for current goods.

What are the effects in the labour market? The increase in the real interest rate leads to a rightward shift of the labour supply curve, from $N^s(r_1)$ to $N^s(r_2)$ in Figure 7.29(a). Therefore, in equilibrium, the quantity of employment increases from N_1 to N_2, and the real wage falls from w_1 to w_2.

In anticipation of a future increase in total factor productivity, firms increase investment expenditure, as the marginal payoff to having a higher future capital stock has increased. The increase in the demand for investment goods raises the market real interest rate, which increases labour supply and employment and generates an increase in aggregate output. The increase in labour supply causes the real wage to fall.

Now that we have gained an understanding of the workings of our real intertemporal model, we can go on to use this model further, adding money and nominal variables in Chapter 9, and then using the model as a basis for studying business cycles in Chapters 10 and 11. In Chapter 8, we will move on to economic growth using a somewhat different model, but with principles we have built up in this and previous chapters.

Chapter Summary

This chapter is built on the microeconomic behaviour studied in Chapters 4–6, to develop a real intertemporal macroeconomic model that is useful for evaluating the macroeconomic effects of shocks to the economy, and which we can build on in later chapters. This model allows us to study the determinants of investment, consumption, aggregate output, the real interest rate, and employment in an intertemporal setting. The model has two periods, the present and the future, and the representative consumer makes a work–leisure decision in each period and a consumption–savings decision in the current period. As the real interest rate increases, the consumer's demand for current consumption goods decreases, and his or her current labour supply increases. These effects are due to the intertemporal substitution of consumption and leisure between the present and the future in response to changes in the real interest rate. The representative firm produces output using labour and capital in each period. The firm's current demand for labour is determined by the usual marginal productivity condition (the marginal product of labour equals the real wage in the current period when the firm optimizes), and the firm invests in new capital in the current period until the net marginal product of capital in the future is equal to the real interest rate. An increase in the real interest rate leads to a decrease in the firm's optimal quantity of investment, and investment will increase if the firm's initial quantity of capital decreases, or there is an anticipated increase in future total factor productivity. In equilibrium, the current goods market and the current labour market clear, and this implies that the credit market clears as well. For simplicity, we ignore markets in the future period.

In the graphical representation of the model, there are two key elements: (i) output demand and supply, determining current aggregate output and the real interest rate; (ii) current labour supply and current labour demand, determining current employment and the current real wage given the real interest rate. We conducted five experiments using the model:

1. If current government purchases increase (a temporary increase in government spending), this increases the present value of taxes for the consumer, reducing lifetime wealth. As a result, the demand for current consumption goods falls, with the demand for current goods rising on net, and labour supply rises given the real interest rate. In equilibrium, current output rises, current employment rises, the current real wage falls, and the real interest rate increases given that a temporary increase in government purchases implies that the output supply effect is small. Consumption and investment are crowded out. This is consistent with observations on Canadian investment during World War II, though the mechanism that caused investment to decrease then was somewhat different from what is depicted in the model.

2. If government spending increases permanently (both current and future government purchases increase), the negative effect on current consumption demand will roughly offset the increase in the current demand for goods resulting from an increase in current government spending. There is then only an output supply effect, and aggregate output increases, the

real interest rate falls, employment rises, the real wage falls, investment increases, and current consumption may rise or fall.

3. If the current capital stock decreases—for example, due to a natural disaster—the optimal quantity of investment increases for the firm, given the real interest rate, so that output demand increases. Current output supply decreases, because the representative firm can produce less current output with a given input of labour. The real interest rate increases in equilibrium, but current aggregate output may rise or fall. If the output demand effect is small, output will fall.

4. If current total factor productivity increases (a temporary increase in total factor productivity), output supply increases, the real interest rate falls, and consumption and investment increase in the current period. Current employment may rise or fall, but it rises provided the interest rate effect on labour supply is small. The current real wage rises. These predictions of the model replicate some of the key business cycle facts from Chapter 3.

5. An anticipated increase in future total factor productivity implies that the representative firm will demand more investment goods, since the future marginal product of capital is expected to be higher. The demand for goods increases, causing the real interest rate and current aggregate output to rise. In the labour market, the real wage falls and employment rises, as the representative consumer substitutes leisure intertemporally in response to the real interest rate increase.

Key Terms

intertemporal substitution of leisure: The substitution of leisure between the current and the future period in response to the market real interest rate.

depreciation: The fraction of capital that wears out in a given period.

marginal cost of investment: The profit forgone by the firm in the current period from investing in an additional unit of capital.

marginal benefit from investment: The future marginal product of capital plus $1 - d$, where d is the depreciation rate.

net marginal product of capital: The marginal product of capital minus the depreciation rate.

optimal investment rule: Rule stating that the firm invests until the future net marginal product of capital is equal to the real interest rate.

optimal investment schedule: A negative relationship between the firm's optimal quantity of investment and the market real interest rate.

output supply curve: A positive relationship between the quantity of output supplied by firms and the real interest rate.

output demand curve: A negative relationship between the quantity of output demanded (in the form of consumption expenditures, investment expenditures, and government expenditures) and the real interest rate.

Questions for Review

All questions refer to the macroeconomic model developed in this chapter.

1. Explain how intertemporal substitution is important for current labour supply and for the current demand for consumption goods.

2. What are three factors that determine current labour supply?

3. What determines the current demand for labour?

4. What is the goal of the representative firm in the real intertemporal model?

5. What rule does the representative firm follow in determining its optimal level of investment?

6. How is optimal investment for the firm affected by an increase in the current capital stock?

7. How is optimal investment affected by an increase in future total factor productivity?

8. What is the government's budget constraint in the real intertemporal model? Can the government run a deficit or run a surplus in the current period?

9. What are the factors that shift the output supply curve?

10. What are the factors that shift the output demand curve?

11. How are aggregate output and the real interest rate determined in competitive equilibrium?

12. What are the effects of a temporary increase in government purchases on the real interest rate, aggregate output, employment, the real wage, consumption, and investment?

13. What are the effects of a permanent increase in government purchases on the real interest rate, aggregate output, employment, the real wage, consumption, and investment? Explain why these results are different from the case in which government purchases increase temporarily.

14. What are the effects of a decrease in the current capital stock on the real interest rate, aggregate output, employment, the real wage, consumption, and investment?

15. What are the effects of an increase in total factor productivity on the real interest rate, aggregate output, employment, the real wage, consumption, and investment? Explain how these results relate to key business cycle facts and the causes of business cycles.

16. Determine the equilibrium effects of an anticipated increase in future total factor productivity in the real intertemporal model. Explain why these effects are different from the effects of an increase in current total factor productivity.

Problems

1. What is the effect of an increase in d, the depreciation rate, on the representative firm's investment decision and on its optimal investment schedule? Explain your results carefully.

2. Tom lives on an island and has 20 coconut trees in the current period, which currently produce 180 coconuts. Tom detests coconuts, but he can trade them with people on other neighbouring islands for things that he wants. Further, Tom can borrow and lend coconuts with neighbouring islands. In the coconut credit market, a loan of 1 coconut in the current period is repaid with 2 coconuts in the future period. Each period, Tom's trees produce, and then 10% of them die. If Tom plants a coconut in the ground in the current period, it will grow into a productive coconut tree in the future period. At the end of the future period, Tom can sell any remaining coconut trees for 1 coconut each. When Tom plants coconuts in the current period, he plants them in successively less fertile ground, and the less fertile the ground, the less productive the coconut tree. For convenience, we will assume here that fractions of coconuts can be produced by trees. Output in the future period, for given numbers of trees in production in the future period, is given in the following table:

Trees in Production in the Future	Future Output of Coconuts
15	155
16	162
17	168
18	173
19	177
20	180
21	182
22	183.8
23	184.8
24	185.2
25	185.4

a. Plot the level of output against the quantity of capital for the future period.

b. Plot the marginal product of capital against the quantity of capital for the future period.

c. Calculate Tom's present value of profits given each quantity of future trees.

d. Calculate the net marginal product of capital for each quantity of future trees.

e. Determine Tom's optimal quantity of investment, and explain your results.

3. The government wishes to bring about an increase in investment expenditures, and is considering two tax policies that policymakers think could bring this about. Under the first tax policy, firms would receive a subsidy in the current period of t per unit of current output produced. Policymakers reason that firms will use this subsidy for investment. The second policy under consideration is an investment tax credit, by which firms would receive a subsidy of s per unit of investment in the current period. Determine which tax policy would be more effective in accomplishing the government's goal of increasing current investment expenditures, and carefully explain your results.

4. Determine how the following will affect the slope of the output demand curve, and explain your results:

a. The marginal propensity to consume increases.

b. The intertemporal substitution effect of the real interest rate on current consumption increases.

c. The demand for investment goods becomes less responsive to the real interest rate.

5. Determine how the following will affect the slope of the output supply curve, and explain your results:

a. The marginal product of labour decreases at a faster rate as the quantity of labour used in production increases.

b. The intertemporal substitution effect of the real interest rate on current leisure decreases.

6. The government announces that an increase in government expenditure will occur next year. Use diagrams to determine the effects this will have on current aggregate output, current employment, the current real wage, the real interest rate, consumption, and investment. Explain your results.

7. Suppose there is a shift in the representative consumer's preferences: namely, the consumer prefers, given the market real interest rate, to consume less current leisure and more current consumption goods.

a. Determine the effects of this on current aggregate output, current employment, the current real wage, current consumption, and current investment.

b. Explain your results. What might cause such a change in the preferences of consumers?

8. Suppose there is a permanent increase in total factor productivity. Determine the implications of this for current macroeconomic variables, and show how the impact differs from the case in which total factor productivity is expected to increase only temporarily. Explain your results.

9. Suppose z' and K increase at the same time. Show that it is possible for the real interest rate to remain constant as a result. What does this say about the model's ability to explain the differences between poor and rich countries and to explain what happens as a country's economy grows?

10. There is a temporary increase in the relative price of energy. Determine how the response of current aggregate output to this shock depends on the marginal propensity to consume, and explain carefully why you get this result.

11. A war breaks out that is widely expected to last only one year. Show how the effect of this shock on aggregate output depends on the size of the intertemporal substitution effect of the real interest rate on current leisure, and carefully explain your results.

12. The nation experiences a major hurricane that destroys significant capital stock. Policymakers in the federal government reason that the destruction caused by the hurricane will reduce national income, and that this should be counteracted through an increase in government expenditures.
    a. Is the action suggested by these policymakers necessary, given what their goals appear to be?
    b. What would be the net effects on the economy if government expenditures were temporarily increased after the hurricane?
    c. Are there any circumstances when this course of action would make sense? Explain.

Working with the Data

1. Calculate percentage quarterly growth rates in real GDP, real investment spending, and real consumption spending in 1997 and 1998. Are these observations consistent with Macroeconomics in Action 7.1? Explain.

2. Calculate the ratio of real investment expenditures to GDP, quarterly, for the period 1961–2002, and also calculate the real interest rate as the 3-month Treasury bill rate minus the inflation rate (be careful that you calculate the inflation rate as an annualized rate), then plot the first variable against the second in a scatter plot. The theory of investment in this chapter predicts an optimal investment schedule that is a negative relationship between investment and the real interest rate. Is this what you observe in the data? Explain.

3. Calculate the ratio of total real government purchases to real GDP, quarterly, from first-quarter 1961 to third-quarter 2002. Also, calculate the real interest rate on a quarterly basis, as the 3-month Treasury bill rate in the last month of the quarter, minus the inflation rate (measured as the percentage increase in the consumer price index from the last month of the previous quarter to the last month of the current quarter, multiplied by four to make this an annual rate).
    a. Construct a scatter plot of the ratio of government purchases to GDP against the real interest rate.
    b. Our real intertemporal model predicts that a temporary increase in government purchases causes an increase in the real interest rate. Is this implication of the model consistent with what you see in the scatter plot from part (a)? Explain why or why not.

CHAPTER 8

Economic Growth

The two primary phenomena macroeconomists study are business cycles and economic growth. Though much macroeconomic research focuses on business cycles, the study of economic growth has also received a good deal of attention, especially since the late 1980s. Robert Lucas[1] has argued that the potential social gains from a greater understanding of business cycles are dwarfed by those from understanding growth. This is because, even if (most optimistically) business cycles could be completely eliminated, the avoided reductions of real GDP below trend would be, at most, on the order of 5% on the basis of post–World War II U.S. data. However, if changes in economic policy could cause the growth rate of real GDP to increase by 1% per year for 100 years, GDP would be 2.7 times higher after 100 years than it would otherwise have been.

The effects of economic growth have been phenomenal. Per capita Canadian income in 2002 was $27 580, but before Confederation in the early 19th century, per capita Canadian income was only several hundred 2002 dollars. Economic growth has not been uniform across countries, however, and there are currently wide disparities in standards of living across the countries of the world. In 2002, income per worker in Mexico was 47% of that in Canada, in Egypt it was 26% of that in Canada, and in Burundi it was about 2% of that in Canada.

The goals of this chapter are to understand the causes and consequences of economic growth. To do this, we will first introduce growth accounting, which is an approach to separating out the sources of economic growth—growth in capital, labour, and total factor productivity—to determine from macroeconomic data how much each of these sources contributed to growth over particular periods of time. Next, we will study the Solow growth model, which is the most widely used model of economic growth, developed by Robert Solow in the 1950s.[2] The Solow growth model makes important predictions concerning the effects of savings rates, population growth, and changes in total factor productivity on a nation's standard of living and growth rate of GDP. We will show that these predictions match economic data quite well.

A key implication of the Solow growth model is that a country's standard of living cannot continue to improve in the long run in the absence of continuing increases in total

[1]See R. Lucas, 1987, *Models of Business Cycles*, Basil Blackwell, Oxford.
[2]See R. Solow, 1956, "A Contribution to the Theory of Economic Growth," *Quarterly Journal of Economics* 70, 65–94.

factor productivity. In the short run, the standard of living can improve if a country's residents save and invest more, thus accumulating more capital. However, the Solow growth model tells us that building more productive capacity will not improve long-run living standards unless the production technology becomes more efficient.

The Solow growth model makes strong predictions concerning the ability of poor countries to catch up with rich countries. That is, in this model income per worker will converge among countries that are initially rich and poor but otherwise identical. The model tells us that countries that are initially poor in terms of income per worker will grow at a faster rate than countries that are initially rich. This prediction is consistent with what we observe happening among the richest countries in the world. Since 1960, income per worker appears to be converging among these countries. Among the poorest countries of the world, however, income per worker does not appear to be converging, and the poorest countries of the world seem to be falling behind the richest ones, rather than catching up. Therefore, the Solow model is not entirely consistent with the way in which the distribution of income is evolving in the world.

The Solow growth model is an **exogenous growth model**, in that growth is caused in the model by forces that are not explained by the model itself. To gain a deeper understanding of economic growth, it is useful to examine the economic factors that cause growth, and this is done in **endogenous growth models**. In this chapter, we will consider a simple model of endogenous growth, and we will show how some of the predictions of this model differ from those of the Solow growth model. The endogenous growth model we study shows how the accumulation of skills and education is important to economic growth. We will use the model to evaluate how economic policy might affect the quantity of resources allocated to skills and education, and how this affects growth.

In contrast to the Solow growth model, the endogenous growth model we study does not predict convergence in levels of per capita income across countries. In fact, the endogenous growth model predicts that differences in per capita income will persist forever. The model indicates which factors are important in explaining the continuing disparities in living standards between the richest and poorest countries of the world.

Growth Accounting

Why do economies grow? Why are some countries growth miracles, and others growth disasters? (See Macroeconomics in Action 8.1 on p. 250.) If aggregate real output is to grow over time, it is necessary for a factor or factors of production to increase over time, or for there to be increases in total factor productivity. Typically, growing economies are experiencing growth in factors of production *and* in total factor productivity. A useful exercise is to measure how much of the growth in aggregate output over a given period of time is accounted for by growth in each of the inputs to production and by increases in total factor productivity. This exercise is called **growth accounting**, and it can be helpful in developing theories of economic growth and for discriminating among different theories. Growth accounting was introduced in the 1950s by Robert Solow, one of the pioneering researchers in modern economic growth.[3]

Growth accounting starts by considering the aggregate production function

$$Y = zF(K, N),$$

where Y is aggregate output, z is total factor productivity, F is a function, K is the capital input, and N is the labour input. To use the aggregate production function to organize our thinking about measured output and factor inputs, we need a specific form for the function F. The widely used Cobb-Douglas production function, as discussed in Chapter 4, provides a good fit to Canadian aggregate data, and to data for other countries and it is also a good analytical tool for growth accounting. For the production function to be Cobb-Douglas, the function F takes the form

$$F(K, N) = K^a N^{1-a}, \tag{8.1}$$

where a is a number between 0 and 1. Recall from Chapter 4 that, in a competitive equilibrium, a is the fraction of national income that goes to the capital input, and $1 - a$ is the fraction that goes to the labour input. In recent Canadian data, the labour share in national income has been roughly constant at 70%, so we can set $a = 0.3$, and our production function is then

$$Y = zK^{0.3}N^{0.7}. \tag{8.2}$$

If we have measures of aggregate output, the capital input, and the labour input, denoted $\hat{Y}$, $\hat{K}$, and $\hat{N}$, respectively, then total factor productivity z can be measured as a residual, as discussed in Chapter 4. The **Solow residual** (named of course after Robert Solow), denoted $\hat{z}$, is measured from the production function, Equation (8.2), as

$$\hat{z} = \frac{\hat{Y}}{\hat{K}^{0.3}\hat{N}^{0.7}}. \tag{8.3}$$

This measure of total factor productivity is a residual, since it is the output that remains to be accounted for after we measure the direct contribution of the capital and labour inputs to output. Total factor productivity has many interpretations, as we studied in Chapters 4 and 5, and hence so does the Solow residual. Increases in measured total factor productivity could be the result of new inventions, good weather, new management techniques, favourable changes in government regulations, decreases in the relative price of energy, or any other factor that causes more aggregate output to be produced given the same quantities of aggregate factor inputs.

SOLOW RESIDUALS AND THE PRODUCTIVITY SLOWDOWN

A first exercise we will work through is to calculate and graph Solow residuals from Canadian data for 1961–2001, and then explain what is interesting in the resulting

---

[3]See R. Solow, 1957, "Technical Change and the Aggregate Production Function," *Review of Economic Statistics* 39, 312–320.

FIGURE 8.1

Natural Log of the Solow Residual, 1961–2001

The Solow residual is a measure of total factor productivity. Growth in total factor productivity slows from the early 1970s to the early 1990s.

Source: Adapted from the Statistics Canada CANSIM database, Series v3860085, v2461119, v3822183, v1078498, and from the Statistics Canada publication *Historical Statistics of Canada*, Catalogue 11-516, 1983, Series D175–189.

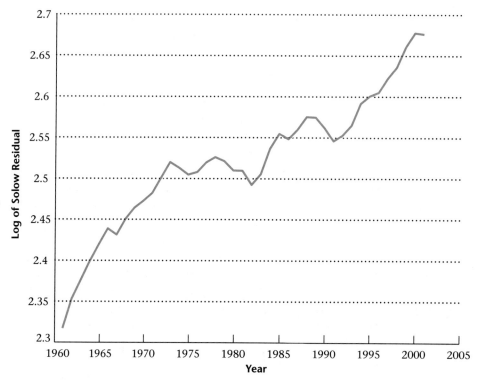

figure. Using GDP for $\hat{Y}$, measured aggregate output, total employment for $\hat{N}$, and a measure of the capital stock for $\hat{K}$, we calculated the Solow residual $\hat{z}$ using Equation (8.3), and plotted its natural logarithm in Figure 8.1, for the period 1961–2001. We can see that growth in total factor productivity was very high from 1961 until the early 1970s, as evidenced by the steep slope in the graph during that period. However, there was a dramatic decrease in total factor productivity growth beginning about 1973 and continuing until the early 1990s, which is referred to as the **productivity slowdown**.[4]

TABLE 8.1 Average Annual Growth Rates in the Solow Residual

Period	Average Annual Growth Rate
1961–1971	1.67%
1971–1981	0.27%
1981–1991	0.36%
1991–2001	1.31%

[4]There was a similar productivity slowdown in the United States, but it continued only until the early 1980s. The slowdown is also seen in Table 8.1, where we show the average percentage growth in the Solow residual during the periods 1961–1971, 1971–1981, 1981–1991, and 1991–2001. Note in the table that total factor productivity growth, as measured by growth in the Solow residual, was low during the periods 1971–81 and 1981–91 and high from 1961–1971, and then was quite high again from 1991 to 2001.

There are at least three reasons given by economists for the productivity slowdown:

1. The measured productivity slowdown might have been a measurement problem. Over this period, there was a shift in Canada from the production of manufactured goods to the production of services. Earlier, in Chapter 2, we discussed the problems associated with measuring real growth in GDP due to changes in the quality of goods and services over time. This measurement problem is especially severe in the service sector. Thus, if production is shifting from goods to services, there will tend to be an increase in the downward bias in measuring growth in GDP. It can appear that GDP growth and total factor productivity growth are low, when they actually are not.

2. The productivity slowdown could have resulted from increases in the relative price of energy. There were two large increases in the world price of oil, in 1973–74 and in 1979–80. An effect of the increase in oil prices was that old capital equipment that was not energy-efficient—for example, buildings with poor insulation—became obsolete. It was possible that obsolete plant and equipment were scrapped or fell out of use, and that this scenario was not adequately captured in the capital stock measure. That is, some of the measured capital stock was not actually productive. Essentially then, this is another type of measurement problem, but it is a problem in measuring inputs, whereas the measurement issue discussed in the first point is a problem in measuring output.

3. The productivity slowdown could have been caused by the costs of adopting new technology. Some economists—for example, Jeremy Greenwood and Mehmet Yorukoglu[5]—mark the early 1970s as the beginning of the information revolution, when computer and other information technology began to be widely adopted in developed countries. With any dramatically new technology, time is required for workers to learn how to use the new technology, which is embodied in new capital equipment like computers. During this learning period, productivity growth can be low, because workers are spending some of their time investing in learning on the job, and they are therefore contributing less to measured output. The fact that productivity growth increased in the 1990s is consistent with this explanation for the productivity slowdown. The argument would be that, by the 1990s, older workers had become accustomed to working in the information age, and younger workers had been educated in how to use computers and other high-tech equipment.

THE CYCLICAL PROPERTIES OF SOLOW RESIDUALS

From Figure 8.1, it is clear that there are cyclical fluctuations in Solow residuals about trend growth. In Figure 8.2 we plot percentage deviations from trend in Solow residuals for the years 1961–2001, along with percentage deviations from trend in real GDP. Note that the fluctuations in Solow residuals about trend are highly positively correlated with the fluctuations in real GDP about trend (recall our discussion of correlations and comovements from Chapter 3). In fact, the Solow residual moves very closely with GDP, so that fluctuations in total factor productivity could be an important explanation for

---

[5]See J. Greenwood and M. Yorukoglu, "1974," University of Rochester working paper.

FIGURE 8.2

Percentage Deviations from Trend in Real GDP (black line) and the Solow Residual (coloured line), 1961–2001

Note that the Solow residual tracks GDP quite closely.

Source: Adapted from the Statistics Canada CANSIM database, Series v3860085, v2461119, v3822183, v1078498, and from the Statistics Canada publication *Historical Statistics of Canada*, Catalogue 11-516, 1983, Series D175–189.

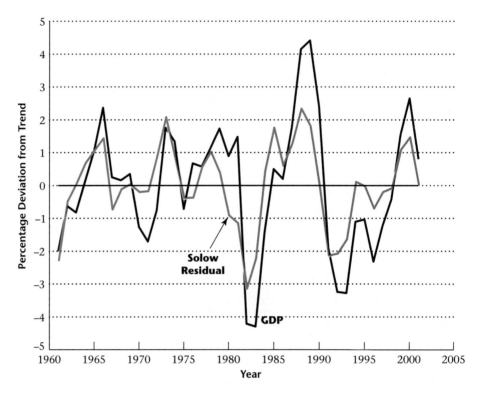

why GDP fluctuates. This is the key idea in real business cycle theory, which we will study in Chapter 11.

A GROWTH ACCOUNTING EXERCISE

Now that we know how the Solow residual is constructed, and what some of its empirical properties are, we can do a full growth accounting exercise. By way of example, we will show here how we can use the Cobb-Douglas production function (8.2), and observations on GDP, the capital stock, and employment, to obtain measures of the contributions to growth in real output of growth in the capital stock, in employment, and in total factor productivity.

To start, first take natural logarithms on both sides of Equation (8.2):

$$\log Y = \log z + 0.3\log K + 0.7\log N. \tag{8.4}$$

Therefore, if we look at changes over time in the natural logarithms of aggregate output, the aggregate capital stock, and aggregate employment, from (8.2) we will have

$$\Delta\log Y = \Delta\log z + 0.3\,\Delta\log K + 0.7\,\Delta\log N, \tag{8.5}$$

where $\Delta\log Y$ denotes the change per unit time in the log of Y, $\Delta\log z$ denotes the change per unit time in the log of z, and so on. Now, recall from Chapter 1 that the change per

TABLE 8.2 Measured GDP, Capital Stock, and Employment

Year	$\hat{Y}$ (billions of 1997 dollars)	$\hat{K}$ (billions of 1997 dollars)	$\hat{N}$ (millions)	$\hat{z}$
1961	245.2	611.3	6.06	10.19
1971	405.9	964.6	8.08	11.97
1981	600.3	1484.7	11.30	12.30
1991	749.3	2079.6	12.85	13.35
2001	1027.5	2605.9	15.08	14.53

unit time in the natural logarithm of an economic time series is approximately the rate of growth in that variable. Therefore, in percentage terms, from (8.5), we have

$$\%\Delta Y \cong \%\Delta z + 0.30(\%\Delta K) + 0.70(\%\Delta N), \tag{8.6}$$

where, for example, $\%\Delta Y$ denotes the percentage change per unit time in aggregate output. Equation (8.6) is a key relationship that shows how the percentage change in total factor productivity, in the capital stock, and in employment, on the right-hand side, contribute to the percentage change in aggregate output on the left-hand side.

Next, to do growth accounting, we can either use Equation (8.3) to calculate the Solow residual $\hat{z}$ directly, or Equation (8.6) can be used to calculate an approximation to the growth rate in the Solow residual. Note that the approximation will not be good if growth rates are large, say over a ten-year period. In Table 8.2 we show data on real GDP, the capital stock, and employment at ten-year intervals from 1961 to 2001. This is the data we will use to carry out our growth accounting exercise. The Solow residual $\hat{z}$ in the table was calculated using Equation (8.3).

Now, taking the data from Table 8.2, we calculate the average annual growth rates for measured output, capital, employment, and the Solow residual for the periods 1961–1971, 1971–1981, 1981–1991, and 1991–2001. If X_n is the value of a variable in year n, and X_m is the value of that variable in year m, where $n > m$, then the average annual growth in X between year m and year n, denoted by g_{mn}, is given by

$$g_{mn} = \left(\frac{X_n}{X_m}\right)^{\frac{1}{n-m}} - 1.$$

For example, in Table 8.2, GDP in 1961 is 245.2 billion 1997 dollars, or $Y_{1961} = 245.2$. Further, $Y_{1971} = 405.9$ from Table 8.2. Then, we have $n - m = 10$, and the average annual growth rate in GDP from 1961 to 1971 in Table 8.3 is $\left(\frac{405.9}{245.2}\right)^{\frac{1}{10}} - 1 = 0.0517$ or 5.17%.

TABLE 8.3 Average Annual Growth Rates

Years	$\hat{Y}$	$\hat{K}$	$\hat{N}$	$\hat{z}$
1961-1971	5.17	4.67	2.92	1.67
1971-1981	3.99	4.41	3.41	0.27
1981-1991	2.24	3.23	1.30	0.36
1991-2001	3.21	2.48	1.61	1.32

East Asian Miracles and Total Factor Productivity Growth

If we examine the recent history of world growth, some countries stand out as growth miracles, and others are growth disasters. A careful study of the causes of growth miracles and growth disasters is instructive, since we would like to know how a growth miracle could be replicated or how a disaster could be avoided. Four countries that stand out as growth miracles are the so-called "East Asian Tigers," which are Hong Kong, Singapore, South Korea, and Taiwan. From the data in Table 8.4, between 1966 and 1991 real GDP grew at an average annual rate of 7.3% in Hong Kong, and between 1966 and 1990 the average annual growth rates of real GDP in Singapore, South Korea, and Taiwan were 8.7%, 10.3%, and 9.4%, respectively. Note in the table that annual average growth in real GDP in Canada over the period 1966–1990 was 3.5%. Thus, it seems extraordinary that such high growth rates could be sustained for about a quarter of a century in East Asia.

A prediction of the Solow growth model, which we will study later in this chapter, is that a country's standard of living can continue to increase over the long run only if there are sustained increases in total factor productivity. Thus, most economists (who are trained to view the world through the lens of the Solow growth model) would tend to think that the very high sustained rates of GDP growth experienced in East Asia had been driven primarily by very high total factor productivity growth.

Alwyn Young, in an article in the *Quarterly Journal of Economics*,[1] did a growth accounting exercise for each of Hong Kong, Singapore, South Korea, and Taiwan to evaluate whether it was high growth in total factor productivity that explained the high growth in real GDP in these countries. Surprisingly, Young found that total factor productivity growth in Hong Kong, Singapore, South Korea, and Taiwan was anything but miraculous. The high rates of GDP growth in these countries

TABLE 8.4   East Asian Growth Miracles (average annual growth rates)

	Output	Capital	Labour	Total Factor Productivity
Hong Kong (1966–91)	7.3%	7.7%	2.6%	2.3%
Singapore (1966–90)	8.7%	10.8%	4.5%	0.2%
South Korea (1966–90)*	10.3%	12.9%	5.4%	1.7%
Taiwan (1966–90)*	9.4%	11.8%	4.6%	2.6%
Canada (1966–90)	3.5%	4.0%	2.6%	0.5%

*Excludes agriculture.

Table 8.3 shows that average annual growth in real GDP was very high during 1961–1971, somewhat lower during 1971–1981, and lowest during 1981–1991. The very high growth during 1961–1971 came from all sources, as growth in capital was very high, growth in employment somewhat high, and growth in total factor productivity (as measured by growth in $\hat{z}$) high. Note that, in spite of the productivity slowdown during 1971–1981, output still grew at a reasonably high rate, due to high growth in

were mainly due to high growth rates in factor inputs.

From Table 8.4, the average growth rates in capital were extremely high in these East Asian countries, ranging from 7.7% per year in Hong Kong to 12.9% per year in South Korea. These growth rates compare with an average growth rate in capital in Canada of 4.0% over the period 1966–1990. High rates of growth in the capital stocks of the East Asian countries were caused by high rates of investment. Also, average rates of growth in the labour force range from 2.6% per year in Hong Kong to 5.4% per year in South Korea, as against 2.6% in Canada over the period 1966–1990. The large increases in the labour force in East Asia were driven partly by population growth, and partly by increases in labour force participation, particularly among women. For example, in Singapore the labour force participation rate for all workers increased from 27% to 51% from 1966 to 1990, and population grew at an average rate of 1.9% per year.

Young concluded that total factor productivity growth during this period in Hong Kong, Singapore, South Korea, and Taiwan was far short of miraculous, ranging from an average growth rate of 0.2% in Singapore to one of 2.6% in Taiwan. In Canada over the period 1966–1990, total factor productivity grew at an average annual rate of 0.5%. While total factor productivity growth exceeded that in Canada for three of these four countries, the difference is not as impressive as the difference in GDP growth rates. Therefore, while GDP growth in these four East Asian countries was extremely impressive, this high growth was mainly the result of unusually high growth rates in capital and labour.

There are two important implications of Young's analysis. The first is that the high growth in East Asia from the mid-1960s to the early 1990s is probably not sustainable over a longer period. There is a limit to how much labour force participation rates can grow, and thus contribute to growth in the labour force; namely, once the labour force participation rate reaches 100%, it cannot increase further. Also, consumers in these countries may not want to continue to forgo large quantities of current consumption to support the high rates of investment required to make the capital stock grow quickly. Second, Young's analysis makes it clear that the East Asian experience would be extremely difficult to replicate in Canada. The labour force participation rate exceeds 66% in Canada, which is much higher than in East Asia, and so there is little scope in Canada for rapid growth in the labour force due to increased labour force participation. To mimic the East Asian experience would require that a very large fraction of Canadian GDP be devoted to investment, and this is not consistent with recent history. Note that growth in the Canadian capital stock averaged 4.0% per year over 1966–1990 and has slowed since then, while average growth in capital stocks ranged from 7.7% in Hong Kong to 12.9% in South Korea during the period of East Asian miracle growth.

---

[1]A. Young, 1995, "The Tyranny of Numbers: Confronting the Statistical Realities of the East Asian Growth Experience," *Quarterly Journal of Economics* 110, 641–680.

factors of production. During the 1970s, capital was accumulated at a high rate. Further, employment growth was unusually high, in part because of rapid increases in the female labour force participation rate. While growth in capital and employment declined during 1981–1991 and 1991–2001, there was a pickup in total factor productivity growth during 1991–2001. This increase in total factor productivity growth was the driving force behind the high growth rate in aggregate output during 1991–2001.

The Solow Model: Exogenous Growth

The Solow growth model is very simple, yet it makes sharp predictions concerning the sources of economic growth, what causes living standards to increase over time, what happens to the level and growth rate of aggregate income when the savings rate or the population growth rate rises, and what we should observe happening to relative living standards across countries over time. In constructing this model, we will begin with a description of the consumers who live in this environment and of the production technology. A key difference from the one-period and two-period models we examined in Chapters 5 to 7 is that we will treat dynamics much more seriously here. We will study how this economy evolves over time in a competitive equilibrium, and a good part of our analysis will concern the **steady state** of the model, which is the rest point or long-run equilibrium of the model.

CONSUMERS

The time horizon in the Solow growth model is infinite; that is, the economy continues forever. However, we will analyze the economy in terms of the "current" and the "future" period, where the current period is any arbitrary period in time, and the future period is the period following this current period. There is a growing population of consumers, and N denotes the population in the current period. As we will show below, N will also be the labour force, or the quantity of employment. The population grows over time, with

$$N' = (1 + n)N, \tag{8.7}$$

where N' is the population in the future period and $n > -1$. Here, n is the rate of growth in the population, which is assumed to be constant over time. Note that we are allowing for the possibility that $n < 0$, in which case the population would be shrinking over time. Each consumer, once born, lives forever. It is obviously not realistic to assume that consumers never die, but we might imagine that the individual economic units in this economy are households, each of which consists of linked generations of finite-lived individuals.

    In each period, a given consumer has one unit of time available, and we will assume that consumers do not value leisure, so that they supply their one unit of time as labour in each period. The fact that the number of units of time is one for each consumer in each period is just a normalization, and it will not matter for our analysis. In this model, the population is identical to the labour force, since we have assumed that all members of the population work. We will then refer to N as the number of workers or the labour force, and to n as the growth rate in the labour force.

    Consumers collectively will receive all current real output Y as income (through wage income and dividend income from firms), since there is no government sector and no taxes, and we assume that consumers consume a constant fraction of income in each period; that is,

$$C = (1 - s)Y, \tag{8.8}$$

where C is current consumption and s is the aggregate savings rate. In Chapter 6, we showed how a consumer's current demand for consumption goods depends on lifetime wealth and the real interest rate, and so it might seem odd that we impose a rule, as in (8.8), whereby consumers simply consume a constant fraction of current income. This rule for consumption simplifies the model, and it turns out that many of the fundamental insights of the Solow growth model do not change if consumers make optimal consumption–savings decisions reflecting the effects of lifetime wealth and interest rates on current consumption and savings.

THE REPRESENTATIVE FIRM

Output is produced by a representative firm, according to the production function

$$Y = zF(K, N), \tag{8.9}$$

where Y is current output, z is current total factor productivity, K is the current capital stock, and N is the current labour input. The production function F has all of the properties that we studied in Chapter 4. One of those properties is constant returns to scale, or

$$xY = zF(xK, xN) \tag{8.10}$$

for any $x > 0$. That is, increasing both factor inputs by a factor x increases output by the same factor x. Equation (8.10) also holds if $x = \frac{1}{N}$ so we can write

$$\frac{Y}{N} = zF\left(\frac{K}{N}, 1\right). \tag{8.11}$$

In Equation (8.11), $\frac{Y}{N}$ is output per worker, and $\frac{K}{N}$ is capital per worker, and so (8.11) tells us that if the production function has constant returns to scale, then output per worker [on the left-hand side of (8.11)] depends only on the quantity of capital per worker [on the right-hand side of (8.11)]. For simplicity, we can rewrite Equation (8.11) as

$$y = zf(k),$$

where y is output per worker, k is capital per worker, and $f(k)$ is the **per-worker production function**, which is defined by $f(k) \equiv F(k, 1)$. We will use lowercase letters in what follows to refer to per-worker quantities. The per-worker production function is graphed in Figure 8.3. A key property of the per-worker production function is that its slope is the marginal product of capital, MP_K. This is because adding one unit to k, the quantity of capital per worker, increases y, output per worker, by the marginal product of capital, since, $f(k) = F(k, 1)$. As the slope of the per-worker production function is MP_K, and since MP_K is diminishing with K, the per-worker production function in the figure is concave—that is, its slope decreases as k increases.

As in Chapter 7, where we introduced investment behaviour, the capital stock changes over time according to

$$K' = (1 - d)K + I, \tag{8.12}$$

where K' is the future capital stock, d is the depreciation rate, with $0 < d < 1$, K is the current capital stock, and I is investment.

FIGURE 8.3

**The Per-Worker
Production Function**

This function is the relationship between aggregate
output per worker and capital
per worker determined by the
constant-returns-to-scale
production function. The slope
of the per-worker production
function is the marginal
product of capital, MP_K.

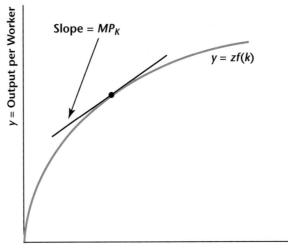

COMPETITIVE EQUILIBRIUM

Now that we have described the behaviour of consumers and firms in the Solow growth
model, we can put this behaviour together and determine how consistency is achieved
in a competitive equilibrium. In this economy, there are two markets in the current
period. In the first market, current consumption goods are traded for current labour;
in the second market, current consumption goods are traded for capital. That is, capital is the asset in this model, and consumers save by accumulating it. The labour market and the capital market must clear in each period. In the labour market, the quantity
of labour is always determined by the inelastic supply of labour, which is N. That is,
since the supply of labour is N no matter what the real wage, the real wage will adjust
in the current period so that the representative firm wishes to hire N workers. Letting
S denote the aggregate quantity of saving in the current period, the capital market will
be in equilibrium in the current period if $S = I$, that is, if what consumers wish to save
equals the quantity of investment. However, since $S = Y - C$ in this economy—that is,
national savings is aggregate income minus consumption as there is no government—
we can write the equilibrium condition as

$$Y = C + I, \tag{8.13}$$

or current output is equal to aggregate consumption plus aggregate investment. From
(8.12) we have that $I = K' - (1 - d)K$, and so using this and Equation (8.8) to substitute for C and I in Equation (8.13), we get

$$Y = (1 - s)Y + K' - (1 - d)K,$$

or, rearranging terms and simplifying,

$$K' = sY + (1 - d)K; \tag{8.14}$$

that is, the capital stock in the future period is the quantity of aggregate savings in the current period ($S = Y - C = sY$) plus the capital stock left over from the current period that has not depreciated. Then if we substitute for Y in Equation (8.14) using the production function from Equation (8.9), we get

$$K' = szF(K, N) + (1 - d)K. \tag{8.15}$$

Equation (8.15) states that the stock of capital in the future period is equal to the quantity of savings in the current period (identical to the quantity of investment) plus the quantity of current capital that remains in the future after depreciation.

Now, it will prove convenient to express Equation (8.15) in per-worker terms by dividing each term on the right-hand and left-hand sides of (8.15) by N, the number of workers, to get

$$\frac{K'}{N} = sz\frac{F(K, N)}{N} + (1 - d)\frac{K}{N},$$

and then multiplying the left-hand side by $1 = \frac{N'}{N'}$, which gives

$$\frac{K'}{N'}\frac{N'}{N} = sz\frac{F(K, N)}{N} + (1 - d)\frac{K}{N}; \tag{8.16}$$

we can rewrite this as

$$k'(1 + n) = szf(k) + (1 - d)k. \tag{8.17}$$

In Equation (8.17), $k' = \frac{K'}{N'}$ is the future quantity of capital per worker, $\frac{N'}{N} = 1 + n$ from Equation (8.7), and the first term on the right-hand side of (8.17) comes from the fact that $\frac{F(K, N)}{N} = F(\frac{K}{N}, 1)$ because the production function has constant returns to scale, and $F(\frac{K}{N}, 1) = f(k)$ by definition. We can then divide the right-hand and left-hand sides of Equation (8.17) by $1 + n$ to obtain

$$k' = \frac{szf(k)}{1 + n} + \frac{(1 - d)k}{1 + n}. \tag{8.18}$$

Equation (8.18) is a key equation that summarizes most of what we need to know about competitive equilibrium in the Solow growth model, and we will use it to derive the important implications of the model. This equation determines the future stock of capital per worker, k', on the left-hand side of the equation, as a function of the current stock of capital per worker, k, on the right-hand side.

In Figure 8.4 we graph the relationship given by (8.18). In the figure, the curve has a decreasing slope because of the decreasing slope of the per-worker production function $f(k)$ in Figure 8.3. In the figure, the 45° line is the line along which $k' = k$, and the point at which the 45° line intersects the curve given by (8.18) is called the steady state. Once the economy reaches the steady state, where current capital per worker $k = k^*$, then future capital per worker $k' = k^*$, and the economy will have k^* units of capital per worker forever after. If the current stock of capital per worker, k, is less than the steady state value, so $k < k^*$, then from the figure $k' > k$, and the capital stock per worker will increase from the current period to the future period. In this situation, current investment is sufficiently large, relative to depreciation and growth in the labour force, that the per-worker quantity of capital increases. However, if $k > k^*$, then we will

FIGURE 8.4

Determination of the Steady State Quantity of Capital per Worker

In the figure the coloured curve is the relationship between current capital per worker, k, and future capital per worker, k', determined in a competitive equilibrium in the Solow growth model. The steady state quantity of capital per worker is k*, given by the intersection of the 45° line (the black line) with the coloured curve.

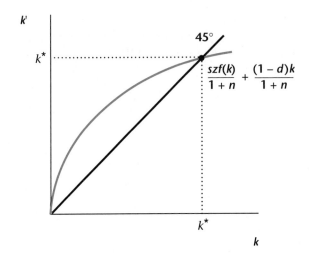

have $k' < k$, and the capital stock per worker will decrease from the current period to the future period. In this situation, investment is sufficiently small that it cannot keep up with depreciation and labour force growth, and the per-worker quantity of capital declines from the current period to the future period. Therefore, if the quantity of capital per worker is smaller than its steady state value, it will increase until it reaches the steady state; and if the quantity of capital per worker is larger than its steady state value, it will decrease until it reaches the steady state.

Since the Solow growth model predicts that the quantity of capital per worker converges to a constant, $k*$, in the long run, it also predicts that the quantity of output per worker converges to a constant, which is $y* = zf(k*)$ from the per-worker production function. The Solow model then tells us that, if the savings rate s, the labour force growth rate n, and the total factor productivity z are constant, then real income per worker cannot grow in the long run. Thus, if we take real GDP per worker as a measure of the standard of living, then there can be no long-run betterment in living standards under these circumstances. Why does this happen? The reason is that the marginal product of capital is diminishing. Output per worker can grow only as long as capital per worker continues to grow. However, the marginal return to investment, which is determined by the marginal product of capital, declines as the per-worker capital stock grows. That is, as the capital stock per worker grows, it takes more and more investment per worker in the current period to produce one unit of additional capital per worker for the future period. Therefore, as the economy grows, new investment will ultimately only just keep up with depreciation and the growth of the labour force, and growth in per-worker output will cease.

In the long run, when the economy converges to the steady state quantity of capital per worker, $k*$, all real aggregate quantities will grow at the rate n, which is the growth rate in the labour force. That is, the aggregate quantity of capital in the steady state will be $K = k*N$, and since $k*$ is a constant and N grows at the rate n, K must also grow at the rate n. Similarly, aggregate real output is $Y = y*N = zf(k*)N$, and so Y also grows at the rate n. Further, the quantity of investment is equal to savings, so that investment in the steady state is $I = sY = szf(k^*)N$, and since $szf(k^*)$ is a constant, I also grows at the rate n in the steady state. As well, aggregate consumption is $C = (1 - s) zf(k^*)N$, so that consumption also grows at the rate n in the steady state. Therefore, in the long run, if the savings rate, the labour force growth rate, and total factor productivity are constant, then growth rates in aggregate quantities are determined by the growth rate in the labour force. This is one sense in which the Solow growth model is an *exogenous* growth model. In the long run, the Solow model tells us that growth in key macroeconomic aggregates is determined by exogenous labour force growth when the savings rate, the labour force growth rate, and total factor productivity are constant.

ANALYSIS OF THE STEADY STATE

In this section, we put the Solow growth model to work. We will perform some experiments with the model, analyzing how the steady state or long-run equilibrium is affected by changes in the savings rate, the population growth rate, and total factor productivity. We will then show how the response of the model to these experiments is consistent with what we see in the data. Finally, we will examine the Solow growth model's predictions concerning relative living standards in different countries, and explore how well these predictions match the data.

To analyze the steady state, we start with Equation (8.18), which determines the future capital stock per worker, k', given the current capital stock per worker, k. In the steady state, we will have $k = k' = k^*$, and so substituting k^* in Equation (8.18) for k and k', we get

$$k^* = \frac{szf(k^*)}{1 + n} + \frac{(1 - d)k^*}{1 + n},$$

multiplying both sides of this equation by $1 + n$ and rearranging, we get

$$szf(k^*) = (n + d)k^*. \tag{8.19}$$

Equation (8.19) solves for the steady state capital stock per worker, k^*. It is this equation we wish to analyze to determine the effects of changes in the savings rate s, in the population growth rate n, and in total factor productivity z on the steady state quantity of capital per worker, k^*.

We graph the left-hand and right-hand sides of Equation (8.19) in Figure 8.5, where the intersection of the two curves determines the steady state quantity of capital per worker, which we denote by k_1^* in the figure. Note that the curve $szf(k^*)$ is the per-worker production function multiplied by the savings rate s, and so this function inherits the properties of the per-worker production function in Figure 8.3. The curve $(n + d)k^*$ in Figure 8.5 is a straight line with slope $n + d$.

The Steady State Effects of an Increase in the Savings Rate A key experiment to consider in the Solow growth model is a change in the savings rate s. We can interpret a change in s as occurring due to a change in the preferences of consumers. For example, if consumers care more about the future, they will save more, and s will increase. A change in s could also be brought about through government policy, for

FIGURE 8.5

**Determination of the
Steady State Quantity of
Capital per Worker**

The steady state quantity of
capital, k_1^* in the figure, is
determined by the intersection
of the curve $szf(k^*)$ with the
line $(n + d)k^*$.

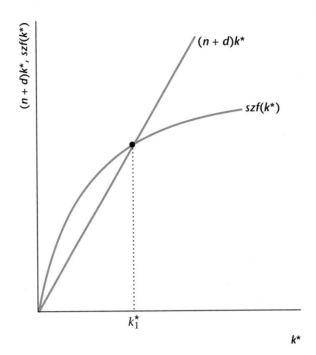

example, if the government were to subsidize savings (though, from Chapter 6, we know that this has opposing income and substitution effects on savings for lenders). With regard to government policy, we need to be careful about interpreting our results, since to be completely rigorous we should actually build a complete description of government behaviour into the model.

In Figure 8.6 we show the effect of an increase in the savings rate, from s_1 to s_2, on the steady state quantity of capital per worker. The increase in s shifts the curve $szf(k^*)$ up, and k^* increases from k_1^* to k_2^*. Therefore, in the new steady state, the quantity of capital per worker is higher, which implies that output per worker is also higher, given the per-worker production function $y = zf(k^*)$. Though the levels of capital per worker and output per worker are higher in the new steady state, the increase in the savings rate has no effect on the growth rates of aggregate variables. Before and after the increase in the savings rate, the aggregate capital stock K, aggregate output Y, aggregate investment I, and aggregate consumption C grow at the rate of growth in the labour force, n. This is perhaps surprising, as we might think that a country that invests and saves more, thus accumulating capital at a higher rate, would grow faster.

Though the growth rates of aggregate variables are unaffected by the increase in the savings rate in the steady state, it may take some time for the adjustment from one steady state to another to take place. In Figure 8.7 we show the path that the natural logarithm of output follows when there is an increase in the savings rate, with time measured along the horizontal axis. Before time T, aggregate output is growing at the constant rate n (recall that if the growth rate is constant, then the time path of the natural logarithm will be a straight line), and then the savings rate increases at time T. Aggregate

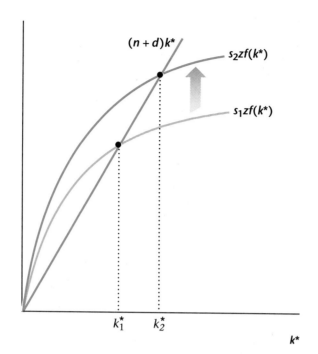

FIGURE 8.6

Effect of an Increase in the Savings Rate on the Steady State Quantity of Capital per Worker

An increase in the savings rate shifts the curve $szf(k*)$ up, resulting in an increase in the quantity of capital per worker from k_1^* to k_2^*.

output then adjusts to its higher growth path after period T, but in the transition to the new growth path, the rate of growth in Y will be higher than n. The temporarily high growth rate in transition results from a higher rate of capital accumulation when the savings rate increases, which translates into a higher growth rate in aggregate output. As capital is accumulated at a higher rate, however, the marginal product of capital diminishes, and growth slows down, ultimately converging to the steady state growth rate n.

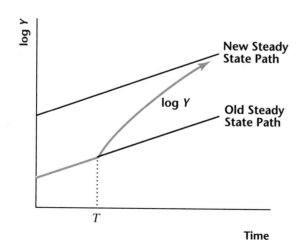

FIGURE 8.7

Effect of an Increase in the Savings Rate at Time T

The figure shows the natural logarithm of aggregate output. Before time T, the economy is in a steady state. At time T, the savings rate increases, and output then converges in the long run to a new higher steady state growth path.

Consumption per Worker and Golden Rule Capital Accumulation We know from Chapter 2 that GDP, or GDP per person, is often used as a measure of aggregate welfare. However, what consumers ultimately care about is their lifetime consumption. In this model, given our focus on steady states, an aggregate welfare measure we might want to consider is the steady state level of consumption per worker. In this subsection, we will show how to determine steady state consumption per worker from a diagram similar to Figure 8.6. Then, we will show that there is a given quantity of capital per worker that maximizes consumption per worker in the steady state. This implies that an increase in the savings rate could cause a *decrease* in steady state consumption per worker, even though an increase in the savings rate always increases output per worker.

Consumption per worker in the steady state is $c = (1 - s)zf(k^*)$, which is the difference between steady state income per worker, $y^* = zf(k^*)$, and steady state savings per worker, which is $szf(k^*)$. If we add the per-worker production function to Figure 8.6, as we have done in Figure 8.8, then the steady state quantity of capital per worker in the figure is k_1^*, and steady state consumption per worker is the distance AB, which is the difference between output per worker and savings per worker. Note that consumption per worker in the steady state is also the difference between output per worker, $y^* = zf(k^*)$, and $(n + d)k^*$.

Next, since consumption per worker in the steady state is

$$c^* = zf(k^*) - (n + d)k^*,$$

in Figure 8.9(a), we have in Figure 8.9(b) plotted c^* against the steady state quantity of capital per worker, k^*. Note that there is a quantity of capital per worker for which consumption per worker is maximized, which we denote by k_{gr}^* in the figure. If the

FIGURE 8.8

Steady State Consumption per Worker

Consumption per worker in the steady state is shown as the distance AB in the figure, given the steady state quantity of capital per worker, k_1^*.

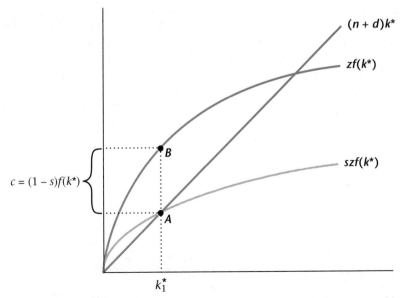

steady state quantity of capital is k_{gr}^*, then maximum consumption per worker is c^{**}. Here, k_{gr}^* is called the **golden rule quantity of capital per worker**. The golden rule has the property, from Figure 8.9(a), that the slope of the per-worker production function where $k^* = k_{gr}^*$ is equal to the slope of the function $(n + d)k^*$. That is, since the slope of the per-worker production function is the marginal product of capital, MP_K, at the golden rule steady state we have

$$MP_K = n + d.$$

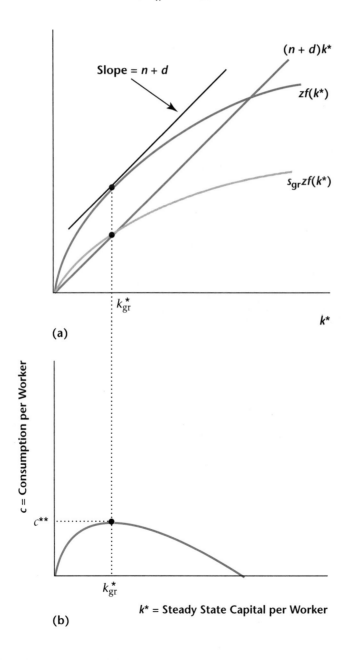

(a)

(b)

k^* = Steady State Capital per Worker

FIGURE 8.9

The Golden Rule Quantity of Capital per Worker

This quantity, which maximizes consumption per worker in the steady state, is k_{gr}^*, and the maximized quantity of consumption per worker is c^{**}. The golden rule savings rate s_{gr} achieves the golden rule quantity of capital per worker in a competitive equilibrium steady state.

Therefore, when capital is accumulated at a rate that maximizes consumption per worker in the steady state, the marginal product of capital will equal the population growth rate plus the depreciation rate.

How can the golden rule be achieved in the steady state? In Figure 8.9(a), we show that if the savings rate is s_{gr}, then the curve $s_{gr}zf(k^*)$ intersects the line $(n + d)k^*$ where $k^* = k^*_{gr}$. Thus, s_{gr} is the **golden rule savings rate**. If savings takes place at the golden rule savings rate, then in the steady state the current population consumes and saves the appropriate amount so that, in each succeeding period, the population can continue to consume this maximum amount per person. "Golden rule" is a biblical reference, the dictum that we should treat others as we ourselves would like to be treated.

Note from Figure 8.9(b) that if the steady state capital stock per worker is less than k^*_{gr}, then an increase in the savings rate s will increase the steady state capital stock per worker and increase consumption per worker. However, if $k^* > k^*_{gr}$, then an increase in the savings rate will increase k^* and cause a *decrease* in consumption per worker.

Suppose that we calculated the golden rule savings rate, and found that the actual savings rate was different from the golden rule rate. For example, suppose we found that the actual savings rate was lower than the golden rule savings rate. Would this necessarily imply that the government should implement a change in policy that would increase the savings rate? The answer is no, for two reasons. First, any increase in the savings rate would come at a cost in current consumption. It would take time to build up a higher stock of capital to support higher consumption per worker in the new steady state, and the current generation may be unwilling to bear this short-term cost. Second, in practice, savings behaviour is the result of optimizing decisions by individual consumers. In general, we should presume that private market outcomes achieve the correct tradeoff between current consumption and savings, unless we have good reason to believe that there exists some market failure that the government can efficiently correct.

The Steady State Effects of an Increase in Labour Force Growth The next experiment we will carry out with the Solow model is to ask what will happen in the long run if the labour force growth rate increases. As labour is a factor of production, it is clear that higher labour force growth will ultimately cause aggregate output to grow at a higher rate. But what is the effect on output per worker in the steady state? With aggregate output growing at a higher rate, there will be a larger and larger "income pie" to split up, but with more and more workers to share this pie. As we will show, the Solow growth model predicts that capital per worker and output per worker will decrease in the steady state when the labour force growth rate increases, but aggregate output will grow at a higher rate, which is the new rate of labour force growth.

In Figure 8.10 we show the steady state effects of an increase in the labour force growth rate, from n_1 to n_2. Initially, the quantity of capital per worker is k^*_1, determined by the intersection of the curves $szf(k^*)$ and $(n_1 + d)k^*$. When the population growth rate increases, this results in a decrease in the quantity of capital per worker to k^*_2 in the figure. Since capital per worker falls, output per worker also falls, from the per-worker production function. That is, output per worker falls from $zf(k^*_1)$ to $zf(k^*_2)$. The reason for this result is that, when the labour force grows at a higher rate, the capital stock must grow faster to keep up with this higher labour force growth, in order to hold

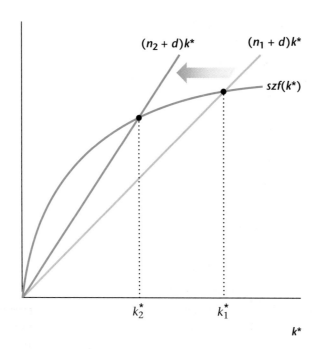

FIGURE 8.10
Steady State Effects of an Increase in the Labour Force Growth Rate n
An increase in the labour force growth rate from n_1 to n_2 causes a decrease in the steady state quantity of capital per worker.

the quantity of capital per worker constant in the long run. This implies that output per worker and capital per worker are ultimately lower in the steady state.

We have already determined that aggregate output, aggregate consumption, and aggregate investment grow at the labour force growth rate n in the steady state. Therefore, when the labour force growth rate increases, growth in all of these variables must also increase. This is an example that shows that higher growth in aggregate income need not be associated, in the long run, with higher income per worker.

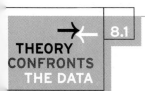

THEORY CONFRONTS THE DATA

8.1 The Solow Growth Model, Investment Rates, and Population Growth

Now that we know something about the predictions that the Solow growth model makes, we can evaluate the model by matching its predictions with the data. It has only been relatively recently that economists have had access to comprehensive national income accounts data for essentially all countries in the world. The Penn World Tables, which are the work of Alan Heston, Robert Summers, and Bettina Aten at the University of Pennsylvania,[1] allow for comparisons of GDP, among other macroeconomic variables, across countries. Making these comparisons is a complicated measurement exercise, as GDP in different countries at a given point in time is measured in different currencies, and simply making adjustments using foreign exchange rates will not give the right answers. A limitation of the Penn World Tables is that they only go back to 1950. A few decades of data may not tell us all we need to know, in terms of matching the long-run predictions of the Solow growth model: can the steady state be achieved within a few decades? However, as we will see, two predictions of the model appear to match the data in the Tables quite well.

Two key predictions of the Solow growth model are that, in the long run, an increase in the savings rate will cause an increase in the quantity of income per worker, and that, in the long run, an increase in the labour force growth rate will cause a decrease in the quantity of income per worker. We will examine in turn the fit of each of these predictions with the data.

The savings rate in the Solow growth model is the ratio of investment expenditures to GDP. The model thus predicts that, if we look at data from a set of countries in the world, we should see a positive correlation between GDP per worker and the ratio of investment to GDP. Figure 8.11 shows a scatter plot for countries in the Penn World Tables. In the scatter plot, we measure investment as a percentage of GDP (for 1995) on the horizontal axis, and on the vertical axis we measure real income per worker in 1995 as a percentage of real income per worker in Canada. Clearly, as the model predicts, countries with high (low) ratios of investment to GDP also have high (low) quantities of income per worker.

Next, the model predicts that, in data for a set of countries, we should observe the labour force growth rate to be negatively correlated with output per worker. Using population growth as a proxy for labour force growth, Figure 8.12 is a scatter plot for the countries in the Penn World Tables, with the average annual population growth rate from 1960 to 1995 on the horizontal axis and income per worker for 1995 as a percentage of that in Canada on the vertical axis. Here again, note the negative correlation in the data, just as the Solow model predicts. ⏮

---

[1]See A. Heston, R. Summers, and B. Aten, Penn World Table Version 6.1, Center for International Comparisons at the University of Pennsylvania (CICUP), October 18, 2002, available **pwt.econ.upenn.edu**, accessed July 11, 2003.

The Steady State Effects of an Increase in Total Factor Productivity If we take real income per worker to be a measure of the standard of living in a country, what we have shown thus far is that an increase in the savings rate or a decrease in the labour force growth rate can increase the standard of living in the long run. However, increases in the savings rate and reductions in the labour force growth rate cannot bring about an ever-increasing standard of living in a country. This is because the savings rate must always be below 1 (no country would have a savings rate equal to 1, as this would imply zero consumption), and the labour force growth rate cannot fall indefinitely. The Solow model predicts that a country's standard of living can continue to increase in the long run only if there are continuing increases in total factor productivity, as we will show here.

In Figure 8.13 we show the effect of increases in total factor productivity. First, an increase in total factor productivity from z_1 to z_2 results in an increase in capital per worker from k_1^* to k_2^*, and an increase in output per worker as a result. A further increase in total factor productivity to z_3 will cause an additional increase in capital per worker to k_3^*, and an additional increase in output per worker. These increases in capital per worker and output per worker can continue indefinitely, as long as the increases in total factor productivity continue.

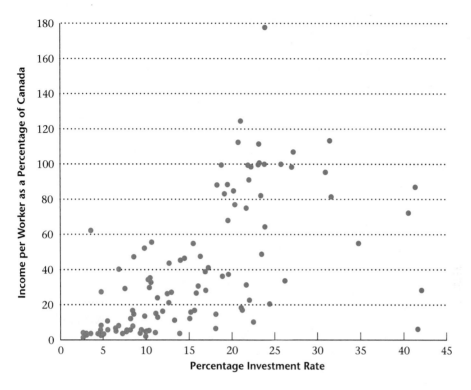

FIGURE 8.11

Income per Worker Versus the Investment Rate

The figure is a scatter plot of income per worker (as a percentage of Canadian income per worker) versus the investment rate in the countries of the world. As the Solow model predicts, income per worker and the investment rate are positively correlated.

Source: Alan Heston, Robert Summers, and Bettina Aten, Penn World Table Version 6.1, Center for International Comparisons at the University of Pennsylvania (CICUP), October 2002.

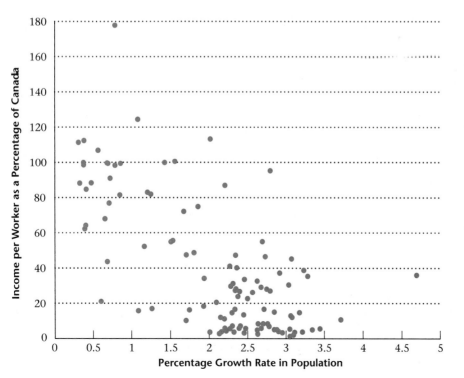

FIGURE 8.12

Income per Worker Versus Population Growth Rate

The figure is a scatter plot of income per worker (as a percentage of Canadian income per worker) versus the percentage growth rate in population in the countries of the world. As the Solow model predicts, the figure shows a negative correlation.

Source: Alan Heston, Robert Summers, and Bettina Aten, Penn World Table Version 6.1, Center for International Comparisons at the University of Pennsylvania (CICUP), October 2002.

FIGURE 8.13

Increases in Total Factor Productivity in the Solow Growth Model

Increases in total factor productivity from z_1 to z_2, and from z_2 to z_3, cause increases in the quantity of capital per worker from k_1^* to k_2^*, and from k_2^* to k_3^*. Thus, increases in total factor productivity lead to increases in output per worker.

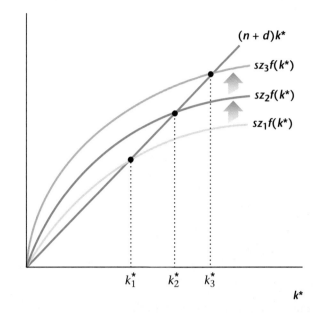

This is a key insight that comes from the Solow growth model. An increase in a country's propensity to save or a decrease in the labour force growth rate imply one-time increases in a country's standard of living, but there can be unbounded growth in the standard of living only if total factor productivity continues to grow. Thus, the source of continual long-run betterment in a country's standard of living can only be the process of devising better methods for putting factor inputs together to produce output, thus generating increases in total factor productivity.

Convergence There are remarkable differences in the levels of income per worker in the countries of the world. In 2000, income per worker in Mexico was 47% of what it was in Canada, in Egypt it was 26%, and in Burundi it was about 2%. The differences in the growth rates of income per worker are no less remarkable. Between 1960 and 2000, when income per worker grew at an average annual rate of 3.2% in Canada, income per worker grew at an average annual rate of 11.1% in Korea and 0.5% in Burundi. While these statistics tell us something about the wide variation in standards of living and in growth experience in the world, we would also like to know whether the distribution of income in the world is becoming more or less equitable. Is there a tendency for poor countries to catch up with rich countries with respect to standards of living?

The Solow growth model makes strong predictions about the ability of poor countries to catch up with rich ones with regard to living standards. For example, suppose two countries are identical with respect to total factor productivities (they share the same technology), labour force growth rates, and savings rates. However, the rich country initially has a higher level of capital per worker than the poor country. Given the per-worker production function, the rich country will also have a higher quantity of output per worker than will the poor country. However, the model predicts that both

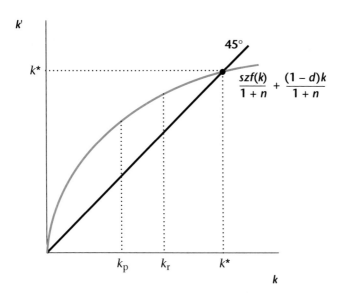

FIGURE 8.14

Rich and Poor Countries and the Steady State

Two otherwise identical countries have initial capital stocks per worker of k_p (the poor country) and k_r (the rich country). The two countries will converge in the long run steady state to the quantity k^* of capital per worker.

countries will converge to the same level of capital per worker and output per worker. Ultimately, the poor country will catch up to the rich country.

In Figure 8.14, we show the relationship between current capital per worker, k, and future capital per worker, k', from the Solow growth model. The poor country initially has quantity k_p of capital per worker, while the rich country initially has quantity k_r of capital per worker. Capital per worker and output per worker will grow in both countries, but in the long run both countries will have k^* units of capital per worker and the same quantity of output per worker. In Figure 8.15 we show the paths followed over time by real income per worker in the rich country and poor country. Note that the initial gap between the rich and poor countries narrows over time and disappears in the long run.

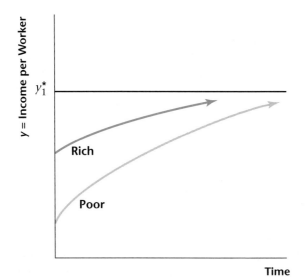

FIGURE 8.15

Convergence in Income per Worker Across Countries in the Solow Growth Model

Two otherwise identical countries, one with lower income per worker (the poor country) than the other (the rich country), converge in the long-run steady state to the same level of income per worker, y_1^*.

FIGURE 8.16

Convergence in Aggregate Output Across Countries in the Solow Growth Model
The initially rich country and the initially poor country converge in the long run to the same long-run growth path, where aggregate output grows at a constant rate.

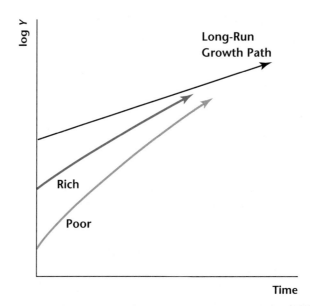

The rich country and poor countries in the example above will also have identical growth rates of aggregate output (equal to their identical labour force growth rates) in the long run. Recall that the Solow growth model predicts aggregate output will grow at the rate of labour force growth in the long run, and so if the rich and poor countries have the same labour force growth rate, their long-run growth rates in aggregate output will be identical. Supposing that the rich and poor countries also have the same initial labour force levels, the growth paths of aggregate output, as predicted by the model, will be the same in the long run. In Figure 8.16 above the black line denotes the long-run growth path of the natural logarithm of aggregate output in the rich and poor countries. As predicted by the Solow growth model, if aggregate output is initially lower in the poor country, its growth rate in aggregate output will be larger than that for the rich country, and this will cause the level of aggregate output in the poor country to catch up to the level in the rich country. In the long run, growth in aggregate output in the rich and poor countries converges to the same rate.

The Solow model is thus quite optimistic about the world distribution of income. It predicts that, left alone, the countries of the world will converge to similar standards of living, with some differences across countries explained by differences in savings rates and population growth rates.

8.2 Is Income per Worker Converging in the World?

The Penn World Tables give us a good deal of data, though perhaps not as much as we would like, to evaluate whether incomes per worker in the countries of the world appear to be converging. As we will see, there is evidence that convergence exists in the group of the richest countries of the world, but there is no evidence of convergence among the group of poorest

countries. Indeed, income per worker may be diverging if we look at the richest countries as a group relative to the poorest countries as a group.

To evaluate whether incomes per worker have been converging across the countries of the world, we can look at statistics from the Penn World Tables on the levels of
income per worker and growth rates of income per worker. The Solow model predicts
that countries with low (high) levels of income per worker should have high (low) rates
of growth of income per worker, so in the data we should observe a negative correlation between the level of income per worker and the growth rate of income per worker
across countries.

Figure 8.17 shows a scatter plot, where we graph the growth rate of income per
worker for all of the countries in the Tables, for the years 1960 to 1995, against the level
of income per worker for the same countries in 1960, as a percentage of income per
worker in Canada. Perhaps surprisingly, the figure shows no apparent correlation
between the two variables, and so there seems to be no evidence of convergence, at least
during 1960–1995, when we look at all the countries in the world.

Does the apparent lack of convergence in incomes per worker in the world imply
that the Solow model is wrong? The answer is no. Suppose we examine data for the
countries that were richest in 1960, which we take to include all countries with incomes
per worker 50% or more of that in Canada. The same data as in Figure 8.17 is plotted
for these rich countries only in Figure 8.18. Note that in this figure there is a clear negative correlation between the rate of growth in income per worker and the level of
income per worker. Therefore, convergence appears to be occurring among the rich

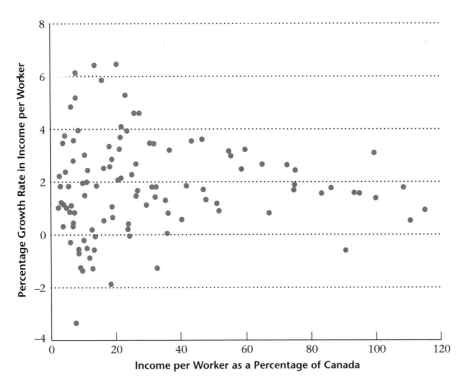

FIGURE 8.17

Growth Rate in Income per Worker vs. Income per Worker for Countries in the World

There appears to be no correlation in the scatter plot for 1960–1995 data, indicating that incomes per worker are not converging among the countries of the world.

Source: Alan Heston, Robert Summers, and Bettina Aten, Penn World Table Version 6.1, Center for International Comparisons at the University of Pennsylvania (CICUP), October 2002.

FIGURE 8.18

Convergence Among the Rich Countries

The negative correlation in the scatter plot indicates convergence in incomes per worker among the richest countries in the world.

Source: Alan Heston, Robert Summers, and Bettina Aten, Penn World Table Version 6.1, Center for International Comparisons at the University of Pennsylvania (CICUP), October 2002.

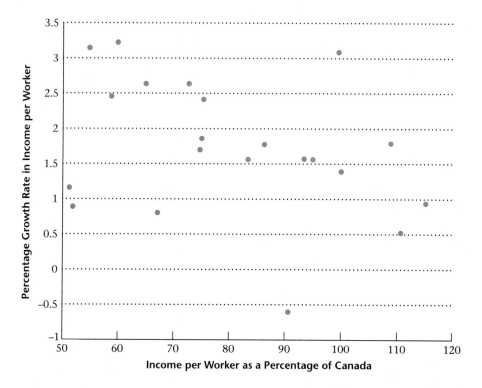

FIGURE 8.19

No Convergence Among the Poor Countries

There is no correlation evident in the scatter plot, indicating no convergence in incomes per worker among the poorest countries in the world.

Source: Alan Heston, Robert Summers, and Bettina Aten, Penn World Table Version 6.1, Center for International Comparisons at the University of Pennsylvania (CICUP), October 2002.

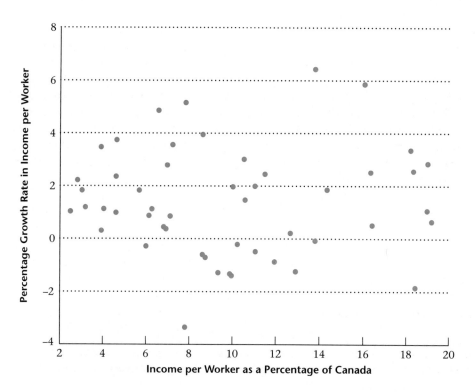

countries. However, if we plot data for the poorest countries, here taken to be those with 20% or less of income per worker in Canada in 1960, and plot the growth rate in income per worker against the level of income per worker in Figure 8.19, we observe no correlation. Therefore, convergence does not appear to be occurring among the poor countries.

The Solow growth model is thus consistent with the convergence that occurred among the rich countries of the world between 1960 and 1995, but it appears inconsistent with the lack of convergence among poor countries. While the most highly developed countries of the world in North America, Western Europe, and the Western Pacific region show evidence of convergence, there seems to be no tendency for the less developed countries of Africa to catch up to the richer countries. While the Solow growth model is simple, tells a compelling story about the sources of economic growth, and is consistent with several features of the data, it is clear that this model cannot explain everything. In the next section, we develop an alternative growth model that rectifies some of the defects in the Solow growth framework, while building on it as well.

Endogenous Growth: A Model of Human Capital Accumulation

Perhaps the primary deficiency of the Solow growth model is that it does not explain a key observation, which is growth itself. The Solow model relies on increases in total factor productivity coming from outside the model to generate long-run increases in per capita output, and this seems unsatisfactory, as we would like to understand the economic forces behind increases in total factor productivity. Total factor productivity growth involves research and development by firms, education, and training on the job, and all of these activities are responsive to the economic environment. We might like an economic growth model to answer the following questions: How does total factor productivity growth respond to the quantity of public funds spent on public education? (See Macroeconomics in Action 8.2 on p. 280.) How is total factor productivity growth affected by subsidies to research and development? Does it make sense to have the government intervene to promote economic growth? While the Solow growth model cannot answer these questions, a model of endogenous growth, where growth rates are explained by the model, potentially can.

The endogenous growth model we will work with here is a simplification of one developed by Robert Lucas.[6] Another important earlier contributor to research on endogenous growth was Paul Romer.[7] In our model, the representative consumer allocates his or her time between supplying labour to produce output, and accumulating **human capital**, where human capital is the accumulated stock of skills and education that a worker has at a point in time. The higher the human capital that workers have, the more they can produce, and the more new human capital they can produce. Thus, a higher level of human capital means that the economy can grow at a faster rate.

---

[6]R. Lucas, 1988, "On the Mechanics of Economic Development," *Journal of Monetary Economics* 22, July, 3–42.
[7]See P. Romer, 1986, "Increasing Returns and Long-Run Growth," *Journal of Political Economy* 94, 500–521.

If we think in terms of real-world economies, at any given time some of the working-age population will be employed, thus producing goods and services, some will be in school, and some will be unemployed or not in the labour force. There is an opportunity cost associated with people of working age who are in school, as these people could otherwise be producing goods and services. By acquiring schooling, however, people accumulate skills (human capital), and a more highly skilled labour force in the future permits more future output to be produced. Also, a more highly skilled population can better pass skills on to others, and so human capital accumulation is more efficient if the level of human capital is higher.

Human capital accumulation is therefore an investment, just like investment in plant and equipment, as there are associated current costs and future benefits. However, there are good reasons to think that physical investment is fundamentally different from human capital investment, in addition to the obvious difference that physical investment is embodied in machines and buildings and human capital investment is embodied in people. Recall that we have assumed in all our models that there are diminishing marginal returns to the accumulation of physical capital, since adding more plant and equipment to a fixed labour force should eventually yield lower increases in output at the margin. Human capital accumulation differs in that there appears to be no limit to human knowledge or to how productive individuals can become given increases in knowledge and skills. Paul Romer has argued that a key feature of knowledge is **nonrivalry**.[8] That is, a given person's acquisition of knowledge does not reduce the ability of someone else to acquire the same knowledge. Most goods are rivalrous; for example, my consumption of hotel services will limit the ability of others to benefit from hotel services, as only a fixed number of hotel rooms is available in a given city at a given time. Physical capital accumulation also involves rivalry, as the acquisition of plant and equipment by a firm uses up resources that could be used by other firms to acquire plant and equipment. Thus, diminishing marginal returns to human capital investment seem unnatural. It is the lack of diminishing returns to human capital investment that will lead to unbounded growth in the model we study here, even though there are no exogenous forces propelling economic growth.

THE REPRESENTATIVE CONSUMER

Our endogenous growth model has a representative consumer, who starts the current period with H^s units of human capital. In each period, the consumer has one unit of time (as in the Solow model, the fact that there is one unit of time is simply a normalization), which can be allocated between work and accumulating human capital. For simplicity, we assume the consumer does not use time for leisure. Let u denote the fraction of time devoted to working in each period, so that the number of **efficiency units of labour** devoted to work is uH^s. That is, the number of units of labour that the consumer effectively supplies is the number of units of time spent working multiplied by the consumer's quantity of human capital. The consumer's quantity of human capital is the measure of the productivity of the consumer's time when he or she is working. For

---

[8]See P. Romer, 1990, "Endogenous Technological Change," *Journal of Political Economy* 98, S71–S102.

each efficiency unit of labour supplied, the consumer receives the current real wage w. For simplicity, we assume the consumer cannot save, and so the consumer's budget constraint in the current period is

$$C = wuH^s. \tag{8.20}$$

Though the consumer cannot save, he or she can trade off current consumption for future consumption by accumulating human capital. Since u units of time are used for work, the remainder, $1 - u$, is used for human capital accumulation. The technology for accumulating human capital is given by

$$H^{s'} = b(1 - u)H^s; \tag{8.21}$$

that is, the stock of human capital in the future period, denoted by $H^{s'}$, varies in proportion to the number of current efficiency units of labour devoted to human capital accumulation, which is $(1 - u)H^s$. Here, b is a parameter that captures the efficiency of the human capital accumulation technology, with $b > 0$. Thus, (8.21) represents the idea that accumulating skills and education is easier, the more skills and education an individual (or society) has.

THE REPRESENTATIVE FIRM

The representative firm produces output using only efficiency units of labour, since for simplicity there is no physical capital in this model. The production function is given by

$$Y = duH^d, \tag{8.22}$$

where Y is current output, $d > 0$ is the marginal product of efficiency units of labour, and uH^d is the current input of efficiency units of labour into production. That is, uH^d is the demand for efficiency units of labour by the representative firm. The production function in Equation (8.22) has constant returns to scale, since there is only one input into production, efficiency units of labour, and increasing the quantity of efficiency units of labour increases output in the same proportion. For example, increasing efficiency units of labour uH^d by 1% will increase current output by 1%.

The representative firm hires the quantity of efficiency units of labour, uH^d, that maximizes current profits, where profits are

$$\pi = Y - wuH^d,$$

which is the quantity of output produced minus the wages paid to workers. Substituting for Y from Equation (8.22), we get

$$\pi = duH^d - wuH^d = (d - w)uH^d. \tag{8.23}$$

Now, if $d - w < 0$, then in Equation (8.23) profits are negative if the firm hires a positive quantity of efficiency units of labour, so that the firm will maximize profits by setting $uH^d = 0$. If $d - w > 0$, then profits are $d - w$ for each efficiency unit hired, so that the firm will want to hire an infinite quantity of workers to maximize profits. If $d = w$, then the firm's profits are zero for any quantity of workers hired, so that the firm will

FIGURE 8.20

**Determination of the
Equilibrium Real Wage in the
Endogenous Growth Model**
The figure shows the demand
and supply of efficiency units
of labour in the endogenous
growth model. The equilibrium
wage will be *d*, the constant
marginal product of efficiency
units of labour.

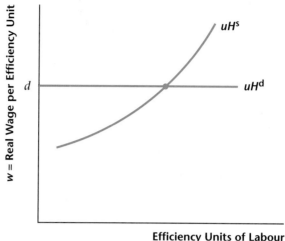

Efficiency Units of Labour

be indifferent about the quantity of efficiency units of labour hired. We conclude that the firm's demand curve for efficiency units of labour is infinitely elastic at $w = d$. In Figure 8.20 above we show the firm's demand curve for efficiency units of labour, which is just a special case of the demand curve being identical to the marginal product schedule for efficiency units of labour. Here, the marginal product of efficiency units of labour is a constant, d. What this implies is that no matter what the supply curve for efficiency units of labour, the intersection between demand and supply will always occur, as in Figure 8.20, at a real wage of $w = d$. That is, the equilibrium real wage per efficiency unit of labour will always be $w = d$. This then implies that the real wage per hour of work is $wH^d = dH^d$, and so the real wage as we would measure it empirically will change in proportion to the quantity of human capital of the representative consumer.

COMPETITIVE EQUILIBRIUM

Working out the competitive equilibrium here is quite straightforward. There is only one market each period, on which consumption goods are traded for efficiency units of labour. We know already that this market always clears at a real wage of $w = d$. Market clearing gives $uH^s = uH^d$ (the supply of efficiency units of labour is equal to the demand), and so $H^s = H^d = H$. Therefore, substituting in Equations (8.20) and (8.21) for w and H^s, we get

$$C = duH, \tag{8.24}$$

and

$$H' = b(1 - u)H. \tag{8.25}$$

Therefore, Equation (8.25) determines future human capital H' given current human capital H, and we show this relationship in Figure 8.21. The slope of the coloured line in the figure is $b(1 - u)$, and if $b(1 - u) > 1$, then we will have $H' > H$, so that future human capital is always greater than current human capital, and therefore human

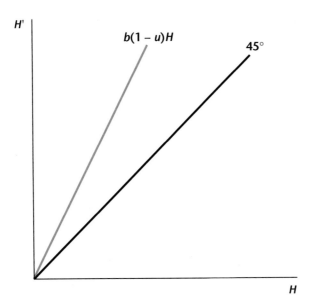

FIGURE 8.21

Human Capital Accumulation in the Endogenous Growth Model

The coloured line shows the quantity of future human capital H' as a function of current human capital H. As drawn $H' > H$ for any H, and so human capital will continue to increase forever.

capital will grow over time without bound. From Equation (8.25), the growth rate of human capital is

$$\frac{H'}{H} - 1 = b(1 - u) - 1, \tag{8.26}$$

which is a constant. What is important here is that the growth rate of human capital will increase if b increases or if u decreases. Recall that b determines the efficiency of the human capital accumulation technology, which could be interpreted as the efficiency of the educational sector. Thus, the model predicts that countries with more efficient education systems should experience higher rates of growth in human capital. If u decreases, more time is devoted to human capital accumulation and less to producing output in each period. As seems natural, this causes the growth rate in human capital to increase.

Now, Equation (8.24) will also hold in the future period, so that $C' = duH'$, where C' is future consumption, and therefore from Equation (8.24) we can determine the growth rate of consumption, which is

$$\frac{C'}{C} - 1 = \frac{buH'}{buH} - 1 = \frac{H'}{H} - 1 = b(1 - u) - 1,$$

that is, the growth rate of consumption is identical to the growth rate of human capital. Further, note from Equations (8.22) and (8.24), that $C = Y$, which we also know must hold in equilibrium, given the income–expenditure identity from Chapter 2 (our model has no investment, no government, and no net exports). Therefore, human capital, consumption, and output all grow at the same rate, $b(1 - u) - 1$, in equilibrium.

Note that this model economy does not grow because of any exogenous forces. There is no population growth (there is a single representative consumer), and the production technology does not change over time (b and d remain fixed). Thus, growth occurs due to endogenous forces, with the growth rate determined by b and u. The key element in the model that leads to unbounded growth is the fact that the production function, given by (8.22), does not exhibit decreasing returns to scale in human capital. That is, the production function has constant returns to scale in human capital, since output will increase in proportion to human capital, given u. For example, if human capital increases by 10%, then, holding u constant, output will increase by 10%. In the Solow growth model, growth is limited because of the decreasing marginal product of physical capital, but here the marginal product of human capital does not decrease as the quantity of human capital used in production increases. The marginal product of human capital does not fall as human capital increases, because knowledge and skills are nonrivalrous; additional education and skills do not reduce the extra output that can be achieved through the acquisition of more education and skills.

ECONOMIC POLICY AND GROWTH

Our endogenous growth model suggests that government policies can affect the growth rates of aggregate output and consumption. Since the common growth rate of human capital, consumption, and output depends on b and u, it is useful to think about how government policy might affect b and u. As b is the efficiency of the human capital accumulation technology, b could be affected by government policies that make the educational system more efficient. For example, this might be accomplished through the implementation of better incentives for performance in the school system, or possibly by changing the mix of public and private education. Exactly what policies the government would have to pursue to increase b we cannot say here without being much more specific in modelling the education system. However, it certainly seems feasible for governments to affect the efficiency of education, and politicians seem to believe this too.

Government policy could also change the rate of economic growth by changing u. For example, this could be done through taxes or subsidies to education. If the government subsidizes education, such a policy would make human capital accumulation more desirable relative to current production, and so u would decrease and the growth rate of output and consumption would increase.

Now, suppose that the government had the power to decrease u or to increase b, increasing the growth rate of consumption and output. Would this be a good idea or not? To answer this question, we would have to ask how the representative consumer's welfare would change as a result. Now, clearly a decrease in u will increase the growth rate of consumption, which is $b(1 - u) - 1$, but there is also a second effect, in that the level of consumption goes down. That is, current consumption is $C = buH$, and so in the very first period if u decreases, then C must also fall, since initial human capital H is given. Recall from Chapter 1 that if we graph the natural logarithm of a variable against time, then the slope of the graph is approximately the growth rate. Since consumption grows at the constant rate $b(1 - u) - 1$ in equilibrium, if we graph the natural log of consumption against time, this will be a straight line. The slope of the graph of consumption will increase as u decreases and the growth rate of consumption increases, and the vertical intercept of the graph will decrease as u decreases, as this reduces consumption in the very first period. There is therefore a tradeoff for the representative consumer when u decreases: consumption is sacrificed early on, but consumption will grow at a higher rate, so that consumption will ultimately be higher than it was with a higher level of u. Thus, the path for consumption shifts as in Figure 8.22. In the figure, consumption will be lower after the change in u until period T, when after-change consumption will be higher.

It is not clear that the consumer would prefer the new consumption path with the higher growth rate of consumption, even though consumption will be higher in the long run. There is a cost to higher growth: consumption in the near future must be forgone. Which consumption path the consumer prefers will depend on how patient he or she is. Preferences could be such that the consumer is very impatient, in which case he or she would tend to prefer the initial consumption path with a low growth rate of consumption. Alternatively, the consumer might be very patient, tending to prefer the new consumption path with a high growth rate of consumption. The conclusion is that, even if the government could engineer a higher rate of growth by causing u to fall— say through education subsidies—this may not be desirable because of the near-term costs involved.

We could do a similar analysis for the case in which the government causes the growth rate of consumption to increase because of an increase in b, the parameter governing the efficiency of human capital accumulation. In this case, the model is not explicit about the near-term costs of increasing the growth rate of consumption by increasing b. That is, current consumption is given by $C = duH$, and so consumption in the very first period does not depend on b. However, if the government were to increase b through education policy, for example, this would entail some real resource

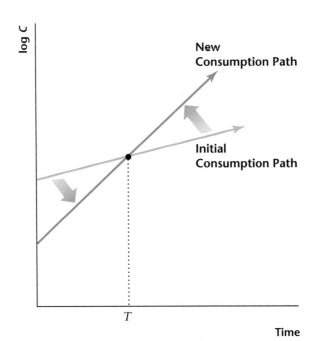

FIGURE 8.22

Effect of a Decrease in u on the Consumption Path in the Endogenous Growth Model
The figure shows the effect of a decrease in u, which increases the fraction of time spent accumulating human capital each period. The growth path for consumption (note that consumption is equal to income) pivots; thus, there is a short-run decrease in consumption, but consumption will be higher in the long run.

costs. Suppose that the government chose to make public education more efficient by increasing monitoring of teacher and student performance. Clearly, there would be a cost attached to this monitoring in terms of labour time. We might represent this cost in our model as a reduction in the level of consumption, as labour is diverted from goods production to government monitoring activities. Therefore, b would increase, which would increase the growth rate of consumption, but, as in the case in which we examined the effects of a decrease in u, there would be a decrease in consumption in the very first period. Thus, the relationship between the new consumption path after the increase in b and the initial consumption path would be just as in Figure 8.22. As in the case where u falls, it is not clear whether the representative consumer is better off when the growth rate of consumption is higher, because there are short-term costs in terms of lost consumption.

CONVERGENCE IN THE ENDOGENOUS GROWTH MODEL

In the Solow growth model, with exogenous growth, countries that are in all respects identical, except for their initial quantities of capital per worker, will in the long run have the same level and growth rate of income per worker. We showed in the previous section that this prediction of the Solow growth model is consistent with data on the evolution of incomes per worker in the richest countries of the world, but not with data for poorer countries. That is, there appears to be no tendency for the poorest countries to catch up with the richest, and the Solow growth model fails to predict this.

In the endogenous growth model we have constructed here, convergence does not occur. To see this, note first that in the endogenous growth model, consumption is equal to income, and there is only one consumer, so that per capita income is identical to aggregate income. From above, current consumption is given by $C = duH$, and consumption grows at a constant rate $b(1 - u) - 1$, so that the natural log of consumption graphed against time is a straight line, as we showed in Figure 8.22. Now, suppose we consider two countries that have the same technology and allocate labour in the same way between goods production and human capital accumulation. That is, b, d, and u are the same in the two countries. However, suppose also that these countries differ according to their initial human capital levels. The rich country has a high level of initial human capital, denoted H_r, and the poor country has a low level of human capital, denoted H_p. This implies that consumption in the rich country is initially $C = duH_r$, which is greater than initial consumption in the poor country, $C = duH_p$. Now, since b and u are identical in the two countries, $b(1 - u) - 1$, the growth rate of consumption, is also identical for the rich and poor countries. Therefore, the growth paths of consumption for the rich country and the poor country are as in Figure 8.23. That is, initial differences in income and consumption across rich and poor countries will persist forever, and there is no convergence.

How do we reconcile the predictions of the endogenous growth model concerning convergence with the facts? The model appears consistent with the fact that there are persistent differences in income per worker among poorer countries, and persistent differences in income per worker between the poorer countries of the world and the

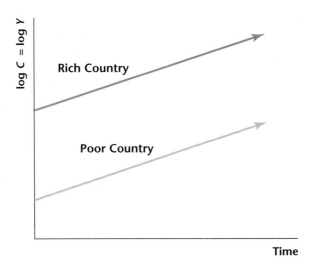

FIGURE 8.23

No Convergence in the Endogenous Growth Model
In the endogenous growth model, two identical countries that differ only in their initial incomes will never converge.

richer countries. However, the model appears inconsistent with the fact that incomes per worker seem to be converging among the richer nations of the world. Perhaps an explanation for this is that, in regions of the world where labour and capital are mobile, and where skills are more easily transferred, there are important **human capital externalities**, as discussed by Robert Lucas.[9] A human capital externality exists when contact with others with high levels of human capital increases our human capital or makes us more productive. Human capital externalities can explain the existence of cities and the specialized activities that take place there. Why, for example, would people specializing in financial activities want to bear the congestion and pollution of New York City unless there were significant positive externalities involved in working there? In highly developed regions of the world where there are greater opportunities for taking advantage of human capital externalities, through business contacts and education in other countries and regions, large differences in the levels of human capital across regions cannot persist. There will be convergence in income per worker. However, less developed countries interact to a low degree with highly developed countries, and people with high levels of human capital tend to move to the highly developed countries from the less developed countries (the "brain drain"). Thus, differences in human capital can persist across very rich and very poor countries.

We have now completed our study of savings, government deficits, investment, and economic growth in this Part, where we considered only the real side of the economy. In Part IV, we will move on to an examination of the interaction between real and monetary factors, and to business cycle analysis.

---

[9]R. Lucas, 1988, "On the Mechanics of Economic Development," *Journal of Monetary Economics* 22, July, 3–42.

Education and Growth

Our endogenous growth model has some interesting implications for the relationship between the growth rate of real GDP and education. In the model, $1 - u$ represents the fraction of time that is devoted to the acquisition of education and skills by the average worker. The higher is $1 - u$, the greater is the growth rate in real GDP, and the greater income per worker will be in the long run. In Figure 8.24 we display a scatter plot of data from Charles Jones' *Introduction to Economic Growth*, with the growth rate in output per worker on the vertical axis and the average number of years of schooling on the horizontal axis. Clearly, this data matches the prediction of the model: there is a positive correlation between the growth rate in income per worker and the average quantity of time spent in school by the average person. Similarly, Figure 8.25 shows a positive correlation between real income per worker (as a percentage of U.S. real income per worker) and educational attainment. The endogenous growth model shows how human capital investment is important for growth, and the data tell us that education (which represents the acquisition of human capital) is strongly positively related to growth in real income per worker and to the standard of living across countries.

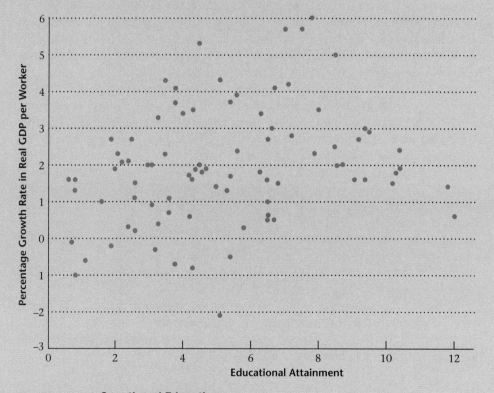

FIGURE 8.24 Growth and Education

This scatter plot shows a positive correlation between the percentage growth rate in real GDP per worker and average educational attainment among the countries of the world. This is consistent with the predictions of the endogenous growth model.

Source: C. Jones, 1998, *Introduction to Economic Growth*, W. W. Norton and Co., New York, Table B.2.

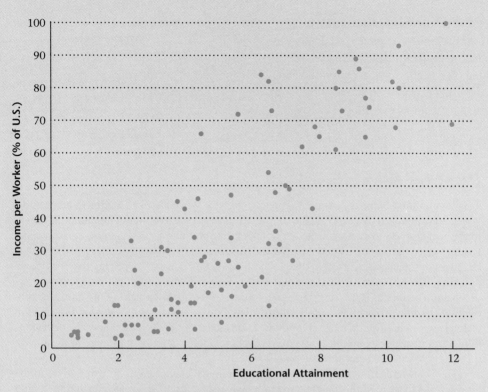

FIGURE 8.25 Income per Worker and Education

This scatter plot shows a positive correlation between income per worker and average educational attainment among the countries of the world. This is consistent with the predictions of the endogenous growth model.

Source: C. Jones, 1998, *Introduction to Economic Growth*, W. W. Norton and Co., New York, Table B.2

While education is important for growth, as the theory and the data tell us, there are many ways education can be delivered. There are key differences among countries, in the public versus private provision of education, and in how public education is financed. The government plays a key role in making decisions determining the public-versus-private mix of education and in financing decisions. These government decisions therefore can play an important role in determining economic growth and long-run living standards.

If we value an equitable distribution of income, public education has an advantage, in that equal access typically applies for elementary and secondary education. Further, public education can be

more efficient. From society's point of view, it is preferable if scarce higher education is allocated by ability, as is typical of public education, rather than by the ability to pay, as can happen with private education. Investment in education will be more productive if the highest-ability people are the ones who receive it. However, a disadvantage of public education is that taxpayers need to be convinced to support it. The benefits of education are indirect for most, and older people will not see any of the benefits, as the acquisition of an education takes decades. Thus, there is a tendency for public education to be underprovided.

Gerhard Glomm and B. Ravikumar[1] construct an endogenous growth model that is similar to ours in its basic structure, but more sophisticated in that it allows for the consideration of public and private education, and the financing of public education. They show that public education produces less income inequality in a country than private education. However, with private education there is a ten-

dency for per capita incomes to be higher in the long run.

[1]See G. Glomm and B. Ravikumar, 1992, "Public vs. Private Investment in Human Capital: Endogenous Growth and Income Inequality," *Journal of Political Economy* 100, 818–834.

Chapter Summary

This chapter introduced the study of economic growth. We first looked at growth accounting, which is an approach to measuring the contributions to growth in aggregate output from growth in the capital stock, in employment, and in total factor productivity. The latter is measured as a residual, given the production function. We call this residual the Solow residual. Measured Solow residuals for Canada using a Cobb-Douglas production function show a productivity slowdown occurring from the early 1970s to the mid-1980s. Suggested reasons for the productivity slowdown are (i) errors in measuring aggregate output; (ii) errors in measuring the inputs to production, particularly capital; (iii) learning costs due to the adoption of new information technology. Cyclically, deviations from trend in the Solow residual track closely the deviations from trend in aggregate output. This empirical observation is important for real business cycle theory, discussed in Chapter 11.

The Solow growth model introduced here is a model of exogenous growth in that, in the long-run steady state of this model, growth in aggregate output, aggregate consumption, and aggregate investment is explained by exogenous growth in the labour force and exogenous changes in total factor productivity. In the model, consumers save a constant fraction of income each period, while the representative firm produces output using a Cobb-Douglas production technology with inputs of labour and capital. In the Solow growth model, output per worker will converge in the long run to a steady state level, in the absence of a change in total factor productivity. The model predicts that output per worker increases in the long run when the savings rate increases, or when the population growth rate decreases. Both of these predictions are consistent with the data. An increase in the savings rate could cause consumption per worker to increase or decrease. The golden rule savings rate maximizes consumption per worker in the steady state. The Solow growth model also predicts that a country's standard of living, as measured by income per worker, cannot increase in the long run unless there is ever-increasing total factor productivity.

A key prediction of the Solow growth model is that poor countries will catch up with rich ones. In the model, countries that are identical except for initial levels of capital will converge to the same level of income per worker and the same growth rate of output. This prediction matches the data well for the rich countries of the world, but there does not appear to be any tendency for convergence among the poor countries of the world, or among all countries of the world. To show how this defect in the Solow growth model can be rectified, we studied an endogenous growth model with human capital accumulation. This model has the property that, even with no increases in total factor productivity and no population growth, there can be unlimited growth in aggregate output and aggregate consumption, fuelled by growth in the stock of human capital (i.e., skills and education). The rate of growth of output and consumption is determined by the efficiency of human capital accumulation and the allocation of labour time between goods production and human capital accumulation. If the government could introduce policies that altered the efficiency of human capital accumulation or the allocation of labour time, it could alter the rate of economic growth. Increasing the rate of economic growth may or may not improve economic welfare, because an increase in the growth rate of aggregate consumption is always associated with lower consumption in the short run. In the endogenous growth model, per capita incomes do not converge across rich and poor countries, as in the Solow growth model.

Key Terms

exogenous growth model: A model in which growth is not caused by forces determined by the model.

endogenous growth model: A model in which growth is caused by forces determined by the model.

growth accounting: uses the production function and data on aggregate output, the capital input, and the labour input, to measure the contribution of growth in capital, the labour force, and total factor productivity to growth in aggregate output.

Solow residual: The aggregate output that remains to be accounted for after measuring the contribution of capital and labour inputs to production; a measure of total factor productivity.

productivity slowdown: A decrease in the rate of measured total factor productivity growth beginning in Canada in the early 1970s and continuing to the mid-1980s.

steady state: A long-run equilibrium; in the Solow growth model the quantity of capital per worker is constant in the steady state.

per-worker production function: $y = zf(k)$, where y is output per worker, z is total factor productivity, k is the quantity of capital per worker, and f is a function. The per-worker production function describes the relationship between output per worker and capital per worker, assuming constant returns to scale in the production function.

golden rule quantity of capital per worker: The quantity of capital per worker that maximizes consumption per worker in the steady state.

golden rule savings rate: The savings rate that will imply consumption per worker is maximized in the steady state of a competitive equilibrium.

human capital: The accumulated stock of skills and education that a worker has at a point in time.

nonrivalry: A feature of knowledge, in that acquisition of knowledge does not reduce the ability of others to acquire it.

efficiency units of labour: The effective number of units of labour input, after adjusting for the quantity of human capital possessed by workers.

human capital externalities: Effects that exist if contact with an individual with higher human capital increases one's own human capital, or makes one more productive.

Questions for Review

1. What is the difference between exogenous growth and endogenous growth?

2. Why is a Cobb-Douglas production function useful for analyzing economic growth?

3. What is the parameter a in the production function in Equation (8.1)?

4. What does the Solow residual measure, and what are its empirical properties?

5. What are three possible causes for the productivity slowdown?

6. What are the three factors that account for growth in GDP?

7. Explain the growth accounting relationship between the growth rate of GDP and the factors that account for growth in GDP.

8. What was miraculous about growth in East Asian countries over the period 1966–1991? What was not miraculous about growth in these countries at this time?

9. What are the characteristics of a steady state in the Solow growth model?

10. In the Solow growth model, what are the steady state effects of an increase in the savings rate, of an increase in the population growth rate, and of an increase in total factor productivity?

11. What are the convergence predictions of the Solow model?

12. What empirical facts does the Solow growth model fit, and which does it not?

13. Why will income per worker not increase indefinitely in the Solow model in the absence of changes in total factor productivity?

14. What causes economic growth in the endogenous growth model?

15. Why is knowledge nonrivalrous?

16. What two factors affect the growth rate of income and consumption in the endogenous growth model?

17. If the government could increase the rate of growth of consumption, should it? Why or why not?

18. Is there convergence in the levels and rates of growth of per capita income in the endogenous growth model? Why or why not?

19. What is the empirical relationship between education and growth, and between education and national living standards?

Problems

1. Consider the following data:

Year	$\hat{Y}$ (billions of 1997 dollars)	$\hat{K}$ (billions of 1997 dollars)	$\hat{N}$ (millions)
1990	765.3	1989.5	13.08
1991	749.3	2039.6	12.85
1992	755.8	2084.3	12.76
1993	773.5	2124.1	12.86
1994	810.7	2171.9	13.11
1995	833.5	2214.5	13.36
1996	847.0	2259.9	13.46
1997	882.7	2323.4	13.77
1998	918.9	2385.9	14.14
1999	968.5	2455.3	14.53
2000	1012.3	2532.8	14.91
2001	1027.5	2605.9	15.08

a. Calculate the Solow residual for each year from 1990 to 2001.

b. Calculate percentage rates of growth in output, capital, employment, and total factor productivity for the years 1990 to 2001. In each year, what contributes the most to growth in aggregate output? What contributes the least? Are there any surprises here? If so, explain.

2. In the Solow growth model, suppose that the marginal product of capital increases for each quantity of the capital input, given the labour input.
   a. Show the effects of this on the aggregate production function.
   b. Using a diagram, determine the effects on the quantity of capital per worker, and on output per worker in the steady state.
   c. Explain your results.

3. Suppose that the depreciation rate increases. In the Solow growth model, determine the effects of this on the quantity of capital per worker, and on output per worker in the steady state. Explain the economic intuition behind your results.

4. Suppose that the economy is initially in a steady state, and that some of the nation's capital stock is destroyed because of a natural disaster or a war.
   a. Determine the long-run effects of this on the quantity of capital per worker, and on output per worker.
   b. In the short run, will aggregate output grow at a rate higher or lower than the growth rate of the labour force?
   c. After World War II, growth in real GDP in Germany and Japan was very high. How do your results in parts (a) and (b) shed light on this historical experience?

5. If total factor productivity decreases, determine using diagrams how this will affect the golden rule quantity of capital per worker, and the golden rule savings rate. Explain your results.

6. Determine the effects of a decrease in the population growth rate on the golden rule quantity of capital per worker and on the golden rule savings rate. Explain your results.

7. Modify the Solow growth model by including government spending as follows. The government purchases G units of consumption goods in the current period, where $G = gN$, and g is a positive constant. The government finances its purchases through lump-sum taxes on consumers, where T denotes total taxes, and the government budget is balanced each period, so that $G = T$. Consumers consume a constant fraction of disposable income—that is, $C = (1 - s)(Y - T)$, where s is the savings rate, with $0 < s < 1$.
   a. Derive equations similar to (8.17), (8.18), and (8.19), and show in a diagram how the steady state quantity of capital per worker, k^*, is determined.
   b. Show that there can be two steady states, one with high k^*, and one with low k^*.
   c. Ignore the steady state with low k^* (it can be shown that this steady state is "unstable"). Determine the effects of an increase in g on capital per worker and on output per worker in the steady state. What are the effects on the growth rates of aggregate output, aggregate consumption, and aggregate investment? Explain your results.

8. Suppose that d, the marginal product of efficiency units of labour, increases in the endogenous growth model. What effects does this have on the rates of growth and the levels of human capital, consumption, and output? Explain your results.

9. Alter the Solow growth model so that the production technology is given by $Y = zK$, where Y is output, K is capital, and z is total factor productivity. Thus, output is produced only with capital.
   a. Show that it is possible for income per person to grow indefinitely.
   b. Also show that an increase in the savings rate will increase the growth rate in per capita income.

   c. From parts (a) and (b), what are the differences between this model and the basic Solow growth model? Account for these differences, and discuss.

10. Introduce government activity in the endogenous growth model as follows. In addition to working u units of time in producing goods, the representative consumer works v units of time for the government, and produces gvH goods for government use in the current period, where $g > 0$. The consumer now spends $1 - u - v$ units of time each period accumulating human capital.

   a. Suppose that v increases, with u decreasing by an equal amount. Determine the effects on the level and the rate of growth of consumption. Draw a diagram showing the initial path followed by the natural logarithm of consumption and the corresponding path after v increases.

   b. Suppose that v increases, with u held constant. Determine the effects on the level and the rate of growth of consumption. Draw a diagram showing the initial path followed by the natural logarithm of consumption and the corresponding path after v increases.

   c. Explain your results, and any differences between parts (a) and (b).

11. Suppose that the government makes a one-time investment in new public school buildings, which results in a one-time reduction in consumption. The new public school buildings increase the efficiency with which human capital is accumulated. Determine the effects of this on the paths of aggregate consumption and aggregate output over time. Is it clear that this investment in new schools is a good idea? Explain.

Working with the Data

1. The total private capital stock consists of residential capital, capital from building construction, capital from engineering construction, and machinery and equipment. Determine the growth rates of each of these components of the capital stock for 1961–1971, 1971–1981, 1981–1991, and 1991–2000. Which component of capital was the most important, and which was the least important, as a contributor to growth in the total capital stock in each period? Comment on your results.

2. For the periods 1961–1971, 1971–1981, 1981–1991, and 1991–2000, determine the growth rates in the total population, in the labour force, and in employment. What explains the differences among these three growth rates for each period?

3. Determine the quantity of capital per worker for the years 1961, 1971, 1981, 1991, and 2001, and calculate the growth rates of capital per worker for the periods 1961–1971, 1971–1981, 1981–1991, and 1991–2000. Relate these growth rates to the data on total factor productivity growth in Table 8.3.

Money and Business Cycles

In this part, our first task is to integrate monetary factors into the real intertemporal model that was developed in Chapter 7. The resulting model, a monetary intertemporal model, will be used in Chapter 9 to study the effects of changes in the quantity of money, the causes of inflation, and the real effects of long-run inflation. We will also examine the determinants of money demand, monetarism, and the implications of instability in money demand for monetary policy. In Chapters 10 and 11, we use the monetary intertemporal model to study the causes of business cycles, and the role of fiscal and monetary policy over the business cycle. Chapter 10 is devoted to the examination of a traditional Keynesian sticky wage model, which implies that the government should smooth business cycles over time. In Chapter 11, we examine three equilibrium models of the business cycle, the first two of which imply that the government can at best make matters worse by smoothing business cycles, whereas the third is a modern Keynesian model with Keynesian-type implications for the role of government. The alternative business cycle models we study will highlight the many possible causes of business cycles, and in Chapters 10 and 11 we will pay careful attention to the match between the predictions of business cycle models and the business cycle facts studied in Chapter 3.

A Monetary Intertemporal Model: The Neutrality of Money, Long-Run Inflation, and Money Demand

Money is important to the economy, for two reasons. First, the economy functions better with money than without it, because carrying out transactions by trading one kind of good for another is difficult, and because using credit in some transactions is costly or impossible. Second, changes in the quantity of money in existence matter for nominal quantities—for example, the price level and the inflation rate—and can also affect real economic activity. The quantity of money in circulation is governed in most countries by a central bank, and the primary monetary policy decisions of the central bank concern how to set the level and growth rate of the money supply.

In this chapter, we will construct a monetary intertemporal model, which builds on the real intertemporal model in Chapter 7. In the monetary intertemporal model, money is held because it is needed to buy some goods that cannot be purchased with credit. This model will serve as the basis for our study of business cycles in Chapters 10 and 11.

The first result we will show using the monetary intertemporal model is the **neutrality of money**, under which a one-time change in the money supply has no real consequences for the economy. Consumption, investment, output, employment, the real interest rate, and economic welfare remain unaffected. The neutrality of money is a good starting point for examining the role of money in the economy, but most macroeconomists agree that money is neutral only in the long run, and that for various reasons, changes in the money supply will have real effects on the economy in the short run. We will study these short-run nonneutralities of money in Chapters 10 and 11.

Next, we will consider the effects of monetary policy changes that bring about permanent increases in the money supply's growth rate. High money supply growth is at the root of most empirical experiences with high inflation, and our model will illustrate the link between inflation and money growth. We will show that money is not neutral when we consider changes in its growth rate. The model shows how inflation is costly, in terms of lost output, employment, and consumption, because of the distortion of intertemporal decisions. Given that inflation is costly, there must be some inflation rate, determined by the growth rate in the money supply, that yields optimal economic welfare, and the central bank should then try to target that rate. The model determines this optimal inflation rate, and the optimal monetary policy that achieves it is called the *Friedman rule*, after Milton Friedman.

Our model determines a **money demand function**, which is a relationship between the quantity of money that economic agents wish to hold and other macroeconomic variables. We then discuss some of the general empirical determinants of money demand, and factors that will cause the demand for money to shift over time. Shifts in the demand for money are a problem for monetary policy, particularly if monetary policy is formulated using monetarist doctrine. We show why monetarist-type monetary policy failed during the 1980s in Canada and other countries.

What Is Money?

A traditional view of money is that it has three important functions. Namely, money is a **medium of exchange**, it is a **store of value**, and it is a **unit of account**. Money is a medium of exchange in that it is accepted in exchange for goods for the sole reason that it can in turn be exchanged for other goods, not because it is wanted for consumption purposes. Money is a store of value, like other assets such as stocks, bonds, housing, and so on. It allows consumers to trade current goods for future goods. Finally, money is a unit of account since essentially all contracts are denominated in terms of money. For example, in Canada a typical labour contract is a promise to pay a specified number of Canadian dollars in exchange for a specified quantity of labour, and a typical loan contract is a promise to pay a specified number of Canadian dollars in the future in exchange for a specified quantity of Canadian dollars in the present. As well, Canadian firms keep their books in terms of Canadian dollars.

The distinguishing economic feature of money is its medium-of-exchange role. As mentioned above, there are other assets such as stocks, bonds, and housing that serve the store-of-value role served by money. However, there are difficulties in using these other assets in exchange. First, there is often imperfect information concerning the quality of assets. For example, it may be difficult to get the clerk in a convenience store to accept a stock certificate in exchange for a newspaper, as the clerk will likely not know the market value of the stock certificate, and it would be costly for him or her to sell the stock certificate. Second, some assets come in large denominations and are therefore difficult to use for small purchases. Even if the clerk in the convenience store knows the market value of a Treasury bill (a short-term debt instrument issued by the government), Treasury bills do not come in denominations of less than $1000, and so the clerk likely cannot make change for the purchase of a newspaper. Third, some assets take time to sell at their market value. For example, if I attempted to sell my house to the convenience store clerk, he or she would likely offer me much less for the house than I would receive if I searched the market for a buyer whose preferences best matched my house.

MEASURING THE MONEY SUPPLY

As we will discuss in more detail in Chapter 14, money has taken many forms historically. Money has circulated as commodity money (primarily silver and gold), circulating private bank notes (as was the case prior to 1935 in Canada), commodity-backed paper currency (e.g., under the gold standard), fiat money (e.g., Canadian currency in Canada), and transactions deposits at private financial institutions. In Canada today, money consists mainly of objects that take the latter two forms, fiat money and transactions deposits at financial institutions.

In modern developed economies, there are potentially many ways to measure the supply of money, depending on where we want to draw the line defining which assets satisfy the medium-of-exchange property and which do not. What is defined as money is somewhat arbitrary, and it is possible that we may want to use different definitions of money for different purposes. Table 9.1 shows measures of the standard **monetary aggregates** for March 2003, taken from the *Bank of Canada Weekly Financial Statistics*. A given monetary aggregate is simply the sum of a number of different assets for the Canadian economy.

TABLE 9.1 **Monetary Aggregates, March 2003 ($ millions)**	
M0	39 087
Gross M1	135 898
M2	566 061
M3	762 290
M1++	363 920
M2++	1 175 120

Source: Bank of Canada, 2003, *Bank of Canada Weekly Financial Statistics*, April 25.

The most narrowly defined monetary aggregate is M0, which is sometimes referred to as the **monetary base, outside money,** or **high-powered money**. The monetary base consists entirely of liabilities of the **Bank of Canada**, which is the central bank of Canada. The chief role of a central bank is to issue outside money. The liabilities making up M0 are Canadian currency outside the Bank of Canada, and the deposits of financial institutions with the Bank of Canada. The quantity of M0 is called outside money because it is the quantity of money *outside* of the financial system. Gross M1 is obtained by adding currency outside banks plus personal chequing accounts in chartered banks, plus current accounts in chartered banks, while M2 is gross M1 plus non-personal notice deposits and personal savings deposits in chartered banks. The quantity of M3 is obtained by adding M2 plus chartered bank non-personal term deposits plus foreign currency deposits of residents of Canada. Finally, there are two modified measures of M1 and M2 that account for transactions deposits and other deposits in financial institutions other than chartered banks, as well as for some kinds of deposits at chartered banks that could be used for transactions, but are not included in M1. The first is M1++, which is M1 plus chequable notice deposits at chartered banks, plus chequable deposits at trust and mortgage loan companies, credit unions, and caisses populaires, plus non-chequable notice deposits at chartered banks, trust and mortgage loan companies, credit unions, and caisses populaires. The second is M2++, obtained by adding M2 plus deposits at trust and mortgage loan companies, credit unions, and caisses populaires, plus life insurance company individual annuities, plus personal deposits at government-owned savings institutions, plus money market mutual funds, plus Canada savings bonds, plus non–money market mutual funds. These last two aggregates, M1++ and M2++, are ones the Bank of Canada focuses on primarily in formulating monetary policy, to the extent that it regards any monetary aggregates as being important in the policy-making process.

The monetary aggregates are important, as they can be useful indirect measures of aggregate economic activity that are available on a more timely basis than GDP. Further, there are key regularities in the relationship between monetary aggregates and other aggregate variables, which make them useful in economic forecasting and in policy analysis. Finally, the paths followed by monetary aggregates over time can be useful in evaluating the performance of the Bank of Canada.

A Monetary Intertemporal Model

Why do we use money in exchange? A useful analogy is that money is to economic exchange as oil is to an engine; money overcomes "frictions." Two important economic frictions that make money useful are the following. First, in modern economies, barter exchange—the exchange of goods for goods—is difficult. As Adam Smith recognized in his *Wealth of Nations*, specialization is key to the efficiency gains that come from economic development. Once economic agents become specialized in what they produce and what they consume, it becomes very time-consuming to trade what one has for what one wants through barter exchange. For example, if Sara specializes in giving economics lectures, and wants to buy car repairs, to make a barter exchange she must not only find someone willing to repair her car—a **single coincidence of wants**—but the car repair person must also want to receive a lecture in economics—a **double coincidence of wants**. Clearly, Sara may have to spend a great deal of time and energy searching for a trading partner! The double coincidence problem was first studied by William Stanley Jevons in the 19th century.[1] Money solves the double-coincidence problem since, if everyone accepts money in exchange, then would-be buyers need only satisfy a single-coincidence problem to buy a good, which is much easier. Sara can sell economics lectures for money, and then exchange this money for car repairs.

A second reason money is useful in exchange is that there are circumstances where credit transactions may be difficult or impossible to make. For example, it would be unlikely that a street vendor in Toronto would accept my personal IOU in exchange for a hot dog. Since the street vendor does not know me or my credit history, he or she cannot evaluate whether my IOU is good or not, and it would be costly for him or her to take legal action should I not be willing to honour my IOU. While modern credit card systems solve some of the information problems connected with the use of personal

---

[1]See S. Jevons, 1910, *Money and the Mechanism of Exchange*, 23rd ed., Kegan Paul, London.

credit in transactions, these systems are costly to operate, and there are sellers of goods who will not accept credit under any circumstances. Since money is easily recognizable, there are essentially no information problems associated with the use of money in exchange, other than the problems that arise from counterfeiting.

There is much heated debate concerning how monetary exchange should be represented in macroeconomic models. According to one view,[2] if we are to understand the role of money in the economy and how monetary policy works, we need to model money at a deep level. That is, we need to model the fundamental reasons money is held—the frictions that make money useful—in order to make progress. In Chapter 14, we will study a model that takes explicit account of the double-coincidence-of-wants problem in barter exchange discussed above, and show how this problem gives rise to a role for money. A problem with deep models of money is that they are sometimes difficult to work with, and such models are not typically useful for matching features of economic data. An alternative view is that, in many circumstances, it is sufficient in modelling money in a macroeconomic context to simply assume that money is used in all or some transactions, and proceed from there. This approach is relatively simple, and it yields a modelling framework more amenable to the problem of matching theory with data. It is this second, more practical approach that we take in this chapter. But the deep approach to modelling money has much merit, particularly in advanced monetary economics.

In the model we construct here, we will assume at the outset that there are some goods that can be purchased with credit cards, while other goods must be purchased with cash on hand. One focus of the model will be on how a consumer makes choices regarding the quantities of goods to buy with credit and with cash. In the macroeconomics literature, this type of model is called a **cash-in-advance model**, and it has been used extensively. The idea behind the cash-in-advance model originated with Robert Clower,[3] and Robert Lucas made important contributions to its development and applications.[4]

The details of the monetary intertemporal model will be used in this chapter to examine the long-run effects of inflation and optimal long-run monetary policy. For those who wish to skip the details of the monetary intertemporal model, however, sufficient background for Chapters 10 through 16 is contained in the next two subsections.

REAL AND NOMINAL INTEREST RATES AND THE FISHER RELATION

In the monetary intertemporal model that we construct, there are many periods, but our analysis will be mainly in terms of an arbitrary current period, the previous period

---

[2]See J. Kareken and N. Wallace, 1980, "Introduction," in J. Kareken and N. Wallace, eds., *Models of Monetary Economies*, Federal Reserve Bank of Minneapolis, Minneapolis, MN, pp. 1–12; and N. Wallace, 1998, "A Dictum for Monetary Theory," *Federal Reserve Bank of Minneapolis Quarterly Review*, Winter, 20–26.

[3]See R. Clower, 1967, "A Reconsideration of the Microfoundations of Monetary Theory," *Western Economic Journal* 6, 1–8.

[4]See R. Lucas, 1980, "Equilibrium in a Pure Currency Economy," in J. Kareken and N. Wallace, eds., *Models of Monetary Economies*, pp. 131–146, Federal Reserve Bank of Minneapolis, Minneapolis, MN; and R. Lucas and N. Stokey, 1987, "Money and Interest in a Cash-in-Advance Economy," *Econometrica* 55, 491–514.

(i.e., the period before the current period), and the following period, which we refer to as the future period. There are two assets, money and nominal bonds. For simplicity, there will not be any banks in the model (we consider banking in Chapter 14), and so the entire money stock will be assumed to consist of currency. We will use money as the numeraire here (recall that the *numeraire* is the object in which all prices are denominated in an economic model) with P denoting the current price level, or the current price of goods in terms of money. Similarly, P' denotes the price level in the future period. A **nominal bond** is an asset that sells for one unit of money (e.g., one dollar in Canada) in the current period and pays off $1 + R$ units of money in the future period. Therefore, R is the rate of return on a bond in units of money, or the **nominal interest rate**. Nominal bonds can be issued by the government, or by consumers, and all bonds bear the same nominal interest rate, as we are assuming that no one defaults on their debts.

As in Chapters 6 and 7, the real rate of interest, r, is the rate of interest in terms of goods. The real interest rate is the real rate of return that someone receives when holding a nominal bond from the current period to the future period. The real interest rate can be determined from the nominal interest rate, and the **inflation rate** i, which is defined by

$$i = \frac{P' - P}{P}.$$
(9.1)

That is, the inflation rate is the rate of increase in the price level from the current period to the future period. Then, the real interest rate is determined by the **Fisher relation**, named after Irving Fisher, which is

$$1 + r = \frac{1 + R}{1 + i}.$$
(9.2)

To derive the Fisher relation, recall that $1 + R$ is the return in terms of money in the future period from giving up one unit of money in the current period to buy a *nominal* bond. In real terms, someone acquiring a nominal bond will give up $\frac{1}{P}$ goods in the current period and receive a payoff of $\frac{1 + R}{P'}$ goods in the future period. Therefore, from (9.1), the gross rate of return on the nominal bond, in real terms, is

$$1 + r = \frac{\frac{(1 + R)}{P'}}{\frac{1}{P}} = \frac{1 + R}{\frac{P'}{P}} = \frac{1 + R}{1 + i},$$

which gives us the Fisher relation (9.2).

Given a positive nominal interest rate on nominal bonds—that is, $R > 0$—the rate of return on nominal bonds exceeds the rate of return on money. The nominal interest rate on money is zero, and the real interest rate on money can be determined just as we determined the real interest rate associated with the nominal bond above. That is, if r^m is the real rate of interest on money, then as in (9.2) we have

$$1 + r^m = \frac{1 + 0}{1 + i} = \frac{1}{1 + i},$$

and so if $R > 0$ then $r^m < r$, or the real interest rate on money is less than the real interest rate on the nominal bond. In our monetary intertemporal model, we will need to explain why people are willing to hold money if they can receive a higher rate of return on the alternative asset, nominal bonds, when the nominal interest rate is positive.

Now, the Fisher relation can be rewritten by multiplying each side of Equation (9.2) by $1 + i$ and rearranging to get

$$r = R - i - iR.$$

Then, if the nominal interest rate and the inflation rate are small, iR will be negligible; for example, if the inflation rate is 10% and the nominal interest rate is 8%, then $i = 0.1$, $R = 0.08$, and $iR = 0.008$. As a result, we can say that, for small inflation rates and interest rates,

$$r \cong R - i; \tag{9.3}$$

that is, the real interest rate is approximately equal to the nominal interest rate minus the inflation rate. For example, if the nominal interest rate is 5%, or 0.05, and the inflation rate is 3%, or 0.03, then the real interest rate is approximately 2%, or 0.02.

Empirically, there is a problem in measuring the real interest rate. Nominal interest rates on many different assets can be observed, but economic agents do not know the inflation rate that will be realized over the time they hold a particular asset. The correct inflation rate to use might be the one that an economic agent expects, but expectations cannot be observed. However, one approach to measuring the real rate of interest is to calculate it based on (9.3), using the realized inflation rate for i. In Figure 9.1 we show data on the nominal interest rate, measured as the interest rate on a 3-month federal government Treasury bill over the period 1962–2002, and the corresponding real rate, calculated as the nominal interest rate minus the inflation rate. Note that the measured real interest rate has varied considerably over time, and that it has sometimes been quite low, dipping below 0% several times over this sample period, particularly during the 1970s.

A PREVIEW OF MONEY DEMAND

For those who wish to skip the remainder of this chapter, and as a preview of some of our results for the monetary intertemporal model, we will explain here the determinants of money demand.

In the model, there will be a representative household, which holds money because there are some goods—cash goods—that must be purchased with money. Other goods—credit goods—can be bought on credit, in that the household has a credit card with which it buys credit goods, and the household always pays its credit card bill at the end of the period. If the household wishes to borrow between the current period and the future period, it does this by selling bonds, not by using its credit card.

At the end of the current period, the money that the representative household has on hand will be used in the future period to buy cash goods. Assuming no uncertainty, the household knows the price of cash goods in the future period and the quantity of cash goods it will buy then, so that it knows exactly how much money will be needed for cash goods purchases. Further, given that the nominal interest rate is positive—that is, $R > 0$—the household would not hold any more money than needed to buy cash

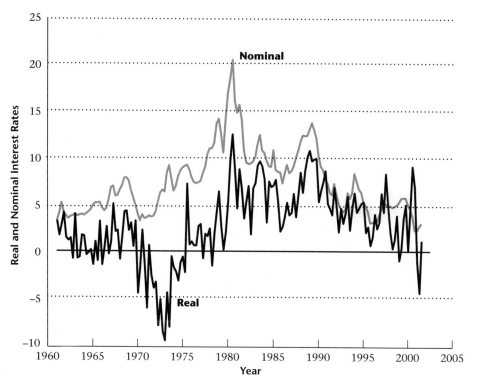

FIGURE 9.1

Real and Nominal Interest Rates, 1962–2002

The figure shows the nominal interest rate on 3-month Canadian Treasury bills, and the corresponding real interest rate, calculated as the nominal interest rate minus the rate of change in the implicit GDP deflator.

Source: Adapted from the Statistics Canada CANSIM database, Series v122531, v1997756.

goods in the future, since holding nominal bonds at a higher rate of return is preferable if money is not used in transactions. This implies that the determinants of the demand for money at the end of the current period are exactly the same as the determinants of the demand for cash goods in the future period.

Some of the determinants of the demand for future cash goods will be the same as the determinants of the demand for future consumption goods that were discussed in Chapter 6. In particular, the demand for future cash goods will increase when lifetime wealth increases, that is, when current income or future income increase. The demand for future cash goods will be affected by the real interest rate r, but we will assume that this effect is small and will ignore it (this will ultimately make no difference for our results). A different effect that we will obtain here is that the nominal interest rate R represents an opportunity cost for purchasing future cash goods. If cash goods are purchased in the future, this requires that the household hold cash between the current and future periods, meaning that the household must forgo holding its assets in the form of nominal bonds, which earn a higher rate of return. The difference in rates of return between nominal bonds and money is the nominal interest rate R. When R increases, the opportunity cost of holding money goes up, and the demand for future cash goods goes down.

Letting M^d denote the demand for money, in nominal terms, at the end of the current period, the current demand for money in real terms, $\frac{M^d}{P}$, will be determined by the factors determining the future demand for cash goods. To summarize, the demand for money in real terms, $\frac{M^d}{P}$, has the following determinants:

1. The current real demand for money increases when current real income Y increases (this increases lifetime wealth, increasing the demand for future cash goods).

2. The current real demand for money increases when future real income Y' increases (this increases lifetime wealth).

3. The current real demand for money decreases when the nominal interest rate R increases (the opportunity cost of holding money rises).

Therefore, the real demand for money, $\frac{M^d}{P}$ can be written as

$$\frac{M^d}{P} = L(Y, R), \tag{9.4}$$

where $L(Y, R)$ is a function that is increasing in current income Y and decreasing in the nominal interest rate R. We omit future income from the function, as none of the experiments we will carry out with the model will involve changes in future income. However, keep in mind that money demand will shift if future income changes.

Then, given the approximate Fisher relation (9.3), which we can take as an equality so that $R = r + i$, we can write the real demand for money as

$$\frac{M^d}{P} = L(Y, r + i), \tag{9.5}$$

so that real money demand increases with real aggregate income Y, and decreases with the real interest rate r and the inflation rate i anticipated between the current and future periods. We can also express money demand in nominal terms, by multiplying both sides of Equation (9.5) by P to get

$$M^d = PL(Y, r + i). \tag{9.6}$$

We graph the nominal money demand curve from Equation (9.6) in Figure 9.2. In the figure, nominal money demand is measured on the horizontal axis, and the price level is measured on the vertical axis. The nominal money demand curve is a straight line from the origin as, given Y, r, and i, money demand is proportional to P, with factor of proportionality $L(Y, r + i)$.

If there is an increase in current income Y, then the nominal money demand curve shifts to the right, as when current income increases from Y_1 to Y_2 in Figure 9.3. The nominal money demand curve would also shift to the right, just as in the figure, if the real interest rate r falls, or the inflation rate i decreases.

The nominal money demand curve, given by Equation (9.6) and shown in Figure 9.2, will be used in the remainder of this text, particularly in studying business cycles in Chapters 10 and 11.

THE REPRESENTATIVE HOUSEHOLD

In constructing the monetary intertemporal model, we start with the behaviour of the representative economic agents in the model, just as in Chapters 4, 5, and 7. In this model, however, instead of having a representative consumer, there will be a representative

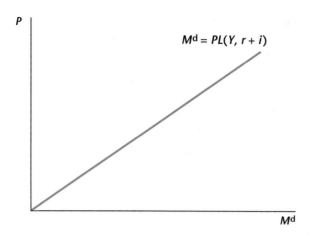

FIGURE 9.2

**The Nominal Money Demand
Curve in the Monetary
Intertemporal Model**
Current nominal money
demand is a straight line and
it will shift with changes in real
income Y, the real interest
rate r, or the inflation rate i.

household that has two members, a *worker* and a *shopper*. The representative household is assumed to have two people here, as we want the household to be doing more than one thing at a time. Indeed, this is realistic, since actual household members typically juggle many activities among themselves.

The household begins the current period with some assets held over from the previous period; namely, it has M^- units of money, and B^- bonds. (We will use "$-$" superscripts to refer to variables in the previous period throughout this chapter.) The household gets utility from consuming three objects during the current period, which are cash goods C^m, credit goods C^c, and leisure l. At the beginning of the period, the shopper and the worker split up to engage in their different activities. We will assume for now that cash goods and credit goods sell at the same price P, and we will show later why this is true in a competitive equilibrium. The shopper purchases cash goods with the money that the household had on hand at the beginning of the period, and the value

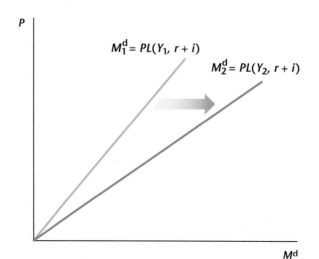

FIGURE 9.3

**The Effect of an Increase
in Current Real Income
on the Nominal Money
Demand Curve**
The current nominal money
demand curve shifts to the
right with an increase in
current real income Y.

of the cash goods that the household purchases cannot exceed the quantity of cash on hand. In other words, the household must abide by a **cash-in-advance constraint**,

$$PC^m = M^-, \qquad (9.7)$$

which states that the nominal quantity of cash goods purchases is equal to cash on hand at the beginning of the period. Note that it would never be the case that $PC^m < M^-$, since this would imply that the household had planned to hold more cash at the beginning of the period than needed to buy cash goods. But this would not be optimal, since a higher return on assets could be earned by holding interest-bearing nominal bonds. Money is held only as a medium of exchange, not as a pure store of value.

To buy credit goods, the shopper has a credit card. The household will receive a credit card bill at the end of the period, after labour earnings are received, and we will assume that the credit card bill is always paid in full. Interest is not charged on credit card balances paid within the period. In the model, cash goods are intended to represent the goods that we typically use money to buy, which are most often small-value items such as newspapers and lunch. Credit goods represent the large-ticket items, such as large-value consumer durables, usually purchased with credit instruments.

The worker has h units of time available during the current period, and he or she takes l units of leisure and supplies $h - l$ units of labour to the representative firm, receiving a real wage of w per unit of time worked, or a nominal wage of Pw. The worker receives payment for his or her labour services in money. After the shopper has purchased cash and credit goods and the worker has received the household's labour earnings, both return home. At this time, the household must pay a lump-sum tax, PT, in money, to the government, where T is the quantity of taxes in terms of goods. The household then receives the interest and principal on the bonds that mature, giving it $(1 + R^-)B^-$ (in units of money), and the household buys B^d nominal bonds maturing in the future period. Note that R^- is the nominal interest rate on bonds maturing in the current period. Also, the household receives nominal dividend income from the representative firm, $P\pi$, at the end of the period. Here, π is real dividend income. At the end of the period, the household then has M^d units of money to carry into the future period. Given all the transactions made by the household, its budget constraint for the current period is then

$$P(C^m + C^c) + PT + B^d + M^d = M^- + (1 + R^-)B^- + Pw(h - l) + P\pi. \qquad (9.8)$$

On the left-hand side of the budget constraint (9.8) are expenditures during the current period, on current goods, current taxes, bond holdings as of the end of the period, and money holdings at the end of the period. On the right-hand side are the money the household has at the beginning of the current period, the interest and principal on maturing bonds, labour earnings, and dividend income. Note that the budget constraint is written in nominal terms, that is, in units of money. As a guide to understanding the timing of transactions that take place within the period, see Figure 9.4.

In the current period, the household chooses current cash goods C^m, current credit goods C^c, leisure l, money balances M^d, and bonds B^d to make itself as well off as possible given the cash-in-advance constraint (9.7) and the budget constraint (9.8). Some of

299

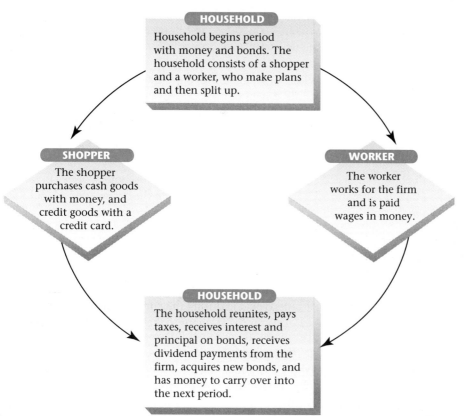

FIGURE 9.4

Timing Within the Period in the Monetary Intertemporal Model
The figure shows the timing of transactions within the current period for the representative household in the monetary intertemporal model.

these decisions will reflect the same factors that we studied in Chapters 4 and 6. For instance, for the household there is a work–leisure decision, as studied in Chapter 4. Also, as in Chapter 6, intertemporal choice is reflected in current consumption choices. What will differ here is that the money demand decision will be reflected in how the household trades off cash goods for credit goods, and cash goods for leisure, as we will see.

Just as in Chapter 4, the optimal tradeoff between current credit goods and current leisure by the household is achieved when

$$MRS_{l,C^c} = w; \quad (9.9)$$

that is, the marginal rate of substitution of leisure for credit goods is equal to the real wage when the household is optimizing. Recall from Chapters 4, 6, and 7 that all marginal conditions, reflecting optimization by a consumer or household, state that the marginal rate of substitution of one good for another is equal to the price of one good relative to the other. Also, as in Chapter 6, the household is optimizing when

$$MRS_{C^c,C^{c'}} = 1 + r; \quad (9.10)$$

that is, the marginal rate of substitution of current credit goods for future credit goods is equal to one plus the real interest rate at the optimum.

In determining the marginal conditions that reflect the optimal tradeoffs between current credit goods and current cash goods, and between leisure and current cash goods, it might seem that the relevant relative prices should be one for credit goods relative to cash goods (both goods sell at the same price P), and w for leisure relative to cash goods. However, things are not as straightforward as this, because the representative household cannot substitute directly in the current period between credit goods and cash goods, nor between leisure and cash goods.

First, consider substitution between current credit goods and current cash goods. If the household consumes less credit goods in the current period, and it wishes to consume more current cash goods, it must carry over more money from the previous period in order to do this. For each extra unit of money that the household acquires in the previous period, it can purchase $\frac{1}{P}$ more units of cash goods in the current period. But holding one more unit of money at the end of the previous period requires giving up one bond, which would have paid off $1 + R^-$ units of money at the end of the current period. This payoff could have been used to purchase $\frac{1 + R^-}{P}$ units of credit goods. Therefore, the effective relative price of current credit goods relative to current cash goods is

$$\frac{\frac{1}{P}}{\frac{1 + R^-}{P}} = \frac{1}{1 + R^-},$$

and so this relative price depends on the nominal interest rate between the previous period and the current period. The higher the nominal interest rate, the lower the relative price of credit goods in terms of cash goods. The intuition behind this is that, as the nominal interest rate rises, the opportunity cost of holding money to purchase cash goods increases. Given this relative price of credit goods and cash goods, one of the marginal conditions that the household will satisfy when it optimizes is

$$MRS_{C^c, C^m} = \frac{1}{1 + R^-}; \tag{9.11}$$

that is, the marginal rate of substitution of current credit goods for current cash goods is equal to the effective relative price of the two goods for the household.

Next, and similarly, if the household wishes to substitute between current leisure and current cash goods, then the household must acquire more money in the previous period. If the household obtains one more unit of money in the previous period, it can purchase $\frac{1}{P}$ units of current cash goods, and it must give up one nominal bond in the previous period, which would have paid off $1 + R^-$ units of money at the end of the current period. To hold everything constant, except M^-, B^-, C^m, and l, in the consumer's budget constraint (Equation 9.8), leisure must then decrease by the amount $1 + \frac{R^-}{wP}$. Therefore, the effective price of current leisure relative to current cash goods is

$$\frac{\frac{1}{P}}{\frac{1 + R^-}{wP}} = \frac{w}{1 + R^-}.$$

That is, the price of current leisure relative to current cash goods falls with an increase in the nominal interest rate as, again, an increase in R^- increases the opportunity cost of holding money from the previous period to the current period in order to buy current cash goods. Thus, at the optimum, the marginal condition for the household, representing the tradeoff between current leisure and current cash goods, is

$$MRS_{l,C^m} = \frac{w}{1 + R}. \qquad (9.12)$$

We will use the above marginal conditions when we set up a graphical apparatus of supply and demand curves to make use of the monetary intertemporal model. This graphical apparatus will build on the real intertemporal model in Chapter 7.

THE REPRESENTATIVE FIRM

Now that we have discussed the behaviour of the representative household, we can move to a description of the representative firm. Just as in the real intertemporal model, the firm supplies consumption goods, demands labour, and demands investment goods during the current period. The only difference in the monetary intertemporal model is that the firm needs to make a decision concerning the quantities of cash goods and credit goods to supply.

The representative firm produces real output in the current period according to the production function

$$Y = zF(K, N),$$

where, as before, Y is real output, z is total factor productivity, K is the capital stock, and N is the labour input. As in Chapter 7, the firm maximizes the real present discounted value of profits, and it hires labour in the current period until the marginal product of labour is equal to the real wage, or

$$MP_N = w. \qquad (9.13)$$

Also as in Chapter 7, the firm makes an investment decision in the current period, and it invests until the future net marginal product of capital is equal to the real interest rate, or

$$MP'_K - d = r, \qquad (9.14)$$

where MP'_K is the future marginal product of capital, and d is the rate at which capital depreciates.

Finally, the firm must choose how much of its output to sell as cash goods, and how much to sell as credit goods. We will assume that it is costless for the firm to convert output one-for-one into either cash goods or credit goods. Then, if P^c is the price of credit goods and P^m is the price of cash goods: if $P^c > P^m$, then the firm will want to sell all of its goods as credit goods, since this maximizes profits; if $P^c < P^m$, it will sell all goods as cash goods; and if $P^c = P^m$, then the firm is indifferent. The representative household always wants to buy some cash goods and some credit goods, no matter what the price, and so it must be the case in equilibrium that $P^c = P^m = P$, and the firm is indifferent about whether it produces cash goods or credit goods.

As in the real intertemporal model, the current profits of the firm, π, are turned over as dividend income to the representative household.

As with the representative household, we will postpone showing how the decisions of the firm fit into our supply–demand graphical apparatus, until after we discuss the government's behaviour.

GOVERNMENT

For our purposes, it will be convenient to assume that there is a single institution in our model called the "government," which is responsible for both fiscal and monetary policy. Therefore, the government entity in this model is essentially what we would get if we merged the federal government with the Bank of Canada, and placed them both under the control of Parliament. In Canada, the Bank of Canada, which is the monetary authority, has some independence from the Department of Finance, which is the federal fiscal authority controlled by the Canadian government. The arrangement between the central bank and the federal government varies considerably across countries. For example, the central bank in the United States, the Federal Reserve System, has somewhat more independence than the Bank of Canada. However, the central banks in some countries have little independence.

In the current period, the government purchases G consumption goods and pays the nominal interest and principal on the government debt outstanding from the last period, $(1 + R^-)B^-$, where B^- is the quantity of one-period nominal bonds issued by the government in the previous period, which come due in the current period, with each of these bonds bearing a nominal interest rate of R^-. Current government purchases and the interest and principal on government debt, which sum to total current government outlays, are financed through taxation, the issue of new bonds, and by printing money. Therefore, the government budget constraint in the current period is given by

$$PG + (1 + R^-)B^- = PT + B + M - M^-. \tag{9.15}$$

The government budget constraint (9.15) is expressed in nominal terms, with the left-hand side denoting total government outlays during the period, and the right-hand side denoting total government receipts. On the right-hand side, PT denotes nominal taxes, B denotes government bonds issued in the current period, which come due in the future period, and the final term, $M - M^-$, is the change in the nominal money supply, where M is the total quantity of money outstanding in the current period, and M^- is the previous period's money supply.

Adding money creation, $M - M^-$, to the government budget constraint is an important step here over the kinds of models we considered in Chapters 5, 6, and 7, where we did not take account of the monetary transactions that take place in the economy. We will now be able to consider the effects of monetary policy, and how monetary and fiscal policy interact.

COMPETITIVE EQUILIBRIUM

Now that we have a complete description of the behaviour of the representative household, the representative firm, and the government, we will proceed to construct a competitive equilibrium for the monetary intertemporal model. This model builds on the real intertemporal model of Chapter 7. The differences between the real intertemporal model and the monetary intertemporal model are that the demand for goods and labour supply will in general be affected by monetary factors in the monetary intertemporal model, and in this model we need to add another market, which is the market for money. In turn, we will consider supply and demand in the current labour market, the current goods market, and the current money market.

The Current Labour Market Figure 9.5 shows the current labour demand curve N^d and the current labour supply curve $N^s(r)$, with the intersection of these two curves determining the current market equilibrium real wage—w^* in the figure—and current employment—N^* in the figure. As in the real intertemporal model in Chapter 7, the labour demand curve N^d is the firm's marginal product of labour schedule, which follows from Equation (9.13) from the representative firm's profit maximization problem. Just as for the real intertemporal model, the labour demand curve will shift as follows:

- The labour demand curve shifts to the right if current total factor productivity z increases.
- The labour demand curve shifts to the right if there is an increase in the current capital stock K.

As in the real intertemporal model, the notation $N^s(r)$ reflects the fact that the labour supply curve shifts with the real interest rate because of the intertemporal substitution of leisure by the representative household. From the household's optimization problem, given the nature of cash transactions, we need to take account of the effects of monetary factors working through the marginal condition (9.12). That is, when the nominal interest rate in the previous period, R^-, rises, this reduces the price of current leisure relative to current cash goods and, assuming that the substitution effect dominates, this causes the household to substitute current leisure for current cash goods. From the approximate Fisher relation (9.3), treated here as an exact relation, we have $R^- = r^- + i^-$;

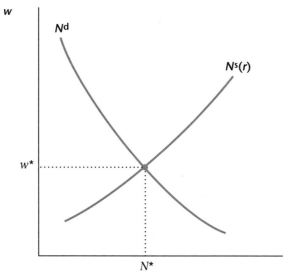

that is, the previous period's nominal interest rate is the previous period's real interest rate plus the inflation rate between the previous period and the current period. Given this, we can conclude that when either r^- or i^- increases, current leisure will increase and the current labour supply curve will shift to the left. To summarize:

- The current labour supply curve $N^s(r)$ shifts to the right when the current real interest rate r increases, as in the real intertemporal model of Chapter 7.

- The current labour supply curve shifts to the right if the present value of taxes increases, as in Chapter 7.

- The current labour supply curve shifts to the left when the previous period's real interest rate r^- increases, because of substitution between current leisure and current cash goods.

- The current labour supply curve shifts to the left when the inflation rate between the previous period and the current period, i^-, increases, because of substitution between current leisure and current cash goods.

This completes our discussion of the labour market in the monetary intertemporal model, and we will now study how the current goods market works.

The Current Goods Market In Figure 9.6 we show the output supply curve Y^s and the output demand curve Y^d, which jointly determine the equilibrium quantity of current output and the equilibrium real interest rate. In the figure, the equilibrium quantity of output is Y^* and the equilibrium real interest rate is r^*. Clearly, the output demand and output supply curves look much as they did in the real intertemporal model of Chapter 7, and they are constructed in the same way. However, as we will see, there are some different factors that will shift these curves.

FIGURE 9.6

The Current Goods Market in the Monetary Intertemporal Model

The figure shows the output demand curve and the output supply curve, which capture behaviour in the goods market in the monetary intertemporal model. The intersection of these curves determines equilibrium current output Y and the equilibrium real interest rate r.

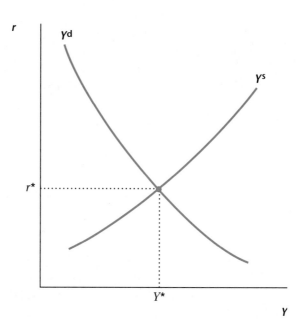

From Chapter 7, we know that anything that shifts the labour supply curve or the labour demand curve to the right (left) will also shift the output supply curve to the right (left). Therefore, from the analysis of the labour market in the previous subsection, we have the following:

- The output supply curve Y^s shifts to the right if current total factor productivity z increases.

- The output supply curve shifts to the right if the current capital stock K increases.

- The output supply curve shifts to the left if the previous period's real interest rate r^- increases.

- The output supply curve shifts to the left if i^-, the inflation rate between the previous period and the current period, increases.

All of the factors that caused shifts in the output demand curve Y^d in the real intertemporal model will have the same effects here, but we also need to account for the effects of monetary factors that can cause substitution among credit goods, cash goods, and leisure. First, from the representative household's optimization problem, the marginal condition (9.11) implies that a change in the previous period's nominal interest rate will cause substitution between current cash goods and current credit goods. However, this type of substitution will have no net effect on the total demand for goods (it is just substitution between different consumption goods), and it will therefore have no effect on the output demand curve. However, the substitution possibilities reflected in Equation (9.12) will be important in terms of shifts in the Y^d curve. In particular, an increase in the previous period's nominal interest rate R^- will cause the price of current leisure relative to current cash goods to fall, so that, assuming the substitution effect dominates the income effect, the household will choose to consume more current leisure and less current cash goods. This will result in a net reduction in the demand for current consumption goods, and it will shift the output demand curve Y^d to the left. Therefore, from the approximate Fisher relation (9.3), which implies that $R^- = r^- + i^-$, an increase in either the previous period's real interest rate r^- or the inflation rate between the previous period and the current period, i^-, will shift the Y^d curve to the left. We can therefore conclude the following concerning shifts in the output demand curve Y^d:

- The output demand curve Y^d shifts to the right if the present value of taxes decreases.

- The output demand curve shifts to the right if current government spending G increases.

- The output demand curve shifts to the right if future income Y' increases.

- The output demand curve shifts to the right if future total factor productivity z' increases.

- The output demand curve shifts to the right if there is a decrease in the current capital stock K.

- The output demand curve shifts to the left if there is an increase in the previous period's real interest rate r^-.

- The output demand curve shifts to the left if there is an increase in the inflation rate i^- between the previous period and the current period.

Of the seven factors listed above that can cause shifts in the output demand curve, the first five are the same as in the real intertemporal model, and are discussed in detail in Chapter 7, while the latter two are new to the monetary intertemporal model.

The Current Money Market Much of the structure of the labour and goods markets discussed above remains the same as in the real intertemporal model of Chapter 7, but the addition of a market for money will be a key difference here.

As discussed above, nominal money demand depends on current real income Y and the nominal interest rate R. That is, nominal money demand M^d is given by

$$M^d = PL(Y, R), \tag{9.16}$$

where $L(Y, R)$ is the demand for money in real terms, and this function is increasing in Y and decreasing in R. We assume that the government determines the nominal supply of money in existence. Recall that in practice it is the job of a country's central bank to determine the quantity of money in circulation, but to simplify here we treat the monetary authority and the fiscal authority as one institution we call the "government." Letting M^s denote the money supply, we have $M^s = M$, where M is an exogenous quantity. In equilibrium the nominal quantity of money supplied is equal to the nominal quantity of money demanded, or $M^s = M^d$, and so from Equation (9.16) the equilibrium condition for the money market is

$$M = PL(Y, R). \tag{9.17}$$

Then, given the approximate Fisher relation (9.3), taken as an equality, we have $R = r + i$, where r is the real interest rate and i is the inflation rate expected to hold from the current period to the future period, and so we can rewrite Equation (9.17) as

$$M = PL(Y, r + i). \tag{9.18}$$

In graphical terms, if we measure the price level P in Figure 9.7 on the vertical axis and the nominal quantity of money on the horizontal axis, the money demand curve is a straight line from the origin given Y, r, and i. The money supply curve is a vertical line at the quantity M, since the money supply is exogenous. The intersection of the nominal money demand and nominal money supply curves determines the price level P. In the figure, the equilibrium price level is P^*.

How is money demand determined? As discussed above, the representative household holds money from one period to the next to allow it to purchase cash goods. The household will hold no more and no less cash at the end of the current period than is required to purchase the planned quantity of future cash goods. Therefore, the demand for current money, in real terms, is identical to the demand for future cash goods. We can therefore conclude the following:

1. The current real demand for money increases with lifetime wealth, because an increase in lifetime wealth increases the demand for future cash goods. Therefore,

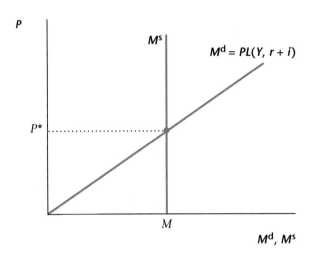

FIGURE 9.7

The Current Money Market in the Monetary Intertemporal Model
The figure shows the current nominal demand for money curve M^d and the money supply curve M^s. The intersection of these two curves determines the equilibrium price level, which is P^* in the figure.

current real money demand increases with current real income Y and future real income Y'.

2. Current real money demand will be affected by the real interest rate r, due to an intertemporal substitution effect on the future quantity of cash goods. For convenience, we will assume this effect is small and ignore it, but this will make no substantial difference for our analysis.

3. Current real money demand decreases with the current nominal interest rate R, since an increase in R causes substitution away from future cash goods and toward future credit goods. In the marginal condition (9.11), the price of current cash goods relative to current credit goods is determined by the previous period's nominal interest rate R^-, and so the price of future cash goods relative to future credit goods is determined by the current nominal interest rate R.

Therefore, given the approximate Fisher relation (9.3) taken as an equality, we can write the current real demand for money as

$$\frac{M^d}{P} = L(Y, r + i),$$

where the function $L(Y, r + i)$ does not take explicit account of the effect of future real income Y' on real money demand, as the experiments we will carry out using the complete monetary intertemporal model will typically not involve changes in Y'.

The Complete Monetary Intertemporal Model Now that we have described the workings of the current labour market, the current goods market, and the current money market, we can put these three elements of the model together to arrive at the complete monetary intertemporal model. In the next sections, we will use this model to address some fundamental questions associated with the role of money in the macroeconomy.

In Figure 9.8 we show how the endogenous variables in the monetary intertemporal model are determined. In Figure 9.8(b), we depict equilibrium in the current

The Complete Monetary Intertemporal Model

In the model, the equilibrium real interest rate r and equilibrium current aggregate output Y are determined in panel (b). Then, the real interest rate determines the position of the labour supply curve in panel (a), where the equilibrium real wage w and equilibrium employment N are determined. Finally, the equilibrium price level P is determined in the money market in panel (c), given the equilibrium real interest rate r and equilibrium output Y.

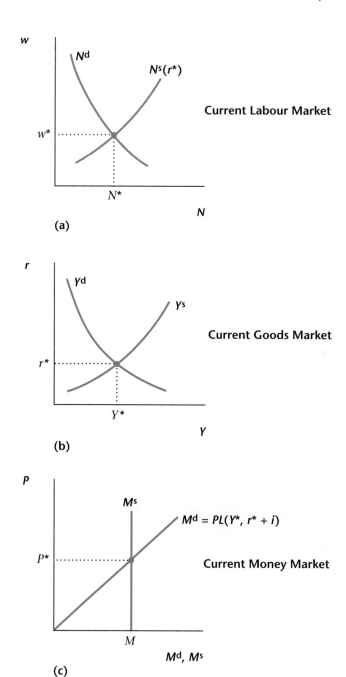

(a) Current Labour Market

(b) Current Goods Market

(c) Current Money Market

$M^d = PL(Y^*, r^* + i)$

goods market, where the output demand curve Y^d and the output supply curve Y^s jointly determine the equilibrium real interest rate r^* and the equilibrium quantity of aggregate output, Y^*. Then, in Figure 9.8(a), given the equilibrium real interest rate r^*, which determines the position of the labour supply curve $N^s(r^*)$, the labour demand curve N^d

and the labour supply curve $N^s(r^*)$ jointly determine the equilibrium real wage w^* and the equilibrium quantity of employment, N^*. Then, in Figure 9.8(c), the equilibrium quantity of output, Y^*, and the equilibrium real interest rate r^* determine the position of the money demand curve M^d. Then, the money demand curve and the money supply curve in Figure 9.8(c) determine the equilibrium price level P^*.

A LEVEL INCREASE IN THE MONEY SUPPLY AND MONETARY NEUTRALITY

A government, through its central bank, has the power to increase the money supply by several different means. Historically, the power of a government to print money has been important, in that this can finance transfers to the private sector, it can involve changing the quantity of interest-bearing assets held by the private sector, and it can finance government expenditures. In this section, we would like to determine the effects on current macroeconomic variables of a one-time increase in the money supply. As we will see, a change in the level of the money supply of this sort will be **neutral**, in that no real variables will change, but all nominal quantities will change in proportion to the change in the money supply. The *neutrality of money* is an important concept in monetary economics, and we want to understand the theory behind it, and what it means in practice.

   In the experiment we will perform in the model, we will suppose that the money supply is fixed at the quantity $M = M_1$ until the current period, as in Figure 9.9. Until the current period, everyone anticipates that the money supply will remain fixed at the quantity M_1 forever. During the current period, however, the money supply increases from M_1 to M_2 and then remains at that level forever. What could cause such an increase in the money supply? From the government budget constraint, Equation (9.15), the change in the money supply in the current period, $M - M^- = M_2 - M_1$, is positive, and

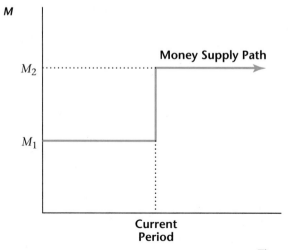

FIGURE 9.9

A Level Increase in the Money Supply in the Current Period

The figure shows a one-time increase in the money supply from M_1 to M_2.

so this positive change in the money supply in the current period needs to be offset by some other term in Equation (9.15). Since the nominal interest rate from the previous period, R^-, and the quantity of bonds issued by the government in the previous period, B^-, were determined last period based on the expectation that the quantity of money in circulation would be M_1 forever, only the other terms in Equation (9.15) could be affected. There are three possibilities:

1. The government could reduce current taxes T. Therefore, the money supply increase is reflected in a decrease in taxes on the household, which is the same as an increase in transfers. Milton Friedman referred to this method of increasing the money stock as a **helicopter drop**, since it is much like having a government helicopter fly over the countryside spewing money.

2. The government could reduce the quantity of bonds, B, that it issues during the current period. This is an **open market operation**, which in practice is carried out when the fiscal authority issues interest-bearing government debt, and then the monetary authority—the central bank—purchases some of this debt by issuing new money. An **open market purchase** is an exchange of money for interest-bearing debt by the monetary authority, and an **open market sale** is the sale of interest-bearing debt initially held by the monetary authority in exchange for money. In the case we examine here, where the money supply increases, there is an open market purchase. The day-to-day control of the money supply is accomplished in Canada mainly through open market operations by the Bank of Canada.

3. The government could temporarily increase the quantity of government spending, G, in the current period. Thus, the government would be printing money in order to finance government spending. When the government does this, it collects **seigniorage**. Seigniorage originally referred to the profit made by a *seigneur*, or ruler, from issuing coinage, but it has come to take on a broader meaning as the revenue earned by the government from issuing money. Seigniorage is also referred to as the revenue from the **inflation tax**, since the extra money that the government prints will in general increase prices. Historically, seigniorage has been an important revenue-generating device and has been a key source of revenue for various governments during times of war.

For our purposes here, it will prove most convenient for now to suppose that the money supply increase occurs through the first method above—a lump-sum transfer of money to the representative household. What happens in equilibrium when the money supply increases in the current period from M_1 to M_2? Here, since the level of the money supply does not matter for labour supply, labour demand, and the demand and supply of goods, the equilibrium determination of N, Y, r, and w in Figure 9.10 is unaffected by the current money supply M. That is, there is a **classical dichotomy**: The model solves for all the real variables (output, employment, the real interest rate, and the real wage) in the labour market and the goods market in Figure 9.10, and the price level is then determined, given real output, in the money market. Real activity is completely separated from nominal variables (the money supply, the price level). In

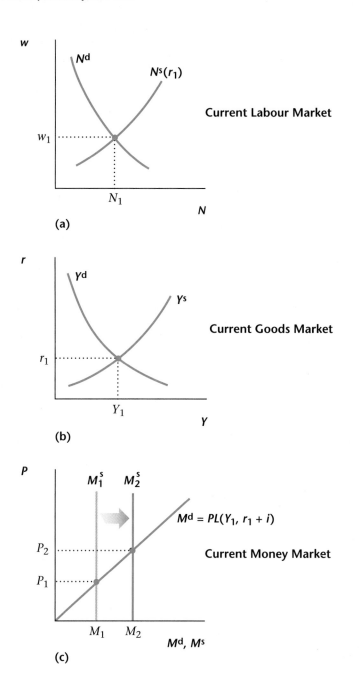

FIGURE 9.10
The Effects of a Level Increase in M—The Neutrality of Money
A level increase in the money supply in the monetary intertemporal model from M_1 to M_2 has no effects on any real variables, but the price level increases in proportion to the increase in the money supply. Money is neutral.

Figure 9.10(b), the real interest rate and current real output are given by r_1 and Y_1, respectively, and in Figure 9.10(a), the equilibrium real wage and level of employment are w_1 and N_1, respectively.

In the model, we want to investigate the effects of having a money supply of M_2 from the current period on, rather than a money supply of M_1. In Figure 9.10 there is no effect on real activity, since the labour market and goods market are unaffected by the level of the money supply. However, there will be an effect on the price level. In Figure 9.10(c), the money supply curve shifts to the right due to the increase in the money supply from M_1 to M_2. The money demand curve is unaffected, since Y does not change, r does not change, and the current inflation rate i will be unaffected because the money supply will not change after the current period. As a result, the price level increases in equilibrium from P_1 to P_2. Further, we can say something about how much the price level increases. Because $M = PL(Y, r + i)$ in equilibrium (money supply equals money demand) and because Y, r, and i are unaffected by the increase in M, P must increase in proportion to M, so that $\frac{M}{P} = L(Y, r + i)$ remains unchanged. That is, if M increases by 10%, then P increases by 10%, so that the real money supply $\frac{M}{P}$ is unaffected. Note that the level increase in the money supply causes a level increase in the price level. There is only a one-time increase in the inflation rate (the rate of change in the price level), from the previous period to the current period, and no long-run increase in the inflation rate.

In this model, then, money is neutral. Money neutrality is said to hold if a change in the level of the money supply results only in a proportionate increase in prices, with no effects on any real variables. Thus, a change in the level of the money supply does not matter here. This does not mean, however, that money does not matter. In this model, if there were no money, then no cash goods could be consumed, since money is necessary to acquire these goods. In the real world, even if money were neutral, we know that if we eliminated it, then people would have to use more cumbersome means to make transactions, such as barter. This would be much less efficient, and in general people would be worse off.

Is monetary neutrality a feature of the real world? In one sense, it almost obviously is. Suppose that the government could magically add a zero to the denominations of all currency. That is, suppose that overnight all $1 bills became $10 bills, $5 bills $50 bills, and so on. Suppose further that this change was announced several months in advance. It seems clear that, on the morning when everyone wakes up with their currency holdings increased tenfold, all sellers of goods would have anticipated this change and would have increased their prices by a factor of ten as well, and that there would be no real change in aggregate economic activity. Though this thought experiment helps us understand the logic behind monetary neutrality, real-world increases in the money supply do not occur in this way, and there is in fact much debate about the extent of money neutrality in the short run.

Later, when we study business cycles, we will explore the role of money in causing short-run fluctuations in real macroeconomic activity. Whether money is neutral in the short run can depend on how changes in the money supply are brought about, for example, through transfer payments, open market operations, or money-financed increases in government purchases. Also, it can matter whether a change in the money supply is widely anticipated. Key macroeconomic debates hinge on whether money is an important contributor to short-run fluctuations in aggregate economic activity, and just what mechanism causes money to be nonneutral in the short run. However, macroeconomists generally agree that money is neutral in the long run.

A GROWING MONEY SUPPLY AND THE EFFECTS
OF LONG-RUN INFLATION

Though money is neutral, in that an increase in the level of the money supply has no real effects in the monetary intertemporal model, changes in the *growth rate* of the money supply will not be neutral. It should not be surprising—since an increase in the level of the money supply causes an increase in the price level—that an increase in the rate of growth in the money supply will cause an increase in the rate of growth in the price level, that is, an increase in the inflation rate. Using our monetary intertemporal model, we will be able to show why money growth and inflation are costly, in terms of lost aggregate output and misallocation of resources. Further, we will determine an optimal prescription for monetary growth, often referred to as the Friedman rule for monetary policy, after Milton Friedman. The Friedman rule for optimal money growth is that money should grow at a rate that implies that the nominal interest rate will be zero. It turns out that the optimal money growth rate and the implied optimal inflation rate will be negative.

There are many factors that can cause changes in the price level, at least some of which we will explore later in this chapter and in Chapters 10 and 11. For example, any factor that causes a change in equilibrium aggregate output Y or in the equilibrium real interest rate r will shift the money demand curve and cause a change in the price level. However, sustained inflations, where the price level continues to increase over a long period of time, are usually the result of sustained growth in the money supply. In Figure 9.11 we plot the rate of inflation in Canada for the period 1968–2002 against the rate of growth in $M1++$. There is a positive relationship between the two, in that a positively sloped straight line would best fit the points in the figure, but the relationship is quite noisy, which reflects the fact that there are factors in addition to money growth affecting the rate of inflation in the short run. The causal link between money growth and inflation was emphasized by Milton Friedman and Anna Schwartz in *A Monetary History of the United States 1867–1960*.[5]

To understand the effects of long-run inflation, we will allow the money supply to grow forever at a constant rate in the monetary intertemporal model. We will suppose that the government permits the money supply to grow by making lump-sum transfers to the representative household each period, with the money supply growing according to

$$M' = (1 + x)M, \qquad (9.19)$$

where M' is the future money supply, M is the current money supply, and x is the growth rate of the money supply from the current period to the future period. For simplicity, we will suppose that the economy looks exactly the same in every period, in that total factor productivity, real government spending, and consumer preferences are identical in every period. The only exogenous variable that changes over time is the money

---

[5]M. Friedman and A. Schwartz, 1960, *A Monetary History of the United States: 1867–1960*, Princeton University Press, Princeton, NJ.

FIGURE 9.11

**Scatter Plot of the Inflation
Rate Versus the Growth Rate
in *M1++* for Canada,
1968–2002**

Clearly, these two variables
are positively correlated.

Source: Adapted from the Statistics
Canada CANSIM database, Series
v37152, v1997756.

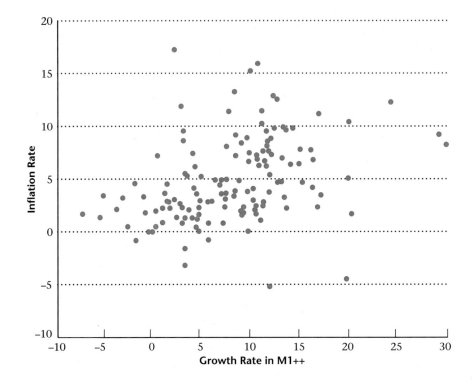

supply, which grows according to Equation (9.19). This implies that all of the endogenous variables in the model, except the price level, will remain the same for all time. That is, the real wage, employment, aggregate output, the real interest rate, and the inflation rate will be constant for all time. In the current period, money supply will be equal to money demand in equilibrium, and so from Equation (9.18), we have

$$M = PL(Y, r + i). \tag{9.20}$$

It must also be true that money supply is equal to money demand in the future period, so that

$$M' = P'L(Y', r' + i'), \tag{9.21}$$

where P' is the price level in the future period, Y' is future aggregate output, r' is the future real interest rate, and i' is the future inflation rate. Then, from Equations (9.20) and (9.21), we will have

$$\frac{M'}{M} = \frac{P'L(Y', r' + i')}{PL(Y, r + i)}. \tag{9.22}$$

But in equilibrium, aggregate output, the real interest rate, and the inflation rate will remain constant over time, which implies that $Y' = Y$, $r' = r$, and $i' = i$. This then gives $L(Y', r' + i') = L(Y, r + i)$, so that the real demand for money is the same in the future and current periods. Then, from (9.22), we get

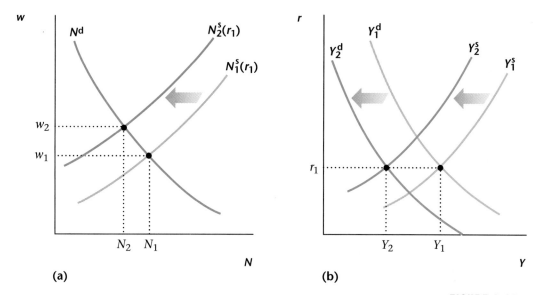

(a)   **(b)**

FIGURE 9.12
The Long-Run Effects of an Increase in the Money Growth Rate
An increase in the money growth rate increases the inflation rate, which shifts the labour supply curve to the left, the output supply curve to the left, and the output demand curve to the left. The real wage rises, employment falls, and output falls. The real interest rate may rise or fall, but for simplicity we show the case where it stays constant.

$$\frac{M'}{M} = \frac{P'}{P},$$

so that the growth rates of the money supply and the price level are the same in equilibrium. This implies, from Equation (9.19), that the inflation rate is given by

$$i = \frac{P'}{P} - 1 = \frac{M'}{M} - 1 = x,$$

so that the inflation rate is equal to the money growth rate. Note that the equality of the money growth rate and the inflation rate is special to this situation where real variables remain constant over time. From Equation (9.22), if the real demand for money changes over time, so that $L(Y', r' + i') \neq L(Y, r + i)$, the money growth rate will not be equal to the inflation rate. However, it will still be true that the inflation rate will increase as the money growth rate increases.

In Figure 9.12 we show the effects in the current period of an increase in the money growth rate from x_1 to x_2, which takes place for all periods, and is anticipated by everyone. The inflation rate in every period increases from x_1 to x_2, and so in particular the previous period's inflation rate rises by this amount. This causes substitution by the representative household from current cash goods to current leisure. Recall that when such substitution occurs, the labour supply curve shifts to the left in Figure 9.12(a), shifting the output supply curve to the left in Figure 9.12(b), and the output demand curve shifts to the left in Figure 9.12(b), as the demand for consumption goods falls. Now, in Figure 9.12(b), it is not clear whether the real interest rate will rise or fall. For simplicity, we show the case where the output demand and output supply effects on the real interest rate just cancel, so that the real interest rate does not change. This also implies that investment and the capital stock will be unaffected (assume that we are in a steady state where the capital stock is constant over time), which also greatly simplifies matters.

In Figure 9.12, in equilibrium output falls from Y_1 to Y_2, employment falls from N_1 to N_2, and the real wage rises from w_1 to w_2. In the figure the real interest rate remains constant, so that investment expenditures are unaffected, but consumption must fall, since from the income–expenditure identity, $Y = C + I + G$, and Y has fallen, I is the same, and G is the same. From the approximate Fisher relation, $R = r + i$, where R is the nominal interest rate. Therefore, since r is constant, and i increases from x_1 to x_2, the nominal interest rate increases by the amount of the money growth rate increase. Also, given equilibrium in the money market,

$$\frac{M}{P} = L(Y, r + i),\qquad\qquad(9.23)$$

real output Y has decreased, r is the same, and i has increased; therefore, real money demand on the right-hand side of Equation (9.23) has decreased, and so the current real money supply on the left-hand side of (9.23) must also decrease. Therefore, because real income falls, there is a lower demand for money to purchase future goods. As well, the higher inflation rate increases the nominal interest rate, which causes the representative household to substitute from future cash goods to future credit goods, thus lowering the current real demand for money.

Though money is neutral in this economy, in that a change in the level of the money supply has no real effects, a change in the growth rate of the money supply is not neutral. If a change in the money growth rate had no real effects, we would say that money was **superneutral**. However, money is not superneutral here, as an increase in the money growth rate leads to decreases in consumption, output, and employment. These effects occur because higher money growth leads to higher inflation, which affects household decisions concerning how much to work in the current period and how much and what to consume. Higher inflation increases the nominal interest rate, which is the opportunity cost of holding money for transactions purposes. As a result, the household economizes on money balances and uses credit to a greater degree in making transactions. The resulting costs of inflation are lost output and consumption. See Macroeconomics in Action 9.1 on p. 318 for some insight into the empirical relationships among money growth, inflation, and output growth.

Optimal Monetary Policy: The Friedman Rule At this point, we would like to demonstrate the key economic inefficiencies that result from inflation, and then show how these inefficiencies can be corrected by the appropriate long-run monetary policy. Recall from Chapter 5 that economic efficiency is achieved when the allocation of resources in an economy is Pareto-optimal, that is, when there is no way to rearrange production or the allocation of goods so that someone is better off and no one worse off. A key condition for Pareto-optimality is that the marginal rate of substitution of any two goods be equal to their marginal rate of transformation. In other words, economic efficiency requires that, in equilibrium, the rate at which consumers trade off one good against another in the market must be equal to the rate at which firms can technologically convert the one good into the other.

What is true in this monetary intertemporal model is that a competitive equilibrium is not in general economically efficient. To show this, first consider cash goods and credit goods. The marginal rate of transformation of credit goods into cash goods is

$$MRT_{C^c,C^m} = 1,$$

since the representative firm can convert credit goods into cash goods one-for-one. However, from (9.11), in equilibrium the household will set

$$MRS_{C^c,C^m} = \frac{1}{1 + R^-};$$

that is, the household optimizes by setting the marginal rate of substitution equal to the reciprocal of one plus the previous period's nominal interest rate. Therefore, as long as $R^- > 0$, we will have $MRS_{C^c,C^m} < MRT_{C^c,C^m}$. Therefore, the positive nominal interest rate on bonds (the opportunity cost of holding money) causes an inefficiency, in that the household tends to consume more credit goods and less cash goods than is optimal. Similarly, if we consider leisure and cash goods, the marginal rate of transformation of leisure into cash goods is the marginal product of labour for the representative firm, and so from condition (9.13), in equilibrium the marginal rate of transformation of leisure into cash goods is

$$MRT_{l,C^m} = w;$$

but, from (9.12), in equilibrium the household will set

$$MRS_{l,C^m} = \frac{w}{1 + R^-}.$$

Again, if $R^- > 0$ we will have $MRS_{l,C^m} < MRT_{l,C^m}$, so that the positive nominal interest rate causes the household to economize too much on cash goods and to consume too much leisure. This is a second inefficiency.

We know that an increase in the money growth rate x causes an increase in the nominal interest rate, so that higher money growth, which is associated with higher inflation, implies larger "wedges" separating marginal rates of transformation from marginal rates of substitution. If the money growth rate and inflation were reduced, then it appears that this would promote economic efficiency; but what would be the best money growth rate for the government to set? Clearly, if the nominal interest rate were reduced to zero, then marginal rates of substitution would be equal to marginal rates of transformation. That is, if $R^- = 0$, then

$$MRT_{C^c,C^m} = MRS_{C^c,C^m} = 1,$$

and

$$MRT_{l,C^m} = MRS_{l,C^m} = w,$$

so that these conditions for economic efficiency would be satisfied. What is the money growth rate x that would drive the nominal interest rate to zero? Since in equilibrium the nominal interest rate in the previous period is $R^- = r^- + i^- = r^- + x$, then if R^- were equal to zero, the money growth rate would be $x = -r^-$. Therefore, it is optimal for the money growth rate to be $x = -r^-$. Since the real interest rate in the previous period is

Money Growth, Inflation, and Output Growth Across Countries

The monetary intertemporal model predicts a one-to-one relationship between money growth and inflation. That is, a permanent increase of one percentage point in the rate of money growth will increase the inflation rate permanently by one percentage point. Also, the model predicts that an increase in the money growth rate will cause a decrease in the level of aggregate output. In a model of endogenous economic growth, related to the endogenous growth model considered in Chapter 8, the inefficiencies associated with inflation will also result in a reduction in the growth rate of aggregate output when the inflation rate increases. This occurs, for example, in the work of Paul Gomme on money and growth.[1]

For the most part, empirical facts fit these predictions fairly well. An article by George McCandless and Warren Weber provides some key evidence and conveniently summarizes the literature on the relationships among money growth, inflation, and output growth across countries.[2] McCandless and Weber look at long-run inflation rates, measured as 30-year average rates of change in consumer prices, long-run rates of growth in some standard measures of money (M0, M1, M2), and long-run growth rates of GDP, for 110 countries. They discuss three important findings. First, long-run money growth and long-run inflation rates are very highly positively correlated across these countries, with correlation coefficients well above 0.9 for most measures of money. The data is consistent with the pre-

diction of our model that the inflation rate increases one-for-one with the money growth rate. Second, long-run money growth and long-run real output growth are negatively correlated across countries, though this correlation is statistically insignificant. This evidence is consistent with other studies of the money-growth/ output-growth relationship, and it is essentially inconclusive concerning the fit of monetary models to the data. Third, long-run inflation and long-run real output growth are negatively correlated across countries, which is consistent with the view that inflationary distortions impede economic growth.

The data therefore provide ample evidence that money growth causes inflation in the long run. However, strong evidence does not exist against the superneutrality of money in the long run. This could be because the real effects of changes in the money growth rate are too small to pick up given the amount of data we have. Uncovering long-run relationships in economic data is extremely difficult, as good economic data has been collected for most countries of the world only since the early-to-mid-20th century.

---

[1]See P. Gomme, 1993, "Money and Growth Revisited: Measuring the Costs of Inflation in an Endogenous Growth Model," *Journal of Monetary Economics* 32, 51–77.

[2]See G. McCandless and W. Weber, 1995, "Some Monetary Facts," *Federal Reserve Bank of Minneapolis Quarterly Review*, Summer, 2–11.

positive (that is, $r^- > 0$), then at the optimum $x < 0$ and the money supply will be decreasing over time. Further, if the money supply is decreasing over time, there will be **deflation**, since the inflation rate is $i^- = x = -r^- < 0$. The same will be true in the current period, since in this equilibrium, $i = i^-$ and $r = r^-$. Thus, it will be optimal for the government to generate a deflation that continues forever, implying that the nominal interest rate is zero in every period.

The fact that the optimal monetary policy drives the nominal interest rate to zero is of prime importance in understanding why this policy works to maximize welfare. A positive nominal interest rate on bonds implies that the representative household economizes too much on money balances in favour of holding bonds. Credit is used too much relative to money in transactions, and the household consumes too much leisure relative to cash goods. If the nominal interest rate is driven to zero through deflation, giving money a higher real return, then the household becomes indifferent between holding bonds and money, and this is optimal.

This type of optimal deflationary monetary policy is called a **Friedman rule**, after Milton Friedman.[6] In practice, the Friedman rule means that the nominal interest rate on riskless securities should always be zero. This does not mean that all nominal interest rates should be zero (this would be impossible), but that the nominal interest rate on short-term government debt (e.g., federal government Treasury bills) should be zero. The Friedman rule is probably the strongest policy conclusion that comes from monetary economics, but it is a policy that essentially no central bank currently follows or has ever followed. No central bank pursues long-run deflation as a goal, and no central bank advocates pushing the nominal interest rate to zero. Thus, either central banks are doing something wrong, or our model leaves out some important aspect(s) of the problem at hand, or inflation just does not matter much.

To pursue the last explanation, one possible reason central banks do not follow the Friedman rule is that, at low levels of inflation, say below 10% per annum, the gains from reducing inflation are very small. Indeed, Thomas Cooley and Gary Hansen[7] conclude that, in a monetary model similar to the one we have studied here, the welfare loss from an inflation rate of 10% per annum is about 0.5% of consumption for the average consumer, and the welfare loss from a monetary rule with 0% inflation versus the Friedman rule rate of deflation is about 0.14% of consumption for the average consumer. Canada has experienced periods of deflation—for example, during the Great Depression—but never a sustained deflation. Therefore, Canadian central bankers may feel—given uncertainty about what might happen during a sustained deflation, because deflation is associated historically with bad economic times, and because the benefits from reducing the inflation rate below zero are potentially only very small—that the most a central bank should do is to reduce the inflation rate to zero. See Macroeconomics in Action 9.2 for more insight into the real-world costs of inflation.

Though most macroeconomic models tell us that the welfare losses from moderate inflations are quite small, the costs of extremely high rates of inflation—that is, **hyperinflations**—are clearly very large. Some prominent hyperinflations occurred in Austria, Hungary, Germany, and Poland in the early 1920s following World War I. For example, the inflation rate in Austria averaged 10 000% per annum between January 1921 and August 1922. Typically, hyperinflations occur because the government is unwilling or

---

[6]See "The Optimum Quantity of Money," in M. Friedman, 1969, *The Optimum Quantity of Money and Other Essays*, pp. 1–50, Aldine Publishing, Hawthorne, NY.

[7]See T. Cooley and G. Hansen, 1989, "The Inflation Tax in a Real Business Cycle Model," *American Economic Review* 79, 733–748.

Should the Bank of Canada Reduce the Inflation Rate to Zero or Less?

Our monetary intertemporal model tells us that the optimal rate of inflation is negative, which implies that the Bank of Canada should engineer a rate of growth in the money supply that would give permanent deflation. However, as we pointed out, no central bank appears to have attempted to bring about a deflation. Currently, the Bank's target for the inflation rate is 2% per year. At most, some policymakers are willing to recommend that the inflation rate be reduced to zero, so that the price level will remain constant over time. Does this imply there is something missing in the monetary intertemporal model in terms of the costs and benefits of inflation? Could the optimal inflation rate be higher than zero? S. Rao Aiyagari makes a case[1] that the costs of reducing the inflation rate to zero would exceed the benefits. In making his argument, Aiyagari appeals to some of the costs of inflation contained in our monetary intertemporal model, but he considers other costs and benefits of inflation as well.

First, as in our model, Aiyagari argues that a cost of inflation arises because the nominal interest rate is positive, which causes people to economize too much on money balances. He points out that some of these costs can be eliminated if interest is paid on some of the components of the money stock. A practice different in Canada from what it is in many countries (including the United States) is that the Bank of Canada pays interest on the component of reserve balances held by financial institutions as deposits at the Bank. The payment of interest on reserves is good for economic efficiency. Indeed, if a central bank could pay interest on currency as well as reserves, then this could implement the Friedman rule. However, it seems impractical for interest to be paid on circulating currency.

While the costs of inflation are very small, as Aiyagari argues, the short-run costs of reducing the inflation rate might potentially be large. Keynesian economists argue that price and wage stickiness can cause short-run decreases in aggregate output if the Bank of Canada were to reduce money supply growth to bring about a reduction in inflation, as we will study in Chapter 10. As well, if the private sector doubts the Bank's resolve to reduce inflation, this can cause a short-run drop in aggregate activity until the Bank proves it is serious, an issue we will address in Chapter 16. Given these potentially large short-run costs, Aiyagari concludes that a reduction in the inflation rate to zero would not be worthwhile, but that relaxing regulations on the financial sector—for example in countries where interest is currently not paid on bank reserves—would certainly be beneficial.

---

[1]See S. R. Aiyagari, 1990, "Deflating the Case for Zero Inflation," *Federal Reserve Bank of Minneapolis Quarterly Review*, Summer, 2–11.

---

unable to finance large government outlays through taxation or borrowing, and so it must resort to seigniorage. For example, the German hyperinflation following World War I occurred in part because the German government financed large war reparations to other European countries by printing money at a very high rate. The key to stopping a hyperinflation, as Thomas Sargent points out,[8] is gaining control over fiscal policy by reducing the government deficit.

---

[8]See "The Ends of Four Big Inflations," in T. Sargent, 1993, *Rational Expectations and Inflation*, 2nd ed., pp. 43–116, Harper Collins.

SHORT-RUN ANALYSIS IN THE INTERTEMPORAL MONETARY MODEL: A TEMPORARY DECREASE IN TOTAL FACTOR PRODUCTIVITY

The monetary intertemporal model developed here will be a basis for the analysis of business cycles in Chapters 10 and 11. Therefore, we must understand how the model is used to analyze short-run issues. As an example, we will examine here the effects in the current period of a temporary decrease in total factor productivity. From Chapter 7, we already know the real effects of such a shock to the economy: a decrease in aggregate output, consumption, investment, the real wage, and employment and an increase in the real interest rate. We will show here that a temporary decrease in total factor productivity also causes an increase in the price level.

A short-run shock to the economy will in general affect the current inflation rate, which will in turn matter for the demand for current consumption goods, current supply of labour, and current money demand. An important simplification is to ignore these effects of changes in the current inflation rate on household behaviour when we analyze the short run using the monetary intertemporal model, as these effects will be small in practice. Then, it will be convenient to consider the case where the current inflation rate is zero, or $i = 0$, so that, given the Fisher relation (9.2), we will have $R = r + i = r$. Therefore, the nominal and real interest rates are equal, and we can write the equilibrium condition for the money market as

$$M = PL(Y, r),$$

The analysis would not change if the inflation rate i were positive or negative; setting $i = 0$ is simply a convenience.

In Chapters 5 and 7, we examined the effects on the real side of the economy of a change in total factor productivity. Recall that a decrease in total factor productivity z could arise because of an increase in the relative price of energy or because of new government regulations. In Figure 9.13 we show the equilibrium effects in the monetary intertemporal model of a temporary decrease in current total factor productivity z. In Figure 9.13(a) and (b), the effects are exactly the same as in the real intertemporal model in Chapter 7. That is, a decrease in z decreases the current marginal product of labour, which shifts the labour demand curve to the left from N_1^d to N_2^d in Figure 9.13(a), and the output supply curve shifts to the left from Y_1^s to Y_2^s in Figure 9.13(b). In equilibrium, the real interest rate will rise from r_1 to r_2, and current aggregate output will fall from Y_1 to Y_2. Because of the increase in the real interest rate, current consumption and current investment will decrease. Also, the higher real interest rate will result in intertemporal substitution of leisure, and the labour supply curve in Figure 9.13(a) will shift to the right, from $N^s(r_1)$ to $N^s(r_2)$. In equilibrium, the shift in the labour supply curve will be sufficiently small that employment will fall from N_1 to N_2, and the real wage will fall from w_1 to w_2.

The effects that are new in the monetary intertemporal model will occur in the money market in Figure 9.13(c). The equilibrium decrease in current real income Y will reduce money demand, and the increase in the real interest rate r will also reduce money demand. Therefore, the money demand curve shifts to the left, from $PL(Y_1, r_1)$ to $PL(Y_2, r_2)$. The money supply is fixed at M, and so in equilibrium the price level must

FIGURE 9.13

Short-Run Analysis of a Temporary Decrease in Total Factor Productivity

This is an example of how to use the monetary intertemporal model to examine the effects of short-run shocks. A decrease in current total factor productivity z reduces real output and raises the real interest rate. The money demand curve shifts to the left, and the equilibrium price level rises.

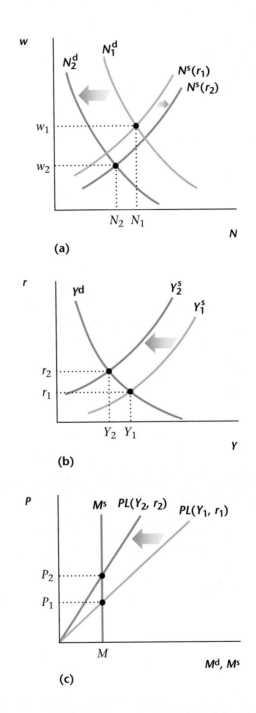

(a)

(b)

(c)

rise from P_1 to P_2. The price level rises because, given the reduced real demand for money and the constant nominal money supply, the price level must rise to reduce the real supply of money so that it is equal to real money demand. Effectively, the same quantity of money is chasing a smaller quantity of goods, and so the price of goods, P, must rise.

Recall from Chapter 7 that the real intertemporal model responded to a change in total factor productivity in a manner consistent with the key business cycle facts that we studied in Chapter 3. That is, in the data, consumption, investment, employment, and the real wage are procyclical, just as the model predicts. The monetary intertemporal model not only matches these real business cycle facts; it is also consistent with observed price level behaviour. That is, the price level is observed to be countercyclical in post–World War II data, from Chapter 3, and the monetary intertemporal model predicts this countercyclical price level behaviour. When total factor productivity decreases, real output falls and the price level increases. Therefore, aggregate output and the price level will move in opposite directions in response to total factor productivity shocks.

THEORY CONFRONTS THE DATA

9.1

Changes in the Relative Price of Energy and the Price Level

The monetary intertemporal model predicts that increases in the price level are associated with decreases in total factor productivity, and in Chapter 7 we discussed how an increase in the relative price of energy can be interpreted as a decrease in total factor productivity. In Figure 9.14 we show the relative price of energy in Canada, as in Chapter 7, and in Figure 9.15 we show data for

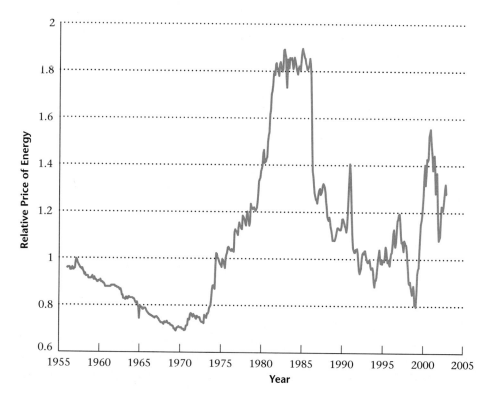

FIGURE 9.14

Relative Price of Energy
This quantity measured here as the price index for petroleum and coal products divided by the consumer price index.

Source: Adapted from the Statistics Canada CANSIM database, Series v3822650, v735319.

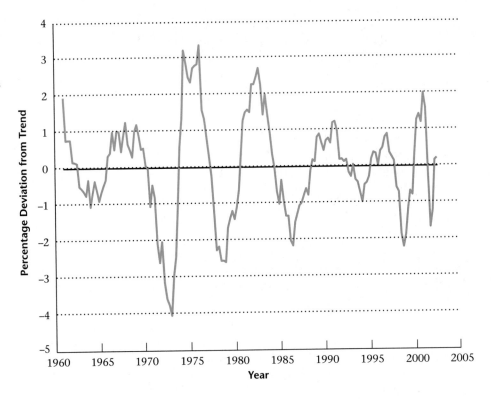

FIGURE 9.15

Percentage Deviations from Trend in the Price Level

This quantity is measured here as percentage deviations from trend in the implicit GDP price deflator.

Source: Adapted from the Statistics Canada CANSIM database, Series v1997756.

a shorter period for the detrended price level, that is, the deviations from trend in the GDP price deflator. Note that there were large positive deviations from trend in the price level following the large increases in the relative price of energy that occurred in 1973–74, 1979–80, and in 2000. However, the positive deviations from trend in the price level tend to lag the increases in the relative price of energy, which is something our theory does not explain. Some macroeconomists would attribute this lag in the response of the price level to "stickiness" in nominal prices, caused by long-term contracting for goods in the economy. However, there is some disagreement concerning whether price stickiness is empirically important and what causes it. These are issues that we will discuss more in Chapter 10.

Further features of the data consistent with the theory are the negative deviations from trend in the price level in the late 1980s, corresponding to a decrease in the relative price of energy, and the small positive deviation from trend in the price level in the early 1990s, corresponding to a small upward blip in the relative price of energy during the Persian Gulf War.

Shifts in Money Demand

In the monetary intertemporal model we worked with above, the money demand relationship, which is determined by the real money demand function $L(Y, R)$, was taken as fixed. In practice, there has been a very unstable relationship between money demand

and aggregate economic variables, and this instability has been quite important for central banks in determining monetary policy. There are many factors that will cause money demand to shift that we have not included in our monetary intertemporal model. In this section, we consider the empirical factors that cause shifts in money demand, and we look at the effects of shifts in money demand and some of their implications for monetary policy.

Shifts in the real demand for money—that is, changes in the function $L(Y, R)$—are associated with money's role as a medium of exchange and store of value. Thus, anything that changes what can be used as a medium of exchange or changes the costs of making transactions will alter the demand for money. As well, in terms of the store-of-value role for money, since money is part of any household's portfolio of assets, changes in factors that affect the desirability of holding money relative to these other assets will also change the demand for money. The most important factors that can lead to shifts in the demand for money are the following:

1. *A change in the costs of using alternatives to currency as means of payment.* If it becomes cheaper to use alternative means of payment (e.g., if the cost of using debit cards falls), then the demand for currency falls, and the money demand curve shifts to the left.

2. *A change in the costs of converting other assets into currency.* If it becomes cheaper to convert other assets into currency, effectively other assets become more liquid relative to money, and households will hold less money. The demand curve for money shifts to the left. An example is the cost of converting a chequing or savings deposit into currency. This cost is essentially the time, and possibly the transaction fee, associated with a trip to the ATM machine. If the costs of visiting the ATM machine are smaller, say because there are more ATMs and a trip to the ATM takes less time, the household will make more frequent trips to the ATM machine and hold less currency on average.

3. *A change in government regulations.* An example is the change in financial regulations in Canada in 1992 that eliminated reserve requirements, minimum quantities of outside money that financial institutions had to hold against particular deposits. If our definition of money is M1, which includes transactions accounts at chartered banks, then the elimination of reserve requirements would increase the demand for money, since it would reduce the costs to chartered banks of offering transactions accounts. This would then imply that chartered banks could offer higher interest rates on these accounts, which would shift the money demand curve to the right.

4. *A change in inflation risk.* Money is a risky asset, in that the real rate of return on money is affected by the inflation rate, and if inflation is uncertain (which it is in practice), then the real rate of return on money is uncertain. Everything else held constant, greater inflation risk implies that the money demand curve shifts to the left. Variability in the inflation rate is typically so small that, given the short holding period of money, it is essentially irrelevant. However, inflation variability tends to rise with the inflation rate, so that, particularly during hyperinflations, inflation variability matters.

FIGURE 9.16

A Shift in the Demand for Money

The money demand curve shifts to the right, causing a decrease in the equilibrium price level P, from P_1 to P_2.

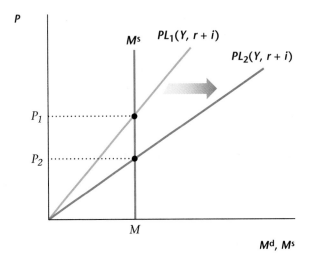

5. *A change in the riskiness of alternative assets.* An increase in the riskiness of alternative assets causes an increase in the demand for money and a shift to the right in the money demand curve. During the Great Depression in the United States, widespread bank failures made households more uncertain about the value of their bank deposits, and there was a dramatic increase in the demand for currency. Greater volatility in the stock market can also lead to an increase in the demand for money.

As an example of the equilibrium effects of a shift in the demand for money, suppose that households perceive that alternative assets are more risky, so that the demand for money increases. We will consider this experiment in the short-run version of the monetary intertemporal model where we set the inflation rate $i = 0$, and the nominal interest rate is equal to the real interest rate, or $R = r$. If the demand for currency increases, the money demand curve will shift to the right in Figure 9.16 above, from $PL_1(Y, r)$ to $PL_2(Y, r)$. Here, Y and r are determined in the goods market and labour market, and they are unaffected by what happens to the supply and demand for money. Thus, the price level falls from P_1 to P_2. That is, since the real demand for money has risen, the real money supply $\frac{M}{P}$ must rise to meet the increased demand, and this can only happen if P falls. This implies that, for example, if the stock market is perceived by the public as being more risky, this should increase the demand for money and reduce the price level.

9.2 The Velocity of Money

THEORY CONFRONTS THE DATA

The velocity of an asset is a measure of how fast that asset circulates. Typically, the most liquid assets (those that can be sold most quickly and at lowest cost for their market value) in the economy will circulate faster (i.e., change hands more frequently) than the least liquid assets. So of all assets money should have the highest velocity, since it is the most liquid. The most common measure of the velocity of money is **income velocity**, defined as the ratio of nominal income to the nominal quantity of money:

$$V = \frac{PY}{M}. \tag{9.24}$$

Since nominal income PY is a measure of the flow of nominal transactions over a given period of time, V is a measure of the number of times the money stock M turns over during the current period.

In studying the behaviour of the velocity of money, we will focus only on the behaviour of M1++ and the velocity of M1++. The velocity of money can behave differently depending on the measure of money we use, but focusing on one monetary aggregate here will allow us to make our essential points. In Figure 9.17 we plot M1++, and in Figure 9.18 we plot the velocity of M1++ for the period 1968–2002. From Figure 9.18, note that the velocity of M1++ has fluctuated considerably over time.

Given our money demand function and market clearing from Equation (9.17), the velocity of money will be

$$V = \frac{PY}{M} = \frac{Y}{L(Y, R)}, \tag{9.25}$$

so that the velocity of money depends on real income Y and the nominal interest rate R. Since money demand decreases with an increase in R, V will increase when R increases. Whether V increases or decreases when Y increases depends on the form of

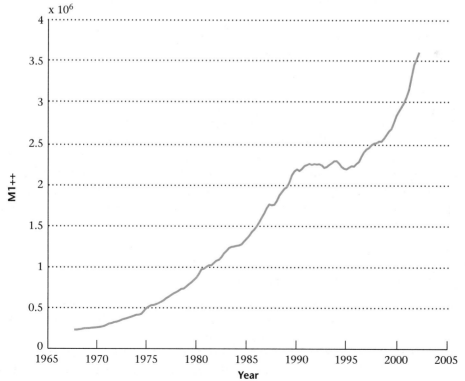

FIGURE 9.17

M1++

The figure shows the quantity, in millions, of M1++ in Canada from 1968 to 2002.

Source: Adapted from the Statistics Canada CANSIM database, Series v37152.

FIGURE 9.18

Velocity of M1++

The figure shows the income velocity of M1++ in Canada from 1968–2002.

Source: Adapted from the Statistics Canada CANSIM database, Series v37152, v498086.

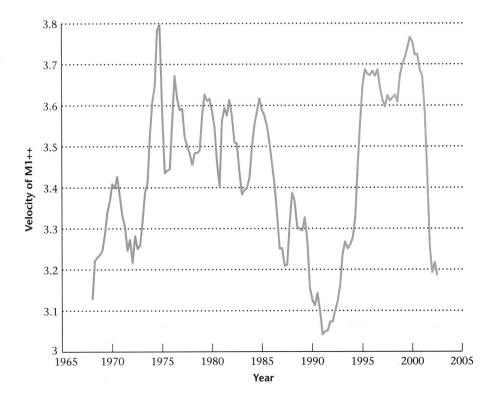

FIGURE 9.19

Scatter Plot of the Velocity of M1++ Versus the Nominal Interest Rate, 1968–2002

As the monetary intertemporal model predicts, the two variables are positively correlated.

Source: Adapted from the Statistics Canada CANSIM database, Series v37152, v498086, v122531.

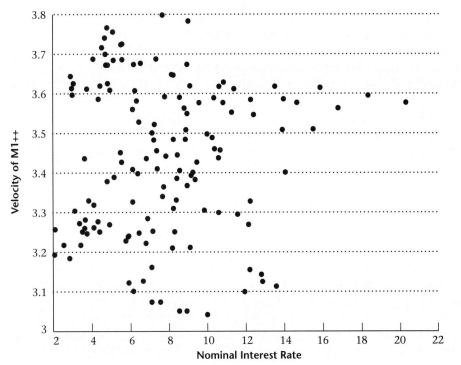

the money demand function $L(Y, R)$. In the special case where $L(Y, R) = aYH(R)$, where $a > 0$ is a constant and H is a decreasing function, we have

$$V = \frac{Y}{L(Y, R)} = \frac{1}{aH(R)},$$

so that the velocity of money does not change when aggregate income changes, as money demand simply increases in proportion to aggregate income. However, there will be a positive relationship between the velocity of money and the nominal interest rate. Therefore, assuming the money demand function takes the form $L(Y, R) = aYH(R)$, if we plot the velocity of money against the nominal interest rate R, we should observe a positive correlation in the data. In Figure 9.19 we plot the velocity of M1++ against the nominal interest rate, given quarterly observations for the period 1968–2002. In the figure, we can indeed observe the predicted positive relationship between the velocity of M1++ and the nominal interest rate. However, this relationship is a noisy one, in that many of the observations fall far from a straight line fit to the data. Part of this noise arises because of the instability in the demand for money.

THE QUANTITY THEORY OF MONEY AND MONETARISM

The quantity theory of money takes many forms, but in modern macroeconomics it is most closely associated with the ideas of Milton Friedman. In its simplest form, the quantity theory starts with the definition of monetary velocity above, rewritten as

$$M = \frac{1}{V}PY. \tag{9.26}$$

Then, if $V = \bar{V}$, a constant, it must be the case that any change in M is reflected in a proportional change in nominal aggregate income PY. Of course, the problem with this simple version of the quantity theory is that we know, from the previous section, that the velocity of money is not constant over time; velocity varies considerably. Thus, more advanced versions of the quantity theory, usually referred to as **monetarism**, argue that the money demand function $L(Y, R)$ is stable, that is, the function does not shift much over time. This then implies that V, from (9.25), is a stable function of Y and R. As a result, in (9.26) there is a predictable relationship between the money supply M and nominal income PY. Based on the assumption that the money demand function is stable, the two key elements of monetarism are as follows:

1. The money supply is the key measure of the level of aggregate economic activity, in that there is a systematic relationship between the money supply and aggregate nominal income.

2. The money supply is the key indicator of monetary policy.

Monetarist ideas became very influential in the 1970s, when many countries, including Canada, experienced high rates of inflation. Central bankers became convinced that the way to control inflation was to control growth in the money supply. Some central banks, including the Bank of Canada, began to implement monetary policy in terms of explicit targets for the growth of specific monetary aggregates. A problem that many central banks encountered, however, particularly in the 1980s and 1990s, was unpredictable shifts in money demand functions. This was part of the reason for the shift in the Bank of Canada's targets from monetary aggregates to inflation rates.

To see how unpredictable money demand shifts can be a problem for monetary policy when the monetary authority adopts a simple rule of controlling the money supply, consider the following example. Suppose that the monetary authority wishes to stabilize the price level—that is, hold the price level constant—in a short-run world where the inflation rate is zero, so that $R = r$. The monetary authority will attempt to do this by setting the money supply appropriately. Suppose first that there is a stable money demand function $L(Y, r)$, and in Figure 9.20 the level of aggregate output is initially Y_1 and the real interest rate (equal to the nominal interest rate, as there is no inflation here) is r_1. Given the initial money supply M_1, the initial price level is P_1. Now suppose there is a change in aggregate output and the real interest rate, and the monetary authority observes these changes, as it has timely information on output and interest rates. However, it takes time for the monetary authority to observe the change in the price level. In the figure, the monetary authority assumes that the money demand function is stable, and here this indicates that, given the changes in output and the interest rate, to Y_2 and r_2, respectively, there is a shift to the right in the money demand curve. Since the monetary authority wants to hold the price level constant at P_1, it increases the money supply from M_1 to M_2. If the money supply had not increased, the price level would have fallen to P_2 in equilibrium. It turns out that in this case the monetary authority was correct in its assumption that the money demand function had not shifted because of factors other than income and the real interest rate, and it was successful in controlling the price level as desired.

However, suppose alternatively that the money demand function shifts to the left, as in Figure 9.21, from $PL_1(Y, r)$ to $PL_2(Y, r)$. If the monetary authority wants to control the price level, it should reduce the money supply from M_1 to M_2. However, the monetary authority does not immediately see the increase in the equilibrium price level that results, from P_1 to P_2, and so it does not change the money supply. Thus, in this

FIGURE 9.20

Central Bank Response Stabilizes Price Level

The central bank observes a change in real income and the real interest rate, and it correctly predicts the shift in the money demand curve to the right. Even though the central bank cannot observe the price level, it increases the money supply appropriately to hold the price level constant.

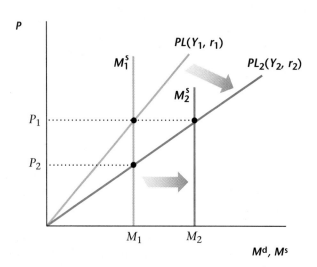

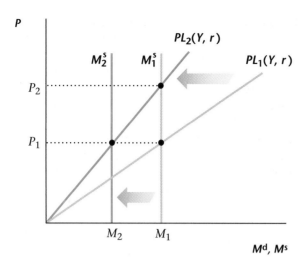

FIGURE 9.21

Central Bank Does Not Observe the Price Level Response to a Shift in Demand for Money

In this case, the central bank cannot observe the increase in the price level or the shift in the money demand curve to the left. The money supply should decrease from M_1 to M_2, but it does not.

case, stabilizing the money supply without somehow accounting for the potential shift of the money demand function will not give the desired result of a stable price level.

Chapter Summary

In this chapter, we first studied three functions of money in the economy—a medium of exchange, a store of value, and a unit of account. Then, we discussed how money is measured in the Canadian economy. The key measures of money are the monetary aggregates, which are the sum of quantities of assets having the functions of money. The monetary base, or M0, is the narrowest monetary aggregate, and it consists only of liabilities of the Bank of Canada, in particular currency and clearing balances. Other broader monetary aggregates, which include bank deposits and other assets, are M1 (broader than M0), M2 (broader than M1), and M3 (broader than M2) as well as M1++ and M2++.

This chapter developed a monetary intertemporal model, which built on the real intertemporal model of Chapter 7 by including supply and demand in the market for money and the effects of monetary factors in the markets for current goods and labour. An important element of the monetary intertemporal model is the cash-in-advance constraint, which states that cash goods must be purchased using cash on hand at the beginning of the period. Credit goods can be bought on credit during the period, with the credit card bill paid by the household at the end of the period. Using the monetary intertemporal model, we showed how money is neutral, in the sense that an increase in the level of the money supply leaves real variables—employment, output, consumption, the real interest rate, the real money supply, and the real wage—unaffected, and causes only a proportionate increase in all money prices. Money is not superneutral, however, in that a change in the growth rate of the money supply will matter for real economic activity. Higher money growth leads to higher inflation and a higher nominal interest rate, given the Fisher relation, which states that the nominal interest rate is approximately equal to the real interest rate plus the inflation rate. With a higher nominal interest rate, the opportunity cost of holding money and making transactions with money rises, and so households substitute away from cash goods and toward credit goods and leisure. In equilibrium, employment and output fall, consumption falls, and the real wage rises. Inflation distorts private decisions, causing economic inefficiency, in that marginal rates of transformation are not equal to marginal rates of substitution. The way to eliminate this inefficiency is for the monetary authority to adopt a Friedman rule for monetary policy, which would drive the nominal interest rate to zero through deflation.

In the model, a short-run decrease in total factor productivity will lead to an increase in the price level, which is consistent with evidence from Canadian historical episodes where the relative price of energy increased. Shifts in money demand can occur because of changes in financial technology, in government regulations, in the properties of money as an asset, and in the properties of alternative assets to money. Money demand shifts can be a particular problem for monetary policy, particularly if it is guided by monetarist principles.

Key Terms

neutrality of money: Money is neutral if a change in its level has no real effects and causes only a proportionate increase in the price level.

money demand function: The relationship between the quantity of money that economic agents wish to hold and other macroeconomic variables.

medium of exchange: A property of money; a medium of exchange is accepted in transactions for the sole reason that it can in turn be exchanged for other goods and services.

store of value: A property of money that is shared with other assets that permit current goods and services to be traded for future goods and services.

unit of account: The object in an economy in which prices and contracts are denominated.

monetary aggregates: These are measures of the money supply; each is the sum of a number of different types of assets in the economy.

monetary base: The quantity of M0, consisting of Canadian currency outside the Bank of Canada, and the clearing balances held with the Bank of Canada.

outside money: This is identical to the monetary base.

high-powered money: This is identical to the monetary base.

Bank of Canada: The central bank of Canada.

single coincidence of wants: Situation in which two people meet, and one person has what the other wants.

double coincidence of wants: Situation in which two people meet, and the first person has what the second person wants, and the second has what the first wants.

cash-in-advance model: A macroeconomic model in which it is assumed that some goods must be purchased with cash on hand at the beginning of the period.

nominal bond: A bond for which the payoff is defined in terms of money.

nominal interest rate: If R is the nominal interest rate on an asset, then if 1 unit of money is exchanged for a given quantity of the asset in the current period, then this quantity of the asset pays off $1 + R$ units of money next period.

inflation rate: The rate of change in the price level.

Fisher relation: Condition stating that $1 + r = \frac{1+R}{1+i}$, where r is the real interest rate from the current period to the future period, R is the nominal interest rate from the current period to the future period, and i is the rate of inflation between the current period and the future period.

cash-in-advance constraint: A condition stating that the household's cash on hand must be at least as large as the nominal quantity of purchases of cash goods it wants to make.

neutral: Describes a government policy that has no real effects.

helicopter drop: Milton Friedman's thought experiment, which corresponds to an increase in the money supply brought about by transfers.

open market operation: A purchase or sale of interest-bearing government debt by the central bank.

open market purchase: An open market operation where interest-bearing government debt is purchased by the central bank, increasing the money supply.

open market sale: An open market operation where interest-bearing government debt is sold by the central bank, decreasing the money supply.

seigniorage: Revenue generated by the government through printing money.

inflation tax: Inflation arising when the government prints money to extract seigniorage; this effectively taxes the private sector.

classical dichotomy: Situation in an economic model where real variables are determined by real factors, and the money supply determines only the price level.

superneutral: Describes money in the situation where a change in the money supply growth rate has no real effects.

deflation: Decrease in the price level over time.

Friedman rule: This rule for monetary policy maximizes welfare for private households, and it sets the path for the money supply so that the nominal interest rate is always zero.

hyperinflations: Situations in which the inflation rate is extremely high.

income velocity: $V = \frac{PY}{M}$, where V is the income velocity of money, P is the price level, Y is real income, and M is the supply of money.

monetarism: The tenets of monetarists, including Milton Friedman, who argue that the money demand function is stable, that money is the key measure of the level of aggregate economic activity, and that money is the key indicator for monetary policy.

Questions for Review

1. What are the three functions of money?

2. List six monetary aggregates and the assets that these monetary aggregates include.

3. Why is money used in exchange when people could carry out transactions by trading goods or using credit?

4. How are the real interest rate, the nominal interest rate, and the inflation rate related to one another?

5. What is the real rate of interest on money?

6. What are the three goods that the representative household consumes in the monetary intertemporal model?

7. How does the cash-in-advance constraint affect the relative prices of the three goods in the monetary intertemporal model?

8. What are the effects of an increase in the money supply in the monetary intertemporal model?

9. What are three ways in which the government could bring about a change in the money supply?

10. What are the effects of an increase in the money supply growth rate in the monetary intertemporal model?

11. What are the costs of inflation?

12. Should the monetary authority manipulate the money supply to hold the price level constant over time?

13. Why don't real-world central banks follow the Friedman rule?

14. What are the effects of a short-run decrease in total factor productivity in the monetary intertemporal model?

15. List five factors that lead to an increase in money demand.

16. How is the velocity of money related to the nominal interest rate?

17. How does the velocity of money behave empirically over short periods of time? Over long periods of time?

18. What are the key principles of monetarism?

19. Why are unpredictable shifts in the money demand function a problem for monetary policy?

Problems

1. In the monetary intertemporal model, suppose that the money supply is fixed for all time.
   a. Determine the effects of a temporary increase in the quantity of government purchases on current equilibrium output, employment, the real wage, the real interest rate, the nominal interest rate, and the price level. Explain your results.
   b. Now suppose that the increase in government spending is permanent. How does this change your answers from part (a)? Explain.

2. In the monetary intertemporal model, suppose that the money supply is fixed for all time, and determine the effects of a decrease in the capital stock, brought about by a war or natural disaster, on current equilibrium output, employment, the real wage, the real interest rate, the nominal interest rate, and the price level. Explain your results.

3. In the monetary intertemporal model, suppose that the level of the money supply is expected to increase in the future period. What effects will this have on current real output, current employment, the current real wage, the current real interest rate, the current nominal interest rate, and the current price level? That is, we want to determine the equilibrium effects today of a money supply increase that will occur in the future. Assume that everyone knows in advance that the money supply increase will occur. Explain your results carefully.

4. Suppose, in the monetary intertemporal model, that the quantity of government purchases increases permanently, and that this increase in government spending is financed by an increase in the growth rate x of the money supply. That is, the increase in government spending is financed through seigniorage. Determine the effects on current equilibrium inflation, employment, output, the real wage, the real interest rate, and the nominal interest rate. Explain your results.

5. A new technological innovation is announced that will come on line in the future period. What are the current effects on aggregate output, consumption, investment, employment, the real wage, the real interest rate, the nominal interest rate, and the price level? Explain your results.

6. Suppose, in the monetary intertemporal model, that the preferences of the representative household change in such a way that the worker in the household becomes more willing to work, in that he or she requires less compensation in terms of consumption goods to supply an extra unit of labour, given any consumption–leisure bundle.
   a. If the money supply is fixed for all time, determine the effects of this change in preferences on current employment, current output, the real interest rate, the nominal interest

rate, and the current price level. (*Hint:* The effect on the real interest rate will be indeterminate; assume that *r* increases.)

b. Now suppose the monetary authority wishes to stabilize the price level (hold the price level constant). How would the money supply change in response to the change in preferences in order to accomplish this?

c. Suppose there is a temporary increase in total factor productivity, and the monetary authority wishes to stabilize the price level. What would be the effects of the increase in total factor productivity on output, employment, the real interest rate, the nominal interest rate, the price level, and the money supply?

d. Now suppose there is an increase in total factor productivity, and the monetary authority cannot observe output, the price level, and employment in the short run but can only observe the nominal interest rate. The monetary authority also cannot observe total factor productivity or household preferences. The monetary authority, in error, guesses that the nominal interest rate moved because there was a change in household preferences toward leisure and consumption. If it attempts to stabilize the price level on the basis of this belief, what will happen to the price level? Discuss the effects of the error the monetary authority makes here.

7. Suppose that there is an increase in the number of ATM machines in service. What are the effects of this innovation on the demand for money and on the price level?

8. The issuers of credit cards demand payment every two weeks instead of every month. Determine the effects on money demand and on the price level, and explain your results.

9. Macroeconomists have observed that, in the past, the demand for money tended to increase during strikes by postal workers. Provide an explanation for this phenomenon.

10. The federal government increases expenditures permanently. Supposing the goal of the central bank is to stabilize the price level, how should the central bank change the money supply in response to this permanent change in government spending? Explain with the aid of diagrams, and discuss what this shows about the importance of coordination between the central bank and the fiscal authority.

11. Suppose the government could pay interest on currency, and this interest on currency is paid at the market interest rate on nominal bonds. The government finances the interest paid on currency through lump-sum taxes on the representative household.

a. In an inflationary environment, what would be the long-run effects of paying interest on currency?

b. Show that paying interest on currency eliminates the inefficiencies resulting from inflation.

c. Do you think that paying interest on currency is a practical solution to eliminating the costs of inflation? Why or why not?

Working with the Data

1. Calculate the ten-year percentage rates of growth in the consumer price index for the periods 1955–1965, 1965–1975, 1975–1985, and 1985–1995, and do the same for the percentage increase in the monetary base. Then plot the growth rates of money against the growth rates of the CPI. What do you see in this scatter plot? Is this evidence consistent with the predictions of the monetary intertemporal model?

2. Calculate the income velocities of M0 and M2++ over the period 1968–2002, and plot these time series. Compare what you get with Figure 9.18, where we show the income velocity of

M1++, and comment on the differences you see. How does the behaviour of these different velocity measures reflect shifts in demand among the monetary aggregates?

3. Construct a scatter plot of M1++ against real GDP for the period 1968–2002.
   a. Is there a positive or negative correlation in the scatter plot?
   b. Is the correlation you observed in part (a) evidence that money is not neutral? Why or why not?

4. Plot the income velocity of M2++ against the 3-month Treasury bill rate for 1968–2002, and compare what you get to Figure 9.19. How would you explain the differences you see, if any?

CHAPTER 10

Keynesian Business Cycle Theory: The Sticky Wage Model

In this chapter, we will study a business cycle model in the spirit of Keynes's *General Theory*.[1] Keynesian business cycle models have been very influential among both academics and policymakers. The basic formal modelling framework underlying these models was developed by Hicks in the late 1930s,[2] and popularized in Paul Samuelson's textbook in the 1950s. In the 1960s, large-scale versions of these Keynesian business cycle models were fit to data, and they are still used by some economists for forecasting and policy analysis. Though Keynesian models certainly have some strong adherents,[3] they have many detractors as well.[4] Part of what we will do in this chapter is to critically evaluate the Keynesian sticky wage model, just as we will evaluate other business cycle models in Chapter 11. We will see how well the Keynesian sticky wage model fits the key business cycle facts we discussed in Chapter 3, and we will examine how useful it is for guiding the formulation of economic policy.

In constructing the Keynesian sticky wage model, we will not start from scratch, but will build on the monetary intertemporal model studied in Chapter 9. The primary feature that makes a Keynesian macroeconomic model different from the models we have examined thus far is that all prices and wages are not completely flexible—that is, some are "sticky." That some prices and wages cannot move so as to clear markets will have important implications for how the economy behaves and for economic policy. The Keynesian sticky wage model studied in this chapter is essentially identical to the monetary intertemporal model in Chapter 9, except that the nominal wage rate is not sufficiently flexible for the labour market to clear in the short run. Given the failure of the labour market to clear, the Keynesian sticky wage model will have far different properties from the monetary intertemporal model, and we will need to take a quite different graphical approach to analyzing how it works.

---

[1]See J. M. Keynes, 1936, *The General Theory of Employment, Interest, and Money*, Macmillan, London.

[2]J. Hicks, 1937, "Mr. Keynes and the Classics: A Suggested Interpretation," *Econometrica* 5, 147–159.

[3]L. Ball and N. G. Mankiw, 1994, "A Sticky-Price Manifesto," *Carnegie-Rochester Conference Series on Public Policy* 41, 127–151.

[4]See R. Lucas, 1980, "Methods and Problems in Business Cycle Theory," *Journal of Money, Credit, and Banking* 12.

In contrast to the monetary intertemporal model in Chapter 9, the Keynesian sticky wage model will have the property that money is not neutral. When the monetary authority increases the money supply, there will be an increase in aggregate output and employment. In general, monetary policy can then be used to improve economic performance and welfare. Keynesians typically believe strongly that the government should play an active role in the economy, through both monetary and fiscal policy, and Keynesian business cycle models support this belief.

Since the nominal wage does not move in the short run to clear the labour market in this model, there may be unemployment in that, given the market real wage, some people who wish to work cannot find employment. This is the first instance in this book of a genuine theory of unemployment; all the macroeconomic models we have studied thus far explain the quantity of employment only, and not unemployment. In Chapter 15, we will study other models of unemployment that take account of the search behaviour of the unemployed and incentive problems in the workplace.

In this chapter, we will first construct the Keynesian sticky wage model, starting with the labour market (where the critical difference in behaviour from the monetary intertemporal model is), and proceed to the construction of the *IS* and *LM* curves, which capture behaviour in the goods market and money market, respectively. Then, we will show how the aggregate demand and aggregate supply curves are constructed, which jointly determine equilibrium aggregate output and the price level. A key feature of the model is that it does not exhibit the classical dichotomy—the price level and real variables are simultaneously determined. Once we have put the Keynesian sticky wage model together, we will put it to work, first in showing that money is not neutral. Then, we will study the match between the model and the key business cycle facts from Chapter 3. Finally, we will show how active monetary and fiscal policy can smooth out business cycles in the model by reacting to extraneous shocks to the economy.

The Labour Market in the Keynesian Sticky Wage Model

What makes the Keynesian sticky wage model different is the functioning of the labour market, and so we will start with a description of how this market works. Keynesians argue that, in the short run, the nominal market wage W is imperfectly flexible. The rationale for this is that there are institutional rigidities in how nominal wages are set. For example, it is costly to get workers and firms together frequently to negotiate wage agreements, so that wages are typically set at a given firm for a year or more. Further, it is also costly for workers and firms to write complicated contracts, that is, contracts that provide for every contingency that might arise during the course of a labour contract. For example, workers might want to have a provision in a labour contract for nominal wages to rise faster in the event that inflation is higher than anticipated, and the firm might want nominal wages to rise at a slower rate if inflation is lower than anticipated. A labour contract in which future wage increases are geared to inflation is an **indexed** contract. Indexation to the inflation rate is relatively simple, since there are observed measures of inflation, such as the consumer price index, that could be used for this purpose. In spite of this, most labour contracts in Canada do not provide for complete indexation to inflation, though indexation was more common when inflation rates were higher, such as in the 1970s and early 1980s.

Given that indexation of wages to observed inflation rates in labour contracts seems relatively low cost and yet is typically not done, we can understand why more complicated types of contingencies do not find their way into labour contracts. For example, consider a bakery negotiating a contract with its workers. It might be efficient for the workers to receive a higher wage over the course of the contractual period in the event that the firm sells an unexpectedly large quantity of bread, or for an individual worker to receive a lower wage in the event that the worker's health is unexpectedly bad. However, it may be difficult for the workers to monitor the firm's output, or for the firm to monitor each worker's health, so that these particular features do not find their way into the labour contract. As well, the more factors that are included in a labour contract, the more difficult it is to negotiate the contract. Simple labour contracts arise in part because contract negotiation is costly.

If workers and firms negotiate wage contracts in nominal terms, we could represent this as a fixed nominal wage W for the economy as a whole. We must recognize that the nominal wage should be thought of as being fixed only in the short run. Though the nominal wage W will not respond to factors affecting the labour market in the short run, we will think of the nominal wage as being flexible over the long run. Given that the nominal wage is fixed in the short run, we could have a situation as in Figure 10.1, where the market-clearing real wage rate is w_{mc}, but the market or actual real wage is w^*, which is greater than w_{mc}. This situation could arise because the nominal wage was negotiated in the past, with the expectation by workers and firms that it would be a market-clearing wage, but then unforeseen circumstances caused unanticipated shifts in the labour supply or labour demand curves. At the real wage w^*, employment is determined by how much labour the representative firm wants to hire, which is N^*. However, the representative consumer wants to supply N^{**} units of labour at the real wage w^*, and we can then think of the difference $N^{**} - N^*$ as **Keynesian unemployment**; that is,

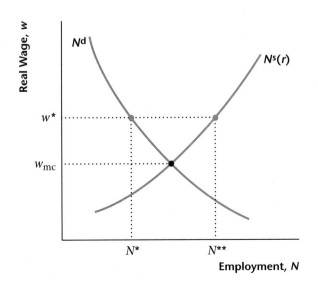

workers cannot work as much as they would like at the going wage. In the sticky wage model, the quantity of labour will always be determined by how much labour the representative firm wants to hire, that is, by the labour demand curve. The justification for this is that, in most employment relationships, the firm determines how many workers will be employed with the firm, and what their hours of work will be.

Though the sticky wage model can capture an element of the phenomenon of unemployment, since in the model there are potentially would-be workers who would like to be employed but cannot find jobs, the Keynesian depiction of unemployment is perhaps unsatisfactory. One problem is that unemployment, as measured by Statistics Canada, is job search activity. In the Keynesian sticky wage model, the representative consumer is not making choices about how hard to search for work or what job offers to accept. A second problem is that, in practice, some unemployment always exists, while in the labour market in the Keynesian sticky wage model, as we have set it up, there are circumstances where there will be no unemployment. If employment is determined as the quantity of labour desired by the representative firm at the market real wage—that is, by the quantity determined by the labour demand curve—then there will be no unemployment if the market real wage is less than the market-clearing real wage. In this case, as in Figure 10.2, the market real wage is w^*, which is less than the market-clearing real wage w_{mc}. At the market real wage, N^* is the quantity of employment determined by the representative firm, but N^{**} is the quantity of labour that the representative consumer wants to supply. Thus, in this case the consumer is working more than he or she would like, which seems unpalatable.

To make the model more palatable, we might suppose instead that, in the situation depicted in Figure 10.2, the quantity of employment is determined by how much the representative consumer wants to work. In this case, employment would be N^{**}, and there would be an excess demand for labour of $N^* - N^{**}$, since the representative firm wants to hire a larger quantity of labour at the market wage than the representative con-

FIGURE 10.2

The Labour Market in the Keynesian Sticky Wage Model When There Is Excess Demand

In this circumstance, the market real wage w^* is less than the market-clearing real wage w_{mc}. The quantity of employment, determined by labour demand, is N^*, which is greater than N^{**}, the quantity of labour that the representative consumer wishes to supply.

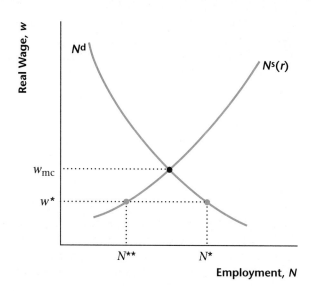

sumer wants to supply. Though this fix is somewhat more appealing, there remains the undesirable feature that in this circumstance there is no unemployment, whereas in practice there are always some people who are not employed but are searching for work. In Chapter 15, we will analyze a model of search and unemployment in which the unemployment rate is determined by the choices of the unemployed concerning what job offers they will take. In that model, the unemployment rate will always be positive.

In the remainder of this chapter, we will stick to circumstances where the market real wage is no lower than the equilibrium real wage, and employment is determined by the labour demand curve. This allows us to consider only cases wherein the model predicts positive unemployment.

The Sticky Wage Aggregate Supply Curve

Now that we have introduced the key element of the Keynesian sticky wage model, which is the labour market, we can fill in the other components of the model. An important difference in the Keynesian model from the monetary intertemporal model in Chapter 9 is that given the fixed nominal wage W, the real wage $\frac{W}{P}$ will depend on the price level. Therefore, since employment is determined by labour demanded at the market real wage, employment and output will depend on the price level. In this section, the component of the model we will construct is the **aggregate supply curve**, which is a positive relationship between real output and the price level.

The aggregate supply curve is derived in Figure 10.3. Since the nominal wage W is fixed in the short run here, the real wage $w = \frac{W}{P}$ will change when the price level changes. In Figure 10.3(a), if the price level is P_1, then the quantity of employment is determined by the labour demand curve N^d, with employment $N = N_1$. Since the labour supply curve is irrelevant for determining employment in the sticky wage model, we leave it out of the diagram. Note that this will also imply that the supply of output will not depend on the real interest rate r, in contrast to the monetary intertemporal model. Given employment equal to N_1, from the production function in Figure 10.3(b) we determine real aggregate output, which is Y_1. Thus, the point (Y_1, P_1) in Figure 10.3(c) represents a level of output and a price level such that the representative firm is willing to supply the quantity of output Y_1 given the nominal wage W and the price level P_1. This point is then on the aggregate supply curve AS.

Suppose that the price level is higher, say $P_2 > P_1$. This implies, since the nominal wage is fixed, that the real wage will be lower, that is, $\frac{W}{P_2} < \frac{W}{P_1}$. Seeing a lower real wage, the representative firm will hire more labour, with the quantity of employment given by the labour demand curve N^d, or employment equal to N_2. Then, from the production function in Figure 10.3(b), output is $Y_2 > Y_1$, and in Figure 10.3(c) we have another point on the aggregate supply curve AS, namely (Y_2, P_2). Similarly, we could ask how much output would be supplied by the representative firm for any value of the price level, and trace out an upward-sloping aggregate supply curve AS. The aggregate supply curve implies that, given a fixed nominal wage W, an increase in the price level reduces the real wage, which increases labour demand and employment, and this implies that more output gets produced. Thus, the AS curve is upward-sloping.

FIGURE 10.3

Construction of the Aggregate Supply Curve

Given the fixed nominal wage W, an increase in the price level will reduce the market real wage, which increases employment as the representative firm hires more labour. This will result in more output being produced. Thus, a higher price level implies that more output is produced, which yields the upward-sloping aggregate supply curve AS in panel (c).

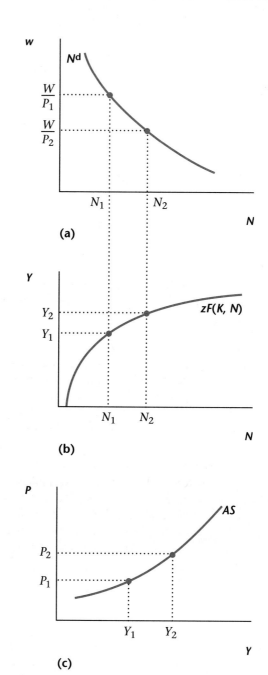

FACTORS SHIFTING THE STICKY WAGE AGGREGATE SUPPLY CURVE

Now that we have constructed the aggregate supply curve, we must determine what factors will shift the curve, so that we can correctly use the curve as part of our model. In general, two factors can shift the AS curve.

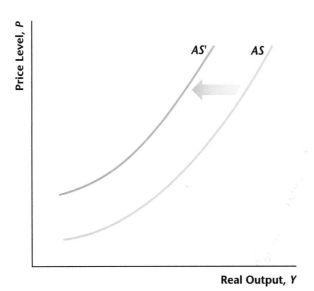

FIGURE 10.4

The Effect of an Increase in W or a Decrease in z
An increase in W or a decrease in z implies that the representative firm will hire less labour given the price level P, and output supplied will therefore decrease. Thus, the aggregate supply curve shifts to the left.

- *An increase in the nominal wage* W *shifts the aggregate supply curve to the left.* If the nominal wage increases, then for any price level P, the real wage, $w = \frac{W}{P}$, is higher. This then implies that labour demand, which equals employment in the sticky wage model, must fall, and therefore output falls. Thus, for any price level, the quantity of output is lower, and so an increase in the nominal wage causes a shift to the left in the aggregate supply curve. In Figure 10.4 above, the aggregate supply curve shifts from AS to AS′.

- *A decrease in current total factor productivity z shifts the aggregate supply curve to the left.* A decrease in z, total factor productivity, causes a downward shift in the production function and a shift to the left in the labour demand function. Given the nominal wage and the price level, which determine the real wage, less labour is demanded, and output supplied falls because employment is lower and because labour and capital are less productive. Again, the aggregate supply curve shifts to the left, as in Figure 10.4.

Aggregate Demand: The *IS* and *LM* Curves

Early Keynesian models often neglected aggregate supply and concentrated on aggregate demand. These aggregate demand Keynesian models are often referred to as *IS–LM* models, because Hicks, in his formalization of Keynes' *General Theory*, used the terms *IS* and *LM* to refer to the curves in his model.

The **IS curve** in the Keynesian sticky wage model is identical to the output demand curve Y^d in the monetary intertemporal model in Chapter 9. As in Chapters 7 and 9, the curve, as depicted in Figure 10.5, is downward-sloping because an increase in the real interest rate *r* causes consumers to substitute future consumption for current

FIGURE 10.5

The *IS* Curve

The *IS* curve is identical to the output demand curve Y^d derived in Chapter 9 in the monetary intertemporal model. The curve represents the demand for current goods given the real interest rate r.

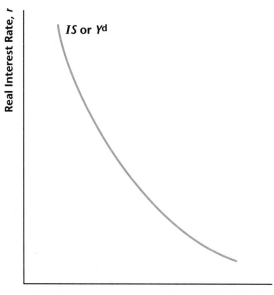

consumption, and causes firms to reduce investment, so that the demands for consumption and investment goods fall when r rises.

Now, to derive the **LM curve**, we need to consider again the approach from the monetary intertemporal model that determines the demand for money. As when we considered short-run analysis in the monetary intertemporal model in Chapter 9, it will be convenient to suppose for now that there is no long-run inflation. This implies, given the Fisher relation from Chapter 9, that the nominal and real interest rates are equal, or $R = r$. Then, from Chapter 9, the demand for real money balances is given by $L(Y, r)$; that is, the real demand for money is increasing in aggregate real income Y and decreasing in the real interest rate r. (Recall from Chapter 9 that an increase in Y increases lifetime wealth, increasing the demand for goods purchased with money, and an increase in r increases the opportunity cost of holding money, so that the demand for real cash balances decreases.) Given that the nominal money supply M is determined exogenously by the government, equilibrium in the money market is determined by

$$M = PL(Y, r),$$

or nominal money supply equals nominal money demand. In Figure 10.6(a), with the real interest rate (rather than the price level; note the difference from Chapter 9) on the vertical axis, the money supply curve is given by the vertical line $M^s = M$, and the current nominal money demand curve $PL(Y_1, r)$ is downward-sloping because the quantity of money demanded falls as the interest rate increases, given the level of real income Y_1 and the price level P. Thus, given real income Y_1 and the price level P, the money market is in equilibrium where money supplied equals money demanded, or where the real interest rate is r_1. We therefore have an output–interest rate pair (Y_1, r_1) for which the money market is in equilibrium (given P), in Figure 10.6(b).

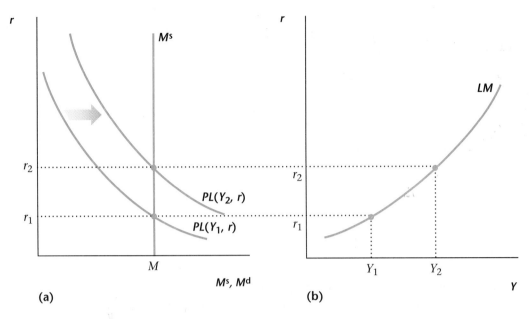

FIGURE 10.6 **Money Demand, Money Supply, and the *LM* Curve**
A shift to the right in the money demand curve in panel (a) occurs because of an increase in income, implying that the real interest rate must rise to restore equilibrium in the money market. This implies that the *LM* curve, representing (Y, r) combinations for which the money market is in equilibrium, is upward-sloping in panel (b).

Now, suppose that the level of real income is higher, say Y_2, while the price level remains the same at P. This implies that money demand increases for each real interest rate, or the current nominal money demand curve shifts rightward to $PL(Y_2, r)$ from $PL(Y_1, r)$. This then implies that the money market will be in equilibrium at a higher real interest rate, $r_2 > r_1$. Now, we have another output–interest rate pair (Y_2, r_2) for which the money market is in equilibrium, given P, in Figure 10.6(b). Similarly, if we consider all possible levels of income and the associated levels of the real interest rate for which the money market is in equilibrium, we will derive an upward-sloping curve, which is the *LM* curve in Figure 10.6(b). The curve is upward-sloping because, given the real money supply $\frac{M}{P}$, real money demand increases when income increases, and so for the money market to be in equilibrium the real interest rate must rise to reduce real money demand.

In Figure 10.7, given the price level P, the goods market and the money market are both in equilibrium at the point where the *IS* and *LM* curves intersect, which is where the real interest rate is r^* and the level of real income is Y^*. The figure then gives a complete picture of the demand side of the model, which determines, given the price level P, the level of aggregate output and the real interest rate.

SHIFTS IN THE *IS* CURVE

The factors we considered previously that lead to shifts in the output demand curve Y^d also shift the *IS* curve, since the *IS* curve is the same thing as the output demand curve.

FIGURE 10.7

FIGURE 10.7

Determination of r and Y

Given P

Given the price level P, the IS and LM curves determine the level of real output and the real interest rate for which the goods market and money market clear.

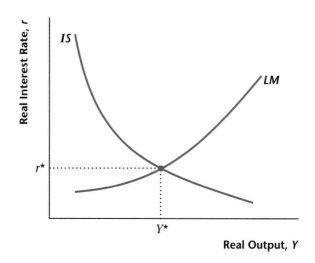

For our short-run analysis, as in Chapter 9, the IS curve will shift to the right as the result of any of the following changes:

- *An increase in current government purchases G.* Recall that this increases the demand for goods consumed by the government.

- *A decrease in the present value of taxes.* This increases the demand for current consumption goods by the representative consumer.

- *An anticipated increase in future income.* This increases lifetime wealth for the consumer, thus increasing the demand for consumption goods.

- *A decrease in the current capital stock K.* Recall that, if the capital stock decreases, then the future marginal product of capital will rise, which will increase the demand for investment goods.

- *An increase in future total factor productivity z′.* If total factor productivity is expected to increase in the future, the future marginal product of capital will rise, and there is an increase in the demand for investment goods.

SHIFTS IN THE *LM* CURVE

In examining factors that shift the LM curve, the key things that we will be interested in are changes in the nominal money supply M, changes in the price level P, and shifts in the money demand function $L(Y, r)$.

- *If the money supply M increases, the LM curve shifts to the right.* In Figure 10.8(a) suppose that the monetary authority increases the money supply from M_1 to M_2 with the price level held constant at P, and aggregate income held constant at Y_1. Initially, the nominal demand for money is given by $PL(Y_1, r)$, and the money market is in equilibrium at the real interest rate r_1. When the money supply increases, the money demand curve does not shift, but the money supply curve shifts to the right from M_1^s to M_2^s. Now, the money market is in equilibrium for a real interest rate of r_2. Therefore, in Figure 10.8(b), the point (Y_1, r_1) is on the initial LM curve, LM_1,

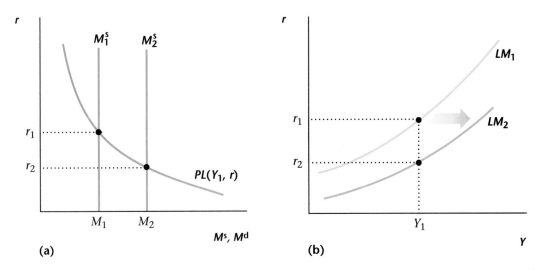

FIGURE 10.8 **The Effect of an Increase in the Money Supply on the *LM* Curve**

An increase in the money supply reduces the real interest rate for which the money market is in equilibrium given the level of real income, which shifts the *LM* curve to the right.

as this is a real income/real interest rate combination such that the money market is in equilibrium. After the money supply increases, the point (Y_1, r_2) is on the new *LM* curve, LM_2. That is, for any level of real income, the real interest rate must now be lower so that money demand will rise to meet the higher money supply. Therefore, the *LM* curve shifts down, or to the right, when the money supply increases.

- *If P increases, the* LM *curve shifts to the left.* In Figure 10.9(a), with the money supply and aggregate income held constant at M and Y_1, respectively, the price level increases from P_1 to P_2. This causes the money demand curve to shift rightward from $P_1L(Y_1, r)$ to $P_2L(Y_1, r)$. Then, in equilibrium, the real interest rate must increase from r_1 to r_2. We then know that, in Figure 10.9(b), a point on the initial *LM* curve, LM_1, is (Y_1, r_1), while a point on the new *LM* curve, LM_2, is (Y_1, r_2). For any level of real income, an increase in the price level increases the demand for money, so that the real interest rate must rise to decrease the demand for money so that this demand will equal the constant supply of money. Therefore, the *LM* curve will shift up or to the left.

- *If there is a positive shift in the money demand function* L(Y, r), *the* LM *curve shifts to the left.* In Figure 10.10(a) the money market is initially in equilibrium, given the price level P and the level of current real income Y_1, for the real interest rate r_1. The initial real demand for money is $L_1(Y_1, r)$. Then, suppose that the demand for money rises, which could occur, for example, if there were an increase in the risk associated with holding alternative assets to money. Then, the nominal demand for money shifts to the right in Figure 10.10(a), from $PL_1(Y_1, r)$ to $PL_2(Y_1, r)$. As a result, given the level of real income Y_1, the equilibrium real interest rate will now be $r_2 > r_1$. Thus, in Figure 10.10(b), (Y_1, r_1) is a point on the initial *LM* curve, LM_1, while (Y_1, r_2) is

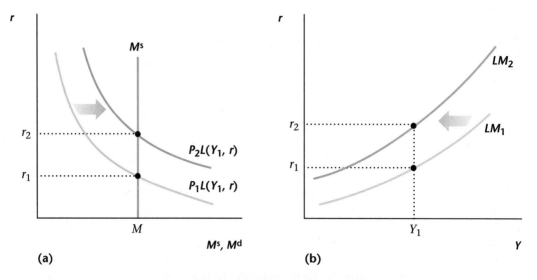

FIGURE 10.9 **The Effect of an Increase in the Price Level on the *LM* Curve**
An increase in the price level increases the real interest rate for which the money market is in equilibrium given the level of the real interest rate, which shifts the *LM* curve to the left.

a point on the new *LM* curve, LM_2. Since money demand is higher for any level of income, given the price level *P*, the real interest rate must be higher in order to reduce money demand to equal the fixed money supply. Thus, the *LM* curve will shift up or to the left with a positive shift in the money demand function.

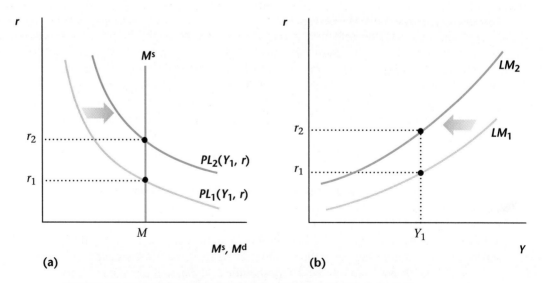

FIGURE 10.10 **A Positive Shift in Money Demand Shifts the *LM* Curve to the Left**
If there is a positive shift in money demand, this has a similar effect to a decrease in the money supply. The real interest rate for which the money market is in equilibrium increases, given the level of real income, shifting the *LM* curve to the left.

The Aggregate Demand Curve

Now that we have constructed the aggregate supply curve, and the IS and LM curves, the final component of the Keynesian sticky wage model is the **aggregate demand curve**, which we derive from the IS–LM diagram. Recall that the IS–LM diagram is constructed for a given price level P. In Figure 10.11(a) the initial LM curve, LM_1, is drawn for price level P_1. Thus, (Y_1, P_1) denotes a real output and price level pair such that the money market and goods market are in equilibrium in Figure 10.11(b). Now, suppose that the price level is higher, say $P_2 > P_1$. Then, the increase in the price level causes the LM curve to shift leftward to LM_2. As a result, the money market and goods market are in equilibrium at a lower level of output, Y_2. Then, in Figure 10.11(b), (Y_2, P_2) is another output and price level combination for which the money market and goods market are in equilibrium. If we considered all possible values for the price level and determined the associated levels of income for which the money market and goods market were in equilibrium, we would trace out the aggregate demand curve AD, which is

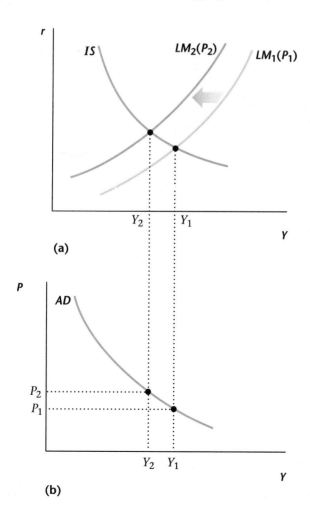

(a)

(b)

FIGURE 10.11

The Aggregate Demand Curve

An increase in the price level reduces the level of real income for which the money market and goods market are in equilibrium in panel (a). This implies that the AD curve, describing (Y, P) combinations for which the goods and money markets are in equilibrium, is downward-sloping, as in panel (b).

a downward-sloping curve in Figure 10.11(b). The curve is downward-sloping because an increase in the price level reduces the real money supply, causing a reduction in the level of output at which the money market and goods market are in equilibrium, given the price level.

SHIFTS IN THE AGGREGATE DEMAND CURVE

To complete our knowledge of how the Keynesian sticky wage model works, we need to know how the aggregate demand curve shifts in response to changes in exogenous variables. Basically, anything that causes a shift in either the *IS* curve or the *LM* curve will also shift the *AD* curve.

- *If the* IS *curve shifts to the right, then the* AD *curve shifts to the right.* In Figure 10.12(a) the *IS* curve shifts to the right. Recall that the *LM* curve depends on the price level, and we will suppose here that the price level is P_1. When the *IS* curve shifts, the level of income for which the goods market and money market are in equilibrium

FIGURE 10.12

A Shift to the Right in the *IS* Curve Shifts the *AD* Curve to the Right

A shift to the right in the *IS* curve implies that, given the price level P, the money and goods markets are in equilibrium for a higher level of real output, which shifts the aggregate demand curve to the right.

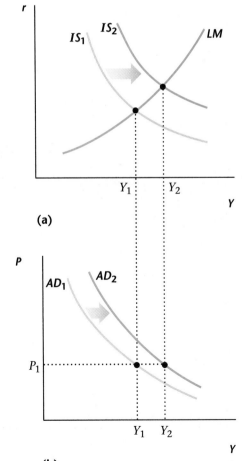

rises from Y_1 to Y_2. Therefore, a point on the initial aggregate demand curve in Figure 10.12(b) is (Y_1, P_1) and a point on the new aggregate demand curve is (Y_2, P_1). The aggregate demand curve must shift to the right from AD_1 to AD_2 as, for any price level, the level of real income at which the money market and goods market are in equilibrium has increased.

- *If the LM curve shifts to the right, then the aggregate demand curve shifts to the right.* In Figure 10.13(a), given the price level P_1, an increase in the money supply or a negative shift in the money demand function shifts the LM curve to the right, from LM_1 to LM_2. Therefore, the money market and goods market are now in equilibrium at the level of income Y_2 rather than at Y_1, as initially. Therefore, the point (Y_1, P_1) in Figure 10.13(b) is on the initial aggregate demand curve AD_1 and the point (Y_2, P_1) is on the new aggregate demand curve AD_2. As we could conduct the same experiment for all possible values for the price level, the new aggregate demand curve AD_2 is to the right of the initial curve AD_1.

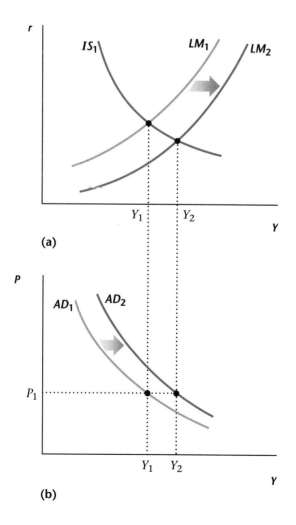

(a)

(b)

FIGURE 10.13

A Shift to the Right in the *LM* Curve Shifts the *AD* Curve to the Right

A shift to the right in the *LM* curve implies that, given the price level *P*, the money and goods markets are in equilibrium for a higher level of real output, which shifts the aggregate demand curve to the right.

Therefore, given what we know from the previous sections about the factors that shift the *IS* and *LM* curves, and the relationship between shifts in the *IS* and *LM* curves and the *AD* curve, we know that the *AD* curve shifts to the right when any of the following occur:

- Government spending *G* increases.
- The present value of taxes decreases.
- The current capital stock *K* decreases.
- Future total factor productivity z^1 will increase.
- The money supply increases.
- There is a negative shift in the money demand function.

The Complete Keynesian Sticky Wage Model

Now that we have constructed the aggregate supply curve, the *IS* and *LM* curves, and the aggregate demand curve, we can put these elements of the Keynesian sticky wage model together into a useful working model. Again, recall that this is the same structure as we worked with in the monetary intertemporal model, except that the sticky nominal wage makes the model work in a quite different way. A key feature of the Keynesian sticky wage model is that the classical dichotomy does not hold, in contrast to the monetary intertemporal model. That is, the price level and real variables are jointly determined, and money will not be neutral, as we will see.

Figure 10.14 shows the complete Keynesian sticky wage model, where we determine the real interest rate, the level of output, the price level, the real wage, and employment, as r^*, Y^*, P^*, $\frac{W}{P^*}$, and N^*, respectively. Here, Y and P are determined by the intersection of the aggregate demand and aggregate supply curves in Figure 10.14(b). Since the nominal wage W is fixed, when we know the price level we know the real wage $w = \frac{W}{P}$, which determines employment in Figure 10.14(c). Given the price level, we know the position of the *LM* curve in Figure 10.14(a), which then determines the real interest rate r from the intersection of the *IS* and *LM* curves.

THE NONNEUTRALITY OF MONEY WHEN WAGES ARE STICKY

Given our complete description of the Keynesian sticky wage model, we can proceed with an experiment, which will illustrate how money fails to be neutral in this model. In general, a change in the supply of money will have real effects in the Keynesian sticky wage model, and the price level will not change in proportion to the change in the money supply.

In Figure 10.15 we show the effects of an increase in the money supply. Initially the money supply is M_1, and it increases to M_2. This increase shifts the aggregate demand curve to the right, from AD_1 to AD_2 in Figure 10.15(b). In equilibrium, the price level rises from P_1 to P_2, and real output rises from Y_1 to Y_2. In the *IS*–*LM* diagram in Figure 10.15(a), the increase in the money supply from M_1 to M_2 shifts the *LM* curve rightward from LM_1 to LM_2. However, we know that in equilibrium the price level rises,

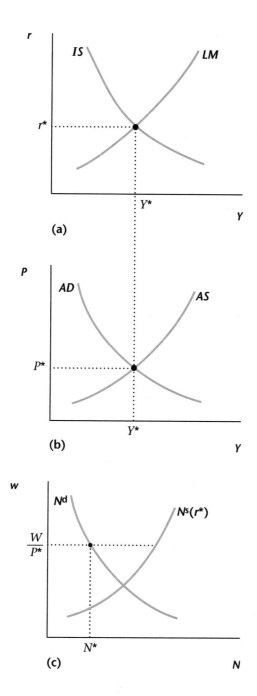

FIGURE 10.14

The Keynesian Sticky Wage Model

The figure shows the complete Keynesian sticky wage model. The AD and AS curves determine the price level P and level of output Y in panel (b). Then, given the nominal wage W, the real wage $\frac{W}{P}$ determines employment from the labour demand curve N^d in panel (c). Finally, given P, the real interest rate is determined by the intersection of the IS and LM curves in panel (a).

and this will shift the LM curve back to the left to LM_3. We know that the leftward shift in LM does not completely offset the rightward shift in LM, as we know from the AD–AS diagram in Figure 10.15(b) that output must increase in equilibrium. Therefore, in equilibrium the real interest rate must fall, from r_1 to r_2. Further, we know that the real money supply $\frac{M}{P}$ must rise in equilibrium, since it is $\frac{M}{P}$ that determines the position of

FIGURE 10.15

An Increase in the Money Supply in the Sticky Wage Model

An increase in the money supply is not neutral. The real interest rate falls, the price level rises less than proportionally to the money supply increase, the real wage falls, and employment and output rise.

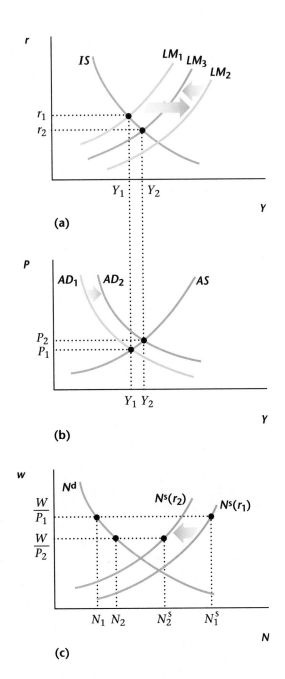

(a)

(b)

(c)

the *LM* curve; if the *LM* curve shifted to the right from LM_1 to LM_3, then $\frac{M}{P}$ must have risen, so that the price level increased less than in proportion to the money supply.

In the labour market diagram in Figure 10.15(c), the real wage falls from $\frac{W}{P_1}$ to $\frac{W}{P_2}$, since the nominal wage W is fixed and the price level has increased. As employment is determined by the labour demand curve, employment increases from N_1 to N_2; that is, firms hire more labour because the real wage has fallen. Further, because the real interest rate falls in equilibrium, workers wish to supply less labour (they wish to supply less labour today and more in the future), and the labour supply curve shifts to the left from $N^s(r_1)$ to $N^s(r_2)$. The result is that, since employment rises from N_1 to N_2, and desired labour supply falls from N_1^s to N_2^s, Keynesian unemployment falls from $N_1^s - N_1$ to $N_2^s - N_2$.

Therefore, to summarize, money is not neutral, because the increase in the money supply has real effects; the real interest rate falls, real output increases, the real wage falls, employment increases, and Keynesian unemployment decreases. Keynesians think of money having these real effects through the **Keynesian transmission mechanism for monetary policy**. That is, an increase in the money supply has its first effects in financial markets; the real interest rate falls to equate money demand with the increased money supply. Since the interest rate is lower, this increases the demand for consumption goods (through intertemporal substitution), and for investment goods. The increase in the demand for goods raises the price level, which lowers the real wage (given the fixed nominal wage), and increases employment.

Most Keynesians regard money as being neutral in the long run. While Keynesians argue that money is not neutral in the short run because of sticky wages (or prices), they also believe that the nominal wage will eventually adjust so that supply equals demand in the labour market, in which case money will be neutral as in the monetary intertemporal model we studied in Chapter 9. See Macroeconomics in Action 10.1 on p. 359 for a discussion of the role of money in the 1981–82 recession.

THEORY CONFRONTS THE DATA 10.1

Can Sticky Wages and Money Supply Fluctuations Explain Business Cycles?

Since changes in the money supply can cause output to change in the Keynesian sticky wage model, a key prediction of the model is that, if the money supply fluctuates, so will aggregate output. The model then gives a monetary theory of business cycles. That is, the model predicts that fluctuations in the money supply could cause business cycles. As economists, we would then like to ask whether this is a good or bad theory of business cycles. To answer this question, we have to ask how the predictions of the model fit the key business cycle regularities that we outlined in Chapter 3.

In Table 10.1 we show how the predictions of the Keynesian sticky wage model with money supply fluctuations fit features of the data we examined in Chapter 3. Some features of the model clearly fit the data. For example, when the money supply increases, output increases, which is consistent with the fact that money is procyclical in the data. As well, when the money supply increases, the fall in the real interest rate causes investment and consumption to rise, so that investment I and consumption C are procyclical, as is true for the data. Further, an increase in the money supply causes an increase in employment, and so employment will be procyclical, as is the case in the data.

However, other results do not fit. When the money supply increases, the price level goes up, so that if money supply fluctuations are a primary cause of business cycles, the price level will be procyclical. However, the price level is countercyclical in the data.

TABLE 10.1 **Data Versus Predictions of the Keynesian Sticky Wage Model with Monetary Shocks**

	Data	Model
Consumption	Procyclical	Procyclical
Investment	Procyclical	Procyclical
Price level	Countercyclical	Procyclical
Money supply	Procyclical	Procyclical
Employment	Procyclical	Procyclical
Real wage	Procyclical	Countercyclical

As well, the real wage falls when the money supply increases and so the model predicts that the real wage is countercyclical, but it is procyclical in the data.

We conclude that, at least for the time period in Canada we examined in Chapter 3, it does not appear that fluctuations in the stock of money could have been the most important cause of business cycles, if money affects the economy as captured in the Keynesian sticky wage model. It is possible, however, that fluctuations in the money supply, acting through the Keynesian transmission mechanism for monetary policy, made significant contributions (though not the primary ones) to fluctuations in GDP over this period. As well, before World War II in Canada, the price level was procyclical, rather than countercyclical as in the later period we examined, which is consistent with monetary shocks being important for business cycles during this earlier period.

We must regard conclusions from Table 10.1 with caution, as in practice the money supply in Canada is controlled by the Bank of Canada, which reacts to events in the economy. Bank of Canada policymakers living in the Keynesian sticky wage world would come to realize that fluctuations in the money supply could cause output and employment to fluctuate. In circumstances where no other shocks were impinging on the economy, the Bank would have no reason to change the money supply, and so we would not observe events where a change in the money supply was the obvious cause of a change in output. As we will study in more detail later in this chapter, the Bank might have good reasons to change the money supply in response to other shocks to the economy, but then it would be hard to disentangle the effects of monetary policy on real activity from the effects of other shocks.

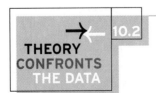

THEORY CONFRONTS THE DATA   10.2   Keynesian Aggregate Demand Shocks as Causes of Business Cycles

Though monetary shocks in the Keynesian sticky wage model may not be able to explain the key business cycle regularities discussed in Chapter 3, some other shock to the economy might successfully explain observed business cycles in this model. Keynes argued in his *General Theory of Employment, Interest, and Money* that a principal cause of business cycles is fluctuations in aggregate demand. What he appears to have had in mind was shocks to investment, which would be captured here as shifts in the *IS* curve. That is, suppose that firms become more optimistic about future total factor productivity, so that they view the future marginal product of capital as having increased (Keynes referred to such waves of optimism as being due to the "animal spirits" of investors). This increases the demand for investment goods, shifts the IS curve to the right, and shifts the AD curve to the right.

An increase in the demand for investment goods leads to a rightward shift in the IS curve from IS_1 to IS_2 in Figure 10.16(a) and a rightward shift in the AD curve from

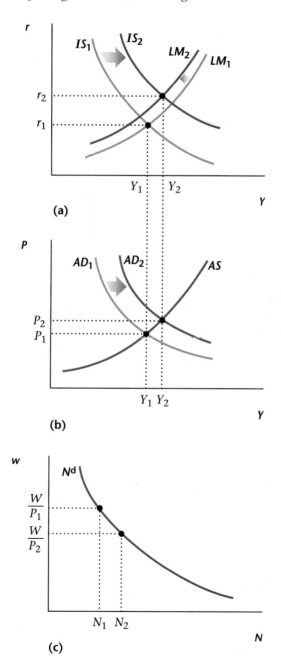

(a)

(b)

(c)

FIGURE 10.16

An Increase in the Demand for Investment Goods in the Sticky Wage Model

An anticipated increase in future total factor productivity increases the demand for investment goods, shifting the IS curve to the right. Output, employment, and the price level increase, and the real wage declines. Consumption and investment may increase or decrease.

TABLE 10.2 **Data Versus Predictions of the Keynesian Sticky Wage Model with Investment Shocks**

	Data	Model
Consumption	Procyclical	?
Investment	Procyclical	Procyclical
Price level	Countercyclical	Procyclical
Money supply	Procyclical	Acyclical
Employment	Procyclical	Procyclical
Real wage	Procyclical	Countercyclical

AD_1 to AD_2 in Figure 10.16 (b). In equilibrium, in Figure 10.16(b), the price level increases from P_1 to P_2, and real output increases from Y_1 to Y_2. In Figure 10.16(a), when the price level increases, this causes the LM curve to shift leftward from LM_1 to LM_2. Ultimately, the real interest rate increases from r_1 to r_2. The increase in the real interest rate will cause investment to fall and consumption to fall. The increase in real income causes consumption to rise, so net consumption could rise or fall, but investment must rise, as it was the initial shock that caused the demand for investment goods to rise. In the labour market, in Figure 10.16(c), the real wage falls from $\frac{W}{P_1}$ to $\frac{W}{P_2}$, and employment increases from N_1 to N_2. We leave the labour supply curve out of Figure 10.16(c) as labour supply is important only for determining unemployment in this model, and this will not be critical for our arguments.

Table 10.2 above summarizes the key business cycle facts from Chapter 3 and the predictions of the Keynesian sticky wage model under investment shocks. From Figure 10.16, an increase in output coincides with an increase in investment, an increase or decrease in consumption, an increase in the price level, an increase in employment, and a decrease in the real wage. Therefore, in contrast to the data, consumption may be countercyclical, the price level is procyclical, and the real wage is countercyclical. As well, the model provides no explanation for why the money supply is procyclical, though as we will see in Chapter 11, there are forces at work in the economy that can cause the money supply to respond to other shocks that cause output to fluctuate. Our conclusion is that the fit to the data is not the best, and so investment shocks in the Keynesian sticky wage model do not appear to adequately explain business cycle facts. ✦

THE ROLE OF GOVERNMENT POLICY IN THE STICKY WAGE MODEL

In macroeconomics, some important disagreements focus on the issue of whether the government should act to smooth out business cycles. This smoothing, or what is sometimes referred to as **stabilization policy**, involves carrying out government actions that will increase aggregate real output when it is below trend, and decrease it when it is above trend. Using government policy to smooth business cycles may appear to be a good idea. For example, we know that a consumer whose income fluctuates will behave optimally by smoothing consumption relative to income, so why shouldn't the government take actions that will smooth aggregate real income over time? As we will see

Monetary Policy and the 1981–82 Recession

Though the evidence from the previous section appears to indicate that monetary policy was relatively unimportant in causing business cycles during the 1961–2002 period, the 1981–82 recession is widely attributed to central bank actions. The inflation rate reached post–World War II highs during the 1970s in Canada. Under a Keynesian interpretation of events, the Bank of Canada decided that inflation had to be reduced through contractionary monetary policy, which had the side-effect of producing a severe recession in 1981–82. Then, according to the story, once Canadian residents had borne the short-run pain of a recession, they could enjoy the relatively low inflation rates of the later 1980s and 1990s.

Typically, there are many different shocks hitting the economy simultaneously, and sophisticated statistical analysis is required to separate out the effects of these shocks from the effects of monetary policy. It turns out that the results from this type of sophisticated statistical analysis are not entirely conclusive.

Work by Eric Leeper, Christopher Sims, and Tao Zha summarizes much of the research in this area, and it generally finds that contractionary monetary policy has significant negative effects on real output.[1] However, Harald Uhlig argues that much of this research is tainted, and he suggests that the evidence is consistent with money being neutral.[2]

During the 1981–82 recession in Canada, most casual observers attributed the severity of the recession to high interest rates, and they assigned responsibility for those high interest rates to the Bank of Canada. The statistical evidence, however, though tending to favour this view of the cause of the 1981–82 recession, is not entirely conclusive.

---

[1]See E. Leeper, C. Sims, and T. Zha, 1996, "What Does Monetary Policy Do?" *Brookings Papers on Economic Activity*, series 2, 1–63.

[2]See H. Uhlig, 2001, "What Are the Effects of Monetary Policy on Output? Results from an Agnostic Identification Procedure," working paper, Humboldt University.

---

in Chapter 11, this logic need not apply when considering the rationale for government policy intervention with respect to macroeconomic events.

An examination of the behaviour of real GDP, the money supply, and interest rates certainly appears to support this view. In Figure 10.17 the money supply dips below trend in 1981–82, though the trough in money supply below trend in this case was reached after GDP began to recover. In Figure 10.18 there is an increase in real and nominal interest rates in 1980–81, which is consistent with monetary tightening. The data in Figures 10.17 and 10.18 therefore appear consistent with the Keynesian sticky wage model, and with the view that monetary policy can have large effects on real output. The evidence from Figures 10.17 and 10.18 is not, however, the end of the story.

Keynesians tend to believe that government intervention to smooth out business cycles is appropriate, and the Keynesian sticky wage model provides a justification for this belief. We will start by considering a situation where an unanticipated shock has hit the economy, causing the real wage to be higher than its equilibrium level in the labour market, as in Figure 10.19(c). For example, there may have been an unanticipated increase in the relative price of energy, which led to a decrease in total factor productivity.

FIGURE 10.17

Money Supply and GDP

The figure shows detrended money supply and detrended real GDP for the 1962–2002 period in Canada. A drop in money below trend is consistent with the 1981–82 recession, though the money supply bottoms out later than does real GDP.

Source: Adapted from the Statistics Canada CANSIM database, Series v37145, v1992067.

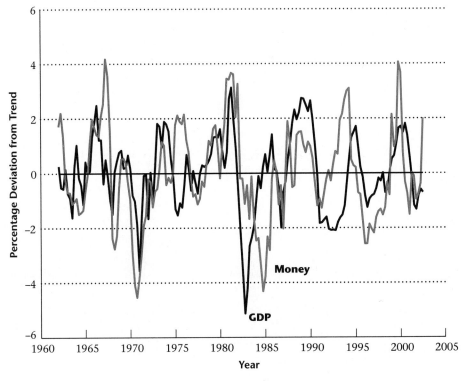

FIGURE 10.18

Real and Nominal Interest Rates

The figure shows the short-term nominal interest rate and the corresponding real interest rate, measured as the nominal rate minus the actual inflation rate, for the 1962–2002 period in Canada. Increases in the real and nominal interest rates precede the 1981–82 recession.

Source: Adapted from the Statistics Canada CANSIM database, Series v122531, v1997756.

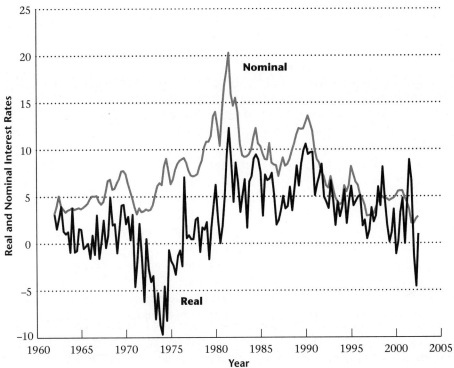

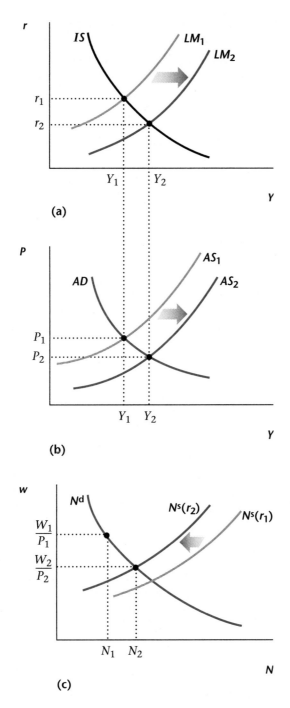

FIGURE 10.19

Long-Run Adjustment of the Nominal Wage
If the real wage is initially higher than its equilibrium value, the nominal wage will tend to fall. In the long run, the nominal wage decreases, the price level decreases, output increases, and the real interest rate falls, until supply is equal to demand in the labour market.

After the shock hits the economy, the nominal wage is W_1, the price level is P_1, and the real wage is $\frac{W_1}{P_1}$, which implies, in Figure 10.19(c), that employment is N_1 and there is Keynesian unemployment, given the labour supply curve $N^s(r_1)$. In Figure 10.19(b) aggregate output is Y_1 and the price level is P_1, while in Figure 10.19(a) the real interest rate is r_1.

Now, after the shock has hit the economy, the allocation of resources is not economically efficient. Recall from Chapter 5 that the first fundamental theorem of welfare economics implies that a competitive equilibrium is Pareto-optimal,[5] but in Figure 10.19 the economy is not in a competitive equilibrium, as initially labour demand is not equal to labour supply. One response of the government to the economic inefficiency caused by the shock to the economy would be to do nothing, and let the problem cure itself. Since the real wage is initially above its equilibrium level, there will be a tendency for the nominal wage to fall. This will cause the aggregate supply curve to shift to the right, which will put downward pressure on the price level. This in turn will cause the LM curve to shift to the right, reducing the real interest rate. In the long run, the nominal wage and the price level will decrease to the point where the price level is P_2 in Figure 10.19(b) and output is Y_2, and in Figure 10.19(c) the nominal wage has fallen to W_2 and the real wage $\frac{W_2}{P_2}$ is such that supply is equal to demand in the labour market. The labour supply curve comes to rest at $N^s(r_2)$ given the decrease in the real interest rate. The fall in the price level will lead to a shift in the LM curve to LM_2 in the long run, and the real interest rate will fall to r_2. Ultimately, then, long-run reductions in the nominal wage and the price level will result in increases in real output, employment, consumption, and investment (since the real interest rate falls).

Keynesian macroeconomists argue that the long run is too long to wait. In Figure 10.20 suppose an initial situation just as in Figure 10.19, where the economy has been hit by a shock that causes the initial real wage, $\frac{W}{P_1}$ in Figure 10.20(c), to be too high relative to its equilibrium level. One possible response to the economic inefficiency that exists would be an increase in the money supply M by the monetary authority. Initially, the LM curve shifts to LM_2 in Figure 10.20(a), given the initial price level P_1, determined by the intersection of the initial aggregate demand curve AD_1 and the aggregate supply curve AS in Figure 10.20(b). If M is increased just the right amount by the monetary authority, the aggregate demand curve will shift to AD_2 and the equilibrium price level will rise to P_2 while output rises to Y_2 from Y_1. The increase in the price level causes a leftward shift in the LM curve from LM_2 to LM_3, the ultimate result being that the real interest rate falls from r_1 to r_2. In the labour market, the labour supply curve shifts from $N^s(r_1)$ to $N^s(r_2)$ because of the fall in the interest rate, and the real wage falls to $\frac{W}{P_2}$ due to the increase in the price level. If the increase in the money supply is just right, then full employment is achieved with the quantity of employment being N_2.

Note that after the increase in the money supply, the economy is in exactly the same situation, in real terms, as it would have been in the long run if the monetary authority did nothing and allowed the nominal wage and price level to fall (compare Figure 10.20 with Figure 10.19). The only difference is that the nominal wage and the price level are higher in the case where the monetary authority intervenes. The advantage of intervention is that an efficient outcome is achieved faster than if the monetary authority let events take their course.

---

[5]Note that we are ignoring the long-run inefficiency that results from an inflation rate that is not optimal, as discussed in Chapter 9.

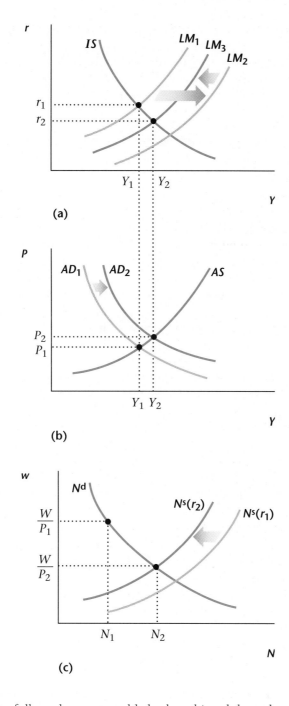

(a)

(b)

(c)

FIGURE 10.20
Stabilization Policy in the Sticky Wage Model—Monetary Policy
A shock to the economy initially causes the real wage to be above its equilibrium value. The monetary authority increases the money supply, causing the real interest rate to fall, the price level to rise, the real wage to fall, and employment and output to rise. An appropriate increase in the money supply restores equilibrium in the labour market.

The return to full employment could also be achieved through an increase in government expenditures G, but with some different results. In Figure 10.21 we show a similar initial situation to Figures 10.19 and 10.20, where initial employment is N_1, which is less than the quantity of labour that the representative consumer wants to

FIGURE 10.21

**Stabilization Policy in the
Sticky Wage Model—
Fiscal Policy**

The figure shows stabilization
policy by way of a temporary
increase in government
spending. Equilibrium is
restored in the labour market
through an increase in G,
which increases the real
interest rate, reduces
consumption and investment,
increases the price level,
reduces the real wage,
and increases employment
and output.

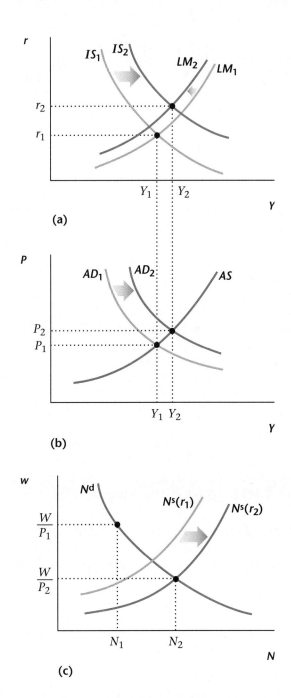

supply at the market real wage $\frac{W}{P_1}$. If the government increases government purchases
G by just the right amount, then the IS curve shifts rightward in Figure 10.21(a) from
IS_1 to IS_2 and the aggregate demand curve in Figure 10.21(b) shifts rightward from AD_1
to AD_2. In equilibrium, the price level increases from P_1 to P_2, and aggregate output
increases from Y_1 to Y_2 in Figure 10.21(b). Then, in Figure 10.21(a), the increase in the

price level causes the *LM* curve to shift leftward from LM_1 to LM_2, just enough that the intersection of IS_2 with LM_2 is at the level of income Y_2, as determined in the aggregate demand/aggregate supply diagram in Figure 10.21(b). In equilibrium, the real interest rate increases from r_1 to r_2. With the increase in the price level, the real wage falls from $\frac{W}{P_1}$ to $\frac{W}{P_2}$, and the increase in the real interest rate causes the labour supply curve to shift to the right, from $N^s(r_1)$ to $N^s(r_2)$ in Figure 10.21(c). Given that the government increases *G* by the right amount, in equilibrium the quantity of employment will be N_2 and supply will be equal to demand in the labour market.

Now, note the differences in final outcomes between Figures 10.21 and 10.20. In Figure 10.21, with the increase in *G* the real interest rate has risen, while it falls in Figure 10.20 when the money supply is increased. The increase in the real interest rate in Figure 10.21 causes investment and consumption to fall; that is, there is crowding-out of private expenditure by government expenditure. In contrast, the decrease in the real interest rate will cause an increase in investment and consumption in Figure 10.20. Note also that the increase in the real interest rate leads to a rightward shift in the labour supply curve in Figure 10.21, while the labour supply curve shifts to the left in Figure 10.20. The conclusion is that, when government expenditures are used to increase employment rather than having the monetary authority increase the money supply, consumption and investment will be lower, and employment will be higher, so that output will also be higher. Thus, it matters whether fiscal or monetary policy is used for stabilization purposes, as this will affect the level of aggregate output, and the public and private uses of that output.

Whether fiscal or monetary policy is used to smooth business cycles, the Keynesian sticky wage model provides a rationale for stabilization policy. If shocks kick the economy out of equilibrium, because of a failure of private markets to clear in the short run, fiscal or monetary policymakers can, if they move fast enough, restore the economy to equilibrium before self-adjusting markets achieve this on their own. Thus, the important elements of the Keynesian view of government's role in the macroeconomy are the following:

1. Private markets fail to operate smoothly on their own, in that not all wages and prices are perfectly flexible, implying that supply is not equal to demand in all markets, and economic efficiency is not always achieved in a world without government intervention.

2. Fiscal policy and/or monetary policy decisions can be made quickly enough, and information on the behaviour of the economy is good enough, that the fiscal or monetary authorities can improve efficiency by countering shocks that cause a deviation from a full-employment equilibrium.

In Macroeconomics in Action 10.2, we discuss the problem of stabilization policy in the face of real-world lags in the implementation and effects of monetary and fiscal policy.

SHIFTS IN MONEY DEMAND AND MONETARY CONTROL

In Chapter 9, we discussed some implications of shifts in money demand for monetary policy in a world where money is neutral and the central bank is interested in controlling

Policy Lags

In the Keynesian sticky wage model, we have shown that either fiscal or monetary policy can stabilize the economy. That is, if government spending is set appropriately by the fiscal authority, then full employment can be achieved; and economic efficiency can also be achieved if the monetary authority acts to set the money supply appropriately in response to shocks that affect aggregate economic activity. In practice, important imperfections—the policy lags in the formulation and implementation of monetary and fiscal policies—matter critically for the absolute and relative effectiveness of monetary and fiscal policies.

Milton Friedman argued that there are three key lags involved in policymaking, "(1) the lag between the need for action and the recognition of this need; (2) the lag between recognition of the need for action and the taking of action; and (3) the lag between the action and its effects."[1] First, policymakers do not have complete information. The national income and expenditure accounts, employment data, and price data are time-consuming to compile, and policymakers in the federal government and at the Bank of Canada have good information only for what was happening in the economy months previously. Second, when information is available, it may take time for policymakers to agree among themselves concerning a course of action. Third, once policy is implemented, there is a lag before policy has its effects on aggregate economic activity.

The first lag is the same for monetary and fiscal policy. In Canada, economists working at the Bank of Canada and the Department of Finance, and the key leaders who are making decisions on fiscal and monetary policies, have essentially identical information. Further, the Governor of the Bank of Canada and the Minister of Finance consult regularly, as do other officials in the Bank of Canada and the Department of Finance. The key differences between the lags in fiscal and monetary policy lie in the second and third stages.

David Dodge, current Governor of the Bank of Canada, has been in the somewhat unusual position of being a practitioner of both fiscal and monetary policy. Before being appointed Governor in 2001, Dodge served as Deputy Minister of Finance (the top civil service position in the Department of Finance) from 1992 to 1997. Dodge's views on the effectiveness of monetary and fiscal policies in stabilization are nicely articulated in his remarks at a symposium held by the Federal Reserve Bank of Kansas City on August 31, 2002.[2] Dodge feels, in terms of the second stage of the policy lag (the lag between the recognition of action and the taking of action), that monetary policy wins out. On the one hand, monetary policy actions can be taken at any time, with decisions made by a small group of people led by the Governor of the Bank of Canada, and there is no need for legislative action. On the other hand, Dodge argues that "I can tell you that the great problem here [with fiscal policy] is that temporary measures are both difficult to initiate quickly when the need arises and extraordinarily difficult to stop once the need is past." For fiscal policy action to be implemented requires that recommendations be formulated at the Department of Finance and passed to the Minister of Finance, following which legislative action needs to be taken by Parliament. All this takes much time and, as Dodge points out, is costly to reverse.

With respect to the third stage, the lag between the action and its effects, Dodge views monetary policy as being somewhat inferior to fiscal policy. He states that "monetary policy ... takes time to work, with the full impact on output normally felt after 12 to 18 months," while "fiscal policy measures could, *in principle*, and under ideal circumstances, shorten the time it takes to move output back to its desired level."

The conclusion is that, even if we believe stabilizing the economy through the use of fiscal and monetary policy is appropriate, as the Keynesian sticky wage model tells us, there is still much that can go wrong. Guiding the economy can be much like trying to steer a car with a faulty steering mechanism; one has to see the bumps and curves in the road well in advance to avoid driving in the ditch or otherwise having a very uncomfortable ride. This is in part why Milton Friedman, among others, has encouraged abstinence from stabilization policy altogether. Friedman argued that well-intentioned stabilization policy could do more harm than good, as the

lags in policy could lead to stimulative action being taken when tightening the screws on the economy would be more appropriate, and vice versa.

[1]See M. Friedman, 1953, *Essays in Positive Economics*, University of Chicago Press, Chicago, p. 145.

[2]See David Dodge, 2002, "Macroeconomic Stabilization Policy in Canada," remarks to a symposium sponsored by the Federal Reserve Bank of Kansas City Jackson Hole, Wyoming, August 31, available **www.bankofcanada.ca/en/speeches/sp02-15.htm**, accessed July 13, 2003.

the price level. The Keynesian sticky wage model implies an important stabilization policy problem for a central bank when the money demand function is unstable. As we will show, a shift in the money demand function will cause output and employment to change. This can be counteracted with an appropriate change in the money supply. Essentially, if money demand increases (decreases), then the money supply should increase (decrease) to accommodate this. With unstable money demand, we will show that in the short run it is preferable for the central bank to target the interest rate rather than the money supply.

Suppose that the economy is initially in a long-run equilibrium with the price level equal to P_1 and output at the level Y_1 as in Figure 10.22(b), given initial aggregate demand and aggregate supply curves AD_1 and AS, respectively. In Figure 10.22(c), the real wage $\frac{W}{P_1}$ initially clears the labour market, given the labour demand curve N^d and the initial labour supply curve $N^s(r_1)$.

Then, suppose there is a positive shift in money demand, for example, because of an increase in the riskiness of alternative assets to money. This will cause the LM curve in Figure 10.22(a) to shift leftward to LM_2, given the initial price level P_1. As a result, the aggregate demand curve in Figure 10.22(b) shifts leftward from AD_1 to AD_2, and in equilibrium the price level falls to P_2 and aggregate output drops to Y_2. The decrease in the price level shifts the LM curve rightward from LM_2 to LM_3, implying an equilibrium level of income of Y_2 in Figure 10.22(a). In equilibrium, the real interest rate rises to r_2. In Figure 10.22(c), the real wage rises to $\frac{W}{P_2}$, and the labour supply curve shifts rightward to $N^s(r_2)$, implying that employment falls from N_1 to N_2 and there is now unemployment. Therefore, the positive shift in money demand leads to a bad short-run outcome where output and employment are inefficiently low.

The central bank can correct the short-run inefficiency resulting from the shift in money demand by changing the money supply appropriately. In this case, the central bank should accommodate the increase in money demand by increasing the money supply. This will shift the LM curve to the right. If the central bank increases the money supply by just the right amount, the LM curve will shift to LM_1 in Figure 10.22(a), the aggregate demand curve will shift to AD_1 in Figure 10.22(b), the real wage will fall to

FIGURE 10.22
**The Equilibrium Effects
of a Positive Money
Demand Shift**
A positive shift in money
demand increases the real
interest rate, reduces the price
level, increases the real wage,
and reduces employment and
aggregate output.

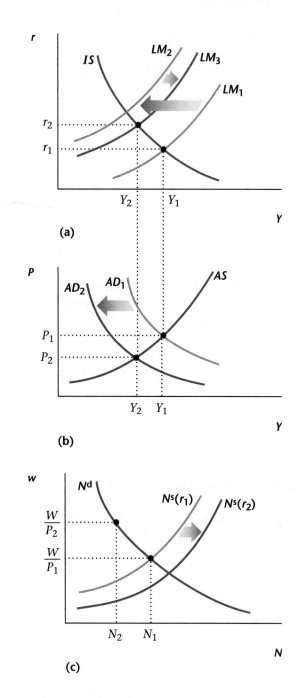

(a)

(b)

(c)

$\frac{W}{P_1}$ in Figure 10.22(c), and the real interest rate will fall to r_1 in Figure 10.22(a), shifting the labour supply curve in Figure 10.22(c) leftward to $N^s(r_1)$. The result is that efficiency is restored, with all real and nominal variables identical to what they were before the shift in money demand.

In the discussion above, it may appear straightforward for a central bank to manipulate the money supply to respond to unexpected shifts in money demand. However, central banks face a problem of imperfect information. The central bank can observe market interest rates on a minute-by-minute basis, but it observes the money supply less frequently, and real variables such as aggregate output are observable even less frequently. For simplicity, suppose the central bank wants to control aggregate output but cannot observe it in the short run. It can, however, observe the money supply and the real interest rate. If unexpected shocks to money demand hit the economy, which of the observable variables should the central bank choose to control as a short-run target, the money supply or the real interest rate? Our analysis above tells us that the central bank should control the interest rate. In Figure 10.22 control of the money supply (i.e., holding it constant) in the short run would imply that the positive shock to money demand would cause output to fall from Y_1 to Y_2, which is undesirable. However, controlling the real interest rate by holding it constant at r_1 implies that the money supply has to increase, and output stays constant at Y_1.

Beginning in the 1970s, many central banks, including the Bank of Canada, experimented with the short-run targeting of monetary aggregates. However, instability in money demand in the 1980s led most of the world's central banks to lessen considerably the attention paid to the behaviour of monetary aggregates in setting monetary policy. In Chapter 9, we showed how the instability of money demand can lead to price level fluctuations when the money stock is targeted, and our analysis here suggests Keynesian arguments that money demand instability can lead to undesirable fluctuations in real variables.

Keynesian Sticky Price Models

In Keynesian macroeconomics, the sticky wage model is not the only approach to studying how the economy functions and for understanding the role of policy. Alternatives to the sticky wage model are models where prices are sticky, so that goods markets do not always clear. These **sticky price models** have properties similar to those of the sticky wage model, in that money is not neutral in the short run and there is a role for government stabilization policy.

Why might goods prices be sticky in the short run? Some Keynesians argue that it is costly for firms to change prices, and even if these costs are small, this could lead firms to fix the prices for their products for long periods of time.[6] Consider a restaurant, which must print new menus whenever it changes its prices. Printing menus is costly, and this causes the restaurant to change prices infrequently. Given that prices change infrequently, there may be periods when the restaurant is full and people are being turned away. If menus were not costly to print, the restaurant might increase its prices under these circumstances. Alternatively, there may be periods when the restaurant is

---

[6]See L. Ball and N. G. Mankiw, 1994, "A Sticky Price Manifesto," *Carnegie-Rochester Conference Series on Public Policy* 41, 127–151.

not full and prices would be lowered if it were not for the costs of changing prices. The restaurant example is a common one in the economic literature on sticky price models. Indeed, sticky price models are often referred to as **menu cost models**.

CRITICISMS OF KEYNESIAN STICKY WAGE AND STICKY PRICE MODELS

Critics of Keynesian sticky wage and sticky price models, whom we will refer to as **classical macroeconomists**, argue that these models fall short in several respects. First, as we have already pointed out, the sticky wage model does not fully replicate the key business cycle regularities. Perhaps most importantly, the model implies that the real wage is countercyclical, which does not fit the facts. Second, classical economists argue that the theory underlying the sticky wage model is poor or nonexistent. In the sticky wage model, it is argued that the nominal wage is fixed because of long-term labour contracts, but the model does not take explicit account of the reasons that firms and workers write such contracts. To properly understand why wages might be sticky and exactly how this will matter for macroeconomic activity, we need to be explicit in our theories about the features of the world that are important to labour contracting, and to show how a model with such features explains reality.

Menu cost models are a response to the criticisms by classical economists of Keynesian models. In these models, firms face explicit costs of changing prices, firms maximize profits in the face of these costs, and the result is that prices are in fact sticky and the models have implications much like those of our sticky wage model. However, menu cost models have certainly not been immune from criticism. Classical economists point out that the costs of changing prices are minuscule compared with the short-run costs of changing the quantity of output. Consider the case of a restaurant. The cost of changing menu prices is the cost of making a few keystrokes on a computer keyboard, and then running off a few copies of the menu on the printer in the back room. Indeed, a restaurant will be printing new menus frequently anyway, since restaurant patrons tend to spill food on the menus. On the other hand, if the restaurant wants to increase output in response to higher demand, it will have to move in more tables and chairs, and hire and train new staff. Why would the restaurant want to change output in response to a temporary increase in demand rather than just increasing prices temporarily?

The questions we have raised above are useful in framing the debate on business cycle models as we consider equilibrium models of the business cycle in Chapter 11. Equilibrium models in general have quite different implications for the role of fiscal and monetary policy from those of the Keynesian sticky wage model, often implying that government intervention is detrimental. However, there are also modern equilibrium Keynesian models that justify active government stabilization policy. The reader may wonder at this point why we should study different business cycle models that appear to have contradictory implications. The reason is that business cycles can have many causes, and each of the business cycle models we will examine contains an element of truth that will be useful in understanding why business cycles occur and what, if anything, can or should be done about them.

Chapter Summary

In this chapter, we constructed a Keynesian sticky wage model of the business cycle. In this model, the nominal wage is fixed in the short run, and it does not move to equate supply and demand in the labour market. As a result there may be Keynesian unemployment, in that the representative consumer wishes to supply more labour than the representative firm wants to hire. Given the fixed nominal wage, there exists an aggregate supply relationship, whereby an increase in the price level reduces the real wage, firms hire more labour (in the model, we assume that the labour demand curve determines employment), and more output is produced. The aggregate supply curve is a positive relationship between the price level and level of output. This curve shifts to the right if the nominal wage falls or if total factor productivity increases. The aggregate demand side of the model is constructed from the *IS–LM* diagram, where the *IS* curve is identical to the output demand curve in the monetary intertemporal model of Chapter 9. The *IS* curve describes real interest rate/real output combinations such that the goods market is in equilibrium. The *LM* curve describes real interest rate/real output combinations such that the money market is in equilibrium, given the price level. The aggregate demand curve is a negative relationship between the price level and the level of aggregate output, which describes price level/output combinations for which the goods market and money market are in equilibrium. The *IS* curve shifts to the right with an increase in government spending, a decrease in the present value of taxes, an increase in future income, a decrease in the current capital stock, or an increase in future total factor productivity. The *LM* curve shifts to the right if the money supply increases, if there is a negative shift in the money demand function, or if the price level decreases. If the *IS* curve or *LM* curve shifts to the right, the aggregate demand curve shifts to the right (excepting changes in the price level, which involve movements along the aggregate demand curve). In the complete Keynesian sticky wage model, the price level and output are determined in the aggregate demand/aggregate supply diagram. Then, given the price level, employment and the real wage are determined in the labour market, and the real interest rate is determined by the *IS–LM* diagram.

Money is not neutral in the Keynesian sticky wage model. An increase in the money supply, through the Keynesian transmission mechanism for monetary policy, causes the real interest rate to fall, which leads to an increase in the demand for investment goods and consumption goods, causing the price level to increase and the real wage to fall (given the fixed nominal wage). As a result, the firm hires more labour and output rises. Money supply shocks in the Keynesian sticky wage model are inconsistent with key business cycle facts, in that the model predicts a procyclical price level and a countercyclical real wage. With investment shocks, the model is also inconsistent with business cycle facts, in that it predicts possibly countercyclical consumption, a procyclical price level, and a countercyclical real wage. Since the nominal wage does not adjust to clear the labour market in the model, there is a role for monetary policy and/or fiscal policy to smooth business cycles over time.

Shifts in money demand in the Keynesian sticky wage model will cause real effects, and these real effects can be offset by the appropriate monetary policy. When the central bank has difficulty observing real output on a timely basis, it is appropriate for the central bank to control the interest rate rather than the money supply in the short run, in the face of an unstable money demand function.

Alternative Keynesian models have sticky prices, motivated by the existence of menu costs. The Keynesian sticky wage model's faults are that it is not entirely consistent with the data, and that the model is silent as to why wages are sticky. Sticky price models are more explicit about the reasons for stickiness.

Key Terms

indexed: Describes the situation in which the rate of increase of a price or wage is tied to the rate of increase in a measure of the price level, such as the consumer price index.

Keynesian unemployment: Given the market real wage, the difference between the quantity of labour that workers want to supply and actual employment (the quantity demanded).

aggregate supply curve: In the Keynesian sticky wage model, a positive relationship between the price level and the level of real output.

IS curve: A curve that is identical to the output demand curve in the monetary intertemporal model of Chapter 9. In the Keynesian sticky wage model, this is a downward-sloping relationship between the real interest rate and the level of output, and it represents a set of (Y, r) combinations such that the goods market is in equilibrium.

LM curve: In the Keynesian sticky wage model, an upward-sloping relationship between the real interest rate and the level of output; a set of (Y, r) combinations such that the money market is in equilibrium, given the price level.

aggregate demand curve: In the Keynesian sticky wage model, a downward-sloping relationship between the price level and the level of real output; a set of (Y, P) combinations such that the goods market and the money market are in equilibrium.

Keynesian transmission mechanism for monetary policy: The real effects of monetary policy in the Keynesian model. In the model, money is not neutral, because an increase in the money supply causes the real interest rate to fall, increasing the demand for consumption and investment, causing the price level to increase. The real wage then falls, the firm hires more labour, and output increases.

stabilization policy: Fiscal or monetary policy justified by Keynesian models, which acts to offset shocks to the economy.

sticky price models: Keynesian models that are closely related to sticky wage models except that there are costs to changing prices, which cause prices to adjust slowly to clear goods markets.

menu cost models: Identical to sticky price models.

classical macroeconomists: The alternative to Keynesian macroeconomists; a classical macroeconomist believes that market-clearing models are useful, and tends to believe that the government should not engage in stabilization policy.

Questions for Review

1. Are Keynesian business cycle models still used? If so, what for?

2. Why is the nominal wage sticky in the sticky wage model?

3. Is there unemployment in the sticky wage model? If so, why?

4. Does the unemployment in the sticky wage model correspond to unemployment as we observe it? Why or why not?

5. What are two factors that shift the aggregate supply curve in the sticky wage model?

6. Give five factors that shift the IS curve.

7. Give three factors that shift the LM curve.

8. What are seven factors that shift the aggregate demand curve in the sticky wage model?

9. Explain why money is not neutral in the sticky wage model.

10. Do money supply shocks explain recent business cycles in Canada? Why or why not?

11. Do investment shocks explain recent business cycles in Canada? Why or why not?

12. Should the government act to stabilize output in the sticky wage model? If so, how should it do this?

13. Does it matter if output is stabilized using fiscal policy or monetary policy? Why or why not?

14. Why should the central bank target the interest rate if money demand is unstable?

15. Why are prices sticky in a sticky price model?

16. Explain what faults Keynesian sticky wage and sticky price models have.

Problems

1. Suppose total factor productivity decreases in the sticky wage model. Determine the effects on output, the real interest rate, consumption, investment, employment, the price level, and the real wage. Compare these predictions with those of the monetary intertemporal model. Are there any important differences? Explain.

2. Suppose nominal wages are negotiated between the representative firm and the representative consumer to be perfectly indexed to the price level; that is, if the price level rises by $x\%$, then the nominal wage will increase by $x\%$. This implies that the real wage will be fixed over the course of the contract.
   a. Determine the aggregate supply curve when the real wage is fixed.
   b. Suppose initially that supply equals demand in the labour market. Then, assume that the money supply increases. Determine the effects on real output, employment, the real interest rate, the real wage, the nominal wage, and Keynesian unemployment, and explain your results.
   c. Now, suppose again that supply initially equals demand in the labour market, and that total factor productivity falls. Determine the effects on real output, employment, the real interest rate, the real wage, the nominal wage, and Keynesian unemployment. Explain your results and any differences from part (b).

3. Suppose government spending increases temporarily in the sticky wage model.
   a. What are the effects on real output, consumption, investment, the price level, employment, and the real wage?
   b. Are these effects consistent with the key business cycle facts from Chapter 3? What does this say about the ability of government spending shocks to explain business cycles?

4. In the Keynesian sticky wage model, suppose that supply is initially equal to demand in the labour market, and that there is a negative shock to the demand for investment goods, because the firm anticipates lower total factor productivity in the future.
   a. Determine the effects on real output, the real interest rate, the price level, employment, and the real wage, if the government did nothing in response to the shock.
   b. Determine the effects if monetary policy is used to stabilize the economy, with the goal of the monetary authority being zero Keynesian unemployment.
   c. Determine the effects if government spending is used to stabilize the economy, with the goal of the fiscal authority being zero Keynesian unemployment.
   d. Explain and comment on the differences in your results among parts (a), (b), and (c).

5. If there is a reduction in government spending in the Keynesian sticky wage model, show what difference it makes if this reduction is temporary or permanent. What do you conclude about how fiscal policy should be used as a stabilization device? If government spending changes to offset a shock to the economy, should this spending change be announced to be temporary or permanent? Why?

6. The nominal interest rate cannot be less than zero, since if the nominal interest rate were negative, then no one would want to hold bonds. In terms of our model, this can be represented as the demand for money being perfectly elastic with respect to the nominal interest rate when the nominal interest rate is zero.

   a. Suppose the nominal interest rate (equal to the real interest rate in the Keynesian sticky wage model) is currently equal to zero. What does this imply about the slope of the *LM* curve?

   b. Suppose the nominal interest rate is currently zero and the monetary authority increases the money supply. What are the short-run equilibrium effects?

   c. At the time of this writing (mid-2003), nominal interest rates are at or close to zero in Japan. What implications does this have for Japanese monetary policy?

7. Suppose that the goal of the fiscal authority is to set government spending so as to achieve zero Keynesian unemployment, while the goal of the monetary authority is to achieve stability of the price level. Now, the economy is hit by a temporary decrease in total factor productivity. Show that the goals of the fiscal authority and monetary authority will be in conflict, suggest a remedy for this conflict, and discuss.

8. Suppose that the monetary authority's goal is to stabilize aggregate output, but that it cannot observe aggregate output in the short run. If there are shocks to the demand for investment goods, would it be preferable for the monetary authority to target the interest rate or the money supply in the short run? Explain your results.

9. Some macroeconomists have argued that it would be beneficial for the government to run a deficit when the economy is in a recession, and a surplus during a boom. Does this make sense? Carefully explain why or why not, using the Keynesian sticky wage model.

10. Suppose that investment and consumption expenditures change very little with a change in the real interest rate. Show what this implies for the slopes of the *IS* curve and the *AD* curve, and for the relative effectiveness of monetary and fiscal policy in stabilizing real output. Explain your results.

Working with the Data

1. Plot the percentage deviations from trend in government spending in a scatter plot against the percentage deviations from trend in real GDP. What do you observe? Does this indicate that the Canadian government has been actively engaged in stabilization policy of the kind that the Keynesian sticky wage model dictates? Explain.

2. The Keynesian sticky wage model predicts that there is a negative relationship between the quantity of Keynesian unemployment and the deviation of real output from potential. Suppose Keynesian unemployment is measured as the deviation from trend in the unemployment rate, and the deviation of output from potential is the percentage deviation of real GDP from trend.

   a. Plot the deviation from trend in the unemployment rate and the percentage deviation from trend in real GDP in a scatter plot.

   b. What do you observe in the scatter plot? Is this consistent with what the Keynesian sticky wage model predicts? Explain.

3. Plot the annual percentage rate of change in real GDP against the annual percentage rate of change in the monetary base (calculated as December-to-December percentage rates of change) in a scatter plot. Is this plot consistent or inconsistent with the nonneutrality of money the Keynesian sticky wage model predicts? Explain.

CHAPTER 11

Market-Clearing Models of the Business Cycle

In the 1960s, macroeconomics had evolved to the point where most macroeconomists accepted Keynesian business cycle models as capturing the behaviour of the economy in the short run. There appeared to be broad agreement that money was not neutral in the short run, and most macroeconomists viewed this nonneutrality as arising from the short-run inflexibility of wages and prices. The main disagreements were between monetarists and Keynesians. Monetarists tended to believe that monetary policy was a more effective stabilization tool than fiscal policy, but they were skeptical about the ability of government policy to fine-tune the economy; some monetarists argued that the short run over which policy could be effective was very short indeed. Keynesians believed that monetary policy was unimportant relative to fiscal policy, and that government policy should take an active role in guiding the economy along a smooth growth path. It may have seemed at the time that all the theoretical issues in macroeconomics had been resolved, in that most everyone agreed that the Keynesian model was a satisfactory model of the macroeconomy, and all that remained was for empirical work to sort out the disagreements between monetarists and Keynesians.

This view changed dramatically, however, with the advent of the rational expectations revolution in the early 1970s. Some important early contributors to the rational expectations revolution were Robert Lucas, Thomas Sargent, Neil Wallace, and Robert Barro. Two important principles coming out of the rational expectations revolution were: (1) macroeconomic models should be based on microeconomic principles—that is, they should be grounded in descriptions of the preferences, endowments, technology, and optimizing behaviour of consumers and firms; (2) equilibrium models are the most productive vehicles for studying macroeconomic phenomena. There was some resistance to following these two principles, but there was wide acceptance of the first principle, at least, by the 1980s. It became clear as well, with respect to the second principle, that equilibrium modelling did not automatically foreclose an active role for government policy. Indeed, as we will see in this chapter, some Keynesian ideas can be exposited using equilibrium models.

In this chapter, we will study three models of the business cycle, which were each developed as explicit equilibrium models with optimizing consumers and firms. These models are the Friedman-Lucas money surprise model, the real business cycle model, and the Keynesian coordination failure model. Each model differs from the others in terms of what is important in causing business cycles and the role implied for government policy. We will show how we can nevertheless describe each of these models by building on the monetary intertemporal model of Chapter 9 in straightforward ways. We will study each model in turn, examine how well each matches the business cycle facts discussed in Chapter 10, and discuss each model's shortcomings.

Why is it necessary to study several different business cycle models? As we discussed in Chapter 3, business cycles are remarkably similar, in terms of the comovements among macroeconomic time series. However, business cycles can have many causes, and fiscal and monetary policymakers are constantly grappling with the question of what macroeconomic shocks are driving the economy and what this implies for future aggregate activity. Each business cycle model we study allows us to understand one or a few features of the economy and some aspects of the economy's response to macroeconomic shocks. Putting all these features into one model would produce an unwieldy mess that would not help us understand the fundamentals of business cycle behaviour and government policy.

But different business cycle models sometimes give contradictory advice concerning the role of government policy. Does this mean that business cycle theory has nothing to say? The contradictory advice that different business cycle models give concerning the role of government policy reflects the reality of macroeconomic policymaking. Policymakers in federal and provincial governments and in central banks often disagree about the direction in which policy should move. To make persuasive arguments, however, policymakers have to ground their arguments in well-articulated macroeconomic models. This chapter shows how we can evaluate and compare macroeconomic models, and come to conclusions about their relative usefulness.

The Friedman-Lucas Money Surprise Model

The theory behind the money surprise model was sketched out by Milton Friedman[1] in 1968, and it was formalized by Robert Lucas in 1972.[2] Lucas's work marked the start of the rational expectations revolution, and Lucas was awarded the Nobel Prize in economics in 1995 for this work.

In the 1960s, macroeconomists had regarded any short-run nonneutralities of money as being the result of out-of-equilibrium behaviour of the economy arising from sticky wages or prices. The Friedman-Lucas model was the first attempt to construct a theory where changes in the level of the money supply could have real effects, with all markets clearing all the time.

The key element of the theory is that workers have imperfect information, in the short run, about aggregate variables that are important to their decision making. In the theory, a worker, whom we will call Bob, has complete information about things that directly concern him, for example, the current nominal wage. However, because Bob is not buying all goods all the time, he has imperfect information about the price level.

---

[1]See M. Friedman, 1968, "The Role of Monetary Policy," *American Economic Review* 58, 1–17.
[2]See R. Lucas, 1972, "Expectations and the Neutrality of Money," *Journal of Economic Theory* 4, 103–124.

Further, Bob cannot immediately observe aggregate shocks, such as changes in total factor productivity and changes in the money supply, that hit the economy. Under these circumstances, Bob might misperceive an increase in his nominal wage as an increase in his real wage, when it is really not, and Bob is fooled into working harder. Money "surprises" can then cause output to fluctuate, but this is a bad thing. The role for the central bank in this model is to make the money supply predictable.

The Friedman-Lucas money surprise model will be a modification of the monetary intertemporal model from Chapter 9, with changes accounting for the imperfect information problem. During the current period, Bob observes his current nominal wage W, where $W = wP$, with w the current real wage and P the price level. In terms of making his current labour supply decision, Bob cares about his real wage, not the nominal wage, and there would be no problem determining the real wage if Bob knew the current price level. Then, he could calculate the real wage as $w = \frac{W}{P}$. The problem is that Bob buys many goods, and he does not purchase all of these goods in any one period. For example, consumers in practice typically buy groceries and restaurant food every week, clothing perhaps monthly or seasonally, and a new car every two years or more. Suppose, for simplicity, that Bob simply does not know the current price level P during the current period. This implies that he also does not observe his current real wage w.

We will suppose there are two shocks that may hit the macroeconomy. The first is a temporary change in z, total factor productivity, and the second is a permanent increase in M, the money supply. We will assume that Bob cannot observe either z or M during the current period. However, he does know that either temporary z-shocks or permanent M-shocks can hit the economy. Though Bob cannot observe the price level or the real wage directly, he can make inferences about the chances of a particular shock having hit the economy, on the basis of how his nominal wage moves in the current period.

Given the environment Bob lives in, how will he make decisions? Suppose that in the current period Bob sees an increase in his nominal wage W. Given what he knows about how the world works, Bob knows that W may have increased because the money supply went up permanently, or because there was a temporary increase in total factor productivity. If Bob knows how frequently total factor productivity shocks and money supply shocks hit the economy, he then knows the chances that W increased in the current period as the result of either shock. Recall from Chapter 9 that if there is perfect information (Bob can observe all variables in the economy), then a permanent increase in the level of the money supply would cause a proportionate increase in the price level and there would be no real effects, so that the current real wage w would remain unchanged. Therefore, Bob would not change labour supply. Also, from Chapter 9, if there were a temporary increase in z under perfect information, then the real wage w would increase and the current price level P would fall. We will assume that the nominal wage, wP, increases. Thus, in this case, Bob would want to increase labour supply in response to the increase in the real wage, and an increase in the nominal wage effectively signals an increase in the real wage.

The problem is that Bob does not know whether the current nominal wage increased because the money supply increased permanently or because total factor productivity increased temporarily. This implies that if the money supply actually went up, causing the nominal wage to increase, then Bob infers that there is some chance the nominal wage increased because of a temporary productivity shock, and therefore he will increase labour supply. Higher labour supply will then cause output to go up.

To show how this works in the monetary intertemporal model, consider Figure 11.1. Initially, the economy is in equilibrium with current real output Y_1, real interest

FIGURE 11.1

The Effects of an Unanticipated Increase in the Money Supply in the Money Surprise Model

An unanticipated increase in the money supply shifts the labour supply curve to the right, as the actual real wage is lower than the real wage that the worker perceives. The output supply curve shifts to the right, output rises, and the real interest rate falls, increasing the demand for money, and causing the price level to rise. Money is not neutral.

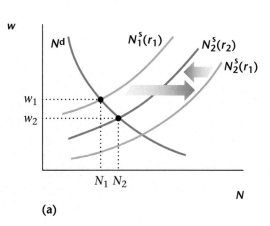

(a)

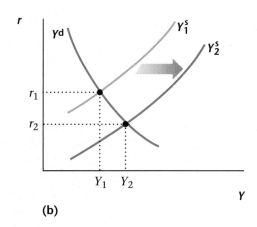

(b)

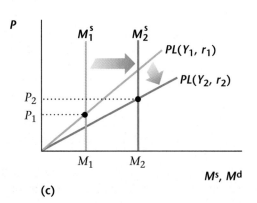

(c)

rate r_1, current price level P_1, current employment N_1, and current real wage w_1. Now, suppose the money supply increases from M_1 to M_2 in Figure 11.1(c). However, Bob infers that z may have increased temporarily when he sees the increase in his nominal wage W. In terms of the *actual* real wage, which is the variable on the vertical axis in Figure 11.1(a), Bob then perceives the real wage to be higher than it actually is, and this implies that the labour supply curve shifts rightward, from $N_1^s(r_1)$ to $N_2^s(r_1)$. That is, a money supply increase does not increase the real wage, a total factor productivity increase causes the real wage to increase, and the consumer thinks there is some chance that either event happened, so that the consumer's estimate is that the real wage increased. Thus, when it was really the money supply that increased, Bob's estimate of the real wage is higher than the actual real wage. We know that when the labour supply curve shifts to the right, the output supply curve also shifts to the right, so there is a shift in Y^s from Y_1^s to Y_2^s in Figure 11.1(b). In equilibrium, the level of output increases to Y_2, and the real interest rate falls to r_2. In Figure 11.1(c), the nominal money demand curve shifts rightward from $PL(Y_1, r_1)$ to $PL(Y_2, r_2)$, because real income has increased and the real interest rate has gone down. The money supply curve has also shifted to the right, with the increase in the money supply from M_1 to M_2, but on net the price level will have to increase, from P_1 to P_2.

In Figure 11.1(a), the labour demand curve shifts leftward from $N_2^s(r_1)$ to $N_2^s(r_2)$ when the real interest rate falls, but the shift to the left in the labour supply curve cannot be greater than the initial rightward shift, since we know that output must increase, and output could not increase unless employment increased. Therefore, employment goes up to N_2 and the actual real wage falls to w_2, though the perceived real wage of the consumer has risen. The perceived real wage of the consumer must have increased, as this is why the consumer is supplying more labour in equilibrium.

The key feature of the money surprise model is that money is not neutral. An increase in the nominal money supply in the short run will cause the real interest rate and the real wage to fall, and real output and employment to rise. Further, since $\frac{M}{P} = L(Y, r)$ in equilibrium, and because real output has increased and the real interest rate has decreased, causing real money demand $L(Y, r)$ to rise, $\frac{M}{P}$ (the real money supply) rises. That is, the price level rises less than proportionally to the increase in the money supply.

IMPLICATIONS OF THE MONEY SURPRISE MODEL FOR MONETARY POLICY

In the Friedman-Lucas money surprise model, an unanticipated increase in the money supply causes employment and output to increase, and it might seem that this is a good thing. It is certainly the case in Keynesian models, such as the Keynesian sticky wage model studied in Chapter 10, that in some circumstances it is economically efficient for the central bank to increase the money supply so as to increase output and employment. In the money surprise model, however, an engineered money surprise by the central bank is always a bad thing.

Output increases as the result of a money supply increase in the money surprise model only because people are fooled. An optimal state of affairs in this model is when consumers and firms are perfectly informed about what is happening to the economy. Under perfect information, all markets clear, the optimal quantity of labour is bought and sold in the labour market, and the optimal quantity of goods is bought and sold in the goods market. That is, if there were perfect information in the money surprise model, then the equilibrium allocation of resources would be Pareto-optimal (recall our discussion from Chapter 5).

Market prices carry important signals about shocks hitting the economy. If those signals are transmitted clearly to market participants, then this aids in the appropriate allocation of resources. For example, an increase in the relative price of peaches signals a scarcity in the quantity of peaches. People who buy peaches respond by buying fewer peaches and substituting other goods, and people who sell peaches respond by trying to bring more peaches to market. Any variability in the money supply adds noise to price signals, and this can mean that market participants receive the wrong messages. For example, in the money surprise model, an increase in the nominal wage that is a purely nominal increase can be misinterpreted as an increase in the real wage.

The appropriate policy for the monetary authority to adopt in an environment like this, as emphasized by Friedman and Lucas, is to make the money supply as predictable as possible. Friedman's recommendation[3] was that the monetary authority should follow a **constant money growth rule**, according to which some monetary aggregate (and Friedman argued that it did not matter which one) should grow at a constant rate over time.

The Keynesian sticky wage model in Chapter 10 and the money surprise model are actually quite similar in their predictions concerning the effects of a short-run increase in the money supply, provided the money supply increase is a genuine surprise. However, the policy implications of these two models could not be more different. The sticky wage model implies that using monetary policy to increase output and employment can be an appropriate thing to do, while the money surprise model implies it is not.

CRITIQUE OF THE FRIEDMAN-LUCAS MONEY SURPRISE MODEL

The money surprise model is certainly more theoretically appealing than the Keynesian sticky wage model in Chapter 10. It is internally consistent, and it leaves no loose ends—such as the unanswered question of exactly why the nominal wage is fixed in the sticky wage model. Further, it has the attractive feature that markets always clear. It is hard to say what should happen when the economy is out of equilibrium, and the usual Keynesian assumption that employment is determined by labour demand seems arbitrary.

However, the ability of the money surprise model to mimic the key business cycle regularities over the period 1961–2002 (see Chapter 3) is no better than that of the sticky wage model. Table 11.1 shows the features of the data from Chapter 3 relative to what the money surprise model predicts. The money surprise model predicts that if money variability is the primary explanation for business cycles, as argued by Lucas,[4]

---

[3]See M. Friedman, 1968, "The Role of Monetary Policy," *American Economic Review* 58, 1–17.

[4]See R. Lucas, 1980, "Methods and Problems in Business Cycle Theory," *Journal of Money, Credit, and Banking* 12.

TABLE 11.1 **Data Versus Predictions of the Money Surprise Model with Monetary Shocks**

	Data	Model
Consumption	Procyclical	Procyclical
Investment	Procyclical	Procyclical
Price level	Countercyclical	Procyclical
Money supply	Procyclical	Procyclical
Employment	Procyclical	Procyclical
Real wage	Procyclical	Countercyclical

then consumption and investment are procyclical (because the real interest rate is countercyclical), money is procyclical, and employment is procyclical, as in the data. But the real wage is countercyclical, and the price level is procyclical, and these two predictions are inconsistent with the data.

It can also be argued that the mechanism by which money affects output in the money surprise model is not plausible. That is, information on aggregate price indices and the money supply is widely available on a timely basis, and so it seems hard for people to be fooled as happens in the model. Further, the Bank of Canada has become increasingly open about how it conducts monetary policy. These factors make it hard to believe that imperfect information about the money supply and/or the price level could contribute much to fluctuations in aggregate GDP in Canada.

In spite of its shortcomings, a key insight of the Friedman-Lucas money surprise model has been quite influential among macroeconomic policymakers: the idea that the economy functions less efficiently when the behaviour of policymakers is not well understood, or when policy decisions are difficult to predict. Since the 1970s, central banks in particular have taken greater pains to provide information about their policy decisions and to help the public understand the reasons for their decisions. The Bank of Canada, for example, is much more open than it once was about what it is doing and why.

The Real Business Cycle Model

Now that we know the basic features of the Friedman-Lucas money surprise model, we can move on to study the real business cycle model, which was developed later. Real business cycle theory was introduced by Finn Kydland and Edward Prescott[5] in the early 1980s. Kydland and Prescott asked whether a standard model of economic growth subjected to random productivity shocks (i.e., "real" shocks as opposed to monetary shocks) could replicate, qualitatively and quantitatively, observed business cycles. Kydland and Prescott were perhaps motivated to pursue this question by the observation we made in Chapter 8, and replicate in Figure 11.2, that the detrended Solow residual (a measure of total factor productivity z) closely tracks detrended real GDP. Thus, productivity shocks appear to be a potential explanation for business cycles.

---

[5]See F. Kydland and E. Prescott, 1982, "Time to Build and Aggregate Fluctuations," *Econometrica* 50, 1345–1370.

FIGURE 11.2

Solow Residuals and GDP

The Solow residual (the
coloured line), a measure of
total factor productivity,
tracks aggregate real GDP
(the black line) quite closely.

Source: Adapted from the Statistics
Canada CANSIM database, Series
v3860085, v2461119, v3822183,
v1078498, and from the Statistics
Canada publication *Historical Statistics
of Canada*, Catalogue 11-516, 1983,
Series D175–189.

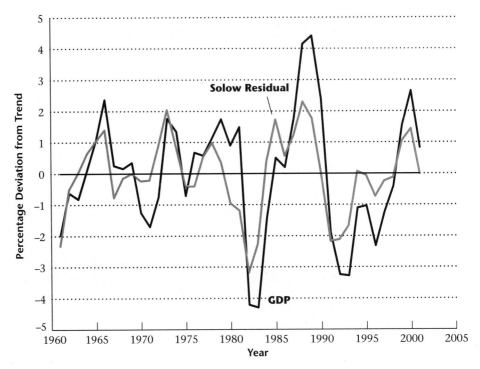

Recall that many factors can lead to changes in total factor productivity. Essentially, any change implying that an economy can produce more aggregate output with the same factor inputs is an increase in total factor productivity, that is, an increase in z. Factors that increase z include good weather, technological innovations, the easing of government regulations, and decreases in the relative price of energy.

The version of the real business cycle model we will study here is the monetary intertemporal model from Chapter 9. Though Kydland and Prescott studied a model where there was no role for money, Thomas Cooley and Gary Hansen showed, in a cash-in-advance real business cycle model, that adding money made little difference to the results.[6]

The Solow residual, as observed in Figure 11.2, is a persistent variable. When it is above (below) trend, it tends to stay there. This tells us that total factor productivity shocks are persistent, so that when there is a current increase in z, we would expect future total factor productivity z' to be higher as well. This implies that, in analyzing how the real business cycle model reacts to a total factor productivity shock, we need to combine the results of two different shocks from Chapter 7, a shock to z and a shock to z'.

Now, suppose there is a persistent increase in total factor productivity in the monetary intertemporal model, so that there are increases in z and z', current and future total factor productivity respectively. In Figure 11.3 we show the equilibrium effects. The increase in current total factor productivity z increases the marginal product of

[6]See T. Cooley and G. Hansen, 1989, "The Inflation Tax in a Real Business Cycle Model," *American Economic Review*
79, 733–748.

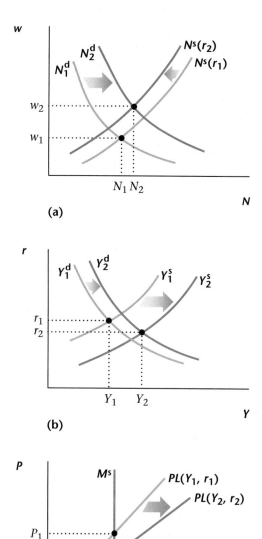

FIGURE 11.3

Effects of a Persistent Increase in Total Factor Productivity in the Real Business Cycle Model

With a persistent increase in total factor productivity, the output supply curve shifts to the right because of the increase in current total factor productivity, and the output demand curve shifts to the right because of the anticipated increase in future total factor productivity. The model replicates the key business cycle facts.

labour for each quantity of labour input, so that the labour demand curve shifts rightward from N_1^d to N_2^d in Figure 11.3(a), and this shifts the output supply curve rightward from Y_1^s to Y_2^s in figure 11.3(b). There are additional effects because of the anticipated increase in future total factor productivity z'. First, the demand for investment goods increases, as the representative firm anticipates an increase in the future marginal productivity of capital. Second, the representative consumer anticipates that higher future total factor productivity will imply higher future income, so that lifetime wealth increases and the demand for consumption goods goes up. Both these factors will cause the output demand curve Y^d to shift rightward from Y_1^d to Y_2^d.

In equilibrium, in Figure 11.3(b), aggregate output must rise, but it is not clear whether the real interest rate will rise or fall. However, the output demand curve will probably shift less than the output supply curve, since the direct effect of the increase in current total factor productivity on the supply of goods is likely to be larger than the effects of the anticipated increase in future total factor productivity on the demand for goods. Thus, the real interest rate falls, as in Figure 11.3(b), from r_1 to r_2. Current consumption expenditures will then increase because of the decrease in the real interest rate and the increase in lifetime wealth. Current investment rises because of the decrease in the real interest rate and the increase in future total factor productivity. In the money market, in Figure 11.3(c), since equilibrium real output rises and the real interest rate falls, money demand increases, and the nominal money demand curve shifts rightward from $PL(Y_1, r_1)$ to $PL(Y_2, r_2)$. Therefore, in equilibrium, the price level falls from P_1 to P_2. In the labour market, in Figure 11.3(a), the labour supply curve shifts leftward from $N^s(r_1)$ to $N^s(r_2)$ because of the fall in the real interest rate. However, as in Chapter 7, the labour supply curve shifts less than the labour demand curve, since the intertemporal substitution effect on labour supply from the change in the real interest rate is relatively small. Hence, current equilibrium employment rises from N_1 to N_2, and the current real wage rises from w_1 to w_2.

Therefore, as shown in Table 11.2, the real business cycle model qualitatively explains essentially all of the key business cycle regularities. Consumption, investment, employment, and the real wage are procyclical, and the price level is countercyclical. Perhaps more importantly, the real business cycle model can also *quantitatively* replicate some important observations about business cycles, as can be shown if a more sophisticated version of this model is put on a computer and simulated. The model can explain the fact that consumption is less variable than output, and that investment is more variable than output. Further, it can approximately replicate the observed relative variabilities in consumption, investment, output, and employment, which were discussed in Chapter 3.[7] As we see in Table 11.2, one feature of the data that the model

TABLE 11.2 **Data Versus Predictions of the Real Business Cycle Model with Productivity Shocks**

	Data	*Model*
Consumption	Procyclical	Procyclical
Investment	Procyclical	Procyclical
Price level	Countercyclical	Countercyclical
Money supply	Procyclical	Acyclical
Employment	Procyclical	Procyclical
Real wage	Procyclical	Procyclical

[7]See E. Prescott, 1986, "Theory Ahead of Business Cycle Measurement," *Federal Reserve Bank of Minneapolis Quarterly Review*, Fall, 9–22.

in this form cannot replicate is the procyclicality of the money supply. We will discuss this further in the next subsection.

REAL BUSINESS CYCLES AND THE BEHAVIOUR OF THE MONEY SUPPLY

In the real business cycle model, money is neutral; level changes in M have no effect on real variables and cause a proportionate increase in the price level. It might seem, then, that the real business cycle model cannot explain two key business cycle regularities from Chapter 3, which are the following:

1. The nominal money supply is procyclical.
2. The nominal money supply tends to lead real GDP.

However, as we will show, the real business cycle model can be made consistent with these two facts through some straightforward extensions.

First, in the real business cycle model, the procyclicality of the nominal money supply can be explained by way of **endogenous money**. That is, in practice, the money supply is not determined exogenously by the monetary authority, but responds to conditions in the economy. Endogenous money can explain the procyclicality of money in two ways, supposing that business cycles are caused by fluctuations in z. First, if our money supply measure is M1, M2, or some broader monetary aggregate, then part of the money supply consists of bank deposits. When aggregate output increases, all sectors in the economy, including the banking sector, tend to experience an increase in activity at the same time. An increase in banking sector activity will be reflected in an increase in the quantity of bank deposits, and therefore in an increase in M1, M2, and the broader monetary aggregates, and we will observe the money supply increasing when total factor productivity increases. Second, the money supply could increase in response to an increase in z because of the response of monetary policy. Suppose that the central bank wishes to stabilize the price level. When there is a persistent increase in total factor productivity, this will cause an equilibrium increase in Y, and the real interest rate will fall, as we showed above. In Figure 11.4 output increases from Y_1 to Y_2 and the real interest rate falls from r_1 to r_2, so that the nominal money demand curve shifts rightward from $PL(Y_1, r_1)$ to $PL(Y_2, r_2)$. If the central bank did nothing, the price level would fall from P_1 to P_2. However, since the central bank wishes to stabilize the price level, it increases the money supply from M_1 to M_2, shifting the money supply curve from M_1^s to M_2^s. As a result, the money supply will be procyclical, as it increases when output increases, in response to the persistent total factor productivity increase.

Fact 2 above, that the nominal money supply tends to lead real GDP, appears to be a particular problem, since this might be viewed as strong evidence that money supply fluctuations cause the fluctuations in real GDP. Indeed, this was the interpretation given to fact 2 by Milton Friedman and Anna Schwartz.[8] However, the weak link in Friedman and Schwartz' interpretation of the data is that **statistical causality** need not tell us

---

[8]See M. Friedman and A. Schwartz, 1963, *A Monetary History of the United States 1867–1960*, National Bureau of Economic Research, Cambridge, MA.

FIGURE 11.4

Procyclical Money Supply in the Real Business Cycle Model with Endogenous Money

A persistent increase in total factor productivity increases aggregate real income and reduces the real interest rate, causing money demand to increase. If the central bank attempts to stabilize the price level, this will increase the money supply in response to the total factor productivity shock.

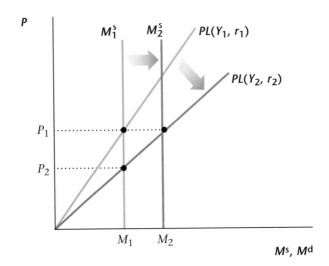

anything about true causality. A variable a statistically causes a variable b if current a helps predict future b. For example, every year we observe birds flying south before the onset of winter, and so the flight patterns of birds statistically predict the winter. However, birds flying south do not cause winter; it is the prospect of winter that is causing the birds to fly south.

There is an explanation for the tendency of money to lead output that is analogous to the example of birds flying south for the winter. Productivity shocks could cause money to lead output for two reasons, again through the process of endogenous money. First, the banking sector tends to lead other sectors of the economy, as banks provide loans for real activity that will occur at a later date. When bank loans increase, so will bank deposits, as a bank borrows by way of bank deposits to finance its lending. Thus, bank deposits will tend to be procyclical and to lead real GDP, and therefore M1, M2, and broader monetary aggregates will tend to lead real GDP. Second, if the monetary authority is trying to stabilize prices, and it uses all available information efficiently, it will be able to predict an increase in output due to an increase in z before the output increase is observed. Since an increase in the money supply may take time to affect prices, the monetary authority may want to act on this information before the increase in output and the decrease in the price level actually occur. Thus, money can lead real GDP due to preemptive monetary policy actions.

IMPLICATIONS OF REAL BUSINESS CYCLE THEORY FOR GOVERNMENT POLICY

Now that we know how the real business cycle model works, and have discussed how it fits the data, we can explore what the model implies for government policy. In the basic real business cycle model, there is no role for government stabilization policy. First, level changes in the money supply are neutral, and so attempts to smooth out business cycles through monetary policy actions will have no effect. Second, since all markets clear, and there are no inefficiencies (e.g., distorting taxes or externalities) in the basic model that government policy should correct for, there is also no reason that the government should vary its spending in response to fluctuations in total factor productivity. Government spending can have an effect on output, but the level of such spending should be set according to the appropriate long-run role of the government in providing public goods (goods and services, such as national defence, that cannot or should not be provided by the private sector), not to smooth short-run fluctuations in aggregate GDP. In the basic real business cycle model, business cycles are essentially optimal responses of the economy to fluctuations in total factor productivity, and nothing should be done about them. Given the first fundamental theorem of welfare economics, from Chapter 5, if the allocation of resources in the economy is Pareto-optimal, there is no need for the government to intervene, unless we think the government should redistribute income and wealth.

Though there is no role for government in the basic real business cycle model, other, more elaborate versions of this model explain a role for government arising from the need to correct market failures and distortions. For example, Cooley and Hansen's model,[9] as well as the model we have sketched here, with a cash-in-advance role for money, implies that the monetary authority should follow a Friedman rule in the long run. That is, the monetary authority should set the money growth rate so that the nominal interest rate is always zero. Note that, if the government is following a Friedman rule for monetary policy, this need not imply that it is stabilizing output.

There are plenty of examples of work on real business cycle models that show how the existence of market failures and distortions can lead to a role for cyclical variations in government policy.[10] For example, in practice all taxes are distorting. Income taxes distort labour supply decisions because firms and workers face different effective wage rates, and sales taxes distort consumer purchasing patterns because firms and consumers do not face the same effective prices for all goods. Over time, it is efficient for the government to smooth out these distortions, or welfare losses, that arise from taxation. This can tell us that tax rates should be smooth over time, which then implies that the government should let total tax revenues rise in booms and fall in recessions, as tax revenue will increase with income if the income tax rate is constant. This is a kind of countercyclical government policy, which may look like it is intended to stabilize output, but is actually aimed at smoothing tax distortions.

CRITIQUE OF REAL BUSINESS CYCLE THEORY

The real business cycle model certainly fits the data better than either the Keynesian sticky wage model or the Friedman-Lucas money surprise model. The theory is internally consistent, and it helps focus our attention on how government policy should act to correct market failures and distortions, rather than on attempting to correct for the fact that prices and wages may not clear markets over short periods of time.

---

[9]See T. Cooley and G. Hansen, 1989, "The Inflation Tax in a Real Business Cycle Model," *American Economic Review* 79, 733–748.

[10]See T. Cooley, 1995, *Frontiers of Business Cycle Research*, Princeton University Press, Princeton, NJ.

Real business cycle theory certainly has shortcomings, however, in its ability to explain business cycles. One problem is that the assessment of whether real business cycle theory fits the data is based on using the Solow residual to measure total factor productivity. There is good reason to believe that there is a large cyclical error in how the Solow residual measures total factor productivity z, and that the close tracking of detrended GDP by the Solow residual in Figure 11.2 might be accounted for mainly by measurement error. During a boom, the aggregate capital stock is close to being fully utilized. Most machinery is running full-time, and many manufacturing plants are in operation 24 hours per day. Further, the workers who are operating the plant and equipment are very busy. These workers are under pressure to produce output, since demand is high. There are few opportunities to take breaks, and overtime work is common. Thus, workers are being fully utilized as well. Alternatively, in a temporary recession, the aggregate capital stock is not fully utilized, in that some machinery is sitting idle and plants are not running 24 hours per day. Further, during a temporary recession, a firm may not wish to lay workers off (even though there is not much for them to do), since this may mean that these workers would get other jobs, and the firm would lose workers having valuable skills that are specific to the firm. Thus, workers employed at the firm during a recession might not be working very hard—they might take long breaks and produce little. In other words, the workforce tends to be underutilized during a recession, just as the aggregate capital stock is. This phenomenon of underutilization of labour during a recession is sometimes called **labour hoarding**.

The underutilization of capital and labour during a recession is a problem for measurement of total factor productivity, since during recessions the capital stock and the labour input would be measured as higher than they actually are. Thus, in terms of measurement, we could see a drop in output during a recession and infer that total factor productivity dropped because the Solow residual decreased. But output may have dropped simply because the quantity of inputs in production dropped, with no change in total factor productivity.

To see how this works, consider the following example. Suppose that the production function is Cobb-Douglas, as we assumed in calculating Solow residuals in Chapter 8. Namely, the production function takes the form

$$Y = zK^{0.3}N^{0.7}, \tag{11.1}$$

where Y is aggregate output, z is total factor productivity, K is the capital stock, and N is employment. Now, suppose initially that $z = 1$, $K = 100$, and $N = 50$, so that, from (11.1), we have $Y = 61.6$, and capital and labour are fully utilized. Now suppose a recession occurs that is not the result of a drop in total factor productivity, so that $z = 1$ as before. Firms still have capital on hand equal to 100 units, and employment is still 50 units, and so measured capital will be $\hat{K} = 100$ and measured employment will be $\hat{N} = 50$. However, suppose only 95% of the capital in existence is actually being used in production (the rest is shut down), so that actual capital is $K = 95$. Further, suppose the employed workforce is being used only 90% as intensively as before, with workers actually only putting in 90% of the time working that they were formerly. Thus, actual employment is $N = 45$. Plugging $z = 1$, $K = 95$, and $N = 45$ into Equation (11.1), we get $Y = 56.3$. Now, if we mistakenly used the measured capital stock, measured employment, and measured output to calculate the Solow residual, we would obtain

$$\hat{z} = \frac{56.3}{(100)^{0.3} (50)^{0.7}} = 0.914,$$

where $\hat{z}$ is the Solow residual or measured total factor productivity. Therefore, we would measure total factor productivity as having decreased by 8.6%, when it really had not changed at all. This shows how decreases in the utilization of factors of production during recessions can lead to biases in the measurement of total factor productivity, and in biases in how we evaluate the importance of total factor productivity shocks for business cycles.

For a discussion of how real business cycle theory and other theories of the business cycle fit data from the Great Depression, see Macroeconomics in Action 11.1 on p. 391.

Recessions in the Mid-1970s and the Early 1980s

A problem with real business cycle theory is that it sometimes does not help us understand the underlying causes of business cycles. The Solow residual may fluctuate over time, but what are the causes of these movements in the Solow residual? A case where the theory helps to explain the data is the 1974–75 recession in Canada. During this period, we see a drop in the Solow residual in Figure 11.2, which tracks closely a drop in real GDP. Further, we can consider what happened to the nominal money supply during this period in Figure 11.5. The nominal money supply actually rises above trend in the 1974–75 recession. During this period, there was a large increase in the price of imported oil, brought on by actions of the OPEC oil cartel. Thus, the 1974–75 recession seems consistent with real business cycle theory. There was an observable real shock to the economy, which shows up as a decrease in measured total factor productivity, real GDP declined, and the increase in money supply is consistent with money being neutral.

However, suppose that we consider another recession, the one that occurred in Canada in 1981–82. In Figure 11.2, we again see a large decrease below trend in the Solow residual in 1981–82, and a somewhat larger percentage decrease in real GDP. In Figure 11.5, there is a decline in the money supply below trend in 1981–82, but the money supply exhibits a large decrease below trend after the 1981–82 recession. In 1981–82 there does not appear to have been any shock to the economy that could have caused total factor productivity to fall to the degree it did, as measured by the Solow residual. However, there is much evidence (not entirely conclusive, though, as we indicated in Chapter 10) to indicate that, prior to the 1981–82 recession, the Bank of Canada tightened monetary policy significantly. This appears to be the likely cause of this recession, though superficially it might appear that a negative productivity shock was the cause.

Therefore, the 1974–75 recession provides empirical evidence that shocks to total factor productivity can be an important cause of business cycles. However, the recession in 1981–82 casts doubt on the role of total factor productivity shocks as a universal explanation for business cycle behaviour.

FIGURE 11.5

Deviations from Trend in the Monetary Base and GDP

The figure shows an increase in the monetary base above trend at the time of the 1974–75 recession, which is consistent with money being neutral, and a decrease below trend around the 1981–82 recession, which is consistent with a tightening of monetary policy at that time.

Source: Adapted from the Statistics Canada CANSIM database, Series v37145, v1992067.

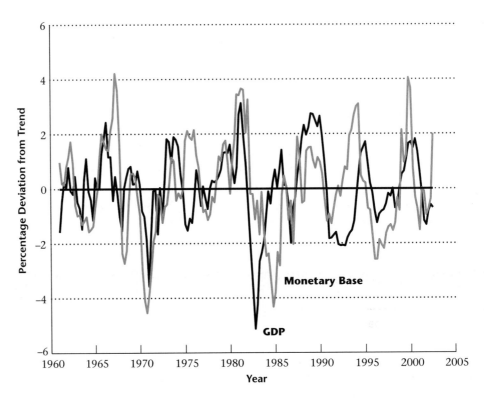

A Keynesian Coordination Failure Model

The two equilibrium theories of the business cycle we have discussed thus far in this chapter—the Friedman-Lucas money surprise theory and real business cycle theory—are in the classical tradition, in that they imply that the government should at best stay out of the way and allow markets to work. However, this does not mean that all equilibrium theories of the business cycle imply no role for the government in smoothing business cycles. Many modern Keynesians adopt an approach to macroeconomics very similar to that of classical economists, in assuming that prices and wages are fully flexible, and that all markets clear. Some of these modern Keynesians explore an idea that one can find in Keynes' *General Theory*, the notion of **coordination failure**. In macroeconomics, coordination failures were first studied rigorously by Peter Diamond in the early 1980s,[11] and later contributions were by Russell Cooper and Andrew John,[12] Jess Benhabib and Roger Farmer,[13] and Roger Farmer and Jang-Ting Guo.[14] The basic idea

---

[11]See P. Diamond, 1982, "Aggregate Demand in Search Equilibrium," *Journal of Political Economy* 90, 881–894.

[12]R. Cooper and A. John, 1988, "Coordinating Coordination Failures in Keynesian Models," *Quarterly Journal of Economics* 103, 441–463.

[13]See J. Benhabib and R. Farmer, 1994, "Indeterminacy and Increasing Returns," *Journal of Economic Theory* 63, 19–41.

[14]See R. Farmer and J. Guo, 1994, "Real Business Cycles and the Animal Spirits Hypothesis," *Journal of Economic Theory* 63, 42–72.

Business Cycle Models and the Great Depression in Canada

The Great Depression was a unique event in Canadian macroeconomic history, and this unique event was the object of an article in the *Review of Economic Dynamics* by Pedro Amaral and James MacGee.[1] The authors compared the economic performance of Canada and the United States during the Great Depression, and evaluated competing explanations for this performance. Between 1929 and 1933, aggregate output in Canada and the United States was about 40% below the trend established prior to the Great Depression. By the end of the 1930s, Canadian output was still 30% below trend, while U.S. output was 25% below trend. Relative to the average post–World War II recession in Canada or the United States, the length and the size of this decline were very large, and the recovery took an especially long time.

Was the Great Depression essentially a larger-scale version of a recession that otherwise looks much like a typical post–World War II recession, or do standard macroeconomic theories of the business cycle fail to explain the behaviour of the U.S. and Canadian economies during the Great Depression? Amaral and MacGee find that some modern business cycle theories, unlike some traditional ones, help to explain the Great Depression in Canada. Some puzzles remain, however.

The authors first consider a real business cycle explanation for the Great Depression. Total factor productivity in Canada declined sharply at the beginning of the Great Depression and took a very long time to recover, roughly matching the downturn and slow recovery of real output. The authors found that movements in total factor productivity account for about 50% of the decline in output, and do well in replicating the slow recovery.

Amaral and MacGee also evaluate sticky wage explanations for the Great Depression. Sticky wages, discussed in Chapter 10, have often been cited as a contributing factor to the Great Depression, since there was a large deflation in both Canada and the United States at the time, which would tend to drive up real wages if nominal wages are sticky. Amaral and MacGee find that sticky wages played a small role in the downturn, and do not help explain the protracted downturn. Further, they argue there was an even larger deflation in Canada in 1920–22 that failed to cause an economic downturn, so it seems hard to believe that deflation was an important contributing factor to the Great Depression.

Amaral and MacGee conclude that there is still much to learn. While they dismiss conventional channels of business cycle transmission working through trade between Canada and other countries, they argue that there may be unexplored avenues by which trade affects total factor productivity.

---

[1] See P. Amaral and J. MacGee, 2002, "The Great Depression in Canada and the United States: A Neoclassical Perspective," *Review of Economic Dynamics* 5, 45–72.

---

in coordination failure models is that it is difficult for private sector workers and producers to coordinate their actions, and there exist **strategic complementarities**, which imply that one person's willingness to engage in some activity increases with the number of other people engaged in that activity.

An example of an activity with a strategic complementarity is a party. If Paul knows that someone wishes to hold a party, and that only a few other people will be going, he will probably not want to go. However, if many people are going, this will be much more fun, and Paul will likely go. Paul's potential enjoyment of the party increases with the number of other people who are likely to go. We might imagine that there are two possible outcomes (equilibria) here. One outcome is that no one goes, and another is that everyone goes. These are equilibria because, if no one goes to the party, then no individual would want to go, and if everyone goes to the party, then no individual would want to stay at home. If Paul could coordinate with other people, then everyone would certainly agree that having everyone go to the party would be a good idea, and they could all agree to go. However, without coordination, possibly no one will go.

If we use the party as an analogy for aggregate economic activity, the willingness of one producer to produce may depend on what other producers are doing. For example, if Jennifer is a computer software producer, the quantity of software she can sell depends on the quantity and quality of computer hardware sold. If more is sold, it is easier for Jennifer to sell software, and if Jennifer sells more software, it is easier to sell hardware. Computer hardware and computer software are complementary. Many such complementarities exist in the economy, and different producers find it difficult to coordinate their actions. Thus, there may be **multiple equilibria** for the aggregate economy, whereby output and employment might be high, or output and employment might be low. Business cycles might simply be fluctuations between these high and low equilibria, driven by waves of optimism and pessimism.

To formalize this idea in an economic model, we start with the notion that there are aggregate **increasing returns to scale**, which implies that output more than doubles if all inputs double. Until now, we have assumed constant returns to scale, which implies that the marginal product of labour is diminishing when the quantity of capital is fixed. Increasing returns to scale at the aggregate level can be due to the strategic complementarities discussed above. We can then have increasing returns to scale at the aggregate level in a situation where, for each individual firm, there are constant returns

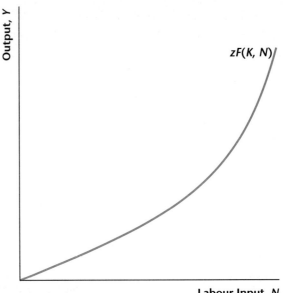

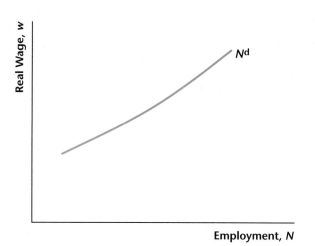

FIGURE 11.7
Aggregate Labour Demand with Sufficient Increasing Returns to Scale
With sufficient increasing returns to scale, the aggregate labour demand curve slopes upward, as the aggregate marginal product of labour increases with aggregate employment.

to scale in production. With sufficient aggregate increasing returns to scale, the aggregate production function, fixing the quantity of capital, can be convex, as in Figure 11.6. Then, since the slope of the production function in the figure increases with the labour input, the marginal product of labour for the aggregate economy will be increasing rather than decreasing. Since the aggregate demand for labour is just the aggregate marginal product of labour schedule, this implies that the aggregate labour demand curve N^d can be upward-sloping, as in Figure 11.7.

Now, for the coordination failure theory to work, the aggregate labour demand curve must have a greater slope than the labour supply curve, as in Figure 11.8. To repeat the exercise from Chapter 7 where we derived the output supply curve Y^s, suppose that the real interest rate is r_1, with the labour supply curve $N^s(r_1)$ in Figure 11.9(c). Then the equilibrium quantity of employment would be N_1, and output would be Y_1, from the production function in Figure 11.9(b). Therefore, an output–real interest rate pair implying equilibrium in the labour market is (Y_1, r_1) in Figure 11.9(a). Now, if the

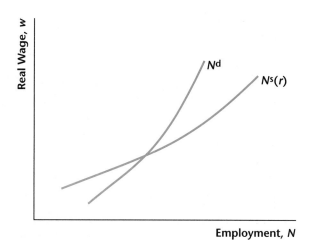

FIGURE 11.8
The Labour Market in the Coordination Failure Model
With sufficient increasing returns, the labour demand curve is steeper than the labour supply curve, which is required for the coordination failure model to work.

FIGURE 11.9

**The Output Supply Curve
in the Coordination
Failure Model**

The figure shows the con-
struction of the output supply
curve Y^s in the coordination
failure model. An increase in
the real interest rate shifts the
labour supply curve to the
right, reducing employment
and output.

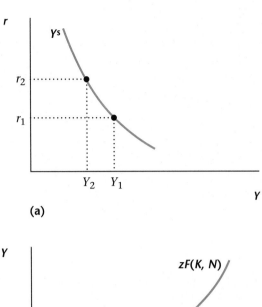

(a)

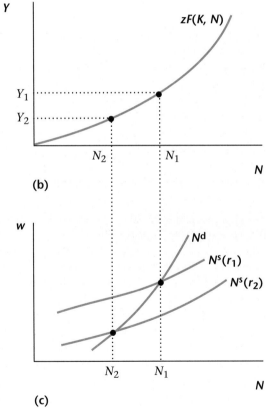

(b)

(c)

real interest rate is higher, say r_2, then the labour supply curve shifts rightward to $N^s(r_2)$
in Figure 11.9(c), because workers wish to substitute future leisure for current leisure.
As a result, the equilibrium quantity of employment falls to N_2, and output falls to Y_2.
Thus, another point on the output supply curve in Figure 11.9(a) is (Y_2, r_2), and the Y^s
curve is downward-sloping.

THE COORDINATION FAILURE MODEL: AN EXAMPLE

We will now consider a simple example that will show some of the key insights that come from coordination failure models. Suppose that the downward-sloping Y^s curve and the downward-sloping Y^d curve intersect in just two places (though this need not be the case; there could be more than two intersections, or there could be only one), as in Figure 11.10(b). Here, the economy could be in one of two equilibria. In the first, the "bad equilibrium," output is Y_1, the real interest rate is r_1, the price level is P_1, the real wage is w_1, and employment is N_1. In the second, the "good equilibrium," output is Y_2, the real interest rate is r_2, the price level is P_2, the real wage is w_2, and employment is N_2. In a more explicit version of this model, which would have a description of consumers' preferences, consumers would be better off in the good equilibrium, with high output and employment, than in the bad equilibrium, with low output and employment.

Will the economy be in the good or the bad equilibrium? Certainly nothing prevents the latter from arising if everyone is pessimistic, even though everyone prefers the good equilibrium. Similarly, the good equilibrium will arise if everyone is optimistic. In this model, business cycles could result if consumers and firms are alternately optimistic and pessimistic, so that the economy alternates between the good and the bad equilibrium. This seems much like what Keynes referred to as "animal spirits," the waves of optimism and pessimism he saw as an important determinant of investment.

In the coordination failure model, it is possible that extraneous events that are completely unrelated to economic fundamentals (technology, preferences, and endowments) can "cause" business cycles. Macroeconomists sometimes call such extraneous events **sunspots**, analogous to the irregular occurrence of dark spots observed on the sun, because a dark spot on the sun does not affect production possibilities, preferences, or available resources (i.e., anything fundamental) on Earth. However, sunspots are in principle observable to everyone. Therefore, if workers and firms all treat the observation of a sunspot as a sign of optimism, then the economy will go to the good equilibrium when a sunspot is observed, and it will go to the bad equilibrium when no sunspot is observed. It will then appear that sunspots are causing business cycles. The behaviour of the stock market is perhaps most indicative of the presence of "sunspot behaviour," in that there is much more variability in stock prices than can be explained by fluctuations in fundamentals (the earnings potential of firms). Alan Greenspan, current chairman of the Federal Reserve Board in the United States, once referred to the stock market as being under the influence of "irrational exuberance." Sunspot behaviour in the economy need not literally be driven by sunspots, but by events with no connection to anything fundamentally important to preferences, endowments, and technology.

PREDICTIONS OF THE COORDINATION FAILURE MODEL

From Figure 11.10, the good equilibrium has a low real interest rate, a high level of output, a low price level, a high level of employment, and a high real wage. The bad equilibrium has a high real interest rate, a low level of output, a high price level, a low level of employment, and a low real wage. Thus, given the low (high) real interest rate, the good (bad) equilibrium has a high (low) level of consumption and investment.

FIGURE 11.10

**Multiple Equilibria in the
Coordination Failure Model**
Because the output supply
curve is downward-sloping in
the coordination failure model,
there can be two equilibria,
as in this example. In one
equilibrium, aggregate output
is low and the real interest
rate is high; in the other,
aggregate output is high and
the real interest rate is low.

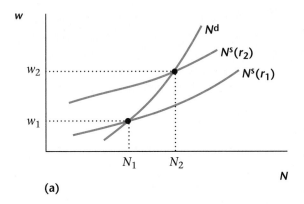

(a)

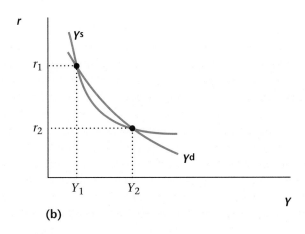

(b)

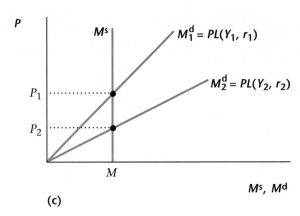

(c)

Therefore, if business cycles are fluctuations between the good and bad equilibrium, then, as in Table 11.3, consumption, investment, and employment will be procyclical, the price level will be countercyclical, and the real wage will be procyclical, just as observed in the data. Further, Roger Farmer and Jang-Ting Guo have shown that a version of the coordination failure model does essentially as well as the real business cycle model in quantitatively replicating U.S. business cycle behaviour.[15]

TABLE 11.3 **Data Versus Predictions of the Coordination Failure Model**

	Data	Model
Consumption	Procyclical	Procyclical
Investment	Procyclical	Procyclical
Price level	Countercyclical	Countercyclical
Money supply	Procyclical	Acyclical
Employment	Procyclical	Procyclical
Real wage	Procyclical	Procyclical

Though money is neutral in the coordination failure model, as it is in the real business cycle model, the coordination failure model can explain why the nominal money supply is procyclical. Suppose the money supply fluctuates between M_1 and M_2, where $M_2 > M_1$. Also, suppose that money acts as a sunspot variable; that is, when consumers and firms observe a high money supply they are optimistic and when they observe a low money supply they are pessimistic. Therefore, when the money supply is high the economy will be in the good equilibrium and when the money supply is low the economy will be in the bad equilibrium—people's expectations will be self-fulfilling. In Figure 11.11, we can still have the price level moving countercyclically, provided money supply does not fluctuate too much. In the good equilibrium, nominal money demand is $PL(Y_2, r_2)$, and in the bad equilibrium, nominal money demand is $PL(Y_1, r_1)$. Money supply increases in the good equilibrium from M_1 to M_2, and the price level falls

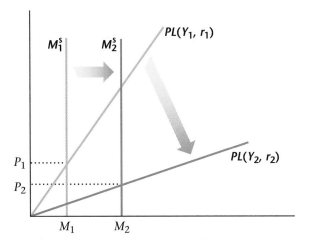

FIGURE 11.11

Procyclical Money Supply in the Coordination Failure Model

If the money supply is a sunspot variable in the coordination failure model, then money may appear to be nonneutral because people believe it to be. When the money supply is high (low), everyone is optimistic (pessimistic), and output is high (low).

[15]See R. Farmer and J. Guo, 1994, "Real Business Cycles and the Animal Spirits Hypothesis," *Journal of Economic Theory* 63, 42–72.

from P_1 to P_2. Here, though money is actually neutral, it can appear to be causing business cycles.

POLICY IMPLICATIONS OF THE COORDINATION FAILURE MODEL

In terms of how they match the data, the coordination failure and real business cycle models are essentially indistinguishable. However, the two models have very different policy implications. In the real business cycle model, decreases in output and employment are just optimal responses to a decline in total factor productivity, while in the coordination failure model, the good equilibrium is in principle an opportunity available in the aggregate economy when the bad equilibrium is realized. Thus, if we believed this model, then government policies that promote optimism would be beneficial. For example, encouraging statements by public officials, such as the Minister of Finance or the Governor of the Bank of Canada, could in principle bump the economy from the bad to the good equilibrium.

Policy could also be designed to smooth business cycles, or to eliminate them altogether in the coordination failure model. As an example, consider Figure 11.12, where there are initially two equilibria, a bad equilibrium where the real interest rate is r_1 and the level of output is Y_1 and a good equilibrium where the real interest rate is r_2 and the level of output is Y_2. Then, suppose the government reduces current government spending G. A decrease in current government spending will reduce the present value of taxes, cause a decrease in current labour supply, and shift the output supply curve to the right, from Y_1^s to Y_2^s in the figure. Further, recall from Chapter 7 that we know that a decrease in G will shift the output demand curve leftward from Y_1^d to Y_2^d. If the government reduces G by just the right amount, then there will be only one equilibrium, where $Y = Y^*$ and $r = r^*$, as in the figure. Effectively, the bad equilibrium gets better, and the good equilibrium gets worse, due to the decrease in G, and there will be no business cycles. It is not clear whether eliminating business cycles in this manner is advantageous. For example, if in the absence of the decrease in G the economy was in the good equilibrium most of the time, then average welfare could go down when business cycles are

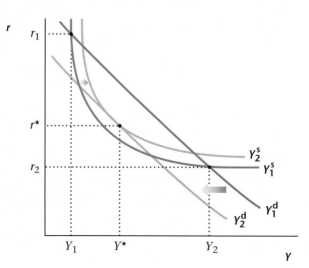

eliminated. It could be, however, that there are benefits from reduced uncertainty when business cycles are eliminated, so that even though average output might go down, the benefits from reduced uncertainty from smoothing business cycles could be beneficial.

The business cycle models we have discussed so far ignore the different effects that shocks to the economy can have across regions of the country. In Canada these different effects can be quite important, and they are discussed in Macroeconomics in Action 11.2.

MACROECONOMICS *IN ACTION* 11.2

Regional Differences in the Response of the Canadian Economy to Aggregate Shocks

The sectoral composition of output in Canada is very different across regions of the country, and this sometimes results in key differences in how regions of the country respond to aggregate shocks. Thus, for example, an important cause of business cycles in the Prairie provinces may not be an important cause of business cycles in Quebec and Ontario. In a recent article in the *Bank of Canada Review*, Brigid Brady and Farid Novin evaluate the varying economic performance of Canadian regions over the period from mid-2000 to mid-2001.[1]

Brady and Novin first look at the sectoral composition of output across regions in Canada. Quebec and Ontario have a high concentration of manufacturing relative to the rest of the country. From 1995 to 1999, manufacturing output accounted for 23% and 20%, respectively, of GDP in Ontario and Quebec, while representing only about 10% of GDP in the rest of Canada. Given the importance of oil and gas production in Alberta, mining, quarrying and oil-well drilling accounts for 14% of GDP in the Prairie provinces, and for only 3% of GDP or less in all other regions. Production of services is relatively predominant in British Columbia and Atlantic Canada (oil and gas and manufacturing represent tangible output in the Prairie provinces,

Quebec, and Ontario). Finally, the fraction of GDP accounted for by logging and forestry in British Columbia is more than four times the fraction for all of Canada (though logging and forestry production is only 2.6% of GDP in British Columbia).

What does the sectoral composition of regional output imply for the responses to aggregate shocks? Brady and Novin isolate three aggregate shocks that played an important role in the Canadian economy in this period. The first was a slowdown in aggregate economic activity in the United States, which is a shock from outside Canadian borders. We will study open economy macroeconomics (of key importance for Canada) in more detail in Chapters 12 and 13, but for now think of there being spillovers from the United States in terms of optimism and pessimism concerning future total factor productivity. In 2000, firms in the United States became increasing pessimistic about future total factor productivity, particularly in high-technology industries, and this pessimism was contagious around the world, particularly in Canada. The second aggregate shock to Canada during this period was an increase in the relative price of energy. Third, there was an expiry of the Softwood Lumber Agreement between Canada and the United States,

(continued)

and a large tariff was imposed in the United States on imports from Canada of softwood lumber. These three shocks affected the regions of Canada in the following ways. First, the slowdown in U.S. aggregate economic activity had its primary negative effect on the manufacturing industry, and this was therefore a relatively more important shock for Ontario and Quebec. Second, the increase in the relative price of energy was a positive shock for the oil and gas industry in the Prairie provinces, but a negative shock that would reduce total factor productivity in the manufacturing industry, thus having a relatively more detrimental effect in Ontario and Quebec. Third, the trade difficulties with the United States over softwood lumber had a negative impact on the British Columbia economy, but were relatively unimportant elsewhere. Therefore, on net British Columbia received a negative shock to GDP, the Prairie provinces received a positive shock, Ontario and Quebec received a negative shock, and the effect on the Atlantic Provinces was more or less neutral.

It is not unusual for aggregate shocks to the Canadian economy to affect different regions in very different ways, and the example of mid-2000 to mid-2001 is no exception. Even if shocks averaged out across regions of the country, for example if total factor productivity increased in one area of the country and decreased in another but average total factor productivity in Canada did not change, there could still be a net negative effect on the economy. This is because factors of production—capital and labour—must move, in this case, from a region of relatively low total factor productivity to a region where total factor productivity is relatively high, in order to take advantage of good opportunities. It takes time for this movement to take place, and in the meantime resources will be unemployed and GDP will be lower than it would be if resources could move instantaneously.

[1]See B. Brady and F. Novin, 2001, "Factors Affecting Regional Economic Performance in Canada," *Bank of Canada Review*, Autumn, 21–29.

CRITIQUE OF THE COORDINATION FAILURE MODEL

The key insight of the coordination failure model is that business cycles can result simply from self-fulfilling waves of optimism and pessimism. As mentioned previously, the existence of these self-fulfilling expectations appears to be most evident in the case of the stock market, where it seems difficult to explain the wild gyrations that occur daily as being the result of changes in fundamental economic factors.

However, there are some potential weaknesses in coordination failure theories of the business cycle. First, a critical element of the coordination failure theory is that there exist sufficient increasing returns to scale in aggregate production that the aggregate labour demand curve slopes upward and is steeper than the aggregate labour supply curve. If aggregate production is subject to constant returns to scale or decreasing returns to scale, then this theory is a nonstarter. In practice, the measurement of returns to scale in aggregate production is very imprecise. Some researchers claim to find evidence of increasing returns in the data, but others do not. A good reference for this issue is the work of Harold Cole and Lee Ohanian.[16] At best, the evidence supporting the existence of increasing returns to scale at the aggregate level is weak.

[16]See H. Cole and L. Ohanian, 1999, "Aggregate Returns to Scale: Why Measurement Is Imprecise," *Federal Reserve Bank of Minneapolis Quarterly Review*, Summer, 19–28.

Second, a problem with this model is that the underlying shocks that cause business cycles are expectations, and expectations are essentially unobservable. This makes it difficult to use the theory to understand historical recessions and booms.

This chapter completes our study of business cycles in the closed economy. In Chapters 12 and 13, we will move on to study how openness in the economy—trade in goods and assets with the outside world—matters for the determination of aggregate variables, for business cycles, and for government policy.

Chapter Summary

In this chapter, we constructed three different equilibrium models of the business cycle, and we evaluated these models in terms of how they fit the data, their policy predictions, and their plausibility. In the first model, the Friedman-Lucas money surprise model, workers in the short run do not have perfect information on aggregate economic variables, in that they do not observe the money supply, the price level, or total factor productivity, but they know that the economy could be hit by permanent shocks to the money supply or temporary shocks to total factor productivity. If the money supply increases, then workers observe an increase in their nominal wage, but they do not know if this is because the money supply increased or there was a positive shock to total factor productivity. In the latter case, the increase in the nominal wage would also signal an increase in the real wage, and so workers increase labour supply, implying that output increases. Therefore, money is not neutral in the money surprise model, because workers can be fooled by unanticipated increases in the money supply. The money surprise model fits most features of the data, but it implies that the price level is procyclical and that the real wage is countercyclical, and these predictions are not consistent with the key business cycle facts from Chapter 3. The policy conclusion implied by the money surprise model is that monetary policy should be carried out in a predictable fashion.

The second model studied in this chapter is the real business cycle model, in which business cycles are explained by persistent fluctuations in total factor productivity. The real business cycle model is consistent with all the business cycle facts from Chapter 3, and endogenous money can explain the regularities in the behaviour of the nominal money supply relative to real aggregate output. The basic real business cycle model has no role for government policy, since business cycles are simply optimal responses to fluctuations in total factor productivity. The real business cycle model is not always successful in explaining historical business cycle events, and there are measurement problems in using the Solow residual as a measure of total factor productivity.

The third model studied here is the Keynesian coordination failure model, which is based on the existence of strategic complementarities giving rise to increasing returns to scale at the aggregate level. This implies that there can be multiple equilibria, and we considered an example where the model had two equilibria: a good equilibrium with high output, consumption, investment, employment, and real wage, and a low real interest rate and price level; and a bad equilibrium with low output, consumption, investment employment, and real wage, and a high real interest rate and price level. The economy could then fluctuate between these two equilibria, with fluctuations driven by waves of optimism and pessimism. Money is neutral in the model, but it could be a sunspot variable that produces optimism and pessimism, making it appear that money is not neutral. The coordination failure model does as well as the real business cycle model in fitting the data. The role for government policy in the coordination failure model could be to produce optimism, and there may be a role for fiscal policy in smoothing out business cycles.

Key Terms

constant money growth rule: A monetary policy rule advocated by Milton Friedman, which specifies that the money supply should grow at a constant rate.

endogenous money: The concept that the money supply is not exogenous, but depends on other aggregate economic variables, due to the behaviour of the banking system and the central bank.

statistical causality: When an economic variable *a* helps predict the future values of an economic variable *b*, we say that *a* statistically causes *b*.

labour hoarding: The process by which firms may not lay off workers during a recession, even though those workers are not as busy as they might be on the job.

coordination failure: Situation in which economic agents cannot coordinate their actions, producing a bad equilibrium.

strategic complementarities: Relationships in which actions taken by others encourage a particular firm or consumer to take the same action.

multiple equilibria: The presence of more than one equilibrium in an economic model.

increasing returns to scale: Situation in which output increases more than proportionally to an increase in factor inputs.

sunspot: An economic variable that has no effect on aggregate production possibilities or on consumers' preferences.

Questions for Review

1. What were the two main principles introduced in the rational expectations revolution?

2. Why is it useful to study different models of the business cycle?

3. Explain why money is nonneutral in the money surprise model.

4. Should the government act to stabilize output in the money surprise model? Why or why not?

5. Does the money surprise model fit the data?

6. What causes output to fluctuate in the real business cycle model?

7. Why is money neutral in the real business cycle model?

8. How can the real business cycle model explain the behaviour of the money supply over the business cycle?

9. Should the government act to stabilize output in the real business cycle model?

10. Does the real business cycle model fit the data?

11. What are the important shortcomings of the real business cycle model?

12. Describe an example of a coordination failure problem.

13. What causes business cycles in the coordination failure model?

14. Why is money neutral in the coordination failure model?

15. Does the coordination failure model fit the data?

16. Which is the better macro model, the real business cycle model or the coordination failure model? Explain.

Problems

1. In the money surprise model, suppose that total factor productivity increases temporarily. What are the equilibrium effects of this, and how does this differ from what happens in the monetary intertemporal model of Chapter 9? Explain your results.

2. Suppose that the central bank wishes to reduce the price level, and announces that it will reduce the money supply to accomplish this. Use the money surprise model to answer the following questions:
   a. Suppose the public does not believe that the central bank is serious about reducing the price level. What happens to real aggregate variables and the price level?
   b. Suppose, alternatively, that the public believes the central bank announcement. What happens to real variables and the price level now?
   c. Compare your results in parts (a) and (b). In which case does the price level change more for a given reduction in the money supply? What do you think a central bank can do to make its policy announcements more credible?

3. In the money surprise model, compare the performance of the economies in two countries that are identical in all respects but one: in country a the money supply is highly variable, while in country b there is little variability in the money supply. For a given surprise increase in the money supply, determine with the aid of diagrams how the economy in country a will respond relative to the economy in country b. Explain your results.

4. In the real business cycle model, suppose government spending increases temporarily. Determine the equilibrium effects of this. Could business cycles be explained by fluctuations in G? That is, does the model replicate the key business cycle facts from Chapter 3 when subjected to temporary shocks to government spending? Explain carefully.

5. Suppose temporary increases in government spending lead to permanent increases in total factor productivity, perhaps because some government spending improves infrastructure and makes private firms more productive. Show that temporary shocks to government spending of this type could lead to business cycles consistent with the key business cycle facts, and explain your results.

6. In the real business cycle model, suppose firms become infected with optimism, and they expect total factor productivity will be much higher in the future.
   a. Determine the equilibrium effects of this expectation.
   b. If waves of optimism and pessimism of this sort cause GDP to fluctuate, does the model explain the key business cycle facts?
   c. Suppose that the monetary authority wants to stabilize the price level in the face of a wave of optimism. Determine what it should do, and explain.

7. Suppose money plays the role of a sunspot variable in the coordination failure model, so that the economy is in the bad equilibrium when the money supply is low and in the good equilibrium when the money supply is high. Explain what the monetary authority could do to make consumers better off. Compare this prescription for monetary policy with the one coming from the money surprise model, and discuss.

8. In the coordination failure model, suppose consumers' preferences shift so that they want to consume less leisure and more consumption goods. Determine the effects on aggregate variables in the good equilibrium and in the bad equilibrium, and explain your results.

9. In the coordination failure model, suppose there is a permanent increase in government spending. Determine how this will affect output, the real interest rate, employment, the real wage, and the price level in the good equilibrium and in the bad equilibrium. Will real output be more or less volatile over time if there are waves of optimism and pessimism? Explain your results.

10. Suppose a natural disaster destroys some of the nation's capital stock. The central bank's goal is to stabilize the price level. Given this goal, what should the central bank do in response to the disaster? Explain with the aid of diagrams.

Working with the Data

1. Plot the December-to-December percentage rates of change in a stock price index against the annual percentage rates of change in real GDP. Are these two variables positively or negatively correlated? What business cycle theories are consistent with this relationship?

2. Calculate and plot average labour productivity, measured as annual real GDP divided by annual total employment. Then plot the annual percentage rate of change in average labour productivity against the annual percentage rate of change in real GDP. Determine whether the money surprise model, the real business cycle model, and the coordination failure model are consistent with the correlation you observe in the scatter plot, and explain your results.

3. Construct time series plots of the percentage deviations from trend in real GDP, the monetary base, M1++, and M2++. What do you observe? What explanations might there be for the differences in the comovements between the monetary base and real GDP, M1++ and real GDP, and M2++ and real GDP?

International Macroeconomics

Because of globalization—the continuing integration of world markets in goods, services, and assets—international factors are increasingly important for the performance of the domestic economy, and for the conduct of fiscal and monetary policy. In this Part, we will study models of open economies in which there is trade between the domestic economy and the rest of the world. We will use these models in Chapter 12 to study the benefits from international trade, the effects of changes in world prices and interest rates, the determinants of the current account surplus, and the implications of current account deficits. In Chapter 13, we will examine the role of money in the world economy, the determination of exchange rates, the effects of fixed and flexible exchange rates, and the implications of shocks occurring abroad for domestic business cycles.

CHAPTER 12

International Trade in Goods and Assets

Our goal in this chapter will be to extend the models developed in Chapters 5, 6, and 7, so that they can address issues in international macroeconomics. Until now, we have looked at closed-economy macroeconomic issues using closed-economy models, but for many interesting macroeconomic problems, we must do our analysis in an open-economy context. This chapter will be confined to issues relating to real international macroeconomics. In Chapter 13, we will address the monetary side of international interaction.

International trade is of key importance for Canada, as is reflected by the fact that, in 2001, exports of goods and services were 43.3% of GDP, and imports were 38.1% of GDP. Thus, the volume of trade between Canada and the rest of the world is close to three times the volume of trade between the United States and its trading partners. Just as trade is important for Canada, international trade in goods and assets has become increasingly important in the 20th and 21st centuries for the world as a whole. This growth in world trade has occurred for two reasons. First, the costs of transporting goods and assets across international boundaries have fallen dramatically, permitting a freer flow of international trade. Second, government-imposed barriers to trade, such as import quotas, tariffs, and restrictions on international financial activity, have been relaxed. A relaxation of trade restrictions was carried out under the General Agreement on Tariffs and Trade (GATT) between 1947 and 1995, when the GATT framework was replaced by the World Trade Organization. Trade restrictions have also been reduced through regional agreements, for example, the Canada–U.S. Free Trade Agreement (1989), the North American Free Trade Agreement (NAFTA) (1994), and the European Union (EU). Given the critical nature of trade for Canada and increasing importance of trade in the world economy, we must understand its implications for domestic macroeconomic activity.

In this chapter, we will study the importance for domestic aggregate economic activity of trade with the rest of the world in goods and assets. We are interested particularly in how the current account surplus and domestic output, employment, consumption, and investment are affected by events in the rest of the world. To study this, we will extend some of the models we have worked with in Chapters 5, 6, and 7.

Throughout this chapter, we will confine attention to small open-economy models, which are models in which actions by consumers and firms in the domestic economy will have no collective effect on world prices. Some countries are clearly small relative to the rest of the world, such as New Zealand, Singapore, and Luxembourg, and for these countries it is clear that the small open-economy assumption is quite realistic. Canada is also sufficiently small in most respects that for macroeconomic analysis the small open economy assumption is a good one. However, for large countries such as the United States, Germany, or Japan, which play a particularly important role in the world economy, the assumption of price-taking on world markets is perhaps less plausible. There are three reasons why using small open-economy models to explain events in large open economies is a useful approach. First, small open-economy models are relatively simple to work with; for example, it is easy to modify closed-economy models so as to construct small open-economy models. Second, many of the conclusions we derive from small open-economy models will be identical to the ones we would obtain in more complicated large open-economy models. Third, as time passes, the small open-economy assumption becomes more realistic for countries such as Germany, Japan, and the United States. Given development in the rest of the world, GDP in these countries relative to GDP in the rest of the world falls, and it becomes a closer approximation to the truth that these countries are price-takers in world goods and asset markets.

In this chapter, we will study three small open-economy models that build, respectively, on the one-period model in Chapter 5, the two-period model in Chapter 6, and the real intertemporal model in Chapter 7. The first model focuses on the determinants of domestic production and consumption of goods, and the volume of trade between the domestic economy and the rest of the world. This model will be used to study how the welfare of domestic consumers can be improved through free trade in goods with the rest of the world, and also to study the effects of changes in world prices on domestic consumption, production, and the volume of trade.

In the second model, there are two periods, so that we can examine the impact of borrowing and lending between the domestic economy and the rest of the world. Here, we are primarily interested in the determinants of the current account surplus, and the importance of the current account surplus in domestic policymaking. An important idea is that international borrowing and lending permits the smoothing of aggregate consumption over time for the domestic economy, just as a single consumer can smooth consumption by borrowing and lending.

In the third and final model, we include investment and production, so that we can study the relationships among domestic consumption, output, investment, government spending, and the current account balance. This model is used to examine the relationship between the current account deficit and the government budget deficit, and we can apply this analysis to understanding the observed relationship between the two deficits in Canada. We also will examine the role of investment in determining the current account deficit, and we will address to what extent a current account deficit is good or bad for a nation's welfare.

A Two-Good Model of a Small Open Economy: Trade in Tinyland

The first international model we will consider is closely related to the one-period model we constructed in Chapter 5, and the analysis we developed there will also be useful here. However, we will use this international model for quite different purposes—to understand why countries trade, and the primary determinants of the volume of trade. This is a model of a **small open economy**. The economy is small, in the sense that economic activity in this country does not affect the world prices of goods. That is, the firms and consumers in this economy are both individual price-takers—they treat market prices as being given—and collective price-takers—their collective actions have no effect on the world prices for goods. The economy is also open, in that we will explore the consequences of trade between this economy and the rest of the world. Until now, we have considered macroeconomic models of closed economies where there is no trade with the rest of the world.

We will call our small open economy Tinyland. In Tinyland, there are two goods that are produced and consumed, which we will call good a and good b. From the viewpoint of people in Tinyland, the price of good a in terms of good b, denoted by TOT_{ab}, is given. This price is the **terms of trade** or the **real exchange rate**, since TOT_{ab} is the rate at which the residents of Tinyland can trade good b for good a on world markets. The model will tell us under what conditions Tinyland will import good a and export good b, or export good a and import good b.

Allowing the two goods in the model, a and b, to stand in for all of the goods produced and consumed in the economy is clearly an important simplification. Clearly, a given country will import and export many different kinds of goods, and so assuming that there are only two goods may seem unrealistic. For many countries, however, the assumption of two broad categories of goods fits the facts of their trade patterns well. For example, New Zealand's exports are primarily agricultural products, and its main imports are manufactured goods. Similarly, Kuwait exports crude oil and imports manufactured goods. For Canada, the story is somewhat more complicated, as we import and export goods that may appear to be the same. For example, a good portion of trade between Canada and the United States is in automobiles. The Ford Motor Company assembles cars in Oakville, Ontario for export to the United States, and it also builds cars in Detroit, Michigan for export to Canada. For our purposes, however, it will prove convenient to think of exports and imports as different goods. However, note that most of the trade between Canada and the United States in automobiles is explained by factors quite specific to the nature of production in the auto industry. These factors will be unimportant for the issues we wish to address.

Tinyland has a production possibilities frontier (PPF), which describes the combinations of good a and good b that Tinyland can produce, and this PPF is depicted in Figure 12.1. The PPF is similar to the ones that we constructed in Chapter 5, where we considered the combinations of consumption and leisure that could be produced in a closed economy. We will not formally derive the PPF for Tinyland in the figure as we did in Chapter 5, but we can give some intuition for why it has the shape that it does. In Tinyland, goods a and b are produced using labour and capital. At point A on the PPF in the figure, only good a is produced; at point B, only good b is produced. Now, consider what happens if we begin at point B, and move along the PPF toward point A. As we do so, more of good a is produced, and less of good b, with labour and capital being reallocated from production of good b to production of good a. Since the PPF

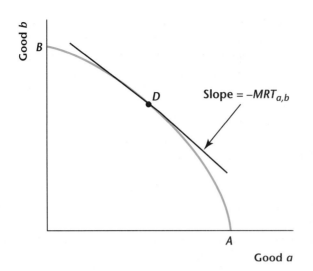

FIGURE 12.1

**Production Possibilities
Frontier for Tinyland**
The figure depicts the production possibilities frontier
(*PPF*) for Tinyland, a small
open economy. The slope of
the *PPF* is minus the marginal
rate of transformation, and
the *PPF* is concave.

represents combinations of goods b and a that can be produced *efficiently* in Tinyland, when labour and capital are reallocated from production of good b to production of good a, these factors of production will be those that are most productive at the margin in producing good a relative to good b. Thus, the *PPF* is not very steep at point B, as only a small amount of good b is sacrificed at the margin to obtain another unit of good a. As we move down the *PPF* from point B to point A, however, the *PPF* becomes steeper, as the labour and capital reallocated from production of good b to production of good a become relatively more productive at the margin in industry b than industry a, and we need to sacrifice more of good b at the margin to obtain another unit of a. Recall that the slope of the *PPF* is minus the marginal rate of transformation, which is denoted by $MRT_{a,b}$. The marginal rate of transformation, $MRT_{a,b}$, is the quantity of good b that must be forgone in the economy if another unit of good a is produced. At point D in Figure 12.1, $MRT_{a,b}$ is minus the slope of a tangent to the *PPF*. Thus, as for the *PPF* in Chapter 5, the marginal rate of transformation increases as we move down the *PPF* from point B to point A. That is, the *PPF* is concave.

The residents of Tinyland consume only goods a and b, and we will assume that we can capture their preferences using the representative consumer device, as in Chapter 4. That is, there is a representative consumer in Tinyland whose preferences are represented by indifference curves, as in Figure 12.2. As we assumed in Chapter 4, the representative consumer prefers more to less and has a preference for diversity, so that the indifference curves in Figure 12.2 slope downward and are convex. Further, goods a and b are both normal, in that an increase in income, holding prices constant, will imply that domestic consumption of both goods increases.

COMPETITIVE EQUILIBRIUM IN TINYLAND WITHOUT TRADE

Now that we know the basic elements of the Tinyland economy, given by the production possibilities frontier and the representative consumer's indifference curves, our first

FIGURE 12.2

**Indifference Curves of the
Representative Consumer
in Tinyland**
The indifference curves of
the representative consumer
in Tinyland are downward-
sloping and convex.

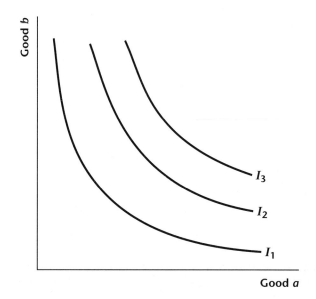

goal will be to understand what determines the pattern of trade in Tinyland. That is, we want to know what factors determine whether Tinyland imports a and exports b, or vice versa, and how this is important for the welfare of consumers in Tinyland.

To show the effects of trade in Tinyland, we want to first determine the characteristics of a competitive equilibrium if Tinyland could not engage in trade. Just as in Chapter 5, a competitive equilibrium for this economy will be Pareto-optimal, and the competitive equilibrium quantities of goods a and b produced and consumed are determined by the point at which an indifference curve is tangent to the *PPF*. That is, the competitive equilibrium is point A in Figure 12.3. Recall that, at the competitive equilibrium point A, the marginal rate of substitution of good a for good b is equal to the marginal rate of transformation, or

$$MRS_{a,b} = MRT_{a,b},$$

since the marginal rate of substitution is minus the slope of the indifference curve at point A, and the marginal rate of transformation is minus the slope of the *PPF* at point A. Further, the equilibrium price of good a relative to good b, or p_{ab}, is minus the slope of a line tangent to the indifference curve and the *PPF* at point A. This is because, first, in equilibrium the representative consumer optimizes by setting

$$MRS_{a,b} = p_{ab}. \tag{12.1}$$

Recall from Chapter 4 that consumer optimization implies that a consumer will set the marginal rate of substitution of one good for another equal to the price of one good relative to the other, which implies that (12.1) holds in this model in equilibrium. Second, optimization by firms will imply that

$$MRT_{a,b} = p_{ab}. \tag{12.2}$$

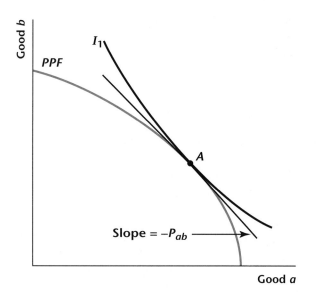

FIGURE 12.3

Equilibrium in Tinyland with No Trade

If there is no trade in Tinyland, equilibrium is determined by the tangency between the production possibilities frontier and an indifference curve for the representative consumer. In equilibrium, the slope of the *PPF* is equal to minus the price of good *a* relative to good *b*.

This second condition holds for the following reason. The marginal rate of transformation, $MRT_{a,b}$, tells us how many units of good b must be given up to produce one additional unit of good a, while p_{ab} is the price that can be received in the market for one unit of good a in units of good b. If $MRT_{a,b} < p_{ab}$, then a firm could profit by taking capital and labour from the production of good b and producing good a, whereas if $MRT_{a,b} < p_{ab}$, then a firm could profit by taking capital and labour from the production of good a and producing good b. Therefore, profit maximization implies that (12.2) holds in equilibrium.

THE EFFECTS OF TRADE ON TINYLAND

We now know the characteristics of a competitive equilibrium in Tinyland in the case where there is no trade with the rest of the world. Of course, our objective is to show the determinants of the pattern and volume of trade between Tinyland and the rest of the world, and to show how trade affects welfare. Thus, at this stage, we will suppose that Tinyland can trade with the rest of the world at world prices given by TOT_{ab}; that is, the relative price of good a in terms of good b is now determined on world markets, rather than in domestic markets in Tinyland. Recall that Tinyland is a price-taker on world markets, so that economic activity in Tinyland will not affect the terms of trade TOT_{ab}.

Trade opens up consumption opportunities not available to the representative consumer in Tinyland in the absence of trade. That is, in equilibrium, the representative consumer need no longer consume the consumption bundle produced in Tinyland, as was the case in Figure 12.3. When Tinyland can trade with the rest of the world, the terms of trade will determine what is produced. Namely, optimization by firms implies that

$$MRT_{a,b} = TOT_{ab},$$

so that the quantities of goods a and b produced in Tinyland are given by point D in Figure 12.4, where the slope of DE is equal to $-TOT_{ab}$. The quantity of good a produced is a_1, and the quantity of good b produced is b_1. To determine what is consumed in a competitive equilibrium with trade, we will think of the consumption bundle produced in Tinyland as being an endowment available to the consumer, which will then determine the representative consumer's budget constraint. Essentially, the representative consumer will receive what is produced as income, through wages and the dividends distributed by firms. Then, if the consumer is endowed with a_1 units of good a and b_1 units of good b, and can exchange good b for good a on world markets at the rate TOT_{ab}, the terms of trade, then the representative consumer's budget constraint will be given by

$$TOT_{ab}q_a + q_b = TOT_{ab}a_1 + b_1. \tag{12.3}$$

In the consumer's budget constraint (12.3), q_a and q_b are the quantities of good a and good b consumed respectively, and the budget constraint is written in terms of good b. Thus, the quantity on the right-hand side of Equation (12.3) is the representative consumer's income in terms of good b, and the quantity on the left-hand side is the consumer's expenditure on goods a and b, again in units of good b. The budget constraint (12.3) is then line DE in Figure 12.4.

Next, the representative consumer will optimize, just as in Chapter 4, by choosing the consumption bundle where an indifference curve is tangent to his or her budget constraint. In Figure 12.4, the consumer chooses point E, where the quantity of good a consumed is $q_a = a_2$, and the quantity of good b consumed is $q_b = b_2$. In the figure, Tinyland will then be an importer of good a and an exporter of good b, since $a_2 > a_1$ and $b_2 < b_1$. The value of imports, in units of good b, is $TOT_{ab}(a_2 - a_1)$, and the value of exports is $b_1 - b_2$. Recalling the definition of the current account surplus from Chapter 2, which is net exports plus net factor payments from abroad, the current

FIGURE 12.4

Production and Consumption in Tinyland with Trade

When Tinyland trades with the rest of the world at market prices given by the terms of trade, consumption occurs at point E, and production occurs at point D, with the slope of DE equal to minus the terms of trade.

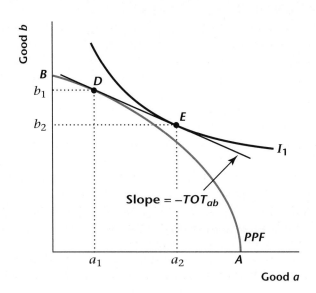

account surplus in Tinyland, in units of good b, will be the value of exports minus the value of imports (since net factor payments are zero here), which is

$$CA = b_1 - b_2 - TOT_{ab}(a_2 - a_1).$$

But from the consumer's budget constraint (12.3), we then have $CA = 0$; that is, the current account surplus is zero. This is a one-period model in which Tinyland cannot borrow and lend abroad, which implies that the current account surplus *must* be zero in equilibrium. In this model, the value of goods exported will always equal the value of goods imported in equilibrium.

The pattern of trade between Tinyland and the rest of the world is determined in part by two factors. The first is the principle of **comparative advantage**. In Figure 12.4, Tinyland imports good a and exports good b, so that Tinyland tends to have a comparative advantage in producing good b. *Comparative advantage is determined by the slope of the production possibilities frontier.* The steeper the production possibilities frontier, the greater Tinyland's comparative advantage in producing good b relative to good a, since more of good b needs to be sacrificed at the margin to produce another unit of good a. A steeper *PPF* will also imply that more of good b is produced, and less of good a is produced, when Tinyland can trade with the rest of the world, and so there will be a tendency to export more of good b.

The second factor that determines the pattern of trade is consumer preferences. Even if Tinyland has a strong comparative advantage in producing a good, if the representative consumer has a strong preference for that good, it could be imported rather than exported. The important characteristic of consumer preferences for determining the pattern of trade is the marginal rate of substitution, $MRS_{a,b}$. As $MRS_{a,b}$ increases, the indifference curves of the representative consumer become steeper, and Tinyland will have a greater tendency to import good a and export good b.

An important result is that the representative consumer will always be better off with trade than without it. To show this, we will consider two cases. In the first case, the domestic price of good a in terms of good b (when there is no trade) is greater than the terms of trade, as in Figure 12.5. Here, when there is no trade, the consumption bundle produced and consumed is given by point A, but when Tinyland is opened up to world trade, production occurs at point B, and the representative consumer chooses point D. The terms of trade are given by minus the slope of the line EF. Note that, with trade, the consumer is on a higher indifference curve; that is, indifference curve I_2 represents a higher level of welfare than indifference curve I_1. In the second case, as in Figure 12.6, the domestic price of good a in terms of good b (when there is no trade) is smaller than the terms of trade. In this case, consumption and production when the economy is closed are at point A, but when the economy is open, production occurs at point B and consumption at point D. Again, the representative consumer's welfare improves with free trade. This result—trade increases opportunities and makes the nation better off—is a fundamental economic principle.

Our model captures the effects of trade on the *average* consumer, showing that trade always makes this average consumer (the representative consumer) better off. In practice, however, eliminating trade restrictions typically harms some people while benefiting

FIGURE 12.5

FIGURE 12.5

An Increase in Welfare when Good *a* Is Imported
When there is no trade, consumption and production occur at point *A*, but when Tinyland trades with the rest of the world, production occurs at *B* and consumption at *D*. In this case, good *a* is imported, and welfare is higher with trade, as the representative consumer attains a higher indifference curve.

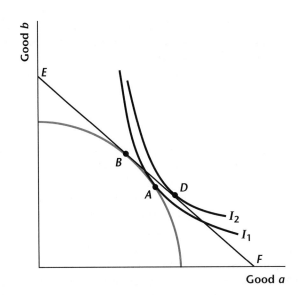

others, though we argue the net effect on welfare is positive. For example, not all Canadian residents were in agreement that the Canada–U.S. Free Trade Agreement (1989) and the North American Free Trade Agreement (NAFTA) were good ideas. NAFTA tended to harm those industries in Canada for which Mexico and the United States had comparative advantages. In those industries, product prices and real wages tended to fall, and workers were displaced. However, in industries for which Canada has a comparative advantage relative to Mexico and the United States, prices and real wages tended to rise, and employment expanded. The fact that someone almost always

FIGURE 12.6

An Increase in Welfare when Good *b* Is Imported
Here, in contrast to Figure 12.5, good *b* is imported when Tinyland can trade with the rest of the world. Trade improves welfare, as the consumer attains a higher indifference curve.

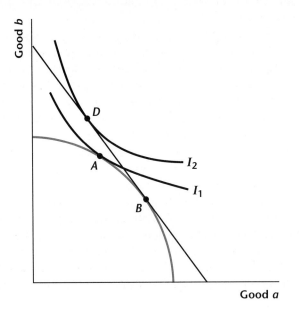

stands to lose in circumstances where trade restrictions are relaxed makes it difficult to pass laws that free up international trade. Also, when particular industries in the United States have been harmed by free trade, this has sometimes led to trade disputes with Canada, for example, trade disputes over lumber and agricultural products.

A CHANGE IN THE TERMS OF TRADE: EFFECTS ON PRODUCTION, CONSUMPTION, AND WELFARE

A key macroeconomic shock for an open economy is a change in the price of imports relative to the price of exports, that is, a change in the terms of trade. The terms of trade could move against a country if imports became more expensive relative to exports, as, for example, in New Zealand if the prices of manufactured goods were to increase relative to the prices of agricultural goods. In this case, economic welfare would decrease in New Zealand. The terms of trade could also move in favour of a country if imports became cheaper relative to exports. This would happen in Kuwait if there were an increase in the relative price of crude oil, which would increase economic welfare for the residents of Kuwait. As we will show in this section, a change in the terms of trade has similarities to a change in total factor productivity in a closed economy, as considered in Chapter 5. This is because there will in general be income and substitution effects associated with a change in the terms of trade.

In an open economy, changes in the terms of trade will affect domestic production, domestic consumption, exports, and imports. In the model, we must consider the two cases where the terms of trade move in favour of, and against Tinyland. In the first case, Tinyland imports good a before an increase in the terms of trade, and in the second, Tinyland initially imports good b. This will matter for the results because of the effects on economic welfare, and because there will be a difference in income effects on consumption of both goods. In the first case, there will be a negative income effect on consumption and in the second case a positive income effect. Substitution effects work in the same way in each case.

In Figure 12.7 we show the first case, where initially the consumption bundle produced is given by point A, and the initial terms of trade are given by the negative of the slope of a line tangent to point A. The initial consumption bundle is at point B, where this line is tangent to indifference curve I_1. With an increase in the terms of trade, production is at point D, where the terms of trade (minus the slope of a line tangent to the PPF at point D) is higher. Note that production of good a must increase, while production of good b decreases, as the relative price of good a has risen, encouraging more production of a and less of b. The new consumption bundle is given by point E, where in this case the representative consumer consumes less of good a and more of good b. In fact, Tinyland now imports b and exports a.

We can separate the effect of the change in the terms of trade on consumption into income and substitution effects. Namely, if we draw a tangent to the initial indifference curve I_1 in Figure 12.7, the slope of which is minus the new terms of trade, then this line will be tangent to I_1 at point F, and the substitution effect of the change in the terms of trade is the movement from B to F. That is, the substitution effect is for consumption of good a to decrease and that of good b to increase. There is a negative income effect,

FIGURE 12.7

An Increase in the Terms of Trade when Good *a* Is Initially Imported

The terms of trade increase, with the price of good *a* increasing relative to good *b*. When good *a* is initially imported, welfare falls. The substitution effect on consumption is the movement from *B* to *F*, the income effect the movement from *F* to *E*. Consumption of good *a* falls, and consumption of good *b* may rise or fall. The production point moves from *A* to *D*.

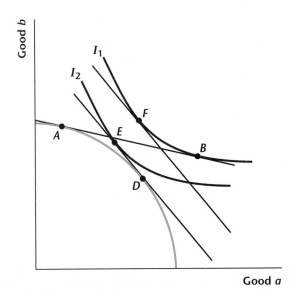

which is the movement from *F* to *E*. Recall that we assumed that both goods are normal, so that the income effect is for consumption of goods *a* and *b* to decrease.

On net, then, the consumption of good *a* must decrease, the consumption of good *b* may increase or decrease, depending on the size of the income effect relative to the substitution effect. Production of good *a* increases, and production of good *b* decreases. The quantity of a good imported is given by consumption minus production. Therefore, we can conclude that the quantity of good *a* imported must decrease, as consumption decreases and production increases. For good *b*, however, there is an ambiguous effect on the quantity imported, as production decreases, but consumption may increase or decrease. However, note that if substitution effects dominate income effects, then the quantity of good *b* imported will rise.

In terms of the value of imports and exports, in units of good *b*, the results are ambiguous. The value of imports is

$$\text{Quantity of imports} \times TOT_{ab},$$

and though we know that the quantity of imports decreases, the terms of trade TOT_{ab} increases, and so the product of quantity and terms of trade could either increase or decrease. Since we have already determined that the quantity of good *b* exported could increase or decrease, we know that the value of good *b* exported, in units of good *b* (which is the same thing), could increase or decrease. Though the effects on the value of exports and imports are ambiguous here, we know that there will be no effect on the current account surplus from a change in the terms of trade, since the current account surplus is always zero in this model.

Now consider the second case, in Figure 12.8 where there is an increase in the terms of trade when Tinyland initially imports good *b* and exports good *a*. Initially, production of goods *a* and *b* is given by point *A*, with consumption at point *B*. The slope

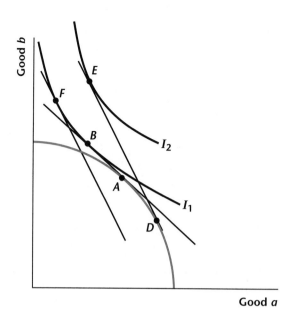

FIGURE 12.8
An Increase in the Terms of Trade when Good b Is Initially Imported
An increase in the terms of trade increases welfare when good b is initially imported. The substitution effect on consumption is the movement from B to F, the income effect the movement from F to E. Consumption of good a may rise or fall, and consumption of good b rises. Production moves from A to D.

of the line AB is equal to minus the initial terms of trade. When the terms of trade increases, the production point shifts to D, with domestic output of good a rising and output of good b falling, just as in the first case. The representative consumer now chooses point E, with the slope of DE equal to minus the new terms of trade. Here, there is a positive income effect on consumption of goods a and b. Separating the effect of the change in the terms of trade into income and substitution effects, the substitution effect is the movement from B to F, while the income effect is the movement from F to E. As before, the substitution effect leads to an increase in consumption of good b and a decrease in consumption of good a. Here, however, the income effect leads to an increase in consumption of both goods a and b (again under the assumption that both goods are normal). Therefore, consumption of good b must rise, but consumption of good a may rise or fall.

In the second case, then, imports of good b rise, since less is produced and more is consumed as well. Exports of good a may rise or fall, since more is produced, but consumption may increase or decrease. What happens to the value of imports and exports is also ambiguous, but again there will be no effect on the current account surplus, which is always zero.

Note that what happens to the representative consumer's welfare differs between the first case and the second. When good a is initially imported, and the terms of trade change so that the relative price of good a increases, the representative consumer will be worse off. That is, in Figure 12.7, the representative consumer initially chooses a consumption bundle on indifference curve I_1, and chooses a consumption bundle on a lower indifference curve, I_2, when the terms of trade changes. This is the case where the terms of trade turn against Tinyland, in the sense that the goods that are being sold abroad (good b) become cheaper relative to the goods that are purchased abroad (good a). In Figure 12.8, however, the change in the terms of trade is favourable to

How Important Are Shocks to the Terms of Trade for Business Cycles?

Since the terms of trade cause changes in the makeup of domestic consumption and production, and they affect aggregate economic welfare, shocks to the terms of trade could be sources of business cycles. Indeed, one of the shocks to the economy that we have previously analyzed as a shock to total factor productivity—a change in the relative price of energy—can also be modelled as an adverse change in the terms of trade for most industrialized countries. That is, most industrialized countries are net importers of oil, so if the world price of crude oil increased relative to other world prices, this would imply that the terms of trade had turned against those countries. For example, the large increases in the world price of crude oil that took place in 1973, 1979–80, and 2000–01 were negative terms of trade shocks for Germany, Great Britain, Japan, and the United States, among other countries. For Canada, the effects of an increase in the world price of oil are somewhat more complicated than in these other industrialized countries, in particular because Canada is a net exporter of energy products. Thus, when the world price of oil increases, this is a favourable term of trade shock for Canada: oil and natural gas production, especially in Alberta, becomes more profitable, and the governments of Alberta and Canada receive higher tax revenues. However, there are negative effects for Canada: energy-using industries, particularly the manufacturing industry centred in eastern Canada, become less profitable. On net, Canada still suffers from an increase in the world price of oil, though the net negative effect on Canadian welfare is smaller than it once was, because Canada's net exports of energy

commodities and products have increased more than sixfold since 1973.[1]

Canada is not as sensitive to changes in the terms of trade as some other countries are, in spite of the fact that exports and imports represent a relatively large fraction of GDP in Canada. Canadian imports and exports have become more diversified across a wide array of goods and services than was once the case. In particular, Canada relies less on exports of raw materials (lumber, metals, wheat) and more on exports of semi-processed and manufactured goods than in the past. In some countries, there is a dependence on one commodity as a major export. For example, Kuwait is primarily an exporter of crude oil, so that fluctuations in the world price of this one commodity can have dramatic effects for the economy of Kuwait.

For all countries of the world, how important are terms of trade shocks for business cycles? Using a real business cycle model, and data from many countries, Enrique Mendoza finds that half of the variability in real GDP is explained by terms of trade shocks.[2] This is a highly significant finding, and it indicates that accounting for shocks from abroad is very important for analyzing business cycles. If attention is confined to a closed-economy analysis of the factors determining business cycles, we lose at least half of the picture.

---

[1] See G. Stuber, 2001, "The Changing Effects of Energy Price Shocks on Economic Activity and Inflation," *Bank of Canada Review*, Summer, pp. 3–14.1

[2] See E. Mendoza, 1993, "The Terms of Trade, the Real Exchange Rate, and Economic Fluctuations," *International Economic Review* 36, 101–138.

Tinyland, in that the representative consumer is on a higher indifference curve after the terms of trade change. In this case, imported goods (good *b*) become cheaper relative to exports, and this is good for economic welfare in Tinyland.

Shocks to the terms of trade can be an important cause of business cycles. Macroeconomics in Action 12.1 contains some evidence on the relative importance of shocks to the terms of trade for business cycles in open economies.

A Two-Period Small Open-Economy Model: The Current Account in Tinyland

The previous one-period model was useful for understanding the benefits from trade and the effects of changes in the terms of trade. However, some important issues in international macroeconomics are related to intertemporal choices. In particular, we would like to study the determinants of the current account surplus. We know from Chapter 2 that a current account surplus must always be reflected in an excess of domestic savings over domestic investment, and by an increase in the net claims of domestic residents on foreign residents. Thus, to analyze the current account, we need a model in which, at minimum, consumers make borrowing and lending and consumption–savings decisions. A useful model of borrowing and lending and consumption–savings decisions is the two-period model we developed in Chapter 6. Here, we will modify that model by having a single representative consumer, capturing the average behaviour of all domestic consumers, and we will allow borrowing and lending between domestic and foreign residents.

We will suppose that there is a single representative consumer in Tinyland, and that this consumer lives for two periods, the current and future periods. For the representative consumer, income is exogenous in both periods, with Y denoting current real income and Y' future real income. The consumer also pays lump-sum taxes to the government of Tinyland of T in the current period and T' in the future period. Since Tinyland is a small open economy, the actions of the representative consumer will not affect the world real interest rate, and so we will assume that the consumer in Tinyland can borrow and lend as much as he or she wishes at the world real interest rate r. Just as in Chapter 6, the representative consumer chooses consumption in the current and future periods, C and C' respectively, to make himself or herself as well off as possible given his or her lifetime budget constraint

$$C + \frac{C'}{1+r} = Y - T + \frac{Y' - T'}{1+r}. \tag{12.4}$$

In Figure 12.9 we show the consumer's lifetime budget constraint as the line AB. Point E is the endowment point, and the representative consumer chooses point D on his or her lifetime budget constraint, which is the point where an indifference curve is tangent to the lifetime budget constraint. In the figure, consumption in the first and second periods is C^* and C'^*, respectively. Private saving in the current period is then given by $S_p = Y - T - C = Y - T - C^*$, and so in the figure the consumer saves a positive amount.

Now, to complete the model, we need to describe the behaviour of the government in Tinyland. Government spending in the current and future periods is G and G', respectively, and these quantities are exogenous. The government then sets current and

FIGURE 12.9

**The Two-Period Small
Open-Economy Model**
The representative consumer's
budget constraint is AB, the
endowment point is E, and
the consumer chooses
point D.

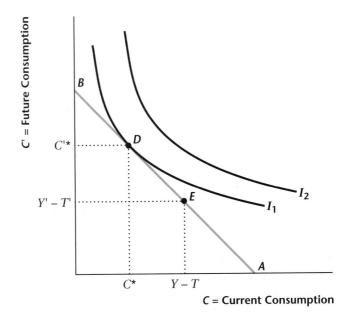

future taxes on the representative consumer, T and T' respectively, to satisfy the government's present-value budget constraint

$$G + \frac{G'}{1 + r} = T + \frac{T'}{1 + r}. \tag{12.5}$$

Then, the quantity of government saving is given by $S_g = T - G$, and in this economy where there is no investment, the current account surplus in the current period, from Chapter 2, is

$$CA = S - I = (S_p + S_g) - 0 = Y - C - G.$$

In this model, we are interested in understanding the key factors that affect the current account surplus CA, which are the following:

- *Current period income.* Recall from Chapter 6 that an increase in current income will increase current consumption and future consumption, and current consumption increases by less than the increase in current income, because the consumer wishes to smooth consumption over his or her lifetime. Therefore, an increase in Y will lead to an increase in the current account surplus. Due to the consumption-smoothing motive, a country that experiences an increase in current income will save more by lending abroad, and this is reflected in an increase in the current account surplus.

- *Current government spending.* An increase in government spending leads, given the government's present-value budget constraint (12.5), to an increase by an equal amount in the present value of taxes for the consumer. Therefore, the consumer's lifetime wealth falls by the increase in government spending. We know then that the consumer's current consumption will fall, but by less than the increase in government spending, since the consumer will smooth consumption between the current and future periods. Therefore, the current account surplus will decrease with an increase in government spending.

- *Taxes.* Given the Ricardian equivalence theorem from Chapter 6, changes in taxes will have no effect on aggregate consumption, since consumers simply adjust savings to account for the change in their future tax liabilities. As consumption is unaffected, there will be no effect on the current account surplus. Just as in the closed-economy model in Chapter 6, however, if there are significant credit market imperfections, then a change in current taxes will in general affect current consumption, and this will matter for the trade balance.

- *The real interest rate.* Recall from Chapter 6 that the effect of a change in the real interest rate on period 1 consumption will depend on whether the representative consumer is initially a net borrower or a net lender. If the consumer is a net lender, then current consumption may rise or fall when the real interest rises, since there is a positive income effect on consumption, and the substitution effect implies that current consumption falls and future consumption rises. If the consumer is a net borrower, the income and substitution effects work in the same direction, and an increase in the real interest rate will cause a decrease in current consumption. In general, then, if income effects are not too large, an increase in the real interest rate will cause a decrease in current consumption and an increase in the current account surplus.

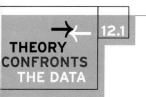

THEORY CONFRONTS THE DATA

12.1

Is a Current Account Deficit a Bad Thing?

It may seem that a current account deficit is undesirable, since if a country runs a current account deficit, it is borrowing from the rest of the world and accumulating debt. However, just as for individual consumers, lending and borrowing is the means by which a nation smooths consumption. If a given country runs current account deficits when aggregate income is low, and runs current account surpluses when aggregate income is high, this allows the residents of that country to smooth their consumption over time. This state of affairs is preferable to one where the country always has a current account surplus of zero and consumption is as variable as income.

Thus, there are good reasons for expecting that countries should run current account surpluses in good times and current account deficits in bad times. Government policy aimed at correcting this tendency could be counterproductive. But do countries actually smooth consumption over time as theory predicts? In Figure 12.10 we show the deviations from trend in real GDP and net exports for Canada over the period 1961–2002. For real GDP, the deviations are percentage deviations from trend, and for net exports these are the absolute deviations from trend, scaled to match reasonably closely the average percentage deviation from trend in real GDP. Note in the figure there is some tendency for net exports to be above (below) trend when real GDP is below (above) trend, so that deviations from trend in GDP and net exports are negatively correlated. This is the opposite of consumption smoothing, in that Canada tended to export

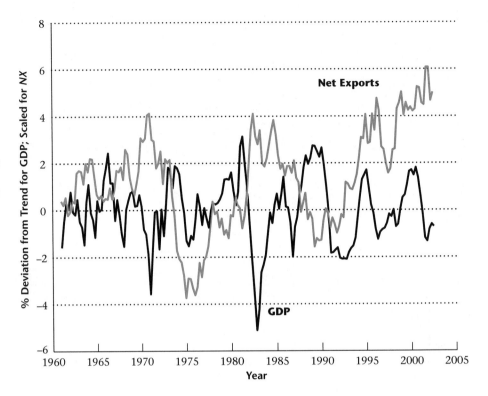

FIGURE 12.10

Deviations from Trend in Net Exports and GDP to Canada, 1961–2002

There does not appear to be evidence of national consumption smoothing for Canada, as deviations from trend in net exports and GDP are negatively correlated. This may be due to synchronization in business cycles across countries.

Source: Adapted from the Statistics Canada CANSIM database, Series v1992067, v1992060, v1992063.

goods and lend more abroad when output was low, and to borrow more abroad when output was high.

Why would the data not exhibit obvious evidence of consumption smoothing when economic theory tells us that nations should smooth consumption by lending (borrowing) abroad when income is high (low)? An explanation may be that the timing and severity of business cycles in the rest of the world and in Canada are similar. For example, the data in Figure 12.10 are consistent with consumption smoothing if, before 1970, output tended to be high (low) in Canada when output was high (low) in the rest of the world, and business cycles were of about the same severity in Canada and in other countries. Then, all countries would want to borrow (lend) at the same times, and interest rates would adjust so that net exports in Canada would be unrelated to GDP. However, after 1970, if business cycles coincided in Canada and the rest of the world, but the upturns and downturns were more severe in the rest of the world, Canada could in equilibrium be lending to other countries when its own output was low, and borrowing from other countries when its own output was high. ⤡

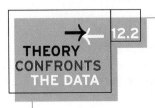

The Twin Deficits

Our two-period small open-economy model predicts that an increase in government spending will cause a decrease in the current account surplus and that, given Ricardian equivalence, a

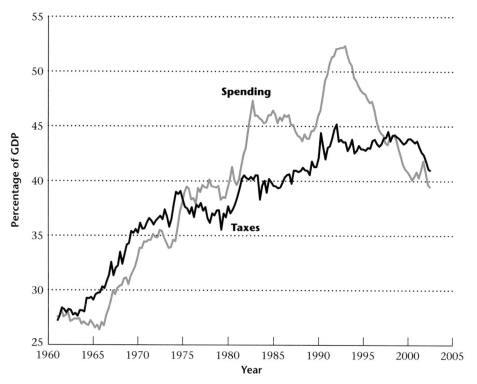

FIGURE 12.11

Government Spending and Taxes in Canada, 1961–2002
Taxes as a fraction of GDP increase relatively smoothly, while government spending fluctuates more.

Source: Adapted from the Statistics Canada CANSIM database, Series v498086, v498316, v498326.

decrease in current taxes will have no effect. With a decrease in current taxes, consumers will understand that their future taxes have increased by an equal amount, in present-value terms, and current consumption will be unaffected, leaving the current account surplus unchanged.

Figure 12.11 shows government spending and taxes as fractions of GDP for the years 1961–2002. First, note that taxes increased on trend over this period relatively smoothly, while there were several sharp short-run changes in government spending. Thus, in Figure 12.12, which shows the government deficit, which is the difference between government spending and taxes, large changes in the government deficit are due primarily to changes in government spending.

Our theory tells us that an increase in government purchases will result in a decrease in the current account surplus. Thus, in Figure 12.12, if the only factor causing the government deficit to fluctuate were government purchases, we should observe the government deficit and net exports moving in opposite directions. There would be a tendency for there to be **twin deficits**, that is, the government deficit would tend to be positive (negative) when the current account is in deficit (surplus), or when net exports are negative (positive). In Figure 12.12, there appears to be a tendency for this to occur. For example, the government deficit increased sharply in 1973–1975 at a time when net exports were decreasing sharply. As well, from the early 1990s to 2002, the government deficit decreased while net exports were increasing.

However, the twin deficits phenomenon is not consistently reflected in the data. In the early 1980s the government deficit and net exports both increased, and there was

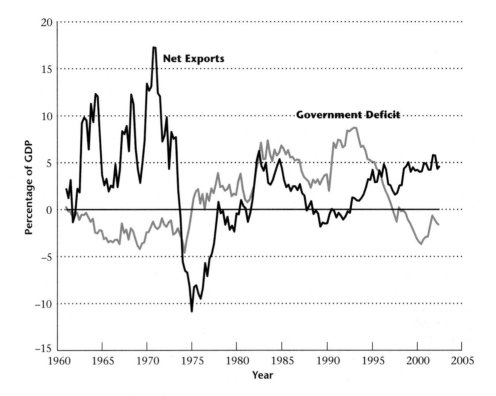

a large increase in the government deficit in the early 1990s with no corresponding significant change in net exports. Recall from Chapter 2 that national income accounts identities imply that

$$CA = S - I;$$

that is, the current account surplus is equal to national saving minus investment expenditures. If private saving and investment are unchanged and there is a decrease in government saving (an increase in the government deficit), then, from this equation, the current account surplus must fall. At any time, there can be many different macroeconomic shocks hitting the economy simultaneously. Some of these shocks can cause large changes in private savings and investment, which could offset changes in the current account surplus resulting from changes in government purchases. This might explain periods of time in Figure 12.12 when the twin deficits phenomenon is not apparent. ⟫

Production, Investment, and the Current Account

While the previous model yields useful insights concerning the role of the current account in national consumption smoothing, and some explanations for the behaviour of the current account, we ought to understand more completely the relationship between the current account surplus and events in the domestic economy. In this section, we will study a model based on the real intertemporal model in Chapter 7, which includes production and investment behaviour.

In this model, just as in the previous one, Tinyland faces a given world real interest rate. As in Chapter 7, output supply is given by the upward-sloping curve Y^s in Figure 12.13. Here, however, we assume that goods can be freely traded with foreign countries, and so from the income-expenditure identity $Y = C + I + G + NX$, the demand for goods also includes net exports, NX. In Figure 12.13, the world real interest rate is r^*, which then determines the domestic demand for consumption goods and investment goods. If total domestic demand, $C + I + G$, exceeds the domestic supply of goods at the world real interest rate, then goods are imported and net exports are negative; and if domestic demand is less than the domestic supply of goods at the world real interest rate, then goods are exported and net exports are positive. The equilibrium quantity of net exports is the quantity NX that implies that the downward-sloping output demand curve Y^d intersects the Y^s curve in Figure 12.13 at the world real interest rate r^*. We have depicted a case in Figure 12.13 where $NX > 0$, that is, if there were no trade in goods with the rest of the world, then the output demand curve would be Y_2^d, to the left of Y_1^d, and the domestic real interest rate would be r_c. In general, it could be that $r^* < r_c$ or $r^* > r_c$. Given the world real interest rate r^*, the quantity of aggregate output produced in Tinyland is Y_1, but in this case the domestic demand for goods, $C + I + G$, is less than Y_1. The domestic demand for goods, $C + I + G$, is sometimes referred to as **absorption**, as this is the quantity of aggregate output that is absorbed by the domestic economy. The quantity NX is then the current account surplus, or net exports. Recall that the current account surplus is net exports plus net factor payments from abroad, but net factor payments from abroad equal zero in this model. In Figure 12.13, Tinyland has a positive current account surplus; that is, $NX > 0$, which implies Tinyland is accumulating assets from the rest of the world.

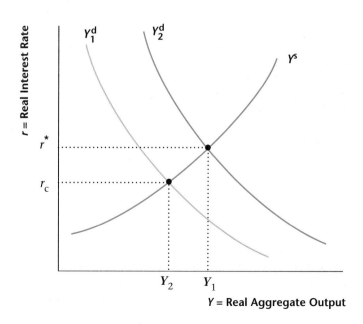

$Y =$ **Real Aggregate Output**

FIGURE 12.13

A Small Open-Economy Model with Production and Investment

The world real interest rate, determined on world credit markets, is r^*. Equilibrium output is Y_1, and there is a current account surplus. If there were no trade, the output demand curve shifts to Y_2^d, and the domestic real interest rate would be r_c.

THE EFFECTS OF AN INCREASE
IN THE WORLD REAL INTEREST RATE

Since the model here is essentially identical to the real intertemporal model with a real interest rate fixed on world credit markets, it is straightforward to use the model to analyze the effects of particular shocks to the domestic economy. The output demand curve and output supply curve will shift in the same ways in response to shocks as in the real intertemporal model of Chapter 7, with the only modification in the analysis being that NX adjusts so that the output demand curve intersects the output supply curve at the world real interest rate r^*. The first experiment we will carry out is to look at the effects in the model of an increase in the world real interest rate. Such a change could have many causes; it could result from, for example, a negative total factor productivity shock in other countries (recall our analysis of domestic total factor productivity shocks from Chapter 7).

Suppose, in Figure 12.14, that the world real interest rate increases from r_1 to r_2. Then the current account surplus increases causing the output demand curve to shift to the right from Y_1^d to Y_2^d. Domestic investment must decrease, as the real interest rate increases, but domestic consumption may rise or fall, as there is a negative effect from the increase in r and a positive effect from the increase in Y.

These results have the interesting implication that a negative total factor productivity shock abroad, which would *decrease* foreign output and cause the world real interest rate to rise, will also cause an *increase* in domestic output. Therefore, a foreign shock of this sort, when transmitted to the domestic economy, will not cause output in the domestic economy and in the rest of the world to move together.

TEMPORARY AND PERMANENT INCREASES IN GOVERNMENT
EXPENDITURE AND THE EFFECTS ON THE CURRENT ACCOUNT

For our second experiment, we will consider the effects of increases in domestic government expenditure. As we will see, the results will depend in important ways on whether the increase in government spending is temporary or permanent, particularly for the response of the current account surplus.

First, we will consider the effects of a temporary increase in government spending, that is, an increase in G. Just as in Chapter 7, there is a negative income effect on leisure for the representative consumer, because of the increase in the present value of taxes, and so labour supply will increase, shifting the output supply curve rightward from Y_1^s to Y_2^s. There is a shift to the right in the output demand curve resulting from the net increase in output demand caused by the increase in G. The current account surplus then adjusts so that the output demand curve ultimately shifts from Y_1^d to Y_2^d (see Figure 12.5). As in Chapter 7, the initial shift in the output supply curve is small relative to the shift in the output demand curve (because the increase in government spending is temporary, so that the effects on lifetime wealth are small). Therefore, the current account surplus must decrease.

Next, suppose that the increase in government spending is permanent. That is, as in Chapter 7, assume that there are equal increases in current government purchases G, and in future government purchases G'. Then, in Figure 12.16, there is no shift in

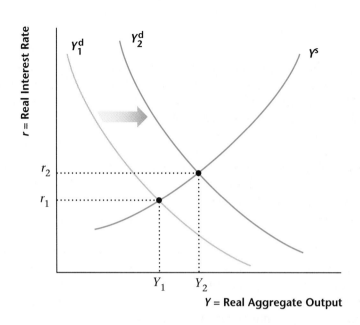

FIGURE 12.14

An Increase in the World Real Interest Rate

An increase in the world real interest rate from r_1 to r_2 causes an increase in output and an increase in the current account surplus.

the output demand curve Y^d due to the change in government spending, as the demand for current consumption falls by as much as current government spending rises, given the reduction in lifetime wealth resulting from the tax increases necessary to finance government spending. The output supply curve shifts rightward from Y_1^s to Y_2^s, because of the negative effect of the decrease in lifetime wealth on current leisure. The current account surplus will increase until the output demand curve has shifted from Y_1^d to Y_2^d.

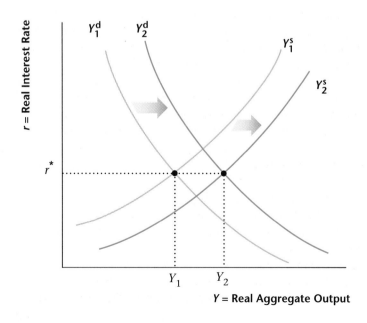

FIGURE 12.15

A Temporary Increase in Government Spending

An increase in current government spending initially shifts the output demand curve and the output supply curve to the right (the output demand curve shifts to a greater extent). Output increases and the current account surplus falls.

FIGURE 12.16

A Permanent Increase in Government Spending

A permanent increase in government spending (current and future spending increase by the same amount) shifts the output supply curve to the right. Domestic output increases, and the current account surplus increases.

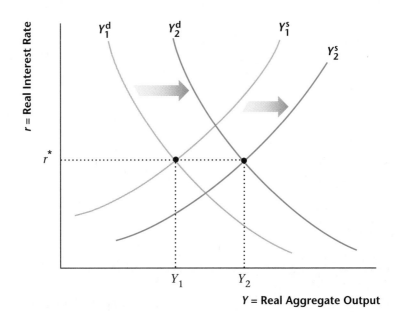

Note that the effect of an increase in government spending is quite different depending on whether the increase in government spending is temporary or permanent. A temporary increase in government spending results in a decrease in the current account surplus, whereas a permanent increase in government spending causes an increase in the current account surplus.

THE EFFECTS OF INCREASES IN CURRENT AND FUTURE TOTAL FACTOR PRODUCTIVITY

In Chapters 5 and 7, we showed how total factor productivity matters for domestic real aggregate activity. An increase in current total factor productivity in a closed economy increases labour demand, and it leads to increases in the real wage, employment, and output, and a decrease in the real interest rate. An anticipated increase in future total factor productivity increases the current demand for investment goods and consumption goods in a closed economy, and it will increase current aggregate output and the real interest rate. In a small open economy, some of these results are somewhat different, as the real interest rate is determined on the world credit market. We will also be able to determine the effects of total factor productivity shocks on the current account.

Suppose first that current total factor productivity increases. Recall from Chapter 7 that this causes a shift to the right in the output supply curve. In Figure 12.17 the output supply curve shifts from Y_1^s to Y_2^s. Then, the current account surplus increases, shifting the output demand curve to the right from Y_1^d to Y_2^d. As a result, aggregate output increases from Y_1 to Y_2, and there is an increase in the current account surplus. Domestic consumption increases due to the increase in real income, but given that the real interest rate is unchanged there is no effect on investment. In a closed economy, the real interest rate falls when total factor productivity increases, causing increases in

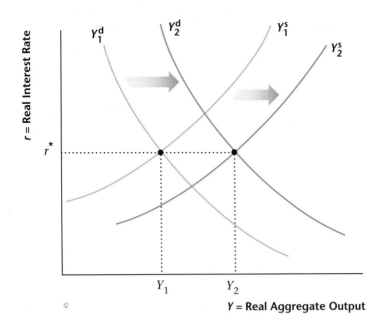

FIGURE 12.17

An Increase in Current Total Factor Productivity

An increase in current total factor productivity shifts the output supply curve to the right. Aggregate output increases, and the current account surplus also increases.

C and I. However, the real interest rate is determined on world markets here, and so an increase in total factor productivity in the domestic economy will have no effect on the real interest rate. Typically, though, different countries will simultaneously experience increases in total factor productivity at the same time, as changes in production technology tend to be transmitted across international borders. Therefore, an increase in total factor productivity domestically would also tend to be associated with a decrease in the world real interest rate and increases in domestic consumption and investment.

Next, suppose an increase in future total factor productivity is anticipated. Recall from Chapter 7 that this implies the representative firm will expect an increase in the future marginal product of capital, which will cause an increase in the demand for investment goods. Further, the representative consumer will anticipate higher future income as the result of the increase in future total factor productivity, and this will cause an increase in the demand for current consumption goods. The increase in the demand for current consumption and investment goods shifts the output demand curve in Figure 12.18 rightward but there will be a corresponding decrease in the current account surplus so that demand equals supply for domestically produced goods. In equilibrium, aggregate output remains fixed at Y_1, but the current account surplus then falls.

The above provides a potential explanation, perhaps more plausible than permanent negative government spending shocks, for some of the features of Figure 12.12 that it was not possible to attribute to government spending shocks alone. In Figure 12.19, note that investment expenditures increase as a fraction of GDP during the 1980s and during the 1990s. Both these periods were times of optimism about future productivity. Thus, the tendency of the government deficit and net exports to move together during the 1980s is consistent with the dominant shock being an anticipated increase

FIGURE 12.18

An Increase in Future Total Factor Productivity

An anticipated increase in future total factor productivity initially shifts the output demand curve to the right. Aggregate output remains unchanged, and the current account surplus declines.

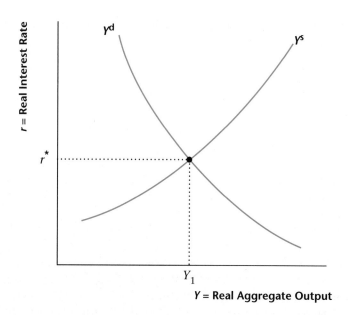

in future total factor productivity, which is reflected in an increase in investment over this period. As well, the fact that net exports increased only modestly during the 1990s in the face of a very large decrease in the government deficit can be accounted for by

FIGURE 12.19

Investment as a Percentage of GDP in Canada, 1961–2002

There were booms in investment during the 1980s and 1990s that have important implications for the current account surplus.

Source: Adapted from the Statistics Canada CANSIM database, Series v1992052, v1992057, v1992067.

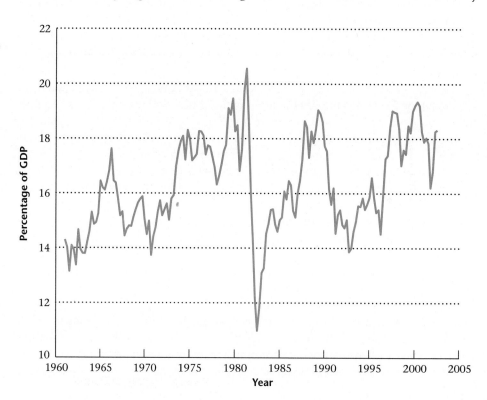

an investment boom in the 1990s resulting from optimism about the prospects for future total factor productivity.

CURRENT ACCOUNT DEFICITS, CONSUMPTION, AND INVESTMENT

We have already discussed how a current account deficit need not be a bad thing, as current account deficits help domestic consumers smooth consumption over time. A current account deficit can also serve another purpose, to finance domestic investment, as was the case when we considered the effects of an anticipated shock to future total factor productivity in the previous subsection. When a country runs a current account deficit so as to finance an increase in domestic investment expenditures, this increases the capital stock and future productive capacity. In the future, the current account deficit can be eliminated because of this higher productive capacity.

In Figure 12.20 Tinyland is initially running a current account deficit. The output demand curve is Y_1^d, the output supply curve is Y_1^s, and current output is Y_1. Now, if the current account deficit is financing domestic investment, in the future the capital stock K will be higher. This will increase the demand for labour and shift the output supply curve to the right, to Y_2^s. Then, the current account surplus increases, shifting the output demand curve to the right to Y_2^d. Thus, if the current account deficit finances domestic investment, this increases future productive capacity, more goods can be sold abroad, and the current account deficit can be eliminated.

Historically, borrowing abroad has been quite useful in promoting development in some countries. For example, the takeoff in economic growth in Canada in the 19th century and the opening up of western Canada to development were spurred in part by the construction of railroads, which were partially financed by borrowing abroad. Current account deficits can finance domestic investment in plants, equipment,

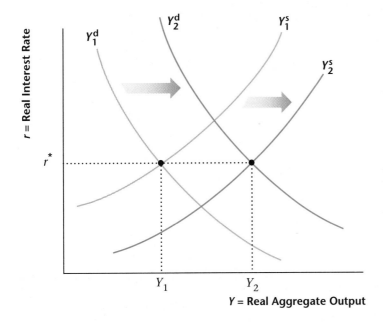

FIGURE 12.20

An Increase in the Capital Stock

The output supply curve shifts to the right, increasing output and potentially eliminating the current account deficit. Thus, investment financed by a current account deficit can eliminate the current account deficit in the long run.

and housing, and this will permit a higher standard of living in the future, and possibly cause a future elimination of the current account deficit.

This chapter explored the real macroeconomic implications of having trade in goods and assets among nations. In Chapter 13, we will integrate money into the third model that we studied in this chapter, so as to understand the determination of nominal exchange rates, the importance of flexible and fixed exchange rates, and why capital controls are important for macroeconomic activity.

Chapter Summary

This chapter studied the implications of international trade in goods and assets for domestic welfare, output, consumption, investment, and the current account surplus. We constructed three small open-economy models and showed how these models can be used to understand the importance of openness for the domestic economy. In a small open economy, domestic residents are price-takers with respect to the rest of the world.

The first model is one in which there are two goods, a and b, consumed and produced in a small open economy called Tinyland. The relative price of good a in terms of good b is the terms of trade, or the real exchange rate, and this is the rate at which good b can be traded for good a on world markets. The representative consumer in Tinyland is always better off by trading on world markets at the terms of trade than by not trading. In equilibrium, domestic production is determined by the condition that the marginal rate of transformation of good a for good b equals the terms of trade, and domestic consumption satisfies the property that the marginal rate of substitution of good a for good b equals the terms of trade. An increase in the terms of trade, which here means that good a becomes more expensive relative to good b, will always imply that production in Tinyland shifts away from production of good b and toward production of good a. However, whether the consumption of goods a or b increases or decreases depends on whether Tinyland was an importer or exporter of good a before the change in the terms of trade, and on income and substitution effects.

The second model we considered was a two-period model of a small open economy, in which the representative consumer has exogenous income in the current and future periods, and the consumer pays taxes to the government in both periods. Government spending is exogenous in each period, and the government and the representative consumer can borrow and lend in the current period. This model permitted us to study the determination of the current account surplus. In the model, the current account surplus increases whenever national saving increases. An increase in current income leads to an increase in the current account surplus in equilibrium, an increase in government spending leads to a decrease in the current account surplus, a change in taxes has no effect under Ricardian equivalence, and a change in the real interest rate has an indeterminate effect. Current account deficits need not be a bad thing, as this implies borrowing abroad, which helps domestic consumers smooth their consumption over time.

In the third small open-economy model, we allowed for the determination of production and investment, with the domestic economy facing an interest rate determined on world markets. Here, the current account surplus is the difference between domestic output and absorption, where absorption is the domestic demand for goods, or consumption plus investment plus government spending. An increase in the world real interest rate increases domestic output, reduces absorption, and increases the current account surplus. A temporary increase in government spending increases domestic absorption and decreases the current account surplus, whereas a permanent increase in government spending increases aggregate output and the current account surplus. An increase in current total factor productivity increases domestic output and increases the current account surplus, whereas an anticipated increase in future total factor productivity causes no change in current aggregate output and reduces the current account surplus. A current account deficit that finances investment will increase the future capital stock and act to increase future output and reduce the current account deficit in the future.

Key Terms

small open economy: An economy that trades with the rest of the world, and for which the collective actions of domestic consumers and firms have negligible effects on prices on world markets.

terms of trade: The relative price at which imports trade for exports on world markets.

real exchange rate: The terms of trade.

comparative advantage: How efficient a country is at producing one good relative to another, as compared with the rest of the world. Comparative advantage is determined by the slope of the production possibilities frontier.

twin deficits: A current account deficit coupled with a government budget deficit.

absorption: Consumption plus investment plus government expenditures; the quantity of domestically produced goods absorbed through domestic spending.

Questions for Review

1. What is a small open economy?

2. Why is it appropriate to use a small open-economy model to explain events in Canada?

3. In the first model in this chapter, with two goods, what are the conditions that determine production and consumption in Tinyland when there is no trade?

4. What are the conditions that determine production and consumption in Tinyland when there is trade with the rest of the world?

5. Are Tinyland residents better or worse off when they can trade with the rest of the world? Why?

6. If the terms of trade increase and Tinyland initially imports good a, what are the effects on consumption and production of goods a and b in Tinyland?

7. If the terms of trade increase and Tinyland initially imports good b, what are the effects on consumption and production of goods a and b in Tinyland?

8. In the second model in this chapter, what are the four determinants of the current account surplus, and how does each of these determinants affect it?

9. Why could it be a good thing for a country to run a current account deficit?

10. Explain the importance of twin deficits.

11. What are the effects of an increase in the world real interest rate on output, absorption, and the current account surplus?

12. What are the effects of temporary and permanent increases in government expenditure on output, absorption, and the current account surplus?

13. What are the effects of an increase in current and future total factor productivity on output, absorption, and the current account balance?

14. If an increase in the current account deficit finances an increase in domestic investment, what implications does this have for the future performance of the economy?

Problems

1. Suppose that, in the model in which two goods a and b are produced domestically and traded internationally, the representative consumer's preferences change so that the marginal rate of substitution of good a for good b increases for each consumption bundle. That is, the consumer is now less willing to give up good a in exchange for good b. Determine the effects of this change in preferences on the production of a and b in Tinyland, on consumption of a and b, and on the quantities of a and b imported and exported. Explain your results.

2. Suppose there is an improvement in the technology for producing good b in Tinyland. This implies that the marginal rate of transformation, $MRT_{a,b}$, increases for each quantity of good a. Determine the effects of this technology change on the consumption of a and b, the production of a and b, and the quantities of a and b imported and exported. Explain your results in terms of income and substitution effects, and interpret.

3. The government imposes a quota on imports. Determine the effect of this on production and consumption of goods a and b in the first model in this chapter. Also determine the effect on the consumer's welfare. Explain your results.

4. Assume a two-period model in which the representative consumer has income of 100 in the current period, income of 120 in the future period, and faces a world real interest rate of 10% per period. The consumer always wishes to set current consumption equal to future consumption, which implies perfect-complements preferences.
   a. Suppose current government expenditures are 15 and 20 in the future. Determine consumption in the current and future periods, and the current account surplus. Draw a diagram to illustrate your results.
   b. Now suppose current government expenditures increase to 25, with everything else unchanged. Again, determine consumption in the current and future periods, and the current account surplus, and show these in your diagram.
   c. Explain the difference in your results in parts (a) and (b).

5. Modify the second model in this chapter as follows: Suppose real interest rates are determined on world markets. The government can borrow and lend on world markets at the interest rate r, but the representative consumer lends at the interest rate r and borrows at the interest rate r^*, which is also determined on world markets. Assume that $r^* > r$, perhaps because of the costs of operating international banks that make loans to consumers.
   a. Suppose r^* increases, with r unchanged. Determine the effects on consumption in the current and future periods, and on the current account balance, and explain your results in terms of income and substitution effects.
   b. Now suppose the government cuts current taxes and increases future taxes, holding constant government spending in periods 1 and 2. Assume, before the tax cut is put into effect, that the current account surplus is zero. Determine the effects of the tax cut in period 1 on consumption in periods 1 and 2, the trade balance, and the welfare of the representative consumer. Explain your results.

6. In the second model in this chapter, determine the effects of an increase in future government spending on current consumption, future consumption, and the current account surplus, and explain your results.

7. Use the third model in this chapter to answer this question. The government in a small open economy is concerned that the current account deficit is too high. One group of economic advisors to the government argues that high government deficits cause the current account

deficit to be high, and that the way to reduce the current account deficit is to increase taxes. A second group of economic advisors argues that the high current account deficit is caused by high domestic investment, and proposes taxing domestic investment and returning these tax revenues to consumers as lump-sum transfers.

    a. Which advice should the government take if its goal is to reduce the current account deficit? Explain.

    b. Is the government's goal of reducing the current account deficit sensible? Why or why not? What will happen if the government takes the advice that achieves its goal, as in part (a)?

8. In Chapter 11, we studied how persistent total factor productivity shocks in a closed economy can provide an explanation for business cycles. In the third model studied in this chapter, determine the effects of a persistent increase in total factor productivity on domestic output, consumption, investment, and the current account surplus. Are the predictions of the model consistent with what you observe in Figure 12.10? Explain why or why not.

9. An increase in government spending is anticipated in the future. What effects does this have on current output, consumption, investment, and the current account surplus? Explain your results.

Working with the Data

1. Answer the following:

    a. Calculate the relative price of energy for 1961–2001, as the ratio of the producer price of petroleum and coal products to the consumer price index, and plot this as a time series.

    b. Calculate the real quantity of net exports of petroleum and petroleum products, as the ratio of net exports of petroleum and petroleum products (nominal) to the consumer price index, for the years 1961–2001, and plot this as a time series.

    c. Calculate the annual percentage increase in the relative price of energy (December to December) and the annual percentage increase in the real quantity of imports of petroleum and petroleum products, and plot one variable against the other in a scatter plot.

    d. Explain what you see in time series and scatter plots from parts (a)–(c), and interpret this in terms of the predictions of the first model in this chapter concerning the effects of changes in the terms of trade.

2. Answer the following:

    a. Calculate consumption (C), investment (I), government spending (G), and net exports (NX), as percentages of GDP (Y) for the years 1961–2001.

    b. Construct scatter plots of NX/Y versus C/Y, NX/Y versus I/Y, and NX/Y versus G/Y for the years 1961–2001. What do you observe? What do these data tell us about the primary causes of fluctuations in the current account?

CHAPTER 13

Money in the Open Economy

Many issues in international macroeconomics can be well understood without the complication of monetary exchange in the picture, as we saw in Chapter 12. However, there are also many intriguing issues in international finance—particularly those involving the determination of nominal exchange rates, the effects of having flexible or fixed exchange rates, the transmission of nominal macroeconomic shocks among countries, the effects of capital controls, and the role of international financial institutions—that we need monetary models to understand. In this chapter, we will build on the third small open-economy model we studied in Chapter 12, to integrate money into a monetary small open-economy model that can address some key issues in international monetary economics.

We will first consider the notion of *purchasing power parity*, or the *law of one price*, which will be a cornerstone of the monetary small open-economy model in this chapter. Purchasing power parity would hold if the prices of all goods in the world economy were equal, corrected for nominal exchange rates, where a nominal exchange rate is the price of one currency in terms of another. While there are economic forces that result in a long-run tendency toward purchasing power parity, in reality there can be fairly large and persistent deviations from purchasing power parity, some examples of which we will study in this chapter. However, although purchasing power parity may not be the best approximation to reality in the short run, it will prove to be very useful in simplifying the model used in this chapter.

The monetary small open-economy model we construct and put to work in this chapter builds on the third small open-economy model from Chapter 12, in that the goods markets in the two models are identical. The model of this chapter will also have much in common with the monetary intertemporal model in Chapter 9. In particular, the monetary small open-economy model features a classical dichotomy, in that nominal variables—in this case, the price level and the nominal exchange rate—are determined independently of real variables. Further, money is neutral. This is a useful starting point for international monetary economics, since adding some of the frictions that we considered in the business cycle models of Chapters 10 and 11—sticky wages, the money surprise mechanism, and coordination failures—involves straightforward extensions of this basic framework.

The first experiments we will carry out with the model in this chapter will emphasize the effects of shocks from abroad under flexible and fixed nominal exchange rates. A flexible exchange rate is free to move according to supply and demand in the market for foreign exchange, whereas under a fixed exchange rate the domestic government commits in some fashion to supporting the nominal exchange rate at a specified value. A flexible exchange rate has the property that monetary policy can be set independently in the domestic economy, and the domestic price level is not affected by changes in foreign prices. Under a fixed exchange rate, however, the domestic central bank cannot control its money supply independently, and price level changes originating abroad are essentially imported to the domestic economy. Flexible and fixed exchange rate regimes each have their own advantages and disadvantages, as we will discuss.

Then, we examine the effects of capital controls on the behaviour of the domestic economy. Capital controls are restrictions on the international flow of assets; such controls tend to dampen the fluctuations that result from some shocks to the economy. However, capital controls are detrimental, in that they reduce economic efficiency. Finally, we will study an open economy extension of the Keynesian sticky wage model that we worked with in Chapter 10. This model is a version of the well-known Mundell-Fleming model, and will be used to study Keynesian stabilization policy in the context of fixed and flexible exchange rates.

The Nominal Exchange Rate, the Real Exchange Rate, and Purchasing Power Parity

The model we will work with in this chapter is a monetary small open-economy model, which builds on the third small open-economy model of Chapter 12 and the monetary intertemporal model in Chapter 9. Key variables in this model will be the nominal exchange rate and the real exchange rate, which will be defined in this section. Further, in this section, we will derive the purchasing power parity relationship, which determines the value of the real exchange rate.

In the model in this chapter, just as in the monetary intertemporal model, all domestically produced goods sell at a price P, in terms of domestic currency. Foreign-produced goods sell at the price P^*, in terms of foreign currency. In the model, there is a market for foreign exchange, on which domestic currency can be traded for foreign currency, and we will let e denote the price of one unit of foreign currency in terms of domestic currency. That is, e is the **nominal exchange rate**. Therefore, if a domestic resident holding domestic currency wished to buy goods abroad, assuming that foreign producers of goods will accept only foreign currency in exchange for their goods, one unit of foreign goods will cost eP^*, in units of domestic currency. This is because the domestic resident must first buy foreign currency with domestic currency, at a price of e, and then buy foreign goods with foreign currency at a price of P^*. To give an example, suppose that a book in the U.S. costs five U.S. dollars, and that the exchange rate between Canadian and U.S. dollars is 1.5 Canadian dollars per U.S. dollar, that is, $e = 1.5$. Then, the cost of the book in Canadian dollars is $1.5 \times 5 = 7.50$.

Since the price of domestic goods in domestic currency is P, and the price of foreign goods in terms of domestic currency is eP^*, the real exchange rate (or the terms of trade), which is the price of foreign goods in terms of domestic goods, is

$$\text{Real exchange rate} = \frac{eP^*}{P}.$$

Now, suppose it is costless to transport goods between foreign countries and the domestic country, and that there are no trade barriers, such as government-set import quotas and tariffs (import taxes). Then, if $eP^* > P$, it would be cheaper to buy goods domestically than abroad, so that foreign consumers would want to buy domestic goods rather than foreign goods, and this would tend to increase P. Alternatively, if $eP^* < P$, then foreign goods would be cheaper than domestic goods, and so domestic consumers would prefer to purchase foreign goods rather than domestic goods, in which case P would tend to fall. Thus, with no transportation costs and no trade barriers, we should expect to observe that

$$P = eP^*, \tag{13.1}$$

and this relationship is called the **law of one price**, or **purchasing power parity (PPP)**. This relationship is called the law of one price because, if it holds, the price of goods is the same, in terms of domestic currency, at home and abroad. Note that if purchasing power parity holds, then the real exchange rate is 1.

In the real world, we would not in general expect PPP to hold exactly if we measure P and P^* as the price levels in two different countries. Any measure of the price level, such as the consumer price index or the implicit GDP price deflator, includes the prices of a large set of goods produced and consumed in the economy. Some of these goods will be traded on world markets, such as agricultural commodities and raw materials, while other goods will only be traded domestically, such as local services like haircuts. While we would expect a tendency for the law of one price to hold for goods that are traded internationally, we would not expect it to hold for nontraded goods. For example, crude oil can be shipped at a relatively low cost over large distances by pipeline and in large oil tankers. There is a well-organized world market for crude oil, so that crude oil sells almost anywhere in the world at close to the same price (plus transport costs). However, there is not a world market in haircuts, as the cost of travelling to another country for a haircut is in most cases very large relative to the cost of the haircut. The law of one price should hold for crude oil, but not for haircuts.

In general, there are strong economic forces that will tend to make market prices and nominal exchange rates adjust so that PPP holds. For example, if PPP does not hold, then even if there are large costs of transporting goods across countries, consumers will want to move to where goods are relatively cheaper, firms will want to move their production where goods are relatively more expensive, and ultimately we would expect PPP to hold over the long run. Unless it is very difficult to move goods, labour, and capital across international borders, purchasing power parity should hold, at least as a long-run relationship. Though PPP may be a poor description of short-run reality, as we will show in the next section, and the adjustment to PPP may be quite slow, it will simplify our models considerably to make the PPP assumption, and this simplification will help us focus on the issues of this chapter.

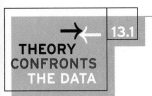

The Big Mac Index and the PPP Relationship for the United States and Canada

If purchasing power parity holds for each good, then a particular good should sell at the same price worldwide, corrected for foreign exchange rates. At the aggregate level, if PPP holds, then the real exchange rate, in terms of price indices, should remain fixed over time. In this section, we will show that there are important deviations from purchasing power parity for Big Macs—a homogeneous good sold worldwide—and that the real exchange rate varies significantly for Canada and the United States, two countries that have a very close trading relationship.

An interesting example of deviations from purchasing power parity for a single good is the **Big Mac index**, published by *The Economist*. The Big Mac is a homogeneous product; it is essentially identical wherever it is sold by McDonald's. Table 13.1 shows data from April 2003 for a set of 17 countries, which shows the price in local currency of a Big Mac (P), the implied purchasing power parity nominal exchange rate $\frac{P}{P*}$, where P^* is the price in U.S. dollars of a Big Mac in the United States, and the actual nominal exchange rate e (the price of U.S. currency in terms of domestic currency). We also show the percentage deviation of real exchange rates from purchasing power parity, where the percentage deviation is equal to $(\frac{eP*}{P} - 1) \times 100\%$.

Table 13.1 shows that there are sometimes large deviations from purchasing power parity in terms of Big Macs. For China, the actual real exchange rate is 126.65% above what purchasing power parity would predict, and for Denmark the real exchange rate is 33.7% below what purchasing power parity would predict. For most of the countries in this sample, there is a positive deviation of the real exchange rate from the value that purchasing power parity predicts, and this perhaps suggests reasons for the deviation from purchasing power parity. While Big Macs are essentially the same product no matter where they are sold, they are not traded between countries, and so it should not be surprising that hamburgers might be relatively more expensive in other countries of the world than in the United States.

A case where we might expect relatively small deviations from PPP involves the relationship between Canada and the United States. Historically, there has been a high volume of trade between these two countries. The United States and Canada signed a free trade agreement in 1989, which was replaced in 1992 by the North American Free Trade Agreement (NAFTA) which included Mexico. An earlier trade agreement was the Canada-U.S. Auto Pact, signed in 1965, which permitted the shipment of autos and auto parts across the Canada-U.S. border by manufacturers. Given the proximity of Canada and the United States, and natural north-south transportation links, transportation costs between the two nations are quite low. Not only are goods easy to move between these two countries, but NAFTA now permits freer movement of labour across the Canada-U.S. border as well. Capital is also relatively free to move between these two countries. Therefore, there are especially strong forces in place in the U.S.-Canada case that would cause us to be surprised if PPP did not hold, at least approximately.

In Figure 13.1 we show the real exchange rate, $\frac{eP*}{P}$, for Canada versus the United States for the years 1945–2002. Here, e is the price of U.S. dollars in terms of Canadian

TABLE 13.1 Purchasing Power Parity and the Big Mac Index

Currency Area	P	$\frac{P}{P^*}$	e	Percentage Deviation
United States	2.71	1	1	0
Argentina	4.10	1.51	2.88	90.4
Australia	3.00	1.11	1.61	45.4
Brazil	4.55	1.68	3.07	82.85
Britain	1.99	0.73	1.58	115.17
Canada	3.20	1.18	1.45	22.80
Chile	1400	516.61	716	38.60
China	9.90	3.65	8.28	126.65
Czech Republic	56.57	20.87	28.9	38.45
Denmark	27.75	10.24	6.78	−33.79
Euro area	2.71	1	1.1	10
Japan	262	96.68	120	24.12
Mexico	23.00	8.49	10.53	24.07
New Zealand	3.95	1.46	1 78	22.12
Russia	41	15.13	31.1	105.56
Sweden	30	11.07	8.34	−24.66
Thailand	59	21.77	42.7	96.13

dollars, P^* is the U.S. consumer price index, and P is the Canadian consumer price index. The real exchange rate has been scaled for convenience, so that its value is 100 in January 1945.

Purchasing power parity predicts that the real exchange rate in the figure should be constant, but it certainly is not. In the figure, the real exchange rate has fluctuated significantly. The fluctuations are not small short-run ones around a constant value, but more persistent in nature. Indeed, there appears to be no tendency for the real exchange rate to fluctuate more closely around some long-run value after the free trade agreement in 1989. Between 1989 and 2002, the real exchange rate increased by about 40%. If there are such large deviations from PPP for Canada and the United States, we should expect PPP relationships to be even more loose in the short run between Canada and other countries of the world. ✦

Flexible and Fixed Exchange Rates

In addition to PPP, another important component of the monetary small open-economy model will be the exchange rate regime. As we will show, a key determinant of how the domestic economy responds to shocks, and an important factor for the conduct of domestic monetary and fiscal policy, is the set of rules for government intervention in foreign exchange markets. Roughly speaking, the polar extremes in foreign exchange market intervention are a **flexible exchange rate regime** and a **fixed exchange rate regime**. Currently, some countries conform closely to an idealized flexible exchange rate regime, others fix the exchange rate, and others mix the two approaches.

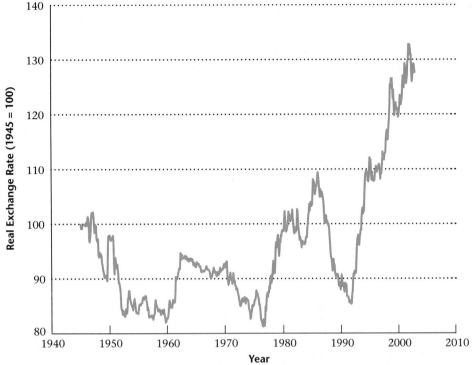

FIGURE 13.1

**The Real Exchange Rate for
Canada vs. the United States**
Purchasing power parity
predicts that the real exchange
rate should be a constant, but
there have been large and
persistent deviations from
PPP in this case.

Under a flexible or floating exchange rate, there is no intervention by the domestic fiscal or monetary authorities to specifically target the nominal exchange rate e. If the nominal exchange rate is truly flexible, it is free to move in response to market forces. Some countries with flexible exchange rates are India, South Korea, Brazil, Australia, New Zealand, Canada, and the United States. For reasons we will discuss below, essentially all countries care about short-run movements in their nominal exchange rate, and they will therefore from time to time intervene through monetary and fiscal policy to influence the value of the nominal exchange rate, even under a flexible exchange rate regime.

There are several different important fixed exchange rate systems, which can be roughly characterized as **hard pegs** and **soft pegs**. Under a hard peg, a country commits to a fixed nominal exchange rate relative to some other currency for the indefinite future. Under a soft peg, there is no long-term commitment to a particular value for the exchange rate, but the exchange rate can be fixed relative to another currency for long periods, with occasional **devaluations** (increases in the nominal exchange rate e) and **revaluations** (decreases in e).

A hard peg can be implemented in basically three ways. First, a country could abandon its national currency and **dollarize**. Dollarization essentially involves using the currency of another country as the national medium of exchange. For example, Ecuador currently uses the U.S. dollar as its national currency, though dollarization can refer to a situation where a country uses a currency other than the U.S. dollar. A disadvantage of dollarizing is that a country relinquishes its ability to collect seignior-age (a concept discussed in Chapter 9); that is, it cannot print money to finance government spending.

The second way to implement a hard peg is through the establishment of a **currency board**. With a currency board, there is a centralized institution, which could be the country's central bank, that holds interest-bearing assets denominated in the currency of the country against which the nominal exchange rate is being fixed. This institution then stands ready to exchange domestic currency for foreign currency at a specified fixed exchange rate, and it can buy and sell interest-bearing assets in order to carry out these exchanges. A country that currently uses a currency board is Hong Kong, which fixes its nominal exchange rate relative to the U.S. dollar. Under a currency board, a country retains its ability to collect seigniorage.

The third approach to implementing a hard peg is through agreement among countries to a common currency, as in the **European Monetary Union (EMU)**, established in 1999. The common currency of the EMU is the **Euro**, and the supply of Euros is managed by the **European Central Bank (ECB)**. The rules governing the operation of the ECB specify how the seigniorage revenue from the printing of new Euros is to be split among the EMU members.

Soft pegs involve various degrees of commitment to a fixed exchange rate or to target bands for the exchange rate. For example, under the **European Monetary System (EMS)**, which was established in 1979, preceding the EMU, member European countries committed over the short run to target their exchange rates within specified ranges. In this arrangement, coordination was required among the EMS members, and there were periodic crises and changes in target bands for exchange rates. Another soft peg was the **Bretton Woods arrangement**, the rules for which were specified in an agreement negotiated at Bretton Woods, New Hampshire in 1944. The Bretton Woods arrangement governed post–World War II international monetary relations until 1971. Under Bretton Woods, the United States fixed the value of the U.S. dollar relative to gold, by agreeing to exchange U.S. dollars for gold at a specified price. All other countries then agreed to fix their exchange rates relative to the U.S. dollar. This was thus a modified gold standard arrangement. For reasons we will discuss later in this chapter, soft peg arrangements have tended to be unstable, typically collapsing and being replaced by alternative systems—as happened with the EMS and the Bretton Woods arrangement.

A key international monetary institution that plays an important role in exchange rate determination is the **International Monetary Fund (IMF)**, the framework for which was discussed at Bretton Woods in 1944, with the IMF established in 1946. The IMF currently has 184 member countries, and it performs a function in some ways similar to that carried out by a central bank relative to the domestic banks under its supervision. Namely, the IMF plays the role of a **lender of last resort** for its member countries, just as a central bank is a lender of last resort for domestic financial institutions (as we will discuss in detail in Chapter 14). However, IMF lending comes with strings attached; typically, the loans are conditional on a member country submitting to a program set up by the IMF, which typically specifies corrective policy actions.

A Monetary Small Open-Economy Model with a Flexible Exchange Rate

Now that we have discussed some of the institutional arrangements governing the determination of exchange rates, we can proceed to work with a monetary small open-economy model in which there is international monetary interaction. This model—in part based on the monetary intertemporal model in Chapter 9—is a small open-economy model that essentially involves adding a money market to the third real small open-economy model in Chapter 12. In this model, we will assume for now that the exchange rate is flexible, and we will study the properties of a fixed exchange rate system in the next section.

In Figure 13.2 we show the goods market for the monetary small open-economy model, which is identical to the goods market for the third real small open-economy model of Chapter 12. The curve Y^d is the output demand curve, which is downward-sloping because of the negative effect of the real interest rate on the demand for consumption and investment goods, and Y^s is the output supply curve, which is upward-sloping because of the intertemporal substitution effect of the real interest rate on labour supply. The output supply and output demand curves will shift as the result of factors discussed in detail in Chapter 12. Just as in Chapter 12, the small open-economy assumption implies that domestic firms and consumers are collectively price-takers on world markets. In equilibrium, the income-expenditure identity holds, so that $Y = C + I + G + NX$. Given that the domestic economy is, as a whole, a price-taker on world markets, any output not absorbed domestically as C, I, or G is exported (if net exports are positive) or any excess of domestic absorption over domestic output is purchased abroad (if net exports are negative).

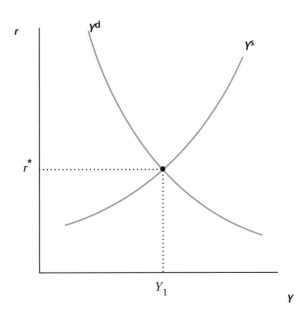

FIGURE 13.2

The Goods Market in the Monetary Small Open-Economy Model

The goods market in this model is identical to the goods market in the real small open-economy model with investment in Chapter 12. The world real interest rate is r^* and equilibrium real output is Y_1.

We will assume that purchasing power parity holds, so that

$$P = eP^*, \qquad\qquad (13.2)$$

where P is the domestic price level, e is the price of foreign exchange in terms of domestic currency, and P^* is the foreign price level. Though we know from above that the PPP relationship typically does not hold in the short run, assuming PPP simplifies our model greatly, and essentially implies that we are ignoring the effects of changes in the terms of trade (discussed in Chapter 12), which would cloud some of the issues we want to discuss here. Given the assumption of a small open economy, events in the domestic economy have no effect on the foreign price level P^*, and so we will treat P^* as exogenous. However, the domestic price level P and the exchange rate e are endogenous variables. The exchange rate is flexible, in that it is determined by market forces, as we will show below.

Next, we want to determine how the money market works in our equilibrium model. As in Chapter 9, money demand is given by

$$M^d = PL(Y, r^*), \qquad\qquad (13.3)$$

where $L(Y, r^*)$ denotes the demand for real money balances, which depends positively on aggregate real income Y and negatively on the nominal interest rate. Here, recall that the domestic real interest rate is identical to the world real interest rate r^*, and we are assuming no long-run money growth, so that the domestic inflation rate is zero and the real interest rate is equal to the nominal interest rate given the Fisher relation (recall Chapter 9). Now, given the purchasing power parity relation (13.2), we can substitute in Equation (13.3) for P to get

$$M^d = eP^*L(Y, r^*).$$

We will take the nominal money supply to be exogenous, with $M^s = M$. In equilibrium, money supply equals money demand, so that $M^s = M^d$, or

$$M = eP^*L(Y, r^*). \qquad\qquad (13.4)$$

In Figure 13.3, money demand and money supply are on the horizontal axis, while e, the exchange rate, is on the vertical axis. Then, given Y and r^*, money demand M^d is a straight line through the origin in the figure, while money supply M^s is a vertical line at $M^s = M$. The intersection of the supply and demand curves for money then determines the nominal exchange rate e, so that the equilibrium exchange rate in the figure is e_1. Note that, once we have determined e, we have also determined the domestic price level P from the purchasing power parity equation, (13.2).

Thus, in this model, the nominal exchange rate is determined by the nominal demand for money relative to the nominal supply of money. Since the nominal exchange rate is a nominal variable, this seems natural. Movements in the exchange rate will be caused either by a shift in money demand or a shift in money supply.

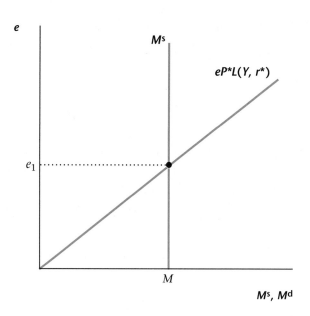

FIGURE 13.3
The Money Market in the Monetary Small Open-Economy Model with a Flexible Exchange Rate
With a flexible exchange rate, and given purchasing power parity, the equilibrium nominal exchange rate is e_1, determined by the intersection of the nominal money supply and nominal money demand curves.

THE NEUTRALITY OF MONEY WITH A FLEXIBLE EXCHANGE RATE

Now that we have set up the model, we can proceed to study its properties. Just as in the monetary intertemporal model we studied in Chapter 9, this model features a classical dichotomy, in that real variables (the level of output, the current account surplus, consumption, and investment) are determined independently of nominal variables (the domestic price level P and the nominal exchange rate e). In Figure 13.3, the nominal exchange rate is determined by the supply and demand for money, and the level of the nominal exchange rate has no bearing on real variables.

If the central bank increases the money supply, say from M_1 to M_2 in Figure 13.4, this has the effect of shifting the money supply curve rightward from M_1^s to M_2^s. In equilibrium, the nominal exchange rate increases from e_1 to e_2, and there is no effect on the level of real output, the real interest rate (which is the real interest rate on world markets, r^*), consumption, investment, or the current account surplus. Since the price of foreign currency has risen in terms of domestic currency, we say that there is a **depreciation** of the domestic currency. Ultimately, since (13.4) implies that

$$\frac{M}{e} = P^*L(Y, r^*),$$

and since P^*, Y, and r^* remain unaffected by the change in the money supply, $\frac{M}{e}$ remains unchanged. Thus, the nominal exchange rate increases in proportion to the money supply; for example, if the money supply increased by 5%, the nominal exchange rate would also increase by 5%. Further, since purchasing power parity holds, or $P = eP^*$, and since P^* is fixed, the price level P also increases in proportion to the increase in the money supply.

Thus, money is neutral in this model economy with a flexible exchange rate. There are no real effects of an increase in the nominal money supply, but all money prices,

FIGURE 13.4
**An Increase in the Money
Supply in the Monetary
Small Open-Economy
Model with a Flexible
Exchange Rate**
Money is neutral in the
monetary small open-
economy model with a
flexible exchange rate. An
increase in the money supply
causes the nominal exchange
rate and the price level to
increase in proportion to the
increase in the money supply,
with no effect on real variables.

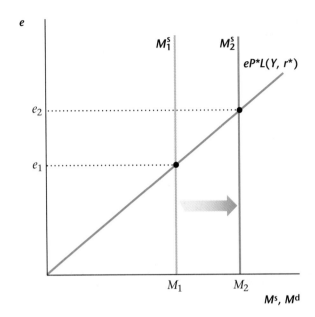

including the nominal exchange rate, increase in proportion to the increase in the money supply. While most macroeconomists adopt the view that money is neutral in the long run in an open economy, there are differences of opinion about the short-run neutrality of money and the explanations for any nonneutralities of money, just as in closed-economy macroeconomics. At the end of this chapter, we will extend this model to include Keynesian sticky wages. It is also possible to extend the model to include other nonneutralities of money, such as the money surprise mechanism studied in Chapter 11.

A NOMINAL SHOCK TO THE DOMESTIC ECONOMY FROM ABROAD: P^* INCREASES

We would like to use the monetary small open-economy model to investigate how the domestic economy is affected by events in the rest of the world. The first example we consider is the case of an increase in the price level in the rest of the world, which is essentially a nominal shock to the domestic economy. We will see that a flexible exchange rate system has an insulating property with respect to increases in the foreign price level. That is, the nominal exchange rate adjusts to exactly offset the increase in the foreign price level, and there are no effects on the domestic price level or domestic real variables. In particular, the temporary foreign inflation resulting from the increase in the foreign price level is not imported to the domestic economy.

Suppose that P^* increases from P_1^* to P_2^*, perhaps because central banks in foreign countries increase the quantity of foreign money in circulation. Then, in Figure 13.5, the money demand curve shifts rightward from $eP_1^*L(Y, r^*)$ to $eP_2^*L(Y, r^*)$. In equilibrium, there will be no effect on real variables, but the nominal exchange rate falls from

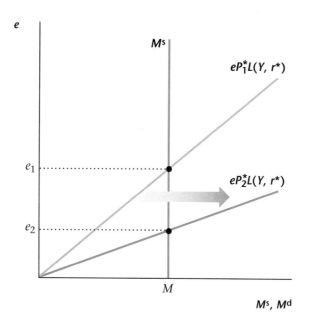

FIGURE 13.5

An Increase in the Foreign Price Level in the Monetary Small Open-Economy Model with a Flexible Exchange Rate

If the foreign price level increases, this shifts the nominal money demand curve to the right, with the nominal exchange rate falling from e_1 to e_2 in equilibrium. The decrease in the nominal exchange rate exactly offsets the increase in the foreign price level, and there is no effect on the domestic price level.

e_1 to e_2, so that there is an **appreciation** of the domestic currency. Since $P = eP^*$, from Equation (13.4) we have

$$\frac{M}{P} = L(Y, r^*),$$

and since M, Y, and r^* remain unchanged, so does P. Therefore, no domestic variables were affected by the price level change in the rest of the world. In particular, the appreciation of the domestic currency was just sufficient to offset the effect of the increase in P^* on the domestic price level. That is, the flexible exchange rate insulated the domestic economy from the nominal shock from abroad. This is certainly a desirable property of a flexible exchange rate regime. Under flexible exchange rates, the domestic price level, and by implication the domestic inflation rate, is determined by the quantity of domestic money supplied by the domestic central bank, and it is not influenced by how monetary policy is conducted by foreign central banks.

A REAL SHOCK TO THE DOMESTIC ECONOMY FROM ABROAD

As an experiment to determine how real domestic variables, the nominal exchange rate, and the price level will respond to a real disturbance transmitted from abroad, we will examine the effects of an increase in the world real interest rate. Such a shock could result, for example, from a decrease in total factor productivity in the rest of the world (recall our analysis of the effects of total factor productivity shocks from Chapter 7). As we will show, a flexible exchange rate cannot shield the domestic economy from the effects of a change in the world real interest rate; the nominal exchange rate appreciates (e falls), and the price level falls.

In Figure 13.6 the world real interest rate increases from r_1^* to r_2^*. The real effects of this are the same as we considered for the third real small open-economy model in

FIGURE 13.6

An Increase in the World Real Interest Rate with a Flexible Exchange Rate

Under a flexible exchange rate, if the world real interest rate increases, this causes real output to rise, and the money demand curve shifts to the right, assuming money demand is much more responsive to real income than to the real interest rate. The nominal exchange rate decreases in equilibrium.

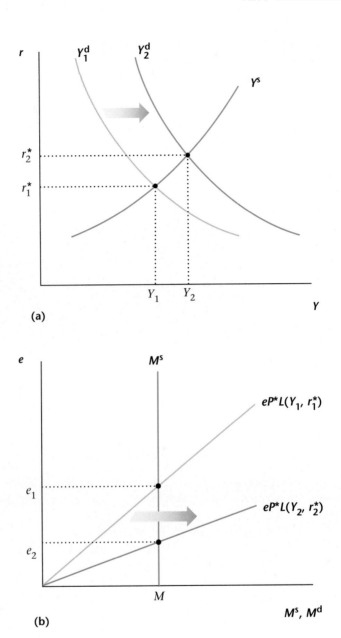

(a)

(b)

Chapter 12. In Figure 13.6(a), the current account surplus increases, shifting the output demand curve to the right until it comes to rest at Y_2^d. Output increases from Y_1 to Y_2 due to the increase in labour supply that results from intertemporal substitution of leisure by the representative consumer. The increase in the real interest rate causes domestic consumption expenditures and investment expenditures to fall, though the increase in current income will cause consumption to rise. On net, consumption may rise or fall. Total domestic absorption, $C + I + G$, may rise or fall, but any increase in absorption is smaller than the increase in domestic output, so that the current account surplus rises.

The nominal effects of the increase in the world real interest rate depend on how the demand for money changes. The increase in the real interest rate causes the demand for money to fall, while the increase in domestic output causes the demand for money to rise. It is not clear whether $L(Y_2, r_2^*) < L(Y_1, r_1^*)$ or $L(Y_2, r_2^*) > L(Y_1, r_1^*)$. However, if real money demand is much more responsive to real income than to the interest rate, then money demand will rise, and the money demand curve in Figure 13.6(b) shifts to the right. In equilibrium, the exchange rate appreciates, with the nominal exchange rate decreasing from e_1 to e_2. As purchasing power parity holds—that is, $P = eP^*$—with P^* constant, P falls in proportion to the decrease in e. Thus, the increase in the world real interest rate leads to an exchange rate appreciation and a decrease in the price level. Clearly, the flexible exchange rate cannot automatically insulate the domestic economy from real shocks that occur abroad. For example, if the central bank wished to stabilize the price level in the face of the increase in the world real interest rate, it would have to increase the money supply in response to the increase in money demand resulting from the shock.

MACROECONOMICS *IN ACTION* 13.1

The Asian Crisis

In 1997, there was a sharp depreciation in nominal exchange rates in East Asia, primarily in Indonesia, South Korea, Malaysia, and Thailand, and these exchange rate depreciations were the first symptoms of what became known as the Asian crisis. From 1996 until the fall of 1997, the nominal exchange rate (the price of a U.S. dollar in terms of domestic currency) increased by 98.5% in Indonesia, 110.7% in South Korea, 54.4% in Malaysia, and 86.5% in Thailand.[1] What could cause nominal exchange rates to depreciate so dramatically in East Asia over so short a time period? Some answers are provided in a National Bureau of Economic Research working paper[2] by Giancarlo Corsetti, Paolo Pesenti, and Nouriel Roubini (hereafter referred to as CPR).

At the time of the Asian crisis, Indonesia, South Korea, Malaysia, and Thailand were under flexible exchange rate regimes; thus, the model we worked with above should be useful in understanding the large exchange rate depreciation that occurred. The model tells us that a large exchange rate depreciation (a large increase in e) would have to occur because the demand for money fell abruptly or because there was a large increase in the domestic money supply. In our model, money demand could fall because real GDP fell, and so let us first consider the possibility that money demand fell because of a reduction in real GDP in East Asia. This was certainly not the case. Economic growth had been quite strong in East Asia before and during the 1990s. Indeed, in Chapter 8, we discussed the miraculous growth performance of the "East Asian Tigers," which included South Korea. From CPR, the growth rates in real GDP in 1996 for Indonesia, South Korea, Malaysia, and Thailand were 7.98%, 7.10%, 8.58%, and 5.52%, respectively. These rates of growth were very high relative to average growth rates in GDP in other countries, and growth continued to be high for most of these countries in 1997, though lower than

(continued)

in 1996. The exception is Thailand, which had negative real GDP growth in 1997. In general, though, for these countries money demand would have been *increasing* rather than decreasing because of growth in real GDP, and so this does not seem to explain the large nominal exchange rate depreciations.

To consider a second possibility, the exchange rate depreciations could have been caused during the Asian crisis by rapid growth in the money supply. However, rapid growth in the money supply typically results in a high domestic inflation rate (recall our analysis from Chapter 9), and inflation rates in Indonesia, South Korea, Malaysia, and Thailand, in 1997, from CPR, were 11.62%, 4.45%, 2.66%, and 5.61%, which are certainly moderate relative to the size of the exchange rate depreciations. Thus, money supply growth does not seem to be a potential explanation.

The only other potential explanation could be a dramatic shift in the demand for the currencies of Indonesia, South Korea, Malaysia, and Thailand, and this explanation appears to be in agreement with the analysis of CPR. They argue that these four countries were running large current account deficits prior to the Asian crisis, and that these current account deficits were financing investment that would ultimately have poor returns. That is, the domestic financial institutions in these countries were badly regulated, and they were borrowing abroad to make loans to finance domestic investment projects that would ultimately have poor returns. In terms of our analysis of current account deficits from Chapter 12, international lenders became concerned that the large current account deficits in East Asia were not sustainable. That is, to ultimately pay off the foreign debt resulting from large current account deficits, these countries would have to generate large current account surpluses in the future. International lenders to these countries did not appear to believe that the capital stocks in these countries would increase sufficiently to produce high enough future current account surpluses.

The result was a loss in confidence in East Asia on the part of international lenders, who discontinued lending to these countries. Effectively, this loss in confidence works much like a loss in confidence in the domestic banking system. In a domestic banking panic, deposits are withdrawn from banks and converted into domestic currency. In the case of the Asian crisis, the deposits of foreign lenders were withdrawn from East Asian banks, and converted into assets denominated in non–East Asian currencies. This is effectively a fall in the demand for East Asian currencies, and it will result in an exchange rate depreciation, as in our model.

Why was the Asian crisis a crisis? The main risk from the large exchange rate depreciations was the possibility of a widespread failure of East Asian financial institutions. These institutions were having difficulty borrowing abroad to finance long-term lending, and the exchange rate depreciation implied that the real value of the liabilities of these institutions had increased a great deal relative to the real value of their assets. East Asian financial institutions could then become insolvent and fail. The Asian crisis had temporary and fairly small effects for countries outside of East Asia, in part because of the intervention of the IMF and the world's central banks.

[1,2]G. Corsetti, P. Pesenti, and N. Roubini, 1998, "What Caused the Asian Currency and Financial Crisis?" working paper, National Bureau of Economic Research.

A Monetary Small Open-Economy Model with a Fixed Exchange Rate

Now that we have studied how the economy behaves under a flexible exchange rate regime, we will explore how real and nominal variables are determined when the exchange rate is fixed. The type of fixed exchange rate regime we will consider is a type of soft peg, where the government fixes the nominal exchange rate for extended periods of time, but might devalue or revalue the domestic currency at some times.

Under the fixed exchange rate regime we model, the government chooses a level at which it wants to fix the nominal exchange rate, which is e_1 in Figure 13.7. The government must then, either through its central bank or some other authority, stand ready to support this exchange rate. For simplicity, we will suppose that the fixed exchange rate is supported through the government standing ready to exchange foreign currency for domestic currency at the fixed exchange rate e_1. To see how this happens, consider the simplified government balance sheet in Table 13.2. This is a consolidated balance sheet for the central bank and the fiscal authority. To support a fixed exchange rate, the government must act to buy or sell its foreign exchange reserves (think of this as foreign currency) for outside money (domestic currency) in foreign exchange markets, whenever there are market forces that would tend to push the exchange rate away from the fixed value the government wants it to have. For example, if there are forces tending to increase the exchange rate and thus cause a depreciation of the domestic currency, the government should sell foreign currency and buy domestic currency in order to offset those forces. If there are forces pushing down the exchange rate (appreciation), the government should buy foreign currency and sell domestic currency.

With a fixed exchange rate, the domestic central bank necessarily loses control over the domestic stock of money. To see this, consider Figure 13.7, where the nominal exchange rate is fixed at e_1. If the domestic central bank attempted to increase the money supply above M, its current value, the effect of this would be to put upward pressure on the exchange rate. Given the tendency for the price of foreign currency to rise in terms of domestic currency as a result, participants in foreign exchange markets would want to trade domestic currency for foreign currency, and the government would have to carry out these exchanges in order to support the fixed exchange rate. This would tend to reduce the stock of domestic money in circulation, and the attempt by the central bank to increase the money supply would be completely undone by actions in the foreign exchange market to support the fixed exchange rate. The money supply would remain at M, with the exchange rate and the domestic price level P unchanged. Similarly, if the domestic central bank attempted to engineer a reduction in the money supply below M, this would put downward pressure on the exchange rate, participants in the foreign exchange market would want to exchange foreign currency for domestic currency, and the government would be forced to exchange domestic currency for foreign currency, thus increasing the supply of money. The money supply could therefore not be reduced below M. The implication of this is that, under a fixed exchange rate regime, the supply of money cannot be determined independently by the central bank. Once the government fixes the exchange rate, this determines the domestic money supply.

TABLE 13.2 **A Simplified Government Balance Sheet**

Assets	Liabilities
Foreign exchange reserves	Outside money
	Interest-bearing government debt

FIGURE 13.7

The Money Market in the Monetary Small Open-Economy Model with a Fixed Exchange Rate

With a fixed exchange rate, the money supply is endogenous. Given the fixed exchange rate e_1, the money supply M is determined so that the money supply curve M^s intersects the money demand curve for an exchange rate equal to e_1.

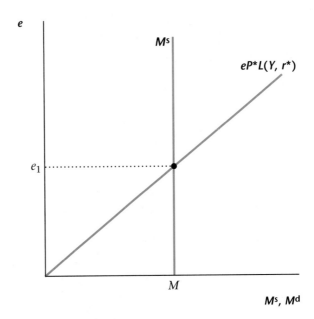

A NOMINAL FOREIGN SHOCK UNDER A FIXED EXCHANGE RATE

Suppose that the foreign price level increases when the domestic economy is under a fixed exchange rate. In Figure 13.8, P^* increases from P_1^* to P_2^*. As a result, the demand for money shifts rightward from $eP_1^*L(Y, r^*)$ to $eP_2^*L(Y, r^*)$. This increase in the demand for money results in downward pressure on the exchange rate, so that domestic currency becomes more attractive relative to foreign currency. On foreign exchange markets, the government must exchange domestic currency for foreign currency, and this will

FIGURE 13.8

An Increase in the Foreign Price Level in the Monetary Small Open-Economy Model with a Fixed Exchange Rate

With a fixed exchange rate, an increase in the foreign price level shifts the money demand curve to the right, which causes the domestic money supply to increase. The domestic price level increases in proportion to the increase in the foreign price level.

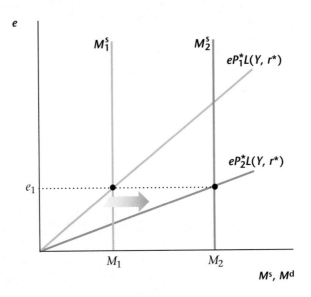

lead to an increase in the domestic money supply from M_1 to M_2. Since $P = eP^*$, and the exchange rate is fixed, the domestic price level will increase in proportion to the increase in the foreign price level. Thus, under a fixed exchange rate regime, in contrast to the flexible exchange rate regime, the domestic economy is not insulated from nominal shocks that occur abroad. When the foreign price level changes, this price level change is imported, and the domestic price level increases in proportion. Because domestic monetary policy is not independent under a fixed exchange rate, the domestic central bank is forced to adopt the world's inflation rate domestically.

A REAL FOREIGN SHOCK UNDER A FIXED EXCHANGE RATE

Now, we consider the effects of an increase in the world real interest rate from r_1^* to r_2^*, just as we did for the case of a flexible exchange rate. In Figure 13.9(a), as under the flexible exchange rate regime, the real effects of the interest rate increase are an increase in domestic output from Y_1 to Y_2, a decrease in investment, consumption may increase or decrease, and the current account surplus increases. Assuming that the effect of the increase in real income on money demand is much larger than that of the increase in the real interest rate, the demand for money will shift rightward in Figure 13.9(b), from $eP^*L\ (Y_1, r_1^*)$ to $eP^*L(Y_2, r_2^*)$. Then, with the exchange rate fixed at e_1, the domestic money supply must rise from M_1 to M_2. Since $P = eP^*$ and e and P^* do not change, the domestic price level does not change. Thus, a fixed exchange rate can insulate the domestic price level from real shocks that occur abroad. The same result could be achieved under a flexible exchange rate, but this would require discretionary action by the domestic central bank, rather than the automatic response that occurs under a fixed exchange rate.

EXCHANGE RATE DEVALUATION

Under a fixed exchange rate regime, a devaluation of the domestic currency (an increase in the fixed exchange rate e) might be a course the government chooses in response to a shock to the economy. In this section, we will show how a temporary reduction in domestic total factor productivity would lead to a reduction in foreign exchange reserves that the government may not desire. In this case, the decrease in foreign exchange reserves can be prevented by a devaluation of the domestic currency. The total factor productivity shock will also cause a decrease in the current account surplus, but the devaluation has no effect in offsetting this current account change.

Suppose in Figure 13.10 that the domestic economy is initially in equilibrium with the output demand curve Y_1^d and the output supply curve Y_1^s determining domestic output Y_1 in panel (a), given the world real interest rate r^*. In Figure 13.10(b), the exchange rate is fixed at e_1 at first, nominal money demand is initially $eP^*L(Y_1, r^*)$, and the money supply is M_1. Now, suppose that there is a temporary negative shock to domestic total factor productivity. This shifts the output supply curve leftward from Y_1^s to Y_2^s in Figure 13.10(a), as in Chapter 7. The current account surplus falls, shifting the output demand curve to the left, until it comes to rest at Y_2^d. In equilibrium, output falls to Y_2, domestic absorption falls due to the decrease in consumption (income falls), and the current account surplus falls. In Figure 13.10(b), the money demand curve shifts leftward to

FIGURE 13.9

An Increase in the World Real Interest Rate with a Fixed Exchange Rate

Under a fixed exchange rate, an increase in the world real interest rate causes an increase in real output and a shift to the right in nominal money demand. The money supply increases to accommodate the increase in money demand, and the domestic price level remains unchanged.

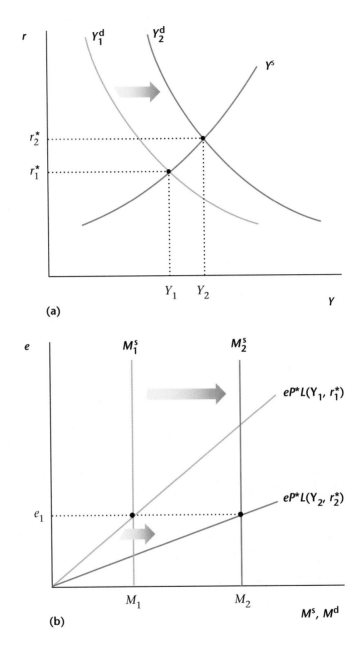

eP*L(Y_2, r*) with the fall in real income. If the government were to continue to support the fixed nominal exchange rate at e_1, this would imply, given the fall in the demand for the domestic currency, that the government would have to sell foreign currency on the foreign exchange market and buy domestic currency. This implies that the money supply would contract from M_1 to M_2.

Suppose, however, that the government does not wish to sell any of its foreign exchange reserves, or that it does not have the foreign exchange reserves to sell, when

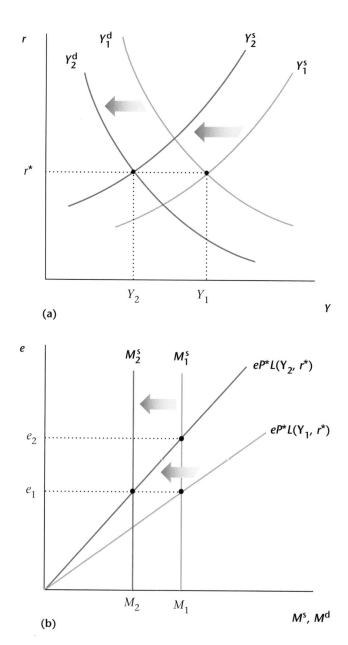

FIGURE 13.10

A Devaluation in Response to a Temporary Total Factor Productivity Shock

A temporary decrease in total factor productivity shifts the output supply curve to the left, reducing output and the current account surplus. The nominal money demand curve shifts to the left. If the government wants to avoid a loss in foreign exchange reserves, it can increase the fixed exchange rate from e_1 to e_2 and devalue the domestic currency.

the demand for domestic money falls. The government can avoid selling foreign exchange by fixing the exchange rate at e_2 in Figure 13.10(b). This implies that the money supply remains fixed at M_1, and there is a devaluation in the exchange rate, as the price of foreign currency has risen relative to domestic currency.

An important point is that the devaluation of the domestic currency has no effect here on the current account deficit. We might think that a devaluation would make domestic goods cheaper relative to foreign goods, thus increasing the real exchange rate, and that this would cause imports to fall, exports to rise, and the current account deficit to fall. While this might be true in the short run in some types of Keynesian analysis with sticky prices (but note that there are income and substitution effects to be concerned with, in terms of the effect on the current account deficit), with purchasing power parity there is no effect on the real exchange rate. Ultimately, if the government determined that the current account deficit that results here is a problem—for example, if the current account deficit is caused by excessive government spending—then this is a real problem that should be corrected through real means. That is, the real current account deficit could be reduced through a reduction in government spending, which we know from Chapter 12 can reduce the current account deficit in Figure 13.10(a). Trying to reduce the current account deficit through a devaluation in the domestic currency essentially involves trying to make a real change through nominal means, which cannot work in the long run.

FLEXIBLE VERSUS FIXED EXCHANGE RATES

Governments face important choices concerning exchange rate policy, and a key choice is whether a flexible or fixed exchange rate regime should be adopted. What are the arguments for the adoption of flexible versus fixed exchange rates? In the previous subsections, we have seen that the exchange rate regime affects how the domestic economy is insulated from shocks from abroad. If a country's central bank seeks to stabilize the price level, then our analysis tells us that if nominal shocks from abroad are important, then a flexible exchange rate is preferable to a fixed exchange rate—because a flexible exchange rate will absorb a shock to the foreign price level and stabilize the domestic price level. Alternatively, if real shocks from abroad are important, then a fixed exchange rate is preferable to a flexible exchange rate, as this acts to prevent the domestic price level from moving in response to real shocks from abroad; the domestic money supply acts as a shock absorber. Thus, in this respect, whether a particular country should choose a fixed or flexible exchange rate depends on its circumstances. A country might want to move from a fixed to a flexible exchange rate over time, and then back again.

It is sometimes argued that a flexible exchange rate allows the domestic central bank to implement a monetary policy independently of what happens in the rest of the world. In our model, with a flexible exchange rate the domestic government can set the domestic money supply independently, but with a fixed exchange rate, the money supply is not under the control of the domestic government. However, giving the domestic central bank the power to implement an independent monetary policy is useful only if the central bank can be trusted with this power. Some central banks, such as those in the United States, Canada, and parts of Europe, have excellent track records in controlling the rate of inflation after World War II. In other countries, the track record is not so good. For example, Argentina suffered very high rates of inflation until its nominal exchange rate was fixed relative to the U.S. dollar. If the central bank is weak, having difficulty controlling the domestic money supply, then a fixed exchange rate can be a very important commitment device. If the exchange rate is fixed against the currency of a country with a strong central bank, then this implies, given purchasing power parity, that the weak central-bank country essentially adopts the monetary policy of the strong central-bank country. With a fixed exchange rate, the price level of the domestic economy is tied to the foreign price level, which is essentially determined by foreign monetary policy.

In conclusion, there is no clear case for flexible versus fixed exchange rates. For Canada, where the central bank is relatively independent of political pressures and appears to be well focused on controlling inflation, a flexible exchange rate seems appropriate. The Bank of Canada appears to be sufficiently trustworthy relative to foreign central banks that allowing it to pursue a monetary policy geared to Canadian interests seems advisable. However, for other countries, particularly some in Latin America and Africa, a fixed exchange rate regime makes good sense.

Note that there are many long-standing instances of fixed exchange rates that we take for granted. For example, rates of exchange between different denominations of Canadian currency have always been fixed in Canada. Why should it necessarily be the case that five one-dollar coins trade for one five-dollar bill in all circumstances in Canada? This is because the Bank of Canada always stands ready to trade one five-dollar bill for five ones; essentially, the Bank of Canada maintains fixed exchange rates among notes of different denominations.

Essentially, all countries maintain fixed exchange rates within their borders. There is a national currency accepted as legal tender, and typically this currency circulates nationally as a medium of exchange, though in some countries foreign currencies, in particular U.S. dollars, circulate widely, as in Canada. What then determines the natural region, or **common currency area**, over which a single currency dominates as a medium of exchange? Clearly, a common currency area need not be the area over which there is a single political or fiscal authority. In Canada, every province has the power to tax provincial residents, but the provinces cede monetary authority to the Bank of Canada. In the European Monetary Union (EMU), member countries maintain their fiscal independence, but monetary policy is in the hands of the European Central Bank (ECB). An advantage of having a large trading area with a common currency is that this simplifies exchange; it is much easier to write contracts and trade across international borders without the complications of converting one currency into another or bearing the risk associated with fluctuating exchange rates. However, in joining a **currency union** such as the EMU, a country must give up its monetary independence to the group. The formation of the EMU has created tensions among EMU members, concerning matters that include the choice of the leaders of the European Central Bank, and the monetary policy stance this central bank should take. Great Britain, which has the world's oldest central bank, the Bank of England, chose not to join the EMU in order to maintain its monetary independence.

Capital Controls

A useful application of the monetary small open-economy model is to the problem of the role of capital controls in the international economy. Capital controls refer broadly to any government restrictions on the trade of assets across international borders. We will show here that capital controls can reduce movements in the nominal exchange rate in response to some shocks under a flexible exchange rate regime, and they can reduce fluctuations in foreign exchange reserves under a fixed exchange rate regime. We will argue, however, that capital controls are in general undesirable, because they introduce welfare-decreasing economic inefficiencies.

THE CAPITAL ACCOUNT AND THE BALANCE OF PAYMENTS

To understand capital controls, we have to first understand the accounting practices behind the **capital account**. The capital account is part of the **balance of payments**, which includes the current account and the capital account. The capital account includes all transactions in assets, where entries in the capital account where a foreign resident purchases a domestic asset are recorded as a positive amount—a **capital inflow**—and entries where a domestic resident purchases a foreign asset are recorded as a negative amount—a **capital outflow**. For example, if a Canadian bank lends to a British firm, this is a capital outflow, as the loan to the British firm is an asset for the Canadian bank. If a U.S. automobile manufacturer builds a new plant in Canada, this is a capital inflow for Canada, and it is part of **foreign direct investment** in Canada. Foreign direct investment is distinct from **portfolio inflows and outflows**, which are capital account transactions involving financial assets, including stocks and debt instruments. A helpful rule of thumb in counting asset transactions in the capital account is that the transaction counts as a capital inflow if funds flow into the domestic country to purchase an asset, and as an outflow if funds flow out of the domestic country to purchase an asset.

The balance of payments is defined to be the current account surplus plus the capital account surplus. That is, letting BP denote the balance of payments, and KA the capital account surplus, we have

$$BP = KA + CA,$$

where CA is the current account surplus. A key element in balance of payments accounting is that the balance of payments is always zero (though it is not measured as such because of measurement error), so that

$$KA = -CA.$$

Therefore, the capital account surplus is always the negative of the current account surplus. If the current account is in deficit (surplus), then the capital account is in surplus (deficit). We have not discussed the capital account until now for this reason—the capital account surplus is just the flip side of the current account surplus, so that when we know the current account surplus we know exactly what the capital account surplus is.

The balance of payments is always zero, because any transaction entering the balance of payments always has equal and opposite entries in the accounts. For example, suppose that a Canadian firm borrows the equivalent of $50 million in British pounds from a British bank so that it can purchase $50 million worth of auto parts in Britain to ship to Canada. The loan from the British bank will enter as a capital inflow, since the British bank has accumulated a Canadian asset, and so there will be an entry of +$50 million in the capital account for Canada. Next, when the auto parts are purchased and imported into Canada, this will enter as –$50 million in the current account. Thus, in this as in all cases, the net effect on the balance of payments is zero. The offsetting entries associated with a given transaction need not be in the current account and the capital account, but in some cases could be all in the current account, or all in the capital account.

THE EFFECTS OF CAPITAL CONTROLS

In practice, capital controls can be imposed in terms of capital inflows or capital out-flows, and they sometimes apply to foreign direct investment and sometimes to port-folio inflows and outflows. For example, restrictions on capital outflows were introduced in Malaysia in 1998 after the Asian crisis, and Chile used controls on capi-tal inflows extensively from 1978 to 1982 and from 1991 to 1998. In both cases, the capital controls were in terms of portfolio inflows and outflows. Countries sometimes also restrict foreign direct investment, which is a control on capital inflows. Controls on foreign direct investment are sometimes put in place because of concern (perhaps misplaced) over the foreign ownership of the domestic capital stock.

What are the macroeconomic effects of capital controls? Essentially, they alter how the domestic economy responds to a shock. For example, suppose that there is a tem-porary negative shock to domestic total factor productivity under a flexible exchange rate. In Figure 13.11(a), suppose that the output demand curve is Y_1^d and the initial out-put supply curve is Y_1^s, and assume that initially the current account surplus is zero with output equal to Y_1 at the world real interest rate r^*. In Figure 13.11(b), the initial money demand curve is $eP^*L(Y_1, r^*)$, and the initial nominal exchange rate is e_1, given the nominal money supply M.

Now, suppose there is a temporary decrease in domestic total factor productivity, which shifts the output supply curve leftward to Y_2^s in Figure 13.11(a). With no capital controls in place, this will imply that the current account surplus falls (with the current account then running a deficit), shifting the output demand curve to the left until it comes to rest at Y_2^d. Real output falls to Y_2 from Y_1, and consumption falls because of the decrease in income. In Figure 13.11(b), nominal money demand shifts leftward to $eP^*L(Y_2, r^*)$, and there is an exchange rate depreciation, with the nominal exchange rate increasing to e_2.

Now, assume an extreme form of capital controls in which the government pro-hibits all capital inflows and outflows. This will imply that the capital account surplus must be zero in equilibrium, and so the current account surplus must be zero as well. With a temporary decrease in domestic total factor productivity in Figure 13.11, the domestic real interest rate will rise to r_1, which is above the world real interest rate r^*. In equilibrium, foreign investors would like to purchase domestic assets, as the return on domestic assets is greater than it is in the rest of the world, but they are prohibited from doing so. Thus, in this case, real output decreases to Y_3 in equilibrium. Assuming that money demand is much more responsive to real income than to the real interest rate, the money demand curve shifts to the left in Figure 13.11(b), though by less than it does in the case with no capital controls. The nominal exchange rate rises to e_3.

The results are that the nominal exchange rate increases by a smaller amount when capital controls are in place than when they are not, output falls by a smaller amount,

FIGURE 13.11

**A Temporary Total Factor
Productivity Shock, With and
Without Capital Controls**

With a temporary decrease in
total factor productivity, under
a flexible exchange rate there
is a larger decrease in aggregate output and the current
account surplus, and a larger
increase in the nominal
exchange rate, in the case
without capital controls.

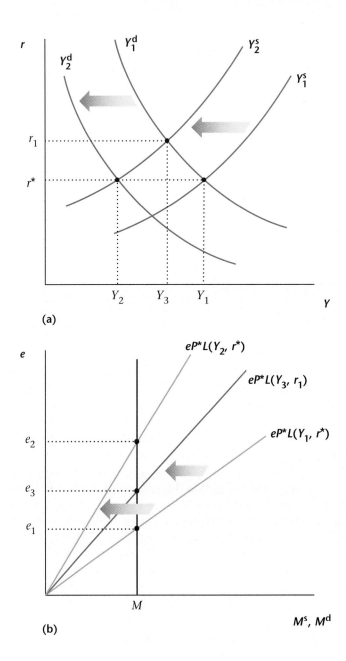

and there is a smaller change in the current account deficit. Thus, capital controls tend
to dampen aggregate fluctuations in output, the current account surplus, and the nominal exchange rate resulting from shocks of this type to the economy. If a country is concerned about the effects of fluctuations in the nominal exchange rate under a flexible
exchange rate regime (for reasons not modelled here), capital controls will tend to mit-
igate this problem, at least if the major source of shocks is temporary changes in total
factor productivity. However, this solution is quite costly, as it produces an economic

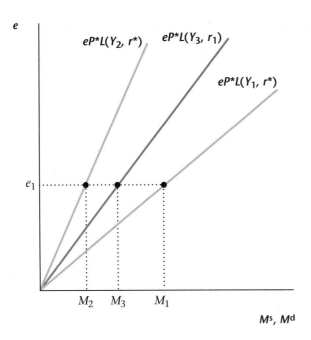

FIGURE 13.12

A Total Factor Productivity Shock Under a Fixed Exchange Rate, With and Without Capital Controls

Under a fixed exchange rate, capital controls dampen the reduction in the money supply that occurs when there is a temporary decline in total factor productivity.

inefficiency. As in Chapter 5, the equilibrium allocation of resources is Pareto-optimal in this model in the absence of capital controls. With no capital controls, in this example, the domestic economy would face a lower real interest rate after the total factor productivity shock, and this means that lenders would be worse off and borrowers better off. Though some would win and some would lose from getting rid of capital controls, there would in general be an average gain in welfare.

Under a fixed exchange rate, Figure 13.11(a) still applies, but the money market works as in Figure 13.12. The nominal exchange rate is assumed to be fixed at e_1. Initially, the money supply is M_1, and in the absence of capital controls, the money supply declines to M_2, but with capital controls there will be a decline in the money supply only to M_3. Here, fluctuations in the money supply are smaller with capital controls, which implies that foreign exchange reserves will drop by a smaller amount with capital controls. Therefore, with capital controls in place a government can better support a fixed exchange rate, if exhausting the stock of foreign exchange reserves on hand is potentially a problem without controls. Again, though, capital controls come at a cost in lost economic efficiency. For a discussion of the effects of capital controls in practice, see Macroeconomics in Action 13.2 on page 462.

A Mundell-Fleming Model: Sticky Wages in the Open Economy

As was mentioned earlier in this chapter, it is straightforward to build on our monetary small open economy model by adding features that will imply that money is not neutral in the short run, or that there is a role for short-run stabilization policy. In this section, we will explore how traditional Keynesian stabilization policy works in an open economy setting, under flexible and fixed exchange rates.

Do Capital Controls Work in Practice?

With regard to how capital controls work in practice, we are primarily interested in two questions: (i) Can capital controls be effectively enforced, so that they have the intended effects? (ii) How large are the economic inefficiencies that capital controls cause? In an article in the *Journal of Economic Perspectives*, Sebastian Edwards sets out to answer these questions, using the example of Chile.[1]

Edwards argues that there is little support by economists for restrictions on capital outflows, but that some economists have pointed to Chile as an example of how restrictions on capital inflows appeared to have worked well. One aim of his article is to dismiss these latter arguments by studying the details of what happened in Chile, where controls on capital inflows were in place from 1978 to 1982 and from 1991 to 1998. These restrictions mainly applied to portfolio inflows of short-maturity securities, and they took the form of reserve requirements on these inflows. That is, if a foreigner purchased short-term interest-bearing Chilean assets (a capital inflow), then a fraction of the value of these assets would have to be held as a non-interest-bearing deposit with the central bank. This had the same effect as a tax on short-term capital inflows, as the non-interest-bearing deposits could otherwise be held in interest-bearing form.

What were the effects of the capital controls in Chile? Edwards finds that apparently many investors learned how to avoid them. While capital inflows appeared to have shifted somewhat toward longer-term from shorter-term inflows, the shift was not very large, and investors seemed to have found many clever schemes for disguising short-term capital inflows as long-term ones. Edwards argues that the controls had severe effects on small and medium-sized Chilean firms, which faced much higher costs of borrowing.

Edwards' conclusion is that the welfare costs of capital controls are small on average, mainly because the controls are ineffective, but the costs are large for some groups in the population. Edwards argues that capital controls should be phased out in countries where they still exist. However, he argues that in some cases this phase-out should be gradual. The inefficiencies caused by capital controls may in some cases be small relative to the inefficiencies arising from a poorly regulated banking system. If restrictions on capital inflows are relaxed quickly, then domestic banks can borrow abroad more easily to finance domestic lending. However, if domestic banks are improperly regulated (as we will study in more depth in Chapter 14), then they will take on too much risk; and this problem can be exacerbated in a wide-open international lending environment. The relaxation of capital controls sometimes needs to be coupled with improvements in the regulation of domestic financial institutions.

---

[1] S. Edwards, 1999, "How Effective Are Capital Controls?" *Journal of Economic Perspectives* 13, 65–84.

The model we will study is a version of the Mundell-Fleming model.[1] Here, we will essentially combine the closed-economy Keynesian sticky-wage model from Chapter 10 with the monetary small open economy model developed earlier in this chapter.

---

[1] See R. Mundell, 1961, "Flexible Exchange Rates and Employment Policy," *Canadian Journal of Economics and Political Science*, 509–517, and J. Fleming, 1962, "Domestic Financial Policies Under Fixed and Floating Exchange Rates," *IMF Staff Papers*, 369–379. The models here take liberties with the approaches of Mundell and Fleming, but are certainly in the spirit of those models.

As in the monetary small open economy model, the real interest rate is determined on world markets, so that $r = r^*$, that is we have perfect capital mobility. As well, purchasing power parity holds, as per Equation (13.2), and money demand equals money supply, which gives Equation (13.4). Just as in Chapter 10, the LM curve is an upward-sloping relationship in Figure 13.3 (a), which is a set of real interest rate–real income pairs for which the money market is in equilibrium. Here, however, since $P = eP^*$ from the purchasing power parity relationship, the LM curve will shift to the left with an increase in the exchange rate e. In Figure 13.3 (a), the curve LM_1 is drawn for a given exchange rate e_1, and curve LM_2 is drawn for a given exchange rate e_2, where $e_2 > e_1$.

Recall from Chapter 10 that the IS curve is identical to the output demand curve. In this open-economy context, then, in Figure 13.13(a) the IS curve is a construct identical to the output demand curve in the monetary small open economy model.

In Figure 13.3 (b), the open economy aggregate demand curve AD is a downward-sloping relationship between the exchange rate e and the level of real income Y. The aggregate demand curve is derived by noting that, for example, if the exchange rate is e_1, then this determines the position of the LM curve in Figure 13.3 (a) at LM_1. In equilibrium, the current account surplus adjusts so that the IS curve is IS_1, intersecting LM_1 at the real interest rate r^*. Then, if the exchange rate were at a higher level, say e_2, then this would imply that the LM curve in Figure 13.3 (a) would shift to the left to LM_2. As a result, the current account surplus would fall, shifting the IS curve to the left until it comes to rest at IS_2. Thus, a higher exchange rate implies that real income must fall to Y_2 to maintain equilibrium in the money market and the domestic goods market. Thus, the AD curve in 13.3 (b) is downward-sloping, on which two points are (Y_1, e_1) and (Y_2, e_2). The AD curve is a set of exchange rate/real income combinations such that the domestic goods market and the money market are in equilibrium.

The upward-sloping aggregate supply curve, AS, in Figure 13.3 (b) is the counterpart of the upward-sloping AS curve in the Keynesian sticky wage model in Chapter 10. Here, since $P = eP^*$, with P^* given, we have output increasing with the exchange rate rather than with the domestic price level, as was the case in Chapter 10.

STABILIZATION POLICY WITH A FLEXIBLE EXCHANGE RATE

Under a flexible exchange rate regime, fiscal policy is completely ineffective in stabilizing real output. To see this, suppose in Figure 13.14 that the economy is initially in equilibrium with curves IS_1, LM_1, AD_1, and AS determining the level of real income Y_1 and the exchange rate e_1 given the world real interest rate r^*. Then suppose that current government expenditures G increase. This will simply result in a decrease in the current account surplus that exactly offsets the increase in G, and there is no shift in the IS curve. This occurs because, given the exchange rate e, equation (13.4) determines the level of income Y. Therefore, there is no effect on real income, the nominal exchange rate, consumption, or investment, while government spending crowds out net exports one-for-one. There are no other effects.

In contrast to fiscal policy, monetary policy has potency with a flexible exchange rate. Suppose again that the economy is initially in equilibrium in Figure 13.14 with curves IS_1, LM_1, AD_1, and AS determining the level of real income Y_1 and the exchange rate e_1 given the world real interest rate r^*. Then, the central bank increases the money

FIGURE 13.13

The Mundell-Fleming Model
The nominal exchange rate is
determined by the *AS* and *AD*
curves in 13.13 (b), which
determines the position of the
LM curve in 13.13 (a). This
determines output given the
world real interest rate, and
net exports adjust so that the
IS and *LM* curves intersect at
the real interest rate *r*.

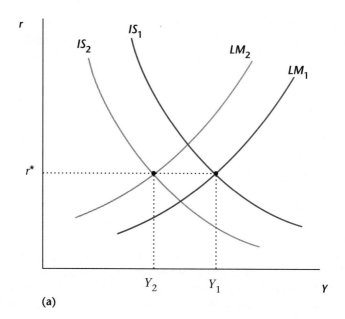

(a)

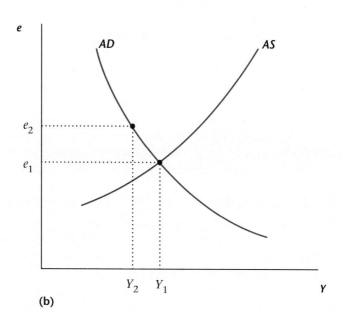

(b)

supply, which, given the initial exchange rate e_1, shifts the *LM* curve to the right to LM_2 and the aggregate demand curve to the right from AD_1 to AD_2. As a result, in Figure 13.14 (b), real income increases in equilibrium from Y_1 to Y_2, and the nominal exchange rate rises from e_1 to e_2. In Figure 13.14 (a), the increase in the exchange rate shifts the *LM* curve to the left from LM_2 to LM_3, and the current account surplus increases, shift-

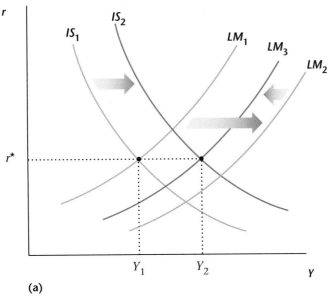

FIGURE 13.14

An Increase in the Money Supply in the Mundell-Fleming Model

An increase in the money supply shifts the aggregate demand curve to the right, and output and the nominal exchange rate increase. The current account surplus increases, with the *IS* and *LM* curves coming to rest at *IS*$_2$ and *LM*$_3$, respectively.

ing the *IS* curve to the right from *IS*$_1$ to *IS*$_2$. Consumption expenditures increase with the increase in equilibrium income.

Note that the money supply must increase in real terms, as the real demand for money increases with real income. Thus, the nominal exchange rate and the domestic price level rise less than in proportion to the increase in the money supply.

If the domestic economy is completely open to the rest of the world, with no barriers to the flows of goods and assets, this dramatically changes the Keynesian view of how stabilization policy works. This analysis is particularly important for Canada, where trade in goods with other countries matters greatly, and where domestic asset markets are highly integrated with world asset markets. Our analysis tells us that, for a country like Canada, if the exchange rate is flexible and we believe that Keynesian-type sticky wages are important, then fiscal policy is ineffective as a stabilization tool and monetary policy is effective.

As an example of how stabilization policy can work under a flexible exchange rate, consider Figure 13.15. Here, suppose initially that equilibrium real income is Y_1 and the equilibrium nominal exchange rate is e_1, with initial curves IS_1, LM_1, AD_1, and AS. Also suppose that there is full employment initially; that is, supply is equal to demand in the labour market. Then, suppose the world real interest rate falls from r_1^* to r_2^*. This has the effect of shifting the aggregate demand curve to the left from AD_1 to AD_2 in Figure 13.15 (a). In equilibrium, real income will fall from Y_1 to Y_2 and the nominal exchange rate falls from e_1 to e_2. In Figure 13.15 (a), the decrease in the nominal exchange rate causes a shift to the right in the LM curve from LM_1 to LM_2, and the current account surplus falls until the IS curve comes to rest at IS_2. Thus, in equilibrium investment will increase (the interest rate falls), and consumption could increase or decrease (because the interest rate falls but income falls as well). Given the decrease in real output, employment will have fallen as well, and there will be Keynesian unemployment.

Now, it is possible for the central bank to completely offset the negative effect of the decrease in r^* on real output and to achieve full employment through an increase in the domestic money supply. If the central bank increases M sufficiently, then the aggregate demand curve will shift to the right to AD_1, and equilibrium output and the nominal exchange rate will be at their initial levels, Y_1 and e_1 respectively, in Figure 13.15 (b). In Figure 13.15 (a), the LM curve shifts to the right to LM_3, and the current account surplus increases until the IS curve comes to rest at IS_3. Note that, though output is the same at point B in Figure 13.15 (a) as at point A, investment and consumption are higher at B than A (the interest rate is lower), and the current account surplus is lower.

STABILIZATION POLICY WITH A FIXED EXCHANGE RATE

Recall from the monetary small open economy model that, under a fixed exchange rate, the money supply becomes endogenous. In our Mundell-Fleming sticky wage model, in Figure 13.16 (b) the exchange rate is fixed at e_1, and this determines output Y_1 from the aggregate supply curve AS. The money supply then adjusts so that the aggregate demand curve AD intersects AS at the level of income Y_1 and the nominal exchange rate e_1. Then, in Figure 13.16 (a) the current account surplus and the money supply adjust so that the IS and LM curves intersect at interest rate r^* and level of income Y_1.

A key property of the model, then, is that neither monetary nor fiscal policy can be effective in stabilizing output against shocks that cause Keynesian unemployment. Increases in government spending, as with a flexible exchange rate, simply displace an equal quantity of net exports and have no other effects. An increase in the money sup-

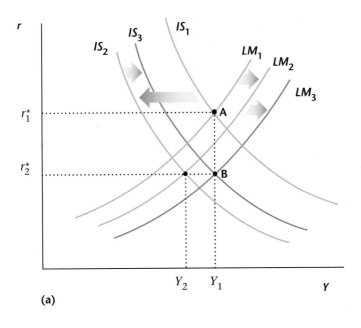

FIGURE 13.15

Stabilization Policy in Response to a Decrease in r*
The world real interest rate falls, which leads to a shift to the left in the aggregate demand curve and a decrease in output and the nominal exchange rate. An increase in the money supply can restore output and employment to their initial levels.

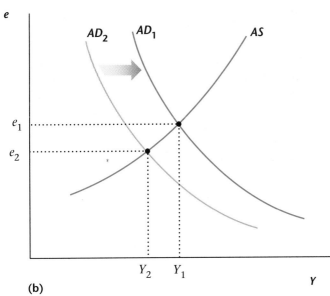

ply acts to shift the aggregate demand curve to the right, but this puts upward pressure on the nominal exchange rate. The authority responsible for defending the exchange rate must sell foreign exchange and buy domestic money, reducing the money supply and completely offsetting the effects of the money supply increase.

Under a fixed exchange rate, and with unrestricted flows of goods and assets across borders, the only stabilization policy open to domestic policymakers is a change in the exchange rate (a devaluation or revaluation). As an example of a stabilizing devaluation,

FIGURE 13.16

The Mundell-Fleming Model with a Fixed Exchange Rate
The exchange rate is fixed at e_1, which determines output from the aggregate supply curve. The money supply adjusts so that the AD curve intersects the AS curve at the fixed exchange rate. The current account surplus adjusts so that the IS and LM curves intersect at the real interest rate r^*.

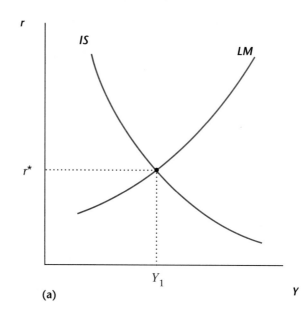

(a)

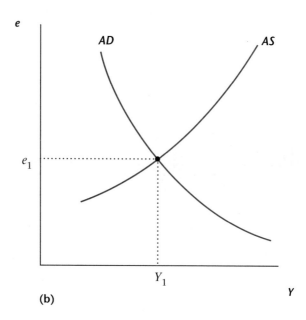

(b)

consider the case where there is a decrease in P^*, the foreign price level. Given the fixed exchange rate and purchasing power parity, this will act to reduce the domestic price level, increase the real wage, reduce employment, and shift the aggregate supply curve in Figure 13.17 (b) to the left from AS_1 to AS_2. There is then downward pressure on the exchange rate, the domestic money supply falls, and the aggregate demand curve shifts to the left from AD_1 to AD_2. Real output declines in equilibrium from Y_1 to Y_2, and there will be Keynesian unemployment in the labour market. In Figure 13.17 (a), the LM

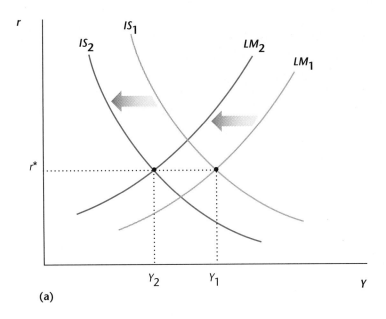

(a)

FIGURE 13.17
Devaluation in Response
to a Decrease in P*
If there is a decrease in the
foreign price level, this will
shift the aggregate supply
curve to the left, leading to a
decrease in output, and the
current account surplus falls.
A devaluation can shift the
aggregate demand curve to
the right and restore all real
variables to their initial levels.

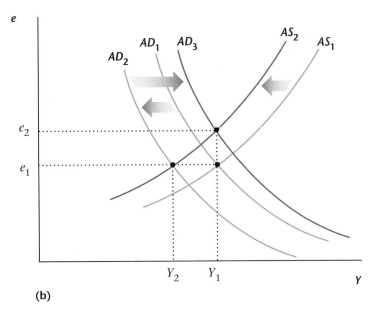

(b)

curve shifts to the left from LM_1 to LM_2, and the current account surplus falls causing the IS curve to shift left from IS_1 to IS_2.

The government could wait for the nominal wage to decrease until, ultimately, the aggregate supply curve shifts back to AS_1 in Figure 13.17 (b). If instead a devaluation of the domestic currency takes place, with e_1 increasing to e_2, then the domestic money supply increases causing the aggregate demand curve to shift to the right to AD_3. In Figure 13.17 (a), the LM curve shifts right to LM_1 and the IS curve shifts to IS_1. The devaluation offsets the decline in $P*$, so that the domestic price level is unaffected on net. After the stabilization, the domestic economy looks identical to its state before $P*$ fell.

While stabilization through devaluation may appear attractive in this example, this also shows how these actions can detract from the virtues of a fixed exchange rate. In countries with weak central banks, a fixed exchange rate can be a useful commitment device, which allows the domestic economy to adopt the inflation policy of a low-inflation country. If a country on a fixed exchange rate goes through continued rounds of devaluation, then it will generate a higher rate of inflation than the outside world.

While there are many more interesting issues to study in international macroeconomics, this chapter ends our discussion of this topic here. In Part 6, we will move on to study topics in money and banking, unemployment, and inflation, which involve in-depth issues in closed-economy macroeconomics.

Chapter Summary

The purpose of this chapter was to study the implications of international monetary relations for the determination of domestic output, the domestic price level, the nominal exchange rate, the current account surplus, and the capital account surplus. We first studied purchasing power parity, or the law of one price, which predicts that prices are equated across countries in terms of the same currency. While there can be large and persistent deviations from purchasing power parity in practice, there are strong economic forces that move prices and exchange rates toward purchasing power parity over the long run. The purchasing power parity assumption is very useful in the model studied in this chapter.

The monetary small open-economy model we studied in this chapter is one in which the real interest rate and the foreign price level are determined on world markets. Under a flexible exchange rate, money is neutral, and the domestic economy is insulated from nominal shocks from abroad—no real or nominal domestic variables are affected by a change in the foreign price level. The nominal exchange rate moves in equilibrium to absorb completely a shock to the foreign price level. However, the flexible exchange rate does not insulate the domestic price level against real shocks from abroad. Alternatively, a fixed exchange rate causes the domestic price level to increase in proportion to an increase in the foreign price level, but the fixed exchange rate regime insulates the domestic price level from foreign real shocks. Under a fixed exchange rate regime, a devaluation of the domestic currency might occur if the government's foreign exchange reserves are depleted. A devaluation raises the domestic price level. Whether a flexible exchange rate regime is preferred to a fixed exchange rate regime depends on a country's circumstances, but a flexible exchange rate regime implies that domestic monetary policy can be independent, whereas a fixed exchange rate regime implies that the domestic economy adopts the monetary policy of a foreign central bank.

Capital controls involve restrictions on capital inflows and outflows, which are items in the capital account, where the asset transactions for a nation are added up. The balance of payments surplus is the sum of the capital account surplus and the current account surplus. The balance of payments surplus is always zero. Capital controls can dampen fluctuations in output, the current account surplus, and the exchange rate (under a flexible exchange rate) or the money supply (under a fixed exchange rate), but these controls reduce economic efficiency. In practice, capital controls appear not to have been very effective, and in this sense they have not had large effects on efficiency.

A version of the Mundell-Fleming model introduced a Keynesian sticky wage mechanism into the monetary small open economy model. In this setup, money is not neutral, and there is generally a role for stabilization policy. However, fiscal policy and monetary policy are limited by the international mobility of goods and assets. Fiscal policy is ineffective under either a flexible or a fixed exchange rate in stabilizing output. Monetary policy can stabilize output under a flexible exchange rate, but is ineffective under a fixed exchange rate, when only devaluation or revaluation of the exchange rate can be used as a stabilization tool.

Key Terms

nominal exchange rate: The price of foreign currency in term of domestic currency, denoted by e in the model of this chapter.

law of one price: $P = eP^*$ where P is the domestic price, P^* is the foreign price, and e is the exchange rate.

purchasing power parity (PPP): The same thing as the law of one price, except that P is the domestic price *level* and P^* is the foreign price *level*.

Big Mac index: The ratio of the prices of Big Macs in two different countries, published by *The Economist*.

flexible exchange rate regime: A system under which a nation's nominal exchange rate is determined by market forces.

fixed exchange rate regime: A system under which the domestic government supports the value of the exchange rate at a specified level in terms of a foreign currency or currencies.

hard pegs: Exchange rate systems under which there is firm commitment to a fixed exchange rate, through either dollarization or a currency board.

soft pegs: Exchange rate systems under which the government commits to a fixed exchange rate for periods of time, but sometimes changes the value at which the exchange rate is fixed.

devaluations: Increases in the price of foreign exchange in terms of domestic currency.

revaluations: Decreases in the price of foreign exchange in terms of domestic currency.

dollarize: For a nation to abandon its own currency and adopt the currency of another country as its medium of exchange.

currency board: An institution that fixes the exchange rate by holding foreign-currency-denominated interest-bearing assets and committing to buying and selling foreign exchange at a fixed rate of exchange.

European Monetary Union (EMU): An organization of European countries, established in 1999, that shares a common currency, the Euro.

Euro: The currency shared by the members of the EMU.

European Central Bank (ECB): The central bank of the EMU countries.

European Monetary System (EMS): A cooperative exchange rate system in place among European countries from 1979 until 1999.

Bretton Woods arrangement: A worldwide cooperative exchange rate system, in place from 1946 to 1971, under which the price of gold was fixed in terms of U.S. dollars, and there were fixed exchange rates for all other currencies in terms of the U.S. dollar.

International Monetary Fund (IMF): An international monetary institution established in 1946, intended as a lender of last resort for its member countries, which now number 184.

lender of last resort: A centralized institution that lends to economic agents in distress; examples are central banks, which lend to domestic banks, and the IMF, which lends to its member countries.

depreciation (of the exchange rate): A rise in the price of foreign currency in terms of domestic currency.

appreciation (of the exchange rate): A fall in the price of foreign currency in terms of domestic currency.

common currency area: A region over which a single currency dominates as a medium of exchange.

currency union: A group of countries that agree to become a common currency area.

capital account: The component of the balance of payments in which all international asset transactions between the domestic economy and foreign countries are added up.

balance of payments: A system of accounts for a country for adding up all international transactions in goods and assets.

capital inflow: The purchase of a domestic asset by a foreign resident, recorded as a positive entry in the capital account.

capital outflow: The purchase of a foreign asset by a domestic resident, recorded as a negative entry in the capital account.

foreign direct investment: A capital inflow that involves the acquisition of a new physical asset by a foreign resident.

portfolio inflows and outflows: Capital account transactions involving international transactions in financial assets.

Questions for Review

1. Does purchasing power parity hold in practice in the short run? Why or why not? Does it hold in the long run? Why or why not?

2. What countries in the world have flexible exchange rates? Which have fixed exchange rates?

3. What are the different systems for fixing the exchange rate? Describe how each works.

4. Describe the role of the International Monetary Fund.

5. In the model constructed in this chapter, what are the effects on the domestic economy of an increase in the foreign price level under a flexible exchange rate, and under a fixed exchange rate?

6. In the model, what are the effects on the domestic economy of an increase in the world real interest rate under a flexible exchange rate, and under a fixed exchange rate?

7. In the model, is money neutral under a flexible exchange rate? Explain why or why not. Can we say that money is neutral under a fixed exchange rate? Explain.

8. Explain why domestic monetary policy is not independent under a flexible exchange rate.

9. What are the effects of a devaluation of the domestic currency under a fixed exchange rate?

10. List the key pros and cons of fixed versus flexible exchange rate regimes.

11. Give two examples of fixed exchange rates within the United States.

12. What are the advantages and disadvantages of a common currency area or currency union?

13. If there is a capital account surplus, what can we say about the current account surplus?

14. Give two examples of countries where capital controls were imposed.

15. What do capital controls imply for the response of the economy to shocks?

16. Are capital controls a good idea? Why or why not?

17. Are capital controls effective in practice? Explain.

18. Is monetary policy effective in affecting the level of output in the Mundell-Fleming model under a flexible exchange rate? What about fiscal policy?

19. How effective are monetary and fiscal policy in the Mundell-Fleming model under a fixed exchange rate?

20. In the Mundell-Fleming model, what role do exchange rate devaluations and revaluations play in stabilization policy under a fixed exchange rate?

Problems

1. In the equilibrium small open-economy model, suppose that total factor productivity increases temporarily.
   a. If the exchange rate is flexible, determine the effects on aggregate output, absorption, the current account surplus, the nominal exchange rate, and the price level.
   b. Repeat part (a) for the case of a fixed exchange rate. If the goal of the domestic government is to stabilize the price level, would it be preferable to have a fixed exchange rate or a flexible exchange rate regime when there is a change in total factor productivity?
   c. Now suppose that under a flexible exchange rate regime the domestic monetary authority controls the money supply so as to stabilize the price level when total factor productivity increases. Explain the differences between the outcome in this case and what happens in part (b) with a fixed exchange rate.

2. Suppose in the model that government expenditures increase temporarily. Determine the effects on aggregate output, absorption, the current account surplus, the nominal exchange rate, and the price level. What difference will it make if the exchange rate is flexible or fixed?

3. Suppose that better transaction technologies are developed that reduce the domestic demand for money. Use the monetary small open-economy model to answer the following:
   a. Suppose that the exchange rate is flexible. What are the equilibrium effects on the price level and the exchange rate?
   b. Suppose that the exchange rate is flexible, and the domestic monetary authority acts to stabilize the price level. Determine how the domestic money supply changes, and the effect on the nominal exchange rate.
   c. Suppose that the exchange rate is fixed. Determine the effects on the exchange rate and the price level, and determine the differences from your results in parts (a) and (b).

4. A country is under a fixed exchange rate regime, and the government decides to reduce government spending permanently.
   a. Show that if the government has no foreign exchange reserves, it must devalue the domestic currency. Determine the equilibrium effects of this.
   b. What effect does the change in government spending have on the current account surplus? Does the exchange rate devaluation affect the current account surplus? Explain your results.

5. Consider a country with a flexible exchange rate, and that initially has a current account surplus of zero. Then suppose there is an anticipated increase in future total factor productivity.
   a. Determine the equilibrium effects on the domestic economy in the case where there are no capital controls. In particular, show that there will be a current account deficit when firms and consumers anticipate the increase in future total factor productivity.

b. Now suppose that the government dislikes current account deficits, and that it imposes capital controls in an attempt to reduce the current account deficit. With the anticipated increase in future total factor productivity, what will the equilibrium effects on the economy be? Do the capital controls have the desired effect on the current account deficit? Do capital controls dampen the effects of the shock to the economy on output and the exchange rate? Are capital controls sound macroeconomic policy in this context? Why or why not?

6. The domestic central bank increases the supply of money under a flexible exchange rate regime, leading to a depreciation of the nominal exchange rate. If the government had imposed capital controls before the increase in the money supply, would this have had any effect on the exchange rate depreciation? Explain your results, and comment on their significance.

7. In the Mundell-Fleming model, suppose that there is a flexible exchange rate regime. The foreign price level decreases. What is the effect on the equilibrium level of output, consumption, investment, employment, the real wage, the price level, the current account surplus, and the nominal exchange rate? Explain your results and compare this to what happens under a fixed exchange rate. What are your conclusions concerning the desirability of flexible versus fixed exchange rates?

8. In the Mundell-Fleming model, suppose there is a temporary decrease in total factor productivity.
   a. Under a flexible exchange rate, what is the effect on output, the nominal exchange rate, the current account surplus, consumption, and investment?
   b. Under a flexible exchange rate, what is the appropriate stabilization policy for the government to pursue?
   c. If the exchange rate is fixed, what is the effect on output, the nominal exchange rate, the current account surplus, consumption, and investment?
   d. Under a fixed exchange rate, what is the appropriate stabilization policy?
   e. Explain your results, and discuss the differences in your answers to parts (a) and (c), and (b) and (d), respectively.

Working with the Data

1. Using the data from Figure 13.1, where e is the value of a Canadian dollar in terms of U.S. dollars, P^* is the U.S. consumer price index, and P is the Canadian consumer price index, construct a time series plot of e, $\frac{P^*}{P}$, and $\frac{eP^*}{P}$. What explains most of the variability in $\frac{eP^*}{P}$? Is it variability in e, or in $\frac{P^*}{P}$? What does this tell us about the causes of changes in the real exchange rate in the short run?

2. Construct a time series plot of the German exchange rate in Canadian dollars, the Japanese exchange rate in Canadian dollars, and the U.S. exchange rate in Canadian dollars. For comparability, scale these exchange rates so that they all are equal to 100 for the first data point. What do you observe in the time series plot? What does this tell us about how the Bank of Canada controls different foreign exchange rates?

3. Construct a scatter plot of the annual percentage changes (December to December) in the U.S. exchange rate in Canadian dollars and the annual percentage changes in the monetary base. What do you observe? Is this consistent with the models constructed in this chapter?

Money, Banking, Unemployment, and Inflation

In this Part, we will deal with some in-depth topics. In Chapter 14, we will study at a more detailed level the role of money in the economy, the forms money has taken historically, and the relationships among the monetary system, the banking system, and the central bank. Chapter 15 looks at two theories of unemployment, the search model and the efficiency wage model. Both models help explain why there are always unemployed people, even in a well-functioning economy, and these models will also help us understand the main determinants of the unemployment rate. Finally, Chapter 16 aims to explain why central banks may cause inflation, even though it is well known that inflation is harmful. We will use recent inflation history in Canada as a backdrop in examining the role of central bank learning and commitment in inflation policy.

CHAPTER 14

Money, Private Banking, and Central Banking

In the monetary analysis we have done so far in this book, particularly in Chapters 9–11 and 13, we began by assuming that money was needed to make transactions, and proceeded from there. This allowed us to understand the effects of changes in the quantity of money, the costs of inflation, the role of money in the business cycle, and how money influences foreign exchange rates. In this chapter, we wish to gain a deeper understanding of the functions of money in the economy, and to examine the relationships among money, banking, and the central bank.

The monetary system generally comprises a wide range of institutions for carrying out transactions, and only a small part of this system is associated with the hand-to-hand currency that we are most familiar with. In this chapter we will first discuss how historical monetary systems worked, and study the basic role of money in the economy in overcoming the difficulty of carrying out exchange using only commodities. Since much of our modern monetary system is dominated by private banks and central banks, we will then explore the functions of these institutions.

Finally, we examine how monetary policy works in Canada. In Canada, the institution that has authority to set monetary policy is the Bank of Canada. Monetary policy consists of decisions by the Bank of Canada concerning the control of the quantity of money in existence, and lending by the Bank of Canada to financial institutions. We will show what the immediate effects of these decisions are in the financial sector, and explain the mechanisms by which monetary control is exercised.

Alternative Forms of Money

In Chapter 9, we discussed how money functions as a medium of exchange, a store of value, and a unit of account, with the key distinguishing feature of money being its medium-of-exchange property. Though all money is a medium of exchange, historically there have been many different objects that have performed this role. The most important forms of money have been commodity money, circulating private bank notes, commodity-backed paper currency, fiat money, and transactions deposits at private banks. We will discuss each of these in turn.

commodity money: This was the earliest money, in common use in Greek and Roman civilizations and in earlier times, and it was typically a precious metal: gold, silver, or copper. In practice, commodity money systems involved having the government operate a mint to produce coins from precious metals, which then circulated as money. Control over the mint by the government was important, since the ability to issue money provided an important source of seigniorage revenue. Commodity money systems had several problems, however. First, the quality of any commodity is difficult to verify. For example, gold can be adulterated with other cheaper metals, so that there is an opportunity for fraud in the production of commodity money. Also, in the exchange of commodity monies, bits could be clipped off coins and melted down, with the hope that this would go undetected. Second, commodity money is costly to produce. For example, gold has to be dug out of the ground, minted, and then reminted when the coins wear out. Third, the use of a commodity as money diverts it from other uses. Gold and silver, for example, can also be used as jewellery, and in industrial applications. In spite of these three problems, at the time commodity monies were used there were no good alternatives, mainly because any laws against the counterfeiting of paper currency would have been difficult or impossible to enforce. What may seem paradoxical is that the high cost of producing a commodity money was a virtue. To avoid inflation, the quantity of money must be in limited supply, and one reason that gold and silver functioned well as commodity monies is that they were scarce.

circulating private bank notes: Before the Bank of Canada was established in 1935, much of the currency in circulation in Canada was issued by Canadian chartered banks. In other countries, monetary systems with private currency issue appeared not to have worked well, as in the United States before 1863. However, the Canadian monetary system before 1935 seemed to have functioned efficiently.[1]

commodity-backed paper currency: In this type of monetary system, there is government-issued paper currency, but the currency is backed by some commodity, the **gold standard** for example. Canada operated under the gold standard before 1929. Under the rules of the gold standard, the Canadian government stood ready to exchange currency for gold at some specified price, so that government currency was always redeemable in gold. Effectively this was a commodity money system, but it saved on some of the costs of a commodity money, in that consumers did not have to carry around large quantities of the commodity (in this case, gold) when they wanted to make large purchases. For two historical examples of commodity-backed currency, see Macroeconomics in Action 14.1 on p. 479.

---

[1]See S. Williamson, 1989, "Restrictions on Financial Intermediaries and Implications for Aggregate Fluctuations: Canada and the United States 1870–1913," in *NBER Macroeconomics Annual 1989*, pp. 303–340, ed. Olivier Blanchard and Stanley Fischer, MIT Press, Cambridge MA; and B. Champ, B. Smith, and S. Williamson, 1996, "Currency Elasticity and Banking Panics: Theory and Evidence," *Canadian Journal of Economics* 29, 828–864.

fiat money: This is at least part of the monetary system in most modern economies. In Canada, fiat money is the stock of notes issued by the Bank of Canada. It consists of pieces of paper that are essentially worthless: for example, most people do not value Canadian currency for its colour or for what is depicted on it. However, fiat money is accepted in exchange for goods. Why? Because people believe others will accept it in exchange for goods in the future. This notion of the value of money supported by belief is intriguing, and it is part of what excites those who study monetary economics.

transactions deposits at private banks: In Canada, widespread deposit banking and the use of cheques in transactions evolved later in the 19th century, and the Canadian financial system (like the financial systems in most developed economies) has evolved to the point where much of the total volume of transactions is carried out through banks. With a chequable bank deposit, consumers can make purchases without the use of fiat money. A cheque is a message that specifies that a given quantity of value is to be debited from the account of the person writing the cheque and credited to the account of the person receiving the cheque. If the accounts of the writer and the receiver are in different banks, the cheque needs to pass through the **cheque-clearing system** for the correct accounts to be debited and credited. Cheque clearing is one mechanism by which banks carry out exchanges with each other. Transactions accounts can also be debited and credited by debit card, which is now a less costly technology than chequing.

Some readers may be concerned that we have not mentioned credit cards as a form of money. There is a good reason we have not done this—money and credit are fundamentally different. When a credit card purchase is made, the vendor of goods or services extends credit to the purchaser, and then this credit is transferred to the credit card issuer (e.g., Visa, MasterCard, or American Express). The credit extended is not money in the sense that currency or a bank deposit is money, since the issuer of credit cannot use what is effectively an IOU of the purchaser as a medium of exchange. Note, however, that forms of credit, particularly credit cards, are a substitute for money in making transactions, and therefore they are important in terms of how we think about the monetary system.

Money and the Absence of Double Coincidence of Wants: The Role of Commodity Money and Fiat Money

Now that we know something about what objects have served as a medium of exchange, we will consider in more detail what it means for some object to be a medium of exchange, which is the distinctive function of money. In this section, we will consider a model that formalizes why money is useful as a medium of exchange. This model will help us understand the role of the two simplest types of money, commodity money and fiat money.

Commodity Money and Commodity-Backed Paper Money: Yap Stones and Playing Cards

A commodity money system that appears unusual on the surface, but has several features common to other commodity money systems, is the exchange of so-called Yap stones on the island of Yap in Micronesia, as studied by the anthropologist William Henry Furness III in 1903.[1]

On Yap, large stones measuring from about 0.3 to 3.7 metres in diameter served as money.[2] The stones were quarried from limestone deposits on another island about 650 kilometres from Yap, and transported back by boat. What the Yap stones had in common with other commodity monies, such as gold and silver, was scarcity. It was quite costly in time and effort to create a new stone, and the value of the stones increased with the difficulty of acquiring them, which might include weathering storms on the trip back to Yap. What seems different about the Yap stones as a commodity money is that they were extremely difficult to move around; an attractive feature of gold and silver as commodity monies was that the quantities of it required to make moderate-sized transactions were extremely portable. However, the islanders did not typically move the Yap stones when transactions were made; they were most often used to make large land transactions and large gifts, but the stones themselves usually stayed put. It was well known to most of the small population of Yap who owned which stones, and a transaction involving one of these stones was public knowledge, but there was no written record of ownership. Thus, it appears that exchange was actually carried out on the island using commodity-backed money. What "changed hands" in a transaction was the record of the ownership of the stone, which was stored in the collective memories of the islanders, and the stones were just the backing for the "currency," which was not physical objects at all, but an entry in public memory.

Yap stones had much in common with the earliest known paper money used in North America, in New France in 1685. There had been difficulties in keeping coins minted in France in circulation in New France, as the coins were often used in payment for imports from France, and thus left the colony. Therefore, the coins constantly had to be replenished by shipments from France in the form of payments to the troops in New France. In 1685, the shipment of coins was late in arriving from France, and De Meulles, the Intendant (governor of the colony) of New France authorized the issue of playing-card money. De Meulles requisitioned the playing cards in the colony, and the cards were issued, signed by him in different denominations, as payment to the troops. These cards were essentially IOUs, which promised payment in coin when the shipment arrived from France. The playing cards then circulated as a medium of exchange in New France, and were subsequently retired as promised. The cards were then issued repeatedly in later years. But ultimately the government of France lost interest in its colony in New France, and the shipments of coins stopped arriving from France in the quantities promised, so that the IOUs the playing cards represented could not be honoured in full. There were problems with inflation, because of the temptation to issue the playing-card money in excess of the promises the Intendant could actually keep.[3]

Like the ownership rights to the Yap stones, playing-card money in New France was a commodity-backed money. However, the New France playing-card monetary system seems to have been less successful than the Yap system, because the commodity backing of the playing-card money was uncertain (due to the inability of public officials to keep their promises), whereas the existence of the

(continued)

Yap stones was well known to essentially everyone on the island of Yap.

[1]W. Furness, 1910, *The Island of Stone Money: Uap of the Carolines,* J. P. Lippincott Co., Philadelphia and London.

[2]The Bank of Canada has an impressive Yap stone in the atrium of its building in Ottawa.

[3]See "'Card Money' 3 Livres, 1749," Currency Museum of the Bank of Canada, Industry Canada **collections.ic.gc.ca/bank/ english/emar76.htm**, accessed July 17, 2003, for a description and photograph of card money in New France.

A fundamental question in monetary economics is why market exchange is typically an exchange of goods for money (monetary exchange) rather than of goods for goods (barter exchange). Jevons[2] argued that money helped to solve a problem of an **absence of double coincidence of wants** associated with barter exchange. To understand the double-coincidence-of-wants problem, imagine a world where there are many goods, and people are specialized in what they wish to produce and consume. For example, suppose person *A* produces corn, but wants to consume wheat. If person *A* meets another person *B* who has wheat, that would be a single coincidence of wants, since *B* has what *A* wants. However, *B* may not want corn in exchange for her wheat. If *B* wanted to consume corn, there would be a double coincidence of wants, since *A* wants what *B* has and *B* wants what *A* has. Barter exchange can only take place if there is a double coincidence. Now, searching for a trading partner is costly in time and resources (e.g., hauling corn from place to place looking for a double coincidence of wants), particularly if there are many goods in the economy, so that there are many would-be sellers to search among. It would be much easier if, in selling corn, person *A* only needs to satisfy a single coincidence of wants, that is, find a person who wants corn. This would be the case if everyone accepted some particular object. Then, in selling corn in exchange for wheat, all person *A* would need to do is sell corn for this particular object in a single-coincidence meeting, then sell the particular object for wheat in another single-coincidence meeting. The "particular object" would then be money.

To see how this might work, consider the following simple economy, depicted in Figure 14.1. The example is from the work of Nobuhiro Kiyotaki and Randall Wright,[3] who formalized Jevons' notion of the role of money using modern dynamic methods. There are three types of people in this economy. Type I people consume good 1 and produce good 2, type II people consume good 2 and produce good 3, and type III people consume good 3 and produce good 1. There are many people of each type in the economy, and everyone lives forever, with people meeting each other pairwise and at random each period. That is, each person meets one other person each period, and that other person is someone he or she bumps into at random. If the people in this economy each produce their good, and then wait until they meet another person with whom they can engage in a barter exchange, everyone will wait forever to trade, since this economy has an absence of double coincidence of wants. This is the simplest type of

[2]See S. Jevons, 1910, *Money and the Mechanism of Exchange,* 23rd ed., Kegan Paul.

[3]N. Kiyotaki and R. Wright, 1989, "On Money as a Medium of Exchange," *Journal of Political Economy* 97, 927–954.

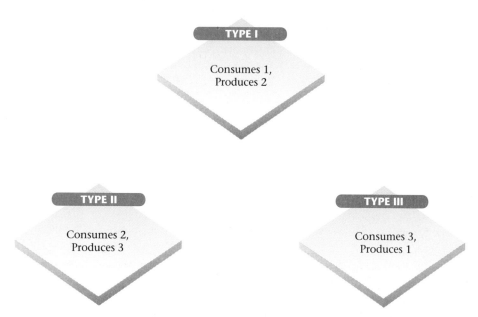

FIGURE 14.1
An Absence-of-Double-Coincidence Economy
In the model there are three types of people. A type I person consumes good 1 and produces good 2, a type II person consumes good 2 and produces good 3, and a type III person consumes good 3 and produces good 1.

example where there are no possible pairwise meetings where a double coincidence of wants occurs.

How might trade be accomplished here? One solution would be for people to use a commodity money. Suppose, for example, that good 1 can be stored at a relatively low cost. Then good 1 might be used as a commodity money, in that type II people accept good 1 in exchange for good 3 when meeting type III people. Why does type II accept good 1 even though it is not something he or she consumes? This situation occurs because type II knows that type I will accept good 1 in exchange for good 2 (this is a double-coincidence trade). Good 1 in this example is then a commodity money—a medium of exchange—as it is accepted in exchange by people who do not ultimately consume it. We show the equilibrium patterns of trade in Figure 14.2.

Another solution to the absence-of-double-coincidence problem would be the introduction of a fourth good, fiat money, which no one consumes but is acceptable to everyone in exchange for goods. A possible equilibrium pattern of exchange is shown in Figure 14.3. Here, when types I and II meet, II buys good 2 with money; when I and III meet, I buys good 1 with money; and when III and II meet, III buys good 3 with money. Thus, money circulates clockwise in Figure 14.3, and goods are passed counter-clockwise.

For this model to say something interesting about the conditions under which commodity money would be useful, and when fiat money would be better than commodity money, we would have to introduce costs of counterfeiting, the resource costs of producing commodity money, and so forth. This would be quite complicated to do. However, this simple model captures the essentials of the absence-of-double-coincidence problem and why this helps to make money socially useful in promoting exchange. Barter exchange is difficult, in fact impossible in this example, unless individuals accept

FIGURE 14.2

Good 1 as a Commodity Money in the Absence-of-Double-Coincidence Economy

Given the absence-of-double-coincidence problem, one solution is to have good 1 serve as a commodity money. A type II person accepts good 1 even though he or she does not consume it. Good 1 is held by type II until he or she can exchange it for good 2 with a type I person.

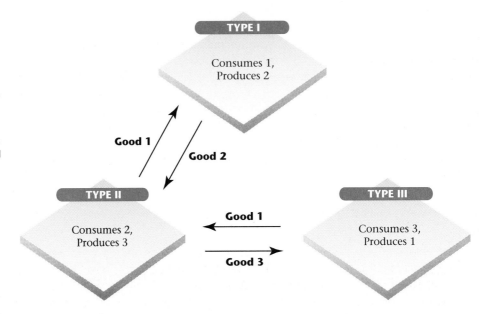

objects that they do not consume. That is, a medium of exchange—money—is essential in allowing people to exchange what they do not want for what they want, and it therefore increases welfare. In fact, in this example the institution of money is a Pareto improvement (recall our discussion from Chapter 5), since it increases welfare for everyone over what it would be otherwise.

FIGURE 14.3

Fiat Money in the Absence-of-Double-Coincidence Economy

The double-coincidence problem can be solved if the people in this economy all accept fiat money. Money circulates clockwise in the figure, while goods are passed counterclockwise.

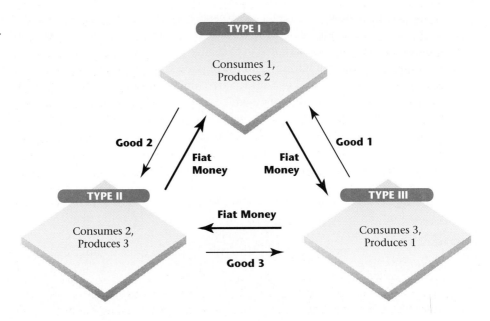

Financial Intermediation and Banking

While the absence-of-double-coincidence model in the previous section tells us something about the role that commodity money and fiat money play in encouraging economic exchange, we need to know more about the place of banking in the monetary system. Earlier, we discussed the historical importance of currency issued by private banks, and how in modern economies much of transactions activity takes place using bank deposits. The role that banks and other financial intermediaries play in the economy is intimately related to the properties of different assets, and so in the following subsection we discuss the characteristics of assets and their economic importance.

PROPERTIES OF ASSETS

The four most important properties of assets are rate of return, risk, maturity, and liquidity; we will discuss each of these in turn.

rate of return: The rate of return on an asset is the payoff on the asset over some specified period of time divided by the initial investment in the asset, minus one. For example, the one-period rate of return on an asset bought at price q_t in period t, sold at price q_{t+1} in period $t+1$, with a payout (say a dividend on a stock) of d in period $t+1$, would be

$$r_t^a = \frac{q_{t+1}+1+d}{q_t} - 1.$$

Everything else held constant, consumers prefer assets that bear higher rates of return.

risk: In modern finance theory, the risk that matters for a consumer's behaviour is the risk an asset contributes to the consumer's entire **portfolio**, where a portfolio is the entire set of assets the consumer holds. For example, a set of stocks might be quite risky on an individual basis, since their rates of return fluctuate a great deal over time. However, when all these stocks are held together in a well-diversified portfolio, the entire portfolio may not be very risky. For instance, holding all one's wealth in shares of Joe's Restaurant might be quite risky, but holding shares in all the restaurants in town might not be very risky at all. Even though diversifying one's portfolio by holding many different assets reduces risk, because the rates of return on some assets can go up while other rates of return go down, there is a limit to the risk reduction that can be gained from diversification. Risk that cannot be diversified away is aggregate or macroeconomic risk, and it is the amount of this **nondiversifiable risk** present in a particular asset that matters for economic behaviour. Here, we will assume that consumers are **risk-averse**, so that, everything else held constant, a consumer will prefer to hold assets with less nondiversifiable risk.

maturity: Maturity refers to the time it takes for an asset to pay off. For some assets, maturity is a straightforward concept. For example, a 3-month Treasury bill is a security issued by the Canadian government that pays its face value three months from the date of issue, and so maturity in this case is three months. For some other assets, however, this is not so clear, as in the case of a long-maturity bond.

Many bonds provide for coupon payments, which are amounts the bearer receives at fixed intervals until the bond matures, when it pays its face value. Thus, a 30-year bond that provides for coupon payments at monthly intervals does not have a maturity of 30 years, but something less than that, since the payoffs on the asset take place during the 30-year period until all payoffs are received. All other things held constant, a consumer will prefer a short-maturity asset to a long-maturity asset. Short-maturity assets imply more flexibility in meeting unanticipated needs for funds, and even if a consumer is certain the funds will not be needed until far into the future (e.g., suppose the consumer is saving for a child's education), it is possible to meet this need by holding a string of short-maturity assets rather than a long-maturity asset.

liquidity: The final asset characteristic is liquidity, which is a measure of how long it takes to sell an asset for its market value, and of how high the costs are of selling the asset. Since money is widely acceptable in exchange and can therefore essentially be sold for its market value instantaneously, it is the most liquid asset. A good example of an illiquid asset is a house, which can often take weeks to sell, with a high transaction fee paid to an intermediary—the real estate agent—to find a buyer. Liquidity is important to an asset holder, since investors face uncertainty about when they want to purchase goods or assets. For example, consumers may face unforeseen expenses such as medical bills, or they may want to take advantage of an unanticipated investment opportunity. All else held constant, consumers prefer more liquidity to less liquidity.

FINANCIAL INTERMEDIATION

Now that we know something about the properties of assets, we can examine the role of financial intermediaries in the monetary system.

A financial intermediary is defined by the following characteristics:

1. It borrows from one group of economic agents and lends to another.
2. The group of economic agents it borrows from is large, and so is the group it lends to. That is, a financial intermediary is well diversified.
3. It transforms assets. That is, the properties of its liabilities are different from the properties of its assets.
4. It processes information.

Examples of financial intermediaries are insurance companies, mutual funds, and depository institutions. The economic role these intermediaries play is intimately related to their four defining characteristics. Consider depository institutions as an example. Depository institutions include chartered banks, mortgage and trust companies, credit unions, and caisses populaires. These institutions exist in part because of difficulties in getting together ultimate borrowers and ultimate lenders. To see why this is so, consider how the borrowing and lending done by a depository institution would take place in the absence of this institution. An individual wanting to borrow to purchase a house, for example, would have to first find a lender willing to lend him or her the funds to make the purchase. Even if the potential borrower were well known to the potential lender, the potential lender may not have good information on the potential borrower's ability to repay the loan, and some time and effort would have to be forgone to acquire this information. Further, given that the loan required is sizable, the potential borrower might have to approach several potential lenders to finance the purchase, and each of these would have to incur information costs to ascertain the riskiness of the loan. Now, supposing the loan is made, each of the lenders would bear some risk, given that there is always some chance the borrower will not repay. Further, unless the lenders had the means to enforce the contract, the borrower might try to abscond without repaying, even though he or she could repay. Finally, after the loan is made, it would be difficult for the lender to sell the loan to someone else should he or she require funds on short notice. That is, the loan is illiquid, in part because it has a long maturity. In fact, given the high value of the loan relative to the potential borrower's income, the maturity of the loan may be so long that few potential lenders would want to tie up funds for this length of time.

To summarize, there are six potential problems with direct lending from ultimate lenders to ultimate borrowers, without the benefit of a financial intermediary:

1. Matching borrowers with lenders is costly in time and effort.

2. The ultimate lenders may not be skilled at evaluating credit risks.

3. Because several lenders would often be required to fund any one borrower, there would be replication of the costs required to evaluate credit risk.

4. Because lenders economize on information costs by lending to few borrowers, lending will be risky.

5. Loans will tend to be illiquid.

6. Loans will tend to have longer maturities than lenders would like.

Without financial intermediaries, few loans would be made, and the only lending would be to the least risky borrowers. However, in our running example, consider what a depository institution can do to alleviate the above six difficulties. First, the depository institution is a well-defined place of business, and people know where to go if they wish to borrow or lend, and so this eliminates the search costs involved in getting borrowers and lenders together. Second, the depository institution specializes in evaluating credit risks, and so can do this at a lower cost per loan than an unspecialized individual. That is, there are economies of scale in acquiring information. Third, because the financial intermediary pools the funds of many lenders, it can avoid the replication of costs that occurs with direct lending. Fourth, because the financial intermediary is well diversified with respect to both its assets and liabilities, it can transform risky, illiquid, long-maturity assets into relatively safe, liquid, short-maturity liabilities.

Taking a depository institution specializing in mortgage lending as an example, each mortgage may be risky, illiquid, and of long maturity. However, because the depository institution holds many mortgages (it is well diversified on the asset side of its balance sheet), the payoff on the bank's entire asset portfolio will be relatively predictable, since the fraction of mortgage loans that default should be predictable. Further, even though all the assets of the depository institution are illiquid and of long maturity, the institution's liabilities can be liquid and of short maturity because of the diversification of its liabilities. That is, suppose that the depository institution has many depositors, all holding transactions accounts. An individual depositor could decide to make withdrawals and deposits or to make debit card transactions at random times, but the behaviour of depositors as a group will be predictable. Thus, though a transactions deposit is highly liquid and has as short a maturity as the depositor could wish for, the institution can make highly illiquid and long-maturity loans on the basis of its ability to predict the aggregate behaviour of a large number of depositors.

Depository Institutions While depository institutions share many features with other financial intermediaries—they borrow from one group of economic agents, lend to another group of economic agents, are well diversified, transform assets, and process information—they are special in that their liabilities are used intensively in transactions. Because of their important role in the transactions system, depository institutions interact more intimately than other financial intermediaries with the central bank, and monetary policy actions typically have their primary, and perhaps most important, effects on depository institutions.

To understand the role played by depository institutions in Canada, we need to understand the unique features of the Canadian financial system. An important element of the Canadian financial system is the set of networks through which financial institutions make transactions among themselves. These financial networks are operated by a not-for-profit organization, the **Canadian Payments Association (CPA)**. Most important financial institutions in Canada, including all chartered banks and the Bank of Canada, are members of the CPA. The CPA runs three payments systems, the **Automated Clearing and Settlement System (ACSS)**, the **U.S. Dollar Bulk Exchange (USBE)**, and the **Large Value Transfer System (LVTS)**. These are all electronic transfer systems for clearing and settling payments among financial institutions. Clearing generally refers to the exchange of assets among financial institutions, while settlement is the debiting and crediting of the accounts of financial institutions that finalizes payment.

To give an example of how financial clearing and settlement takes place, consider the clearing of debit card transactions that takes place through the ACSS. Every day, some consumers with transactions deposits in the Bank of Montreal make debit card purchases from retailers, and some of these retailers hold transactions accounts with the Royal Bank. Similarly, some consumers with transactions deposits in the Royal Bank make debit card purchases from retailers who have transactions accounts at the Bank of Montreal. Every day, through the ACSS, the total quantity of such transactions is determined electronically. Suppose that, on a given day, consumers with Bank of Montreal accounts make $50 million in debit card purchases from retailers with Royal Bank accounts, and consumers with Royal Bank accounts make $48 million in debit card purchases from retailers with Bank of Montreal accounts. One way for the Bank of Montreal and the Royal Bank to settle these transactions would be for the Bank of Montreal to transfer $50 million to the Royal Bank, and the Royal Bank to transfer $48 million to the Bank of Montreal. Of course, this is inefficient, and would in general result in greater transactions costs than if the Bank of Montreal simply made a payment of $2 million to the Royal Bank. This is called **net settlement**, and is key to how all of the payments systems in Canada operate.

In the ACSS, the key players are 11 **direct clearers**, including the major chartered banks and the Bank of Canada, who settle among themselves using their deposits with the Bank of Canada. Indirect clearers settle by transferring account balances they hold with direct clearers. The USBE is a payment system for clearing and settling U.S. dollar transactions among financial institutions. The LVTS has 14 members that, as with the ACSS, include the major chartered banks and the Bank of Canada. Settlement through the LVTS takes place through transfers of deposits held with the Bank of Canada.

To better understand the role played by the key depository institutions that are members of the LVTS, it is useful to consider the simplified balance sheet of such an institution shown in Table 14.1. We will discuss each of the entries in Table 14.1 in turn.

settlement balances: Settlement balances are deposits with the Bank of Canada, held by direct clearers in the ACSS and by members of the LVTS. These deposits bear interest, and are transferred at the end of the day in LVTS settlement and at the beginning of the day in ACSS settlement.

currency: Depository institutions hold currency on hand so that their depositors can withdraw currency as needed. Together, settlement balances and currency on hand make up reserves, which is part of the stock of outside money.

loans: The loans made by a depository institution typically consist of consumer lending (including auto loans), mortgage lending, and lending to firms.

overnight lending: Members of the LVTS can borrow funds overnight if they have insufficient settlement balances on hand to settle with the LVTS at the end of the day.

government securities: These are interest-bearing government securities, the most liquid of which are short-term federal government Treasury bills.

transactions deposits: In considering how the monetary system functions, we are primarily interested in the liabilities of financial institutions that are used in transactions. Depository institutions also issue other kinds of deposits, such as savings deposits and time deposits. These other deposits are not used directly in transactions; but they bear on how the monetary system works, since they can be converted with relative ease into currency or transactions deposits, which can then be used in transactions.

overnight borrowing: If a member of the LVTS has more funds available at the end of the day than is required to make settlement, this can be lent overnight to other members.

TABLE 14.1 Simplified Depository Institution's Balance Sheet

Assets	Liabilities
Settlement balances	Transaction deposits
Currency	Overnight borrowing
Loans	Advances from the Bank of Canada
Overnight lending	
Government securities	

advances from the Bank of Canada: Members of the LVTS and direct clearers in the ACSS can borrow overnight from the Bank of Canada.

The problem a depository institution solves if a member of LVTS is to maximize its profits (the total return on its assets minus the total return on its liabilities) while having sufficient currency and settlement balances (reserves) on hand to satisfy withdrawal demand from depositors and to settle transactions with other members of the LVTS, respectively. Short-term government securities play the role of secondary reserves, since they are easy to sell at short notice to replenish reserves. There may be times when withdrawals are unexpectedly large, and the depository institution will need to borrow overnight or from the Bank of Canada in order to have sufficient reserves.

Central Banking

The central bank of Canada, the Bank of Canada, is a Crown corporation. The Bank Act of July 3, 1934 stated that the role of the Bank of Canada would be "to regulate credit and currency in the best interests of the economic life of the nation." The Bank of Canada officially commenced operations in 1935, and was thus a relative latecomer to the world of central banking. The central bank of the United States, the Federal Reserve System, was set up in 1913, and the first central bank, the Bank of England, was founded in 1694.

The key group of people at the Bank of Canada that makes decisions on monetary policy consists of the Governor (currently David Dodge), the Senior Deputy Governor, four Deputy Governors, the Board of Directors (a group of non-specialists from the private sector), and the Deputy Minister of Finance, who is an ex officio member of the Board of Directors. The Bank of Canada sets eight dates during the year at which it will make a new announcement about the course of monetary policy. Policy is specified in terms of a particular **target rate for the overnight rate**, the interest rate at which funds are lent overnight among the LVTS members. While policy is announced in terms of a nominal interest rate target, this operating procedure effectively controls the money supply, as will be explained.

The target for the overnight rate specifies an **operating band** of 0.5 percentage points within which the overnight rate will fall. The interest rate at which the Bank of Canada lends to LVTS members, the **Bank Rate**, is 0.25 percentage points above the target for the overnight rate, and the interest rate at which the Bank of Canada pays interest on settlement balances is 0.25 percentage points below the target for the overnight rate. Thus, if the target for the overnight rate was 3%, the Bank Rate would be 3.25% and the Bank of Canada would pay an interest rate of 2.75% on settlement balances. The Bank Rate and the interest rate on settlement balances specify the operating band outside of which the overnight rate cannot stray. The operating band is set this way because no member of the LVTS would borrow at an interest rate above the Bank Rate, as it would be unprofitable to borrow at rate greater than what the Bank of Canada will lend at, and because it would also be unprofitable for a member of the LVTS to lend at an interest rate below the interest rate on settlement balances.

TABLE 14.2 Bank of Canada Balance Sheet, May 21, 2003 ($ millions)

Assets	
Government securities	40 047
Advances	256
Foreign currency deposits	276
Other assets	880
Total assets	41 459

Liabilities	
Currency in circulation	39 108
Government of Canada deposits	1 258
CPA member settlement balances	307
Other deposits	305
Foreign currency liabilities	135
Other liabilities	346
Total liabilities	41 459

Source: Bank of Canada, 2003, *Bank of Canada Weekly Financial Statistics*, May 21.

To begin to understand how the Bank of Canada conducts monetary policy, it is useful to consider the balance sheet of the Bank of Canada, which is shown in Table 14.2 for May, 21, 2003.

A key feature reflected in the Bank of Canada's balance sheet is that the Bank of Canada is a financial intermediary. It borrows from one set of economic agents, lends to another, is well diversified on both sides of the balance sheet, transforms assets, and processes information. Indeed, the private financial institutions that most closely resemble the Bank of Canada are depository institutions. The largest borrower at the Bank of Canada is the federal government, in that almost all of the Bank of Canada's assets are securities issued by the government of Canada, and more than two-thirds of those securities are Treasury bills. The Bank of Canada also lends to LVTS members and direct clearers in the ACSS (advances on the balance sheet in Table 14.2). The Bank of Canada is like a depository institution in that most of its liabilities are used for transactions purposes. Just like the note-issuing chartered banks in Canada prior to 1935, the Bank of Canada issues pieces of paper, Canadian currency, that circulate as a medium of exchange. The settlement balances of LVTS members and direct clearers in the ACSS (deposits of CPA members in Table 14.2) at the Bank of Canada also serve as a medium of exchange in settling transactions among financial institutions. In addition, the Government of Canada holds accounts with the Bank of Canada for transactions purposes, and foreign currency-denominated accounts are held at the Bank of Canada for executing foreign transactions.

MONETARY POLICY

Most simply stated, the Bank of Canada's job is to manage the nation's money supply. As a Crown corporation, it has considerable independence from the government of Canada, but the Bank of Canada Act gives the Bank of Canada somewhat less independence than what some central banks in the world have, in particular the Federal Reserve System in the United States. The Governor of the Bank of Canada is appointed by the Board of Directors, and his or her appointment is approved by the federal government. The Governor serves a renewable seven-year term. In practice, the Governor acts independently from the federal government, though he or she is expected to consult frequently with the Minister of Finance, and must make reports to Parliament.

The relationship between the Bank of Canada and the federal government has not been without friction. In 1961, Governor Coyne of the Bank of Canada resigned after a difference of opinion with the Diefenbaker government on the conduct of monetary policy. The Bank of Canada Act was revised in 1967 in light of the "Coyne affair," to in part allow the federal government to essentially dictate monetary policy to the Bank of Canada, should it choose to do so. To date, this power has never been invoked by the federal government, but the fact that the option is there must clearly constrain the behaviour of the Bank.

The Bank has two key instruments at its disposal to control the money supply. These instruments are open market operations and the target for the overnight rate.

Open Market Operations The day-to-day control of the quantity of money in existence is carried out mainly through open market operations by the Bank of Canada. An open market operation is any purchase or sale of assets by a central bank. The sale of an asset by a central bank is an **open market sale**, and the purchase of an asset by a central bank is an **open market purchase**. In Canada, most open market operations are **Special Purchase and Resale Agreements (SPRAs or repos)** and **Sale and Repurchase Agreements (SRAs)**. In a SPRA transaction, the Bank of Canada purchases a federal government security from a financial institution with the agreement that the financial institution will buy the security back the next day. Here, the price at which the financial institution buys back the security is higher than the price at which the Bank of Canada purchased the security, so that effectively this is an overnight loan with an implied interest rate, and with the security held by the Bank of Canada as collateral. Under a SRA, the Bank of Canada sells a federal government security to a financial institution with the agreement that it will buy the security back the next day.

To show the immediate effects of an open market operation, we will consider an example where the Bank of Canada arranges a SPRA of $10 million in government securities initially held by members of the CPA. We will show how the balance sheets of CPA members and the Bank of Canada initially change as a result of the open market operation.

When the Bank of Canada purchases $10 million in government securities from a CPA member, the Bank makes the purchase by increasing the settlement balances of CPA members by $10 million. On the Bank's balance sheet, shown in Table 14.3, government securities increase by $10 million on the asset side, and the settlement balances of CPA members increase by $10 million on the liabilities side of the balance sheet. Thus, by making the SPRA, the Bank of Canada has created outside money; that is, the quantity of M0 in existence has increased by $10 million. On the consolidated balance sheet of CPA members in Table 14.4, settlement balances increase by $10 million, and government securities decrease by $10 million.

TABLE 14.3 **Initial Effects on the Bank of Canada's Balance Sheet of an Open Market Purchase of $10 Million**

Assets	Liabilities
Government securities + $10 million	Settlement balances + $10 million

---

TABLE 14.4 **Initial Effects on the Consolidated Balance Sheet of CPA Members of an Open Market Purchase of $10 Million**

Assets	Liabilities
Settlement balances + $10 million	
Government securities – $10 million	

Now, how the economy adjusts to the asset swap that the Bank carried out cannot be predicted without constructing a complete model of the economy, one that specifies the behaviour of consumers, firms, and financial institutions. Perhaps depository institutions will find they have more reserves than they desire, and they will attempt to make more loans, or buy more government securities, which might cause market interest rates (on loans and government securities) to change. Perhaps the consumers or firms who receive new loans or who exchange government securities for the new money held by banks will exchange this money for deposits with depository institutions, currency, or other assets. Thus, there could be an expansion in **inside money** (transactions deposits at depository institutions—money created *inside* the system of depository institutions), currency, and other intermediary deposits. Thus, the initial increase in M0 engineered by the Bank of Canada can lead also to an expansion of the quantities of M1, M2, and M3. Traditional accounts of the effects of open market operations often rely on **money multiplier** stories to describe how an open market purchase can lead to a multiple expansion of intermediary deposits and yield an increase in M1, for example, that is a multiple of the initial increase in M0. These stories are misleading, because they are told under the assumption that market prices and interest rates are unaffected by the open market operation. We emphasize that a complete model of the macroeconomy is needed to predict the equilibrium effects of an open market operation, for example, by building on the models used in Chapters 9, 10, 11, and 13.

Target for the Overnight Rate As mentioned previously, the announcement of a target for the overnight rate implies an operating band for the overnight lending rate, with the Bank Rate at the top of this band. Now, one approach to increasing the money supply might be to lower the target for the overnight rate from its existing level, which would imply a lowering of the Bank Rate. At the point where the actual overnight rate and the Bank Rate become the same (the overnight rate is at the top of the operating band), members of the LVTS who have a shortage of settlement balances at the end of the day will have an incentive to borrow overnight from the Bank of Canada.

To see how lending by the Bank of Canada increases the money supply, consider the following example, where the Bank of Canada makes loans of $50 million to members of the LVTS. In Table 14.5, the Bank of Canada's assets will increase by $50 million due to the central bank lending, and its liabilities increase by $50 million because of the creation of additional outside money. Thus, M0 increases by $50 million. On the consolidated balance sheet of CPA members in Table 14.6, settlement balances increase by $50 million and advances from the Bank of Canada increase on the liability side by the same amount. As with an open market purchase, the equilibrium effects of an increase in central bank lending will depend on the behaviour of financial institutions, firms, and consumers. However, we know that the initial effect is to increase the quantity of outside money in existence.

In practice, the Bank of Canada does not manipulate the target for the overnight rate so as to force LVTS members to borrow from the Bank of Canada. In fact, Bank of Canada advances are rare, as open market operations are usually conducted so as to keep the overnight rate very close to its target. Lending at the Bank Rate is always available though, as the Bank of Canada needs to perform its role as **lender of last resort** to the financial sector. In times of critical financial stress, central bank lending may be key to helping the financial sector operate smoothly. For example, when the New York financial district was effectively shut down on September 11, 2001, intervention by the Federal Reserve System through central bank lending was crucial to smoothing out the adverse effects of terrorist attacks on the U.S. and world financial system.

DEPOSIT INSURANCE

In Canada, the **Canada Deposit Insurance Corporation (CDIC)** is a Crown corporation that insures deposits at chartered banks and trust and loan companies, up to $60 000 per depositor. The CDIC was established in 1967, which was much later than deposit insurance arrangements were introduced in some other countries. For example, the United States introduced deposit insurance during the 1930s Great Depression. One reason deposit insurance is new in Canada is that Canada did not experience the episodes of widespread bank failures and banking panics that occurred, for example, in the United States in the late 19th and early 20th centuries and during the Great Depression (see Macroeconomics in Action 14.2).

TABLE 14.5   **Initial Effects on the Bank of Canada's Balance Sheet of an Increase in Advances of $50 Million**

Assets	Liabilities
Advances + $50 million	CPA member settlement balances + $50 million

---

TABLE 14.6   **Initial Effects on the Consolidated Balance Sheet of CPA members of an Increase in Advances of $50 Million**

Assets	Liabilities
Settlement balances + $50 million	Advances from the Bank of Canada + $50 million

Bank Failures and Banking Panics in Canada and the United States[1]

Though their respective citizens are fond of pointing out differences, Canada and the United States are similar in many ways. However, the two countries do have very different banking systems. While the United States has a unit banking system, with thousands of banks that typically serve small geographical areas (an arrangement that is changing), Canada has a branch banking system, with only a handful of chartered banks that branch nationally. On the one hand, the United States has a network of regulations designed to keep banks small, and it is relatively easy to open a new bank. On the other hand, in Canada banks are typically not prevented from becoming large, and it requires an act of Parliament to obtain a bank charter.

United States banking history has many episodes of widespread bank failures and banking panics. During the National Banking era in the United States, from 1863 to 1913, there were several banking panics, typically set off by the failure of some large financial institution or institutions. During a panic, there were widespread efforts of depositors to convert their deposits into currency, apparently contagious runs on banks, suspension of convertibility of deposits into currency by banks, and an interruption of payments. These panics were associated with significant downturns in aggregate economic activity. The Federal Reserve System, established in 1914, was supposed to correct the institutional problems that caused the panics, but missteps in monetary policy in the Great Depression contributed to a situation in which about one-third of U.S. banks failed between 1929 and 1933.

Before the establishment of the Bank of Canada in 1935, there were no banking panics of note in Canada. Even in the absence of deposit insurance before 1967, there were few bank failures. No chartered banks failed in the Great Depression in Canada, and the most recent bank failure before 1985 was the failure of the Home Bank in 1923. The most recent chartered bank failures were those of the Northland Bank and the Canadian Commercial Bank in 1985.

Why have the experiences with bank failures and panics been so different in Canada and the United States? The evidence points to two factors. First, in the period before 1935, much of the circulating currency in Canada was issued by chartered banks (see the discussion earlier in this chapter). This private currency was viewed by the public as quite safe. At times of the year when the demand for currency was particularly high (typically during the fall harvest) relative to bank deposits, it was easy for the chartered banks to convert deposit liabilities into notes in circulation by printing more notes to issue when depositors chose to withdraw. In periods of high demand for currency a panic could result in the United States, but this was averted in Canada due to the note-issuing ability of Canadian chartered banks. Bank failures are also averted in Canada by the fact that Canadian banks are relatively large and well diversified geographically. One of the reasons for the failures of the Northland Bank and Canadian Commercial Bank in 1985 was that these banks did most of their lending in Alberta, which exposed them to the risks associated with local shocks. In this case the local shock was a sharp drop in the prices of oil and natural gas that caused a reduction in local asset prices, resulting in borrowers at these banks defaulting on their loans. U.S. banks, which are typically not well diversified geographically, are exposed to the same kind of risk, and thus more likely to fail than a well-diversified Canadian branch bank.

[1]The material here relies heavily on S. Williamson, 1989, "Restrictions on Financial Intermediaries and Implications for Aggregate Fluctuations: Canada and the United States, 1870–1913," in *NBER Macroeconomics Annual 1989*, O. Blanchard and S. Fischer, eds., NBER, Cambridge, MA; and B. Champ, B. Smith, and S. Williamson, 1996, "Currency Elasticity and Banking Panics: Theory and Evidence," *Canadian Journal of Economics 29*, 828–864.

An argument for deposit insurance is that it can prevent the failure of an otherwise sound depository institution. Suppose, for example, that there is no deposit insurance. Because a depository institution has highly illiquid assets, it is not possible for it to quickly liquidate its loans when there is heavy unexpected demand for withdrawals. Therefore, suppose that depositors lose faith in a depository institution, perhaps because other depository institutions have failed, and these depositors do not have good information on the quality of the institution's assets. From an individual depositor's point of view, even if he or she still believes the bank is sound, if other depositors are running to the bank to withdraw their deposits, he or she will want to run to the bank to withdraw as well. It then could become optimal for all depositors to run to the bank, resulting in a failure of the bank to satisfy all its depositors, due to the illiquidity of its assets. This bank failure is a self-fulfilling phenomenon, and it need not have occurred.

Now, supposing that there is deposit insurance, all depositors know that their deposits are safe, even if the bank should fail. The fact that a few depositors choose to withdraw their deposits therefore need not trigger a run on the depository institution. In this view, deposit insurance can prevent incipient banking panics.

The main cost of deposit insurance is that it creates a **moral hazard** problem. Moral hazard arises in essentially all insurance situations, because the insured individual will tend to take less care in preventing the event against which he or she is insured. For example, if the owner of a car is completely insured against damages to his or her car, he or she will take less care in driving in parking lots, and will therefore be more likely to have an accident. It is difficult for the insurance company to correct for this problem, because the amount of care taken by the driver of the car is hard to observe. Moral hazard can explain the existence of deductibles in insurance contracts, which require the insured party to bear the cost of small losses.

For a depository institution, moral hazard arises because deposit insurance encourages the depository institution to take on more risk. This happens because the riskiness of the bank's assets is difficult to observe, and with deposit insurance the depositors have no interest in whether the depository institution is risky. Therefore, though deposit insurance can prevent the failures of sound depository institutions that might occur due to self-fulfilling panics, it could produce more failures because of the increased riskiness of banks. Thus, the existence of deposit insurance requires that the regulators of depository institutions impose restrictions on depository institution activities to assure that these institutions do not take on too much risk.

This completes our study of money, banking, and central banking in this book. In the next two chapters, we will go on to examine some topics in unemployment and inflation.

Chapter Summary

This chapter examined the role of money, private financial intermediaries, and the central bank in the economy. Money functions as a medium of exchange, a store of value, and a unit of account. Historically, money has taken the form of commodity money, circulating private bank notes, commodity-backed paper currency, fiat money, and transactions deposits at private banks. We considered a simple model capturing the absence-of-double-coincidence-of-wants problem that can exist in barter economies where people only have goods to trade. We showed how commodity money or fiat money can overcome this problem by providing a universally acceptable medium of exchange.

To address financial intermediation issues, we first discussed the properties of assets, which are rate of return, risk, maturity, and liquidity. A financial intermediary is an institution that borrows from one group of ultimate lenders, lends to another group of ultimate borrowers, is well diversified on both sides of its balance sheet, transforms assets, and processes information. Examples of financial intermediaries are depository institutions, insurance companies, and mutual funds. Depository institutions include chartered banks, trust and mortgage loan companies, credit unions, and caisses populaires.

Our primary interest is in depository institutions, because some of the liabilities of these institutions (transactions deposits) play the role of a medium of exchange, and because they interact in important ways with the Bank of Canada. Financial intermediaries exist because they economize on the costs of matching lenders with borrowers, they specialize in evaluating credit risks, they avoid the replication of information acquisition costs, they reduce risk, they enhance the liquidity of assets, and they reduce the effective maturity of assets. In Canada, the key financial institutions for our purposes are the members of the Canadian Payments Association (CPA), which includes the key depository institutions. Depository institutions make loans, they hold government securities, they hold settlement balances with the Bank of Canada if they are members of the Large Value Transactions System (LVTS) or are direct clearers in the Automated Clearing and Settlement System (ACSS), and they can engage in overnight lending to other financial institutions. On the liability side, depository institutions issue transactions deposits (in addition to savings deposits and time deposits), they can borrow overnight from other financial institutions, and they can borrow from the Bank of Canada if they are a member of the LVTS or a direct clearer in the ACSS.

The Bank of Canada is Canada's central bank, and it controls the money supply through open market operations and the setting of the target for the overnight rate. The overnight rate is the interest rate charged between members of the LVTS on overnight loans. Setting the overnight right implies an operating band of 0.5 percentage points around the target overnight rate. The Bank of Canada lends at the Bank Rate, which is 0.25 percentage points above the target, and it pays interest on settlement balances at 0.25 percentage points below the target.

Deposit insurance is provided in Canada by the Canada Deposit Insurance Corporation (CDIC), which insures deposits in banks and trust and loan companies up to $60 000. Deposit insurance is intended in part to prevent banking panics, but it creates a moral hazard problem whereby banks tend to take on too much risk if they are not appropriately regulated.

Key Terms

gold standard: An arrangement whereby a country stands ready to exchange its money for gold at a fixed price.

cheque-clearing system: The system that allows for debiting and crediting of the appropriate bank deposit accounts when a cheque deposited in a bank is written on an account in another bank.

absence of double coincidence of wants: A situation in which there are two would-be trading partners, but it is not true that each has what the other wants.

portfolio: A collection of assets.

nondiversifiable risk: Risk that an individual cannot diversify away by holding a large portfolio of assets.

risk-averse: Describes an individual who does not like risk.

Canadian Payments Association (CPA): A not-for-profit organization of financial institutions, including the chartered banks and the Bank of Canada, that operates the key electronic payments systems in Canada.

Automated Clearing and Settlement System (ACSS): An electronic payments system operated by the CPA, which handles mainly smaller transactions among financial institutions.

U.S. Dollar Bulk Exchange (USBE): An electronic payments system operated by the CPA, which handles transactions among financial institutions denominated in U.S. dollars.

Large Value Transfer System (LVTS): An electronic payments system operated by the CPA, handling large transactions among the 14 members, including the Bank of Canada and the major chartered banks. Most of the Bank of Canada's intervention in financial markets occurs in the LVTS.

net settlement: A system by which financial institutions settle only in terms of the net claims of one institution on the other, and not the gross claims.

direct clearers: Members of the ACSS who hold settlement balances with the Bank of Canada and thus can clear transactions directly using these balances.

settlement balances: The deposits held by direct clearers in the ACSS and members of the LVTS with the Bank of Canada.

overnight lending and borrowing: Loans between financial institutions that are taken out at the end of one day and repaid the next.

advances from the Bank of Canada: Loans by the Bank of Canada to LVTS members or to the direct clearers in the ACSS.

target for the overnight rate: The Bank of Canada's target interest rate on overnight loans among financial institutions.

operating band: A band of ±0.25% around the target overnight rate. The target overnight rate plus 0.25% is the Bank Rate, and the target overnight rate minus 0.25% is the rate of interest the Bank of Canada pays on settlement balances.

Bank Rate: The rate of interest at which the Bank of Canada lends to members of the LVTS.

special purchase and resale agreements (SPRAs or repos): Agreements to purchase a government security today on the understanding that it will be purchased back by the seller at a specified price the next day; used extensively in the Bank of Canada's open market operations.

sale and repurchase agreement (SRA): An agreement to sell a government security today on the understanding that it will be bought back tomorrow at a specified price; used extensively in the Bank of Canada's open market operations.

money multiplier: The somewhat misleading notion that an increase in outside money is multiplied by a given factor (the multiplier) in equilibrium to yield a given increase in the total money supply (M1, M2, or M3).

lender of last resort: The role that a central bank plays in lending to depository institutions unable to secure critical funds elsewhere.

Canada Deposit Insurance Corporation (CDIC): A Crown corporation that insures deposits at banks and trust and loan companies up to $60 000 per depositor.

moral hazard: The tendency of insured individuals to take less care to prevent a loss against which they are insured.

Questions for Review

1. What are five forms money has taken historically?

2. What do Yap stones and the playing-card money of New France have in common? What are the differences?

3. How does an absence of double coincidence of wants make money socially useful?

4. List four properties of assets, and explain why these properties are important.

5. What are the four defining characteristics of a financial intermediary?

6. What are three types of financial intermediaries?

7. What is unusual about depository institutions relative to other financial intermediaries?

8. List three types of depository institutions.

9. List six features that make financial intermediaries socially useful.

10. What are the principal assets and liabilities of depository institutions?

11. What are the three key payments systems in Canada, who operates them, and in which system does the Bank of Canada intervene, primarily?

12. Why is the Bank of Canada a financial intermediary?

13. What is the Bank of Canada's goal, and what two instruments can it use to accomplish its goal?

14. Explain what moral hazard is, and why and how deposit insurance gives rise to a moral hazard problem.

Problems

1. Consider the absence-of-double-coincidence economy depicted in Figure 14.1. Determine who would trade what with whom if good 2 were used as a commodity money. Explain your results.

2. As an alternative to the economy depicted in Figure 14.1, suppose there are three types of people, but now the person who consumes good 1 produces good 3, the person who consumes good 2 produces good 1, and the person who consumes good 3 produces good 2.
   a. Determine who trades what with whom if good 1 is used as a commodity money, and compare this with what happens when good 1 is used as a commodity money in the economy in Figure 14.1. Explain.
   b. Determine who trades what with whom if fiat money is used in exchange, and commodity money is not used. Explain.

3. Consider the following assets: (i) a work of art; (ii) a federal government Treasury bill; (iii) a share in Microsoft; (iv) a loan to a close relative; (v) a loan to Bell Canada. For each asset, answer the following questions:
   a. Does the asset have a high rate of return or a low rate of return (on average)?
   b. Is the asset high risk or low risk?
   c. Is the asset a long-maturity asset or a short-maturity asset?
   d. Is the asset highly liquid, less liquid, somewhat illiquid, or highly illiquid?
   e. Explain why the asset has the above four properties.

f. Which of the properties of money (medium of exchange, store of value, unit of account) does the asset have? Would we consider it money, and why or why not?

4. A money market mutual fund is a financial intermediary that holds as assets relatively liquid money market financial instruments such as short-term certificates of deposit issued by banks, short-term commercial paper issued by private firms, and short-term government securities. People can buy shares in the mutual fund, which give them a proportional share in the total return on the fund over the period the share is held. The shareholders can sell the shares by writing large-denomination cheques, or through electronic transfers.
   a. Explain why a money market mutual fund is a financial intermediary.
   b. In what ways is a money market mutual fund different from a depository institution?
   c. In what ways is a money market mutual fund like a depository institution?
   d. Should the shares in money market mutual funds be considered money? Why or why not?

5. Suppose that there are two banks in the economy, bank A and bank B. The Bank of Canada sells $10 million in government securities to bank A, and bank A then borrows $10 million from bank B on the overnight market.
   a. Show what changes take place in the balance sheets of bank A, bank B, and the Bank of Canada. What change in outside money occurs?
   b. Now, suppose that in addition to the above transactions, bank B borrows $10 million as an advance from the Bank of Canada. Show the net changes on the balance sheets of bank A, bank B, and the Bank of Canada. What change in outside money occurs?

6. The Bank of Canada purchases $40 million in government securities from members of the CPA. Members of the CPA then make additional loans of $30 million, and they purchase $10 million in government securities in transactions with private consumers. Private consumers, having received $40 million in outside money, then deposit this money in depository institutions.
   a. Determine the changes on the Bank of Canada's balance sheet and the consolidated balance sheet of members of the CPA.
   b. What is the change in outside money, and in M1? Explain your results.

7. Explain how moral hazard arises in each of the following situations:
   a. A parent has his or her child mow the grass.
   b. An individual's house is insured against damage by fire for its full value.
   c. An individual is appointed to manage an investment portfolio for a group of coworkers.
   d. The same individual in part (c) is appointed to manage the investment portfolio, and the government guarantees that all investors in the group will receive a 5% return per year. That is, the government will make up the difference if the return on the portfolio falls below 5% in a given year.

Working with the Data

1. Construct a time series plot of the target overnight rate and the 3-month Treasury bill rate. What do you notice here, and how would you explain it?

2. Plot the target rate, the overnight rate, and the high and low points of the operating band. How close does the Bank of Canada typically come to its target?

3. Plot in a time series the 3-month Treasury bill rate and the interest rate on government of Canada marketable bonds over ten years. Which interest rate tends to be higher? Why is this so? Which interest rate tends to be more variable? Explain why.

CHAPTER 15

Unemployment: Search and Efficiency Wages

To study the reasons for unemployment, we need to understand in more detail how people use their time. In the macroeconomic models we have used in previous chapters, consumers typically divide their time between leisure and market work, but in this chapter we would like to explore explanations for a third activity—unemployment—which, as measured by Statistics Canada, is neither leisure nor market work. Two key features of unemployment set it apart. One is that unemployment entails searching for work, which is costly. The reason the unemployed are willing to bear the costs of searching for work is that there is a chance they will find a job and be better off. Thus, the fact that searching for work is painful implies the second key feature of unemployment: that the unemployed are, in some sense, worse off than the employed. Though unemployment is painful, and the unemployed would typically be better off working, unemployment is a necessary evil in modern economies. Indeed, it would be impossible to eliminate all unemployment, and some government policies that might reduce unemployment would in fact be detrimental to overall economic welfare.

Our first goal in this chapter will be to examine the behaviour of the unemployment rate in Canada. As well, we will study the behaviour of another key labour market variable, the participation rate. We will show how the unemployment rate and participation rate move over the business cycle, and discuss some of the determinants of these two variables.

Next, we will study two models that will permit us to organize our thinking about the determinants of the unemployment rate. The first is a search model, in which unemployed workers look for jobs, and will accept a job when the welfare they receive from working at the wage offered exceeds the welfare from turning down the job offer and continuing to search. This model allows us to show how unemployment insurance benefits, taxation, and other government interventions affect the behaviour of unemployed workers and the unemployment rate.

The second model we consider is the efficiency wage model, which builds on the idea that workers' effort on the job depends on the real wage they receive. This can imply that, in equilibrium, the real wage is higher than the market-clearing real wage, because the higher real wage allows the firm to elicit more effort from its workers. Thus, the real wage is "sticky," and there can be equilibrium unemployment. This model thus is related to the Keynesian sticky wage model in Chapter 10, though in that model it was the nominal wage rather than the real wage that was sticky. Once we have constructed the efficiency wage model and have showed how it works, we will examine how well it fits the business cycle facts discussed in Chapter 3.

The Behaviour of the Unemployment Rate and the Participation Rate in Canada

Before studying models of unemployment, we will explore the empirical behaviour of the unemployment rate and the participation rate in Canada. Recall from Chapter 2 that, if E is the number of working age persons who are employed, U is the number of unemployed, and NL denotes those who are not in the labour force, the unemployment rate and participation rate are defined by

$$\text{unemployment rate} = \frac{U}{E + U},$$

$$\text{participation rate} = \frac{E + U}{E + U + NL},$$

where the total labour force is equal to $E + U$.

Figure 15.1 shows a plot of the annual unemployment rate for Canada for the years 1946–2002. The unemployment rate is a countercyclical variable: high during

FIGURE 15.1

The Canadian Unemployment Rate, 1946–2002

The unemployment rate shows considerable cyclical volatility. In Canada, there was also a trend increase in the unemployment rate from the late 1960s until the mid-1980s, and a small trend decrease from the mid-1980s through the 1990s.

Source: Adapted from the Statistics Canada CANSIM database, Series v2461224, and from the Statistics Canada publication *Historical Statistics of Canada*, Catalogue 11-516, 1983, Series D491.

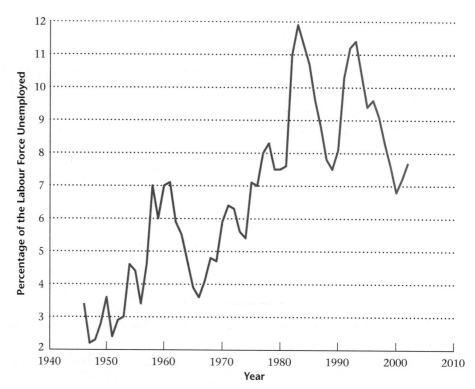

recessions and low during booms. In particular, note in the figure that the unemployment rate spiked during the recessions of 1973–75, 1981–82, and 1990–92, and decreased during the economic booms of the late 1970s, the late 1980s, and the 1990s following the 1991–92 recession. In addition to the cyclical behaviour of the unemployment rate, there also appear to be longer-run movements in the unemployment rate in the figure. For example, from the late 1960s until the mid-1980s, there was a trend increase in the unemployment rate, and a slight trend decrease from the mid-1980s through the 1990s. We would like to understand the reasons for both the cyclical behaviour and long-run behaviour of the unemployment rate.

The key determinants of the unemployment rate are the following:

- *Aggregate economic activity.* When aggregate real GDP is high relative to trend, the unemployment rate tends to be low. As mentioned above, the unemployment rate is a countercyclical variable. In Figure 15.2, which shows the deviations from trend in the unemployment rate and in real GDP (percentages in this case), we see that the unemployment rate tends to be below (above) trend when real GDP is above (below) trend.

- *Demographics.* **Demography** is the study of population. The age structure of the population matters a great deal for the unemployment rate, as workers of different ages behave quite differently in the labour market. The unemployment rate for the young tends to be higher than that for the old, as younger workers have a weaker attachment to the labour force and switch jobs more frequently early in their

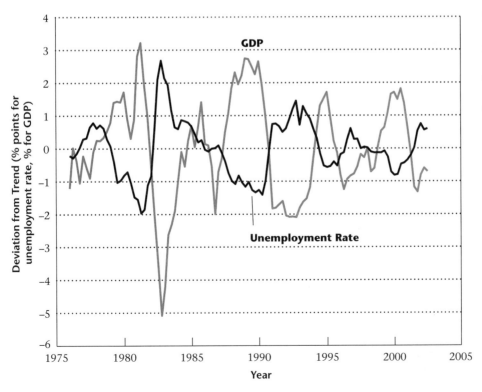

FIGURE 15.2

Deviations from Trend in the Unemployment Rate, and Percentage Deviations from Trend in Real GDP for 1976–2002

The unemployment rate is countercyclical, as it tends to be above (below) trend when real GDP is below (above) trend.

Source: Adapted from the Statistics Canada CANSIM database, Series v2062815, v1992067.

careers, thus suffering more frequent spells of unemployment. In Figure 15.1, part of the cause of the increase in the average unemployment rate in the 1970s was many members of the post–World War II baby boom generation entered the labour force at that time. Then, the average unemployment rate fell during the 1980s and 1990s as baby boomers aged.

- *Government intervention.* A key government program that affects the unemployment rate over the long run is government-provided unemployment insurance. Workers who suffer a spell of unemployment typically experience a drop in their consumption. Why shouldn't this loss be insurable, just as is the loss from an automobile accident, a fire, or ill health? The problem is that unemployment insurance is not supplied by private firms, and the government has taken on this role in most developed countries. Unemployment insurance was introduced in Canada in 1941 under the Unemployment Insurance Act. Its scope was widened and the level of benefits was increased significantly in 1971. Since then, there has been a tightening of the rules for eligibility for such insurance, and a lowering of the level of benefits, culminating in the last major program changes in 1996, when the program was renamed Employment Insurance (EI).

  As with other types of insurance, there is moral hazard associated with EI. That is, the behaviour of an insured person changes in a way that makes a loss more likely, as we discussed in connection with deposit insurance in Chapter 14. In the case of EI programs, more generous EI benefits will tend to make unemployed workers more picky concerning the kinds of jobs they will take, and this will tend to increase the duration of unemployment spells and increase the unemployment rate, as we will show in a search model of unemployment later in this chapter. Part of the increase in the unemployment rate from 1971 until the 1980s and part of the slight trend decrease in the unemployment rate from the early 1980s to the late 1990s in Figure 15.1 can be attributed to the increase in the generosity of the program in 1971 and the later tightening.

- *Sectoral shifts.* A **sectoral shift** is a change in the economy's aggregate structure of production. For example, in Canada recently, there has been a shift away from manufacturing (the production of tangible goods) and toward services (intangible goods). As a result, workers in manufacturing industries have been displaced. Displacement can imply a long period of unemployment, particularly for older workers, as displaced workers may have obsolete skills and will need to acquire new ones, and finding work in a different sector of the economy will take time.

  In Canada, displacement can be a regional phenomenon. When fish stocks became depleted in the Atlantic, there was high unemployment in the Atlantic provinces, which are highly specialized in fishing and fish processing. For these displaced workers to find jobs would require costly migration to other regions. Given the level of aggregate economic activity, the greater the restructuring occurring among industries in the economy, the higher the unemployment rate will tend to be.

We have gained some understanding of the determinants of the unemployment rate, which will be reinforced by our study of models of unemployment later in this chapter. Let us now turn to the other key labour market variable, the participation

FIGURE 15.3

The Canadian Participation Rate, 1946–2002
The participation rate has increased in Canada from about 55% in 1946 to about 67% in 2002.

Source: Adapted from the Statistics Canada CANSIM database, Series v2461245, and from the Statistics Canada publication *Historical Statistics of Canada*, Catalogue 11-516, 1983, Series D484.

rate, depicted in Figure 15.3 for the years 1946–2002. Here, note that the fraction of the working-age population in the labour force increased substantially, from about 55% in 1946 to about 67% in 2002. In Figure 15.4 we show the participation rates of men and women, which show a decline for men and a huge increase for women. Therefore, the increase in the total participation rate in Figure 15.3 is accounted for solely by an increase in the labour force participation rate for women. Some point to sociological explanations for the increase in the participation rate of women, but economists do not find it surprising that more women would choose market work in the face of large increases in market real wages in the post–World War II period. The declining participation rate of men is closely connected to the increasing participation rate of women, since family decisions concerning labour market participation are made jointly.

The cyclical behaviour of the participation rate will be reflected mainly in the behaviour of the labour force, as the total population, which is the denominator in the participation rate, moves very slowly over time. In Figure 15.5 we show the percentage deviations from trend in the labour force and real GDP in Canada. The labour force is a procyclical variable, in that it tends to be above trend when real GDP is above trend. With increases in aggregate economic activity, more workers tend to enter the labour force. That is, when GDP increases, employment tends to go up, and naturally some of this increase in employment arises because of a flow of people from the unemployment pool to the employment pool. However, some of the increased employment also arises because people who were formerly not in the labour force choose to work when aggregate economic activity increases.

FIGURE 15.4

Labour Force Participation of Women and Men

While the labour force participation rate of women has increased almost continuously since 1946, the participation rate of men has decreased.

Source: Adapted from the Statistics Canada CANSIM database, Series v2461445, v2461665, and from the Statistics Canada publication *Historical Statistics of Canada*, Catalogue 11-516, 1983, Series D221, D222.

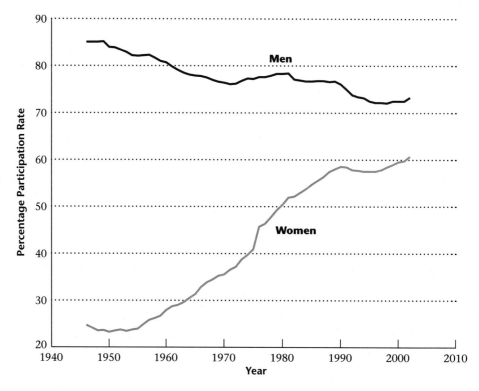

FIGURE 15.5

Deviations from Trend in Labour Force and GDP

The labour force is procyclical: an increase (decrease) in aggregate economic activity tends to cause an increase (decrease) in labour force participation.

Source: Adapted from the Statistics Canada CANSIM database, Series v2062810, v1992067.

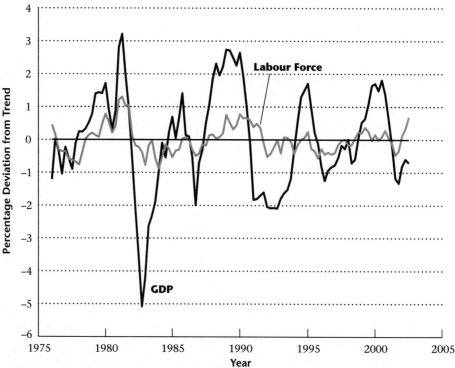

A Search Model of Unemployment

Now that we know some of the features of labour market data, we can proceed to study models that explain the behaviour of the unemployment rate. In explaining the unemployment rate, we need to construct a more complicated model of how people use their time. In the models we have worked with to this point, consumers typically use their time for only two different purposes, market work and leisure. Unemployment, however, is an economic activity distinct from either work or leisure, being an activity that involves search. The first search models were developed in the late 1960s,[1] and they have since been refined and put into wide use in labour economics and macroeconomics. This model will allow us to think about the factors that motivate the search behaviour of unemployed workers, and it will permit us to analyze the determinants of the unemployment rate.

THE WELFARE OF EMPLOYED AND UNEMPLOYED WORKERS

For simplicity, the workers in our model will all be in the labour force; that is, they will be either employed or unemployed, with U denoting the fraction of workers who are unemployed, and $1 - U$ the fraction who are employed. The jobs of the employed differ according to the wages that they pay, where w will denote the real wage associated with a particular job. Let $V_e(w)$ denote the value of being employed. This is the welfare of a worker who is employed and earning a real wage w, and it takes into account the taxes that a worker pays, and all possible future events, including the chances of the worker being separated from his or her job, and what will happen to the worker in such an event. We will let s denote the **separation rate**; that is, s is the fraction of workers who will become randomly separated from their jobs every period. This is a simple way to capture job separations that occur in practice due to firings and quits arising from poor matches between workers and firms. We depict the function $V_e(w)$ in Figure 15.6. Note that $V_e(w)$ increases with w, as the worker is better off with higher-paying jobs, and $V_e(w)$ is concave because the worker experiences diminishing marginal utility from higher-paying jobs. That is, the increase in welfare for the worker from an extra unit of real wage income becomes smaller as real wage income increases, reflected in the declining slope of $V_e(w)$.

Shifts in the function $V_e(w)$ will result as follows:

- The function $V_e(w)$ shifts down if the separation rate s increases. Given an increase in the separation rate, there is a greater chance of an employed worker losing his or her job and becoming unemployed. This makes employment less attractive, and the welfare from being employed at any wage must fall.

- The function $V_e(w)$ shifts down if taxes on wage income increase. Clearly, an increase in such taxes implies that effective wages are lower, which will decrease the welfare of an employed worker for each real wage.

Now, we want to consider the welfare of an unemployed worker, which we denote by V_u. The key determinant of V_u is the size of the EI benefit that an unemployed worker

---

[1]See J. McCall, 1970, "Economics of Information and Job Search," *Quarterly Journal of Economics* 84, 113–126.

FIGURE 15.6

The Welfare of an Employed Worker

The worker's welfare is increasing in the real wage w that he or she earns on the job, and the function is concave because the marginal benefit from a higher real wage declines as the real wage increases.

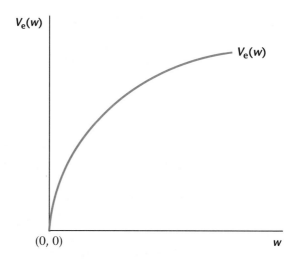

receives. For simplicity, we will assume that the EI benefit is a constant real amount b that does not depend on the wage the unemployed worker earned when he or she was employed. Another important determinant of V_u is the frequency with which the unemployed worker receives job offers, and we will denote this frequency by p. That is, each period a fraction p of all the unemployed workers will receive job offers. Three important facts are the following:

- V_u increases when b increases. An increase in the EI benefit increases an unemployed worker's welfare.

- V_u increases when p increases. With a higher p, the chances are better for the unemployed worker of receiving a job offer he or she will take, and this will increase welfare.

- V_u decreases if taxes on EI benefits increase. This decreases the effective unemployment benefit and reduces the welfare of the unemployed.

THE RESERVATION WAGE

Now that we know how a worker's welfare is determined when employed and unemployed, we can work out how the unemployed worker will make choices. When an unemployed worker receives a job offer, it will be a job offer at a particular wage, w. The key decision for the unemployed worker on receiving a job offer is whether to take the offer or continue searching for work. If a low-wage job is turned down, there is some possibility of receiving a higher-wage offer in the future, but the worker must bear a period of unemployment and uncertainty before such an offer is received. Therefore, if a bad job is turned down, this involves a tradeoff between the short-run losses from unemployment and the uncertain long-run benefits from a good job. Clearly, some wage offer will be sufficiently high that the unemployed worker will accept it, and he or she would also accept any wage offer that was higher than this amount. We call this the **reservation wage**, and denote it by w^*.

Unemployment in Europe and the United States

A common view of unemployment in Europe versus the United States is that unemployment is high in Europe and low in the United States because European labour markets are overregulated and therefore unnecessarily rigid. In an article in the *Journal of Economic Perspectives*, Stephen Nickell argues that this view is in part correct, but that the story is considerably more complicated.[1]

Table 15.1 shows average unemployment rates in the member countries of the Organization for Economic Co-operation and Development (OECD) for the period 1983–96, from Table 1 of Nickell's article. While it is true that, of the 15 European countries in the table, 9 had average unemployment rates greater than the 6.5% U.S. rate, ranging as high as 19.7% for Spain, there were 6 countries with lower average unemployment rates than the U.S.

rate. Further, as Nickell points out, these low-unemployment-rate countries have labour markets with considerably more rigidity than that in the United States, which appears to be inconsistent with the idea that greater labour market rigidities create greater unemployment. The greater labour market rigidities present in most European countries include laws that encourage the formation of labour unions, tougher legal restrictions on the hiring and firing of employees, relatively generous unemployment compensation, high minimum wages, and high taxes. In general, we would expect all these factors to make it more difficult for those searching for jobs to find them, but Nickell shows that this need not always be the case.

Nickell's empirical work shows that high unemployment tends to be associated with poorly designed unemployment insurance systems, a high degree of unionization, high taxes on labour, high minimum wages, and poor educational standards. One of Nickell's surprising findings is that unemployment insurance compensation can be quite generous and still have little effect on the unemployment rate, provided the benefits are limited in duration, and sufficient incentives are given for finding employment when unemployed. Also, high unionization does not always mean higher unemployment, if there is a high degree of coordination among employers in wage negotiations; presumably, this prevents inefficiencies such as costly strikes.

TABLE 15.1 Average Unemployment Rates in OECD Countries, 1983-96

Australia	8.7%
Austria	3.8%
Belgium	9.7%
Canada	9.8%
Denmark	9.9%
Finland	9.1%
France	10.4%
West Germany	6.2%
Ireland	15.1%
Italy	7.6%
Japan	2.6%
Netherlands	8.4%
Norway	4.2%
Portugal	6.4%
Spain	19.7%
Sweden	4.3%
Switzerland	1.8%
United Kingdom	9.7%
United States	6.5%
New Zealand	6.8%

---

[1]S. Nickell, 1997, "Unemployment and Labour Market Rigidities: Europe Versus North America," *Journal of Economic Perspectives* 11, 55–74.

FIGURE 15.7

The Reservation Wage

The reservation wage w^* is determined by the intersection of the $V_e(w)$ curve (the welfare from employment) and the V_u curve (the welfare from unemployment).

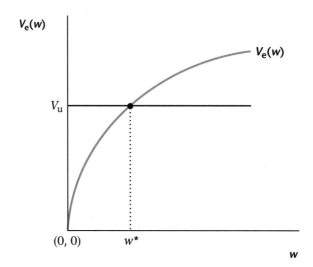

When a wage offer w is received, this implies a level of welfare for the job, $V_e(w)$. The unemployed worker will accept the job if the welfare from taking it is higher than the welfare of being unemployed, and will decline it otherwise. That is, the worker will accept the job if $V_e(w) \geq V_u$ and will turn it down if $V_e(w) < V_u$. In Figure 15.7 we have $V_e(w) \geq V_u$ if $w \geq w^*$ and $V_e(w) < V_u$ if $w < w^*$, and so w^* is the reservation wage that determines acceptance or rejection of job offers.

The reservation wage will change if there are shifts in either $V_e(w)$ or V_u. We will consider two examples. First, suppose that the unemployment benefit increases. This causes an increase in V_u from V_u^1 to V_u^2 in Figure 15.8. As a result, the reservation wage increases from w_1^* to w_2^*. Therefore, with an increase in the unemployment benefit, there is a smaller cost to turning down a job to hold out for a higher wage offer, and an unemployed worker will then become more picky concerning the jobs that he or she will take. Second, suppose that there is an increase in the tax on wage income, which in

FIGURE 15.8

An Increase in the Unemployment Insurance Benefit *b*

The increase in benefits increases the welfare from unemployment from V_u^1 to V_u^2. The reservation wage then increases from w_1^* to w_2^*.

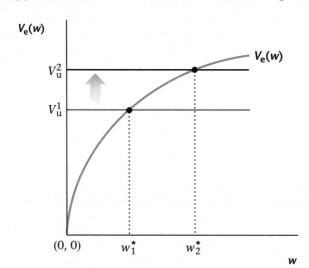

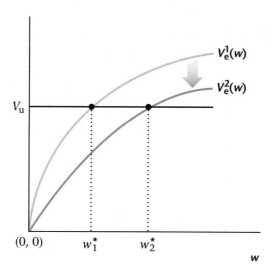

FIGURE 15.9
An Increase in the Taxes on the Wage Income of the Employed
The tax increase reduces the welfare from employment, and increases the reservation wage from w_1^* to w_2^*.

Figure 15.9 causes a shift down in the welfare of an employed worker from $V_e^1(w)$ to $V_e^2(w)$. As a result, the reservation wage increases from w_1^* to w_2^*. This occurs because, for a given wage offer w, there is now a smaller difference between welfare when employed and when unemployed, and so the net loss from turning down any job offer and waiting for a better one is now smaller. Unemployed workers will then be more picky and therefore have a higher reservation wage.

THE DETERMINATION OF THE UNEMPLOYMENT RATE

Having shown how an unemployed worker chooses his or her reservation wage, we can complete our search model of unemployment and show how it determines the long-run rate of unemployment. In the model, there will be flows between the pool of employed workers and the pool of unemployed workers each period. Some employed workers will be separated from their jobs and become unemployed, while some unemployed workers will receive job offers that are sufficiently attractive to accept. If U is the unemployment rate—that is, the fraction of the labour force that is unemployed—then given that the separation rate is s, the flow of workers from employment to unemployment will be $s(1-U)$. Now, let $H(w)$ denote the fraction of unemployed workers receiving a wage offer whose offer is greater than w, where $H(w)$ is depicted in Figure 15.10. Note that $H(w)$ is decreasing in w. Now, if unemployed workers choose a reservation wage w^*, then, given that a fraction p of the unemployed receive a job offer and that a fraction $H(w^*)$ of those receiving an offer are offered a wage greater than w^*, the portion of the unemployed who will be employed next period will be the fraction who receive a wage offer at or above their reservation wage. Therefore, the flow of workers from unemployment to employment will be $UpH(w^*)$.

In a long-run equilibrium, the flow of workers from employment to unemployment must be equal to the flow of workers from unemployment to employment, and so we must have

$$s(1 - U) = UpH(w^*). \tag{15.1}$$

FIGURE 15.10

The Fraction of Unemployed
Workers Receiving a Wage
Offer Greater than *w*

As *w* increases, the fraction of
unemployed workers, *H(w)*,
who will receive a wage offer
greater than *w* falls.

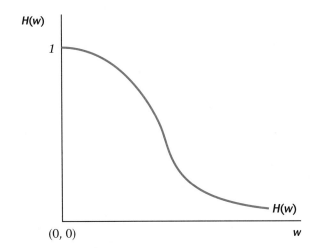

FIGURE 15.10

The Fraction of Unemployed Workers Receiving a Wage Offer Greater than *w*

As *w* increases, the fraction of unemployed workers, *H(w)*, who will receive a wage offer greater than *w* falls.

This equation determines the unemployment rate U given s, p, and the reservation wage w^*. In Figure 15.11 we depict the left-hand and right-hand sides of Equation (15.1), with the intersection of these two curves determining the long-run equilibrium unemployment rate, denoted by U^*.

Now, Figure 15.12 shows how the reservation wage and the unemployment rate are determined in equilibrium. In Figure 15.12(a), the reservation wage w^* is determined by the intersection of the V_u and $V_e(w)$ curves, while Figure 15.12(b) determines the unemployment rate given the reservation wage w^*.

Now that we have a complete model that determines the reservation wage and the long-run unemployment rate, we can use this model to analyze the effects on these two variables of changes in the economic environment. See Macroeconomics in Action 15.2 on page 515 for a discussion of the importance of search theory for the determination of the "natural rate of unemployment."

FIGURE 15.11

The Determination of the Unemployment Rate *U** in the Search Model

In the figure, $s(1 - U)$ is the flow of workers from employment to unemployment, and $UpH(w^*)$ is the flow of workers from unemployment to employment. The long-run unemployment rate U^* is determined by the intersection of the two lines.

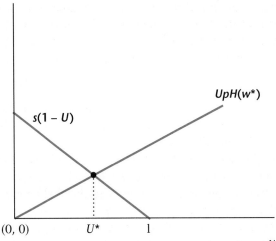

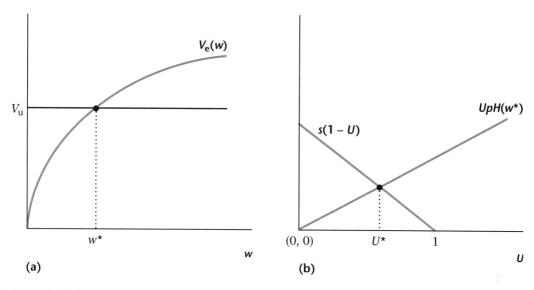

FIGURE 15.12 **The Determination of the Reservation Wage and the Unemployment Rate in the Search Model**
The reservation wage w^* is determined in panel (a) by the intersection of the curves $V_e(w)$ and V_u. Then, given the reservation wage, the long-run unemployment rate is determined in panel (b).

An Increase in Unemployment Insurance Benefits The first experiment we will carry out is to look at the effects of a change in EI benefits. In Figure 15.13(a) an increase in benefits b increases the welfare of the unemployed, V_u, from V_u^1 to V_u^2. The effect of this is to increase the reservation wage from w_1^* to w_2^*. This then implies that the fraction of unemployed workers receiving an acceptable wage offer is smaller. That is, since $H(w)$ is decreasing in w, we have $H(w_2^*) < H(w_1^*)$. In Figure 15.13(b), this implies that the line $UpH(w_1^*)$ shifts down to $UpH(w_2^*)$. As a result, the unemployment rate increases from U_1 to U_2 in the long run.

The intuition behind this result is that more generous EI benefits imply that unemployed workers can afford to be more picky about the jobs they accept. On average, then, spells of employment will tend to be longer, and the long-run unemployment rate must increase. Relatively higher unemployment insurance benefits in part explain higher average unemployment rates in Europe and Canada than in the United States.

An Increase in the Job Offer Rate A second experiment is to look at the effects of an increase in the job offer rate p on the reservation wage and the long-run unemployment rate. Suppose the job offer rate p increases. Such a change would result from an increase in the efficiency with which firms and unemployed workers are matched. This could occur for two reasons. First, there might be technological change, such as better information technology, which could increase the likelihood of matches between unemployed workers and firms with vacancies. For example, the Internet greatly increases an unemployed worker's ability to find work at low cost. Second, p could increase because of government intervention. In many countries, including Canada, the

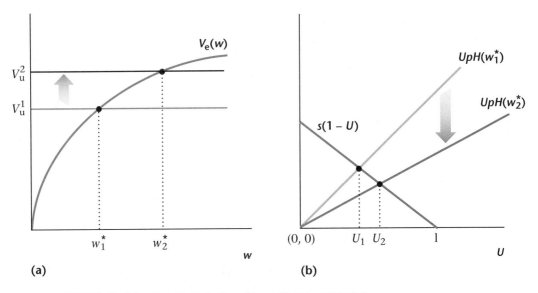

FIGURE 15.13 An Increase in the Unemployment Insurance Benefit *b*

The rise in EI benefit increases the value of unemployment from V_u^1 to V_u^2 in panel (a), causing the reservation wage to increase. This decreases the flow of workers from unemployment to employment in panel (b), and the unemployment rate rises in the long run.

government plays an active role in finding work for unemployed workers, through government-run employment centres and the like.

In Figure 15.14 we show the long-run equilibrium effects of an increase in p. Here, when p increases, this raises the welfare of the unemployed from V_u^1 to V_u^2 in Figure 15.14(a). As a result, the reservation wage increases from w_1^* to w_2^*, since unemployed workers can now afford to be more picky, as they will not have to wait so long for another wage offer if the current offer is turned down. In Figure 15.14(b), there are two effects on the flow of workers from unemployment to employment. The direct effect is that an increase in p from p_1 to p_2 increases the flow of workers from unemployment to employment, since job offers are now received at a higher rate. This shifts the line $UpH(w^*)$ up. The indirect effect is that the reservation wage rises, reducing $H(w^*)$, the fraction of workers receiving a job offer who accept the offer. On net, it is not clear whether $UpH(w^*)$ will rise or fall, but in Figure 15.14 we show it increasing from $Up_1H(w_1^*)$ to $Up_2H(w_2^*)$, which implies that the unemployment rate falls in long-run equilibrium from U_1 to U_2. However, if the indirect effect is greater than the direct effect, the unemployment rate will rise.

The implications of this for government policy are important. If the government uses resources to find work for unemployed workers, then this may be counterproductive if its goal is to decrease the unemployment rate. It may be the case that unemployed workers simply become more picky about acceptable jobs, causing the unemployment rate to rise. Also, workers may or may not be better off as a result. The welfare of the unemployed is affected positively, because unemployed workers have bet-

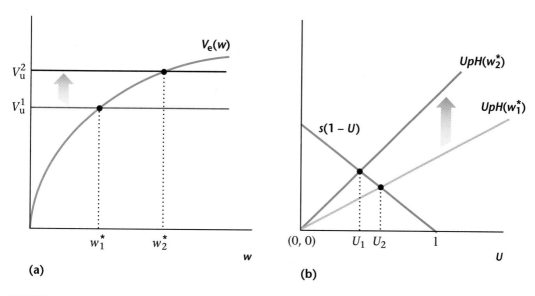

FIGURE 15.14 **An Increase in the Job Offer Rate *p***

When *p* increases, this increases the welfare of the unemployed, who are now more likely to find work, and the reservation wage increases from w_1^* to w_2^* in panel (a). In panel (b), there are two effects on $UpH(w^*)$, in that *p* has increased, which increases the flow of workers from unemployment to employment, but w^* has increased, which reduces this flow. It is not clear how the unemployment rate is affected, but we show it decreasing in the figure.

ter choices, and the employed will in general be working at higher-paying jobs, but there is a cost of the government's unemployment program that will ultimately have to be financed through taxation, and this will reduce the welfare of those taxed. The net effect on economic welfare is therefore uncertain.

Taxes on Labour Income and Unemployment Insurance Benefits Our next set of experiments will involve looking at the effects of taxing the labour income of the employed and the EI benefits of the unemployed. First, in Figure 15.15 we show the effects of a tax on labour income. This reduces the welfare of the employed in Figure 15.15(a), with $V_e^1(w)$ shifting down to $V_e^2(w)$. Therefore, the reservation wage will increase from w_1* to w_2^*. Then, the fraction of workers receiving wage offers who accept them will fall from $H(w_1^*)$ to $H(w_2^*)$, which implies that, in Figure 15.15(b), the line $UpH(w_1^*)$ shifts down to $UpH(w_2^*)$. In equilibrium, the unemployment rate increases from U_1 to U_2.

The effect of the labour income tax is to discourage employment, so that in the long run the unemployment rate increases. This effect is neutralized if the income tax is levied on both labour income and EI benefits. In this case, $V_e(w)$ and V_u both shift down by the same amount, in Figure 15.16(a), so that the reservation wage remains unchanged at w^*. Then, in Figure 15.16(b), the long-run unemployment rate also stays constant at U^*. In Canada, unemployment insurance benefits are taxed at the same rates as other income, so that employment is not discouraged.

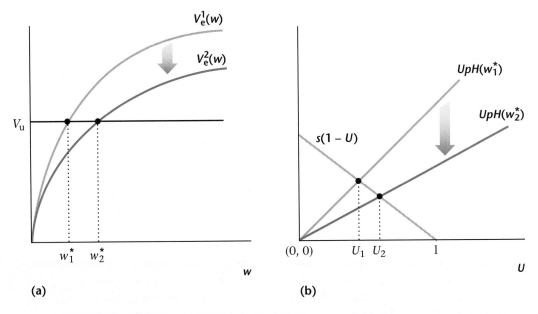

FIGURE 15.15 An Increase in Taxes on Labour Income

This tax increase reduces the welfare of the employed, increasing the reservation wage from w_1^* to w_2^* in panel (a). In panel (b), the flow of workers from unemployment to employment goes down, which causes the unemployment rate to rise in the long run.

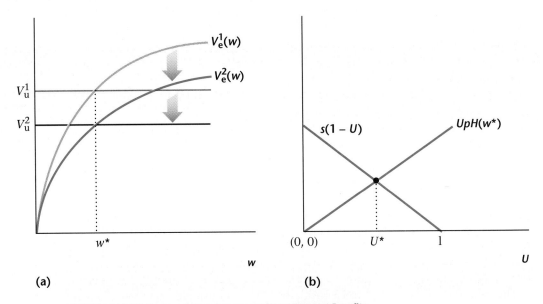

FIGURE 15.16 Taxes on Labour Income and Unemployment Benefits

If taxes fall equally on labour income and unemployment benefits, there is no effect on the reservation wage, and no effect on the unemployment rate.

The Natural Rate of Unemployment and Search Theory

The term "natural rate of unemployment" was first used by Milton Friedman, in his Presidential address to the American Economic Association in 1968. Friedman stated that "the natural rate of unemployment ... is the level that would be ground out by the Walrasian system of general equilibrium equations, provided there is imbedded in them the actual structural characteristics of the labor and commodity markets. ..."[1] Friedman appeared to have in mind that the natural rate of unemployment was a long-run rate of unemployment for the economy, and that there could be short-run fluctuations around this natural rate because of money surprises, working according to the Friedman-Lucas money surprise theory we studied in Chapter 11. Richard Rogerson, in an article in the *Journal of Economic Perspectives*,[2] evaluates the usefulness of the natural rate of unemployment concept in the context of modern search theory.

The search model of unemployment tells us that the unemployment rate can fluctuate over time for many reasons. In the search model, there is a long-run equilibrium unemployment rate determined by factors affecting the choices of unemployed workers, by the rate at which the unemployed receive job offers, and by the rate at which job separations occur. Changes in the unemployment rate may occur in the short run because the economy is moving toward a long-run equilibrium, or because there has been a shock to the economy that has changed the long-run equilibrium itself. In any case, it does not appear to be particularly useful to introduce another economic concept, such as the natural rate of unemployment; it seems sufficient to focus our attention on the *actual* rate and its determinants.

Since Friedman's address, there has been much empirical work that attempts to measure the natural rate of unemployment. Some economists believe that if they could obtain accurate estimates of it, this would be a good guide for monetary policy, since the natural rate might help predict the inflation rate. As Rogerson argues, to best predict the inflation rate we need to look at many economic variables, though this set of variables may include the unemployment rate. Rogerson concludes that the natural rate of unemployment is an outmoded concept that economists would be better off ignoring, in the interests of formulating better economic models and better policy.

---

[1] See M. Friedman, 1968, "The Role of Monetary Policy," *American Economic Review* 58, 1–17.

[2] R. Rogerson, 1997, "Theory Ahead of Language in the Economics of Unemployment," *Journal of Economic Perspectives* 11, 73–92.

The Efficiency Wage Model

An alternative to search theory in modelling unemployment is the efficiency wage model, which takes seriously the notion that workers' wages affect their on-the-job performance.[2] In the efficiency wage model, a firm may be willing to pay its workers a real wage higher than that which would be competitively determined, because this will induce the firm's employees to work harder. In equilibrium, more workers than are

---

[2] For a survey, see L. Katz, 1986, "Efficiency Wage Theories: A Partial Evaluation," *NBER Macroeconomics Annual* 1, 235–276.

employed would like to work, but it is not efficient for firms to hire them; thus, there is unemployment. Efficiency wage considerations will make the labour market work quite differently from the standard competitive labour market we studied in previous chapters, as we will see.

In the efficiency wage model, a worker's effort will increase with the wage he or she receives. To capture this, we let $e(w)$ denote the effort of each worker on the job, where w is the real wage, and the function $e(w)$, an increasing function, is depicted in Figure 15.17. Then, if N denotes hours worked by all workers, the effective labour input for the firm will be $e(w)N$, or effort per worker multiplied by the total hours worked, which gives total effort.

There are two reasons worker effort would tend to increase with the real wage, both of which are associated with information problems in the labour market. First, there can be problems of **adverse selection** in the labour market. Adverse selection problems generally occur in markets where there are different types of market participants and it is difficult for other market participants to distinguish among these different types. In a labour market context, there can be workers of different abilities, but firms may have difficulty distinguishing high-ability workers from low-ability workers. Now, if high-ability workers tend to have higher reservation wages than low-ability workers, because in general they have better options in the labour market, then a higher wage offered by a particular firm will imply that the quality of the firm's job applicants will increase. Therefore, a higher real wage implies that average effort by workers will be higher. Second, there may be a moral hazard problem in the relationship between a firm and its workers (recall our earlier discussions of moral hazard in this chapter and in Chapter 14). A moral hazard problem can arise if a firm has difficulty in monitoring the on-the-job effort of its workers. However, if the firm can threaten to fire a worker if it detects shirking, then the loss to the worker from being fired is larger the greater the

FIGURE 15.17

Effort of the Worker as a Function of His or Her Wage
The curve $e(w)$ gives the effort of the worker as a function of the real wage w. Effort increases because of adverse selection and moral hazard problems.

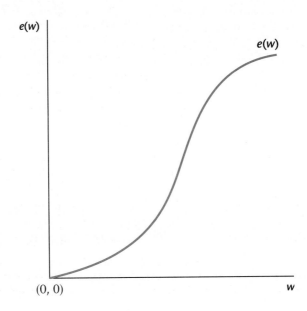

gap between market real wages and the real wage offered by the firm. Therefore, effort by the worker will increase with the real wage paid by the firm.

OPTIMIZATION BY THE FIRM: THE CHOICE OF EMPLOYMENT AND THE EFFICIENCY WAGE

Now, given that the effective quantity of labour hired by the firm is $e(w)N$, the production function for the firm is given by

$$Y = zF(K, e(w)N),$$

where Y is output, z is total factor productivity, and K is the capital stock, assumed fixed in the short run. The firm's goal is to maximize profits. In a competitive environment where a firm is a price-taker, typically the firm will not want to offer a real wage to its workers above the market real wage, as this would not be profit-maximizing. In the efficiency wage model, however, it may be profit-maximizing for the firm to pay a real wage higher than the market wage. Therefore, one of the choices for the firm here will concern what real wage it should pay. The firm then chooses the wage rate w and employment N to maximize profits, where profits are given by

$$\pi = F(K, e(w)N) - wN.$$

The firm will hire labour N until the marginal product of labour is equal to the real wage. In this case, the marginal product of labour is

$$MP_N = e(w)MP_{e(w)N}.$$

That is, the marginal product of labour is the effort of the worker at the real wage offered by the firm, multiplied by the marginal product of effective units of labour. Then, the firm hires labour until $MP_N = w$, or

$$e(w)MP_{e(w)N} = w. \tag{15.2}$$

Equation (15.2) describes a relationship between w and N that we can interpret as the firm's demand curve for labour. Under certain conditions, this demand curve will not slope downward everywhere, but we will assume that $e(w)$ and the production function have properties that guarantee that the implied demand curve for labour N^d is downward-sloping, as in Figure 15.18. The demand curve tells us how much labour N the firm wants to hire given any real wage w.

Now, in choosing the real wage, the firm wants to minimize the cost of inducing each worker to supply effort. If the firm offers its workers a higher wage, this induces more effort on the part of workers, but this is of course more costly for the firm. What the firm wants to do is to maximize $\frac{e(w)}{w}$, which is the effort received from the worker per unit of real wages paid to the worker. In Figure 15.19, if a worker receives a real wage w', then effort is $e(w')$. Then, $\frac{e(w')}{w'}$ is the slope of a line from the origin to point A in Figure 15.19. Now, given that the goal of the firm is to maximize $\frac{e(w)}{w}$, the firm will choose a wage such that a line from the origin to a point on the curve $e(w)$ is just tangent to the curve, as in Figure 15.20. Here, w^* is the optimal wage for the firm to

FIGURE 15.18

The Demand for Labour in the Efficiency Wage Model
The demand curve for labour, N^d, is downward-sloping in this model.

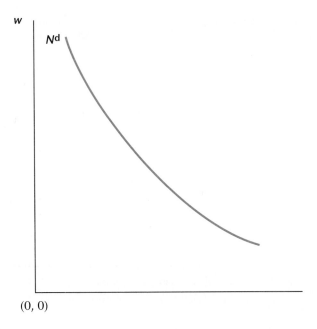

choose, and we call this wage the **efficiency wage**. If the firm sets the real wage at the efficiency wage, then workers will be supplying the optimal amount of effort on the job.

LABOUR MARKET EQUILIBRIUM IN THE EFFICIENCY WAGE MODEL

The efficiency wage model implies that there can be unemployment in equilibrium. In Figure 15.21(a) the efficiency wage is w^*, which is above the market-clearing wage w^{**}, which would imply equality between the supply and demand for labour. The repre-

FIGURE 15.19

The Ratio of Effort to the Real Wage
Given the real wage w', the ratio of effort to the real wage is the slope of a line from the origin to point A.

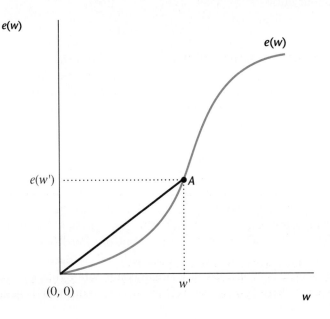

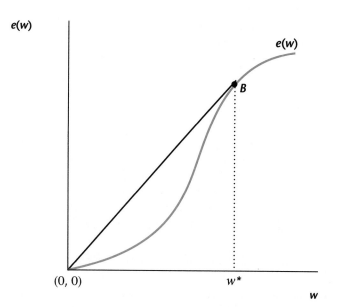

FIGURE 15.20

**Determination of
the Efficiency Wage**
The efficiency wage w^* is
chosen so as to maximize the
ratio of effort to the real wage,
$\frac{e(w)}{w}$. Point B is the point of
tangency between the curve
$e(w)$ and a line from the origin.

sentative firm does not reduce the real wage to w^{**} because this would decrease its
profits, as workers would supply an inefficient quantity of effort. In equilibrium, the
firm sets the real wage at the efficiency wage w^*, which implies that the equilibrium

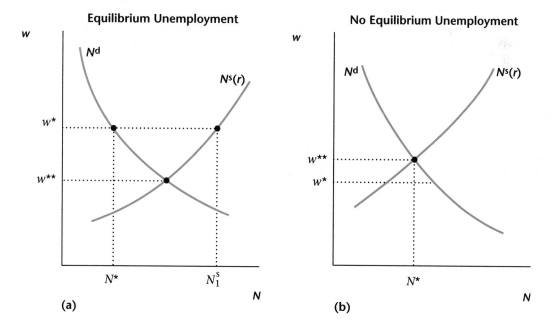

FIGURE 15.21 Unemployment in the Efficiency Wage Model
In panel (a), the efficiency wage is higher than the market-clearing real wage, and there is equilibrium unemployment,
whereas in panel (b), the efficiency wage is lower than the market-clearing wage and there is no unemployment.

quantity of employment is N^*, and the quantity of unemployment is $N_1^s - N^*$, which is equal to quantity of labour that workers want to supply at the efficiency wage minus the quantity of labour firms want to hire. This looks very similar to Keynesian unemployment, though in the efficiency wage model we can have permanent real wage rigidity, as opposed to the temporary nominal wage rigidity in the Keynesian sticky wage model. In the Keynesian model, unemployment disappears in the long run as the nominal wage adjusts.

Alternatively, it is possible for the efficiency wage to be smaller than the market-clearing real wage, as in Figure 15.21(b). Here, the equilibrium quantity of employment is N^* and the equilibrium real wage is w^{**}. In this case, at the efficiency wage the firm cannot hire all the labour it would like to, and therefore it is forced to bid up wages to the point where the market real wage implies that the quantity of labour the firm wants to hire is equal to the quantity workers want to supply.

THE EFFICIENCY WAGE MODEL AND BUSINESS CYCLES

Unemployment in the efficiency wage model implies that the quantity of employment is determined by the labour demand curve. Therefore, labour supply will have no effect on employment and output. As a result, the output supply curve will be vertical, as in Figure 15.22(c), since the real interest rate does not affect the labour demand curve. In the figure, the equilibrium real interest rate is r^*, aggregate output is Y^* [in panels (b) and (c)], employment is N^*, and the equilibrium real wage is the efficiency wage w^* [in panels (a) and (b)].

Given the vertical output supply curve, aggregate output will change only if there is a shift in the output supply curve. If there is a shock that increases some component of output demand—for example, if government spending G increases—then this will shift the output demand curve rightward in Figure 15.23(b) from Y_1^d to Y_2^d. The labour supply curve will shift rightward from $N_1^s(r_1)$ to $N_2^s(r_1)$ because of the negative wealth effect of an increase in government spending. In equilibrium, the real interest rate will increase from r_1 to r_2, with output remaining unchanged at Y_1. In Figure 15.23(a), the labour supply curve shifts rightward from $N_2^s(r_1)$ to $N_2^s(r_2)$ given the increase in the real interest rate, as consumers substitute leisure in the future for leisure in the present. There is then an increase in unemployment, with no change in employment.

The only shock to the economy that can cause aggregate output to fluctuate in the efficiency wage model is one that shifts the output supply curve. A candidate shock is a change in total factor productivity. Now, suppose that total factor productivity increases. In Figure 15.24(a) the labour demand curve then shifts rightward from N_1^d to N_2^d. However, there is no change in the efficiency wage w^*, since the efficiency wage is determined by the schedule $e(w)$, as in Figure 15.20. The output supply curve shifts rightward from Y_1^s to Y_2^s in Figure 15.24(b), which implies that the real interest rate falls from r_1 to r_2, causing a leftward shift in the labour supply curve from $N^s(r_1)$ to $N^s(r_2)$. In equilibrium, the level of employment rises from N_1 to N_2 and unemployment falls. The model is thus consistent with most of the business cycle facts discussed in Chapter 3. That is, the model predicts that, under productivity shocks, consumption and investment are procyclical (because the decrease in r in Figure 15.24(b) causes C

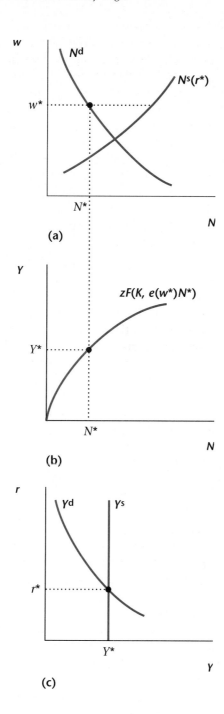

FIGURE 15.22
The Output Supply Curve in the Efficiency Wage Model
The output supply curve in panel (c) is vertical, since in panel (a) the quantity of employment is determined by the labour demand curve, which does not depend on the real interest rate.

and I to increase), and employment is procyclical. However, the model does not predict the procyclicality of the real wage, since the efficiency wage does not respond to productivity shocks.

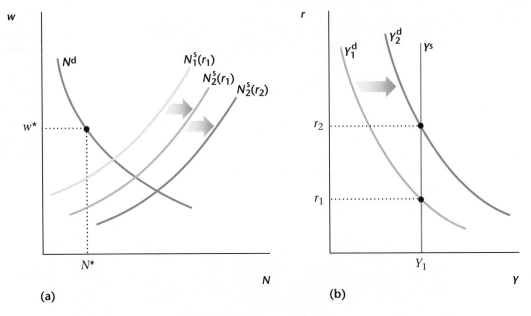

(a)   **(b)**

FIGURE 15.23   An Increase in *G* in the Efficiency Wage Model
An increase in government spending shifts the output demand curve to the right in panel (b) of the figure. This
increases the real interest rate, but has no effect on aggregate output in equilibrium.

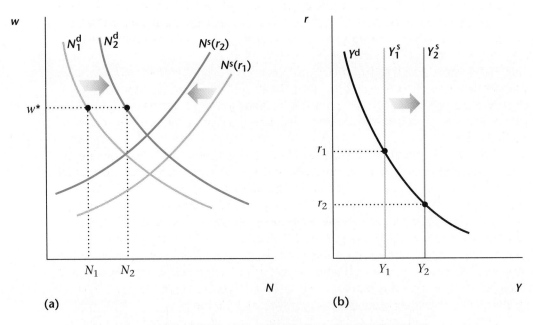

(a)   **(b)**

FIGURE 15.24   An Increase in Total Factor Productivity in the Efficiency Wage Model
An increase in total factor productivity shifts the labour demand curve in panel (a) to the right, and the output supply
curve in panel (b) to the right. The efficiency wage remains unchanged, and employment and output increase.

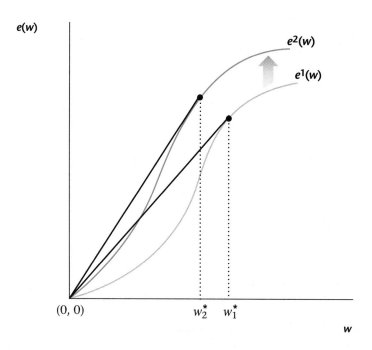

FIGURE 15.25

An Increase in the Effectiveness of Monitoring by the Firm

If firms can more effectively monitor workers, this will cause the effort function $e(w)$ to shift up, and this will reduce the efficiency wage from w_1^* to w_2^*.

The only way the efficiency wage model could be consistent with a procyclical real wage under total factor productivity shocks would be if the change in total factor productivity somehow affected the efficiency wage. It would be useful to explore this possibility. If an increase in total factor productivity is due to better management practices, this change might also imply that firms develop improved methods for monitoring workers in the firm, and this could change $e(w)$. Effort will then increase for each level of the real wage. In Figure 15.25 the effort function shifts up from $e^1(w)$ to $e^2(w)$, which implies that the efficiency wage will decrease from w_1^* to w_2^*. Therefore, this would result in a decrease in the real wage in conjunction with an increase in aggregate output. Then, the model would predict that the real wage is countercyclical, which is inconsistent with the data.

To conclude, the efficiency wage model is not consistent with all the business cycle regularities, though in this respect it is no worse than the Keynesian sticky wage model studied in Chapter 10, or the Friedman-Lucas money surprise model in Chapter 11. A perhaps unexpected feature of the efficiency wage model is that it has a Keynesian-type sticky real wage, but the other properties of the model are actually quite different from those of the Keynesian sticky wage model. We typically think of Keynesian models as having the feature that shocks to the demand for output will cause aggregate output to fluctuate. In the efficiency wage model, however, shocks that affect output demand will have no effect on aggregate output, and changes in government spending will be completely ineffective in changing the quantity of output produced.

This chapter ends our detailed study of the causes of unemployment. In Chapter 16, we will examine how well-intentioned policymakers can generate inflation, and the problems in obtaining commitment by a central bank to low inflation.

Chapter Summary

This chapter examined the behaviour of two key labour market variables, the unemployment rate and the participation rate, and studied the determinants of the unemployment rate using two models of unemployment, a search model and an efficiency wage model. We first looked at the unemployment rate and the participation rate. The key determinants of the unemployment rate are aggregate economic activity, demographics, government intervention, and sectoral shifts. The participation rate is also affected by demographics, and by the different labour market behaviour of men and women. The unemployment rate is a countercyclical variable, whereas the participation rate is procyclical.

In the search model of unemployment, the welfare of an employed worker increases with the real wage the worker earns, decreases with the chances of separation from his or her current job, and decreases as taxes on wage income increase. The welfare of an unemployed worker increases as unemployment insurance benefits increase, increases as the chances of receiving job offers increase, and decreases as taxes on unemployment benefits rise. The reservation wage is the wage at which an unemployed worker is indifferent between accepting a job offer and continuing to search for work. When an unemployed worker receives a wage offer, the wage offer will be accepted if that wage offer is at or above the worker's reservation wage. The reservation wage increases as UI benefits increase and as taxes on wage income increase.

In the search model, the long-run unemployment rate is determined by the condition that the flow of workers between unemployment and employment is equal to the flow in the opposite direction. An increase in EI benefits increases the unemployment rate, but an increase in the job offer rate has an indeterminate effect on the unemployment rate. Thus, government intervention designed to make it easier for unemployed workers to find jobs may not reduce the unemployment rate. Taxes on labour income increase the unemployment rate, but if labour income and unemployment benefits are taxed equally, then there is no effect on the unemployment rate.

In the efficiency wage model, worker effort increases with the real wage as a result of adverse selection in the labour market and moral hazard on the job. The efficiency wage is the wage set by the firm that maximizes the ratio of worker effort to the real wage. In equilibrium, there may be unemployment, but the firm does not lower its wages, as this will reduce worker effort and cause profits to fall. The efficiency wage model has the property that, if there is unemployment in equilibrium, then aggregate output is determined by the vertical output supply curve, and labour supply does not matter for employment. An increase in government spending has no effect on output and employment, and an increase in total factor productivity increases output and employment but has no effect on the efficiency wage or the equilibrium real wage. The efficiency wage model is not entirely consistent with the key business cycle facts.

Key Terms

demography: The study of population.
sectoral shift: A change in an economy's structure of production.
separation rate: The rate at which employed workers become separated from their jobs.
reservation wage: The wage such that an unemployed worker will accept any job offering this wage or more.
adverse selection: Phenomenon that occurs in a market where there are different types of market participants, and other market participants have difficulty distinguishing among them.
efficiency wage: In the efficiency wage model, this is the wage the firm sets to maximize the effort of workers relative to the wage they are paid.

Questions for Review

1. What are the four key determinants of the unemployment rate?

2. Is the unemployment rate procyclical or countercyclical?

3. How do demographic factors affect the participation rate?

4. Is the participation rate procyclical or countercyclical?

5. What causes shifts in the welfare of the employed in the search model?

6. What causes shifts in the welfare of the unemployed in the search model?

7. What determines the reservation wage in the search model?

8. How does an increase in the EI benefit affect the reservation wage in the search model, and why?

9. How does an increase in the tax on wage income affect the reservation wage in the search model, and why?

10. How will an increase in the EI benefit affect the long-run unemployment rate in the search model, and why?

11. How will an increase in the job offer rate affect the reservation wage and the long-run unemployment rate in the search model? What implications does this have for government policy?

12. Explain why it matters whether EI benefits are taxed.

13. Give two reasons why the effort of workers on the job can depend on the real wage workers are paid.

14. Why can there be unemployment in the efficiency wage model?

15. What are the effects of an increase in government spending in the efficiency wage model?

16. What are the effects of an increase in total factor productivity in the efficiency wage model?

17. Which business cycle facts does the efficiency wage model fit, and which does it not?

Problems

1. Determine the effects of an increase in the separation rate s on the reservation wage and on the long-run unemployment rate in the search model of unemployment. Explain your results.

2. Suppose that there is an increase in total factor productivity, which implies that all firms offer higher wages. In the search model of unemployment, determine the effects of this on the reservation wage and on the long-run unemployment rate. Explain your results.

3. Suppose that the government introduces an unemployment insurance program in which benefits are financed by taxes on employed workers. Determine the effects on the reservation wage and on the long-run unemployment rate in the search model of unemployment, and explain your results.

4. Suppose that the government makes it more difficult to qualify for unemployment insurance, for example by increasing the duration of employment required before collecting EI benefits during an unemployment spell. Determine the effects of this change in government policy on the reservation wage and the long-run unemployment rate in the search model of unemployment.

5. Suppose that, in the efficiency wage model, it becomes more difficult for the firm to distinguish high-ability workers from low-ability workers in the labour market. What effects will this have on $e(w)$ and the efficiency wage? Explain your results.

6. Suppose in the efficiency wage model that some of the firm's capital stock is destroyed. Determine the effects on aggregate output, employment, unemployment, the real wage, and the real interest rate, and explain your results.

7. Because the real wage is sticky in the efficiency wage model, does this mean efficiency wages will imply that money is not neutral, as was the case in the Keynesian sticky wage model? Explain with the use of diagrams.

8. Suppose government spending increases temporarily in the efficiency wage model. What are the effects on equilibrium output, employment, the real wage, consumption, investment, and the real interest rate? Is there crowding-out caused by government spending? Explain your results, and discuss.

Working with the Data

1. Construct time series plots of the Canadian and the U.S. unemployment rate. How do the two compare? Provide explanations for any differences you notice in terms of the factors affecting the unemployment rate.

2. Construct time series plots of the unemployment rates of males and females. What are the key differences between the two time series? Have these differences changed over time? How would you explain these features?

3. Construct time series plots of the unemployment rates for the following age groups: 15–24, 25–44, and 45+. Explain what you see in these plots, and discuss.

CHAPTER 16

Inflation, the Phillips Curve, and Central Bank Commitment

Recently, the inflation rate has been quite low in Canada. Using the rate of growth in the implicit GDP price deflator as a measure of inflation, the quarterly inflation rate, at annual rates, has been mainly in the 0% to 5% range, and an inflation rate in excess of 10% was last seen in Canada in the early 1980s. Further, Canada has never had a hyperinflationary episode on the order of the 10 000% inflation rate achieved in Austria in 1921–22, or the 20 000% inflation rate in Argentina in 1989–90. Inflation is of little public concern currently in Canada, and Canadians have been able to avoid some of the truly calamitous experiences with inflation of other countries.

From Chapter 9, we know some of the economic costs of inflation, which arise from the distortions inflation causes in intertemporal rates of return. Inflation causes the public to hold an inefficiently low aggregate stock of real money balances, and it reduces aggregate output and employment below their efficient levels. The costs of inflation are certainly obvious to anyone who has lived through a hyperinflation. Significant public concern can even arise about inflation during relatively moderate inflations, such as what occurred in Canada during the 1970s, when the average inflation rate was below 10%.

If it is widely recognized that inflation is undesirable, why then do governments let it happen? In some circumstances, it is clear that inflation results from problems associated with fiscal policy. Indeed, essentially all hyperinflations can be traced to the existence of large government budget deficits. A government may have high expenditures, perhaps because it must fight a war. However, the public may be unwilling to pay for these expenditures through taxation, or the government may be unwilling to increase taxes. As a result, the government may resort to printing money to finance the government deficit. Moderate inflations, though, need not result from high government budget deficits and the necessity of resorting to the inflation tax. For example, the moderate inflation in Canada in the 1970s was not associated with large government budget deficits, and would not have generated much seigniorage, so what motivated the Bank of Canada to increase the money supply at a high rate and cause what appeared to be excessive inflation? In this chapter, we use a version of the Friedman-Lucas money surprise model studied in Chapter 11 to evaluate two explanations for the behaviour of the Bank of Canada in the post-1960 period. The post-1960 inflation will serve as a convenient example to illustrate some principles concerning the causes of inflation.

The Friedman-Lucas model provides an explanation for the **Phillips curve**, which is the sometimes-observed positive relationship between the inflation rate and real aggregate economic activity. In Canadian data, the Phillips curve is readily discernible during some time periods, while during other periods it is not. The Friedman-Lucas money surprise model is a useful aid in understanding why we should sometimes observe a Phillips curve, and sometimes not. The model tells us that the Phillips curve is an unstable relationship that shifts with the inflation rate that the private sector expects.

Two competing explanations for the behaviour of the Bank of Canada over the post–World War II period are the "central bank learning story," and the "central bank commitment story." In the central bank learning story, high inflation in the 1970s was caused by a lack of knowledge on the part of the Bank of Canada concerning how the economy works. Once the Bank of Canada understood, by the early 1980s, that higher inflation could not permanently increase aggregate output, it acted quickly to reduce inflation. In the central bank commitment story, high inflation in the 1970s was caused by an inability of the Bank of Canada to commit to not using surprise inflation to increase output in the short run.

Ultimately, we will conclude that central bank commitment was probably not an important element in recent Canadian inflation history. However, this does not mean that commitment is unimportant for central banks in all countries and under all circumstances. Indeed, as we will discuss, central bank commitment appears to have been critical in reducing inflation in Argentina in the 1990s after decades of disastrously high inflation rates, and commitment is a key element in the recent poor economic performance of Argentina.

The Phillips Curve

In the 1950s, A. W. Phillips noticed, in data for the United Kingdom,[1] that there was a negative relationship between the rate of change in nominal wages and the unemployment rate. Other researchers found that such a relationship existed in data for other countries. Further, since the rate of change in nominal wages is highly positively correlated with the rate of change in other money prices, and the unemployment rate is highly negatively correlated with the deviation of aggregate economic activity from trend, it should not be surprising that if there is a negative correlation between the rate of change in nominal wages and the unemployment rate, there will also be a positive correlation between the inflation rate and the deviation of aggregate economic activity from trend. Indeed, the term *Phillips curve* has come to denote any positive correlation between aggregate economic activity and the inflation rate. For our purposes, it will be convenient to define the Phillips curve to be a positive relationship between the rate of inflation and the deviation of real aggregate output from trend. If we let Y^T denote trend

---

[1]See A. W. Phillips, 1958, "The Relationship Between Unemployment and the Rate of Change of Money Wages in the United Kingdom, 1861–1957," *Economica* 25, 283–299.

real aggregate output, and Y denote actual real aggregate output, then a Phillips curve is described by the relationship

$$i = H(Y - Y^T),$$

where i is the inflation rate and H is an increasing function. We depict this relationship in Figure 16.1.

Is there a clear Phillips curve relationship in Canadian data? As we will show, this depends on what time period we examine. It is instructive to look at the data in this respect for the periods 1961–1969, 1970–1979, 1980–1989, and 1990–2002. In each of Figures 16.2 through 16.5, we graph the inflation rate, measured as the quarterly percentage change in the implicit GDP price deflator, against the percentage deviation of real GDP from trend. Figures 16.2–16.5 show this data for each of the four periods. In each figure, the solid coloured line represents the best statistical fit to the scatter plot. Figures 16.2, 16.3, and 16.5 show a clear Phillips curve correlation in the data for the periods 1961–1969, 1970–1979, and 1990–2002. That is, for these periods, a positively-sloped line best fits the data in the scatter plots. However, in Figure 16.4 there is no statistically significant Phillips curve.

Now, if we show the data in their time series form in Figures 16.6 and 16.7, we see in Figure 16.6 that there was a large increase in the inflation rate from low levels in the 1960s to very high levels during the 1970s. In the early 1980s, the inflation rate began to fall, and it continued to fall until the late 1990s. This average behaviour of inflation appears unrelated to the behaviour of the deviations of GDP from trend in Figure 16.7. That is, the fact that inflation is high or low for an extended period of time does not seem to matter for how output moves about trend. Therefore, we can make two observations about empirical Phillips curve relations:

1. Clear Phillips curve relations do not exist in all data sets. In Canadian data, we can observe a Phillips curve for the periods 1961–1969, 1970–1979, and 1990–2002, but not for 1980–1989.

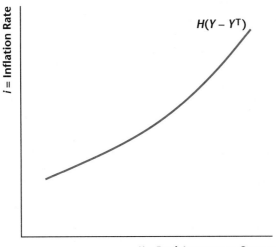

$H(Y - Y^T)$

i = Inflation Rate

Y = **Real Aggregate Output**

FIGURE 16.1

The Phillips Curve
This is an idealized Phillips curve, which is a positive relationship between the inflation rate and aggregate real output.

FIGURE 16.2

The Phillips Curve for 1961–1969

During 1961–1969 there was a clear Phillips curve relationship in the Canadian data, represented by the positively sloped line, which is the best statistical fit to the scatter plot.

Source: Adapted from the Statistics Canada CANSIM database, Series v1992067, v1997756.

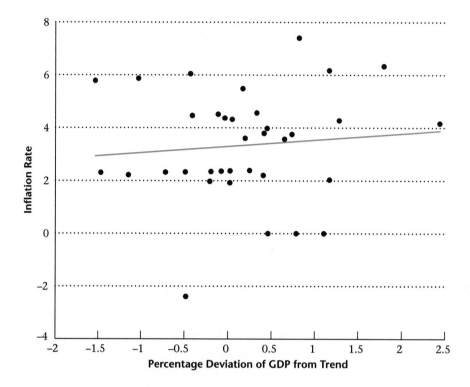

FIGURE 16.3

The Phillips Curve for 1970–1979

In the 1970s, the Phillips curve was more pronounced than in the 1960s, though there is a fairly wide scatter of points around the positively sloped line that is the best statistical fit to the data.

Source: Adapted from the Statistics Canada CANSIM database, Series v1992067, v1997756.

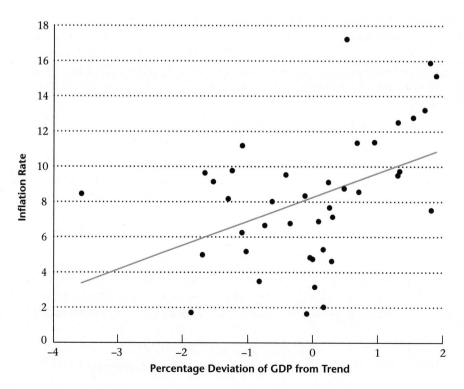

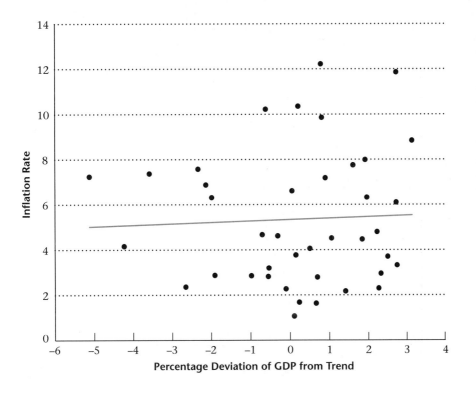

FIGURE 16.4

The Phillips Curve for 1980–1989

During this period, the Phillips curve disintegrated. The correlation between the inflation rate and the percentage deviation of GDP from trend is essentially zero.

Source: Adapted from the Statistics Canada CANSIM database, Series v1992067, v1997756.

2. The Phillips curve relation, where it does exist, appears to shift over time. Over some extended periods the inflation rate is high, but it is low over other extended periods. However, this average behaviour of the inflation rate seems unrelated to the behaviour of deviations of real GDP from trend.

The Friedman-Lucas Money Surprise Model and the Phillips Curve

Now that we have studied empirical Phillips curve relations for Canada, and uncovered the important characteristics of the relationship between cyclical aggregate economic activity and inflation, our goal is to construct a version of the Friedman-Lucas money surprise model that we will ultimately use to understand this data. In Chapter 11, we showed that money is not neutral in the Friedman-Lucas money surprise model. If the central bank brings about a surprise increase in the money supply, then because workers have imperfect information on aggregate variables, the increase in money wages is mistaken for an increase in the real wage, and labour supply, employment, and output increase. The money surprises we studied in Chapter 12 were unanticipated changes in the level of the money supply, but in an environment where there is long-run growth in the money supply, it is straightforward to extend the Friedman-Lucas money surprise model to address the effects of surprise changes in the money supply growth rate.

FIGURE 16.5

The Phillips Curve for 1990–2002

Over this period, the Phillips curve reappeared.

Source: Adapted from the Statistics Canada CANSIM database, Series v1992067, v1997756.

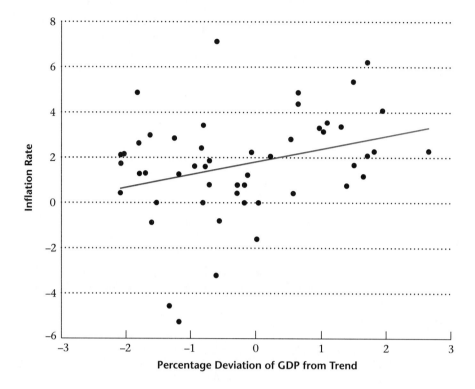

FIGURE 16.6

The Inflation Rate in Canada, 1961–2002

The Canadian inflation rate increased substantially during the 1970s, and then declined through the 1980s and 1990s.

Source: Adapted from the Statistics Canada CANSIM database, Series v1997756.

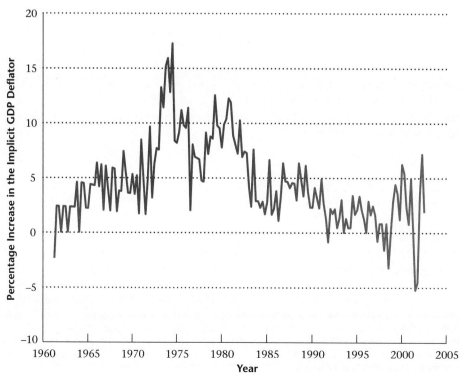

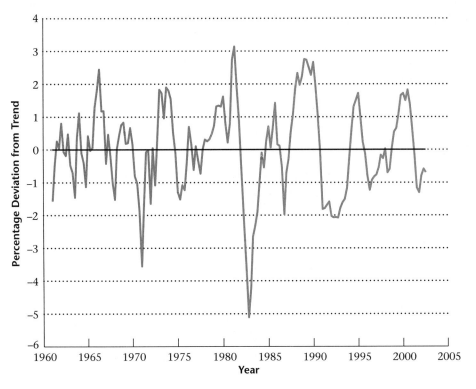

FIGURE 16.7

Deviations from Trend in Real GDP, 1961–2002

The deviations of GDP from trend appear to be unrelated to the behaviour of the inflation rate over long periods of time (compare this figure with Figure 16.6).

Source: Adapted from the Statistics Canada CANSIM database, Series v1992067.

Then, if there is a surprise change in the money supply growth rate, this will imply that there is a surprise increase in the inflation rate, and workers will mistake the increase in the growth rate of money wages for an increase in the growth rate of real wages. Consequently labour supply, employment, and output will increase above trend.

Then, in an environment where there is trend growth in the money supply and the price level, the Friedman-Lucas money surprise model can be summarized by the simplified relationship

$$i - i^e = a(Y - Y^T), \tag{16.1}$$

where i is the actual inflation rate, i^e is the expected inflation rate, or the inflation rate perceived by the private sector, a is a positive constant, Y is aggregate output, and Y^T is trend aggregate output.[2] Equation (16.1) states that there is a positive relationship between the deviation of the inflation rate from what it is expected to be, and the deviation of real output from trend. This relationship arises because real output will only deviate from trend in the model if the central bank increases the growth rate of the

---

[2]There are dangers in representing the Friedman-Lucas money surprise model by Equation (16.1). For example, the constant a in general will depend, as Lucas pointed out, on particular features of central bank behaviour. However, for what we wish to accomplish in this chapter, there will not be much harm in using (16.1) as a reduced form for the Friedman-Lucas money surprise model.

money supply in a surprise way, causing a surprise increase in the inflation rate. We can rewrite (16.1) as

$$i = i^e + a(Y - Y^T), \tag{16.2}$$

which is a Phillips curve relationship, graphed in Figure 16.8. Note that, when $Y = Y^T$, we have $i = i^e$. That is, if workers are not surprised by the current inflation rate, then output is equal to its trend value.

From (16.2), the position of the Phillips curve depends on i^e, the expected inflation rate. In Figure 16.9 we show the effects of an increase in the expected inflation rate from i_1^e to i_2^e. As a result, the Phillips curve shifts up, by the change in the expected inflation rate, $i_2^e - i_1^e$. This provides an explanation for why the Phillips curve is difficult to find in the data over some periods of time. If the expected inflation rate fluctuates significantly, so that there are frequent sizable shifts in the Phillips curve, we may observe no discernible Phillips curve relation, as in Figure 16.4.

UNDERSTANDING THE BEHAVIOUR OF THE INFLATION RATE IN CANADA

The reduction in the inflation rate in Canada from the early 1980s through the late 1990s is viewed as an important success in the implementation of monetary policy by the Bank of Canada. If it was so clear to the Bank of Canada early in the 1980s that the high inflation rate at that time was too costly and should be reduced through reduction in money growth, why was inflation not reduced earlier, and why did the inflation rate increase in the 1970s? We will consider two possible answers to this question, which we call the "central bank learning story" and the "central bank commitment story."

The Central Bank Learning Story   In the late 1950s and the 1960s, the Bank of Canada became aware of the existence of the Phillips curve, through the work of A. W.

FIGURE 16.8

Model Phillips Curve Relationship

This is a linear Phillips curve relationship, from the version of the Friedman-Lucas money surprise model used in this chapter. When the inflation rate is equal to the expected inflation rate, then output is equal to trend output.

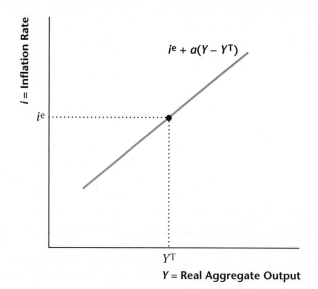

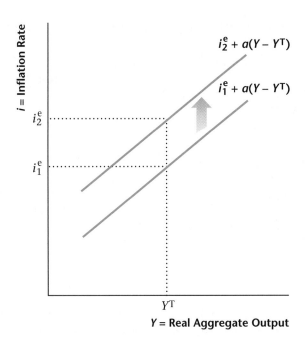

FIGURE 16.9

The Effects of an Increase in the Expected Inflation Rate
The increase in i^e shifts the Phillips curve up.

Phillips and others. The Bank may have become convinced, even though a good theory was not yet available to explain the existence of the Phillips curve, that it represented a stable relationship between the rate of inflation and the level of real aggregate output.

Now, to determine how the Bank of Canada would behave if it operated under the belief that the Phillips curve was stable, we need a device for representing the goals of the central bank. In general, a central bank should be concerned with the welfare of private citizens, though of course there is nothing to guarantee this, since central bank decision makers are guided by their own selfish motives, such as career advancement and the acquisition of more power. We will assume, however, that the framers of the acts of Parliament governing the Bank of Canada's behaviour understood how to correctly align the selfish goals of the Bank of Canada officials with the public good. Then, assuming that the Bank of Canada's goal is to maximize public welfare, it must decide how to further this goal indirectly by controlling some observable economic variables. For our purposes, we will suppose that the Bank of Canada has indirect policy goals relating to inflation and aggregate output. First, there is some inflation rate i^* that is regarded as optimal by the Bank. Some economic models tell us that i^* should be minus the real interest rate (the Friedman rule; see Chapter 9), though in practice many central banks appear to behave as if $i^* = 0$ or $i^* > 0$ but small. If $i > i^*$, the Bank of Canada views more inflation as being more costly, so that less inflation is preferred to more. However, if $i < i^*$, then more inflation is preferred to less. In addition, the Bank always prefers more aggregate output to less, as higher GDP is assumed to be preferred by the public.

We can then represent the Bank of Canada's preferences over inflation and aggregate output by indifference curves, as in Figure 16.10. When $i > i^*$, the Bank is happier if

FIGURE 16.10

**The Bank of Canada's
Preferences over Inflation
Rates and Output**
The figure shows indifference
curves for the Bank of
Canada, capturing the Bank's
preferences over output and
inflation. The inflation rate i^* is
optimal for the Bank, and the
Bank always prefers more
output to less. If $i < i^*$, then
the Bank prefers more inflation
to less, and if $i > i^*$, the Bank
prefers less inflation to more.

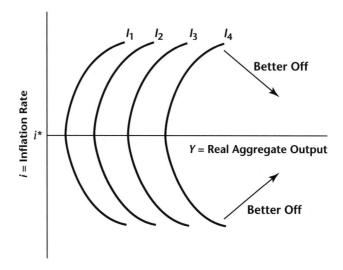

inflation falls and output increases, and when $i < i^*$, it is happier when inflation rises
and output increases. Further, the indifference curves capture a preference for diversity: they are concave when $i > i^*$ and convex when $i < i^*$. That is, as we move up and
to the right along a particular indifference curve where $i > i^*$, output is rising and the
inflation rate is rising. The slope of the indifference curve falls because the higher the
inflation rate the smaller the increase in the inflation rate the Bank is willing to tolerate
for a given increase in aggregate output. However, when $i < i^*$, as we move down the
indifference curve and the inflation rate falls, the Bank is willing to tolerate smaller
decreases in the inflation rate for a given increase in output.

In Figure 16.11 we show the Phillips curve relationship (16.2) along with the Bank
of Canada's indifference curves. If the Bank treats the Phillips curve as a fixed relationship, then it thinks that it can simply choose the point on the Phillips curve that best
suits it. Therefore, if we suppose that the indifference curve that passes through point
A, where $i = i^e$ and $Y = Y^T$, is steeper than the Phillips curve at point A, then the Bank
is willing to increase the money supply growth rate so as to surprise workers with a
higher than expected inflation rate and generate a level of aggregate output above trend
output Y^T. That is, the optimal choice for the Bank of Canada is point B, where an indifference curve is just tangent to the Phillips curve. At B, the inflation rate is i_1 and the
level of aggregate output is Y_1. Note that $i_1 > i^e$, so that the actual inflation rate is greater
than what is expected by the private sector, and $Y_1 > Y^T$, so that output is above trend.

This will not be the end of the story, since the public is being fooled at point B in
Figure 16.11. If the Bank of Canada attempts to hold output permanently at Y_1, then
the public will eventually learn that the actual inflation rate is higher than what they
perceived, and they will revise upward their expected inflation rate. In Figure 16.12,
the Bank of Canada initially chooses point A on Phillips curve PC_1, but as the public
observes that the actual inflation rate is higher than the expected inflation rate i_1^e, the
expected inflation rate is revised upward, say to i_2^e. This then implies that the Phillips
curve shifts up to PC_2, and the Bank will now choose point B, where again the public

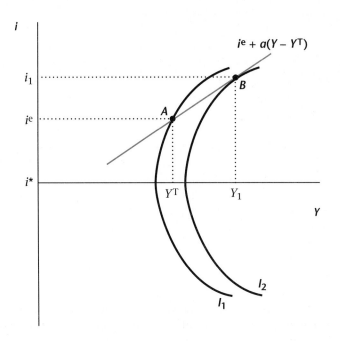

FIGURE 16.11
The Bank of Canada Exploits the Phillips Curve
Facing a Phillips curve that it believes to be stable, the Bank of Canada optimizes by choosing point B, where an indifference curve is tangent to the Phillips curve.

sector is fooled, since the actual inflation rate is still higher than the expected inflation rate i_2^e. Again, the public will eventually catch on, and will revise upward the expected rate of inflation. Ultimately, the economy will come to rest at point D, where $i = i^e = i_3^e$, so that public expectations about inflation prove to be correct, and the Bank has no incentive at point D to change money growth so as to change the inflation rate.

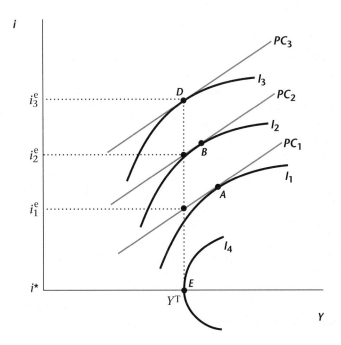

FIGURE 16.12
The Bank of Canada Attempts to Increase Y Permanently
If the Bank of Canada attempts to increase Y above Y^T permanently, then initially it chooses A; but an upward revision in i^e shifts the Phillips curve up, so that the Bank chooses B on the Phillips curve PC_2. Ultimately, the economy comes to rest at D, where $i = i^e$ and $Y = Y^T$.

After experiencing the movement from point A to point D in Figure 16.12, and also after reading Friedman and Lucas's work,[3] the Bank now realizes that the Phillips curve is not a stable relationship, and that it shifts with changes in expected inflation. This implies that there is no long-run tradeoff between inflation and aggregate output; in the long run when the public is not fooled, output will always settle down to its trend level, Y^T. Once the Bank realizes this, it will not optimize by choosing a point along the upward-sloping short-run Phillips curve, but will choose the optimal inflation rate given that the long-run level of output will be Y^T. Therefore, once the Bank of Canada understands the theory correctly, it will want to set the money growth rate so that $i = i^*$, and the economy will in the long run be at point E, after expected inflation adjusts downward again.

This story fits the data on 16.2 through 16.7 in the following sense. During the 1960s and the early 1970s, the Bank of Canada felt that it could exploit a stable Phillips curve, which produced outcomes like the movement from point E to points A and B in Figure 16.12, but by 1980 the Canadian economy was in a position like point D. By then, the Bank understood what was happening, and began the move from D to E in Figure 16.12.

This is a sanguine view of central banking in Canada, since it reflects the attitude that the Bank of Canada will learn from its mistakes and act fairly quickly to correct them. In this view, the inflation of the 1970s was an experiment gone wrong, and an event that is not likely to be repeated. In the central bank learning story, the Bank of Canada is fundamentally sound in that it has the ability to absorb new economic thinking, to efficiently make sense of the new data it is constantly receiving, and to use all this information to make better decisions. See Macroeconomics in Action 16.1 for a discussion of the somewhat different approach to controlling inflation followed in New Zealand.

The Central Bank Commitment Story The second possible explanation for the reduction in inflation that occurred over the 1980s and 1990s in Canada is the central bank commitment story. The theory behind central bank commitment and inflation was first exposited by Kydland and Prescott,[4] who did the first work on the **time consistency problem** in macroeconomics. The fundamentals of the time consistency problem can be explained through a simple example. A teacher is giving a one-semester course in macroeconomics, and his or her goal is to make sure that the students in the class learn as much as possible. The students wish to get high grades, but with as little effort as possible, since they have other things to do with their time than learning macroeconomics. If there is a final exam in the course, the students will work hard in order to get good grades, they will learn, and their teacher will be happy.

However, a problem is that the teacher does not like to grade exams. He or she can promise at the beginning of the semester to give a final exam, but by the end of the

---

[3]See M. Friedman, 1968, "The Role of Monetary Policy," *American Economic Review* 58, 1–17; and R. Lucas, 1972, "Expectations and the Neutrality of Money," *Journal of Economic Theory* 4, 103–124.

[4]See F. Kydland and E. Prescott, 1977, "Rules Rather than Discretion: The Inconsistency of Optimal Plans," *Journal of Political Economy* 87, 473–492.

Learning to Control Inflation in New Zealand: Inflation Targeting

Before reductions in the inflation rate occurred in New Zealand in the late 1970s, this country experienced inflation that was relatively high among developed countries. The average inflation rate in New Zealand between 1977 and 1986 was 13% per year—much higher than in Canada, for example (see Figure 16.6). However, the inflation rate was reduced in New Zealand to 3.3% per year in the 1990–92 period and to 2.3% in the 1993–96 period. In part, this reduction in inflation was brought about through changes in the legal structure within which the Reserve Bank of New Zealand (RBNZ)—the central bank of New Zealand—was constrained to operate, as discussed in a working paper by Michael Hutchison and Carl Walsh.[1]

The changes in the rules governing the operation of the RBNZ were enacted in the RBNZ Act in December 1989, which went into effect in February 1990. Under the Act, "the primary function of the Bank [the RBNZ] is to formulate and implement monetary policy directed to the economic objective of achieving and maintaining stability in the general level of prices." This statement of the goals of the central bank is quite restrictive, since left out are any Keynesian-type objectives, such as "full employment" or "sustained growth," goals that often find their way into the language of central bankers. Given that the objective of the RBNZ as defined by the RBNZ Act is to achieve price stability, how should this be done? The Act also specifies that the finance minister (a cabinet member in the government of New Zealand) will negotiate a Policy Target Agreement (PTA) with the governor of the RBNZ at the beginning of the governor's term of office. This PTA will specify explicitly what price stability means, in terms of numerical objectives, for the governor's term. These objectives are then publicly announced. Should the governor be judged by the prime minister of New Zealand to have failed to meet the goals set out in the PTA, he or she can be removed from office.

In practice, the PTAs that have been negotiated consist of explicit inflation targets. For example, the first PTA agreed to under the RBNZ Act specified a target range for the inflation rate of 0–2% per annum to be achieved by December 1992. As mentioned above, the RBNZ Act appears to have been very successful in meeting its intended goal of reducing inflation in New Zealand. Inflation targeting in this instance seems to have been much more successful than was the targeting of monetary aggregates in some countries in the 1970s and 1980s.

The rules in the RBNZ Act governing the operation of New Zealand's central bank put an unusual amount of structure on monetary policy relative to what governs most central banks in the world. For example, while the Bank of Canada sets inflation rate targets, the Governor of the Bank of Canada would not be fired by the Prime Minister for failing to meet those targets. New Zealand was highly innovative in central banking by setting up explicit objectives and penalties for its central bank. Other central banks, including the Bank of Canada and the Bank of England, have since introduced inflation targeting, though in a less restrictive structure than in New Zealand.

---

[1] See M. Hutchison and C. Walsh, 1998, "Disinflation in New Zealand," working paper, University of California, Santa Cruz.

semester the students will have learned the course material anyway, in expectation of having to write an exam. Therefore, the teacher need not give the exam, as his or her goal has been accomplished, and he or she can avoid the work of grading exams. The plan made at the beginning of the semester to give a final exam is not time-consistent. That is, when the time comes to have the exam, the teacher has no incentive to give it.

However, the students are not stupid. They understand the teacher's motives, and recognize that he or she has no incentive to give a final exam, even if he or she has promised to do so. They will therefore not learn anything. Thus, the outcome is that the students do not learn, and the teacher does not give the final exam. The teacher would prefer to have to grade the exam and have the students learn than to not grade the exam and have no learning, and so the outcome is clearly bad.

Essentially, there is a commitment problem here. A better outcome would be achieved if the teacher could tie his or her hands at the beginning of the semester by somehow committing to giving the final exam. Of course, in practice such commitment is achieved through university rules that bind the teacher to carrying out the promises made in the course outline distributed at the beginning of the semester.

An analogous problem exists for the Bank of Canada if we make some modifications to our model. Suppose that each period there is a game being played between the private sector and the Bank of Canada. At the beginning of the period, the private sector chooses the expected rate of inflation, i^e. Then, the Bank chooses the rate of money growth, which effectively involves determining i. Thus, given i^e, the Bank chooses i satisfying the Phillips curve relationship

$$i - i^e = a(Y - Y^T),$$

so as to be as well off as possible. However, since the public sector is forward-looking and understands the motivation of the Bank of Canada, it must be true in equilibrium that the public cannot be fooled—that is, $i = i^e$. The assumption that $i = i^e$ is a version of the **rational expectations hypothesis**, which states that economic agents cannot make systematic errors; that is, they use all information efficiently. In this case, using information efficiently means the public sector understands the Bank of Canada's preferences over output and inflation, and uses this information efficiently to predict how the Bank will behave.

In Figure 16.13, since $i = i^e$ in equilibrium, this implies that $Y = Y^T$ in equilibrium. Therefore, if the Bank of Canada could commit in advance to an inflation rate, it would choose $i = i^*$, and the equilibrium would be at point A. However, if $i^e = i^*$, then the Phillips curve running through point A is PC_1, and the Bank will then choose point D, where $i > i^e = i^*$; so point A is not an equilibrium. In equilibrium, the Bank's indifference curve must be tangent to the Phillips curve where $i = i_1^e$. That is, the equilibrium point will be at B, on Phillips curve PC_2. Note that point A is strictly preferred by the Bank to B, but A cannot be achieved because of the Bank's inability to commit in advance.

Kydland and Prescott interpreted this exercise as indicating that central bank discretion is dangerous, and that there is something inherently wrong with letting central banks make decisions on an ad hoc basis. The solution to the lack of commitment problem, in their view, is to tie a central bank's hands by imposing some rule to govern monetary policy that would prevent the central bank from using discretion. One such rule for monetary policy, advocated by Milton Friedman and adopted in the 1970s by

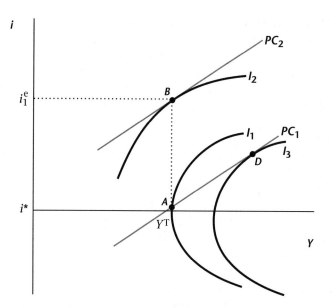

FIGURE 16.13
The Commitment Problem
If the Bank of Canada could commit to an inflation rate, it would choose i^*, and the equilibrium would be at A. However, without commitment, the equilibrium is at B, where inflation is too high, and where an indifference curve is tangent to the Phillips curve at $i = i^e$ (rational expectations holds).

many central banks in the world including the Bank of Canada, was money growth rate targeting. However, increasing instability in the relationships among monetary aggregates, prices, and real activity, which occurred in the 1980s, led to the abandonment of money growth rate targeting in favour of inflation targeting by the Bank of Canada. Inflation targets for monetary policy have been in place in Canada since 1992. Whether these targets represent a firm commitment is debatable. They could easily go the way of money growth targets if the Bank of Canada does not like the outcomes.

A problem with the central bank commitment story is that it does not explain the run-up in inflation in the 1970s, or why inflation decreased in the 1980s and 1990s. Did the Bank of Canada suddenly lose its ability to commit in the late 1960s and then find it again in the early 1980s? This seems unlikely. Further, as Robert Barro and David Gordon have argued,[5] if the Bank of Canada is playing a repeated game with the private sector, then its long-term reputation becomes important, and the long-run equilibrium can be point A in Figure 16.13. That is, the Bank understands that if it attempts to use surprise inflation to generate more aggregate output in the short run, then it will destroy its reputation for producing low inflation. Therefore, a long-run equilibrium can exist at point A in Figure 16.13, since the Bank understands that if it loses its reputation, then the equilibrium will be at point B forever.

Of course, if we accept the importance of the Bank of Canada's concern for its reputation in determining its behaviour, what was it about the 1970s that made the Bank of Canada willing to lose its reputation for low money growth and low inflation at that time?

---

[5]See R. Barro and D. Gordon, 1983, "A Positive Theory of Monetary Policy in a Natural Rate Model," *Journal of Political Economy* 91, 589–610; and R. Barro and D. Gordon, 1983, "Rules, Discretion and Reputation in a Model of Monetary Policy," *Journal of Monetary Economics* 12, 101–121.

Commitment and Inflation in Argentina

From World War II until 1990, Argentina was an inflationary disaster. Table 16.1, from an article by Domingo Cavallo,[1] shows that, in each decade from 1950 until 1990, the average inflation rate was very high in Argentina, ranging from 23.3% per year in 1960–69 to 750.4% per year in 1980–89. In March 1990, a hyperinflation was under way, as the inflation rate exceeded 20 000% per year.

What caused the exceedingly high rates of inflation in Argentina? The root of the problem was a chronically high government budget deficit financed through seigniorage (seigniorage is discussed in Chapter 9). In 1989, the government budget deficit in Argentina was 7.6% of GDP, quite high by any standard. Inflation in Argentina was brought under control by reducing the government budget deficit, and by putting in place a key monetary reform in 1990 that essentially eliminated any discretion in monetary policy on the part of Argentina's central bank.

In 1990, the value of the Argentine peso was fixed in terms of U.S. dollars, and a currency board was established. Recall from Chapter 13 that a currency board stands ready to exchange domestic for foreign currency at a fixed exchange rate, essentially backing the domestic currency one-for-one with foreign exchange reserves or assets denominated in the currency against which the currency is fixed, which is U.S. dollars in the case of Argentina. The currency board is thus a kind of commitment device establishing strict rules for monetary policy that are feasible to execute; since the domestic currency is backed one-for-one with foreign-currency-denominated assets, it is always possible to convert domestic currency into foreign currency, and vice versa.

As we showed in Chapter 13, a fixed exchange rate implies that a country effectively adopts the inflation rate of the country against which it fixes its exchange rate. That is, in 1990 Argentina made a choice to adopt the inflation rate of the United States and to abide by the effects of U.S. monetary policy. The advantage of a fixed exchange rate is that a country commits to the monetary policy of, hopefully, a low-inflation country, but the disadvantage is that monetary independence is abandoned.

In the case of Argentina, the adoption of a fixed exchange rate against the U.S. dollar, enforced by a currency board, was for a time very successful in reducing inflation. The inflation rate declined in Argentina in each year following 1990, reaching 0% in 1996. However, large government deficits led to a crisis that culminated in the abandonment of the currency board in January 2002. The experience of Argentina indicates that monetary policy commitment is not sufficient for the control of inflation. If there are sufficient fiscal policy pressures, then sound monetary policy commitments will ultimately be abandoned.

---

[1]D. Cavallo, 1996, "Lessons from the Stabilization Process in Argentina, 1990–1996," from Achieving Price Stability, a symposium sponsored by the Federal Reserve Bank of Kansas City, Jackson Hole, Wyoming, August 29–31, available **www.kc.frb.org/PUBLICAT/SYMPOS/1996/Sym96prg.htm**, accessed July 19, 2003.

TABLE 16.1 Average Annual Rate of Change in the Consumer Price Index for Argentina

1950–59	30.3%
1960–69	23.3%
1970–79	132.9%
1980–89	750.4%

In summary, several arguments cast doubt on the central bank commitment story as an explanation for recent Canadian inflation history. It seems that commitment issues are probably not very important in the behaviour of the Bank of Canada. The central bank learning story seems to give a more plausible account of the run-up in inflation in the 1970s, and the subsequent decline in the inflation rate in the 1980s and 1990s. However, see Macroeconomics in Action 16.2 on page 542 for a discussion of the importance of commitment in the case of Argentina.

Chapter Summary

This chapter studied the relationship between inflation and real aggregate economic activity, and provided an explanation for the behaviour of the inflation rate during the period 1961–2002 Canada. We first examined the Phillips curve relationship, which, as we study it, is a positive relationship between the inflation rate and the deviation of real aggregate output from trend. For some periods, in particular 1961–1969, 1970–1979, and 1990–2002, a Phillips curve can be observed in Canadian data, but the Phillips curve is not discernible for 1980–1989. We use a version of the Friedman-Lucas money surprise model to explain these facts.

In the version of the Friedman-Lucas money surprise model we use, the deviation of real aggregate output from trend is positively related to the difference between the actual and expected inflation rates. If the Bank of Canada generates a surprise increase in money growth, leading to a surprise increase in inflation, this causes an increase in labour supply, employment, and real output. The money surprise model predicts that the Phillips curve is unstable, as it shifts with changes in the expected rate of inflation.

In Canada, the rate of inflation was moderate during the 1960s, it increased substantially for the 1970s, and it then declined over the 1980s and 1990s. We considered two possible explanations for this. The first was the central bank learning story, whereby the Bank of Canada discovered the existence of the Phillips curve in the 1960s and, assuming the Phillips curve was stable, attempted to exploit this relationship in the 1970s. However, the increased inflation in the 1970s did not generate permanently higher output, and it became clear to the Bank of Canada that there was no long-run tradeoff between output and inflation. Higher inflation simply shifts up the Phillips curve relationship as expected inflation adjusts upward. Once the Bank of Canada discovered that there was no long-run tradeoff between output and inflation, it could then, in the early 1980s, focus solely on the goal of reducing inflation.

The second possible explanation for recent Canadian inflation history is the central bank commitment story. According to this story, high inflation is caused by the inability of the central bank to commit to a policy of not generating surprise inflation in an attempt to exploit the short-run Phillips curve. The central bank learning story provides a more plausible explanation than this, for it seems difficult to argue that the Bank found it difficult to commit in the 1970s but easy to commit itself otherwise. However, for some countries, such as Argentina, a commitment mechanism—a fixed exchange rate enforced by a currency board—appears to have been important in reducing inflation. But Argentina was unable to maintain commitment, and abandoned the currency board in 2002.

Key Terms

Phillips curve: A positive relationship between the rate of inflation and the level of aggregate economic activity.

time consistency problem: Situation that occurs when it proves optimal to abandon a previously announced plan.

rational expectations hypothesis: Hypothesis asserting that economic agents do not make systematic errors, that they use information efficiently.

Questions for Review

1. Why is the "Phillips curve" so called?

2. The Phillips curve relationship examined in this chapter is a positive relationship between what two variables?

3. During what periods over 1961–2002 for Canada can a Phillips curve be observed, and when can it not be observed?

4. What are two observations about empirical Phillips curve relations?

5. Explain how the Friedman-Lucas money surprise model works.

6. What is the relationship that summarizes the Friedman-Lucas money surprise model in this chapter?

7. When real aggregate output is equal to trend output, what is the inflation rate equal to?

8. What is the effect of an increase in expected inflation on the Phillips curve?

9. Describe the course of the inflation rate Canada from 1961 until late 2002.

10. What are two possible explanations for the Canadian inflation rate history after 1961?

11. Why can the central bank have an incentive to increase the inflation rate if it believes that the Phillips curve is stable?

12. Can the Bank of Canada permanently increase the level of aggregate output? Explain why or why not.

13. What was different about the ways in which inflation was reduced in Canada and in New Zealand?

14. Why will the inflation rate be high in the long run if the central bank cannot commit itself?

15. Explain why, if the central bank is concerned about its reputation, inflation can be low in the long run.

16. Which is a more satisfactory explanation of recent Canadian inflation, the central bank learning story or the central bank commitment story? Why?

17. Explain why commitment was important in reducing inflation in Argentina.

Problems

1. Suppose that the private sector does not have rational expectations, but instead follows an "adaptive expectations" scheme. That is, the private sector's expected inflation rate is what the inflation rate was last period. Show in a diagram how the inflation rate and output move over time if the initial inflation rate is the optimal rate i^*, and then the central bank acts to exploit the Phillips curve. Explain your results.

2. Suppose that the economy is in a long-run equilibrium where the inflation rate is greater than the optimal rate i^*, and then the central bank acts to reduce the inflation rate to i^*.

   a. Suppose that the central bank decides to take drastic action, and reduces the inflation rate within one period to i^*. Also, suppose that the private sector has adaptive expectations, so the current expected inflation rate is last period's actual inflation rate. Show in a diagram the path real aggregate output and the inflation rate take over time.

   b. Now, suppose that the central bank takes the drastic strategy in part (a), but that the private sector has rational expectations, so that $i = i^e$. Again, show in a diagram the path followed by output and the inflation rate over time.

   c. Now, suppose that the central bank takes a gradual strategy of reducing the inflation rate in a number of steps to i^*. Under a gradual strategy, show what differences there are between adaptive and rational expectations for the path of output and the inflation rate over time.

   d. Explain your results in parts (a)–(c), and comment on what light this sheds on Figures 16.7 and 16.8 for the early 1980s.

3. Suppose that the inflation rate is higher than i^*, that the central bank announces it will reduce the inflation rate, and that it actually proceeds to do this. Answer the following:

   a. Suppose that the private sector believes the central bank announcement. What are the effects on the inflation rate and real output? Show this in a diagram.

   b. Suppose that the private sector does not believe the central bank announcement. What are the effects on the inflation rate and real output now? Show this in a diagram.

   c. Explain your results in parts (a) and (b).

Working with the Data

1. Calculate the annual percentage rate of change in the consumer price index (December to December), and graph this in scatter plots against the unemployment rate for the 1950s, 1960s, 1970s, 1980s, and 1990s. For which decades do you observe a Phillips curve relationship, and for which do you not? What reasons could there be for a shift in this Phillips curve relationship, other than shifts in inflationary expectations?

2. Calculate annual inflation rates for the United States and Canada, using the consumer price index, and graph these in a time series plot, for the available time period. How does inflation experience in the United States compare with recent inflation history in Canada?

MATHEMATICAL APPENDIX

This appendix provides more formal treatments of some of the models in the book, and it is intended for students with a knowledge of calculus and more advanced algebraic techniques who wish to study some of the topics of this book in more depth. The appendix assumes an understanding of mathematical methods in economics at the level of Alpha C. Chiang's *Fundamental Methods of Mathematical Economics*, 3rd ed. (New York: McGraw-Hill, 1984). We will proceed by working through results for selected models from selected chapters.

Chapter 4: Consumer and Firm Behaviour

Chapter 4 dealt with the representative consumer's and representative firm's optimization problems in the closed-economy one-period model. We will set up the consumer's and firm's problems and derive the main results of Chapter 4 formally.

THE REPRESENTATIVE CONSUMER

The representative consumer's preferences are defined by the utility function $U(C, l)$, where C is consumption and l is leisure, with $U(\cdot, \cdot)$ a function that is increasing in both arguments, strictly quasiconcave, and twice differentiable. These properties of the utility function imply that indifference curves are downward-sloping and convex, and that the consumer strictly prefers more to less. The consumer's optimization problem is to choose C and l so as to maximize $U(C, l)$ subject to his or her budget constraint—that is,

$$\max_{C,\, l} U(C, l)$$

subject to

$$C = w(h - l) + \pi - T,$$

and $C \geq 0$, $0 \leq l \leq h$, where w is the real wage, h is the quantity of time the consumer has available, π is dividend income, and T is the lump-sum tax. The above problem is a constrained optimization problem, with the associated Lagrangian

$$L = U(C, l) + \lambda[w(h - l) + \pi - T - C],$$

where λ is the Lagrange multiplier.

We will assume that there is an interior solution to the consumer's problem where $C > 0$ and $0 < l < h$. This can be guaranteed by assuming that $U_1(0, l) = \infty$ (i.e., the derivative of the utility function with respect to the first argument goes to infinity in the limit as consumption goes to zero), and $U_2(C, 0) = \infty$. These assumptions imply that $C > 0$ and $l > 0$ at the optimum. In a competitive equilibrium we cannot have $l = h$, as this would imply that nothing would be produced and $C = 0$. Given an interior solution to the consumer's problem, we can characterize the solution by the first-order conditions from the problem of choosing C, l, and λ to maximize L. These first-order conditions are (differentiating L with respect to C, l, and λ, respectively, and setting each of these first derivatives equal to zero)

$$U_1(C, l) - \lambda = 0, \tag{A.1}$$

$$U_2(C, l) - \lambda w = 0, \tag{A.2}$$

$$w(h - l) + \pi - T - C = 0. \tag{A.3}$$

In (A.1) and (A.2), $U_i(C, l)$ denotes the first derivative with respect to the ith argument of $U(\cdot, \cdot)$, evaluated at (C, l). From Equations (A.1) and (A.2), we can obtain the condition

$$\frac{U_2(C, l)}{U_1(C, l)} = w, \tag{A.4}$$

which is the optimization condition for the consumer that we showed graphically in Chapter 4, Figure 4.5. Equation (A.4) states that the marginal rate of substitution of leisure for consumption (on the left-hand side of the equation) is equal to the real wage (on the right-hand side) at the optimum. For our purposes, we can rewrite Equation (A.4) as

$$U_2(C, l) - wU_1(C, l) = 0, \tag{A.5}$$

and then (A.3) and (A.5) are two equations determining the optimal choices of C and l given w, π, and T.

In general, we cannot obtain explicit closed-form solutions for C and l from (A.3) and (A.5) without assuming an explicit form for the utility function $U(\cdot, \cdot)$, but we can use comparative statics techniques to determine how C and l will change when any of w, π, or T change. To do this, we totally differentiate (A.3) and (A.5), obtaining

$$-dC - wdl + (h - l)dw + d\pi - dT = 0, \tag{A.6}$$

$$[U_{12} - wU_{11}]\, dC + [U_{22} - wU_{12}]\, dl - U_1\, dw = 0. \tag{A.7}$$

In Equation (A.7), U_{ij} denotes the second derivative with respect to the ith and jth arguments of $U(\cdot, \cdot)$. Now, it will prove useful to write (A.6) and (A.7) in matrix form, as

$$\begin{bmatrix} -1 & -w \\ U_{12} - wU_{11} & U_{22} - wU_{12} \end{bmatrix} \begin{bmatrix} dC \\ dl \end{bmatrix} = \begin{bmatrix} -(h - l)dw - d\pi + dT \\ U_1 dw \end{bmatrix}. \tag{A.8}$$

Then, we can solve for the derivatives of interest by using Cramer's rule.

First, consider the effects of a change in dividend income π. Using Cramer's rule, from (A.8) we get

$$\frac{dC}{d\pi} = \frac{-U_{22} + wU_{12}}{\nabla}, \tag{A.9}$$

$$\frac{dl}{d\pi} = \frac{U_{12} - wU_{11}}{\nabla}, \tag{A.10}$$

where

$$V = -U_{22} + 2wU_{12} - w^2 U_{11}.$$

Now, V is the determinant of the bordered Hessian associated with the constrained optimization problem for the consumer, and the quasiconcavity of the utility function implies that $V > 0$. This, however, does not allow us to sign the derivatives in (A.9) and (A.10). Our assumption from Chapter 4 that consumption and leisure are normal goods is equivalent to the conditions $-U_{22} + wU_{12} > 0$ and $U_{12} - wU_{11} > 0$. Thus, given normal goods, we have $\frac{dC}{d\pi} > 0$ and $\frac{dl}{d\pi} > 0$, so that the quantities of consumption and leisure chosen by the consumer increase when dividend income increases. It is straightforward to show that $\frac{dC}{dT} = -\frac{dC}{d\pi}$ and $\frac{dl}{dT} = -\frac{dl}{d\pi}$, so that the effects of a decrease in taxes are equivalent to the effects of an increase in dividend income.

Next, we can derive the effects of a change in the real wage, again using Cramer's rule to obtain, from (A.8),

$$\frac{dC}{dw} = \frac{wU_1 + (h - l)(-U_{22} + wU_{12})}{V}, \tag{A.11}$$

$$\frac{dl}{dw} = \frac{-U_1 + (h - l)(U_{12} - wU_{11})}{V}. \tag{A.12}$$

Now, assuming that consumption is a normal good, we have $-U_{22} + wU_{12} > 0$, and since $V > 0$ and $U_1 > 0$ (utility increases as consumption increases), we know from (A.11) that $\frac{dC}{dw} > 0$, so that consumption increases when the real wage increases. However, we cannot determine the sign of $\frac{dl}{dw}$ from (A.12), and this is because of the opposing income and substitution effects of a change in the real wage on leisure. It is possible to separate algebraically the income and substitution effects in Equation (A.12), by determining the response of leisure to a change in the real wage, holding utility constant. This gives a substitution effect, which can be expressed as

$$\frac{dl}{dw}(subst) = \frac{-U_1}{V} < 0,$$

so that the substitution effect is for leisure to fall and hours worked to rise when the real wage increases. This implies that, from (A.12), the income effect is

$$\frac{dl}{dw}(inc) = \frac{dl}{dw} - \frac{dl}{dw}(subst) = \frac{(h - l)(U_{12} - wU_{11})}{V} > 0,$$

assuming that leisure is a normal good, which implies that $U_{12} - wU_{11} > 0$. Therefore, the income effect is for leisure to increase when the real wage increases. In general, without putting additional restrictions on the utility function, we do not know the sign of $\frac{dl}{dw}$.

THE REPRESENTATIVE FIRM

We assumed in Chapter 4 that the production function for the representative firm is described by

$$Y = zF(K, N^d),$$

where Y is output, z is total factor productivity, $F(\cdot, \cdot)$ is a function, K is the capital stock, and N^d is the firm's labour input. The function $F(\cdot, \cdot)$ is assumed to be quasiconcave, strictly increasing in both arguments, homogeneous of degree one or constant-returns-to-scale, and twice differentiable. We also assume that $F_2(K, 0) = \infty$ and $F_2(K, \infty) = 0$ to guarantee that there is always an interior solution to the firm's profit maximization problem, where $F_2(K, N^d)$ is the first derivative with respect to the second argument of the function $F(\cdot, \cdot)$. The firm's profit maximization problem is to choose the labour input N^d so as to maximize

$$\pi = zF(K, N^d) - wN^d,$$

subject to $N^d \geq 0$, where π is the difference between revenue and labour costs, in terms of consumption goods. That is, the firm solves

$$\max_{N^d}\left[zF(K, N^d) - wN^d\right]. \tag{A.13}$$

The restrictions on the function $F(\cdot, \cdot)$ imply that there is a unique interior solution to problem (A.13), characterized by the first-order condition

$$zF_2(K, N^d) = w, \tag{A.14}$$

which states that the firm hires labour until the marginal product of labour $zF_2(K, N^d)$ equals the real wage w.

We can determine the effects of changes in w, z, and K on labour demand N^d through comparative statics techniques. Totally differentiating Equation (A.14), which determines N^d implicitly as a function of w, z, and K, we obtain

$$zF_{22}dN^d - dw + F_2\,dz + zF_{12}dK = 0.$$

Then, solving for the appropriate derivatives, we have

$$\frac{dN^d}{dw} = \frac{1}{zF_{22}} < 0,$$

$$\frac{dN^d}{dz} = \frac{-F_2}{zF_{22}} > 0,$$

$$\frac{dN^d}{dK} = \frac{-zF_{12}}{zF_{22}} > 0.$$

We can sign the above derivatives since $F_{22} < 0$ (the marginal product of labour decreases as the quantity of labour increases), $F_2 > 0$ (the marginal product of labour is positive), and $F_{12} > 0$ (the marginal product of labour increases as the capital input increases). These are restrictions on the production function discussed in Chapter 4. Since $\frac{dN^d}{dw} < 0$, the labour demand curve is downward-sloping. Further, $\frac{dN^d}{dz} > 0$ and $\frac{dN^d}{dK} > 0$ imply that the labour demand curve shifts to the right when z or K increases.

Problems

1. Suppose that the consumer's preferences are given by the utility function $U(C, l) = \ln C + \alpha \ln l$. Determine the consumer's choice of consumption and leisure and interpret your solutions.

2. In the consumer's choice problem, show that at least one good must be normal.

3. Suppose that the firm's production technology is given by $Y = zF(K, N) = zK^\alpha N^{1-\alpha}$, where $0 < \alpha < 1$. Determine the firm's demand for labour as a function of z, K, α, and w, and interpret.

4. Suppose that the firm's production technology is given by $Y = z\min(K, \alpha N)$, where $\alpha > 0$. As in problem 3, determine the firm's demand for labour as a function of z, K, α, and w, and interpret.

Chapter 5: A Closed-Economy One-Period Macroeconomic Model

Here, we will show formally the equivalence between the competitive equilibrium and the Pareto optimum in the one-period model, and then determine, using comparative statics, the equilibrium effects of a change in government spending and in total factor productivity.

COMPETITIVE EQUILIBRIUM

In a competitive equilibrium, the representative consumer maximizes utility subject to his or her budget constraint, the representative firm maximizes profits, the government budget constraint holds, and the market on which labour is exchanged for consumption goods clears. From the previous section, the two equations describing consumer optimization are the budget constraint, (A.3), or

$$w(h - l) + \pi - T - C = 0, \tag{A.15}$$

and condition (A.5), or

$$U_2(C, l) - wU_1(C, l) = 0. \tag{A.16}$$

Optimization by the representative firm implies (A.14), or

$$zF_2(K, N^d) = w, \tag{A.17}$$

and profits for the firm are

$$\pi = zF(K, N^d) - wN^d. \tag{A.18}$$

The government budget constraint states that government spending is equal to taxes; that is,

$$G = T. \tag{A.19}$$

Finally, the market-clearing condition is

$$h - l = N^d, \tag{A.20}$$

or the supply of labour is equal to the demand for labour. Equations (A.15)–(A.20) are six equations which solve for the six endogenous variables C, l, N^d, T, π, and w, given the exogenous variables z and G. To make this system of equations more manageable, we can simplify as follows. First, using Equations (A.18)–(A.20) to substitute for π, T, and N^d in Equation (A.15), we obtain

$$C = zF(K, h - l) - G. \tag{A.21}$$

Then, substituting in Equation (17.18) for N^d using equation (17.20), and then in turn for w in (17.16) using equation (17.18), we obtain

$$U_2(C, l) - zF_2(K, h - l)U_1(C, l) = 0. \tag{A.22}$$

Equations (A.21) and (A.22) then solve for equilibrium C and l. Then, the real wage w can be determined from (A.17), after substituting for N^d from (A.20), to get

$$w = zF_2(K, h - l). \tag{A.23}$$

Finally, aggregate output is given from the production function by

$$Y = zF(K, h - l).$$

PARETO OPTIMUM

To determine the Pareto optimum, we need to ask how a fictitious social planner would choose consumption and leisure so as to maximize welfare for the representative consumer, given the production technology. The social planner solves

$$\max_{C, l} U(C, l)$$

subject to

$$C = zF(K, h - l) - G.$$

To solve the social planner's problem, set up the Lagrangian associated with the constrained optimization problem above, which is

$$L = U(C, l) + \lambda [zF(K, h - l) - G - C].$$

The first-order conditions for an optimum are then

$$U_1(C, l) - \lambda = 0, \tag{A.24}$$

$$U_2(C, l) - \lambda zF_2(K, h - l) = 0, \tag{A.25}$$

$$zF(K, h - l) - G - C = 0. \tag{A.26}$$

From Equations (A.24) and (A.25), we obtain

$$U_2(C, l) - zF_2(K, h - l)U_1(C, l) = 0. \tag{A.27}$$

Now, note that Equations (A.26) and (A.27), which solve for the Pareto-optimal quantities of leisure l and consumption C, are identical to Equations (A.21) and (A.22), so that the Pareto-optimal quantities of leisure and consumption are identical to the competitive equilibrium quantities of leisure and consumption. As a result, the competitive equilibrium and the Pareto optimum are the same thing in this model, so the first and second welfare theorems hold.

Note also that Equation (A.27) can be written (suppressing arguments for convenience) as

$$\frac{U_2}{U_1} = zF_2,$$

which states that the marginal rate of substitution of leisure for consumption is equal to the marginal product of labour (the marginal rate of transformation) at the optimum.

COMPARATIVE STATICS

We would like to determine the effects of changes in G and z on equilibrium C, l, Y, and w. To do this, we totally differentiate Equations (A.26) and (A.27), obtaining

$$-dC - zF_2 \, dl + F \, dz - dG = 0,$$

$$(U_{12} - zF_2U_{11}) \, dC + (U_{22} + zF_{22}U_1 - zF_2U_{12}) \, dl - F_2U_1 \, dz = 0.$$

Then, putting these two equations in matrix form, we get

$$\begin{bmatrix} -1 & -zF_2 \\ U_{12} - zF_2U_{11} & U_{22} + zF_{22}U_1 - zF_2U_{12} \end{bmatrix} \begin{bmatrix} dC \\ dl \end{bmatrix} = \begin{bmatrix} -F \, dz + dG \\ F_2U_1 dz \end{bmatrix}. \tag{A.28}$$

Using Cramer's rule to determine the effects of a change in government spending G, from (A.28) we then get

$$\frac{dC}{dG} = \frac{U_{22} + zF_{22}U_1 - zF_2U_{12}}{\nabla},$$

$$\frac{dl}{dG} = \frac{-U_{12} + zF_2U_{11}}{\nabla},$$

where

$$\nabla = -z^2F_2^2U_{11} + 2zF_2U_{12} - U_{22} - zF_{22}U_1.$$

Here, ∇ is the determinant of the bordered Hessian associated with the social planner's constrained optimization problem, and the quasiconcavity of the utility function and the production function guarantees that $\nabla > 0$. To sign the derivatives above, note that in equilibrium $zF_2 = w$, from (A.17). This then implies, given our assumption that consumption and leisure are normal goods, that $U_{22} - zF_2U_{12} < 0$ and $-U_{12} + zF_2U_{11} < 0$ (recall our discussion from the previous section); since $F_{22} < 0$ (the marginal product of labour declines as the labour input increases), we have $\frac{dC}{dG} < 0$ and $\frac{dl}{dG} < 0$, so that consumption and leisure decline when government purchases increase, due to negative income effects. For the effect on the real wage w, since $w = zF_2(K, h - l)$, we have

$$\frac{dw}{dG} = -zF_{22}\frac{dl}{dG} < 0,$$

and so the real wage decreases. For the effect on aggregate output, since $Y = C + G$, we have

$$\frac{dY}{dG} = \frac{dC}{dG} + 1 = \frac{-z^2F_2^2U_{11} + zF_2U_{12}}{\nabla} > 0,$$

as leisure is assumed to be normal, implying $zF_2U_{11} - U_{12} < 0$.

Now, to determine the effects of a change in z, again we use Cramer's rule in conjunction with (A.28), obtaining

$$\frac{dC}{dz} = \frac{-F(U_{22} + zF_{22}U_1 - zF_2U_{12}) + F_2^2zU_1}{\nabla},$$

$$\frac{dl}{dz} = \frac{-F_2U_1 + F(U_{12} - zF_2U_{11})}{\nabla}.$$

Here, since consumption is a normal good, $U_{22} - zF_2U_{12} < 0$, and given $F_{22} < 0$, $F > 0$, and $U_1 > 0$, we have $\frac{dC}{dz} > 0$ and consumption increases with an increase in total factor productivity, as we showed diagrammatically in Chapter 5, Figure 5.9. However, we cannot sign $\frac{dl}{dz}$, as there are opposing income and substitution effects. We can separate out the income and substitution effects on leisure by determining the response of leisure to a change in z holding utility constant. This will give a substitution effect, which is

$$\frac{dl}{dz}(subst) = \frac{-F_2U_1}{\nabla} < 0,$$

so that the substitution effect is for leisure to decrease and employment ($= h - l$) to increase. The income effect of the change in z is then

$$\frac{dl}{dz}(inc) = \frac{dl}{dz} - \frac{dl}{dz}(subst) = \frac{F(U_{12} - zF_2U_{11})}{\nabla} > 0,$$

since leisure is a normal good. Therefore, an increase in z has a positive income effect on leisure.

Problems

1. For the closed-economy one-period model, suppose that $U(C, l) = \ln C + \beta l$, and $F(K, N) = zK^\alpha N^{1-\alpha}$, where $\beta > 0$ and $0 < \alpha < 1$. Determine consumption, employment, output, leisure, and the real wage in a competitive equilibrium, and explain your solutions.

2. For the closed-economy one-period model, suppose that $U(C, l) = min(C, \beta l)$, and $F(K, N) = \alpha K + dN$, where $\beta > 0$, $\alpha > 0$, and $d > 0$. Determine consumption, employment, output, leisure, and the real wage in a competitive equilibrium, and explain your solutions. Also draw a diagram with the consumer's preferences and the production possibilities frontier, and show the competitive equilibrium in this diagram.

Chapter 6: Two-Period Model

In this section we will formally derive the results for individual consumer behaviour, showing how a consumer optimizes by choosing consumption and savings over two periods, and how the consumer responds to changes in income and the market real interest rate.

THE CONSUMER'S OPTIMIZATION PROBLEM

The consumer has preferences defined by a utility function $U(c, c')$, where c is current period consumption, c' is future consumption, and $U(\cdot, \cdot)$ is strictly quasiconcave, increasing in both arguments, and twice differentiable. To guarantee an interior solution to the consumer's problem, we assume that the marginal utilities of current and future consumption each go to infinity in the limit as current and future consumption go to zero, respectively. The consumer chooses c and c' to maximize $U(c, c')$ subject to the consumer's lifetime budget constraint—that is,

$$\max_{c, c'} U(c, c')$$

subject to

$$c + \frac{c'}{1 + r} = y + \frac{y'}{1 + r} - t - \frac{t'}{1 + r},$$

where y is current income, y' is future income, t is the current tax, and t' is the future tax. The Lagrangian associated with this constrained optimization problem is

$$L = U(c, c') + \lambda\left(y + \frac{y'}{1 + r} - t - \frac{t'}{1 + r} - c - \frac{c'}{1 + r}\right),$$

where λ is the Lagrange multiplier. Therefore, the first-order conditions for an optimum are

$$U_1(c, c') - \lambda = 0, \tag{A.29}$$

$$U_2(c, c') - \frac{\lambda}{1 + r} = 0, \tag{A.30}$$

$$y + \frac{y'}{1 + r} - t - \frac{t'}{1 + r} - c - \frac{c'}{1 + r} = 0. \tag{A.31}$$

Then, in (A.29) and (A.30), we can eliminate λ to obtain

$$U_1(c, c') - (1 + r)U_2(c, c') = 0, \tag{A.32}$$

or, rewriting (A.32),

$$\frac{U_1(c, c')}{U_2(c, c')} = 1 + r,$$

which states that the intertemporal marginal rate of substitution (the marginal rate of substitution of current consumption for future consumption) is equal to one plus the real interest rate at the optimum.

For convenience, we can rewrite (A.31) as

$$y(1 + r) + y' - t(1 + r) - t' - c(1 + r) - c' = 0. \tag{A.33}$$

Then, Equations (A.32) and (A.33) determine the quantities of c and c' the consumer will choose given current and future incomes y and y', current and future taxes t and t', and the real interest rate r.

COMPARATIVE STATICS

To determine the effects of changes in current and future income and the real interest rate on current and future consumption and savings, we totally differentiate Equations (A.32) and (A.33), obtaining

$$[U_{11} - (1 + r)U_{12}]dc + [U_{12} - (1 + r)U_{22}]dc' - U_2 dr = 0,$$

$$-(1 + r)dc - dc' + (y - t - c)dr + (1 + r)dy + dy' - (1 + r)dt - dt' = 0;$$

these two equations can be written in matrix form as

$$\begin{bmatrix} U_{11} - (1+r)U_{12} & U_{12} - (1+r)U_{22} \\ -(1+r) & -1 \end{bmatrix} \begin{bmatrix} dc \\ dc' \end{bmatrix} =$$

$$\begin{bmatrix} U_2 dr \\ -(y - t - c)dr - (1 + r)dy - dy' - (1 + r)dt - dt' \end{bmatrix} \tag{A.34}$$

First, we will determine the effects of a change in current income y. Applying Cramer's rule to (A.34), we obtain

$$\frac{dc}{dy} = \frac{(1 + r)[U_{12} - (1 + r)U_{22}]}{\nabla},$$

$$\frac{dc'}{dy} = \frac{(1 + r)[-U_{11} + (1 + r)U_{12}]}{\nabla},$$

where

$$\nabla = -U_{11} + 2(1 + r)U_{12} - (1 + r)^2 U_{22}.$$

Given our restrictions on the utility function, ∇, which is the determinant of the bordered Hessian associated with the consumer's constrained optimization problem, is strictly positive. Further, assuming current and future consumption are normal goods, we have $U_{12} - (1 + r)U_{22} > 0$ and $-U_{11} + (1 + r)U_{12} > 0$, and so $\frac{dc}{dy} > 0$ and $\frac{dc'}{dy} > 0$. Thus, an increase in current income causes increases in both current and future consumption. Saving in the current period is given by $s = y - c - t$, so that

$$\frac{ds}{dy} = 1 - \frac{dc}{dy} = \frac{-U_{11} + (1 + r)U_{12}}{\nabla} > 0,$$

since the assumption that goods are normal gives $-U_{11} + (1 + r)U_{12} > 0$. Therefore, saving increases in the current period when y increases.

To determine the effects of a change in future income y', we again apply Cramer's rule to (A.34), getting

$$\frac{dc}{dy'} = \frac{1}{1 + r} \frac{dc}{dy} > 0,$$

$$\frac{dc'}{dy'} = \frac{1}{1 + r} \frac{dc'}{dy} > 0,$$

so that the effects of a change in y' are identical qualitatively to the effects of a change in y, except that the derivatives are discounted, using the one-period discount factor $\frac{1}{1+r}$. The effect on saving is given by

$$\frac{ds}{dy'} = -\frac{dc}{dy'} < 0,$$

and so saving decreases when future income increases.

Finally, to determine the effects of a change in the real interest rate r on current and future consumption, we again apply Cramer's rule to (A.34), getting

$$\frac{dc}{dr} = \frac{-U_2 + [U_{12} - (1 + r)U_{22}](y - t - c)}{\nabla},$$

$$\frac{dc'}{dr} = \frac{(1 + r)U_2 - [U_{11} - (1 + r)U_{12}](y - t - c)}{\nabla}.$$

The signs of both of these derivatives are indeterminate, because the income and substitution effects may be opposing. As above, we can separate the income and substitution effects by determining the responses of c and c' to a change in r holding utility constant. The substitution effects are

$$\frac{dc}{dr}(subst) = \frac{-U_2}{\nabla} < 0,$$

$$\frac{dc'}{dr}(subst) = \frac{(1 + r)U_2}{\nabla} > 0,$$

so that the substitution effect is for current consumption to decrease and future consumption to increase when the real interest rate increases. The income effects are

$$\frac{dc}{dr}(inc) = \frac{dc}{dr} - \frac{dc}{dr}(subst) = \frac{[U_{12} - (1 + r)U_{22}](y - t - c)}{\nabla},$$

$$\frac{dc'}{dr}(inc) = \frac{dc'}{dr} - \frac{dc'}{dr}(subst) = \frac{[U_{11} - (1 + r)U_{12}](y - t - c)}{\nabla}.$$

Here, the assumption that goods are normal gives $U_{12} - (1 + r)U_{22} > 0$ and $U_{11} - (1 + r)U_{12} < 0$, and so given this assumption the signs of the income effects are determined by whether the consumer is a lender or a borrower, that is, by the sign of $y - t - c$. If the consumer is a lender, so that $y - t - c > 0$, then the income effects are for current consumption to increase and future consumption to decrease. However, if $y - t - c < 0$, so that consumer is a borrower, then the income effect is for current consumption to decrease and future consumption to increase.

Since saving is $s = y - c - t$, the effect on savings of a change in the real interest rate is determined by the effect on current consumption, namely,

$$\frac{ds}{dr} = \frac{dc}{dr}.$$

Problems

1. Suppose that $U(c, c') = \ln c + \beta \ln c'$, where $\beta > 0$. Determine consumption in the current and future periods for the consumer, and interpret your solutions in terms of income and substitution effects.

2. Suppose that $U(c, c') = \ln c + \beta \ln c'$, where $\beta > 0$, and assume that the consumer lends at the real interest rate r_1, and borrows at the interest rate r_2, where $r_1 < r_2$. Under what conditions will the consumer be (i) a borrower, (ii) a lender, (iii) neither a borrower nor a lender? Explain your results.

Chapter 7: A Real Intertemporal Model with Investment

There is not much to be gained from analyzing the model developed in this chapter algebraically. It is possible to linearize the model so as to make it amenable to an explicit solution, but to do analysis with this linearized model requires a good deal of tedious algebra. For this chapter, we will confine attention to a formal treatment of the representative firm's investment problem.

The current and future production functions for the firm are given, respectively, by

$$Y = zF(K, N) \tag{A.35}$$

and

$$Y' = z'F(K', N'), \tag{A.36}$$

where Y and Y' are current and future outputs, respectively, z and z' are current and future total factor productivities, K and K' are current and future capital stocks, and N and N' are current and future labour inputs. The capital stock evolves according to

$$K' = (1 - d)K + I, \tag{A.37}$$

where d is the depreciation rate and I is investment in capital in period 1. The present value of profits for the firm is

$$V = Y - I - wN + \frac{Y' - w'N' + (1 - d)K'}{1 + r}, \tag{A.38}$$

where w is the current real wage, w' is the future real wage, and r is the real interest rate. We can substitute in (A.38) for Y, Y', and K' using (A.35)–(A.37) to obtain

$$V = zF(K, N) - I - wN + \frac{z'F[(1 - d)K + I, N'] - w'N' + (1 - d)[(1 - d)K + I]}{1 + r}. \tag{A.39}$$

The objective of the firm is to choose N, N', and I to maximize V. The first-order conditions for an optimum, obtained by differentiating Equation (A.39) with respect to N, N', and I, are

$$\frac{\partial V}{\partial N} = zF_2(K, N) - w = 0, \tag{A.40}$$

$$\frac{\partial V}{\partial N'} = \frac{z'F_2[(1 - d)K + I, N'] - w'}{1 + r} = 0, \tag{A.41}$$

$$\frac{\partial V}{\partial I} = -1 + \frac{z'F_1[(1 - d)K + I, N'] + 1 - d}{1 + r} = 0. \tag{A.42}$$

Equations (A.40) and (A.41) state, respectively, that the firm optimizes by setting the marginal product of labour equal to the real wage in the current period and in the future period. We can simplify Equation (A.42) by writing it as

$$z'F_1[(1 - d)K + I, N'] - d = r, \tag{A.43}$$

or the firm chooses investment optimally by setting the future net marginal product of capital equal to the real interest rate, given N'. To determine how changes in z', K, d, and r affect the investment decision, given future employment N', we totally differentiate (A.43), getting

$$z'F_{11} \, dI + z'(1 - d)F_{11} \, dK + F_1 \, dz - (z'KF_{11} + 1) \, dd - dr = 0.$$

Then, we have

$$\frac{dI}{dr} = \frac{1}{z'F_{11}} < 0,$$

so that investment declines when the real interest rate increases;

$$\frac{dI}{dK} = d - 1 < 0,$$

so that investment is lower the higher is the initial capital stock K;

$$\frac{dI}{dz'} = \frac{-F_1}{z'F_{11}} > 0,$$

so that investment increases when future total factor productivity increases; and

$$\frac{dI}{dd} = \frac{z'KF_{11} + 1}{z'F_{11}},$$

which has an indeterminate sign, so that the effect of a change in the depreciation rate on investment is ambiguous.

Problem

1. Suppose that the firm produces output only from capital. Current output is given by $Y = zK^\alpha$, and future output is given by $Y' = z'(K')^\alpha$, where $0 < \alpha < 1$. Determine investment for the firm, and show how investment depends on the real interest rate, future total factor productivity, the depreciation rate, and α. Explain your results.

Chapter 8: Economic Growth

In this section we will work out explicitly the effects of changes in the savings rate, the labour force growth rate, and total factor productivity on the steady state quantity of capital per worker and output per worker in the Solow growth model. Then, we will determine the golden rule for capital accumulation in the Solow model. Finally, we will develop a growth model where consumption–savings decisions are made endogenously. In solving this model, we will introduce dynamic programming techniques, which will prove useful later in this appendix.

EXPLICIT RESULTS FOR THE SOLOW GROWTH MODEL

Recall from Chapter 8 that the aggregate quantity of capital in the Solow growth model evolves according to

$$K' = (1 - d)K + I, \tag{A.44}$$

where K' is future period capital, d is the depreciation rate, K is current period capital, and I is current period investment. In equilibrium, saving is equal to investment, and so $sY = I$, where s is the savings rate and Y is aggregate income. Further, the production function is given by $Y = zF(K, N)$, where z is total factor productivity and N is the labour force, so that substituting in Equation (A.44), we have

$$K' = (1 - d)K + szF(K, N). \tag{A.45}$$

Then, dividing the right-hand and left-hand sides of Equation (A.45) by N, using the relationship $N' = (1 + n)N$, which describes labour force growth, with N' denoting the future labour force and n the population growth rate, and rewriting in the form of lowercase variables that denote per-worker quantities, we have

$$k' = \frac{szf(k)}{1 + n} + \frac{(1 - d)k}{1 + n}. \tag{A.46}$$

Equation (A.46) then determines the evolution of the per-worker capital stock from the current period to the future period, where k is the current stock of capital per worker, k' is the stock of future capital per worker, and $f(k)$ is the per-worker production function.

In the steady state, $k' = k = k^*$, where k^* is the steady state quantity of capital per worker, which, from (A.46), satisfies

$$szf(k^*) - (n + d)k^* = 0. \tag{A.47}$$

Now, to determine the effects of changes in s, n, and z on the steady state quantity of capital per worker, we totally differentiate Equation (A.47), getting

$$[szf'(k^*) - n - d] \, dk^* + zf(k^*) \, ds - k^* \, dn + sf(k^*) \, dz = 0. \tag{A.48}$$

Then, solving for the appropriate derivatives, we obtain

$$\frac{dk^*}{ds} = \frac{-zf(k^*)}{szf'(k^*) - n - d} > 0,$$

$$\frac{dk^*}{dn} = \frac{k^*}{szf'(k^*) - n - d} < 0, \tag{A.49}$$

$$\frac{dk^*}{dz} = \frac{-sf(k^*)}{szf'(k^*) - n - d} > 0.$$

Here, capital per worker increases with increases in s and z, and decreases with an increase in n. We get these results since $szf'(k^*) - n - d < 0$ in the steady state. Since output per worker in the steady state is $y^* = zf(k^*)$, for each of these experiments steady state output per worker moves in the same direction as steady state capital per worker.

In the steady state, the quantity of consumption per worker is

$$c^* = zf(k^*) - (n + d)k^*.$$

Now, note that when the savings rate changes, the response of consumption per worker in the steady state is given by

$$\frac{dc^*}{ds} = [zf'(k^*) - n - d]\frac{dk^*}{ds}.$$

Though $\frac{dk^*}{ds} > 0$, the sign of $zf'(k^*) - n - d$ is ambiguous, so that consumption per worker could increase or decrease with an increase in the savings rate. The golden rule savings rate is the savings rate s_{gr} that maximizes consumption per worker in the steady state. The golden rule steady state quantity of capital per worker solves the problem

$$\max_{k^*}[zf(k^*) - (n + d)k^*];$$

letting k_{gr}^* denote this quantity of capital per worker, k_{gr}^* solves

$$zf'(k_{gr}^*) - n - d = 0,$$

and then s_{gr} is determined from (A.47) by

$$s_{gr} = \frac{(n + d)k_{gr}^*}{zf(k_{gr}^*)}.$$

For example, if $F(K, N) = K^\alpha N^{1-\alpha}$, where $0 < \alpha < 1$ (a Cobb-Douglas production function), then $f(k) = k^\alpha$, and we get

$$k_{gr}^* = \left(\frac{z\alpha}{n + d}\right)^{\frac{1}{1-\alpha}},$$

$$s_{gr} = \alpha.$$

Problem

1. Suppose in the Solow growth model that there is government spending financed by lump-sum taxes, with total government spending $G = gY$, where $0 < g < 1$. Solve for steady state capital per worker, consumption per worker, and output per worker, and determine how each depends on g. Can g be set so as to maximize steady state consumption per worker? If so, determine the optimal fraction of output purchased by the government, g^*, and explain your results.

OPTIMAL GROWTH: ENDOGENOUS CONSUMPTION–SAVINGS DECISIONS

In this model, we will relax the assumption made in the Solow growth model that the savings rate is exogenous, and allow consumption to be determined optimally over time. The model we develop here is a version of the optimal growth theory originally developed by David Cass and Tjalling Koopmans.[1] In this model, the second welfare theorem will hold, and so we can solve the social planner's problem to determine the competitive equilibrium. We will set the model up as simply as possible, leaving out population growth and changes in total factor productivity, but these features are easy to add.

There is a representative infinitely lived consumer with preferences given by

$$\sum_{t=0}^{\infty} \beta^t U(C_t), \tag{A.50}$$

---

[1]See D. Cass, 1965, "Optimum Growth in an Aggregative Model of Capital Accumulation," *Review of Economic Studies* 32, 233–240; and T. Koopmans, 1965, "On the Concept of Optimal Growth," in *The Econometric Approach to Development Planning*, North Holland, Amsterdam.

where β is the subjective discount factor of the representative consumer, with $0 < \beta < 1$, and C_t is consumption in period t. Throughout, t subscripts will denote the time period. The period utility function $U(\cdot)$ is continuously differentiable, strictly increasing, strictly concave, and bounded. Assume that $\lim_{c \to 0} U'(C) = \infty$. Each period, the consumer is endowed with one unit of time, which can be supplied as labour.

The production function is given by

$$Y_t = F(K_t, N_t),$$

where Y_t is output, K_t is the capital input, and N_t is the labour input. The production function $F(\cdot, \cdot)$ is continuously differentiable, strictly increasing in both arguments, homogeneous of degree one, and strictly quasiconcave. Assume that $F(0, N) = 0$, $\lim_{K \to 0} F_1(K, 1) = \infty$, and $\lim_{K \to \infty} F_1(K, 1) = 0$.

The capital stock obeys the law of motion

$$K_{t+1} = (1 - d)K_t + I_t, \tag{A.51}$$

where I_t is investment and d is the depreciation rate, with $0 \geq d \leq 1$, and K_0 is the initial capital stock, which is given. In equilibrium, we will have $N_t = 1$ for all t, and so it will prove convenient to define the function $H(K_t)$ by $H(K_t) \equiv F(K_t, 1)$. The resource constraint for the economy is

$$C_t + I_t = H(K_t), \tag{A.52}$$

or consumption plus investment is equal to the total quantity of output produced. It is convenient to substitute for I_t in (A.52) using (A.51) and to rearrange, obtaining a single constraint

$$C_t + K_{t+1} = H(K_t) + (1 - d)K_t; \tag{A.53}$$

we can think of the resources available in period t to the social planner on the right-hand side of Equation (A.53) as being period t output plus the undepreciated portion of the capital stock, which is then split up (on the left-hand side of the equation) between period t consumption and the capital stock for period $t + 1$.

The social planner's problem for this economy is to determine consumption and the capital stock in each period so as to maximize (A.50) subject to the constraint (A.53). Again, the solution to this problem is equivalent to the competitive equilibrium solution. The social planner solves

$$\max_{\{C_t, K_{t+1}\}_{t=0}^{\infty}} \sum_{t=0}^{\infty} \beta^t U(C_t), \tag{A.54}$$

given K_0 and (A.53) for $t = 0, 1, 2, \ldots \infty$.

Now, the problem of solving (A.54) subject to (A.53) may appear quite formidable, as we need to solve for an infinite sequence of choice variables. However, dynamic programming techniques essentially allow us to turn this infinite-dimensional problem into a two-dimensional problem.[2] To see how this works, note from the right-hand side of (A.53) that the current capital stock K_t determines the resources that are available to the social planner at the beginning of period t. Thus, K_t will determine how much utility the social planner can give to the consumer from period t on. Suppose that the social planner knows $v(K_t)$, which is the maximum utility that the social planner

---

[2]For more detail on dynamic programming methods in economics, see N. Stokey, R. Lucas, and E. Prescott, 1989, *Recursive Methods in Economic Dynamics*, Harvard University Press, Cambridge, MA.

could provide for the representative consumer from period t on. Then, the problem that the social planner would solve in any period t would be

$$\max_{C_t,\, K_{t+1}} [U(C_t) + \beta v(K_{t+1})]$$

subject to

$$C_t + K_{t+1} = H(K_t) + (1 - d)K_t.$$

That is, the social planner chooses current period consumption and the capital stock for the following period so as to maximize the sum of current period utility and the discounted value of utility from the next period on, subject to the resource constraint.

Now, since the problem of the social planner looks the same in every period, it will be true that

$$v(K_t) = \max_{C_t,\, K_{t+1}} [U(C_t) + \beta v(K_{t+1})] \tag{A.55}$$

subject to

$$C_t + K_{t+1} = H(K_t) + (1 - d)K_t. \tag{A.56}$$

Then, Equation (A.55) is called a *Bellman equation*, or *functional equation*, and it determines what $v(\cdot)$ is. We call $v(K_t)$ the *value function*, as this tells us the value of the problem at time t to the social planner, as a function of the *state variable* K_t. Given the assumptions we have made, there is a unique function $v(\cdot)$ that solves the Bellman equation. There are some circumstances where we can obtain an explicit solution for $v(\cdot)$ (See the problem at the end of this section), but in any case the dynamic programming formulation of the social planner's problem, (A.55) subject to (A.56), can be convenient for characterizing solutions, if we assume that $v(\cdot)$ is differentiable and strictly concave (which it is here, given our assumptions).

We can simplify the problem above by substituting for C_t in the objective function (A.55) using the constraint (A.56), getting

$$v(K_t) = \max_{K_{t+1}} \{U[H(K_t) + (1 - d)K_t - K_{t+1}] + \beta v(K_{t+1})\}. \tag{A.57}$$

Then, given that the value function $v(\cdot)$ is concave and differentiable, we can differentiate on the right-hand side of (A.57) to get the first-order condition for an optimum, which is

$$-U'[H(K_t) + (1 - d)K_t - K_{t+1}] + \beta v'(K_{t+1}) = 0. \tag{A.58}$$

Now, to determine $v'(K_{t+1})$, we apply the envelope theorem in differentiating Equation (A.57), obtaining

$$v'(K_t) = [H'(K_t) + 1 - d]U'[H(K_t) + (1 - d)K_t - K_{t+1}];$$

then, we update one period, and substitute for $v'(K_{t+1})$ in (A.58), getting

$$-U'[H(K_t) + (1 - d)K_t - K_{t+1}] + \beta[H'(K_{t+1}) + 1 - d]U'[H(K_{t+1}) + (1 - d)K_{t+1} - K_{t+2}] = 0. \tag{A.59}$$

Now, it can be shown that, in this model, the quantity of capital converges to a constant steady state value, K^*. Equation (A.59) can be used to solve for K^* by substituting $K_{t+1} = K_t = K^*$ in (A.59), which gives, after simplifying,

$$-1 + \beta[H'(K^*) + 1 - d] = 0, \tag{A.60}$$

or

$$H'(K^*) - d = \frac{1}{\beta} - 1$$

in the optimal steady state. That is, in the optimal steady state, the net marginal product of capital is equal to the subjective discount rate of the representative consumer.

In the model, the savings rate is given by

$$s_t = \frac{I_t}{Y_t} = \frac{K_{t+1} - (1-d)K_t}{H(K_t)},$$

and so in the steady state the savings rate is

$$s^* = \frac{dK^*}{H(K^*)}.$$

In this model, since the savings rate is optimally chosen over time, choosing a "golden rule savings rate" makes no sense. Indeed, note that the steady state optimal savings rate in this model does not maximize steady state consumption. Steady state consumption would be maximized for a value of the steady state capital stock K^* such that $H'(K^*) = d$, but this is different from the optimal steady state capital stock determined by (A.60).

Problem

1. In the optimal growth model, suppose that $U(C_t) = \ln C_t$, and $F(K_t, N_t) = K_t^\alpha N_t^{1-\alpha}$, with $d = 1$ (100% depreciation).
   a. Guess that the value function takes the form $v(K_t) = A + B \ln K_t$, where A and B are undetermined constants.
   b. Substitute your guess for the value function on the right-hand side of equation (A.57), solve the optimization problem, and verify that your guess was correct.
   c. Solve for A and B by substituting your optimal solution from part (b) on the right-hand side of equation (A.57) and equating coefficients on the left and right-hand sides of the equation.
   d. Determine the solutions for K_{t+1} and C_t as functions of K_t, and interpret these solutions.

Chapter 9: A Monetary Intertemporal Model

Here, we will develop an explicit cash-in-advance model and show some of the implications of this model that we derived more informally in Chapter 9. The model will in some ways be simplified relative to the monetary intertemporal model of Chapter 9, but this will allow a clearer derivation of the results.

In the cash-in-advance model there is a representative consumer, who lives forever, and has preferences given by the utility function

$$\sum_{t=0}^{\infty} \beta^t [U(C_t) - V(N_t)], \tag{A.61}$$

where β is the subjective discount factor, with $0 < \beta < 1$, C_t is consumption in period t, N_t is labour supply in period t, $U(\cdot)$ is a strictly increasing and strictly concave function with $U'(0) = \infty$, and $V(\cdot)$ is a strictly increasing and strictly convex function with $V'(0) = 0$. Assume that $U(\cdot)$ and $V(\cdot)$ are twice continuously differentiable.

For simplicity we will not have capital or investment in the model, to focus on the key results, and the production function will be given by

$$Y_t = zN_t, \tag{A.62}$$

where Y_t is output in period t, and z is the marginal product of labour. Note that the linear production function has the constant-returns-to-scale property.

Within any period t, timing works as follows. At the beginning of the period, the representative consumer has M_t units of money carried over from the previous period, B_t nominal bonds, and X_t real bonds. Each nominal bond issued in period t is a promise to pay one unit of money in period $t + 1$, and each real bond issued in period t is a promise to pay one unit of the consumption good in period $t + 1$. With nominal and real bonds in the model, we can determine explicitly the nominal and real interest rates. A nominal bond issued in period t sells for q_t units of money, while a real bond sells for s_t units of period t consumption goods.

At the beginning of the period, the asset market opens, the consumer receives the payoffs on the bonds held over from the previous period, and the consumer can exchange money for nominal and real bonds that come due in period $t + 1$. The consumer must also pay a real lump-sum tax of T_t at this time. After the asset market closes, the consumer supplies N_t units of labour to the firm and buys consumption goods on the goods market, but he or she must purchase these consumption goods with money held over after the asset market closes. Consumption goods are sold at the money price P_t in period t. Therefore, the representative consumer must abide by the cash-in-advance constraint

$$P_t C_t + q_t B_{t+1} + P_t s_t X_{t+1} + P_t T_t = M_t + B_t + P_t X_t. \tag{A.63}$$

When the goods market closes, the consumer receives his or her labour earnings from the representative firm in cash. The consumer then faces the budget constraint

$$P_t C_t + q_t B_{t+1} + P_t s_t X_{t+1} + P_t T_t + M_{t+1} = M_t + B_t + P_t X_t + P_t z N_t, \tag{A.64}$$

where M_{t+1} is the quantity of money held by the consumer at the end of the period and z is the real wage in period t, which must be equal to the constant marginal product of labour in equilibrium.

Letting $\bar{M}_t$ denote the supply of money at the beginning of period t, the government budget constraint is given by

$$\bar{M}_{t+1} - \bar{M}_t = -P_t T_t, \tag{A.65}$$

and the government sets taxes so that the money supply grows at a constant rate α. That is, we have $\bar{M}_{t+1} = (1 + \alpha) \bar{M}_t$ for all t. This then implies, from (A.65), that

$$\alpha \bar{M}_t = -P_t T_t. \tag{A.66}$$

Now, it will prove convenient to scale the constraints (A.63) and (A.64) by multiplying through by $\frac{1}{\bar{M}_t}$, and letting lowercase letters denote scaled nominal variables—for example, $p_t = \frac{P_t}{\bar{M}_t}$. Then, we can rewrite (A.63) and (A.64) as

$$p_t C_t + q_t b_{t+1}(1 + \alpha) + p_t s_t X_{t+1} + p_t T_t = m_t + b_t + p_t X_t \tag{A.67}$$

and

$$p_t C_t + q_t b_{t+1}(1 + \alpha) + p_t s_t X_{t+1} + p_t T_t + m_{t+1}(1 + \alpha) = m_t + b_t + p_t X_t + p_t z N_t. \tag{A.68}$$

The representative consumer's problem is to choose C_t, N_t, b_{t+1}, X_{t+1}, and m_{t+1} in each period $t = 0, 1, 2, \ldots, \infty$, to maximize (A.61) subject to the constraints (A.67) and (A.68). We can simplify the problem by formulating it as a dynamic program. Letting $v(m_t, b_t, X_t; p_t, q_t, s_t)$ denote the value function, the Bellman equation associated with the consumer's problem is

$$v(m_t, b_t, X_t; p_t, q_t, s_t) = \max_{C_t, N_t, b_{t+1}, X_{t+1}, m_{t+1}} [U(C_t) - V(N_t) + \beta v(m_{t+1}, b_{t+1}, X_{t+1}; p_{t+1}, q_{t+1}, s_{t+1},)]$$

subject to (A.67) and (A.68). Letting λ_t and μ_t denote the Lagrange multipliers associated with the constraints (A.67) and (A.68), the first-order conditions for an optimum are

$$U'(C_t) - (\lambda_t + \mu_t)p_t = 0, \tag{A.69}$$

$$-V'(N_t) + \mu_t p_t z = 0, \tag{A.70}$$

$$-q_{t+1}(1 + \alpha)(\lambda_t + \mu_t) + \beta\frac{\partial v}{\partial b_{t+1}} = 0, \tag{A.71}$$

$$-p_t s_t(\lambda_t + \mu_t) + \beta\frac{\partial v}{\partial X_{t+1}} = 0, \tag{A.72}$$

$$-(1 + \alpha)\mu_t + \beta\frac{\partial v}{\partial m_{t+1}} = 0. \tag{A.73}$$

We can also derive the following envelope conditions by differentiating the Bellman equation above and applying the envelope theorem:

$$\frac{\partial v}{\partial b_t} = \lambda_t + \mu_t; \tag{A.74}$$

$$\frac{\partial v}{\partial X_t} = p_t(\lambda_t + \mu_t); \tag{A.75}$$

$$\frac{\partial v}{\partial m_t} = \lambda_t + \mu_t. \tag{A.76}$$

Now, we can use the envelope conditions, (A.74)–(A.76), updated one period, to substitute for the derivatives of the value function in (A.71)–(A.73), and then use (A.69) and (A.70) to substitute for Lagrange multipliers in (A.71)–(A.73), obtaining

$$\frac{-q_t(1 + \alpha)U'(C_t)}{p_t} = \beta\frac{U'(C_{t+1})}{p_{t+1}} = 0, \tag{A.77}$$

$$-s_t U'(C_t) + \beta U'(C_{t+1}) = 0, \tag{A.78}$$

$$\frac{-(1 + \alpha)V'(N_t)}{p_t z} + \beta\frac{U'(C_{t+1})}{p_{t+1}} = 0. \tag{A.79}$$

Next, the market-clearing conditions are

$$m_t = 1, b_t = 0, X_t = 0,$$

for all t. Money demand equals money supply, the demand for nominal bonds equals the zero net supply of nominal bonds, and the demand for real bonds equals the zero net supply of these bonds as well, in each period. Substituting the market-clearing conditions in Equations (A.67) and (A.68), and using Equation (A.66) to substitute for T_t, we obtain

$$p_t C_t = 1 + \alpha, \tag{A.80}$$

$$C_t = zN_t. \tag{A.81}$$

Equations (A.80) and (A.81) state, respectively, that all money is held in equilibrium at the beginning of the period by the representative consumer, and is used to purchase consumption goods, and that in equilibrium all output produced is consumed.

Now, there is an equilibrium where $C_t = C$, $N_t = N$, $p_t = p$, $q_t = q$, and $s_t = s$, for all t, and we can use Equations (A.77)–(A.81) to solve for C, N, p, q, and s. We obtain

$$q = \frac{\beta}{1 + \alpha},$$ (A.82)

$$s = \beta,$$ (A.83)

$$(1 + \alpha)V'(N) - bzU'(zN) = 0,$$ (A.84)

$$C = zN,$$ (A.85)

$$p = \frac{1 + \alpha}{C}.$$ (A.86)

Here, Equations (A.82) and (A.83) give solutions for q and s respectively, while Equation (A.84) solves implicitly for N. Then, given the solution for N, we can solve recursively for C and p from (A.85) and (A.86). Note as well that we can solve for the Lagrange multiplier λ using (A.69), (A.70), (A.80), (A.81), and (A.84), to get

$$\lambda = \frac{CU'(C)}{1 + \alpha}\left(1 - \frac{\beta}{1 + \alpha}\right) = \frac{CU'(C)}{1 + \alpha}(1 - q).$$ (A.87)

Now, note that the nominal interest rate is determined by the price of the nominal bond q, as $R = \frac{1}{q} - 1$, so that the nominal interest rate is positive as long as $q < 1$. From (A.82), the nominal interest rate is positive when $\alpha > \beta - 1$, that is, as long as the money growth rate is sufficiently large. Note also that the Lagrange multiplier associated with the cash-in-advance constraint is positive—that is, $\lambda > 0$—if and only if $q < 1$. Thus, a positive nominal interest rate is associated with a binding cash-in-advance constraint. From Equation (A.82), the nominal interest rate is

$$R = \frac{1 + \alpha}{\beta} - 1.$$

The real interest rate is $\frac{1}{s} - 1$; from Equation (A.83), this is

$$r = \frac{1}{\beta} - 1,$$

which is the representative consumer's subjective rate of time preference. Further, the inflation rate is

$$i = \frac{P_{t+1}}{P_t} - 1 = \frac{p_{t+1}\bar{M}_{t+1}}{p_t\bar{M}_t} = \alpha,$$

so that the inflation rate is equal to the money growth rate. Now, from the above, it is clear that the Fisher relation holds, as

$$1 + r = \frac{1 + R}{1 + i}.$$

The effects of money growth on real variables can be obtained by totally differentiating Equation (A.84) with respect to N and α, and solving to obtain

$$\frac{dN}{d\alpha} = \frac{-V'}{(1 + \alpha)V'' - \beta z^2 U''} < 0;$$

thus, employment declines with an increase in the money growth rate, and since $Y = C = zN$ in equilibrium, output and consumption also decline. This effect arises because inflation distorts intertemporal decisions. Period t labour income is held as cash and not spent on consumption until period $t + 1$, and it is therefore eroded by inflation. Higher inflation then reduces labour supply, output, and consumption.

What is the optimal rate of inflation? To determine a Pareto optimum, we solve the social planner's problem, which is to solve

$$\max_{\{C_t, N_t\}_{t=0}^{\infty}} \sum_{t=0}^{\infty} \beta^t [U(C_t) - V(N_t)]$$

subject to $C_t = zN_t$ for all t. The solution to this problem is characterized by the first-order condition

$$zU'(zN^*) - V'(N^*) = 0,$$

where N^* is optimal employment in each period t. In equilibrium, employment N is determined by (A.84), and note that equilibrium employment will be equal to N^* for the case where $\alpha = \beta - 1$. The optimal money growth rate $\beta - 1$ characterizes a Friedman rule, as this implies from (A.82) that the nominal interest rate is zero, and that the inflation rate is $\beta - 1$, so that the rate of return on money is $\frac{1}{\beta} - 1$, which is identical to the real interest rate r. Note also, from (A.87), that the cash-in-advance constraint does not bind when $\alpha = \beta - 1$, since $\lambda = 0$. Thus, a Friedman rule relaxes the cash-in-advance constraint, and causes the rates of return on all assets to be equated in equilibrium.

Problem

1. Suppose in the monetary intertemporal model that $U(C) = 2C^{1/2}$ and $V(N) = (1/2)N^2$. Determine closed-form solutions for consumption, employment, output, the nominal interest rate, and the real interest rate. What are the effects of changes in z and α in equilibrium? Explain your results.

Chapter 14: Money, Private Banking, and Central Banking

Here, we will develop a version of the Kiyotaki–Wright random matching model, to show how fiat money can overcome an absence-of-double-coincidence-of-wants problem. This model is closely related to the one constructed by Alberto Trejos and Randall Wright in an article in the *Journal of Political Economy*,[3] and it generalizes the model of Chapter 14 to a case where there are n different goods rather than 3. To work through this model requires an elementary knowledge of probability.

In the model, there are n different types of consumers and n different goods, where $n \geq 3$. Each consumer is infinite-lived and maximizes

$$E_0 \sum_{t=0}^{\infty} \left(\frac{1}{1+r}\right)^t U_t,$$

where E_0 is the expectations operator conditional on information at $t = 0$, r is the consumer's subjective discount rate, and U_t is the utility from consuming in period t, where $U_t = 0$ if nothing is

---

[3]See A. Trejos and R. Wright, 1995, "Search, Bargaining, Money, and Prices," *Journal of Political Economy* 103, 118–141.

consumed. Given that the consumer will face uncertainty, we have assumed that he or she is an expected-utility maximizer. A consumer of type i produces good i and consumes good $i + 1$, for $i = 1, 2, 3, \ldots, n - 1$, and a type n consumer produces good n and consumes good 1. Note that if $n = 3$, then this is the same setup as we considered in Chapter 14. In this n-good model, there is an absence-of-double-coincidence problem, as no two consumers produce what each other wants.

Goods are indivisible, so that when a good is produced, the consumer produces only one unit. At $t = 0$, a fraction M of the population is endowed with one unit of fiat money each, and fiat money is also indivisible. Further, a consumer can hold at most one unit of some object at a time, so that at the end of any period a consumer will be holding one unit of a good, one unit of money, or nothing. It is costless to produce a good and costless to hold one unit of a good or money as inventory.

At the end of period 0, each consumer not holding money produces a good, and then he or she holds this in inventory until period 1. In period 1, consumers are matched two-by-two and at random, so that a given consumer meets only one other consumer during period 1. Two consumers who meet inspect each other's goods, and announce whether they are willing to trade. If both are willing, they trade, and any consumer receiving his or her consumption good in a trade consumes it (this is optimal), receives utility $u > 0$ from consumption, and produces another good. Then consumers move on to period 2, and so on. No two consumers will meet more than once, since there are infinitely many consumers in the population. We will assume that there are equal numbers of each type of consumer, so that the fraction of the population who are of a given type is $\frac{1}{n}$. Then, in any period, the probability that a consumer meets another consumer of a particular type is $\frac{1}{n}$.

What can be an equilibrium in this model? One equilibrium is where money is not valued. That is, if no one accepts money, then no one will want to hold it and, because of the absence-of-double-coincidence problem, there will be no exchange and everyone's utility will be zero. If no one has faith that money will have value in exchange, then this expectation will be self-fulfilling. A more interesting equilibrium is one where everyone accepts money. Here, we will let μ denote the fraction of the population that holds money in equilibrium, V_g will denote the value of holding a good in equilibrium, and V_m will be the value of holding money. Though there are n different goods, the optimization problems of all consumers will be identical in equilibrium, and so the value of holding any good will be the same for each consumer. The Bellman equations associated with a consumer's optimization problem are

$$V_g = \frac{1}{1 + r}\left[(1 - \mu)V_g + \mu(1 - \frac{1}{n})V_g + \mu\frac{1}{n}(V_m - V_g)\right], \tag{A.88}$$

$$V_m = \frac{1}{1 + r}\left[(1 - \mu)(1 - \frac{1}{n})V_m + (1 - \mu)\frac{1}{n}(u + V_g) + \mu V_m\right]. \tag{A.89}$$

In Equation (A.88), the value of holding a good at the end of the current period is equal to the discounted sum of the expected payoff in the following period. In the following period, the consumer meets another agent with a good with probability $1 - m$, in which case trade does not take place, and the consumer will be holding a good at the end of the next period and will receive value V_g. With probability $\mu(1 - \frac{1}{n})$, the consumer meets another consumer with money who does not wish to purchase the consumer's good, and again trade does not take place. With probability $\mu\frac{1}{n}$, the consumer meets a consumer with money who wants his or her good, trade takes place, and the consumer is holding money at the end of the next period. In Equation (A.89), a consumer with money does not trade with another consumer who has money, or with another consumer who has a good that he or she does not consume. However, with probability $(1 - \mu)\frac{1}{n}$ the consumer meets another consumer with his or her consumption good, in which case trade takes place, the consumer gets utility u from consuming the good, and then he or she produces another good.

We can solve for V_g and V_m from (A.88) and (A.89), which give

$$V_g = \frac{\mu(1 - \mu)u}{rn(1 + rn)},$$

$$V_m = \frac{(rn + \mu)(1 - \mu)u}{rn(1 + rn)},$$

so that

$$V_m - V_g = \frac{(1 - \mu)u}{1 + rn} > 0.$$

Therefore, the value of holding money is greater than the value of holding a good, so that everyone will accept money (as conjectured) in equilibrium. Further, consumers who have money in any period will prefer to hold it rather than producing a good, and so we will have $\mu = M$ in equilibrium.

The values of V_g and V_m are the utilities that consumers receive from holding goods and money, respectively. As $V_g > 0$ and $V_m > 0$, everyone is better off in an economy where money is used than in one where it is not used.

Problem

1. Suppose a search economy with the possibility of double coincidences. That is, assume that when an agent produces a good, that he or she cannot consume it herself. In a random match where two agents meet and each has the good that they produced, the first agent has what the second consumes with probability x, the second has what the first consumes with probability x, and each has what the other consumes with probability x^2.

    a. In this economy, show that there are three equilibria, a barter equilibrium where money is not accepted, an equilibrium where an agent with a good is indifferent between accepting and not accepting money, and an equilibrium where agents with goods always accept money.

    b. Show that x needs to be sufficiently small before having money in this economy actually increases welfare over having barter, and explain this result.

Chapter 15: Unemployment: Search and Efficiency Wages

In this section we will formally set up the search model of unemployment from Chapter 15, derive some of the results for that model, and construct an illustrative example. For this model, an elementary knowledge of probability is useful.

In the search model, the infinite-lived worker has preferences given by

$$E_0 \sum_{t=0}^{\infty} \left(\frac{1}{1 + r}\right)^t U(C_t),$$

where E_0 is the expectation operator conditional on information known in period 0, r is the subjective discount rate, C_t is consumption, and $U(\cdot)$ is the period utility function, which is strictly increasing, continuous, and strictly concave. Here, because the worker will face uncertainty, we have assumed that he or she is an expected-utility maximizer.

A worker who is employed at a job paying the real wage w supplies one unit of labour during the period and consumes his or her labour earnings (we assume no savings). There is a probability s, where $0 < s < 1$, that the worker will be separated from his or her job and become unemployed at the end of the period. We let $V_e(w)$ denote the value of being employed at the real wage w, and V_u the value of being unemployed, where both values are calculated as of the end of the current period. Then, the Bellman equation for an employed worker is

$$V_e(w) = \frac{1}{1+r}[U(w) + sV_u + (1-s)V_e(w)]; \qquad (A.90)$$

that is, the value of being employed at the end of the current period is the present discounted value of the utility from employment next period, plus the expected value at the end of the period, given the separation rate s.

Next, a worker who is unemployed receives the employment insurance benefit b at the beginning of the period, and then with probability p receives a wage offer, which is a random draw from the probability distribution $F(w)$, which has the associated probability density function $f(w)$. Assume that $w \in [0, \bar{w}]$, where $\bar{w} > 0$. The unemployed worker must decide whether to accept a given wage offer or turn it down. Thus, the value of unemployment is given by

$$V_u = \frac{1}{1+r}\left\{U(b) + (1-p)V_u + p\int_0^{\bar{w}} \max[V_u, V_e(w)]\, f(w)\, dw\right\}, \qquad (A.91)$$

so that the value of being unemployed at the end of the current period is equal to the discounted value of the utility from consuming the employment insurance benefit, plus the probability of remaining unemployed times the value of remaining unemployed, plus the probability of receiving a job offer, times the expected value of the job offer.

Equations (A.90) and (A.91) can be simplified, respectively, as follows:

$$rV_e(w) = U(w) + s[V_U - V_e(w)]; \qquad (A.92)$$

$$rV_u = U(b) + p\int_0^{\bar{w}} \max[0, V_e(w) - V_u]\, f(w)\, dw. \qquad (A.93)$$

From Equation (A.92), we can solve for $V_e(w)$ to get

$$V_e(w) = \frac{U(w) + sV_u}{r + s},$$

so that $V_e(w)$ inherits the properties of $U(w)$—that is, it is strictly increasing, continuous, and strictly concave. This implies that the worker will accept any wage offer greater than or equal to w^*, and reject any offer less than w^*, where w^* solves

$$V_e(w^*) = V_u.$$

That is w^* is the reservation wage at which the worker is just indifferent between accepting the job offer and remaining unemployed.

To determine the unemployment rate, note that the flow of workers from employment to unemployment must be equal to the flow from unemployment to employment in the steady state, or

$$s(1 - U) = p[1 - F(w^*)]U;$$

solving for the unemployment rate U, we obtain

$$U = \frac{s}{p[1 - F(w^*)] + s}.$$

An example will show how the model works. Suppose that, conditional on receiving a wage offer, an unemployed worker receives a wage offer w_1 with probability π, and a wage offer of zero with probability $1 - \pi$, where $0 < \pi < 1$. Then, conjecturing that a wage offer of w_1 is always accepted and a wage offer of zero is always turned down, (A.92) and (A.93) in this case give

$$rV_e = U(w_1) + s(V_u - V_e),$$

$$rV_u = U(b) + p\pi(V_e - V_u),$$

where V_e is the value of being employed at the real wage w_1. Then, solving the above two equations for V_e and V_u, we get

$$V_e = \frac{(p\pi + r)U(w_1) + sU(b)}{r(s + p\pi + r)},$$

$$V_u = \frac{(s + r)U(w_1) + p\pi U(b)}{r(s + p\pi + r)},$$

with

$$V_e - V_u = \frac{U(w_1) - U(b)}{s + p\pi + r}.$$

Therefore, we have $V_u > 0$, so that a wage offer of zero will be turned down as conjectured, even if the unemployment insurance benefit b is zero. Further, the wage offer of w_1 will be accepted if and only if $w_1 \geq b$, that is, if the wage on the job is higher than the unemployment insurance benefit. The unemployment rate will be

$$U = \frac{s}{p\pi + s},$$

but if $b > w_1$, then no one would accept jobs, and we would have $U = 1$ and everyone would be unemployed. This is an extreme example of how an increase in the employment insurance benefit can increase the unemployment rate.

Problem

1. Suppose in the search model that an employed worker receives a wage offer with probability π. Then, conditional on receiving a wage offer, the offer is w_1 with probability α_1, w_2 with probability α_2, and zero with probability $1 - \alpha_1 - \alpha_2$, where $0 < w_1 < w_2$. Determine under what conditions an unemployed worker would turn down a wage offer of w_1, accepting a wage offer of w_2, and under what conditions an unemployed worker will accept any wage offer greater than zero. Interpret these conditions.

Chapter 16: Inflation, the Phillips Curve, and Central Bank Commitment

In this section we construct a somewhat more explicit version of the model we worked with in Chapter 16, to show some of the results of that chapter more formally.

The first component of the model is the Phillips curve relationship, which captures the key idea in the Friedman–Lucas money surprise model of Chapter 11. That is,

$$i - i^e = a(Y - Y^T), \tag{A.94}$$

where i is the inflation rate, i^e is the private sector's anticipated inflation rate, $a > 0$, Y is aggregate output, and Y^T is trend output. The second component of the model is the preferences of the central bank, which we will represent by supposing that the central bank maximizes $\phi(Y, i)$, where $\phi(\cdot, \cdot)$ is a function. That is, the central bank cares about the level of output and the inflation rate. It is convenient to express $\phi(Y, i)$ as a quadratic function—that is,

$$\phi(Y, i) = \alpha(i - i^*)^2 + \beta(Y - Y^*)^2, \tag{A.95}$$

where α and β are positive constants, i^* is the target inflation rate for the central bank, and Y^* is the target level of aggregate output for the central bank.

Now, suppose, according to the central bank learning story, that the central bank treats the anticipated inflation rate i^e as being given, and chooses i and Y to maximize (A.95) given (A.94). Solving this optimization problem, the central bank will then choose

$$i = \frac{\alpha a^2 i^* + \beta i^e - \beta a(Y^T - Y^*)}{\alpha a^2 + \beta}. \tag{A.96}$$

We will then have

$$i - i^e = \frac{\alpha a^2(i^* - i^e) - \beta a(Y^T - Y^*)}{\alpha a^2 + \beta}.$$

In this circumstance, if the central bank had a target level of output that was higher than trend output—that is, $Y^T - Y^* < 0$—then even if $i^e > i^*$, in which case anticipated inflation is higher than the target inflation rate, the central bank may want to have $i > i^e$ so that the private sector is fooled by positive surprise inflation. Ultimately, though, the private sector is not fooled in the long run, so that $i = i^e$, and if the central bank learns this, then it realizes that, from (A.94), it cannot engineer a level of output other than Y^T, and the best strategy for the central bank is to set $i = i^*$.

Under the central bank commitment story, the central bank cannot commit to an inflation rate, and it is playing a game with the private sector. The private sector first chooses i^e, then the central bank chooses i, and in equilibrium $i = i^e$. In this case Equation (A.96) is the central bank's reaction function, and we can solve for the equilibrium inflation rate by substituting $i = i^e$ in (A.96), getting

$$i = i^* + \frac{\beta}{\alpha a}(Y^* - Y^T);$$

hence, if $Y^* > Y^T$, in equilibrium the inflation rate can be higher than i^*, which is the inflation rate the central bank would choose if it could tie its hands and commit itself to an inflation policy

Problem

1. Suppose that, instead of expectations being rational, expectations are adaptive. That is, each period the private sector expects that the inflation rate will be what it was the previous period. That is, $i^e = i_{-1}$, where i_{-1} the actual inflation rate last period. Under these circumstances, determine what the actual inflation rate and the level of output will be, given i_{-1}. How will the inflation rate and output evolve over time? What will the inflation rate and the level of output be in the long run? Explain your results.

INDEX

Page numbers followed by f and t and n refer to figures and tables and notes, respectively. Key terms and their page numbers are boldface.

macroeconomics